Bertrand's Toyshop in Bath

Luxury Retailing 1685–1765

Monogram in a floral surround, feathers on canvas, Nicholas le Normand, signed, *c.* 1720–35. Height 50.8 cm (20 in); width 40.6 cm (16 in). (Private coll)

Bertrand's Toyshop in Bath

Luxury Retailing 1685–1765

VANESSA BRETT

Oblong

2014

Published in 2014 by
Oblong Creative Ltd
416b Thorp Arch Estate
Wetherby ls23 7fg
UK

Bertrand's Toyshop in Bath: Luxury Retailing 1685–1765
Text © 2014 Vanessa Brett
Illustrations © 2014, see Picture Credits (p. 333) for copyright holders
isbn 978 0 9575992 4 6
All rights reserved. No part of this publication may be reproduced, stored in a retrieval system, or transmitted, in any form or by any means, electronic, mechanical, photocopying, recording, or otherwise without the consent of the copyright owner. Only written permission from the publisher and the copyright owner will be accepted as evidence of such consent.

DESIGNED AND PRODUCED IN THE UK BY OBLONG CREATIVE LTD

Contents

Acknowledgements	6
Timeline	9
Facts and Figures	12
Introduction	15
Part 1: Paul Bertrand and Mary Deards	25
Paul Bertrand in London	27
Marriage to Mary Deards	37
Partnerships	45
Customer of Hoare & Co.	53
Employees	59
Part of Bath's community	65
Part 2: Bath as a resort	73
Bath in the early eighteenth century	79
The assembly rooms	93
When to go and how to get there	105
Where to stay	115
What to do: the daily round	121
Royalty and their retinues	143
Summer at Bristol	165
Other shopkeepers and artists in Bath	171
Part 3: Retirement	193
Part 4: Paul Bertrand's bank account	205
Bibliography	325
Picture acknowledgements	333
Endnotes	335
Index	349

Acknowledgements

Brian Beet, who died in 2003 aged 55.

IT WAS MY GREAT GOOD FORTUNE to edit the journal of the Silver Society for many years, during which time I received encouragement, help and numerous kindnesses from the Society's members, many of whom I count among my friends: words cannot do justice to my gratitude to them. Out of those associations came Brian Beet's request to continue his research into toyshops: this legacy of his hard-won and pioneering work, which underpins my own, has directed the last ten years of my life.

The generosity of the partners of C. Hoare & Co. in allowing me access to their archive has enabled me to learn more than they will ever realise. Obtaining permission to look at the bank's archives and then receiving permission to publish has proved crucial, and caused the focus of the research to shift in an unexpected direction. I have spent many days in the bank in Fleet Street, and have had the unstinting assistance of the archivist Pamela Hunter. This has been a quite extraordinary privilege, for which I am most grateful.

Philippa Glanville, Lisa White, Charles Truman and Matthew Winterbottom have read drafts, listened through many lunches to discoveries and uncertainties, persuaded me to continue, and given advice. From the day on which he handed me Brian Beet's notes, I have received constant encouragement from Peter Cameron, who has also been generous in passing on findings from his own research. This generosity with information and expertise has come from many others also: Gale Glynn has spent untold hours answering genealogical queries; after a lifetime of delving into archives John Culme keeps me on track; Hazel Forsyth and Eileen Goodway have given of their own research. Julia Clarke's generosity and guidance as I tentatively explore her field of vertu and gold boxes, is unstinting.

Time, friendship and guidance such as this, so generously given by them all, are beyond price or thanks.

Mike Chapman and Elizabeth Holland have contributed decades of their own research through Mr Chapman's maps: I acknowledge their scholastic generosity in collaboration. They see it as an opportunity to introduce their interest in the development of Bath to a new audience, and it has been a delight to work with them. Illustrations that flesh out those maps have largely come from Bath's City Library, where Anne Buchanan and Dan Brown (founder of the website Bathintime) could not have been more helpful and generous with their time and knowledge. At the Record Office Colin Johnston and his colleagues have been outstandingly helpful over many years. Also in Bath, Trevor Quartermaine allowed access to the Masonic archives, and Michael Rowe has facilitated many introductions; conversations with Amina Wright, at the Holburne Museum, never fail to enlighten.

Olive Baldwin and Thelma Wilson's knowledge of early eighteenth-century opera has been invaluable: they have advised me on Mary Lindsey's career and identity in lengthy emails, generously giving of their wide experience. In the field of ceramics longstanding friendships with Simon Spero and Gillian Darby have made it easy for me to ask questions about this enormous subject. Nick Panes has shared his research into china-men; Maureen Cassidy-Geiger and Patricia Ferguson have responded to many emails with generosity. By asking me to speak to the English Ceramic Circle early on, Felicity Marno encouraged me to focus on porcelain. In other areas of expertise, David Thompson and Sir George White have advised on watches, Sheila O'Connell on the engravers Simon and Samuel Gribelin; Tessa Murdoch has answered numerous questions, made suggestions and given constant encouragement, as have David Beasley and Eleni Bide at the Goldsmiths' Company.

Many others have helped me also over cups of coffee or tea, via email and telephone, made introductions or provided images. In some cases their information or advice relates to areas of this research not included here, but which I hope to publish later. They are acknowledged now nonetheless, for the future is unpredictable. They include Ellenor Alcorn (Metropolitan Museum); Brian Allen; Robert Barker; Elizabeth Bellord; Helen Clifford; Howard Coutts; Timothy Cox; Barbara Deards; Richard Edgcumbe, Hilary Young, Heike Zech and Kirstin Kennedy (V&A); Hazel Forsyth (Museum of London); Gordon Glanville; Jonathan Gray; Antony Griffiths; Bevis Hillier; Bruce Jones; Christopher Hartop; Timothy Kent; Lowell Libson; James Lomax; Patrick Mannix of Motco; David Mitchell; Jet Pijzel-Dommisse; Stephen Porter (Charterhouse); David Posnett; Pamela Roditi; Anthony Sale; Luke Schrager; Stephanie Tiley; Richard Chenevix Trench; Katherine Wall (Victoria Art Gallery, Bath); Julia Weber; Timothy Wilson (Ashmolean Museum). In addition to those already mentioned at Sotheby's, Cynthia Harris has been unfailingly helpful; so too have

Anthony Phillips, Harry Williams-Bulkeley, Jeffrey Lassaline and David McLachlan at Christie's; Loraine Turner and Michael Moorcroft at Bonhams; and Lucy Chalmers at Woolley & Wallis.

Without exception, owners, curators and archivists at the private and public collections and libraries that I have visited have most helpfully given of their time and expertise. Those who appreciate the cost of work such as this, and keep research and illustration fees to a minimum, make a particular contribution to scholarship: this book would not have been possible without their enlightened approach. Some owners have corresponded directly, in other houses I have been helped by archivists. They include: the Duke of Buccleuch; Sir Lyonel Tollemache; Lady Walpole; Anna Semler (Althorp); Christopher Hunwick (Alnwick); Elizabeth Mence (Guildhall, Bath); Elaine Milsom (Badminton); Gareth Fitzpatrick, Charles Lister and Crispin Powell (Boughton); Stephen Porter (Charterhouse); Stuart Band, Diane Naylor and Hannah Obee (Chatsworth); Elizabeth Stuart and Elizabeth Lomas (Duchy of Cornwall); Tracy Earl (Coutts & Co.); Diane Clements (Grand Lodge); Christine Hiskey (Holkham); Kate Harris (Longleat); Jeremy Smith (LMA); Andrew McLean (Mount Stewart); Timothy Cox (Newmarket); Roderick Smith and Robert Welsh (Company of Playing Card Makers); Nancy Shawcross (University of Pennsylvania library); Alison McCann (Petworth/West Sussex Record Office); Anne Mitchell (Woburn). Members of staff at the record offices listed in the bibliography and illustration acknowledgements have all contributed to this research through their assistance – as have the staff of the London Library.

Several institutions now make images available via the Internet: without this facility, and the generosity of other photographic archives and owners, a work such as this would not be feasible for an independent author.

My family have lived for some years with someone whose mind has often been focussed in another era. It has been a test of endurance for them, but they have loyally supported me throughout this project. My brother Simon Brett never fails me, not only with loving encouragement, but also with his skill with words and sense of what is 'right' on a page.

Lastly, there are those who have helped to bring clarity to the book in its final stages. Suzanne Drown brought order to my text. At Oblong, Derek Brown and Jackie Maidment have been patient and professional throughout the publication process. That which you hold in your hands is the result of their experience and the generosity of many.

VANESSA BRETT

Timeline

	Paul and Mary Bertrand	Deards family and friends	Bath	Politics
1662		John Deards snr born		
1684		John Deards snr marries Mary Bloxom		
1685	Paul Bertrand snr marries Marie Gribelin	Shop in Fleet Street		Death of Charles II; accession of James II
c. 1689	Paul Bertrand jnr born in Maryland			1688: Accession of William III and Mary II
1691–92	Bertrand snr dies, Bertrand jnr and mother return to England	January 1691/2: Mary Deards baptised		
1694		Elizabeth Deards baptised	Gilmore's map of Bath published	Death of Mary II
1699		William Deards baptised		
1702			Queen Anne visits Bath, and again in 1703	Accession of Queen Anne; War of Spanish Succession 1701–14
1705			1704 Richard Nash in Bath; John Wood snr born; Pump Room built	
1707			Charles Delamain mortgages his 'room'	Act of Union: England & Scotland [Union with Ireland 1801]
1702–09			Shops in Gravel Walks (later Orange Grove) developed	
1708/09			Harrison's assembly rooms opened, extended 1720	
1709	Bertrand naturalised			
1712	Francis Neale apprenticed to Bertrand			
1713	Bertrand marries Mary le Maitre		Mary Lindsey takes over Delamain's business	Treaty of Utrecht
1714				Queen Anne dies; accession of George I
1714–19	Three children born, died young			
1715				Jacobite uprising, Old Pretender
1716–29		Seasonal shop in Bath, possibly earlier		

	Paul and Mary Bertrand	Deards family and friends	Bath	Politics
1720				South Sea Bubble 'bursts'
1721				Robert Walpole Lord of the Treasury
1722			James Leake opens bookshop	
1726		Elizabeth Deards marries Daniel Chenevix		Britain at war with Spain 1727–29
1727				Accession of George II
1728			Terrace Walk widened and Thayer's assembly rooms built, managed by Mary Lindsey to 1736; Chandos lodgings completed	Frederick Prince of Wales arrives in England
Feb 1729/30	Bertrand marries Mary Deards; moves to Bath	Daniel and Elizabeth Chenevix open shop in Charing Cross		
1729–36			Queen Square built	
1731		John Deards snr dies	Thomas Harrison retires	Treaty of Vienna ends Anglo-French alliance. Start of Anglo-Austrian alliance
1732	John Wiltshire apprenticed			
1733	Bertrand freeman of Bath			
1733/34			Prince of Orange visit	
1736, May	Bertrand opens bank account with Hoare & Co.			
1737–39	Bertrands begin to live in Barton Street			Death of Queen Caroline, wife of George II 1737
1738		Death of Mary Deards, wife of John snr; will proved 1739	Prince of Wales visit	Gaming Act (followed by others in 1739 & 1744/5)
1739	Probable partnership between Bertrand and Wiltshire family	William Hoare moves to Bath	Building of North and South Parades, completed 1748	No wrought plate officially imported into England to 1750
1740		Peter Russel marries Hannah Hoare		
1740–48				War of Austrian succession
1742		William Hoare marries Elizabeth Barker. William Deards moves from Fleet Street to the Strand	Mineral Water Hospital opens	Robert Walpole resigns

	Paul and Mary Bertrand	Deards family and friends	Bath	Politics
1742/3		Daniel Chenevix dies; shop continued by Elizabeth		
1744			*Bath Journal* begins publication	
1745–46			The game EO introduced to Bath by Nash	Jacobite uprising, Young Pretender
1746			Princess Caroline visit	
1747/48	Bertrand retires; John Wiltshire takes over assembly rooms		Bertrand's employees, Moyse Roubel, John Pyke and James Tilley open shops	
1749		Hannah Russel dies		
1750		Elizabeth Chenevix marries Peter Russel		
1751			Pump Room extended	Death of Prince of Wales; Clive in India
1752				Adoption of Gregorian calendar
1753				Marriage Act. [Women's rights are improved again under the Married Women's Property Acts of 1870 & 1882]
1754			John Wood snr dies	
1755	Paul Bertrand dies; auction of his goods; Mary Bertrand moves to Ealing at unknown date		Kingston excavations for new baths	
1756–62				Seven years' war Britain and Prussia against France, Austria and Spain
1757		William Deards moves from the Strand to Piccadilly	Nash sues the Wiltshire family	
1760				Accession of George III
1761		William Deards dies; shop continued by his son John jnr	Richard Nash dies	Marriage of George III
1762			John Wiltshire dies Goldsmith's life of Nash published	
1763		Russel advertises sale of stock		
1765		Elizabeth Chenevix dies; Peter Russel retires		
1773		Peter Russel dies		
1774	Mary Bertrand dies			
1783		John Deards retires from Piccadilly shop		
1794		John Deards dies		

Facts and figures

Note

There is considerable variety in the way in which dates and money are written in account books and invoices. For the sake of clarity figures have been standardised and may not accurately reflect the original document. The widespread use of capitals, and eccentric or non-existent punctuation in advertisements and letters, has sometimes been simplified for ease of reading; therefore quoted extracts may not be entirely accurate transcriptions.

Calendar

Britain was one of the last countries in Europe to adopt the Gregorian calendar. The Act of Parliament that authorised the change from the Julian calendar to the Gregorian was steered through parliament by the Earl of Chesterfield in 1752. It entailed the loss of eleven days. Wednesday 2 September 1752 was followed by Thursday 14 September. Thereafter the year began on 1 January instead of 25 March.

The system had been confusing for some time, as people wrote the dates for January to March in two different ways, some using what became the new style [NS] for many years before it officially came into force. Taking the years 1710 and 1711 as an example, the old style [OS] was written as follows:

> 1 January – 24 March 1709/10
> 25 March – 31 December 1710
> 1 January – 24 March 1710/11
> 25 March – 31 December 1711
> 1 January – 24 March 1711/12

Dates from 1 January to 24 March in the years before 1753 have, wherever possible, been written in the old style [e.g. 1709/10], however readers should be alert to errors that may have crept into this text where the original source was unclear, as sometimes the months of January to March were written (using the same example) as 1709 and sometimes as 1710.

In hallmarking gold and silver, the London assay office changed the date letter stamped on precious metals annually. During the period covered by this research, the change-over day was usually 29 May, or close to it.[1] The assay year is written here as: 1714/5.

Currency

English currency (pound sterling) was divided into pounds, shillings and pence until 15 February 1971, when a decimal system was introduced. Before 1971, as an alternative, items were often priced in guineas:

1 guinea = £1 1s.
half a guinea = 10s 6d.
1 pound sterling (£ or written as 'l' in the eighteenth century) = 20 shillings (s)
1 shilling = 12 pennies (d)
£1 = 240 pennies
Other commonly found divisions of a pound were:
crown (5s) and half-crown (2s 6d), and division into thirds: 6s 8d and 13s 4d.

Weights

Gold and silver are weighed using the troy system, rather than avoirdupois:

1 troy pound = 12 troy ounces
1 troy ounce (oz) = 20 pennyweights (dwt) = 480 grains
1 dwt = 24 grains
1 troy pound = 240 pennyweights
1 troy ounce = 1.09714 avoirdupois ounces
1kg = 32,1507466 troy ounces

(To convert troy ounces to avoirdupois ounces multiply by 1.0971; to convert avoirdupois ounces to troy ounces multiply by 0.9115)

Conversion of troy weight to grammes:
1 troy ounce = 31.103 grammes
1 dwt = 1.555 grammes
1 gramme = 0.03215 troy oz = 0.643 dwt
Avoirdupois
1 pound (lb) = 16 ounces = 0.453 kilogram (kg)
1 stone = 14 lb = 6.350 kg
1 hundredweight (cwt) = 112 lb = 50.80 kg

Quantities

1 dozen = 12
1 double dozen = 12 dozen = 1 gross = 144
1 score = 20

Distance

12 inches = 1 foot = 0.3048 metre
3 feet = 1 yard = 0.9144 metre
1 furlong = 40 rods = 220 yards = 201.168 metres
1 mile = 1,760 yards = 1.60993 kilometres

Guinea, gold, 1689, William III and Mary II, r. 1688–94.

Paul Bertrand's time in London spanned five reigns, represented here by currency. As a goldsmith, whether operating as a banker, a maker of gold snuff boxes, or as a retailer, Bertrand would have handled precious metals daily. (BM)

Half-crown, silver, 1700, William III, r. 1694–1702.

Guinea, gold, 1702, Queen Anne, r. 1702–14.

Half-guinea, gold, 1726, George I, r. 1714–27.

Five guineas, gold, 1729, George II, r. 1727–60.

To this fam'd shop all loitring people run,
Where with incessant noise themselves they stun

RICHARD PERCIVAL, *BERTRAND'S SHOP AT BATH*

Introduction

BETWEEN 1730 AND 1747 Paul Bertrand and his second wife Mary Deards ran a toyshop in Bath. The story of their life as luxury retailers reveals a hitherto unresearched view of England's most fashionable resort during the first half of the eighteenth century, before its development into the city we know today.

Much has been written on Bath but Paul and Mary Bertrand are unknown today apart from references in Susan Sloman's *Gainsborough in Bath*, in an article by Brian Beet, both published in 2002 and by Trevor Fawcett.[2] Through his bank account and other archive material researched here for the first time, it has been possible to piece together Bertrand's dealings with his customers, his fellow shopkeepers and with his partner John Wiltshire, whose family ran one of the assembly rooms in Bath. Their connection to Bertrand adds to the story of Richard Nash, Master of Ceremonies in Bath and Tunbridge Wells at this time, and the undercurrents of seasonal life in Bath. Paul Bertrand's name appears alongside aristocrats and city worthies in the 1748 list of governors of Bath's Mineral Water Hospital (published by John Wood snr), and yet he sank into obscurity.

It is impossible to understand the luxury trinkets known as toys without delving into the reasons for their manufacture, the people who made and sold them, and the society whose behaviour created the demand for them. Richard Percival's poem *Bertrand's Shop at Bath* says more about the customers than the shop's contents.[3] Those who led fashion, who held the strings of power and who owned most of Britain's acreage, travelled a considerable amount. One of their favourite destinations was Bath, where they went for their health and to escape from heat and overspending in London, or the isolation of the country. At Bath they relaxed amongst friends, read books, ate and drank, rode, danced, gambled and shopped and consulted doctors.

They shopped at Bertrand's toyshop. It was at the heart of Bath, within a few paces of the two assembly rooms, the Pump Room and the river. It appears that Bertrand also operated as a banker. Everyone who visited Bath would have passed the shop nearly

p. 132

Snuff box, silver, the lid mounted with vellum under glass, English, *c.* 1725. Width: 8 cm (3⅛ in). (Albert)

every day; most of those who could afford to would undoubtedly have crossed its threshold. Bertrand's bank account shows us the people who lived in and visited Bath.

In 1981 R. S. Neale wrote, '… there were many elements in early eighteenth-century society shaping the market for Bath. … What really mattered in the production of the city were the myriad responses to the market by thousands of obscure and little known persons and the social and economic milieu in which they moved.'[4] Paul Bertrand and his wife Mary Deards can be counted amongst those 'obscure and little known persons' who contributed so much to the development of Bath. In London, Mary's sister Elizabeth Chenevix and her brother William Deards were less obscure, in that they feature in contemporary letters and literature. They do so because of their personalities and because their toyshops were the best: they knew the importance of location, of fashion, and of liquidity — somehow they got their aristocratic customers to pay their bills.

The eighteenth-century use of the word toy is now largely redundant. A toy was a small and desirable luxury item. It had a function, such as a box to hold snuff, scent or patches, but could vary widely in the materials from which it was made and its practicality, and in its cost. From the seventeenth century the terms toyshop and India Warehouse were used to describe a shop whose stock encompassed a great variety of objects made in many different materials, some useful but many purely decorative. An India Warehouse mainly stocked porcelain, lacquer and textiles from the East (items imported from China and Japan via India by the East India Company), whereas a toyshop's stock leaned towards small metalwares. It is difficult to determine how individual shopkeepers who specialised but also stocked a wide range of goods, described their business. Some sold children's toys, some did not, and no doubt there were those that had a reputation for specialising in certain types of objects. It is very often impossible to distinguish between a jeweller, goldsmith, silversmith, cutler and a toyman, terms that were used fluidly by shopkeepers depending on the particular emphasis of their stock.

Ownership of luxury goods, and the cost and quality of those trinkets, is, and always has been, an indicator of wealth, status and taste — and on another level, is emblematic of power.[5] A toyshop supplied such things, but many toymen were ridiculed for selling objects that became increasingly decorative and non-functional. Wills and other papers reveal the significance of personal possessions both for sentimental reasons and as bankable wealth — which is why so many are quoted here. Regardless of whether their owner came from the lower or middling classes, lesser gentry or aristocracy, possessions were (and are) a route to understanding individuals and a period.

The discovery of Paul Bertrand's bank account transformed this research from a narrow summary of the lives of the Deards family into a wide-ranging study of the creators, retailers and consumers of toys, of which the present volume is the first part. The only comparable business records found so far are those of the Wickes/Wakelin/Garrard firm of silversmiths and the Webb family of jewellers.[6] Previous authors on the subject have veered toward the last four decades of the eighteenth century because of the paucity of earlier material. Bertrand's bank account redresses the balance and has made viable a study of luxury retailing in the first half of the century. It reveals much, but tantalises with information that cannot properly be pursued. Nonetheless, the daily life of Bath springs from the ledgers' pages.

The 'old' bank, or shop, of Hoare & Co., watercolour, T. H. Shepherd. Depicted before demolition and rebuilding in 1829. The sign of the Golden Bottle is in the pediment over the door. Deards' toyshop was immediately to the right of the bank until 1742. (Hoare) [▶ p. 211/10 map]

Roger Jones has written that 'it behoves anyone sitting down to write a book and add one more to the print mountain, to ask themselves the careful and sober question, "Why am I doing this?"'[7] Unlike much writing of this genre today, this research is unconnected to any academic thesis, formal research project or gainful employment — so I have asked myself this question many times. I subscribe to Mr Jones's response to the question:

Reality is a walled and secret garden and we are on the outside, trying to see in. We peep through holes and cracks, we dangle precariously from branches of overhanging trees, we balance on wobbly ladders, we stand on each others' shoulders … Our reward is snatched and fuzzy glimpses, no two the same, no one complete. So, trying always to construct a larger picture of the world, we compare notes. That is why people talk to each other. And that is why people write books. And why other people read them.

Bath was a walled city with secret gardens. The toyshop, hitherto misunderstood or forgotten, is proving to be the honeypot that attracted people (patrons, shopkeepers and craftsmen), skills and raw materials that are usually looked at today in isolation. There seems also to have been an affinity between toymen and toywomen, who knew about 'show', and entertainers — actors, singers, writers and puppeteers. Theatre and writing require a backdrop, a scene needs to be set for the reader: 'fuzzy glimpses' can be made clearer by maps and by images of 'then and now'. And so the following seven pages position the principal buildings and shops of Bath in the first half of the eighteenth century, and place the Bertrands' toyshop in Terrace Walk centre stage.

INTRODUCTION   17

Location of the toyshop in Terrace Walk, Bath

Terrace Walk in 2013. The newsagent (with an awning) was part of Leake's bookshop; Paul and Mary Bertrand's toyshop was to its left. The bookshop also comprised the next shop in the row, which was part of the projecting corner building seen in the watercolour opposite and on p. 192. Wiltshire's assembly rooms (the lower rooms) were next to the shop at the left of this photograph [▶ p. 23 map].

The rear of the buildings in Terrace Walk in 2013. The building with the bay was Leake's bookshop. To the right was Paul and Mary Bertrand's toyshop.

Detail of the trade card of Benjamin Cole who, with his wife Martha, kept a lace shop in St Paul's Churchyard, London. The toyshop in Bath would have had a similar layout. (BM)

18 BERTRAND'S TOYSHOP IN BATH

Terrace Walk, watercolour, early nineteenth century, by an unknown artist. (VAG)

Changes to the layout of Terrace Walk are illustrated on pp. 40–41. The surviving row of shops was built in 1728 but was considerably altered in the nineteenth century. Four houses, as described by the architect John Wood, can be seen between the assembly rooms (with three high round windows) and the bookshop of James Leake (partly at right angles to the other shops). In the photographs opposite taken in 2013, the newsagent's shop (with the awning) has a bay at the rear, which was the reading area of the bookshop. The projecting building, also part of the bookshop, was demolished c. 1830, by which time the archway to Orange Grove had already gone. The shops were then re-faced and re-fenestrated. At the time the watercolour was executed, Leake's shop [▶ p. 178] had been taken over by Lewis Bull.

The watercolour is deceptive, as it makes Terrace Walk look wider than the 8.25 m (27 ft) mentioned by John Wood. Today, the shop's frontage is approximately 4.5 m wide (14 ft 9 in); it no longer has the window set high in the basement behind a grille, which gave light to the kitchen. The overall depth of the building is about 12 m (39 ft). Deliveries must have arrived at the rear of the building, to be taken directly into the basement or into a vault under the garden. The vault is approximately 5.8 m × 3.65 m (19 ft × 12 ft). Inside the shop, there is an arch between the front room and the rear, which may be original. The way the shop space was utilised and how the stock was divided between the front and back rooms can only be guessed, but there would have been show cases and counters, with a room for private transactions behind, like those in Benjamin Cole's trade card. The first floor could have had retail space also, and there must have been a workbench near a window for the craftsmen, and a desk or desks for the book-keeping involved in running any shop.

INTRODUCTION 19

Joseph Gilmore's map of Bath, detail, 1694, published in 1717. Created to assist visitors, the map is bordered with images of lodging houses and inns. (Bath in Time, 27286/30558)
▶ pp. 118, 142, 153

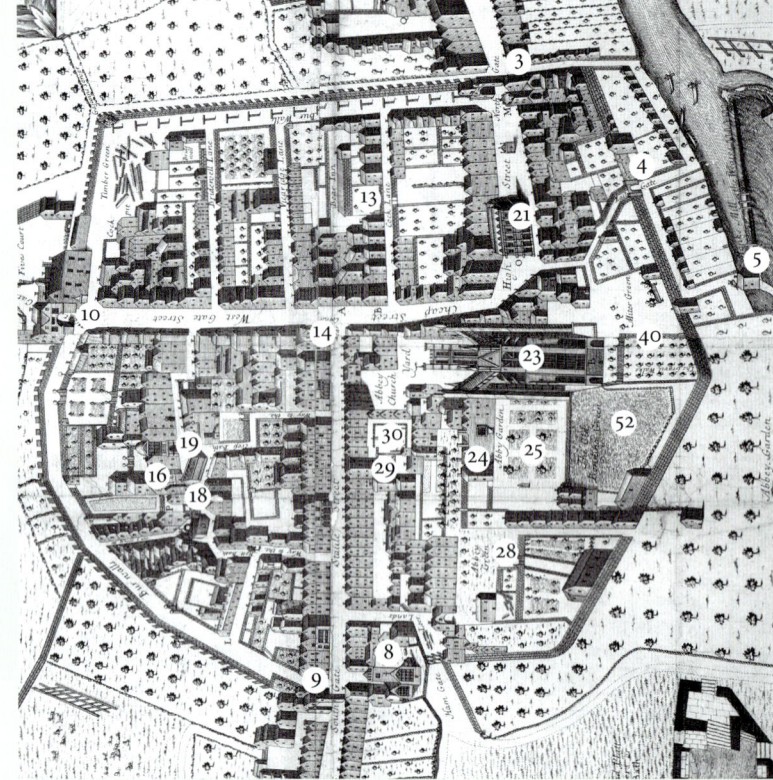

John Wood's map of Bath, detail, 1735.
▶ p. 24

p. 21 Map of Bath, detail, Jacob Henry Cotterell, 1852. Cotterell's office in Terrace Walk was formerly Paul and Mary Bertrand's shop. (Bath in Time, 30569)

pp. 22–23 Map, Mike Chapman 2013, drawn to show the centre of Bath *c.* 1730–55, when Paul and Mary Bertrand were there.

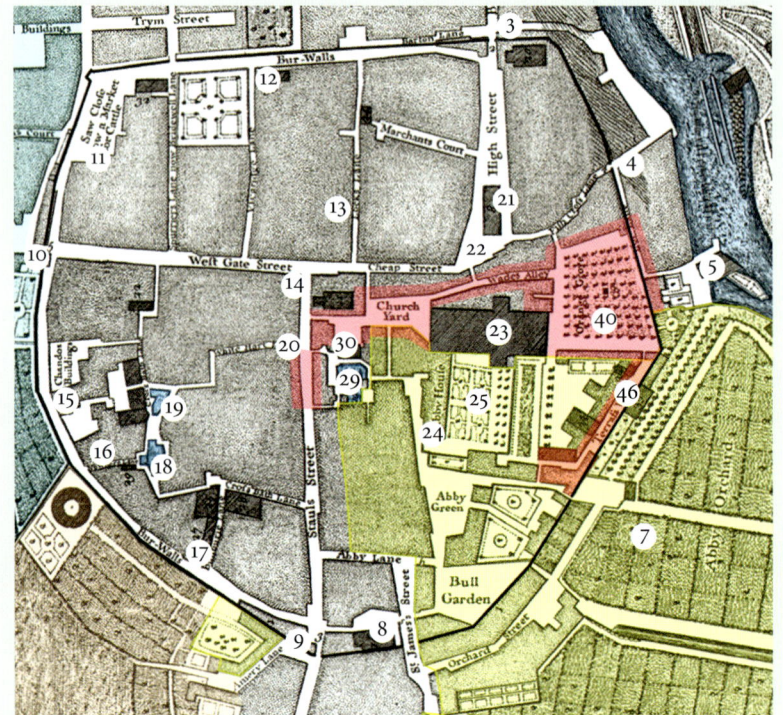

20   BERTRAND'S TOYSHOP IN BATH

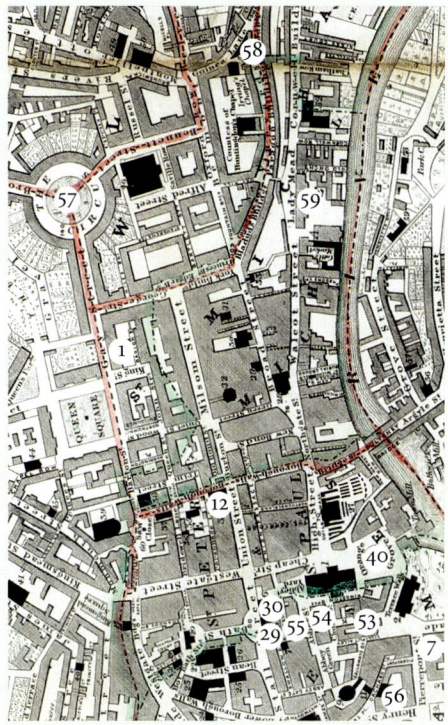

Key to the maps on pp. 20–24.

01　Houses of Paul Bertrand and William Hoare
02　Lady Inchiquin's garden
03　North Gate
04　East Gate
05　Monks Mill
06　Summerhouse
07　South and North Parade, built 1740–48
08　St James's Church
09　South Gate
10　West Gate
11　Richard Nash's house
12　Playhouse, later the Mineral Water Hospital
13　Bear Inn
14　Bear Corner, generally regarded as the 'centre' of Bath
15　Chandos lodging house
16　Savile/Skrine lodging house
17　Bell Tree, Catholic lodging house
18　Hot Bath
19　Cross Bath
20　White Hart Inn
21　Guildhall and Market House
22　Market Place: shops included Francis Bennet, Philip Masters, Jacob Skinner, Samuel Howse
23　Abbey Church of St Peter
24　Abbey House, royal lodgings; later the site of the Kingston Bath (54)
25　Abbey House gardens and walks
26　Ralph Allen's house
27　Old Post House
28　Abbey Green
29　Queen's bath
30　King's bath
31　Pump room
32　Mrs Taylor
33　Abbey churchyard
34　William Rogers
35　Wades Passage: shops included William Clement, Philip Masters
36　Moses Roubel
37　Morgan's coffee house
38　Lord Hawley's house
39　Nassau House, next to steps leading to the ferry across the river to Spring Gardens
40　Orange Grove, formerly The Gravel Walks. On Gilmore's map, the label 'Mitre Green' should probably have been 'Outer Green'
41　Orange Grove shops, at different periods, included Benjamin Axford, Walton sisters, George Speren, John Wickstead, William Frederick
42　Phillip Hayes, next to the archway between Orange Grove and Terrace Walk
43　Assembly rooms: Harrison, then Elizabeth Hayes and, later, Simpson
44　Harrison's walks and gardens
45　James Leake's bookshop, later Lewis Bull
46　Paul and Mary Bertrand's toyshop
47　Terrace Walk shops included: Leonard Coward, John & Joanna Davis; John Pyke
48　Lower assembly rooms: Mary Lindsey, Catherine Lovelace, Wiltshire family. Demolished 1805 to create York Street
49　Site of Charles Delamain's house, demolished 1728.
50　Benjoy's coffee house
51　Concert room and puppet theatre
52　Old Bowling Green
53　Ralph Allen's garden, formerly part of the bowling green
54　Kingston Baths, built 1763–66 on the site of Abbey House (24)
55　Site of Roman baths, excavated in the 1880s
56　Orchard Street theatre, built 1750
57　The Circus, 1755–67
58　St Swithin's church, rebuilt 1777–80
59　Ladymead

INTRODUCTION　21

The red strip represents the line of the first row of shops in Terrace Walk, before it was rebuilt in 1728 [▶ pp. 41 and 76]. The white horizontal line shows York Street, created in 1805, when the lower assembly rooms were demolished.

INTRODUCTION 23

A plan of the City of Bath in the County of Somerset. Copied from the Original Survey of Mr John Wood of BATH Architect. 1735. Engraved by J. Pine, published by J. Leake October 27, 1736. The original map is rotated to show north at the top and is adapted to show land ownership within the city [▶ key on p. 21]: GREY: *City corporation, including a few freeholds;* RED: *luxury shops area;* YELLOW: *John Hall/ Duke of Kingston;* GREEN: *Robert Gay (Walcot Parish);* BROWN: *Robert Gay (St James's Parish);* BLUE: *St John's Hospital, Bath (Walcot Parish). (Bath in Time, 30560/Mike Chapman)*

Part One

Paul Bertrand and Mary Deards

Monument to Paul Bertrand in St Swithin's Church, Walcot, Bath.

A virtuoso seeks painted trifles and fantastic toys
And eagerly pursues imaginary joys

MARK ARKENSIDE, *THE VIRTUOSO*

Paul Bertrand in London

PAUL BERTRAND DESCRIBED HIMSELF as a goldsmith when he was naturalised in London in 1709. It is possible to piece together the bare outline of his early life in London, but whether he trained as a maker of objects, a trader in them, or as a banker, is an unanswered question. Once in Bath following his second marriage in 1730, the evidence of Bertrand's bank account suggests he may have been involved in markets other than luxury goods, in addition to the toyshop. The spread of his interests, and of his business partners, will emerge later in this book. These early chapters chart the few facts that are known of the first four decades of his life.

In crossing the Channel from France to England, Bertrand's parents had followed a course taken by numerous Protestants in the run up to, and following, the revocation of the Edict of Nantes by Louis XIV in 1685.[8] England, and London in particular, had long been a place where the skills of foreign craftsmen and merchants were appreciated. It was the number of people who came with their families, and the range of their skills, that made the Huguenot influx of the late seventeenth century different from earlier generations of immigrants.

Paul Bertrand's father, also Paul, was born in Saintonge, a district of France just north of Bordeaux, on 5 January 1657. He became a clergyman. On 20 October 1685 he married Marie Gribelin at St Mary's, the French Church of the Savoy in London; he was aged about twenty-eight, she was eighteen.[9] Her family came from Blois (on the Loire) where they were engaged in the making and decoration of watches and their cases.[10] Her brother Simon (1661/2–1733) was one of the most gifted engravers of his generation working in London. His son Samuel (Bertrand's cousin, 1694–1784) was also in the engraving and print-selling business. The cousins remained in contact and had financial dealings, as evidenced by Bertrand jnr's later bank account.

pp. 33–35

Shortly after their marriage Paul snr and Marie Bertrand, together with his brother John (also a minister), crossed the Atlantic. Presumably aware of the risks this involved, Paul Bertrand snr made a will in 1686/7. He and his wife settled at 'Cox-Hay' on the Patuxent River in Calvert County, Maryland, where their son Paul was born. The year of his birth, probably 1689, has to be

p. 30 map

THE FAMILY OF PAUL BERTRAND

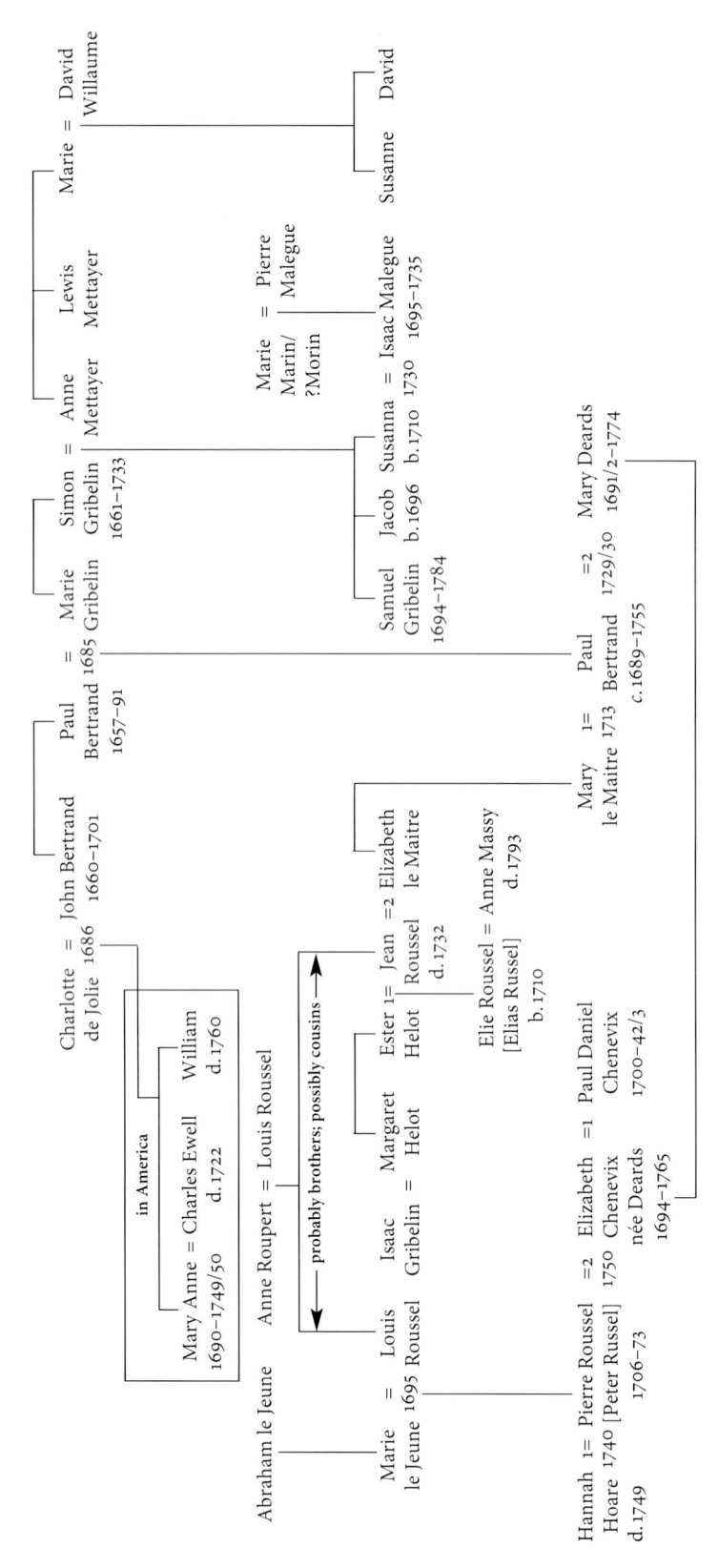

calculated from conflicting information about his later life and from his monument. The family's attempt at a new life in America did not last long: Paul snr's will was proved in 1691 and his widow and Paul jnr must have returned to England shortly after his death.[11] In 1694 Marie Bertrand was godmother to her nephew Samuel Gribelin at La Patente chapel, Soho.

p. 26 illus.

Whereas Paul snr and Marie Bertrand settled in Maryland, his brother John (b. 1660) went to Rappahanock, Virginia. Before leaving London he had married Charlotte de Jolie in September 1686 at St Paul's Cathedral. John's will was proved in August 1701, in which his nephew Paul jnr was a beneficiary.[12] John and Charlotte had two children: William (d. 1760), and Mary Ann (1690 – February 1749/50) who in 1710 married Charles Ewell, known as the probable builder of the first capitol building in Williamsburg.

Apart from one documented mention,[13] Paul Bertrand jnr is off record for the whole of his childhood and adolescence. In London, if an apprentice was bound for no consideration outside the jurisdiction of the City, it was not necessary to record the apprenticeship with the Inland Revenue — which is probably why there appears to be no record of Bertrand being apprenticed. The usual age to complete an apprenticeship was about twenty-one or twenty-two; he must have been only about twenty when he took English nationality on 3 July 1709. He described himself as a goldsmith living in the parish of St Martin-in-the-Fields. He may have trained as a practising goldsmith or in banking or retailing, with a member of his mother's family (a Gribelin) or the family of his future wife (the Roussels), with Isaac Gribelin (a goldsmith at the Savoy in 1706 and Leicester Fields in 1710), or with a jeweller called John Bertrand — but no relationship to the last two has been established.[14] Bertrand's witnesses at his naturalisation were Michel Cabaret Lagarene and Antoine Rigal. Both men, like Bertrand, gave their occupation as a goldsmith (Rigal was a mounter of boxes and other small items) — each man acted as witness for the other two.[15]

No record has been found of Bertrand becoming a freeman of a livery company or of the City of London, but this would not have been necessary if he was working outside the City or within a liberty.[16] In 1712 he took as apprentice Francis Neale, whose father Francis, of Tower Hamlets, belonged to the Company of Turners. This was probably a private arrangement.[17] Francis Neale might subsequently have been the 'Mr Neal' who was the proprietor of a toyshop at the sign of the Blue Last and Comb, 'over against' the White Hart Inn in The Borough, Southwark.[18] He might have been Bertrand's link with this area of London, as Bertrand is recorded

LONDON

The liberty of the Savoy, the church of St Mary le Strand and part of the parish of St Clement Danes, taken from John Strype's 1720 edition of John Stow's *Survey of London*. The church of St Clement is to the east and not shown; most of the parish was east of the Savoy and Somerset House, but small areas were west of the Savoy and north of the Strand, taking in Exeter Exchange. (Motco)

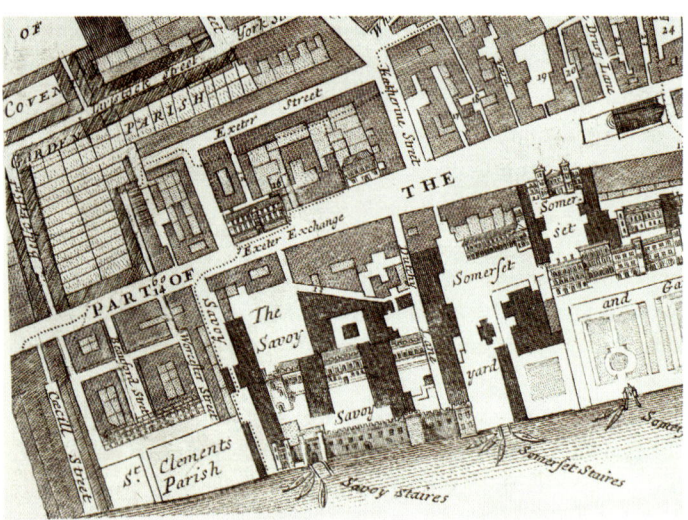

AMERICA

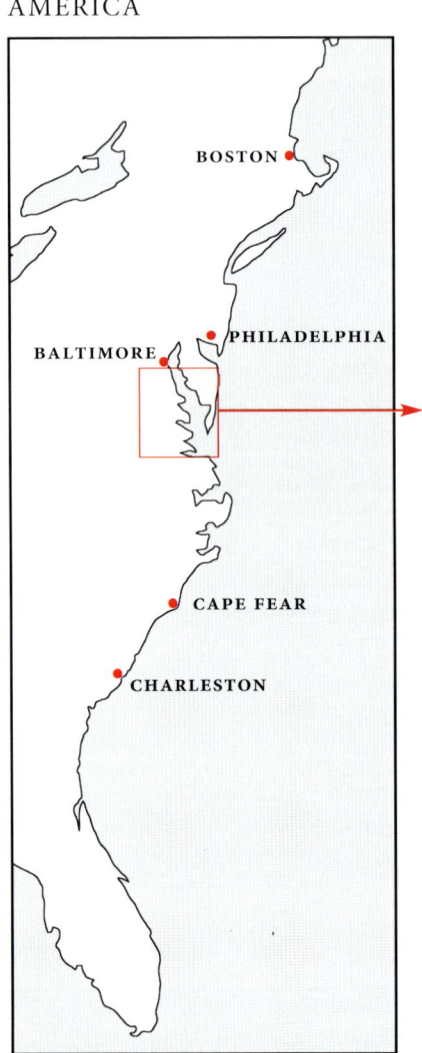

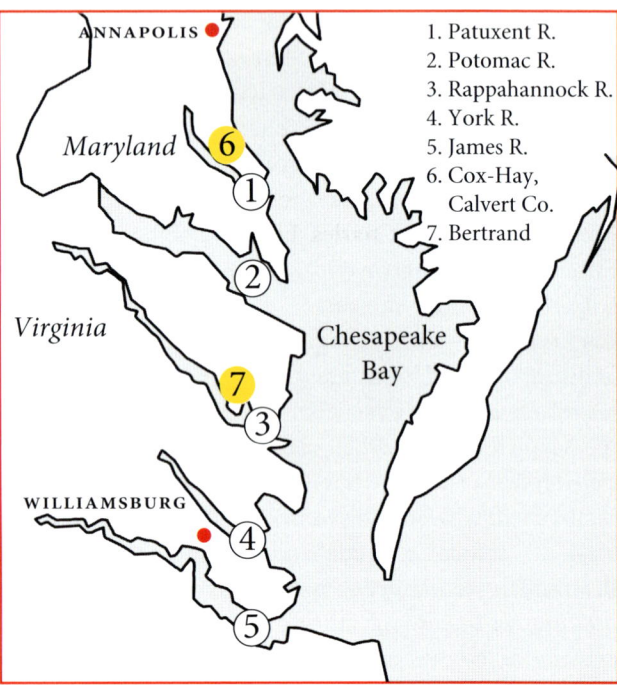

1. Patuxent R.
2. Potomac R.
3. Rappahannock R.
4. York R.
5. James R.
6. Cox-Hay, Calvert Co.
7. Bertrand

Paul Bertrand's parents and uncle went to America, where Paul was born in Calvert County, Maryland, *c.*1689. His uncle was minister in the settlement of Bertrand, Virginia. Paul Bertrand's second wife, Mary Deards, bequeathed their house in Bath to the daughter of Peter Russel and Hannah Hoare [▶p.202] whose husband, George Lewis, saw active service at Louisburg (1758) and Bunker's Hill (1775). Mary Bertrand's nephew, William Deards, went to Annapolis. One of Bertrand's customers, Mary Dering [▶p.162], spent her childhood in America and bequeathed toys to friends in Charleston and Cape Fear, Carolina.

at a lodge meeting of freemasons in Southwark in November 1725, held at the Bull's Head.[19] Some of the men closest to Bertrand were freemasons, such as William Deards and members of the Roussel family. When Francis Neale was apprenticed to him, Bertrand gave his address as in the parish of St Clement Danes and he was living in the same parish when he married for the first time the following year. The marriage licence records him as 'Gent', which adds to the uncertainty about the precise nature of his work. It may refer to his status as the son of a clergyman, and certainly suggests he was of higher status than a mere artisan. Frustratingly his name does not appear in rate books for St Clement Danes during the period he described himself as living there — so he must have rented rooms from a rate-payer and/or worked for someone else. His invisibility might be explained if he was within the liberty of the Savoy (which covered parts of the parishes of St Clement Danes and St Mary le Strand as well as the precinct of the Savoy), for which records have not survived. p. 30 map

His most likely connection in the parish was the Prosser family. William Prosser worked for the Deards family and is mentioned in the wills of Mary Deards and her son William. Thomas Prosser was in Milford Lane, which runs from St Clement Danes church down to the river.[20] Further possible connections are the toymen Peter Parquot and Charles Lilley, who had adjacent shops in Fountaine Court, just west of the Savoy.[21] Others who are in the St Clement Danes rate books of the 1720s, and became better known as toymen in later decades, are 'Ragdale' and Robert Chadd,[22] who had shops in Exeter Market. A John Neale was there too, and in 1717 a 'Mr Neale' in the precinct of the Savoy just might be of interest because of Bertrand's apprentice.[23] Bertrand could have been associated with any of these men. pp. 180 and 304

Bertrand was twenty-four years of age when he married Mary Magdalen Lemaitre on 9 December 1713 at St James's Piccadilly. She was about nineteen, and required the permission of Paul Dufour to marry, as her parents were living in Paris.[24] The marriage linked Bertrand to the Roussel [Russel] family.[25] Paul and Mary Magdalen Bertrand had three children. The first child, Samuel, was baptised on 19 September 1714; his godparents were his grandmother, Marie Bertrand, and Nicolas Rousselet. On 29 April 1718 Magdelaine le Maitre and 'Mr Gribelin' (possibly Simon or Isaac) were godparents to the second child, Marie Magdelaine. Thirdly came Elizabeth, baptised on 15 May 1719, whose godparents were Samuel Gribelin and Elizabeth Roussel. All three baptisms took place in the chapel of the Savoy where, in 1723, Bertrand was in turn godfather to Jean and Elizabeth Roussel's son, Paul.[26] None of Paul and Mary Magdalen's children appears to have survived pp. 28 tree and 227 into adulthood and Mary Magdalen died some time before 1730, when Bertrand remarried.

Bertrand's circle was established in these years in London: friendships that would last for the rest of his life and extend, through Pierre Roussel (hereafter written as Peter Russel) to include the Hoare family in Bath and, through his own second marriage, the Deards family. Whether through the circumstances of his move to Bath in 1730 or because of compatibility of temperament, Bertrand seems not to have been as close to the Deards as to the Russels and Hoares, his closest friends in later years.

pp. 203 and 239

Given the location of where he spent this first part of his life, centred on the Savoy, it seems entirely likely that, if Bertrand was a working goldsmith, he supplied John and William Deards with boxes and similar smallwork. If Bertrand was instead, or perhaps also, acting as a retailer, merchant or banker in London, he might still have had dealings with the Deards family, whose Fleet Street toyshop was one of the best in London.

The only further clue to Bertrand's occupation in London is his monument, which reveals conventions used by portraitists. A merchant or banker would usually have been depicted wearing a wig. A cap such as the one worn by Bertrand denotes an artist, a craftsman or, in some examples, an aristocrat who chose to be depicted as a patron of the arts and science. The monument could be confirmation that Bertrand did indeed begin life as a maker of gold boxes, or at the very least, that he did not regard himself as a 'money man'.

Monuments, documents and bank ledgers establish the existence of a man such as Paul Bertrand. But the glimpses of his life afforded by such records leave gaps, like dots on a blank sheet, and many dots remain unlinked. The temptation to join the dots by speculation has been reined in, and so in a series of short chapters the first part of this book outlines the bare facts of Bertrand's family and associates. In later parts of the book it has been possible to join more of the dots and make links to contemporary society, and so portray the lives of Paul and Mary Bertrand as a window into the life of eighteenth-century Bath.

Detail from an album of pulls from his own engraving compiled by Simon Gribelin, early eighteenth century. (BM)

The Gribelin family

The reason for the large number and high monetary value of Paul Bertrand's payments through his bank account to Samuel Gribelin [▶ p. 278], cannot at present be explained. They must be too great for engraving work, given that in 1735 Gribelin was advertising prints by his father Simon Gribelin (sold also by Bertrand) at 8s, or 16s, for a set of six.[27] Between 1738 and 1746 there are 34 debit entries in the bank account amounting to £2,396.

There were several branches of the Gribelin family in London; they came from Blois about 1680.[28] Isaac Gribelin was a goldsmith who in 1706 married Margaret Helot (from a family of watch casemakers) at the Huguenot Chapel in Spring Gardens. Simon Gribelin (1661/62–1733) was an engraver, naturalised in 1682 and free of the Clockmakers' Company in 1686. He married Anne Mettayer [▶ p. 28]. Her brother Lewis was a silversmith and her sister Mary married the silversmith David Willaume; their father, Samuel Mettayer was pastor of the church of La Patent, Soho. The Mettayer/Willaume/Gribelin families were at the heart of the Huguenot community.

Simon Gribelin lived in Long Acre; in 1710 he was at 'Mr Glovers up two pair of stairs being the figure of the Lock and Three Keys', and in October 1716 he was 'at Mr Henry Friths a scrivener up the two pair of stairs Corner of Banbury Court in Long Acre'.[29] He engraved watch cases, reproductions of paintings, and plate, which he occasionally signed. He assembled pulls of his engraved work into albums now in the British Museum, Strawberry Hill and Christchurch, Oxford.[30]

Samuel Gribelin, the son of Simon and Anne, was born in 1694; Paul Bertrand's mother was a godparent. He was apprenticed to the silversmith Philip Rollos in April 1710 and then to his uncle, the silversmith Lewis Mettayer, in March 1710/11 for seven years, but it is likely that he was trained by his father as an engraver. Charles Oman attributed the engraving on the seal salvers of Sir Robert Eyre to Samuel on the grounds that, although it was in his father's manner 'the general effect lacks his vigour'.[31]

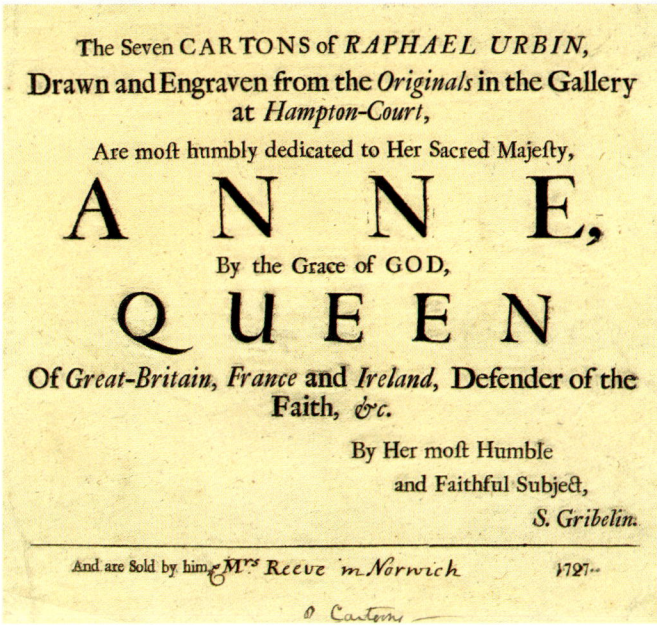

Printed title to The Seven Cartoons of Raphael Urbin, Simon Gribelin, 1707; this set sold by the jeweller Mrs Reeve in Norwich. In 1735 Samuel Gribelin advertised that the engravings were for sale at Paul Bertrand's shop in Bath, priced at 15s.
(BM, 1980.U.1589)

PAUL BERTRAND IN LONDON

 Engraving signed SG for Simon Gribelin. From a wine cistern, silver, Philip Rollos I, London 1699/1700. The arms are those of Evelyn Pierrepont, 5th Earl and later 1st Duke of Kingston-upon-Hull. (Hermitage) [▶ p. 92]

Snuff box, gold, unmarked, English *c.* 1720. Width: 7.6 cm (3 in). The base has a monogram RK below a viscount's coronet, in a decorative surround engraved in the manner of Simon Gribelin. (SL, 2.6.1992/5)

According to the engraver and antiquary George Vertue (1684–1756), Samuel 'had no great success and on that account engaged himself to the Earl of Kinnoul' (ambassador to Constantinople 1729–34).[32] On his return from Turkey he lived in Long Acre, where he advertised himself at 'Mr Pascall's, gilder, at the Golden Head over-against Hanover Street' [▶ pp. 186, 211/20 map]. One of the apprentices of James Pascall (c. 1697–1746) was Joshua Ross, who was later in Bath. Gribelin was godparent to Bertrand's third child, but appears not to have married or gained the freedom of a livery company. In 1750 'Samuel Griblin' was admitted to Charterhouse; he lived to be ninety and died there in 1784.[33] He is unlikely to have been admitted as a Brother in Charterhouse unless his circumstances required it, but it is not known what those circumstances were.

One explanation for the financial transactions between Samuel Gribelin and Bertrand could be that Gribelin was acting as some kind of London agent for Bertrand, who was his first cousin. A further possibility is that transactions were in some way linked to Pascall's workshop. It is still a mystery, but it is worth noting that until December 1746 the payments through Bertrand's bank account were debit entries: i.e. Bertrand was making payments to Gribelin. After Bertrand closed the shop in Bath money went in the other direction: Gribelin made five payments to Bertrand (credit entries in the ledgers), the last in 1752.

Title page to A Book of Severall Ornaments, engraving, Simon Gribelin, 1682. (BM, Gg,6.2.1)

An Ode for Musick on St Cecilia's Day, engraving, Samuel Gribelin. For the cantata composed by George Frederick Handel in 1739 as a setting of John Dryden's poem to the patron saint of music.
(BM, 1876.11.11.645)

PAUL BERTRAND IN LONDON 35

THE DEARDS
FAMILY IN
LONDON

John Strype's 1720 edition of John Stow's map of London, numbered to show the shops of the Deards family and Paul Bertrand's associates. (Motco)

See the family tree on p. 38 and larger map pp. 211–13.

N.B. The positioning of the numbers gives approximate, not exact, locations.

1 John Deards followed by his son William Deards, in Fleet Street *c.* 1685–1742 [▶ p. 19].
2 Clerkenwell: Elizabeth Deards/Chenevix, probable seasonal shop.
3 Westminster Hall: John and William Deards, when Parliament in session [▶ p. 210].
4 William Wiltshire's office in Fleet Street 1772 [▶ p. 44].
5 Paul Bertrand, unknown locations in the parishes of Savoy, St Clement Danes and St Martin-in-the-Fields, before 1730 [▶ p. 30].
6 & 6a Peter Russel in Villiers Street, *c.* 1740s; moved to Suffolk Street *c.* 1748, then to Chenevix's. Sampson Bishop also in Villers Street and Suffolk Street.
7 William Deards, corner of Craven Street and the Strand, 1742–57.
8 Paul Daniel and Elizabeth Chenevix, Charing Cross, 1729 to his death 1742/43, continued by his widow alone until 1750, then with her second husband Peter Russel until her death in 1765 [▶ p. 259].
9 William and Mary Deards, Pall Mall, *c.* 1752–65.
10 William Deards followed by his son John Deards, corner of Dover Street and Piccadilly, 1757–83.
12 The Swan Inn, Holborn, terminus for Wiltshire's waggons [▶ p. 44].

Farewel to Deard's and all her toys,
Which glitter in her shop
Deluding traps to girls and boys,
The warehouse of the fop.

LADY MARY WORTLEY MONTAGU

Marriage to Mary Deards

PAUL BERTRAND'S INTENTION to marry for a second time was recorded on 27 January 1729/30:

> Appeared personally Paul Bertrand of the parish of St Clement Danes in the co. of Middx aged about forty years a widower and alledged that he intends to marry Mary Deards of the parish of St Dunstans in the West, London upwards of thirty years a spinster.

The ceremony took place a month later, on 24 February at Chelsea, the parish to which Mary's parents had retired.[34] The newly married couple went to live in Bath.

Interestingly, both Mary and her younger sister Elizabeth married at quite a late age. Elizabeth was thirty-two when she married Daniel Chenevix in 1726. Mary (baptised on 17 January 1691/92) was thirty-eight: 'upwards of thirty years' was correct, but she was nearer forty than thirty. The sisters had presumably spent their late teens and twenties working in the family business. Mary knew how to run a shop. Unfortunately, there are few clues as to how she and her new husband shared the work when they joined forces.

p. 38 tree

When Mary's father, John Deards, died in 1731 he was described as 'a Man well known at Newmarket, Bath and Tunbridge'.[35] He certainly had connections to Bath from 1716, when his name appears in Thomas Harrison's bank account on 6 December. Between then and December 1729 it seems that members of the Deards family and their staff took their turn to work in Bath. Mary Deards first features in July and September 1725 with Joseph Barker, and William Deards is listed in November that year; Joseph Creswell (who was apprenticed to John Deards in 1720) follows in May 1727 and in December 1728 Mrs Deards. Mary Deards and Paul Bertrand were there during the autumn season of 1729, shortly before their marriage.[36]

p. 202 tree

p. 222

There is nothing to indicate where Deards' seasonal shop was located in Bath, but he probably traded in Terrace Walk, close to the jeweller Charles Delamain, and it may be significant that they jointly advertised as early as 1700:[37]

p. 23 map

Grain Chains for Ladies to wear with Gold Watches, wholly Novel, exceeding fine and richly gilt, appearing to be and wearing like right Gold;

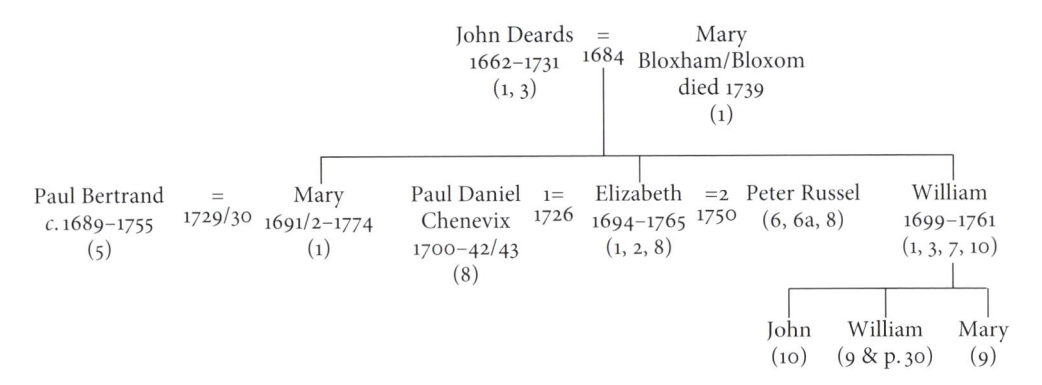

```
                John Deards    =    Mary
                1662–1731    1684   Bloxham/Bloxom
                  (1, 3)            died 1739
                                      (1)
```

Paul Bertrand	=	Mary	Paul Daniel	1=	Elizabeth	=2	Peter Russel	William
c. 1689–1755	1729/30	1691/2–1774	Chenevix	1726	1694–1765	1750	(6, 6a, 8)	1699–1761
(5)		(1)	1700–42/43		(1, 2, 8)			(1, 3, 7, 10)
			(8)					

                                                    John   William   Mary
                                                    (10)   (9 & p.30)   (9)

The family tree is numbered to match locations on p. 36.

The Deards family had shops in London for nearly a century, through three generations. The map shows locations of their seasonal shops in Tunbridge Wells, Newmarket and Scarborough, in addition to Paul and Mary Bertrand's shop in Bath. It also shows production centres and ports.

38   PART ONE: PAUL BERTRAND AND MARY DEARDS

together with a gilt Hook, curiously wrought, not made of a cast Brass, but of a fine composed metal, the Hook and Grain Chain are both stamped on the back side with this Mar [—] the Cypher Wallis his name, who is the only inventor and maker, and are sold by Mr Deards Toy-man under St Dunstans Church in Fleetstreet, and at his Shop at Tunbridge Wells, and Mr Delemain Goldsmith in Bristol, and at his Shop in the Walks at the Bath. The price is thirty shillings. Curious Prints of the said work are given gratis.

The 'fine composed metal' was probably the alloy known as Bath Metal. Delamain's role, not just as a jeweller, but also in the entertainments offered in Bath at the beginning of the century, is discussed on p. 99.

Mary Deards must have been aware of the building projects that were taking place in the city before her marriage. In 1728 Terrace Walk was widened and improved — here is John Wood's description:[38]

It is 27 feet broad in the Middle; contains four fourth Rate Houses, besides the two that are appropriated for General Assembly; and the whole Line of Building is Part of the new Works at the South East Corner of the City …

The key phrase here is 'the whole line of building is part of the new works'. As the series of maps of Terrace Walk shows, the first row of shops was demolished and rebuilt in order to widen the road. Charles Delamain's building was replaced with the new, lower, assembly rooms. At the other end was 'Mr Leake's Shop, the grand Museum of Bath', next to which was the Bertrands' shop — presumably one of the 'fourth rate houses'.[39]

The development of Bath at this time must surely have influenced Paul Bertrand's decision to move there when he re-married. Coupled with the financial prospects that would arise from John Deards' death the following year, it might have spurred him into this second marriage, which as Brian Beet commented, 'lifted Bertrand into the first rank of retailers'. Another factor may have been the death of a possible rival: John Hayward 'toyman of Bath' died in 1730.[40]

Bertrand had married into the first family of toymen. It is not known whether members of the Deards family were linked by a financial arrangement under which they ran their individual shops, or whether each operated entirely independently. The latter seems most likely, although there were clearly business dealings between them. In the months leading up to John Deards' death in 1731 there must have been discussion among his three children about the division of the business.

p. 166

pp. 40–41 maps

p. 19 illus.

Gold, enamel and lapis lazuli cased verge watch with quarter repeat, detail of the movement, signed 'P. D. Chenevix 851' as retailer of the watch. Provenance: The Dukes of Newcastle (Ashmolean, WA1947.191.110)

MARRIAGE TO MARY DEARDS 39

pp. 42–43

The earliest invoices for the shop in Bath that have been found so far are from October 1730: one dated 16 October to the Hon. Charles Fairfax, for £23 13s 11d, 'bought of P. Bertrand', and another receipted by Mary Bertrand on 30 October.[41] So the newlyweds were certainly in business in Bath eight months after their marriage. Their earliest advertisement dates from the spring of 1731, and tells us that Bertrand was selling in a way that was obviously not universal practice:[42]

Bath. March 20. The Nobility and Gentry, who frequent this Place, seem to be greatly pleased with the new and elegant Toyshop lately open'd by Mr Bertrand; and what is the more agreeable to them is the Manner in which all the Toys, Curiosities and Plate are sold; and that is by the price being mark'd upon the Goods, and sold at a Word.

Mary Bertrand's father died intestate in June 1731; her mother was granted administration of his estate in July 1732. Seven months after John snr's death, in January 1731/32, and exactly two years after Bertrand's second marriage, Bertrand borrowed £1,000 from his mother-in-law, presumably to expand the business. Her will refers to the arrangement:[43]

… Also I give the sum of One thousand pounds Secured to me by Bond from the said Paul Bertrand bearing date the Eighth day of January 1732 to my son William Deards Citizen and Cutler of London In trust to pay the Interest of the said Sum of One thousand pounds to the sole and separate use of my said Daughter Mary during her Life and after her

Map of Bath, Henry Savile, *c.* 1600. The line of the city walls can clearly be seen; the site of the shops in what became Orange Grove and Terrace Walk is undeveloped. The Abbey was begun in 1502, incorporating elements from the much larger Norman church, but is shown here with no roof to the nave and the south transept open and without windows – the result of its dissolution in 1539. Reconstruction began following the visit of Queen Elizabeth I to Bath in 1574. (Bath in Time, 25960)

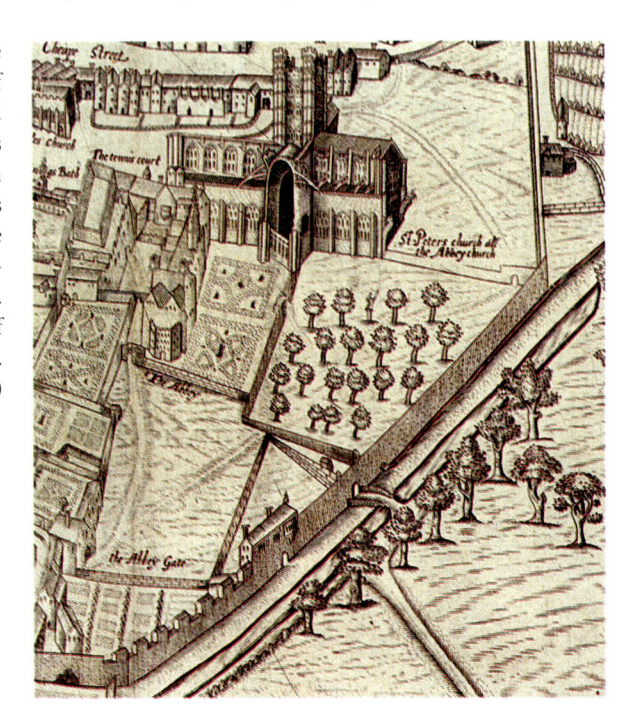

decease to pay five hundred pounds … to such Person or persons as [she] … shall direct and appoint and the rest … to my said Son William Deards for his own use and benefit …

Although part of the money could have been put aside in anticipation of acquiring a house that would soon become available in Barton Street, where Paul and Mary Bertrand were to live, most of the £1,000 would have gone into the business. Fitting out a toyshop could cost anything between £200 and £2,000 and some of the long-term loan could have been used for furnishings and stock. However, the real expense of setting up a top-end shop was the need to have sufficient capital to extend credit. It seems likely that quite soon after his move to Bath Bertrand entered into some kind of partnership with the Wiltshire family and this continued until his retirement. Bertrand took the scion of the family as apprentice: 'John Wiltshire son of Walter Wiltshire to Paul Bertrand Toyman & Jeweller pr 7 years' on 25 September 1732; the premium was £30.[44] John Wiltshire would have been taken on to learn the business of shopkeeping and banking, rather than to be a craftsman.

p. 70 illus.

For the sake of simplicity, in the following pages Paul Bertrand takes centre stage as shopkeeper, but the constant presence of his wife Mary Deards cannot be ignored. Although little survives to record her contribution, she must have had an important role. It was her inheritance that enabled the couple to set up shop, and she must have had at least twenty years' experience of working in Fleet Street before her marriage.

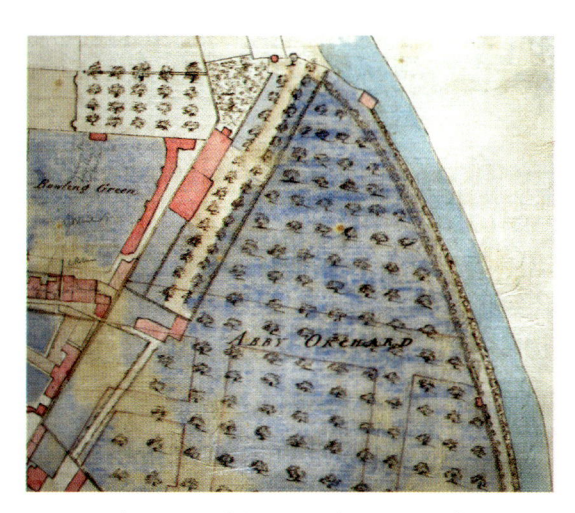

Copy made in 1882 of the original 1725 map of the estate of the Duke of Kingston in Bath. Kingston properties are shown in red; the Orange Grove shops are not depicted as they were not part of the duke's estate. The site of the Parades (completed 1748) is outlined over Abbey Orchard. (Bath in Time, 11409)

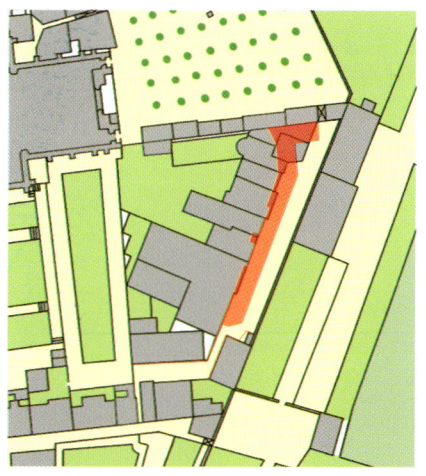

Terrace Walk, detail p. 23. The line of Terrace Walk shops shown on the Kingston map is overlaid in red on the 1728 rebuilding that survives today.

MARRIAGE TO MARY DEARDS 41

An early customer

Charles, 9th Viscount Fairfax, inherited the title on the death of his father in 1738. His first wife, Elizabeth, contracted smallpox in Bath and died there in 1721 aged 32; she is buried in Bath Abbey. A year later he was married again, to his cousin Mary Fairfax.

Lord Fairfax was obviously in Bath in October 1730, the date of the earliest invoices from the Bertrands' shop. From the date on a bill for lodgings [▶ p. 118], he seems to have returned to Bath the following spring.

A later invoice and an entry in Bertrand's bank account are interesting because of the unhappy background to the transaction.[45] On 26 May 1741 Lord Fairfax bought a diamond buckle and a chased silver tea kettle, which he paid for the next day in cash and by trading in some diamonds. His wife died on 1 July and was buried at Gilling five days later. Lord Fairfax must have gone back to Bath almost immediately, or sent an agent, for the ledgers at Hoare & Co. record on 30 July that Bertrand paid out £130 to Fairfax. It seems possible that Fairfax returned the buckle and kettle — possibly his last gifts to his wife — and took a ten per cent loss on the transaction.

Only one of the couple's nine children, Anne, outlived Lord Fairfax. In 1762 father and daughter moved into Fairfax House in York, but she sold it when her father died ten years later and went to live at the family estate, Gilling Castle. The family was staunchly Catholic. Among the artists and craftsmen they patronised in order to furnish the rococo interiors of Gilling and Fairfax House, was the London silversmith Frederick Kandler, who also worked for several other Catholic families.[46]

Invoice dated 16 October 1730 to 'Fairfax Esqr', the future 9th Viscount Fairfax. Bertrand charged the silver at 6s 2½d per ounce. The fashioning of the sauceboats was charged at 3s per ounce, whereas the fashioning of the candlesticks in a second invoice was charged at 2s 6d per ounce. (N. Yorks., micr 1128)

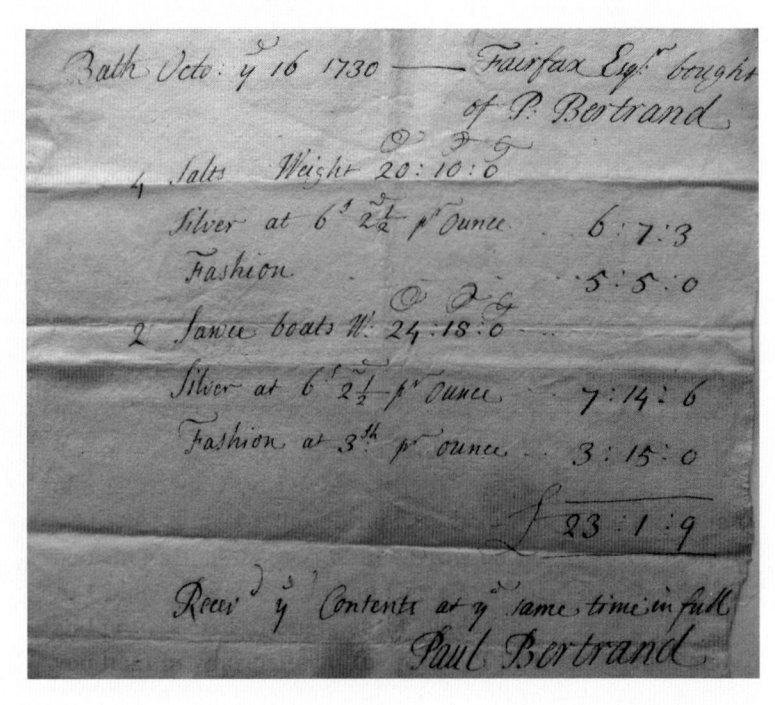

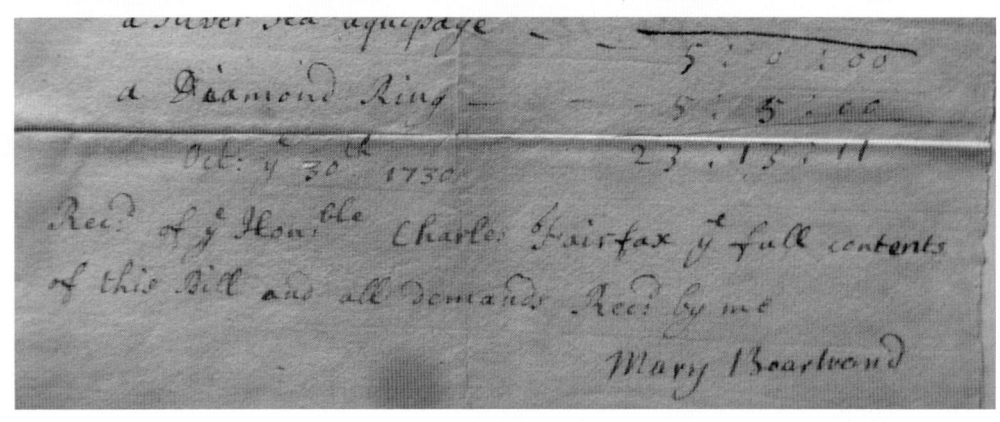

Invoice dated 30 October 1730 (detail). The Hon Charles Fairfax became 9th Viscount Fairfax in 1738. Only a few months after her marriage, Mary Bertrand has spelled her new surname phonetically, 'Beartrand', in the only known example of her handwriting. (N. Yorks., micr 1128)

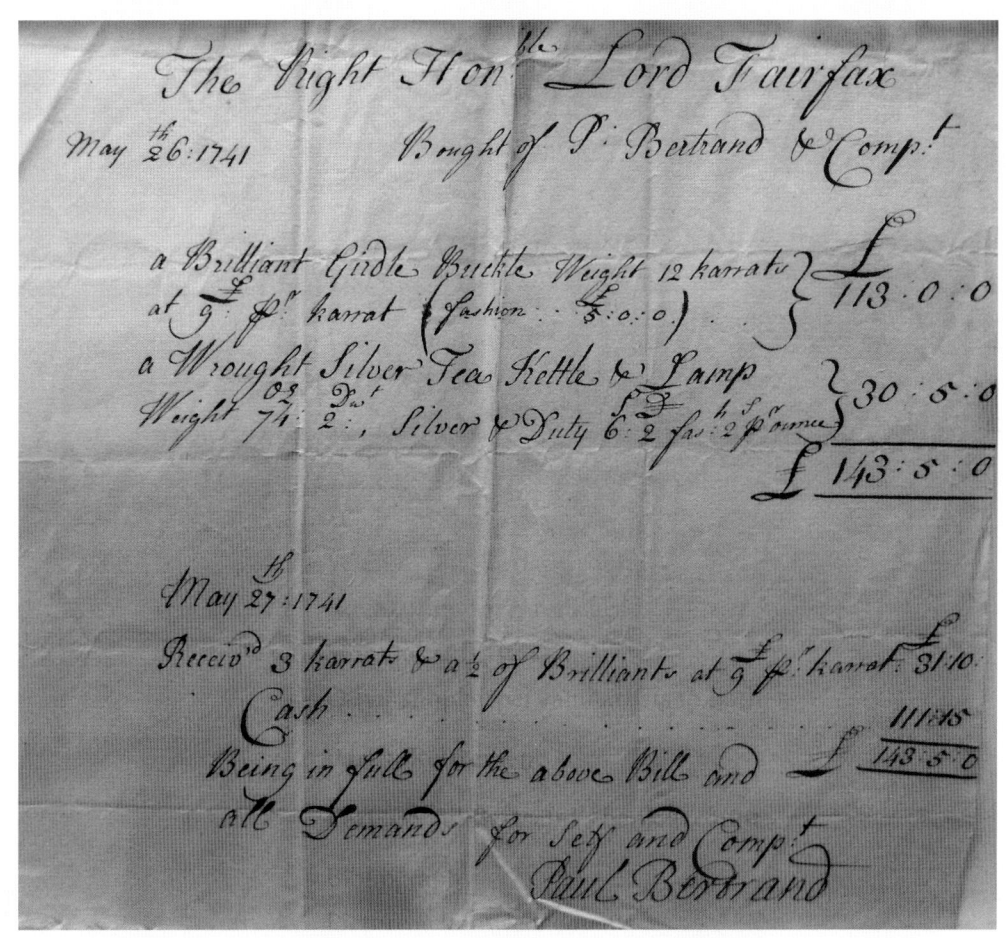

Invoice dated May 1741 to Viscount Fairfax. Bertrand signed for himself 'and compy': evidence of some kind of partnership. (N. Yorks.)

MARRIAGE TO MARY DEARDS 43

The North Side of Fleet Street, watercolour, William Capon (1757–1827), dated 1798. Temple Bar is at the left, the narrow street on the right is Bell Yard. It is a scene that would have been very familiar to Paul Bertrand and the Deards family. The corner building, once the residence of the writer Izaak Walton, has 'Willshire' painted above the door. William Wiltshire, younger brother of John and Walter, took on the building in 1772, indicating the continuing need for a London base for the carrier's business. Benjamin Rackstrow's Museum of Anatomy and Curiosities was two doors to the left, having previously been further east in Fleet Street. (LMA, 2346) [▶ p. 36/4 map]

The Swan Inn, Holborn Bridge, pen and ink on paper, A. Crosby, dated 1839. (LMA, 24478) [▶ p. 36/12 map]

44   PART ONE: PAUL BERTRAND AND MARY DEARDS

Being in full for the above Bill and all Demands for self and Compy

PAUL BERTRAND, *INVOICE TO VISCOUNT FAIRFAX*

Partnerships

THE WILTSHIRE FAMILY were 'common carriers' or waggoners in Bath, not toymen. They earn a place in this tale of toyshops because of a business relationship with Paul Bertrand. In London their main depot was at the Swan Inn in Holborn where their waggons came in on Tuesdays and Fridays and went out at 6 a.m. on Wednesdays and 12 noon on Fridays.[47] Later in the century they had an office in Fleet Street almost opposite Hoare & Co., where the family held several bank accounts. Their waggons would have carried supplies of all kinds to and from Bath, for tradesmen and for visitors, for which they charged by weight. For example when Gertrude Savile went to Bath in September 1746 she noted: 'Bringing by the carriers my chest & a hamper we 2hd 3q 14pd, at ¾d a pd 19s 11d'.[48]

The Wiltshires' business developed beyond that of a carrier. Their finances and widespread interests interweave with Bertrand's and skew the information culled from Hoare & Co.'s ledgers, so that instead of being a straightforward record of shopkeeping, the bank's accounts reveal a partnership of some complexity. It is possible that a man named Thomas Pomfret also had an interest in the business — he features in Paul Bertrand's will and appears to have lent Bertrand £500 at some stage; his signature 'For Self & Co.' is on a receipt from Bertrand & Co. dated 1746/47.[49]

p. 48 illus.

At the beginning of the eighteenth century there were four brothers: John, Walter, Thomas and Edward Wiltshire, of whom Walter plays a large part in Bertrand's story.[50] When Thomas Harrison retired from running his Bath assembly rooms in 1731, he may have left a vacuum that created an opportunity for Walter Wiltshire and for Bertrand. Like many goldsmiths of the day Bertrand would naturally have been drawn into banking, and no doubt many of the agents and brokers listed in his bank account were performing a similar service: 'There was hardly a big merchant in London between 1740 and 1800 whose business, if successful, did not ultimately carry him on to the confines, or even into the very centre, of pure finance. They turned from "merchandising" to banking and broking.'[51]

p. 46 tree

In 1732 Walter Wiltshire opened an account with Hoare & Co. that, over the following years, shows the names of many people who also feature in Bertrand's account and have no bearing on the toy business. Bertrand himself did not open an account with

THE WILTSHIRE FAMILY

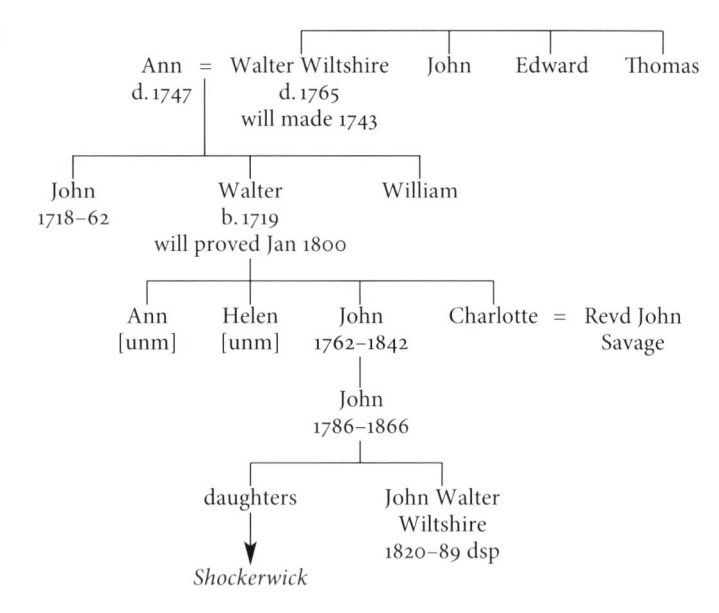

```
                    Ann  =  Walter Wiltshire    John    Edward   Thomas
                   d.1747    d.1765
                            will made 1743

          John          Walter          William
         1718–62        b.1719
                    will proved Jan 1800

       Ann      Helen      John       Charlotte  =  Revd John
      [unm]     [unm]    1762–1842                   Savage
                            |
                          John
                        1786–1866

              daughters        John Walter
                                Wiltshire
                               1820–89 dsp
              Shockerwick
```

Monument to Ann Wiltshire, Bath Abbey.

In the Choir of this Church, lieth interred the Body of Mrs ANN WILTSHIRE, who departed this Life, June 11th 1747; Aged 53 Years.

She left Issue three Sons, who caused this Monument to be erected to her Memory

Shockerwick House, built in the 1770s for Walter Wiltshire to the designs of John Palmer. John Wiltshire purchased part of the estate and after his death his brother Walter acquired further land.

46   PART ONE: PAUL BERTRAND AND MARY DEARDS

Hoare's until 1736. It may be that a business relationship between Bertrand and the Wiltshire family began quite soon after Bertrand's arrival in Bath; Walter's son John was apprenticed to Bertrand on 25 September 1732. The fact that Walter apprenticed his eldest son away from the carrier's business must be an indication of his wider ambitions; and it might say something about the character and abilities of John who, born in 1718, would have been fourteen years of age when apprenticed and twenty-one on completion of his term in 1739. If Paul and Mary Bertrand employed men of the calibre of Moses Roubel as assistants in the toyshop, perhaps John Wiltshire's apprenticeship was not aimed at retailing toys (though he would have had to learn something of it) but at banking. John Wiltshire might have become Bertrand's partner when he completed his apprenticeship, but any partnership arrangement could also have included his father or his brother Walter. Entries on the debit side of Bertrand's bank account to Ann, John and Walter Wiltshire all begin in 1739.[52] *p. 58 illus.*

It is possible that relations were strained between Walter and his wife Ann. There is no mention of her in his will and no mention of him on her monument in Bath Abbey.[53] When Ann Wiltshire took over management of the lower rooms in 1741 John may have divided his time between the toyshop and helping his mother. The earliest invoice found with the mention of 'P. Bertrand & Compy' (to Lord Fairfax) is dated May 1741. Following Bertrand's retirement James Tilley advertised himself as 'French Jeweller from Mess Bertrand and Wiltshire', and the business was also referred to as 'Bertrand & Co.' or 'Messrs Bertrand's and Wiltshire's' in advertisements during November 1747.[54] *p. 46 illus.*

The year 1743 was a turning point in the way the business operated. Walter snr seems to have been putting his affairs in order (including making a will) before handing over to his three sons.[55] A steep rise in transactions through Bertrand's bank account began in 1743 and continued to 1747, the year in which Ann Wiltshire died and the shop in Terrace Walk was closed.[56] In the last four years of the shop's trading it seems that transactions unrelated to the toyshop which might previously have gone through Walter snr's account were put through Bertrand's instead.[57] *pp. 54–55 graphs*

Following the closure of the shop John Wiltshire went to run his mother's assembly rooms — which he did until his death in 1762. His brother Walter opened an account with Hoare & Co. in his own name and continued the carrier's business. Although they shared out the family's interests, they worked closely together and with their brother William. In retirement Bertrand continued to receive irregular payments from Walter; so did Samuel Gribelin and Bath tradespeople familiar through Bertrand's own dealings

PARTNERSHIPS 47

Approximately once a year Bertrand went to his bankers in London to sign the record of his account. Here he signs the account of Walter Wiltshire – proof of a close business relationship. 'I Paul Bertrand by vertue of an order under ye hand of Mr Walter Wiltshire, have examined ye accot & find ye same to be true & just & have recd from Mr Ben: Hoare & Co all ye vouchers for mony paid in ye same, Witness my hand ye 20th Augt 1740, Paul Bertrand.' (Hoare)

Invoice to Sir Richard Hoare for rappee and other items. Receipted 4 March 1746/47 'for Self & Co:' by Thomas Pomfret, whose connection with the business of P. Bertrand & Co. is unclear. (Hoare)

48   PART ONE: PAUL BERTRAND AND MARY DEARDS

such as Leake, Coward and the Walton sisters. The Wiltshires continued the banking side of Bertrand's business.[58]

During the 1740s events were unfolding outside the shop that had an impact on the assembly rooms and exposed the Wiltshire family's association with Richard Nash. There is no evidence that Bertrand played any part in this, other than the fact that the names of three of Richard Nash's associates feature in his bank account.

In 1738 … the Gaming Act made it an offence to keep any place where games such as ace of hearts, faro, basset and hazard were played. So the gamblers invented new games. In 1739 the government went further and banned all dice games; the gamblers turned to roulette, though this in turn was banned, if not always successfully, in 1745.[59]

The initial ban was on games using numbers, so one of the newly invented games used letters in place of numbers and was called EO (evens and odds). The game was first established at Tunbridge Wells in the rooms run there by Metcalf Ashe; Nash became involved in the syndicate formed to share profits from the game. Another 'table' was established there by Thomas Joye, and in order to prevent potentially disastrous clashes between the rival establishments in Tunbridge, Nash brought them together, taking a financial share for himself. In 1745 Nash introduced the game to Bath, ordering two EO tables for the assembly rooms from William Fenton, a cabinet-maker in Suffolk Street, London. If Joye had regularly spent time in Bath up to this time, his pattern of life seems to have changed, for his possessions were advertised to be sold from a house in the Grove in June 1745, and 'Any Person who has any Demands on Mr Joye, are desir'd to bring them in, in order to be paid, he being to remove from Bath.'[60]

Nash involved the Wiltshires in his scheme: he was to have a one-fifth share of the profits from the tables at their assembly room. At first this was paid. As Oliver Goldsmith writes 'The first year [1746] they paid him what he thought just; the next [1747] the woman of the room dying, her son paid him and showed his books'.[61] The son was John Wiltshire, who at that time was still a partner of Paul Bertrand.[62] Goldsmith goes on to explain that 'Some time after the people of the rooms offered him [i.e. Nash] one hundred pounds a year each for his share, which he refused; every succeeding year they continued to pay him less and less, till at length he found, as he pretends, that he had thus lost not less than twenty thousand pounds.'

The assembly rooms were not the only place where EO was played. 'It was by Mr Nash's influence that a table was admitted at Morgan's [the coffee house at the corner of Orange Grove and Wade's Passage] and the operating partners were Ashe, Joye, Cesar

p. 320 and Wheatley, who paid £1,200 rent.' These men feature in Bertrand's bank account. The statement quoted is among notes made by Roland Leffever, a gambler who acted as an intermediary for Nash, and who gathered evidence for litigation.[63]

In 1754 Nash brought a suit in chancery against Ashe and Joye and, in 1757, against the Wiltshires (Bertrand died in 1755.) It was this legal action that confirmed what many had suspected, and exposed Nash as having profited from gambling. It destroyed his reputation and social standing — his financial position was already perilous. People had known, and accepted, that he was financially involved in the running of both assembly rooms in Bath and that he was himself a heavy gambler, but did not like the fact that he gained personally from the profits of the 'bank' at the gaming tables. It is as well to remember here the age of Nash at the time of salient events: he was 31 in 1705 when he became Bath's Master of Ceremonies; 56 when the Bertrands moved to Bath; 71 in 1745 at the crackdown on gambling; 80 when he went to court; and 87 when he died in 1762, the same year as John Wiltshire. Nash was fifteen or sixteen years older than Bertrand, who died seven years before him.

In 1752 Nash had been advised not to pursue litigation: 'Your case ... arises from a Partnership founded on a Gaming Plan — there is no ground to encourage you to hope for ye Justice wch you certainly have a right to agt those you are concern'd wth but ye current of ye times if not ye law, is agt you.' The case involved dealings at Tunbridge and Bath (the latter involved both the Assembly Rooms and Morgan's Coffee House) and was continued until

Fan leaf depicting the interior of the lower assembly rooms, uncoloured etching, George Speren, published June 1737. Width: 49 cm (19¼ in). (BM, 1891,0713.455)

50   PART ONE: PAUL BERTRAND AND MARY DEARDS

Nash's death. Leffever dealt with Nash's solicitor in London (Bristowe), who they inevitably accused of neglecting the business. Leffever's memoranda and letters to Nash are testimony to the large sums of money involved in gambling and the penury to which Leffever himself was reduced through his addiction — he regularly sponged off Nash. He also had dealings with the London toyman Christopher Pinchbeck who, by June 1753, had taken over Ashe's rooms in Tunbridge and who clearly had little time for a man such as Leffever, who begged for financial assistance to avoid self-inflicted woes: 'Mr Ashley was going to make a Gathering for me t'other Day but that despicable malicious wretch Pinchbeck dissuaded him by saying I did not deserve such a Favour.'

This may make it difficult to believe all that Leffever noted, but gamblers understand mathematics and money; the sums that he records are substantial, interlaced with gossipy comments. He noted that it was 'Nash against the three Wiltshires' and that 'I believe Mr W wou'd be very unwilling to have the extraordinary Gain of the Latter season 1749, come to the ears of his Brothers.'[64]

There is a further puzzle that emerges from Bertrand's bank account, namely the large sums paid to Philip Baker, John Jesser and Robert Neale [▶ p. 56 table]. Baker and Jesser had links to the cloth trade and, although it has so far proved impossible to be sure of Neale's identity, it is possible that he did too. Whether Bertrand and the Wiltshires were in some kind of business relationship with these men is an open question which this present research does not try to answer, as it focusses on the toy business.[65]

Bill of exchange: a payment from Lord Ilchester, countersigned by John Wiltshire asking for payment to be made to the account of Walter Wiltshire, his brother. The central hole was made when the paper was filed on a spike. (Dorset, D/FSI/239)

John Wiltshire's bookplate [▶ p. 182] designed by Thomas Ross and engraved by Jacob Skinner, dated 1740. (Bath in Time, 35695)

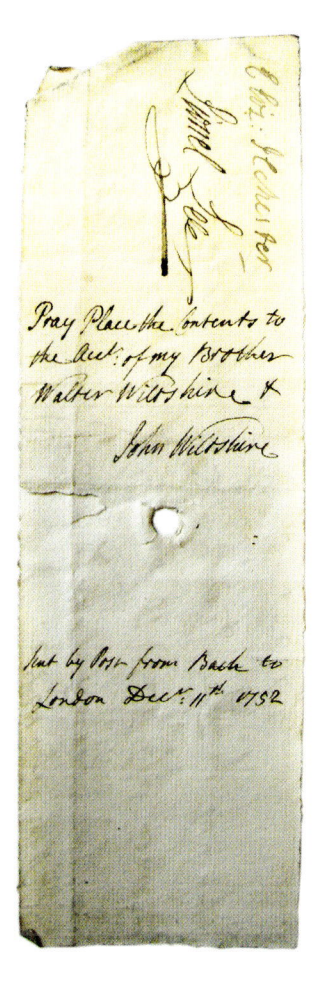

PARTNERSHIPS   51

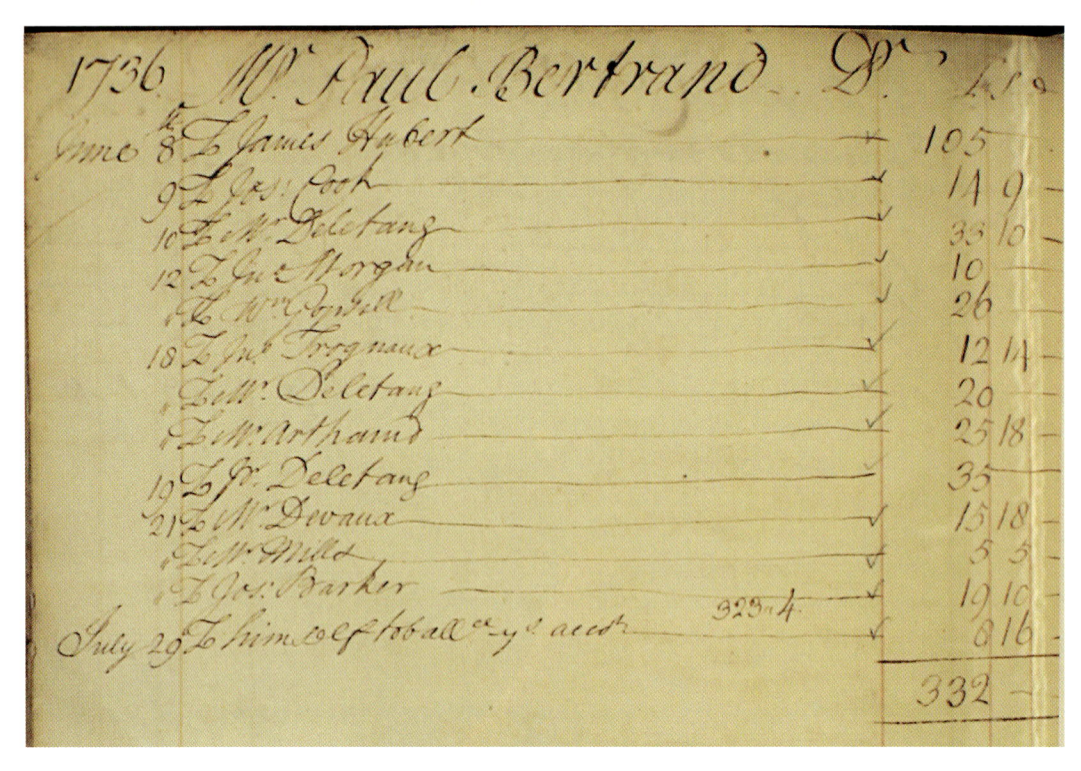

The first debit entries in the ledgers at Hoare & Co. for Paul Bertrand's account. (Hoare)

Charles Wray, oil on canvas, Nathaniel Hone. Wray witnessed the signatures of William Hoare and Peter Russel when they signed off Bertrand's bank account in 1755. He was head clerk at Hoare & Co. 1766–91, and the portrait clearly shows the paperwork involved in running a bank. Before the death of Henry Hoare in 1725, there were two clerks, John Arnold and his son Christopher. William Turner was taken on as a clerk as part of a re-organisation in 1725, when Christopher Arnold was made a salaried partner, and the number of clerks was increased to four. Part of their work would have been to write up the ledgers. (Hoare) [▶ pp. 204, 208 illus.]

Those who are guilty of Prodigality, Pride, Vanity and Luxury, do cause more wealth to the Kingdom, than Loss to their own Estates.

JOHN HOUGHTON[66]

Customer of Hoare & Co.

THE HOARE FAMILY had strong connections to Bath and Wiltshire: Richard Hoare (1709–54) was appointed banker to the Royal Mineral Water Hospital in 1737.

In London, various members of the family lived at the 'shop' (the bank) in Fleet Street. They also bought and developed a number of country estates. In 1717 Henry Hoare acquired property at Stourton, Wiltshire, and built Stourhead. His brother Benjamin purchased New Hall, in Essex, from the Duke and Duchess of Montagu in 1730 and proceeded to use the fittings of this former royal palace for a new house nearby at Boreham. Henry had two sons who ran the bank during Paul Bertrand's time as a customer: Henry, nicknamed 'the magnificent' (who inherited Stourhead) and Richard, Lord Mayor of London 1745–46 (who bought Barn Elms in Barnes, close to London, in 1750).[67]

Bertrand's account begins in May 1736, covers the next eleven years until the closure of the shop in February 1747/48 and continues (but with very different and fewer entries) until it was signed off by his executors, William Hoare and Peter Russel, on 19 January 1756. The account does not cover the first years of the shop in Bath nor his earlier life in London. Nor do the ledger entries in Bertrand's account reveal the whole story: his name is found in the accounts of customers of the bank other than those who are in his own account, as are those of other toymen such as Deards and Chenevix.[68] There must have been a great many transactions that did not go through the London bank, or are hidden in the round numbers of notes of exchange.

The information in the accounts covers five broad groups with whom Bertrand dealt: suppliers of luxury goods who were mainly London-based; tradesmen in Bath; merchants and bankers whose entries relate to financial transactions; customers; Bertrand's family and friends. Bertrand's account certainly relates to more than the selling of toys and, if read in conjunction with accounts of the Wiltshire family, suggests a business partnership that had a wider remit than the toyshop. It is not easy to assess how much of the account relates to Wiltshire's assembly rooms rather than the toyshop.

Bertrand was not the only retailer in Bath who kept running cashes. In 1728, for example, Marmaduke Alington's [▶ p. 246] account with Hoare & Co. shows payments of £50 to Leonard

p. 17 illus.

pp. 52, 208–09 illus.

Sir Richard Hoare, oil on canvas, unknown artist, c. 1745–46. Hoare is wearing his gold chain of office as Lord Mayor of London. The chain, together with one for his wife, was supplied by John Kemp at a total cost of £184 8s 6d. (Hoare)

pp. 175 and 258

Graphs to show approximate totals of transactions 1736–1747 through Paul Bertrand's bank account with Hoare & Co.

Blue = debit (DR).
Red = credit (CR).

BELOW: monthly totals, April to March.
OPPOSITE PAGE: annual totals.

Coward and £100 to Mary Chandler, which can presumably be interpreted as involving a note of some kind, as the amounts are in round numbers. No doubt numerous other shops offered a similar service. Several of the merchants and bankers whose names are in Bertrand's bank account (presumably because of the bills of exchange they handled) had links with the West Country. Several were Georgia Trustees, most were connected with one or more of the big companies of the period: the South Sea Company, East India Company, Levant Company, London Assurance, Royal Exchange Company, Sun Fire Insurance.

Bertrand's evident association with the Wiltshire family, and through them with the assembly rooms, require the overview of Bath that has been attempted in the following pages. The city provided the conditions in which Bertrand was able to trade. Numerous books and articles published on Bath, its architecture and its society, include relatively little about visitors to the city and those who worked there in the first decades of the eighteenth century other than the justifiably famous trio of Ralph Allen, John Wood and Richard Nash, and the foundation of the hospital. Those who people Hoare's ledgers force a different approach: they demand to be taken note of. It is disappointing that so few of the celebrities of the period who are known to have visited Bath are named in the ledgers, but this void can be filled with information from other sources (the letters of Elizabeth Montagu are but one), as the many quotations and invoices scattered through this work show.

Clearly, only some of those listed in the bank account actually set foot in the Bath shop. Most of the bankers and merchants are listed because their names were on bills of exchange. Few, if any, of the London craftsmen would have visited Bath.

The monetary entries in the account have been analysed on a monthly basis. The resulting graph (opposite page) confirms that the busiest times of the year in the shop match the most popular months for visitors. There may have been some delay between a transaction in Bath and it being entered into Hoare's ledgers in London, but the trend is broadly what should be expected: from September there was a steady rise to a peak in December with another highpoint in May. The quietest month was August. Perhaps surprisingly the credit and debit entries follow a roughly similar pattern, however if Bertrand spent time in January/February and July/August in London visiting his suppliers to re-stock for the season, the bills for his orders would not have entered the bank's ledgers for several weeks, by which time the season was in full swing.

A second graph (below) shows the annual balance of the bank account — or more accurately the balance when Bertrand was in London to sign the accounts. This is more problematic. One analysis, suggested above, is that the figures denote a partnership and that Bertrand's business encompassed more than retailing toys. There may be different ways of interpreting the information: ways that could take the story beyond the present research.

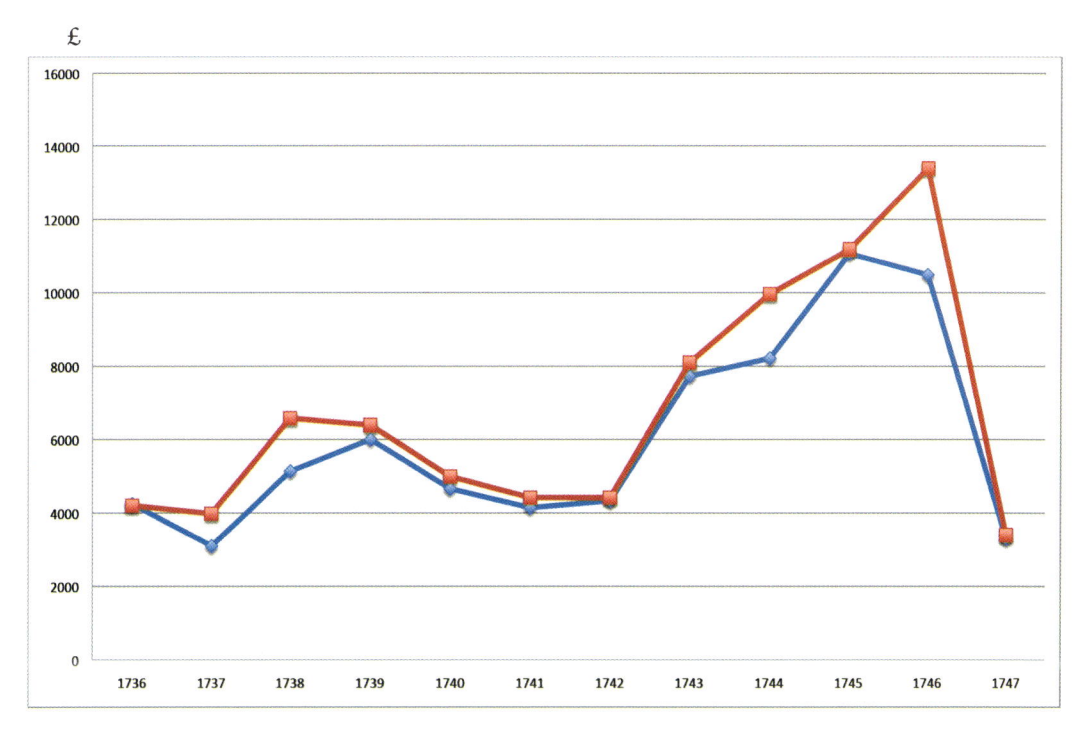

Selected names from debit entries in Bertrand's bank account

	1736	1737	1738	1739	1740	1741	1742	1743	1744	1745	1746	1747	TOTAL
Jesser, J				291	237	696	384	50	662	1206	470		3996
Neale, R.		100	79		142			255	590	924	1065		3155
Gribelin, S.		14		30		289	107	880	670	585	221		2796
Baker, P.					373					223	900		1496
Graham, J.					100		116	292	385	205	328		1426
Thomas, E.				257	100	100	200	400		300	21		1378
Russel, P.	215	121	644	156	29	47	31	72		26			1341
Leake, J.	82	96	36	39	50	25	23	24	128	244	204	239	1190
Mulford, J.	57	62	145	189	30	38	128	100		188	38	28	1003
Feline, E.	145	167	238	131		48							729
Bishop, S.	170	67	54	100	50	20		50	75		125		711
Barker, J.	65	50	86	35		40	200	142		44		45	707
Coward, L.								79	144	364		53	640
Moore, W.									610				610
Harford, C.										72	307	228	607
Margas, P.		85		75	50		84	116			52	91	553
Barbot, J.	33	78	220	63	63						41		498
Hoare, W.					283	87	24		94				488
Masters, B.												400	400
le Maitre, P.	375			9									384
Chandler, M.			50	130		180							360
Trognaux	139	84	81	22	20	10							356
Cotterell, J.	47	21	47		48	55	20	40		50			328
De Vic, I.							91	80	14	77	24		286
Hubert, J.	187	40			9	42							278
Deletang, P.	208			39		10							257
Chenevix, P.	220	22					14						256
Coles, H.					180							71	251
Pomfret, T.							200			13			213
Aumonier	54	66	72		18								210
Hopkins, W.	40	18		150									208
Bowden, J.					50	30				100			180
Bernardeau	50	50			20	22							142
Turner, T.											130		130
Jones, G.				53	76								129
Shruder, J.				113									113
King, J.			95		8					5			108

The banking transactions of Hoare & Co. are recorded in ledgers such as these, and other volumes, from the foundation of the business in 1673. (Hoare)

	1736	1737	1738	1739	1740	1741	1742	1743	1744	1745	1746	1747	TOTAL
Dupont, L.				92									92
Jacob, J.	40					27		23					90
Hillan, C.			18	70									88
Duvall, J.				30		56							86
Brifaut, J.	25	61											86
Tabart, D.				26		31	20						77
Thibault, T.			40	25									65
Callard, I.	25			15	20								60
Pugh, H.	10		41										51
Ross, T.				24					23				47
Allen, J.												35	35
Bellis, J.											18		18
Pantin, L.	17												17
TOTAL	2204	1301	2205	2263	1499	2053	1442	2603	3495	4526	3944	1190	28725

Entries in Paul Bertrand's bank account for the Wiltshire family.
The Wiltshires also had their own accounts at Hoare & Co.

Ann	DR							500	400	165	762	62	1889
Ann	CR			70									70
John	DR			500		89		723	1376	2264	1191	674	6817
Walter/Wm	DR		100	200	120	295	717	370	252	160		606	2820
Walter	CR							550	402	300	745	509	2506
TOTAL DR			100	700	120	384	717	1593	2028	2589	1953	1342	11526
TOTAL CR				70				550	402	300	745	509	2576

CUSTOMER OF HOARE & CO.

Portrait of a family, thought to be the family of Moses Roubel, oil on canvas, unknown artist, probably *c.* 1752. Formerly attributed to Stephen Slaughter. Roubel and his wife Sarah had two sons, Paul and John, and a daughter Catherine who died aged six in 1752. The following year another daughter, Jane, was born. (Geffrye)

A standish, steel and golden pen;
It came from Bertrand's not the skies;
I gave it you to write again.

ALEXANDER POPE

Employees

FOLLOWING THE CLOSURE of the shop, three men advertised themselves as having worked for Bertrand: James Tilly, Moses Roubel and John Pyke. There seems to be no way of knowing for how long they had been employed in Terrace Walk but, by following their fortunes after they lost their jobs with him, it is possible to gauge their skills and what they contributed to Bertrand's toyshop.

Moses Roubel

Moses (or Moyse) Roubel was the only one of the three who made a success of his independent venture. Neither Roubel's will nor his several advertisements give any hint that he was actually named Charles Moyse. Research, by his descendants, reveals that he was born in Ruffec, in the Poitou-Charente district of France, and that as Huguenots his family came to England, where Roubel settled in Bath.[69] He and his wife Sarah Salmon (1718–91) had three children who lived to adulthood, Paul (1742–94), John (1744–1826), and Jane Catherine (1746–87); another daughter died in 1752. When he signed his will in 1776, Roubel appointed as executors Robert Salmon, cabinet-maker of Bristol (described as 'my cousin') and William Purdie, wine merchant of Bath.

From December 1747 Roubel advertised in the *Bath Journal* regularly, by 1750 describing himself as 'From the Prince of Wales's Jeweller in London, and was Chief in the Working-Part to Mr. Bertrand for several Years'.[70] His former employer was Mr Lock of Pall Mall. Roubel advertised from King's Mead Square in 1747 and then from his shop 'the Hand and Solitaire' at the corner of Wade's passage and Orange Grove, opposite Morgan's coffee house. He also retained a 'messuage or tenement' in Lady Mead (Walcot Street), where his sister Elizabeth was living in 1776 and which he described as 'my workshop'.[71] He seems to have worked hard to extend the range of his wares: in 1748 his advertisements were headed by 'exceeding cheap Gold and Silver Watch Toys'; in 1753 he advertised:[72]

pp. 22–23 map

Roubel, Jeweller and Diamond-setter (In the Newest Taste) Lately returned from his Travelling, at the Hand and Solitaire, the Corner of

Gravel Walks: Orange Grove

When Paul Bertrand's employees set up in business on their own account following his retirement, they took shops in Orange Grove and Terrace Walk.

The open space in front of the Abbey [▶ pp. 40 illus., 22–23 map] was laid out in the late seventeenth century as a place for outside entertainment and included an area for playing bowls. It was renamed Orange Grove following the visit of the Prince of Orange in 1734. There were lodging houses and private houses on the north side and on the east side, overlooking the river. In the early eighteenth century the area was full of shops and coffee houses.

Surviving images show that various alterations were made to the building at the corner of Orange Grove and Terrace Walk over the years. There was a passage through an archway to allow access between them, near which there was a stand for chairmen. The corner building was truncated in 1832 and there were further alterations in the late 1880s.

Orange Grove looking west to the Abbey. Copy of a now lost eighteenth-century drawing. Executed after Paul Bertrand's time, it shows at the left, the row of shops on the south side of the Grove. (Bath in Time, 15249)

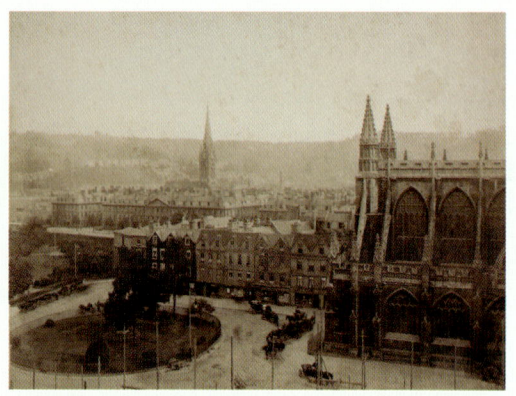

Orange Grove looking to the south, photograph, c. 1896. (Bath in Time, 15248)

Fan leaf, etching, published by J. Pinchbeck. (Bath in Time, 11636-9) [▶ details pp. 80, 104, 147]

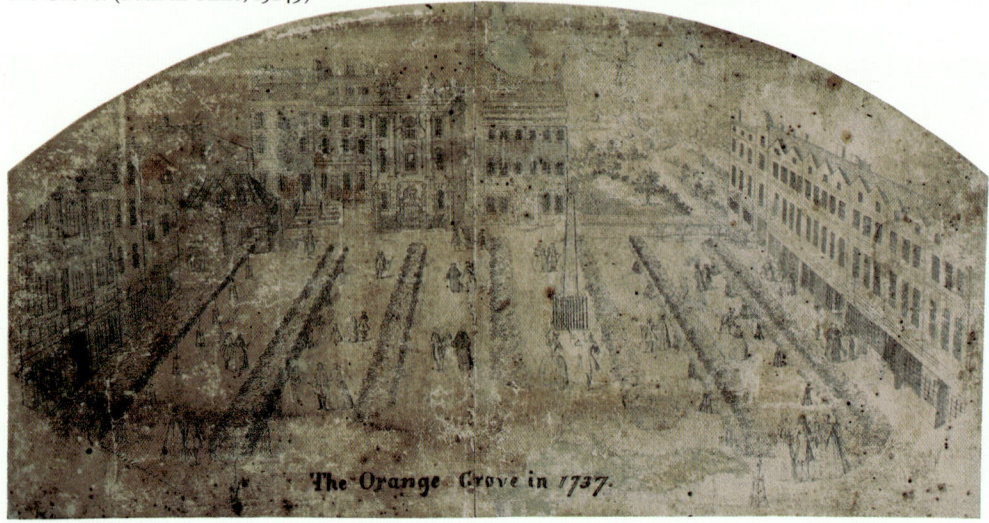

Wade's Passage, in the Grove, has furnish'd himself with several curious Jewels, Gold and Silver Toys, and several Gold and Silversmith Goods; Gold and Silver Second-hand and New Watches: He give Notice to the Publick (to have a quick Sale of his Goods) that he resolves to sell for very small Profit. Gentlemen and Ladies may be supply'd with Diamonds, and Colour'd Stones for their Jewels. — Country Shopkeepers may be supply'd with small Silver Plate and Jewels, Wholesale and Retail. — He gives most Money for Old Gold and Silver; 5s 8d per Ounce for Gold burnt Lace.

The following year 'Mr Corton, painter of perspective views' displayed an example of his work at Wiltshire's Assembly Rooms; he was 'in attendance at the Rooms for several hours every day and could otherwise be contacted through Moses Roubel'. In 1755 Roubel was advertising watches by William Bathe 'clock and watch-maker from Paris' and that his shop was 'Where all Sorts of Jewels are made in the newest Fashion, having fresh Hands from Paris and London, and cuts Rose-Diamonds into Brilliants'. He did a brisk trade in second-hand jewellery. It is hard to judge the size of his establishment and the number of employees, but jewellery was clearly a specialty.[73] He was prepared to act as an agent for those wishing to dispose of jewellery, rather than buying outright:[74]

A lady left the following Jewels for sale — a pair of Brilliant Night Earrings, a double cluster Brilliant Ring; a ditto Heart, rose and emerald ditto; a Brilliant and Ruby shirt Buckle, a Pearl Necklace, 14 Rows, to be sold at Mr Roubel's, Jeweller…

By 1758 Moses Roubel was for a time in Bristol, where his son John was apprenticed to Bathe, leaving Paul to maintain the shop in Bath; but Moses returned to Bath and his two sons worked with him and continued the business.[75] John appears to have helped Paul financially when the latter, although married, had two children by a servant. In May 1773 Paul Roubel was required to sign a bond to indemnify the parish against expenditure on the second child; John, described as a watchmaker, also signed the indemnity by which the brothers were to forfeit £40 should they renege on the agreement. Susanna Savage received 2s a week for each child in 1774.[76] By his will, proved in May 1777, Moses Roubel bequeathed 'sundry articles in my way of Business of which I have no Memorandum, viz Buckles Ear Rings a China Clock shew glasses and other things … to my said son John … also I give to my son Paul Roubel all the working tools Stones and old Jewels which at my decease shall be in my workshop in my house in Lady Mead to and for his own proper use and benefit …'. He had further stock including diamonds, securities and properties in Brock Street and Beaufort Square in Bath as well as those already mentioned. He clearly had a successful business.

One of a pair of buckles, silver and steel, unidentified mark IR, *c.* 1760. Height 3.5 cm (1⅜ in). (Private coll)

EMPLOYEES 61

In the first decade of the nineteenth century William Blathwaite of Dyrham was buying from John Roubel and also from James Williams, who advertised himself as successor to Roubel, at the shop in Wade's Passage.

James Tilley

In January 1747/48, James Tilley advertised himself as having been for many years Bertrand's 'principal workman' when he opened a shop on his own at the Kings Arms in Orange Grove. Further similar advertisements the following October explained that he was next door to Mr Frederick, bookseller in the Grove; his stock had extended beyond jewellery and watches to include plate and snuff

Trade card of John Pyke, toyman in Orange Grove, Bath, engraved by Jacob Skinner, dated 1753.
(Bath in Time, 18639)

62 PART ONE: PAUL BERTRAND AND MARY DEARDS

boxes. He seems not to have flourished, worked for a time with his former colleague Moses Roubel, and then may have gone to London. It is difficult to know whether it was he, or someone with the same surname, who was at a trial in 1756 when the valet of Joseph Ricciarelli was acquitted of stealing some shirts and jewellery. A 'Mr Tilley' gave evidence along with the silversmith and toyman Thomas Harache at the trial:[77]

Thomas Harrache: On the 8th of March, about eleven at night, I came home, and heard the prosecutor's servant had robbed him; he lodged in my house. I examined the prisoner myself, who own'd he had pawn'd ten of his master's shirts. I was present before the magistrate, where he owned the same, and also his taking the two rings. The prosecutor is first singer at the opera.

Mr. Tilley: I have known him 4 or 5 months; I have trusted him alone in my shop, where there were many jewels and other goods, and he never wrong'd me.

John Pyke

John Pyke, like James Tilley, ran into difficulties. He set up shop at the 'Golden Flower D'Luce' in Orange Grove and had his trade card engraved by Jacob Skinner. In 1754 he moved to Terrace Walk, where he advertised himself two years later:[78]

p. 181

John Pyke, Toyman | At the Fleur-de-Luce on the Walks, Bath | Begs Leave to acquaint the Nobility and Gentry, that he continues his Shop as usual and hath laid in an entire new Assortment of Goods, which are all mark'd at the lowest Price. — The best of jewellers and Plate-Workers employ'd as usual.

By that time his business was already in trouble, and notices appeared in the *London Gazette* in 1756–57 about his bankruptcy. Pyke appears to have moved to London, where in 1759 'all persons who are indebted to the Estate of Mr John Pyke, late of Bath, Jeweller & Toyman' were asked to contact his acting trustees, John Barbot and James Bellis.[79] Whereas Tilley and Roubel advertised themselves as craftsmen when they set up their own businesses, Pyke did not, and his exact role at the shop in Terrace Walk remains unclear. His stock in trade was advertised in January 1760.[80] There is a possibility that Pyke then had to seek employment with John Wiltshire — the following notice appeared in 1769:[81]

p. 214

Yesterday Morning John Pyke, Waiter at one of the Assembly Rooms in this City, hung himself with a small Cord. The Coroner's Inquest being taken on the Body, they brought in their Verdict Lunacy.

But Pyke is a common name.

EMPLOYEES 63

Rus in urbe

These images depict the same view of the semi-rural walks — *rus in urbe* — near the River Avon and looking towards the assembly rooms — a scene that would have been very familiar to Paul and Mary Bertrand.

Paul Bertrand must have sold fans (although none has been found in invoices) — they were popular as souvenirs of a visit to Bath. Visitors could choose from a wide range of engraved or hand-painted designs, stocked by many of the toyshops in and around Orange Grove.

Fan leaf, engraving, published by G. Speren, 1737. The view shows the summerhouse and walks laid out by Thomas Harrison between the assembly rooms and the River Avon, seen also in the drawing by Thomas Robins [▶ p. 78]. The assembly rooms and the Bertrands' shop were behind the trees.
(Bath in Time, 11539)

Fan leaf, hand painted, Thomas Loggan, *c.* 1749. Richard Nash (with white hat under his arm) is among the group; Loggan is the small figure to the right.
(Bath in Time, 12885)

Oh be thou blest with all that Heav'n can send
Long Health, long Youth long Pleasure and a Friend:
Not with those toys the Woman-World admire
Riches that vex, and Vanities that tire

ALEXANDER POPE

Part of Bath's community

AS THE OWNERS of a prominent retail business, it would have been crucial for Paul and Mary Bertrand to be accepted into, and take part in, the community life of Bath. Bertrand achieved this in several ways: as a freemason, as a freeman, through the hospital and, most probably, through a local society of artists.

The Bertrands had properties in Bath in addition to the shop. An understanding of their locations within the rapidly developing city makes it easier to visualise the couple's daily activity.

James Leake's bookshop was on the corner of Orange Grove and Terrace Walk; the Bertrands' shop was next to it in Terrace Walk, which runs roughly north-east to south-west. The row of shops on the south side of Orange Grove was built in 1705–08 and extended, following the line of the medieval wall round an awkward corner, to create Terrace Walk — a plan of the Duke of Kingston's estates in Bath shows the outline. Parish records have not survived: the 1766 City Rate Book is the first record of shopkeepers in St James's, the parish in which Terrace Walk was situated.[82] By then, eighteen years after Bertrand retired, there were eleven shops in Orange Grove and nine in Terrace Walk; Bertrand's shop was in the name of 'Mrs Walton'.[83]

p. 19 illus.

pp. 40–41 maps

p. 201 illus.

During their first years in Bath the Bertrands probably lived above the shop in Terrace Walk. From 1739 they are recorded in a terrace of houses between Queen Square and George Street that was originally called Barton Street but is now part of Gay Street — although they could have taken possession earlier. Barton Street ran to the south, north and through the east side of Queen Square. This particular group of eleven houses was begun in 1733 and completed in 1740, to the designs of John Wood. William Hoare took the house next to Bertrand to the north — they are now nos. 37 and 38 Gay Street.[84] These two houses have nothing blocking their view — their prospect is over the gardens of the houses at the north-eastern corner of the square, one of which was occupied by Lady Hotham (Lord Chesterfield's sister), one of Bertrand's customers. It is easy to imagine the friends standing at adjacent windows as they looked west to the setting sun, perhaps

p. 70 illus.

p. 283

occasionally glancing left to some activity in the square. The Bertrands' immediate neighbours to the south were Mr Bowerbank and the Revd James Sparrow, respectively curate and rector of St Swithin's Walcot (the parish comprised most of Bath outside the medieval walls at the time). With such neighbours it would surely have been difficult for Paul Bertrand to avoid involvement in his parish.

By 1749 the houses at the George Street end of the terrace had been taken by Sir John Cope and Sir Edward Stanley — both of whom were customers of the shop in Terrace Walk.[85] They must have lived against a background of builders' noise, for the street was soon being extended northward to what would become the Circus: perhaps the Bertrands walked up the street to witness the laying of its foundation stone in 1754. The street was renamed Gay Street after the landowner, Robert Gay, and leases for the new houses became available in the year Bertrand died, 1755.

Mary Bertrand remained in the house in 1756, no doubt sorting out her affairs and deciding what to do next. There are no available records for the next ten years, but by 1766 she had moved to Ealing and William Hoare had moved round the corner to 4 Edgar's Buildings, part of a terrace for which leases became available in 1761.[86] This, too, had a good aspect: south down Milsom Street, which was built originally as private houses. Mary Bertrand obviously retained the lease of the house in Barton Street, for it was the first bequest in her will: 'I give devise and bequeath my messuage or tenement with the appurtenances situate and being in Barton Street in the City of Bath to the wife of Captain Lewis now at Gibralter … during the residue of the term of ninety nine years which I have therein …'.[87] Mrs Lewis was the daughter of Peter Russel and Hannah Hoare.

Paul Bertrand's name also appears in the rate books for Queen Street between 1746 and 1754. Queen Street does not feature on either the 1735 or 1754 map of Bath and the most likely location for this property is in what is now Barton Buildings, immediately behind the house in Barton Street, the back yard of which probably gave direct access to this second property. Bertrand began to pay rates on this during 1746 and maintained it through his retirement. Presumably he anticipated the closure of the shop and needed extra space at his house.[88]

Bertrand's will shows that in addition to the shop and the Barton Street house, he had invested in two further properties. He left one in Pierrepont Street to William Hoare. The location of the other, which he left to Prince Hoare, is not mentioned but it was rented to 'Mrs Hervey and her sister Mrs Noise' — both feature in Bertrand's bank account.[89]

Freeman of Bath

The Guildhall, drawing attributed to James Vertue, c.1750. There was a market beneath the council chamber. The building was extended on the south side (to the right of the drawing) in 1724–25. (Bath in Time, 10824)

Bertrand became a freeman of Bath in April 1733.[90] The minutes of the Corporation show that he paid a high entry fee:

30 April 1733. Whether Mr Paul Bertrand shall be made a ffreeman of this City paying such ffine for the Same as this Corporation shall think fit. Agreed he shall.
What fine shall he pay for the same: 20 guineas – 16/17; 15 guineas – 4/6; 10 guineas – 2; 30 guineas – 1.
Agreed that Mr Bertrand shall pay twenty guineas for his ffreedome of this City and the other Customary fees.

Although the apprentice system and the Corporation's control over trading was slowly breaking down in the early eighteenth-century, records were still kept of those who undertook a seven-year apprenticeship to attain freedom of the city, and of those who paid for their freedom or were awarded it by gift. Links between tradesmen in Bath and livery companies in London are unclear, but Bath's Corporation attempted to stick to the old system of regulation. In 1689 Joseph Cary had his shop shut down because he was not a freeman, and in 1717 it was agreed that 'the Corporation shall pay half the charge of prosecuting several persons who follow trades in this City not being qualified to do so'. By 1730 Bertrand appears to have had no difficulty in opening his shop, but obviously thought it was appropriate to apply for freedom of the city.[91]

Freemen 'had rights to practice trades [in the city] and to a share in the income from the commons but no right to or share in power, except in the administration of the three parishes in the city.'[92] The Corporation, which was 'closed and self perpetuating', comprised a mayor, councillors and aldermen; they controlled much of the property within the city walls and set the rates. Although they approached the management of the city and its visitors from very different perspectives, the corporation, their Master of Ceremonies, and shopkeepers like Bertrand, had the mutual aim of greater prosperity. The medieval Guildhall was where much business was done, and many corporate dinners eaten. It was decided that it should be 'sashed and wainscotted' in 1710.

Many of the aristocratic visitors to Bath were made honorary freemen, and so were craftsmen and others who had rendered a service to the community. For example, the clockmaker Thomas Tompion was made an honorary freeman in October 1707 (he presented a long case clock to the Pump Room two years later) and Richard Nash in 1716.

Trustee of the Hospital

The need for a hospital, and its subsequent management, brought together in common cause both permanent residents of Bath and its visitors; fundraising had started in the early 1720s. The foundation stone was laid in July 1738. Bertrand is recorded as giving £30 on 16 February 1737/38 towards the 'subscription taken for raising the sum of six thousand pounds for the purchase of ground and erecting a general hospital'. The King gave £200 through Richard Nash, the Prince of Wales £100. Over the years Bertrand also took in donations, presumably through the shop: the cutler James Bernardeau gave a guinea on several occasions; Lord Romney £20 in 1743; Lady Betty Germain ten guineas and Lord Palmerston five guineas in 1748.[93] Most generous of all was Ralph Allen, who not only donated £1,000 to the hospital but also gave the stone with which it was built.

Bertrand was a trustee of the hospital from January 1737/38,[94] and attended trustees' meetings very regularly. Trustees included members of the aristocracy (useful for raising the profile of the hospital and funds), the medical staff and tradesmen like Bertrand. The hospital had an account with Hoare & Co. but Bertrand may have been responsible for day-to-day moneys and for dealing with the staff of the hospital, as the hospital minutes record him being repaid sums expended on its behalf. For example:

The Treasurers have this day paid tradesmens Bills servants wages &c by Mr Paul Bertrand one hundred & thirteen pounds one shilling & nine pence ... The Honbl B. Bathurst reported that he had paid to Mr Paul Bertrand the several sums paid by Mr Bertrand since July the 27th 1748 on Accot of the G Hosp Bath. Also that Mr Bathurst had received of Mr Bertrand the several sums rec'd by Mr Bertrand on accot of the said Hospital which sums were therefore placed to the Mr Bathurst accot amt to £681 18s.

Bertrand's links with various trades in the city also came in useful: he was asked in June 1739 to 'purchase an Iron Chest of about 150lb weight for the use of the hospital' for which he was reimbursed in September the sum of £6 10s. And he very probably had a hand in the acquisition of a seal for the hospital from Jacob Skinner at the cost of two and half guineas in April 1740.[95]

In addition to his role as a trustee, when the hospital opened in 1742 Bertrand became a House Visitor, and he continued to do this until 1755, when on 30 July his (rather shaky) signature appears in the Committee Book for the last time. Sometimes he signed as 'P. Bertrand', sometimes 'Paul Bertrand'. William Hoare also undertook this voluntary work which, as Evelyn Newby described, '… was no sinecure as their duties involved checking on patients, their treatment and progress, on the Hospital's amenities, staff and suppliers.'[96]

Shortly after the hospital began to accept patients Bertrand was involved in a curious episode. By this time he had lived in Bath for thirteen years and would have been well known, which must have helped his case. An assistant surgeon, Archibald Cleland, was found guilty of 'misbehaviour' by a committee of seventeen of the hospital's governors. The records of the hospital are detailed:[97]

On the 7th of Sepr 1743 at the weekly Court of Committee held at the General Hospital at Bath, Mr Bertrand, one of the Governors, moved that an Enquiry should be made into certain indecent practices laid to the charge of Mr Cleland, one of the surgeons in the said Hospital by two of the female Patients, belonging to the Princess's Ward (viz) Mary Hudson and Mary Hooke, the former being Dr Oliver's patient, troubled with Hysteric fits, the latter Dr Rayners afflicted with a Leprosy and both under the Care of Mr Wrigt as their Surgeon … frequent examinations both internal and external … Mary Hooke … suspicion she was with Child …

Cleland defended himself vigorously and may not have liked Bertrand, who he described as 'a French Toyman'. Whether or not this remark shows some kind of prejudice, Cleland was suspicious of Bertrand's motives when the latter requested to attend the post mortem of one of the female patients and asked Cleland if he considered she had been a virgin. In Cleland's words:

It may here not improperly be asked, From what Sort of Principle this extraordinary Curiosity of Mr Bertrand's did proceed? Since he had, or might have fully satisfied a more modest Degree of it, in his frequent Examinations, or at least viewing of naked Women, in the Academy of Painting.[98]

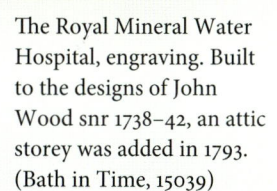

The Royal Mineral Water Hospital, engraving. Built to the designs of John Wood snr 1738–42, an attic storey was added in 1793. (Bath in Time, 15039)

Parishioner of Walcot

The parish of Walcot was the largest in Bath, lying outside the old walls of the city. Its small church, dedicated to St Swithin (Bishop of Winchester and confessor to King Ethelred), measured some 36½ × 26 ft (approximately 11.1 × 7.9 m). In January 1738/39 the congregation voted to build a new church but John Wood's plans for it were not accepted and nothing more was done for some forty years, during which time Paul Bertrand was buried at the church. Today's building, which contains his monument, was designed by Jelly & Palmer and built 1777–80. The father of the novelist Jane Austen is also buried here.

In 1670 the parish contained eighty houses and two cloth mills. In the second quarter of the eighteenth century Walcot attracted the attention of developers who wanted land that was outside the control of the corporation and aldermen. Building began in 1727; Robert Gay leased a large area of Barton Farm to John Wood to build Queen Square, and the area continued to be developed during and after the Bertrands' time in Bath. By 1775 there were some 1,100 houses in the parish.

In 1740 Bertrand's contribution to the Walcot First Church Rate was 16s (at 2s in the pound); in 1741 he insured his house in Barton Street for £500. He is recorded attending vestry meetings of the parish on 2 April 1746 and 23 April 1747, when he signed the churchwardens' accounts.[99] He clearly played his part in parish life.

The houses in which Paul Bertrand and William Hoare lived in Barton Street (now Gay Street), and the rear of the buildings [▶ p. 21/1 map].

Freemason

Freemasonry would have introduced Paul Bertrand to a circle of acquaintance outside his immediate family group among gentry and tradesmen — it was one of the organisations in which social barriers were overcome, and a great many people belonged to the Order at this time.

In London Bertrand attended a lodge that met at The Cardigan Head at Charing Cross. He was one of the wardens at a meeting on 25 November 1723, and he was there again on 27 November 1725, the last year this lodge is listed.[100]

Once initiated into the Order, Bertrand was able to attend the meetings of any lodge as a visitor, and he appears not to have been a member of the lodge in Bath.

The first lodge formed outside London met in Bath in 1724.[101] Among the aristocrats who were its founding members were the dukes of Bedford and St Albans [▶ p. 106]; the master was Viscount Cobham. This lodge appears to have been of short duration and a lodge was subsequently re-formed: its earliest surviving minutes are for a meeting at 'Brother Robinsons, the Bear' on 28 December 1732.

Several of the men listed in Bertrand's bank account attended Masonic meetings in Bath. Bertrand himself is first listed there on 2 November 1737, together with Hugh Kennedy, Henry Bridges, James Leake, Edward Cockey and John Stillingfleet. Howell Gwynn, who presented a trowel to the Lodge in 1742 when he was Master, appears in Bertrand's account in April and June that year. Among those who also attended the lodge during the 1730s was John Wiltshire, presumably the uncle of Bertrand's apprentice. There are a number of payments between 1744 and 1747 in Bertrand's bank account to William Kirkpatrick, later Master Mason.

During Bertrand's time the lodge met at the Bear Inn in Cheap Street; it later moved to the White Hart Inn. The Masonic Hall is today in Orchard Street, in a building that was opened as the theatre on 27 October 1750 — during Bertrand's retirement. He would surely have been to plays there. Between 1809 and 1863 the building was the centre of Catholicism in Bath: mass was celebrated on the spot where Sarah Siddons (1755–1831) had made her name as Lady Macbeth.[102]

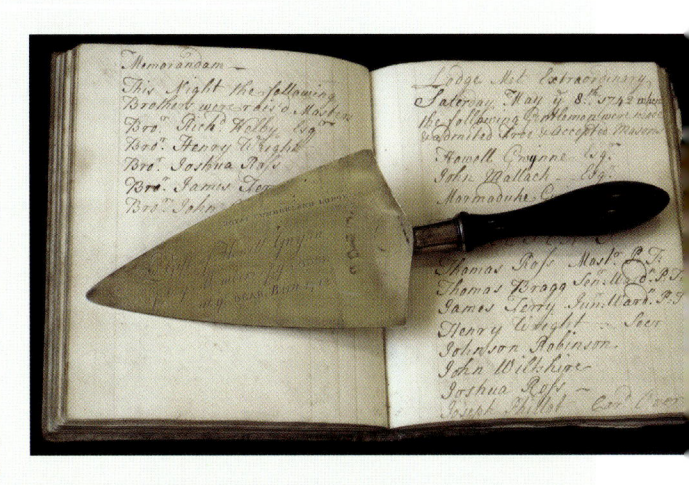

Trowel, silver, unidentified maker WW a star above, London 1741/2; and the attendance book showing a lodge meeting in Bath on 8 May 1742. The page lists Thomas Ross, Henry Wright, John Wiltshire, Joshua Ross and Howell Gwynne. The trowel is inscribed: 'The Gift of Howell Gwynn Esq to ye Members of ye Lodge at ye Bear BATH 1742. Royal Cumberland lodge No 48'. A trowel is one of the working tools that under-pins the installation ceremonies of freemasonry, linked to the third (and final) degree of membership. In a system similar to guilds, a man first becomes an apprentice, then a craftsman, then master mason (which he cannot attain before the age of twenty-one). (Lodge 41)

PART OF BATH'S COMMUNITY   71

The 'Makers of Bath'

Three men are credited with masterminding the development of Bath: Ralph Allen, Richard Nash and John Wood. Allen was the entrepreneurial businessman with a strong social conscience; Nash was Master of Ceremonies; John Wood was the planner and architect who transformed the city's built environment. Of very different temperaments and ambitions, they worked alongside the aldermen and townspeople; they must have recognised that shopkeepers of the calibre of Paul Bertrand and Mary Deards were crucial to their plans to create a successful and fashionable resort. As part of Bath's community, the Bertrands would have known all three men.

RALPH ALLEN (1694–1764) was universally admired. He worked in the postal services in Cornwall before settling in Bath, where he made his fortune by devising and managing cross-country posts in England and Wales. He recognised the opportunities that would result from making the River Avon navigable and bought stone quarries at Combe Down to diversify his interests. Other than supplying stone for St Bartholomew's Hospital in London, he was largely unsuccessful in his attempts to sell stone outside Bath. His town house was in Lilliput Alley and John Wood designed Prior Park for him (begun in 1735) as a showcase for Bath stone, where he entertained liberally. Allen was made a freeman of Bath in 1725 and was elected to the Council in 1734; he was a generous supporter of the Mineral Water Hospital, donating £1,000 and stone for its building; and was a governor in 1748. He married Elizabeth Buckeridge in 1721, and secondly Elizabeth Holder in 1737. He had no surviving children; his heir was his niece, Gertrude Tucker, who married the Revd William Warburton.

Ralph Allen, oil on canvas, attributed to Jonathan Richardson. (MWH, Bath in Time, 14031)

JOHN WOOD SNR (1704–54) was born in Bath, the son of a local builder. He began his career working on the Cavendish/Harley estate in London, north of Oxford Street, and returned to Bath in 1727 to work for the Duke of Chandos. Queen Square, his first important development in Bath, was completed in 1736. He went on to work elsewhere as well as in Bath, where his last major project was the Circus, completed by his son after his death. In 1742 (revised 1749) he published *An essay towards a description of Bath*. John Wood jnr (1728–81) subsequently built the Royal Crescent and the new (upper) Assembly Rooms between 1767 and 1775, projects that Mary Bertrand might have seen if she ever returned to Bath from Ealing.[103]

RICHARD NASH (1674–1762) was in his early thirties when he arrived in Bath in the first decade of the eighteenth century. He came to gamble and he earned a living as a gambler for the rest of his life. Shortly after he settled in the city he took on the voluntary role of Master of Ceremonies and worked with the City Corporation to improve facilities for visitors. He introduced codes of behaviour; he welcomed visitors to the city; he was their guide and facilitator, and laid on entertainments for them.

Nash was familiarly known as the 'king of Bath' — his commanding stature, and the white hat he habitually wore, made him easily recognisable, so few would have had difficulty in identifying him with the initials 'B.N.' for Beau Nash, in this advertisement:[104]

John Wood snr, detail from The Four Bath Worthies, oil on canvas, unknown artist, c. 1735. The group also includes Richard Jones, Ralph Allen and Robert Gay, and are not thought to be accurate likenesses. (BPT, Bath in Time, 18245)

This day is publish'd on a Fan Mount, fit for Second Mourning, or in Colours, An accurate and lively Prospect of the celebrated Grove at Bath; whereon the rural Pleasures and exact Decorum of the Company are curiously represented, with some curious observations on the Behaviour of sundry Persons, particularly the famous B.N. Likewise the rural Harmony and delightful Pleasures of Vaux-Hall Gardens, wherein is shewn the grand Pavillion, the Orchestra, the Organ and the Statue of Mr Handel. Sold wholesale or Retail at Pinchbeck's Fan Warehouse at the Fan and Crown in New Round Court in the Strand, London; and at Mr Delassol's and Mr Wicksteed's shops in the Grove at Bath.

Several authors have already written about Richard Nash's financial involvement in gaming at Tunbridge Wells and Bath. [▶ p. 49][105] He was involved on two levels. The first (considered acceptable) was to play at the tables as a means of obtaining an income. The second, by which he took a percentage of the profits from the assembly room owners who ran the tables, was not liked and ultimately led to his downfall. By 1748 (about the time Bertrand's shop closed) Nash's influence was lessened by rumours of embezzlement, and the lawsuits he filed in the mid-1750s revealed the extent of his monetary involvement in the assembly rooms in Tunbridge Wells and Bath.[106]

Nash's bank account reveals just how much he earned at the height of his success and the extent of his financial downfall. On 8 February 1731/32, for example, he paid into the bank five notes of 1,000 guineas each and fourteen of 50 guineas (a total of £5,985), followed on 7 March by one of 500 and ten of 50 gn each. The following season a sample of credit entries reads: 11 September 1732,

Richard Nash aged seventy-six, portrait miniature, enamel on copper, Nathaniel Hone, dated 1750. Height: 5.2 cm (2 in). (Holburne)

PART OF BATH'S COMMUNITY   73

The 'Makers of Bath', continued

Detail [▶ p. 50]

fourteen notes of 50gn each (£735); 16 January 1732/33, one note of 500 and two of 50 gn (£630); 5 February 1732/33, notes of 2,100, 210, three of 100 and one of 50 (£2,660) and on 19 March, notes of 1,000 gn, 500 gn, three of 100 gn, four of 50gn (£2,100). In August 1741 he received a bill on the banker Albert Nesbitt of £3,652 19s 4d. By any standards this was big money. How much of it represents gambling debts or his personal finances is unlikely to be discovered.

Sometimes, when Nash won very large sums, he negotiated an arrangement for a reduced payment. A bond survives relating to debts due to him dated 5 February 1731, for the sum of £6,000, most probably a gambling debt. It shows how formally such transactions were treated:[107] Wriothesley Russell, 3rd Duke of Bedford (1708–33) is said to have gambled away in the region of £100,000, and on his death he left debts of some £71,000.[108] The duke married Anne Egerton, daughter of the Duke of Bridgwater and grand-daughter of the 1st Duke of Marlborough in 1725 and died at Corunna, in Spain, where he had gone for his health, in October 1732.

Another peer who lost a serious sum to Nash was the Earl of Thomond (1691–1741) — as described by Oliver Goldsmith:[109]

When the late Earl of T—d was a youth he was passionately fond of play and never better pleased than with having Mr Nash for his antagonist. Nash saw with concern his lordship's foible and undertook to cure him, though by a very disagreeable remedy. Conscious of his own superior skill, he determined to engage him in single play for a very considerable sum. His lordship, in proportion as he lost his game, lost his temper too, and as he approached the gulf seemed still more eager for ruin. He lost his estate; some writings were put into the winner's possession; his very equipage was deposited as a last stake, and he lost that also. But when our generous gamester had found his lordship sufficiently punished for his temerity, he returned all, only stipulating that he should be paid five thousand pounds whenever he should think proper to make the demand. However, he never made any such demand during his lordship's life, but some time after his decease, Mr Nash's affairs being on the wane, he demanded the money of his lordship's heirs, who honourably paid it without any hesitation.

> Poor Nash farewell! may Fortune's smile
> Thy drooping soul revive;
> My heart is full, I can no more —
> John, bid the coachman drive.
>
> LADY MARY WORTLEY MONTAGU

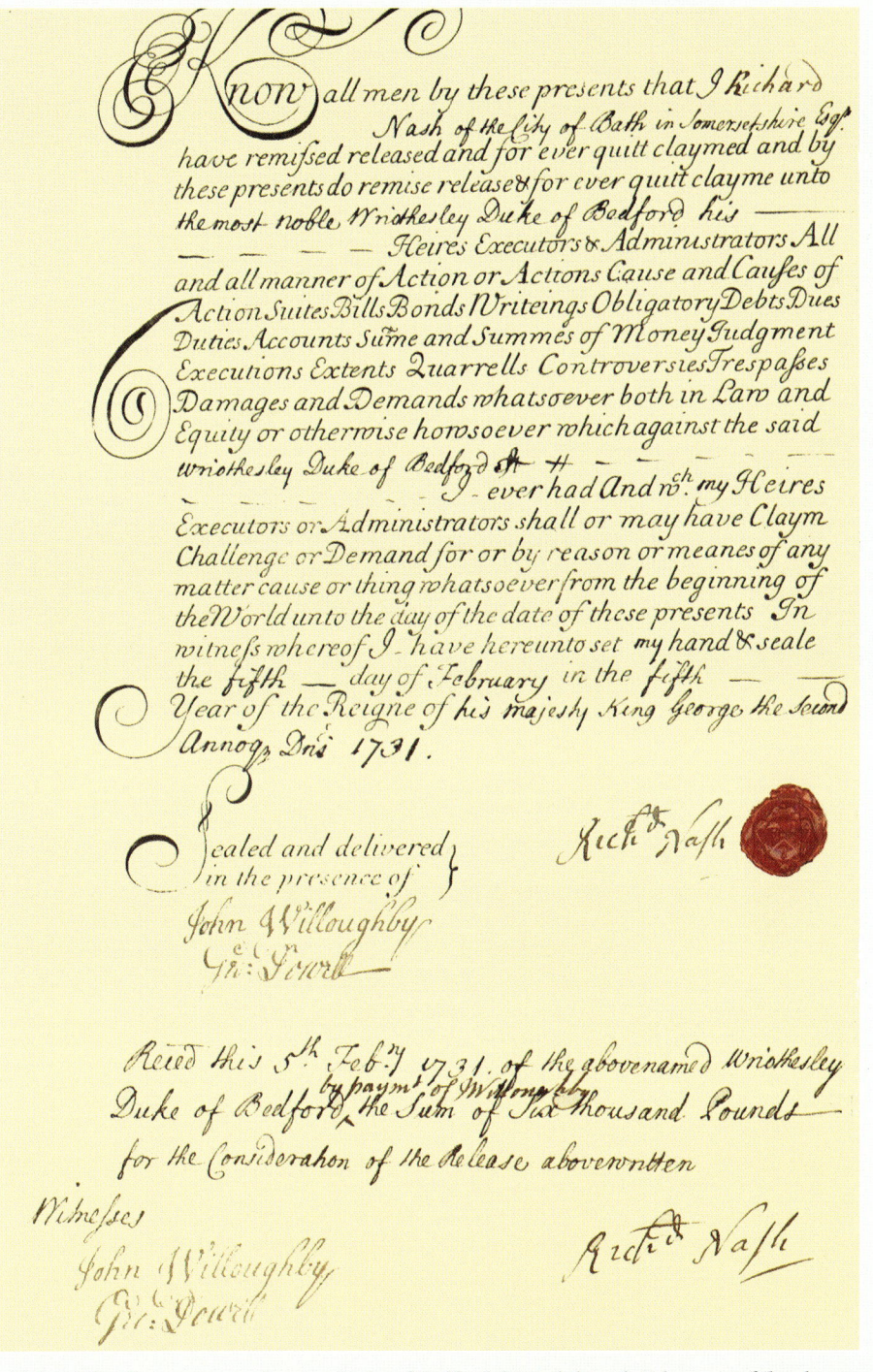

Richard Nash's monetary release to Duke of Bedford. 'Reced this 5th Febry 1731 of the above named Wriothesley Duke of Bedford by paymt of Willoughby the sum of Six Thousand Pounds for the Consideration of the Release above written. Signed Richd Nash; Witnesses John Willoughby, George Jowell.' (Bedford)

The East View of the Bath.

The East View of the Bath, looking north-east, drawing on paper, Bernard Lens, early eighteenth century (VAG).

The summerhouse by the river, and the trees in the Green Walk and Orange Grove, are to the right [▶ pp. 64 and 20–23]. In front of and just to the east of the Abbey, Lens shows the single-storey row of shops in Terrace Walk that was replaced in 1728. To the left of the shops, the tall building (four storeys plus an attic storey) might be the house built by Charles Delamain.

Some years later Thomas Robins took his drawing [▶ p. 78] from a slightly different angle, so that the row of shops is obscured by the river-side assembly rooms. Delamain's building had by this time been replaced by the lower assembly rooms (with high round windows).

Part Two

Bath as a resort

View of Bath looking West, drawing with bodycolour, Thomas Robins (1716–70). The riverside assembly rooms overlook the Green Walk, with the summerhouse in the foreground, near the river. To the left are the Parades with the tower of St James's church in the distance. (BM, 1875,0710.60)

Dispell those Clouds that damp your Fire,
Shew Bath like Tunbridge can inspire

LINES TO THE EARL OF ORRERY[110]

Bath in the early eighteenth century

IT IS IMPOSSIBLE to appreciate the trinkets that have come down to us without some understanding of why they exist. Divorced from the social context of their owners and creators toys can be perceived as beautiful but rather futile objects. Context gives them purpose. An understanding of the setting, the daily round, the opportunities for county folk who seldom went to the capital to see sophisticated shops, the challenges and costs involved in reaching such shops, helps to explain how a toyman's business could flourish outside the capital. The success of Bath in the first half of the eighteenth century depended as much on people like the Deards family who traded there season after season, as on those who funded the building of this remarkable resort and those, from all levels of society, who went there.

Bath was a building site throughout the years Paul and Mary Bertrand lived there. The Bath they knew was not the Bath we know today, nor even the Bath of Thomas Gainsborough or Jane Austen. It was focussed on what is now called the old town: the Abbey, the river, the baths and the market place were its heart. The town retained its medieval layout; most of the buildings dated from the seventeenth century or earlier — a muddle of gabled roofs and back yards. During the Bertrands' lifetime the countryside was very close: it was easy to walk or ride into fields and to the Downs, and it would have been possible to see that rural landscape from almost every street in the city. At the time Bertrand died and his wife moved to Ealing, the buildings of John Wood jnr and Thomas Baldwin were being planned or not yet thought of. The Royal Crescent, the residential streets and squares of the upper town, the new assembly rooms, Pulteney Bridge, Great Pulteney Street and its environs, the present Guildhall, Milsom Street — all these were unknown to the Bertrands and their customers. What they did see, and no doubt marvelled at, was the work of John Wood snr, in particular the creation of Queen Square and the Parades. Wood was born in 1704 (the year before Richard Nash arrived in the city) and died in 1754, the year before Bertrand died.

pp. 126, 129

Moving at a leisurely pace today, neither dawdling nor going briskly, it takes not more than five minutes to walk either the north-south or east-west axis of the old walled city. The walls contained some thirty-two acres and fifteen streets. The majority *p. 20 map*

of the area of expansion in the early eighteenth century, the parts of Bath that were to become the city we know today, was in the parish of St Swithin's Walcot and outside the medieval walls – Paul and Mary Bertrand were among its parishioners. No image survives of the church the Bertrands knew, but the map created by Gilmore in the 1690s depicts the parish churches of St James and St Michael within the walls.[111]

Members of Bath's Corporation owned much of the property within the city walls; they were largely able to control the issuing of leases and keep the sale of such property within their own circle of intimates. Bath was one of the constituencies that were later termed 'rotten boroughs', and the thirty-two aldermen were its only voters at elections for two members to represent the city in the House of Commons.[112] As they also voted for members of the Corporation (i.e. themselves) the governance of Bath was in the hands of a small group of men whose self-interest was paramount. These were the men with whom Richard Nash dealt in his attempts to improve facilities for Bath's visitors, but a start had been made before he arrived. In August 1702 the Corporation decided that '10 convex lights shall be set up in this City at the cost of the inhabitants' and in February 1706/07 it was agreed to build near the Abbey 'a Pass House for the use of ladies frequenting this City'.[113] This would have been of comfort to ladies who wished to spend time in shops on the south side of the Gravel Walks (later named Orange Grove), which at this time were being built independently by members of the Corporation and 'before which a handsome Pavement was then made, with large flat stones for the Company to walk upon'.[114] Buildings on the other sides of the Grove were largely completed by 1740. Because of the Corporation's controlling interests, major development was easier on land owned by individuals who had no association with the Corporation, such as John Gay and the Duke of Kingston.

Bath residents, divided by their different interests, moved in circles that came into contact with each other only fleetingly. Nash's circle was quite different to that of Ralph Allen. Their skills and personalities enabled them to contribute to Bath's success, and their own, without impinging too much on each other's sphere of influence. What brought these two very different men together, uniting them in common cause with tradesmen like Bertrand and aristocratic visitors, was the fund-raising for, founding, and administration of, the Royal Mineral Water Hospital.

The years between 1695 and 1725 — during which Bath was building its reputation as a resort for good company, improved health and gaming — were the years when its visitors were the cream of the aristocracy. They lodged for the most part in

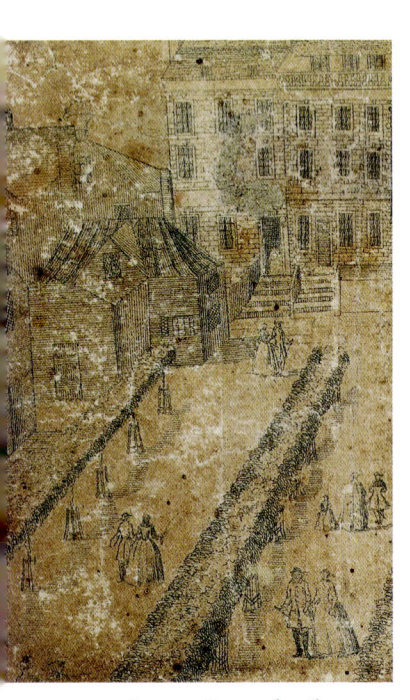

Orange Grove, detail ▶ p. 60.

conditions that were not what they were used to at home. In the first decades of the eighteenth century the Duke of Chandos was one of those who recognised the need for improvement and he invested in property in Bath in the hope it would be profitable. The Duke of Kingston already owned substantial land holdings — not just in Bath, but also in neighbouring areas such as Bradford-on-Avon — and he, too, turned developer. The map of his estate dated 1725 is the earliest known eighteenth-century depiction of the city.

p. 120

p. 92

p. 41 map

Although Nikolaus Pevsner acknowledged the problems in envisaging the early city ('... Of the Bath before 1725 it is much more difficult to speak'), sufficient images survive showing Bath in the first half of the eighteenth century, for us to recreate the settings of the main buildings in which these people gossiped and gambled, consulted doctors and spent money in shops such as Bertrand's. But in that period of transition it is the houses in between that are more difficult to envisage — the mix of the sixteenth and seventeenth centuries, the cramped streets, yards and passages of what was still, in essence, a medieval town. It is also difficult to envisage the daily routine of working men and women, which would have varied so much with the seasons. Celia Fiennes recorded in 1698 that

The streetes are faire and well pitch'd, they carry most things on sledges.

Such a small comment, and yet it reveals so much.

These first fifty years of the eighteenth century can be divided exactly in half, for it was in 1725 that work began on the scheme to make the River Avon navigable and John Wood submitted plans for building on lands belonging to the Duke of Kingston and John Gay. That was when the physical transformation of the city took off, and Bath began to take a lead in architectural fashions that spread throughout the country.

Builders were not idle during the first twenty-five years, however, for Richard Nash and Bath's Corporation encouraged the erection of buildings for the entertainment of seasonal visitors. Several of these early buildings later succumbed to changes in fashion or to fire. In the years between 1704 and 1709 the social heart of the city was improved by the building of a Cold Bath by

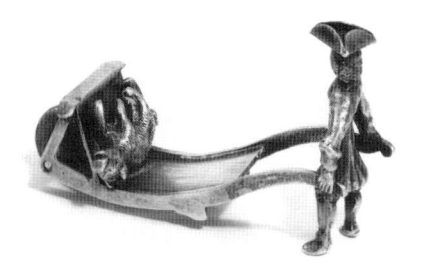

Model of a man pushing a dead boar on a sledge, silver, Amsterdam, *c.* 1740. Length: 5.7 cm (2¼ in). (SL, 4.5.1978/43)

BATH IN THE EARLY EIGHTEENTH CENTURY 81

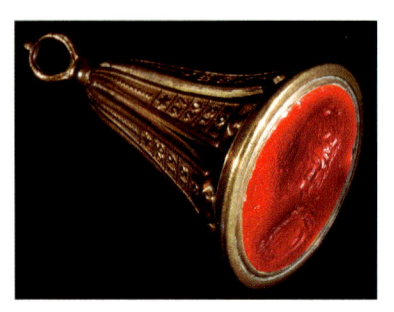

Seal, gilt metal, *c.* 1780. Length: 4.4 cm (1¾ in). The seal is a commemorative head of Alexander Pope (1688–1744); the seven panels of the shaft are stamped with a calendar. (Private coll) [▶ p. 302]

the river, John Harvey's Pump Room, the shops on the south side of Orange Grove and Thomas Harrison's gardens and assembly rooms. Many of the seasonal shops around the Abbey were possibly no more than booths, similar to those shown in Gilmore's map. Whether the Deards' seasonal shop was one of these, or something more substantial, can only be surmised, but it seems likely that it was in the first Terrace Walk development. There were spurts of energy in the development of the city, as new plots became available, notably between 1728 and 1734, but there must also have been a steady stream of work as properties were upgraded, particularly during the months outside the season.

A few names stand out among the many craftsmen working in Bath during the first half century, most of whom were builders (not many would have called themselves 'architect'): William Killigrew, Thomas Greenway, Richard Jones, John Strahan and, of course, John Wood. The last three feature in Bertrand's bank account. Their buildings form the backdrop to the story of Bertrand's shop and the city's visitors, and are crucial to visualising and understanding that era.

In 1724 Ralph Allen and members of his family acquired shares in the scheme developed by John Hobbs, a Bristol merchant, to make the River Avon navigable to Bath. Work began the following year and was completed by 1729.[115] It enabled Allen to transport stone from his quarries and brought goods and people to and from Bristol. It must have altered radically the way the city operated. The last years of that decade saw not just the work on the river and improvements to Terrace Walk, but also the start of Queen Square (built 1729–36) and, as we have seen, what was to be the Bertrands' house in Barton Street. From the shop they would have watched the erection of North (originally Grand) and South Parade (completed in 1748, the year Bertrand retired), using Allen's stone from Combe Down. The noise must have been considerable:

In the year 1739 began the great work in Bath Garden for the Parades, the north side begun first and the common sewer under the directions of Mr Wood, architect. The stone ... was brought up by water ... in two barges, and came with two carriages in each barge four times a day ... All the time Bath Garden work was going on (which was the Parades) four carriages were going [to] the hill constant ...

RICHARD JONES

The main function of the Parade buildings was to provide additional accommodation, and until their completion there was usually a shortage of lodgings, particularly for those who brought their own servants and horses. The logistics of provisioning this influx of humans and animals during winter months, of finding space for people and their horses, must have been demanding. The 2nd Duke of Bedford (1680–1711), for example, brought his coursing dogs; the 3rd duke (1708–32) rode on the Downs each day, presumably using his own horses. The cost of keeping horses at Bath was clearly laid out by Thomas King in a bill submitted to the Duke of Somerset in October 1749:[116]

20 nights hay for 7 Coach horses at 8*d* pr night each 8 Sept – 24 Oct:	£4	13*s*	4*d*
7 Coach Horses	24	13	00
Saddle Horses, between 4 and 13 pr night	25	19	08
Coach hire	12	05	00

The resident population of the city has been variously estimated at 2–3,000 in 1700 and 6–8,000 in 1750, or 9,000 in the mid-1720s. At that time, attempts to count visitors were doubted:[117]

I was yesterday in Bedlam, which is Harrison's room; tis much beyond whatever you saw or can imagine, they pretend to calculate that there is near 7000 strangers here, and out of every 100, 99 that never were seen before; but I got out of this hurly burly very soon … and went … to Lindseys (who never has any company of a Sunday) …

Other estimates allow 8,000 visitors during the season in the early part of the century, rising to some 12,000 in the 1740s.[118] They must have created all the logistical difficulties that face any modern resort, at the mercy of climate and occasionally poor harvests, exacerbated by poor transport facilities. Writing in 1981, Neale calculated the relevant statistics at the beginning of the eighteenth century in these terms: 'In all some 335 households totalling, perhaps, 2,000 persons, serviced the twenty-nine lodging houses, the 324 inn beds, the fifty-eight licensed alehouses, the assembly room, the pump room, the theatre and the five small open baths which supplied most of the lusts and vanities of all its company.'[119]

In the 1720s Lady Bristol wrote that Bath was full of visitors, but that none of them were the type of person ('company') she would expect to mix with:

… ye town is so full as was never known, yet by what I can guess no company …

One of the attractions of Bath, however, was that a blurring of class divisions was acceptable there, but not in London. The circle of people with whom Lord Egmont spent time in Bath included the Speaker of the House of Commons, and others who were not all his social equals:[120]

I spend every day two hours in the evening at the Coffee House, with pleasure and improvement, especially in such public places as the Bath

Obelisk erected by Richard Nash in Orange Grove to commemorate the visit of the Prince of Orange in 1734 [▶ p. 147 illus].

BATH IN THE EARLY EIGHTEENTH CENTURY

Benn's Club of Aldermen, oil on canvas, Thomas Hudson, dated 1752. The painting depicts (left to right, with their livery company): Sir Thomas Rawlinson (grocer), Robert Alsop (ironmonger), Edward Ironside, Sir Henry Marshall (draper, who preceded Richard Hoare as Lord Mayor of London), William Benn (fletcher, who followed Hoare as Lord Mayor) and John Blachford (goldsmith). Ironside and Marshall feature in Bertrand's bank account, [▶ pp. 285, 292] as do many other City merchants and bankers. (GH)

Robert, Lord Nugent, oil on canvas, Thomas Gainsborough, c.1761. (Holburne)

and Tunbridge, because of the great resort of gentlemen thither for their health or amusement, out of whom a few who are of the same turn of conversation (after the ceremonies at making acquaintance are over) naturally select one another out and form a sort of society; when the season is over if we think it worth the while, we preserve the acquaintance; if not, there is no harm done, no offence is taken. The ease with which gentlemen converse, and the variety of their respective knowledge and experience is equally pleasing and instructive.

Who were the seasonal visitors to Bath and how many would have been customers of a toyshop? Itinerant gamblers and beggars would have accounted for quite a few, particularly the latter, who proved a nuisance for visitors and a troublesome expense for the Corporation. Most visitors would have brought a husband, wife or travelling companion, some came with their children, and many would have brought one or two servants at least. In 1703 John Verney travelled to Bath 'in my Calesh' with three servants. In 1752 Lady Luxborough, visiting the city alone, brought four servants, two female and two male. Earl Fitzwalter not only kept account of how much he spent on his visits to Bath and Tunbridge Wells, but also the number in his 'family' (meaning his household: family and servants) who travelled with him and his wife. In 1747 he took fifteen servants and fifteen horses. In the early years some shopkeepers, such as the Deards and their assistants, would have counted as seasonal visitors; they, like innkeepers and lodging-house keepers, must have employed extra servants locally. The markets and fairs were additional attractions for those living within easy reach of the city — Bristolians could make a day trip. If the visitor numbers quoted are to be believed, a good proportion must have been those termed 'the middling sort'.

p. 110

pp. 113–14

It is all too easy to be elitist and focus on the few who left some kind of record, and to ignore the silent majority, about whom we know so little but who would assuredly have gone to a toyshop to buy souvenirs of their visit. The 'middling sort' may or may not have gone into Bertrand's shop, but their presence in Bath explains how so many other toyshops, watchmakers and jewellers stayed in business. It seems more likely that customers of high-end shops such as Bertrand's were 'quality': a small percentage of visitors to Bath, but the percentage that had real money and the percentage on whose letters and diaries we largely rely for our knowledge of the period. They were the people who most attracted Richard Nash, and who in turn were attracted to the events he orchestrated for their entertainment.

The landed gentry and aristocracy are sometimes bracketed under the term 'quality', but the word also embraced wealthy merchants, bankers and clergy — what used to be called, in respect

(ABOVE AND TOP RIGHT) Snuffbox, gold, unmarked, with a glazed miniature inside the lid and armorials on the outside, Bernard Lens II, *c.* 1710. Width: 8.3 cm (3¼ in). The armorials are Hay-Drummond, probably for the 7th or 8th Earl of Kinnoull. The 9th Earl (1710–88) was called Viscount Dupplin between the deaths of his grandfather (in 1718/19) and father (in 1758). He features in Bertrand's bank account in the 1740s. [▶ p. 270] In 1734 his cousin the Duchess of Portland wrote to Mrs Delany of '… poor Dup's misfortune, or more properly, narrow escape; that affair is quite at an end, for as soon as he proposed himself she said "she never wou'd marry but with an equivalent estate". She was treated by all at the Bath just as she deserved, and I hear was hissed as she went along the streets, which pleased me much.' (Gilbert 317-2008)

(MIDDLE AND BOTTOM RIGHT) Etui, silver and shagreen, lacking its contents, *c.* 1755. Length: 10 cm (4 in). Inscribed inside the lid '1757 Peter Gaussen London'; he features in Bertrand's bank account. [▶ p. 276] Etuis (etwees) like this, containing a variety of implements, were among the most popular items in a toyshop. (W&W, 25.1.2011/505)

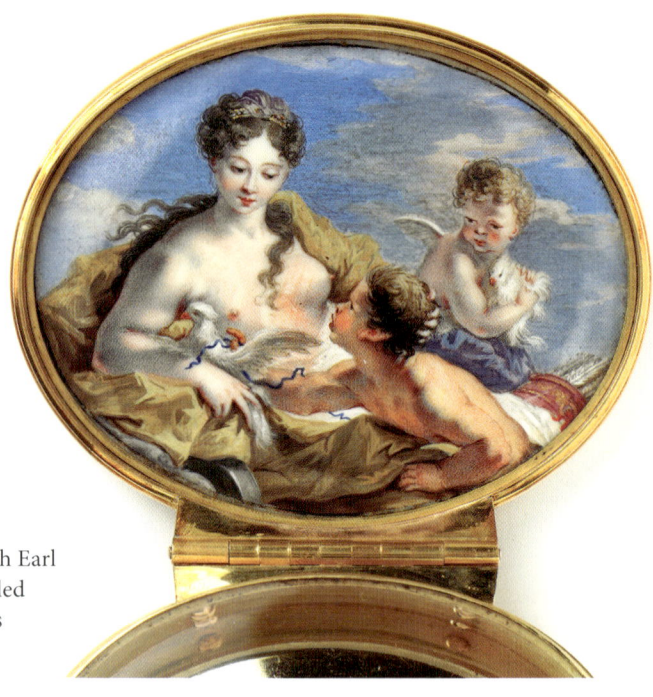

86   PART TWO: BATH AS A RESORT

of later generations, the upper ten thousand. It embraced members of both houses of parliament, graduates of Oxford and Cambridge, pupils of Eton, Harrow, Winchester and Westminster, and the scions of estates scattered throughout the country, from the great mansions to relatively small, but ancient, farmhouses. But in the early eighteenth century, countrywide the numbers of 'quality' were much smaller, perhaps no more than 2,000–3,000; Henry Fielding reckoned 'the ton' at about 1,200. The movements of the most eminent visitors were reported in the London newspapers and from 1744 the *Bath Journal* published the names of new arrivals. In 1746 510 were listed, a substantial increase over the previous year, however newspapers relied on the keepers of lodging houses and inns for information and made no claims of accuracy.[121]

The increase in published numbers occurred just as Bertrand was about to close his shop. Following the defeat of Prince Charles Edward Stuart at Culloden in April 1746, people would have felt it was safer to travel; the road from London and the number of lodgings in Bath had both been greatly improved; Princess Caroline was in the city for a prolonged visit; and the new game of EO had been introduced following the Gaming Act the previous year.

pp. 154–55

'This Day that Truly Great Man and Eminent Patriot the Earl of Chesterfield, is expected to arrive in this City, Lodgings being taken for his Lordship at Mr Leake's.'[122] Among others who lodged at Leake's bookshop, next to Bertrand's, were Viscount Perceval and Earl Cowper, but Chesterfield and Cowper are not in Bertrand's bank account. Chesterfield's correspondence shows that he was certainly in the city in 1734 (for two months), 1739, 1740, 1742, 1746 and 1748 (twice). It is inconceivable that he did not go into the toyshop. On the one hand Lord Chesterfield was exactly the kind of wealthy aristocrat who typified Bertrand's patrons, but on the other his renowned abstemiousness was not what Bertrand would have wanted in too many customers: Chesterfield advised his son that one snuff box and one cane handle from a toy store were enough for a man of fashion.

p. 176

Bath's Corporation may have suffered from provincialism, but people like Richard Nash, Ralph Allen and William Hoare (who settled in Bath in 1739) extended its horizons and from the 1730s onwards the city expanded physically, intellectually and socially. By the 1740s Allen and John Wood had their sights on making Bath a place to live rather than merely to visit. This, surely, is one reason to look objectively at this period in the city's history, for although 'the idea of corruption seemed to be naturally associated with the name of Bath', to view Bath only through novels and newspapers can distort the picture:[123]

If Bath had really been the sink of iniquity they would lead us to suppose, the excellent persons … would never have visited, and above all, revisited the town; they would have turned away from it in disgust. The very suspicion of contagion would have kept away or put to flight the respectable county families who were regular visitors to the town. Finally, the letters and memoirs in which Bath is so constantly mentioned would be filled, if not with indignant denunciations, at least with scandalous anecdotes and allusions. But, on the contrary, these are conspicuous by their absence …

The biggest change came at about the time the Bertrands closed their shop, and in the years of his retirement (1746–55). The differing tastes of Bath's widening clientele may well have partially influenced the Bertrands' decision to retire. They may have seen the city's developing attractions as further competition for their business. Bertrand would have needed to visit London regularly to keep up with the latest fashions and keep one step ahead of many of Bath's visitors, anticipating what they would wish to buy, perhaps himself influencing taste through his stock, ensuring that he had something to offer that other shops did not. Paul and Mary Bertrand and their staff would have been expected to recognise their customers from one year to the next, to know their likes and dislikes. The central position of their shop ensured that all visitors would pass by it frequently, if not daily, perhaps several times a day, during their stay. The challenge must have been to tempt people to buy, rather than just window-shop or treat the shop as a meeting place to gossip — and to make them buy in Bath rather than wait until they returned to London. With increasing competition from other shops and entertainments where people could part with money, the Bertrands must have worked long hours to maintain the footfall through their door.

Playing card, *c.* 1720.(LMA/WCMPC, 244) During 1720 and 1721, as a result of the South Sea Bubble, several advertisements promoted 'Bubble Cards', for example:

Saturday, December 24, 1720. Just published, A new Pack of Stockjobbing Cards … and Bubble Cards, spotted with their proper Colours, so that they may be played with as well as common Cards. Price 2s. 6d.

> In future Times 'twill hardly be believ'd,
> So wise an Age shou'd be so much deceiv'd
> By empty Bubbles : but, too late we find,
> That Avarice and Pride hath made us blind.

Printed for Tho. Bowles Printseller, next to the Chapter-House in St. Paul's Church-yard, Eman. Bowen, in St. Catherine's, where such as take a Quantity may have considerable Allowance; sold likewise by … Mr. Deard's a Toy-shop, at the King's Arms against St. Dunstan's Church, Fleet-street … at which Places are to be had the Bubble Cards. Price 2s. 6d.

Lady Hertford

The manner in which the 'Proud' Duke of Somerset and his duchess formally greeted their future daughter-in-law, Frances Thynne, the evening before her marriage in March 1714/15 to Algernon Seymour, Earl of Hertford and later 7th Duke of Somerset, is revealing of aristocratic behaviour in the early eighteenth century.[124]

… The Duke and Duchess of Somerset came to Mrs Thynne's with each of them a chagreen box in their hand, which they presented to Miss Thynne, who having had previous instructions from her mother not to open them in their presence, she forebore doing … One of them was a pair of diamond earrings from the Duke; the other a diamond necklace from the Duchess; both of them very fine for those days, when fine diamonds were not so frequently seen as they have been since.

In the early years of their marriage, Mary Wortley Montagu placed the couple at the heart of one of her six town eclogues, 'Tuesday, St James's Coffee-house', written in 1716. The character of Patch was the Earl of Hertford. Here is one of the verses under his name:

> My Countess is more nice, more artfull too,
> Affects to fly, that I may fierce persue.
> This Snuff box, while I begg'd, she still deny'd,
> And when I strove to snatch it, seem'd to hide,
> She laugh'd, and fled, and as I sought to seize
> With Affectation cramm'd it down her Stays:
> Yet hoped she did not place it there unseen;
> I press'd her Breasts, and pull'd it from between.

Frances Thynne and her sister Mary (who married 7th Lord Brooke) were daughters of Henry Thynne, son of 1st Viscount Weymouth, and his wife Grace, daughter of Sir George Strode. Mary was the mother of Francis, later Earl of Warwick. The Earl and Countess of Hertford had two children. Elizabeth (Betty) married on 16 July 1740 Sir Hugh Smithson, later Duke of Northumberland. George (called Beauchamp) died of smallpox on his nineteenth birthday in September 1744, a blow from which his mother never quite recovered.

Playing card, early eighteenth century, depicting the Duchess of Somerset. Elizabeth Percy (1666/7–1722) married the 6th Duke of Somerset as her third husband in 1682. She was made a Lady of the Bedchamber to Queen Anne in 1702 at a salary of £1,000, and was Groom of the Stole 1711–14, following the Duchess of Marlborough. She was chief mourner at the funerals of Queen Mary and Queen Anne. Her son Algernon, Earl of Hertford, succeeded as 7th Duke of Somerset in 1748. (LMA/WCMPC)

Lady Hertford, continued

On a visit to Bath in October 1747, Lord Hertford bought from John and Joanna Davis two Dresden figures for three guineas, a silver sliding pencil for 8s and a silver 'sprig for the hair' for 12s.[125] These modest purchases do not in any way reflect the standing of Lord and Lady Hertford, whose lives are well recorded; toys and jewels feature in a small way in their correspondence.

Little Brook is to be an Earl; I want to bespeak him a Lilliputian coronet at Chenevix's.

HORACE WALPOLE

Francis Greville, Lord Brooke (later 1st Earl of Warwick), oil on canvas, Jean Marc Nattier, signed and dated 1740. (Northumberland/Syon)

'Little Brook' was Francis Greville, 8th Baron Brooke (1719–73), who was created Earl Brooke in 1746 and Earl of Warwick in 1759.[126] His parents died when he was a child and Lady Hertford, his mother's sister, became one of his guardians. He married on 16 May 1742 Elizabeth, daughter of Lord Archibald Hamilton. Clearly a regular visitor to Bath, his arrival was listed, for example, on 22 October 1744 [▶p. 254]. He died at Warwick Castle.

While on his Grand Tour, which lasted from 1734 to 1740, he sent presents to his aunt and her family from Geneva. Clearly pleased with her new snuffbox, Lady Hertford showed it off to her friends at Court:

London, 5 Oct 1736 [Lord Hertford to his wife]

Mr Clark our next door neighbour came last night & has brought wth him from Lord Brooke two snuff boxes for you & Betty & two Pick tooth cases for Beauchamp & myself, they are all very pritty, I wont venture to send for fear of accidents.

Geneva, 5 Nov 1736

Dear Aunt

... I am exceedingly glad the Box pleased you & the rest of the Court. I am sure that was all my ambition. I wonder my Dear Aunt how you can talk about my Buying things for you the expence & such stuff I am sure I don't know how I can lay out my money better than in obliging my friends & if the sum was twenty times as much if it pleased them it would be the greatest pleasure alive to me. So if I ever find any little thing that I think you will like I shall send it to you. I believe you think me as poor as a church mouse.

Two years previously Lady Hertford's daughter Betty had been a train-bearer at the wedding of the Princess Royal to the Prince of Orange. Lady Hertford had given the prince and his party food and shelter in Marlborough, on his way to Bath [▶p. 145].

Algernon Seymour, Lord Hertford (later 7th Duke of Somerset), with family and friends, oil on canvas, Charles Philips. From left to right: Miss Herbert; Lady Elizabeth Seymour (later 1st Duchess of Northumberland); Frances, Lady Hertford; Lord Beauchamp; Colonel Browne; Lord Hertford; Colonel Tomkins Wardour. (Northumberland/Alnwick)

Several of the items depicted above could have come from a toyshop. In the 1730s and '40s a pair of scissors cost on average between 2s and 4s, but if in silver and cased, between 10s and 13s 6d. William Deards charged 2s 6d for putting a new side on scissors or 6d for re-setting a pair. A child's drum could cost as little as 6d, although a fringed pair such as Lord Beauchamp's would be more costly. A pair of garters cost on average between 2s 6d and 5s. In 1744 and 1745 the Duke of Gordon spent 6 guineas on a 'fine ivory and ebony backgammon table with ivory dice boxes and ivory and ebony chessmen', 3s for a 'set of common men for backgammon', and 3s 6d and 7s 6d for two pairs of dice — all from Elizabeth Chenevix.

The Kingston Estate

Terrace Walk was part of the Kingston Estate [▶ p. 24 map]. Evelyn Pierrepont, 1st Duke of Kingston, died a couple of years before the row of buildings that contained Paul and Mary Bertrand's shop was redeveloped [▶ p. 76]. A substantial amount of property in Bath and Bradford-on-Avon came to the Kingston family when the 1st Duke's son (who predeceased him in 1713) married Rachel Hall in 1711. The duke was succeeded by his grandson (1711–73), renowned for his marriage in 1769 to Elizabeth Chudleigh; she had married the Earl of Bristol in 1744, who was still alive at the time of her bigamous marriage to the duke. Mary Wortley Montagu was the daughter of the 1st Duke of Kingston and thus the 2nd Duke's aunt.

Thomas Cromp, the agent of the Kingston estates, features in Bertrand's bank account between 1737 and 1739. It is tempting to speculate whether the monetary transactions related to the assembly rooms that the Wiltshire family took over, but Cromp might also have been in Bath to negotiate with John Wood over the site of North and South Parades, the lease of which was signed in 1739.

Tureen, one of a pair, silver, made for the 2nd Duke of Kingston after designs by Juste-Aurèle Meissonnier, Paris 1735–40. Length: 45.7 cm (18 in). (SNY, 13.5.1998)

The actions of the 1st Duke's trustees demonstrate the high priority given to plate and trinkets when dealing with the investments, land and personal property of grandees. Among his personal effects were many items that might have been acquired at a toyshop. The duke was buried on 8 March 1725/26; on 24 March his trustees met in Arlington Street and the duke's keys, his pocket book, etwee and purse, were handed over to them. On 28 March the gold and silver plate was sent for safekeeping to Hoare & Co.,[127] to be followed two days later by personal effects that included 'a large gold seal with the late Lord Pierrepont's arms'. One of the duke's gentlemen then handed over 'two pair of Gold Shoe Buckles, & one pair for the Knees of Britches & one for the Garter of the Order two pair of Sleeve Buttons & Two Georges, a small silver Case of Instruments for the Teeth & a reading Glass & an old silver Watch' and 'Mr Cromp delivered from her Grace his late Grace's repeating Watch by Tompion & two seals one with his Graces Arms & the other with two heads, a Gold toothpick Case, an Agate Snuff box sett in Gold a mother of Pearl Box sett in Gold & a Tortoiseshell box studded with gold, a gold hinge & rim' all of which went into a strong box to go to the bank. Some of the plate left by the 1st Duke might have been sent to France by his grandson to be refashioned into a pair of soup tureens made in Paris 1735–40 (part of a table setting designed by Juste Aurèle Meissonnier that was never completed) but a considerable quantity was taken to Russia by Elizabeth Chudleigh.[128]

It is worth noting that in 1755, the year Paul Bertrand died, important Roman remains were discovered during the course of excavations for new baths on the Kingston estate in Bath. Bertrand may have witnessed this just as, when they were in Bath for the season, members of his wife's family may have admired the bronze head of Sulis Minerva, which was discovered in 1727.

Lindsays and Hayes's both farewel
Where in the spacious hall,
With bounding steps and sprightly air,
I've led up many a ball.

LADY MARY WORTLEY MONTAGU

The assembly rooms

THE TWO ASSEMBLY ROOMS in Terrace Walk were each known by the name of their current proprietor. Lady Mary Wortley Montagu encapsulated Bath society, and neatly linked the toyshop and both rooms, in verses published in 1731.[129] More than physical proximity in Terrace Walk connected them. The story of the proprietors of the two Bath assembly rooms, their lives and the possessions they mention in their wills, are part of the background to the culture of toys and toyshops in Bath. The assembly rooms were run by some particularly colourful personalities during the time that John Deards, and later Paul and Mary Bertrand, traded there. What went on in the rooms was important to shopkeepers: who lost money to whom, who danced with whom, the gossip, the prevailing mood, whether visitors were pleased or critical of the management. All this would have affected a day's trade.

It is now possible to expand on information in the writings of John Wood (1749) and Francis Fleming (1771). Fleming arrived in Bath in 1732 and was leader of the Pump Room band until his death.[130] He was in Scarborough in 1736, the year after Mary Bertrand's brother, William Deards, is first known to have traded there, and became a friend of Deards' son John (Mary Bertrand's nephew), who continued the family's seasonal shop in Scarborough as well as their principal shop in London.[131] Describing events in Bath that took place some forty years earlier, Fleming wrote:[132]

pp. 19 illus., 23 map

Mr Harrison's being the only house of amusement, he made what exactions he pleased, till the company grew much dissatisfied, and applied to Mr Nash to get another room built at the lower end of the Walks, which was done accordingly at the expense of Mr Theyer, on some ground belonging to the Duke of Kingston, and Mrs Lindsey, a person who sung in the opera, was fixed on to conduct it. The balls were held Tuesdays and Fridays alternately at each room, beginning at six o'clock and ending at eleven …

When Mr Harrison died, Mrs Lindsey (with the consent of Mr Nash) sent for her sister Mrs Hayes, to take upon her the management of his rooms;

Assembly rooms and gaming houses

	RIVER SIDE ROOMS		LOWER ROOMS
1708/09	Site leased from John Hall, by Thomas Harrison, who built the rooms and developed walks by the river.	1706	Charles Delamain built a 'room' and had gaming tables at the southern end of Terrace Walk.
1711	John Hall's illegitimate daughter married Viscount Newark (died 1713), son of the 1st Duke of Kingston (died 1725/26). Hall died later in 1711; his properties in Bath and Bradford-on-Avon passed into the Kingston family.	1713	Mary Lindsey in Charles Delamain's building.
1720	Ballroom added to the designs of William Killigrew.	1728–30	Built by Humphrey Thayer to designs of John Wood on land belonging to the 2nd Duke of Kingston.
1731–45	Elizabeth Hayes, Lady Hawley	1730–36	Mary Lindsey
		1736–40	Catherine Lovelace
1745–55	William Simpson; the rooms extended again in 1750.	1740–47	Ann Wiltshire
1755–71	Charles Simpson	1747–62	John Wiltshire
		1762–67	Walter Wiltshire
		1767–71	Cam Gyde
1771–85	Cam Gyde	1771	Rooms closed
1785–1820	Thomas, then James Heaven. Burned December 1820	1805	Demolished to form York Street [▶ pp. 22–23 map]
1824–1933	Rebuilt as Bath Royal Literary and Scientific Institution		
1933	Demolished		

The New or Upper rooms that exist today were built after Paul Bertrand's time in Bath. They were opened in 1771, given to the National Trust in 1931, bombed in 1942 and restored 1956–63.

but they played into each other's hands, in such a manner, as greatly displeased the company, who found themselves not in the least relieved from the exactions they before complained of. Mr Nash accordingly interposed, and the two sisters were under a necessity of lowering their charges. Soon after an enmity arose between them, which was never got over, and Mrs Lindsey at her death left the whole of her fortune to her house-keeper Mrs Lovelace, who continued mistress of the room until her death. After this Mr Nash, for political reasons, prevented as much as possible the least intimacy between the two rooms.

Harrison's rooms were not 'the only house of amusement', but there seems no reason to disbelieve Fleming's description of high prices and family dispute. Richard Nash's attempts to prevent intimacy between the two rooms were undermined by his own involvement through gambling.

Hitherto, the identities of the women who ran the assembly rooms have been muddled: they have been named as Dame Catherine Lindsey and Elizabeth Hayes or Hawley. John Wood wrote of two sisters: 'The Dame's Wit and Humour, with the Appearance of Sanctity in a Sister that Lived with her … Kitty was the familiar Name of that Pattern of Piety', and their wills prove that Lindsey's name was Mary not Catherine. Catherine (Kitty) Hayes died in 1731, leaving her property to 'my dear sister Mary Lindsey'. So there were three women, but Catherine Hayes plays no part in events related here. Fleming described the women who ran the two rooms as sisters. It is likely that Mary Lindsey's maiden name was Hayes, but Elizabeth could have been a sister-in-law rather than sibling, as she was described as a widow when she married Francis Hawley in 1718/19.

Both Mary Lindsey and Elizabeth Hayes may have had links with the theatre in London, but these are as yet unproven. Clues are given here as a possible backdrop to their activities in Bath.

Detail p. 50, showing the distinctive high round windows of the lower assembly rooms.

THE EAST OR RIVER-SIDE ROOMS
Thomas Harrison followed by Elizabeth Hayes

In the first years of the eighteenth century, improvements were being made to many of the city's buildings, but[133]

… the Company were driven to the necessity of meeting in a booth to drink their tea and chocolate and to divert themselves at cards, till Mr Thomas Harrison, at the instigation of the new King of Bath, erected a handsome Assembly House for those purposes.

Thomas Harrison was a liveryman of the Cutlers' Company in London, as were John and William Deards. He opened his rooms in Terrace Walk, facing the river, in 1708/09. His account with

Hoare & Co. shows that from 1710 he was handling financial transactions for many well-known figures in Bath: the names of several re-appear in Bertrand's account later on.

In April 1730 Lord Perceval noted in his diary that:[134]

I went this morning to Mr. Hore's the banker, and left with him 930 l of my brother Dering's money and took a note for his use of the other 70 l drawn by Mr. Hore on Harrison, of the Bath. I also caused the 20 l paid by Hore to a woman in Bath last year on my brother Dering's account to be entered in my account with Mr. Hore and my brother Dering is to account with me for it.

pp. 37, 74, 93

Harrison's account ceased in May 1731, and Bertrand and Wiltshire may have picked up the banking side of Harrison's affairs at that time. When Lady Mary Montagu's verses were published two months later in July, Elizabeth Hayes and Lord Hawley had the management of Harrison's rooms — which Harrison mentions in the will he made on 24 December 1734.[135]

Elizabeth Hayes' identity is problematic. As she seems to have been in both London and Bath, the possibility that there were two women with this name cannot be discounted, but the seasonal life of Bath, and of the theatre, would have enabled her to operate in several spheres.[136] She was married twice (two documents dating from 1719 describe her as a widow), but no evidence of her first marriage has been found. It is also possible that she used her maiden name throughout her two marriages.

Hayes is a relatively common surname: in Bath there was a goldsmith named Phillip, a barber and periwig maker named Robert,[137] and there was Samuel, who in 1700 was one of a group who took advantage of a young and inexperienced man and 'persuaded him to drink and play hazard, backgammon and other games and extorted bonds for gaming debts from him with menaces'.[138]

In 1700 the Council, realising that it was desirable to have a freeman who was a goldsmith, appointed Phillip Hayes.[139] The last known evidence of him is on a lease in 1713: he had the end shop in Orange Grove, close to the archway that led from the Grove into Terrace Walk, until about 1718–19.[140] In October 1719 Elizabeth Hayes, a widow, was the plaintiff in a case relating to the lease of a shop and a room with the use of a kitchen in the Grove in Bath, which she had 'caused to be furnished and bought in vast quantities of valuable goods for sale in her way of trade'.[141] What that trade was, is not explained, but she could have been in Phillip Hayes' premises.

Elizabeth Hayes was described as 'widow' when, on 11 March 1718/19 she married Francis, 2nd Baron Hawley at All Hallows,

Detail ▶ p. 60. There was a rank for sedan chairs near the archway that gave access between Orange Grove and Terrace Walk. The watercolour [▶ p. 19] shows the Terrace Walk side of the same arch.

London Wall. A son, Samuel, was born at about this time.[142] It seems safe to assume that she is the Elizabeth Hayes who had a bank account with Hoare & Co. during the 1720s, and she used the name Hayes to run the riverside assembly rooms that she took over from Thomas Harrison in 1731. Harrison described his rooms as 'in the possession of Lord Hawley', but Hawley's daughter Rachel called her 'Mrs Elizabeth Hayes' in her will.

In the early 1720s Lord Hawley had a house in Bath in Orange Grove, abutting the Abbey.[143] It was at about this time that Mary Delany, then unhappily married to her first husband Alexander Pendarves, learned of one of Lord Hawley's daughters from his first marriage. Her story may typify the pitfalls that some young people fell victim to, particularly in Bath where they easily made friends with (in Mrs Delany's words) 'wild and unprincipled people', just as 'Miss Sylvia' was to do a few years later. Mrs Delany wrote at considerable length of [144]

Miss H —, daughter of Lord —, the Earl of —'s son, who had been so reduced in his circumstances that he married Mrs Hays, who kept the rooms at Bath, for a maintenance. Lady Pendarves, when at Bath, was moved with compassion at seeing a young creature like Miss H— exposed to every danger that beauty, high spirits, and no education must necessarily subject her to, without a prudent relation or friend to guard and admonish her.

Mrs Delany's wording is not entirely clear. In addition to her other activities, Hayes was tenant of a property (demolished in 1738 to make way for the new hospital) that housed Bath's playhouse, for which she took a percentage of the takings. Mrs Delany may have been referring to the facilities there, where private parties were probably also held, in rather simpler surroundings than the assembly rooms.[145] John Wood linked the closure of the theatre to 'the suppression of play houses by the Act of Parliament which took place the 24th of June 1737 and the death of Mr Thayer the 9th of the following December'. However it seems that performances were moved to Elizabeth Hayes' assembly rooms in 1732, shortly after she took them over.[146]

She made a will (as Lady Hawley) only a few days before her death: its brevity suggests that she may by then have been very weak. The will was witnessed by Paul Bertrand, Thomas Pomfret and Samuel Hemming: it is easy to imagine them crossing the road between Bertrand's shop and the assembly rooms to do so. The *Bath Journal* of 4 February 1744/45 noted that 'Last Tuesday night died Lady Hawley (relict of Lord Hawley) who has for several Years past kept one of the Houses here for Publick Assemblies, Balls etc known by the name of Mrs. Hayes's.' She left everything to her son

THE ASSEMBLY ROOMS 97

The Long Room at the river side assembly rooms, pencil on paper, Thomas Robins snr (1716–70). Thomas Harrison opened the rooms in 1708/09, and enlarged them to the designs of Thomas Killigrew in 1720. They were extended again in 1749 after the death of Elizabeth Hayes, who managed the rooms 1731–45. (V&A, Bath in Time, 13081)

The Long Room of the lower assembly rooms, pen and ink, Thomas Robins snr. The rooms were designed by John Wood and opened in 1730. In Paul Bertrand's time they were managed by Mary Lindsey, then by Catherine Lovelace, Ann Wiltshire and John Wiltshire. (V&A, Bath in Time, 13075)[▶ p. 187 illus.]

Samuel, and the following October Bertrand made two payments to him totalling £752.[147]

Francis Hawley's daughter Rachel died in 1743. She bequeathed an amethyst ring set with her father's and her brother's hair and 'a cornelian seal with a head cut on it' to Elizabeth Hayes. Her niece received 'my watch and chain and all the things hanging at it except what I shall otherways dispose of' together with her snuff boxes; she also bequeathed a mother-of-pearl snuff box, gold buttons, a ring set with little diamonds and rubies. To her half-brother Samuel she left 'my father's picture that is set with diamonds and my gold tweezer case and my iron snuff box sett in gold and a silver seal'. At least some of these things might well have been acquired in Bertrand's shop.[148]

THE LOWER ROOMS
Charles Delamain and Mary Lindsey

The lower rooms were opened with a public breakfast on 6 April 1730 and a ball the next day — the season in which Paul and Mary Bertrand opened their shop — and were run by Mary Lindsey. The rooms were on the same side of Terrace Walk as the Bertrands' shop, a little to the south, in a building designed by John Wood. However Lindsey had been in business before then, in premises built by Charles Delamain.

Many writers on Bath have repeated John Wood's sad tale of 'Sylvia', who was driven to suicide, but they have largely overlooked Mr Delamain:[149]

p. 103

> This unfortunate young Lady was particularly attach'd to the Interest of Dame Lindsey; and when I first came down to Bath in the Year 1727, Sylvia was entirely at the Dame's Command, whenever a Person was wanting to make up a Party for Play at her House, which went by the Name of De la Mains, from the Builder and former Occupier of it.

As a jeweller and goldsmith, Charles Delamain sold toys: he therefore has a place in this story.

p. 37

Delamain took on a lease of a property at the lower end of Terrace Walk in 1706. There, he was encouraged to build a 'room … with freestone the expense whereof cost him considerable sums of money'.[150] Richard Nash's recent arrival in Bath may have had some bearing on this. Delamain:

p. 76 illus.

> … did there carry on the trade of a Jeweller and also for the Entertainment of Quallity in the Summer Season did under the permission of the Groom Porter keep severall Gaming Tables but the situation of the premises being not so convenient as other houses thereabout the said Delamain could not obtain Trade and Custom sufficient to support him …

He would have faced stiff competition from the better-located, and probably more lavishly appointed, rooms built by Harrison at much the same time. Delamain had over-extended himself, and in 1707 had to mortgage the property for £300 to Colonel John Pocock, a sum that he was unable to repay. Delamain died in 1711 and his lease devolved to Pocock.[151] Now Mary Lindsey enters the story: she took Pocock and Delamain's executors to court on behalf of his younger daughter, a minor, claiming that the executors 'possessed themselves of [his] personal estate consisting of haberdasher's hardwares, money, security for money, plate, jewels and household goods'. She continued litigating on her own account until 1716.[152]

She was litigating because she fell out with Pocock and those who took on Delamain's lease, Henry Smith and Humphrey Thayer. In 1713 Pocock contacted Lindsey 'who was an inhabitant in London and requested her to become his tenant ' — which she did. Pocock had earlier rejected an application from Mr Powell, who had a puppet show, because he thought he would prove insolvent, and clearly thought Mary Lindsey would be a better tenant. However, a dispute arose over the extension of her initial lease and because of Henry Smith, who was

p. 131

> … an inhabitant near and adjoining to and carrying on the business of a Toyshop of the like nature with that in which your Oratrix [Lindsey] is Imployed.

Complaining also of Delamain's executors and others who she thought had been charged 'to molest and incommode' her, Lindsey protested that she had

> brought her trade into a flourishing state or condition and that … Henry Smith, perceiving that … by her care and diligence has obtained a better trade than himself is become uneasy thereat.

Clearly there was rivalry, but the interesting point is that Mary Lindsey seems to have taken on Delamain's retail business as well as the gaming-tables. The two went hand-in-hand. If Lindsey was related to the goldsmith Phillip Hayes, she would have been familiar with luxury retailing. Interesting, too, is the fact that Pocock approached her in 1713, for this is the year that an opera singer in London of the same name goes off record.[153]

Previous writers have repeated without comment Fleming's description of Mrs Lindsey, 'a person who sang in the opera'. There was an opera singer called Mary Lindsey who enjoyed considerable fame between 1697 and 1713 in London. In 1705 a petition from a number of London actors and actresses, protesting against a proposed union between the two London theatre companies, included the signature of Mary Lindsey.[154] It cannot be proved that the singer in London and the proprietor of a Bath assembly room were the same person, and opera historians have hitherto been sceptical of any connection, but such a link seems very possible.[155]

The London singer performed before Queen Anne on four known occasions and was regularly in the Haymarket, often working with the singer and composer Richard Leveridge, specialising in the entertainments between acts ('comical dialogues') and performing works by Purcell. They sang together during the summer season at Tunbridge Wells and she gave benefit concerts in London in York Buildings, the concert room owned at one time by Sir Richard Steele in Villiers Street (off the Strand). This was a favoured area for numerous luxury shops and goldsmiths including, a few years later, Paul Bertrand's close friend the goldsmith Peter Russel.[156]

In taking her dispute with John Pocock and Henry Smith to court, Lindsey had support from an interesting group of men who either knew her in London, or visited Bath. Richard Nash approached Smith, and Pocock 'was applied to by Sir John Lambert Mr Swarts Mr Nun Mr Moteux & several others'. Sir John Lambert, 'an opulent London merchant', was given a baronetcy in February 1710/11 'as a reward for his exertions to uphold the public credit in that year, by supplying the Treasury with large sums of money'. He died in February 1722/23.[157] Mr Swarts is probably 'Baron Swartz the great Jew', who in 1720 purchased items from the sale of the Arundel Collection. An enthusiast of horse racing, he was assaulted and wounded at a gaming table at Epsom by Lord Muskerry, in September 1721.[158] Mr Nun may be the Mr Noon who features in Elizabeth Hayes' bank account in the 1720s. Motteux is best known as the translator of *Don Quixote*. In 1704 Mary Lindsey and Richard Leveridge performed in 'a Dialogue which was originally perform'd by them in the opera of The Island Princess'; the libretto was by Pierre Motteux. From around 1711, Motteux turned away from his career as a writer and opened a luxury goods shop in Leadenhall Street, the stock of which included toys and India wares. He died in dubious circumstances in a brothel in 1718.[159]

It is unclear how the litigation was resolved, however Charles Delamain's property devolved to Humphrey Thayer and Mary Lindsey remained in business. She is mentioned in Thomas Coke's account book at Holkham, in 1720, which documents:[160]

Peter Motteux and his family, pen and brown ink with grey wash, Giovanni Antonio Pellegrini. (BM, 1874-0808.43)

THE ASSEMBLY ROOMS 101

Codes of conduct

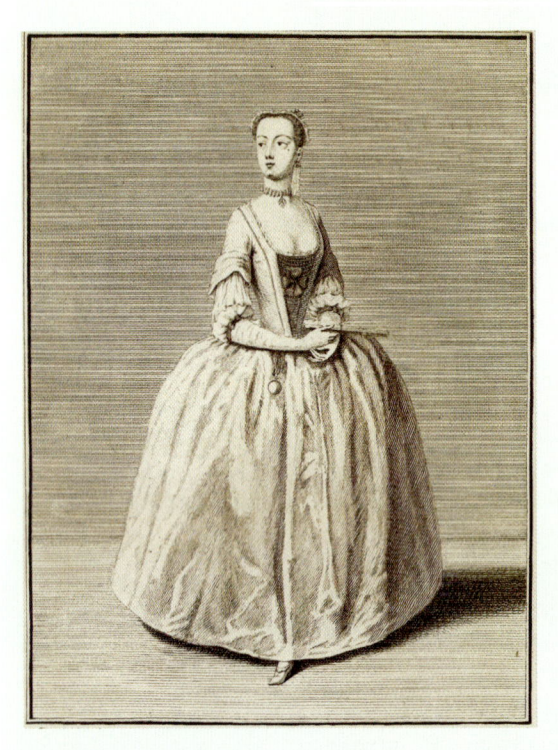

For the ingénue making a first appearance at a ball, dowagers and fortune hunters were every bit as formidable in Bath as they were in London. In purchasing from a toyshop the accoutrements dictated by fashion, both ladies and gentlemen had to learn what was considered good taste, as well as how to wear and use a range of objects.

Before being launched into society a young person had lessons in deportment, in dancing, genteel behaviour and etiquette, for which tutors generally came to a pupil's house or lodgings. A gentleman had to bow correctly, present his snuffbox elegantly, carry and use his sword in a manly fashion. A lady had to respond with the right depth of curtsey and 'bridle' when entering a room; she had to learn how to wear jewellery, hold a fan, place patches and just how many toys were thought appropriate on a watch chain.

The social mix of visitors to Bath was one of the features that made it an interesting place to visit. But the manners of the aristocracy, the country squire, the town beau and an ambitious lawyer or merchant did not easily blend, and the behaviour of some (from all classes) threatened to destroy the city's reputation. Thus it was that when Richard Nash became Master of Ceremonies one of his first tasks was to publish a set of rules that covered dress code and the hours for balls, among a variety of other matters.

As the central role of gambling in the pleasures on offer in Bath dissolved, so too did the influence of the nobility on its culture. Their desire to move within a small circle of intimates as they peregrinated between London and various resorts was understandable at a time when their lives were largely lived in public. When at home their houses were filled with staff, hangers-on and the wider family. When in Bath they would have spent more time in the pump room, coffee houses, assembly rooms and the Grove, than in their lodgings, unless they were very unwell. On holiday from politics and management of their estates, some escaped from stultifying and inconsequential gossip into drink, cards and dice; others enjoyed the opportunity, both in Bath and in Tunbridge Wells, for discussion with people with whom they would not usually mix.

One of a twelve plates from F. Nivelon's The Rudiments of Genteel Behaviour demonstrating 'Standing', etching and engraving after Bartolomew Dandridge, published 1737. Other plates show 'The courtsie', 'To give or receive', 'Walking', 'Dancing', 'Giving a hand in a minuet', 'Giving both hands in a minuet', 'Walking and saluting passing by', 'The bow', 'The complement retiring', 'To offer or receive', 'Dancing the minuet'. The lady's cap, earrings, necklace, fan, watch, ribbons and patch might all have come from a toyshop. (BM, 1882,1209.753-765)

					£	s	d
1720	Entertainmts at Bath						
26 May	To Dame Lindsey for an Entertainment & supper				18	16	0
	For ye Use of her Rooms	3	3	0			
	& to ye Musick	3	3	0	6	6	0
	Given to her Servants for their trouble at ye Ball				1	1	0
					26	3	0
13 June	To Mr Harrison for having a Ball in his Room				27	0	0
	And to his servants for their trouble					10	6
					£27	10	6

In August 1721 Lady Bristol reported that Betty Southel [Southwell] 'came back from Lindseys loaded with silver and a bitt or two of gold she had nickd Syms out off at hasard' and that she herself had been 'but three times at Lindseys since I came and once at Harrisons to see a medly ye Duke of Warton bespoke'.[161]

Charles Delamain's building may have been incorporated into the planning of the new assembly rooms when, according to John Wood, in 1727 'Mr Thayer directed me to contrive such an Assembly House for the famous Dame Lindsey as could be turned to other Uses for a small Expenditure', and that she was 'zealously bent upon a House'. Once the new (lower) rooms opened in 1730, according to Wood they 'proved so very successful that she [Lindsey] in a few years amass'd in it at least £8,000.[162]

She was not universally popular. Oliver Goldsmith related the same story as John Wood about 'Miss Sylvia S---', and is less than flattering to Lindsey — the episode caused a considerable scandal at the time:

This woman's name was Dame Lindsey, a creature who, though vicious, was in appearance sanctified, and, though designing, had some wit and humour. She began by the humblest assiduity to ingratiate herself with Miss S .... Whenever a person was wanting to make up a party for play at Dame Lindsey's, Sylvia ... was sent for and was obliged to suffer all those slights which the rich but too often let fall upon their inferiors in point of fortune.

Goldsmith's aim was to show how Richard Nash attempted to rescue the girl who, though 'descended from one of the best families in the kingdom', was ruined financially and morally by her affection for a man whose life ended in gaol. Her tale (and those of others like her) was seen as symptomatic of the seamier side of resort life.[163]

Clearly the job of running such establishments was a tough one, requiring a head for business, an ability to deal with and pander to the inflated egos of visitors and, it seems, a lack of scruples over how these aims were achieved. Mrs Pendarves wrote to her sister six days after Lindsey's death.[164]

p. 99

Dial plate for a toy watch, lead alloy, first half eighteenth century. Diameter: 4.6 cm (1¾ in). (London, 98.2/462)

p. 249   … as to her [Mrs Barber] undertaking Dame Lindseys, she is the unfittest person for it in the world, she would be cheated by everybody, and not able to keep herself, and her daughter is too young and unexperienced to be of any great use to her in the management of so difficult a sort of business … I think it too hazardous an undertaking to persuade her to it.

Writing in 1771, Fleming reported that there was 'an enmity' between Mary Lindsey and Elizabeth Hayes. The rift must have occurred within months of Hayes's succession to Harrison's rooms, as Lindsey signed a new will on 1 August 1732 leaving her property to Catharine Lovelace, who lived with her. Lindsey died in 1736 and Lovelace had the assembly rooms until her own death in 1740; she bequeathed 'a little picture of Mrs Mary Lyndsey set in Gold'.[165]

p. 46 illus.   Lovelace may have handed the day-to-day management of the rooms to another. This would explain Mrs Pendarves's piece of gossip and, as the Mrs Barber she referred to is not heard of again, the Wiltshire family in the person of Ann Wiltshire, mother of John and Walter jnr, may have become involved in management of the lower assembly rooms at this stage, before taking them over following Lovelace's death.[166]

▶ pp. 23/39 and 41
Orange Grove, detail ▶ p. 60

The Expences of the Journey to Bath in 3 days of my Lady: £25 6s 3d
HOUSEHOLD ACCOUNTS, THOMAS COKE[167]

When to go and how to get there

EARLY IN THE EIGHTEENTH CENTURY Bath's season was in the summer, but this was also the time of Tunbridge Wells' season. The attractions of the two resorts were very similar but the Wells had the advantage of being closer to London, and so Bath's season was moved. The annual round of social events — how and where the aristocracy and gentry spent their time — was dictated primarily by the London season during November to May (which meant the royal family's Courts, when Parliament was sitting, legal terms) and then by field sports and the racing calendar. In Bath, for example, race meetings were held towards the end of September, when the season was under way and the ground still hard. In the provinces assize weeks (when judges were on circuit to dispense justice outside London) were a social focus too.

During the period that the Deards family and Paul Bertrand were trading, September and October were the months of the greatest number of arrivals in the city (when it was usual to stay until early December), followed by March and April. Early in September and March the start of balls in the assembly rooms and music in the Pump Room was announced, indicating that there was a break in the organised entertainments in January and February, between the main seasons; but in one sense the seasons merged and regular visitors came and went at any time between the end of August and early May. Virtually nobody arrived in June or July and the number of entries in Bertrand's accounts reflect this, with on average a month's delay to allow for the receipt of payments and their processing in London.

Newspapers were upbeat about the prospects for each coming season: 'We have Reason to believe that this Season will be the fullest that we have had these many Years, most of our Lodgings being taken for the latter End of this month' was a sentence that appeared regularly in early September in reports from Bath published in London papers, and in the *Bath Journal*.

Men travelling alone would have been better able to tolerate the discomforts of a crowded and slow public conveyance than a family with servants, but sufficient endured that discomfort, and found the resources, to make the journey. In the seventeenth century it took on average about sixty hours to travel from London to Bath;

Miniature model of a horse and carriage, silver, Arnoldus van Geffen, Amsterdam, c. 1734. Width: 11.5 cm (4½ in). In 1734 Sir Richard Hoare bought from William Deards 'a chase and a pair of horses' for 4s, but the material was not specified in the invoice. (SL)

Equipment for travel

The logistics and cost of travelling to Bath must have inhibited many who might otherwise have benefited from taking the waters, and both men and women were assiduous in keeping records of their journeys. Any journey involved several changes of horses, which were hired for each stage. The cost of travelling by coach and keeping horses, together with the time a journey took, were noted in detail as a reminder, in case a trip had to be repeated. Those who owned coaches were taxed but, like the tax on plate, many people were slow to pay.[168]

Many of the items stocked by toyshops were specifically designed for use when travelling. Eating equipment and toiletries were cased for carrying in a pocket or as hand luggage. Maps, compasses and pocket dials were needed. Lamps and watches were designed to accommodate the swaying of a coach. Toyshops also supplied some of the accoutrements of a horseman: whips, spurs, and flasks for brandy. The Duke of Gordon purchased a travelling dispensary from William Deards in 1748; portable writing desks and inkwells with secure caps were also a necessity.

Spirit flask, silver, unmarked, *c.* 1690. Height: 13.7 cm (5⅜ in). Engraved with the arms and monogram of Charles, 1st Duke of St Albans (1670–1726), illegitimate son of Charles II and Eleanor Gwynne. He died at Bath [▶ p. 71]. Sold by toyshops, small and portable flasks such as this were used when hunting and travelling. (SL, 9.6.1994/327)

the time steadily shortened as the roads were improved and by 1750 had been cut to about thirty-six hours. Most of Bertrand's clients would have used their own or a hired coach; horses were hired at each stage of the journey. A few would have travelled in the same style as Sir John Finch in 1680: 'My brother Sr John has bin at Bath and will be tomorrow at Tunbridge with his chariot and six Flanders horses and all things suitable thereunto; so that he will be the chief spark there.'[169] The family account book of the Earls of Rockingham [▶ p. 110] shows how high was the cost of travel, and the care of horses, in comparison to the price of lodgings or food, and also gives an indication of the advance planning required for a woman travelling on her own from Northamptonshire to Somerset.[170] At the other end of the social spectrum some visitors walked, but not those who would have been Bertrand's customers.

In the early 1740s there were seventeen weekly coaches from London to Bath, twenty-three in 1757. Conditions greatly improved for travellers from London from 1745. In March of that year advertisements announced that the journey by stage coach took two days,[171] by August a stretch of road from Beckhampton, near Marlborough, through Calne and Chippenham to Pickwick, was completed, a more level route than the one previously available. It boasted 'watering places every two or three miles'.[172] Only what we would now term 'hand luggage' could be taken on a coach; additional luggage would have been sent ahead by carrier. The roads would have been full of waggons as well as coaches, together with those travelling on foot and those herding livestock. Baggage would, for the most part, have been sent in advance, and servants (often referred to as 'my family') might also have travelled separately.

The vicinity of Newbury or Reading was the most convenient for an overnight stop, and those who had houses en route, where it was possible to break the journey, were no doubt frequently called upon for accommodation. These included the Duke of Chandos (Shaw Hall, near Reading), Lady Orkney (Cliveden), and Mr Poyntz, near Newbury, at whose house the Princess of Hesse broke her return journey to London in October 1746.[173] Sandy Lane, near Calne, was the Prince of Orange's last overnight stop before reaching Bath in 1732, having had an unpleasant journey via Marlborough. During the winter the Marlborough Downs were a particularly treacherous stretch of the route:[174]

[24 December 1726] Last Monday the Coach was set fast in the Snow, and forced to stay all Night on the Downs beyond Marlborough; the Horses were taken out, and put into a Stable at Marlborough, and the poor Passengers left to make the best of themselves in the Coach all Night.

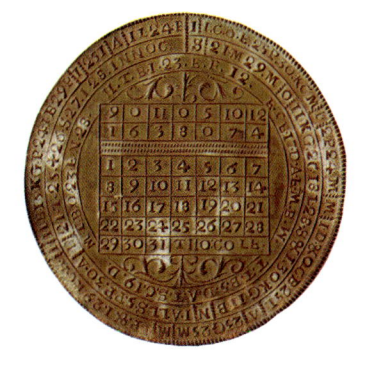

Calendar, brass, *c.* 1735. Diameter: 5 cm (2 in). Perpetual calendars made in silver, ivory, or base metals, were devised to give a variety of information, such as phases of the moon, tides, a monthly and weekly calendar, sunrise and sunset. (Private coll)

pp. 298, 157 and 302

p. 145

WHEN TO GO AND HOW TO GET THERE 107

Transport of goods

A trip to Bath usually involved more than a single person travelling alone — many took a substantial household. Family and servants needed to be transported, together with clothing, linen and other necessaries, which were usually sent separately. This was the lifeblood of the Wiltshire family's business as carriers. Transporting valuable property over considerable distances required experience: in addition to difficulties caused by weather conditions, goods and personal luggage attracted opportunist thieves. During the visit of Princess Caroline in April 1746 the *Bath Journal* reported:

p. 45

p. 154

p. 163

A trunk has been missing ever since the 2nd Instant directed to the Right Hon Lady Isabella Finch, which was sent with HRH Pr Caroline's baggage. Reward of 5 guineas. [the luggage included] a white onyx seal with three griffins set in gold + her maid's clothes.

The theft of relatively modest personal baggage in 1752, which included toys, is another example:[175]

Isaac Odaway was indicted for stealing one hair trunk, two iron padlocks, fifteen holland shirts, eleven pair of cotton stockings, six pair of thread ditto, seventeen handkerchiefs, three pair of velvet breeches, one pair of cloth breeches, nine pair of dresden and worked ruffes, a gold chain, a gold watch, three seals, a velvet cap, a set of pebble buckles for shoes and knees; the goods of Walter Wiltshire …

Walter Wiltshire. I am owner of the Bath waggon; the goods mentioned were the property of William Coleman, Esq; the trunk with the other goods in it, and 130 l. which was not laid in the indictment, was delivered to the book-keeper belonging to the waggon, to go down to Bath on the 15th of May 1752, and loaded in the waggon the same evening, but was taken out and missed before the waggon was got off the stones.

Figures with a waggon and horses, pen and grey wash on paper, Thomas Ross (active c. 1730–45). (Mellon, B2001.2.1129)

PART TWO: BATH AS A RESORT

[23 February 1746/47] The Snow has been very deep in some parts of the county, so as to render the Roads impassable … six feet deep in some places on Marlborough Downs last Wednesday night, by which the Post was several Hours later here than usual.

It seems extraordinary that anyone attempted the journey to Bath in snowy conditions, but travelling in winter, when the ground was hard, was sometimes preferable to horses and carriages getting stuck in mud. Visitors did arrive in the depths of winter; others stayed on after the autumn season was over. However mid-December to February were quieter months for the resort, giving shopkeepers a respite and a chance to restock and send out bills. English weather ensured that conditions could be difficult throughout the year of course, and newspapers regularly reported on the state of the roads and the weather that caused travellers such hardship. In July 1747, for example, there was the most 'violent storm of rain ever known. One hailstone measured 5½ in; when dissolved = ¼ pt'.[176] Such rain would have turned roads into a quagmire, but on the other hand dry weather caused a different discomfort: despite having her own coach, Lady Bristol wrote that she had had 'a terable dusty jurney' on her way to Bath in 1721.[177]

The weather was not, of course, the only challenge facing those seeking Bath's attractions — Hounslow Heath, on the edge of London, had to be crossed (if possible with blinds down to avoid seeing the gibbets) and was a particular challenge when newspapers publicised the travel arrangements of the wealthiest visitors: 'The Day their Royal Highnesses the Prince and Princess of Wales set out for the Bath there were seven Coaches robb'd on Hounslow Heath.'[178] Lady Bristol was full of admiration for the courage of Lady Stamford when set upon by highwaymen in Marlborough Forest.[179]

Transport for goods and for letters was as integral to the resort's development as the need to transport people. Letter writing occupied a considerable amount of the time many visitors spent at 'the Bath' (Lady Bristol wrote to her husband every other day) and the delivery of letters to and from visitors was perhaps almost as important to the enjoyment of their visit as the delivery of goods to stock its shops. Letters were the best means of obtaining advice from friends about where to stay and then booking accommodation in advance of the trip. Often, however, letters failed to reach their destination, causing misunderstandings between correspondents and frustrating loss of time. In January 1721, for example 'the Bristol & Bath Bags were broke, and above 600 letters taken out'; in a letter that did reach its destination later that year Lady Bristol wrote nervously: 'I can't depend on your having this or what I writt

	£	s	d

Sir John Verney. Expences to Bath with my wife, daughter & servts 1700.

Sept 9 – Oct 30.
Stopped at Kennet, Oxford, Faringdon, Tetbury. arr Bath 12th

	£	s	d
At Bath the first night		13	10
Horse & servants bills	1	01	00
Trumpets, Fiddle, Harp		07	00
Chair hire		05	06
Ivory snuff box to Lady Verney		05	00
Bath rings to Lady Verny		05	00
Coffee 6s; Chocolate & tea 9s		15	00
Oct. Widdow Child for 5 weekes lodgings at 20s.			
Dyet for 3 of us at 10s each, do for 2 servts at 5s each	15	00	00
Given her 4 servts		15	00
To the water pumper		02	06

Viscountess Sondes. Rockingham. Bath Journey, 20 October 1723 and November

	£	s	d
Pd for a Coach horse at the Bath	20	00	00
Pd Travailing Charges from Rockm to Bath	36	00	00
Givn Dr Farrer going wth me to Bath	26	05	00
Givn Anth Frisby setting up at Rockm & on ye Road	1	06	00
Pd Causson two Bills	2	01	06
Given Dr Bave at Bath	14	14	00
Pd Rob Dainty 5 wks Bills includg ye Butcher's &c at Bath	49	11	08
Pd Mr Billing for Lodging 5 Wks at Bath	28	03	00
pd him a Bill for Wine	4	13	00
pd Mr Boyes a Bill for hors keeping in Stable & at Grass	31	13	00
pd Mr Bave the Apothecry bill 4.13.6. & given hm 1.11.6	6	05	00
pd the Brewer's bill at Bath	6	10	00
pd the Farrier's bill & giv'n him 2s 6d	2	19	06
Givn to the poor housekeepers at Bath	2	01	00
Givn to ye 2 women servs where I lodg'd at Bath	3	01	00
Pd Mr Russell 3 bills for wine	8	11	06
Givn ye pumper £1.1. the Serv 10s pumpers maid 5s	1	16	00
pd John Frisby setting up at Rockm 6 nights	0	06	00
Given Dr Farrer meeting me at Oxford	0	10	00
Givn Mr Rushworth at Northton	1	01	00
Pd travelling charges back from Bath to Rockm	51	08	06
pd for hire of 3 coach & 2 Saddle horses back from Bath to Rockm	12	10	00
pd Hen: Lacy 5 wks board wages at Bath	1	15	00
Givn him towds his loss wh robbd	2	02	00
pd for wood & coal at Bath	7	13	11
pd for Green & Bohee tea	2	09	06
pd Severall other small Expences at Bath amountg to	14	15	02
Given Causson for going before to ye Bath to take lodgings	2	02	00

upon ye road, for ye mail has been robd this week and all ye letters thrown in a ditch'.[180]

Transportation of valuable stock must have been a real concern for the Deards during the season and for Bertrand throughout the year: a fragile stock whose nearest origins were London, Birmingham or Bristol, but which came also from Europe or even more distant parts of the world via merchant intermediaries. Bertrand's close business relationship with the Wiltshire family would have ensured particular care for his goods. Every Wednesday and Sunday evening the Wiltshires' waggons began their 2½ days' journey from Bath to the depot in Holborn. Alternatively Bertrand's stock might have come by boat via Bristol, using the newly navigable River Avon for the last part of the journey, although water transport was chiefly used for bringing in raw materials, food and the full range of goods necessary to supply a burgeoning city.[181]

The mode of transport for visitors within Bath was on foot or by sedan chair — there were chairs specially designed for those using the baths. By the middle of the century the *Bath and Bristol Guide* gave the rate and distance between venues in yards: 500 yards = 6*d*, 1760 yards (1 mile) = 1*s*. One of the stands for chairmen was just by the passageway leading from Orange Grove to Terrace Walk.

p.96 illus.

The cost of travelling to Bath

Extracts from the accounts of four families have been transcribed in some detail in order to give a flavour of the cost of lengthy journeys in search of medical treatment and pleasure: they are Sir John Verney, Stephen Fox, Earl and Countess Fitzwalter, and the Furnese family.

Unfortunately few people bothered to include in their accounts what they spent on trinkets once arrived at their destination. Sir John Verney did so in 1700, when his expenses totalled £54 14*s* 3*d*.[182]

In 1701, travelling only with three servants, a trip to Bath between mid-August and October cost Sir John £29 0*s* 5*d*. He was there again in 1703 'in my Calesh with 3 servants'. On that visit he bought a 'China tea pott' for 18*s* and an ivory teapot for 9*d*. In 1705 he acquired 'silver playthings' (at 10½*s* and 1½*s*).

Stephen Fox used a different method to calculate costs in 1712.[183]

My Son began his journey upon Monday the 11th of May and ended it on Saturday the 15th August 1713 being 97 dayes, viz: Five nights on the road to Bath, sixty nine at the Bath, ten at Redlinch, one at Hindon, six at Sarum. Five on the road back with eight servants & seven horses, besides Hired horses. Accompanied with his Father and eighteen in family with

Folding lantern, ebony, silver and paper, unmarked, English c. 1700. Diameter: 7.6 cm (3 in). (Albert)

The Furnese family

Catherine Furnese was one of three half-sisters. Their father, Sir Robert Furnese, had three daughters by three wives: the youngest, Selina, was born between 1729 and 1733. In 1729 the eldest, Anne, married the Hon. John St John, brother of Lord Bolingbroke, at her father's house in Dover Street.[184] The house was the venue for the marriage in April 1736, of the middle sister, Catherine (born between 1714 and 1722), to the 2nd Earl of Rockingham; she was said to have a fortune of £200,000.[185]

Catherine and Selina sat to Christian Friedrich Zincke for miniatures that are mounted into an unmarked gold box. The reason for the box is not known: it is possible that the miniatures were mounted between 1747 and 1755, after the death of Anne in 1747 when the younger sisters were both single, but the box is stylistically closer to 1740. The Earl of Rockingham died in 1745 aged 31 and Catherine re-married in 1751. Selina married in 1755 Edward Dering, who was a few years younger than her: Elizabeth Montagu wrote to her sister at the time 'Miss Furnese is to be married to Mr Dering in about a fortnight. Sir Edward is very happy in it.' She died a month after giving birth to their second child in 1757.

Several relations of the Furnese sisters visited Bath. Their grandfather Earl Ferrers, who died there on Christmas Day 1717, had twenty-seven legitimate children 'besides some thirty natural children which his mistresses have born him'. Selina Furnese was cousin to Selina, Countess of Huntington, who in 1765 built a chapel in the Vineyards at Bath 'to protect the residents from the evils of Bath society'.

Snuff box, gold, unmarked, English, *c.* 1740. Length: 6.2 cm (2½ in). Set with two portrait miniatures by Christian Friedrich Zincke (died 1767) of Selina Furnese, later Lady Dering (in a blue dress) and her sister Catherine, Lady Rockingham, later Lady Guildford (wearing green). (Gilbert, 388-2008)

nine Horses eighty-two Nights to Saturday the 1st of August. The Expence of which Journey as by an abstract hereof doth amount to: Total of House expenses, 9½ weeks: £148 0s 5½d on food & drink 16 May – 23 July 1713

The expenses listed on p. 110 relate to a visit to Bath made by the widow of Viscount Sondes, heir to the 1st Earl of Rockingham. The distance from Rockingham, in Northamptonshire, to Bath is about 150 miles. A stay of five weeks cost some £340 in 1723. Five months later, in March 1723/24, her son succeeded his grandfather as 2nd Earl; he married Catherine Furnese in 1736.[186]   p. 112

Between 1726 and 1754 Earl Fitzwalter (1672–1756) recorded expenditure of some £5,300 on visits to Bath and Tunbridge Wells, primarily in search of treatment for his wife's gout and rheumatism; she died on 7 August 1751.[187] They spent a lot of time on the road, travelling between Schomberg House in London, Bath, Tunbridge Wells and Moulsham Hall, his house in Essex. Benjamin Mildmay was Chief Commissioner of the Salt Duties 1714–20 and Commissioner of Excise 1720–28; he succeeded his brother as Lord Fitzwalter and was elevated to Earl Fitzwalter in 1730. At the age of 51 he married the widow of the 3rd Earl of Holderness, grand-daughter of Marshal Schomberg and of the Elector Palatine. Fitzwalter became closely attached to her two children (her daughter married Lord Ancram) and grandchildren, Lord Newbattle and Lady Louisa Kerr – who very often accompanied the Fitzwalters to Bath and Tunbridge.   p. 114

It is inconceivable that Lord and Lady Fitzwalter did not go into the shop of Paul and Mary Bertrand during their visits to Bath, but there is no mention of toyshops in his careful record of expenses – unfortunately the separate 'Bath book' that might have contained the detail of his expenditure there does not survive. Fitzwalter banked with Snow & Denne, so it is possible that transactions are disguised in that bank's entries in Bertrand's account at Hoare & Co. Presumably his orders for lace from Mr Harford are noted because it was delivered and paid for after his return home, whereas other bills would have been settled before leaving Bath; the Harford family feature in Bertrand's bank account.   p. 310

   p. 280

Like numerous men of his social milieu, Fitzwalter gave his wife generous pin money – at Midsummer 1745 her quarterly allowance was £125.

Earl Fitzwalter: Expenses relating to Bath and Tunbridge Wells

			£	s	d
1727	6 Nov	Spent in my journey to and from the Bath with a coach and six horses and 7 saddle horses.			
		To the carriage by the wagon to and from the Bath. Spent at the Bath in ten weeks in expenses of all sorts, gaming excepted	316	15	01
1742	26 Aug	Spent at Tunbridge 6 July to 16 August — not less than:	200	00	00
1745	6 July	Go to Tunbridge wth my Lady Fitzwalter & my Lady Ancram			
	16 Aug	Retund again to London			
	19 Aug	Pd Tunbridge Carrier for bring up my Baggage to London att 45 pr lb wt	2	19	09
		Pd the T. carrier for carrying down my baggage	4	00	00
1747	30 Sept	Set out for Bath. Nov 27 Returned to Pall Mall spent	340	12	11
		Gave to the Hospital at Bath	10	10	00
1747/48	2 Feb	Returned to London from Bath with my Lady Fitzwalter and my Lord and my Lady Ancram, who had been there with us a month, besides my Lord and my Lady Holderness, who came down and stayed with us above a fortnight. My own family consisted also of fifteen in number. I had also there fifteen horses, and from my setting out from this place to my return was eleven weeks, in which expedition I spent (sending down 16 dozen of my own wine)	366	00	00
1748	7 Oct	Set out for Bath; returned 18 November (6 weeks and 1 day)	245	07	05
	28 Nov	Pd for my Goods bringing from Bath	4	10	0
	19 July	Go to Tunbridge wth my Lady Fitzwalter and my Lady Ancram with us			
	21 Aug	The waters not agreeing with my Lady Fitzwalter we return'd from Tunbridge this day and my lady Ancram with us.			
		NB spent at Tunbridge during that time	200	13	03
1749	12 Oct	Set out for Bath wth my Lady Fitzwalter			
	29 Nov	Returned with Mr Tindal; spent at Bath in six weeks	290	00	6½
1749/50	6 March	Set out with Lady Fitzwalter for Bath			
	27 April	Returned. Spent there and in going and coming & carriers wagons	343	12	03
1750/51	9 Janr	Set out with Dr Pringle			
1751	19 May	Arrived from Bath and my Lady Louisa. Spent on road & carriage of goods with Doctors fees there for Lady F. besides fifty pounds I gave to Pringle for only going down with us & staying but 2 days	962	00	00
	1 July	To Tunbridge wth Lady F & Lady Louisa. 22nd returned. Spent	169	00	00
		Dr Pringle there also	21	00	00
1753	17 Jan	Pd Mr Harford of Bath for Cloth at 8d 3d pyd for my Livery servts and in full	11	06	00
	19 Nov	Pd Mr Harford of Bath his bill in full for Frock and Blew Livery Cloth. Cloth not good	20	02	00
1754	5 May	Set out and carry wth me to Bath in Bank bills about 1200£ and some mony I think about 70 G-S.			
	4 Aug	Returnd from Bath to Pall Mall this day having spent in my Journy thither, during my stay there and in my Journy back to Town in all	635	02	04
	18 Nov	Pd Mr Harford of Bath in full for Cloth for my serts for this year 60th for Liveries as also for their frocks	20	02	00

We shall be greatly oblig'd to those Persons that lett Lodgings in this City if they would send the Names of the Gentry that arrive at their respective Houses to the Printer of this Journal.

BATH JOURNAL, 1745

Where to stay

SOME OF THE REGULAR VISITORS to Bath, and those who had estates nearby (such as Viscount Thynne and the Duke of Beaufort), had houses in the city. Many county families maintained a residence in their local town so that they could attend the assizes, visit fairs, or carry out duties in respect of a position as Justice of the Peace, Councillor or Member of Parliament. A few of these private houses in Bath were large establishments. Other quite large properties were built or acquired by a wealthy tradesman or professional man, so that his family could inhabit part of the house and also take lodgers.

Reports in London newspapers and the *Bath Journal* (from May 1744) name those who would have been Bertrand's customers: they reported the movements of people of rank when they left London to go abroad or to their estates, and those who arrived at Bath. For example in 1732:[188]

Bath. Sept 11. We have already a great deal of Company in this Place; particularly, the duke of Montague, Lord and Lady Cardigan, Lord and Lady Lauderdale, Lord Mountcashell, Lady Hinchingbrook, Lady Londonderry, Baron Comyns, Sir John Buckworth, Sir Seymer Pyle, Mr Justic Tracey; Sir Robert Rich, Sir John Ingleby &c.

As at any seasonal resort, there was difficulty in providing sufficient accommodation.

Lady Elizabeth Finch wrote to her husband in July 1667, telling him not to come to fetch her 'because the lodgings are very unpleasant'.[189] Lodgings probably did not significantly improve over the next forty years, and similar comments were made in letters home well into the 1730s from those who failed to obtain the best accommodation. Gilmore's map of the 1690s shows the main places to stay in the city, amounting to some 25 lodging houses and 23 inns. A survey in the 1680s calculated that the inns of Bath could accommodate 324 beds and 451 horses; in 1694 there were 29 lodging houses.[190]

Some visitors who were making only a short visit preferred to stay at an inn. The disadvantage was the noise — the constant bustle of coaches arriving and horses being stabled — for inns were the points of arrival and departure for coaches to London, Bristol and Oxford. But inns were useful places to put up on first arrival

Cane handle, porcelain, Chantilly, *c.* 1730–40. (Spero)

pp.20, 118, 142, 153 illus.

A good location

Many who came to Bath were elderly or infirm: they needed the canes and walking sticks that were sold in toyshops. Many visitors were unable to walk even the short distances between their lodgings and the pump room or baths.

The area of the old town is relatively flat and the hills surrounding Bath were not extensively built over until after the Bertrands' time, but it was better to move round the narrow and slippery streets by sedan chair than by carriage if infirmity made walking difficult. A central location reduced the cost and discomfort of using chairs, the tariffs for which were set according to distance. Chairs were designed so that they could be brought indoors, enabling an invalid to be taken directly from lodgings to the baths. Some houses have wide stairs with shallow treads, so a patient could be carried to and from a bedroom; hallways were wide enough to turn a chair. The chairs used in Bath had to withstand not only the weather but also the damp costumes of those who had bathed.

p.144

Those who suffered from carriage sickness (Princess Amelia was a notable victim) preferred to travel by chair and were carried considerable distances. The wealthy fitted out their own chairs in some luxury, including specially designed timepieces. Toyshops sold travelling goods of all descriptions.

An ill woman lifted from a sedan chair, etching and engraving, Hubert Gravelot after Francis Hayman, *c.* 1732–45. (BM, 1857,0217.136)

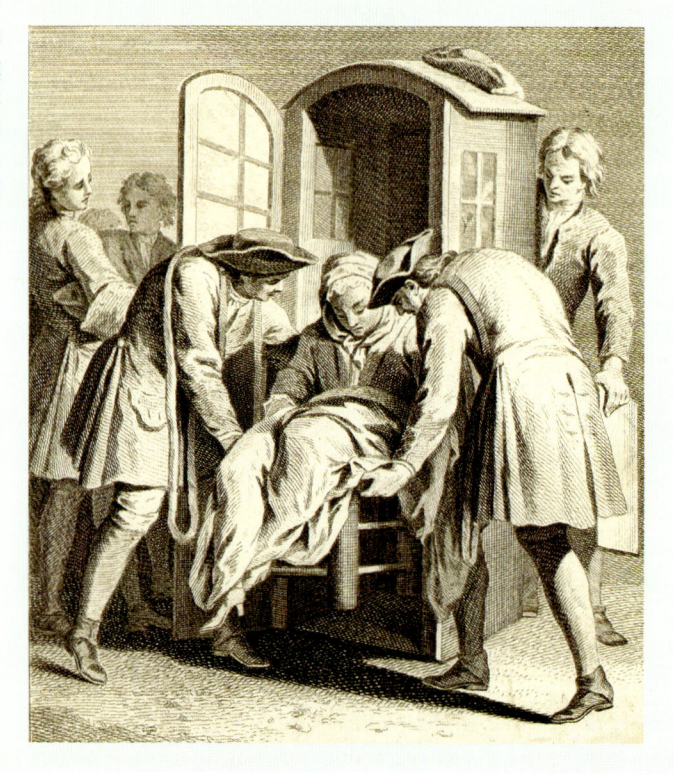

116   PART TWO: BATH AS A RESORT

while looking for lodgings, if these had not been booked in advance. Inns would also have better suited those who came without their own servants or those who wanted the high standards of comfort and service for which the larger inns, such as The Bear, were renowned.

An inn offered an inclusive service similar to an hotel today, whereas many lodgings were largely self-catering, although some offered 'full board'. Some lodgings had a communal parlour, in others it was possible to rent a private one; some provided services such as dressing meat. Day-to-day necessities had to be hired: a number of shopkeepers advertised that they hired china and glass.[191] In 1721 Thomas Coke paid 6s for the use of knives and forks, and spent £1 2 3½d on candles for eight weeks when he lodged at Mrs Atwood's in Orange Grove. In May 1724 a week's lodgings cost him £2.[192] In September 1723 Lady Bristol complained that her lodgings were 'really extream inconvenient, but … there is not a room to be got …'. A week later she wrote to her husband that 'Our company increases daily, so that people of fashion is forcd to be content with garrets, and I shall remain where I am …'.[193]

The Duke of Chandos recognised the need for better accommodation and hoped to improve his income by investing in new development. One of his earliest projects in Bath (and the scheme that launched John Wood's architectural career despite the fact that the buildings were not an unqualified success) was to employ Wood to rebuild Mrs Phillips' lodging house on the site of St John's almshouse, finished in March 1728. The acrimonious correspondence between the architect, the duke and his landladies, has been described as follows:[194]

p. 120

> … a very high proportion of the houses behind the fine facades which Wood was to erect were intended to accommodate lodgers in the season. … In the Preface to his Essay Wood boasted of the huge advance in the standard of lodging between 1727 and 1742: 'the best Chambers for Gentlemen were then just what the Garrets for Servants now are'. He did not mention that it was Chandos who pioneered the way to bedrooms with en suite dressing rooms and who fought in the teeth of Wood's own incompetence to have decent toilet facilities on every floor and soundproof partitions between rooms.

Other than those few who owned houses, visitors came first to hope for, and then to expect, conditions such as these. No wonder the best lodgings had to be booked early. Those who ran them must have been kept busy in the off-season summer months renovating, re-stocking and generally improving facilities, so that they continued to attract the best clients. Joanna and Ann Phillips, Chandos's tenants, are both listed in Bertrand's accounts. They ran substantial establishments: in the 1720s Mrs Phillips' house was estimated by

p. 301

Lodgings

Invoice from Aletheia Pigott to the Hon Charles Fairfax for lodgings, dated 3 March 1730/1. (N. Yorks)

In high season accommodation was still in short supply in the 1740s, and those who arrived in the city without reserving rooms in advance had a worrying time, as Mary Hayne and her mother discovered, having come from near Newbury. She wrote to her father (without punctuation):[195]

Alderman Bush's lodging house at the Bear Corner, engraving, from the map by Joseph Gilmore, 1694. The houses are typical of the gabled buildings of the seventeenth century and earlier, with shops at street level. The map made it easy for visitors to identify lodgings. (Bath in Time, 13818)

Bath March ye 12 1749

Dear Sir, My Mother and I got to Bath yesterday very well but not soon enough to get Lodgings to our likeing. We did not go to any Inn but was set down at the Bear Corner. All ye Lodgings in ye Grove was full but a Room up two pair of Stairs at Mrs Fishers. She desired us to stay with Her till we could fitt our selves & we thought it as well or better then to be at an inn. Ye Room of shelters was to be filled next Tusday or Wenesay so yt we could not take Lodgings at ye House. Mrs Fisher sent us to severall Houses but my Mother was to Fagued to walk much so we did not fix till in the second time of going out Sunday about 10. We have a Room up two Pair of Stairs at Mr Smiths a confectionar in West Gate Street. We have a Bed that is not seen in ye day so we have ye shew of a Dining Room, there is no Reason to dislike ye People at ye House yet & there is a Bed to be taken if you please. My Mother & I went to Mr Normans & he sent ye things by a Porter with us to ye Lodgings

118 PART TWO: BATH AS A RESORT

Neale to have had 40 rooms, 17 garrets and 7 kitchens; Susan Jenkins calculated that it comprised 64 rooms, made up of 30 to 34 lodging and dining rooms that could be rented for 10s a week each, twelve garrets (rented for 5s per week) and three pantries (rentable for 5s per week). Mrs Phillips' weekly earnings amounted to about £26, thus £520 during the five months of the main seasons. Of Mrs Jones's lodgings (another tenant), Chandos wrote that it contained '28 rooms which according to the Bath way of reckoning will let for £14 a week for the Seasons'.[196]

Between November 1745 and March 1745/46 Lady Jernegan was charged 38s per week for lodgings by Thomas and Sarah King; a set of four horses was charged at 30s a day and two saddle horses at 8s a day; 'standing the coach' at The Bear Inn for 17 weeks cost £1 14s plus 2s for 'oyling' it. This compares with the £32 10s she paid for 10 weeks' lodgings in Pall Mall, in London, in May 1740.[197]

p. 83

The Chandos development at St John's Hospital was, of course, slightly away from the heart of the city, but close to the Cross Baths and the Hot Bath. Those who took lodgings in Orange Grove, on the other hand, had Bath's principal social activities (and Bertrand's shop) on their doorstep. On the east side of the Grove there were lodgings in Nassau house and Winchester House (built by Bennet Stevenson, who features in Bertrand's accounts), Bush's lodgings were also on this side of the Grove as were Mrs Atwood's — favoured by many of the aristocracy perhaps because they overlooked the river. On the north side of the Grove was Susannah Axford, on the west side Sheyler's coffee house, then Morgan's.[198] The south side comprised the range of shops built in the first decade of the eighteenth century, with Leake's bookshop (also with lodgings) and Bertrand's toyshop at the corner of the Grove and Terrace Walk.

p. 23 map
p. 312
p. 248

In fine weather tables and chairs were set outside the assembly rooms and coffee houses; if there was no breeze, a pack of cards or dice was produced, or letters written and newspapers read — daylight would have been welcome in preference to poorly-lit interiors. Breakfast was taken out, or in lodgings if clothes needed to be changed after bathing; dinner was usually eaten at an inn or in lodgings.

The Duke of Chandos

He was a bauble to every project.

C. H. C. AND M. I. BAKER, 1949

It is indicative of how long the language of a toyshop persisted that Chandos's biographers should so describe him. Sadly, when publishing their research on the duke's life they failed to footnote their findings, and it has proved impossible to rediscover the references they make to Chandos's purchases from toyshops. Chandos does not feature in Bertrand's bank account, but bills from Chenevix survive somewhere in the duke's vast archive.[199]

James Brydges (1674–1744) may have made his fortune in dubious ways: he held the lucrative office of Paymaster-General of the Forces between 1705 and 1713, through which office he profited to the tune of some £600,000. Like many men of his standing he was far from idle. He was created Duke of Chandos in 1719. Thereafter 'the experiences of the Brydges family were peculiarly frenetic':[200]

Double snuff box, gold, unmarked, *c.*1725. Width: 6.6 cm (2⅝ in). Provenance: The Duke of Chandos. (Walters, 57.102)

He managed to dent his vast fortune, losing heavily in the South Seas Bubble and proving the softest of touches for confidence men of every kind. He invested in building projects in Bath and Bridgwater, in oyster fishing, in bottle manufacture, copper-bottoming, lead, gold, American lands, coal … and everywhere he lost … his schemes form a kind of compendium of early eighteenth-century bucket shops.

He was a regular visitor to Bath and in 1727 commissioned the young and inexperienced John Wood to build four lodging houses on the site of St John's Hospital. The name of one of the landladies, Mrs Phillips, features in Hoare & Co.'s ledgers and it is possible that the 'Wm Bridges' listed in 1744 was a cousin. When travelling to and from Bath the duke and duchess were able to stay at Shaw Hall, near Newbury, which he acquired in the 1720s.

Chandos lavished his fortune on his house in Edgware, Middlesex, called Cannons, acquired in 1712 following the death of his first wife. He maintained a full choir for the chapel and for two years employed Handel at the house. After the duke's death Cannons was broken up and sold for its materials at auction in 1747–48.[201]

120 PART TWO: BATH AS A RESORT

From the Pump House, the Ladies from time to time withdraw to a neighbouring Toy Shop, Amusing themselves there with Reading the News; and from thence they return to their Lodgings to Breakfast.

JOHN WOOD

What to do: the daily round

SHOPPING AND WINDOW-SHOPPING were among Bath's chief attractions, but many other activities were on offer to help visitors pass the time. Like any successful resort, Bath's attractions were sufficiently varied to cater for visitors with very different interests. It is easy to fall into the trap of thinking that everyone who came to Bath did the same things and crammed all that the city had to offer into each and every day of their stay. To do so over a long period would have left them exhausted and lacking sleep, for the baths were generally visited very early in the morning, whereas dancing and gambling continued long into the evening (bathing began at 6 am, balls finished at 11 pm). People paced themselves according to the entertainment on offer; for example on 30 October 1734, 'Being his Majesty's birthday, little company appeared in the morning, all being resolved to look well at night'.[202] Many visitors would never have got wet in any of the baths, others would never have joined the delights or tedium of a ball. Some might have avoided the temptations of Bertrand's shop but surely everyone walked past it, just as most would have entered a coffee shop at some stage in their stay.

The quality and range of the shops in Bath were one of its chief attractions, particularly for those who seldom visited the capital and wanted to spend time amongst fashionable society and keep up with the latest trends. Although expensive Bath was cheaper than London, despite the large number of subscriptions that needed to be paid in order to gain access to the best coffee houses, bookshops and circulating libraries, to the pump room and the assembly rooms.[203] Experience or good advice must have been necessary to understand the city's (and Richard Nash's) rules and traditions, to know how to fend off tradesmen who called, know whom to tip and when, and which doctors were frauds and which had a cure that might work. As early as 1700 Sir John Verney's expenses included trumpets, fiddle and harp. The cost of balls and concerts seem to have been surprisingly high, presumably to keep them exclusive, although those held to celebrate special occasions were regularly reported to have between 300 and 400 gentlemen and ladies present. Such costs would not have troubled the majority of Bertrand's clients, whose pocket books were easily

p. 110

Doctors

Dr George Cheyne (1671–1743), engraving, unknown artist. (Bath in Time, 25894) [▶ p. 259]

Dr Oliver and Mr Peirce Examining Patients, oil on canvas, William Hoare, 1761. (MWH, Bath in Time, 14025) [▶ p. 298]

Henry Wright, oil on canvas, William Hoare, 1742. (MWH, Bath in Time, 14024) [▶ p. 322]

John Morris, oil on canvas, Benjamin Morris, 1742. (MWH, Bath in Time, 14032) [▶ p. 295]

replenished from substantial incomes — their only concern would have been large losses at the gaming.

However, the need for medical treatment was the reason why most visitors undertook the expensive and arduous journey to Bath. In days before effective medication, the use of warm mineral waters was considered a major weapon against illness, alongside herbal remedies. So were diet, rest and exercise. The expectation — the sometimes desperate hope — that a visit of several weeks to Bath might at least alleviate, if not cure, a range of medical conditions, is vividly expressed in letters and diaries of the period.

Bathing and drinking the waters

Numerous visitors wrote about the hopes and fears, the pleasures and perils, associated with using the baths for the treatment of many ailments. The principal bath that visitors see today was not discovered until the nineteenth century; in the 1730s and '40s there were five baths: King's, Queen's, Hot, Cross and Leper's. The hours for bathing were 6–9 am, after which the sluices were opened and the water drained into the River Avon. The King's Bath took about 9½ hours to fill, the Hot Bath and the Cross Bath about 11½ hours each.

With the help of attendants who prevented them stumbling, slipping (or drowning due to the weight of clothing) as they went down steps into the steaming water, those who immersed themselves made their way to a seat round the edge, walked round the pool chatting to others in the baths or avoiding them, and steadied themselves with the help of rings attached to the walls. They wore specially designed garments that withstood the minerals in the water and were easy to remove when wet — but once submerged the weight would have been considerable. Gertrude Savile recorded the cost:[204]

1746 Oct 6:

Gave according to custome upon first going into the Bath, for a breakfast as they call it, to the guide, & slip woman 2s 6d, & to the two maids of the lodgins 2s 6d, & to the chair men 1s. Total: 6s.

A canvas shift & pallereen £1 1s, a canvas hatt with ribon 4s, a flanell shift 8s, a bowl & ribons 6s. Total: £1 19s 0d.

The bowl that cost 6s was an accessory described by Daniel Defoe:[205]

a little floating wooden Dish like a Bason, in which the lady puts her Handkerchief, and a Nosegay, of late the Snuff-Box is added, and some Patches; tho' the Bath occasioning a little Perspiration, the Patches do not stick so kindly as they should.

Fan leaf depicting the interior of the Pump Room, George Speren, 1736. (Bath in Time, 13398)

The king's and queen's baths, watercolour and pen and ink on paper, Thomas Robins, 1747. (V&A, Bath in Time, 13057)

They could be purchased from one of Bertrand's neighbours, Rebecca Griffith, 'milliner and tirewoman at the lower end of Orange Grove', who advertised that she sold 'all sorts of Bathing Linnen and Bath Bowls'.[206] How many trinkets were lost in the water will never be known, nor how many found when the baths were drained each day.

There are many descriptions of the experience of bathing and the concerns of those using the baths about being infected by other bathers. In 1734 Lord Chesterfield gossiped about a different type of peril:

... the Duchess of Norfolk, had like the other day to have been no innocent cause of Mrs Buckley's death. Mrs Buckley was bathing in the Cross Bath, as she thought, in perfect security, when of a sudden her Grace, who is considerably increased in bulk even since you saw her, came, and, like the great leviathan, rais'd the waters so high, that Mrs Buckley's guide was obliged to hold her up in her arms to save her from drowning and carry her about like a child.

The Ladies with their floating Japann Bowles, freighted with confectionary, knick knacks, essences & Perfumes, wade about like Neptun's courtiers, suppling their Industrious Joynts

A STEP TO BATH

The duchess did not change her ways or her size, for in January 1739/40 Elizabeth Robinson related:[207]

The dowager Dutchess of Norfolk bathes, and being very tall, had nearly drowned a few women in the Cross Bath, for she ordered it to be filled till it reached her chin, and so all those who were below her stature, as well as her rank, were forced to come out or drown; and finding it, according to the proverb, in vain to strive against the stream, they left the bath rather than swallow so large a draught of water.

The ritual drinking of Bath's water in the pump room was also usually undertaken before breakfast, between about 8 am and 10 am. The room was built in 1706, shortly after Richard Nash's arrival in the city, and the Bertrands would have watched it being extended in 1751 when a fifth bay was added. The water could also be purchased in bottles and delivered to lodgings so that the water could be taken privately — and wine was also delivered to lodgings. Glasses could be hired from china shops or bought at toyshops. Bath's water, like that of other spas, was bottled and sent up to London weekly by waggon. Henry Eyre, 'Purveyor for Mineral

WHAT TO DO: THE DAILY ROUND

"What I do with myself"

The 4th Duke of Bedford, in a letter written to his wife in April 1746, describes his daily routine.[208] He was at Bath for his gout and, unlike his father and elder brother, was able to restrain himself at the gaming tables.

As you seem desirous of knowing what I do with myself, I will tell you, as well as an idle Bath life can be described in writing.

In the first place, I get up early in a morning, sometimes before 7 o'clock, and drink the waters or bath in their respective turns, so as to be able to be at the coffee house at breakfast at 10 o'clock. This morning after breakfast I rode out. Other mornings I saunter about this town till I am footsore, and then lounge till the time of dressing in the booksellers shop or at home with Pere Daniel. Two or three people generally dine here, always Lord Fane (which, by the way, is the only comfortable thing I have yet mentioned). After dinner one glass of Bath water, a very short walk, and then home to write letters or read.

Now comes the gaiety. At close of the evening I sit down to Guinea Whist, either with Lord Winchelsea [▶ p. 136] or Lady Bell, and have made a shift already to win 16 guineas. How long they will last God knows. At half past 10 I regularly return to my old woman to pump my hand; by the by she has a daughter but don't be jealous. After the lightest of suppers and one glass of Bath water, I get to bed soon after 11. Does not this agreeable life make you wish to be here?

Two Women and a Man Walking on a Terrace, drypoint, John Theodore Heins jnr after Thomas Worlidge. (BM, 1861,0518.133)

Waters to their Majesties at his Water Warehouse in Fleet Street' was one of many who traded in water from Holt, Bristol, Scarborough and Spa.[209]

Exercise and entertainment

Walking, riding, dancing, playing bowls, going to the play or a lecture, regular church going: a variety of activities were on offer both in Bath and Tunbridge Wells for which it was essential to be dressed appropriately and to carry fashionable accessories. Regardless of their station in life (and the 'middling sort' came in great numbers), taking a stroll in Orange Grove and the Walks, by the river or further afield, was a popular pastime and an opportunity to show off trinkets recently acquired in the abundance of shops. The parade, or parading — the business of seeing and being seen – was as integral to seasonal life in Bath as it was in Pall Mall or St James's Park in London. Nor was it confined to outdoors: dressing for the opera and the play was equally important and those who attended balls in the assembly rooms dressed as carefully and as richly in Bath as in London.

Sporting activities were not entirely forgotten by those who were in Bath for more urban pursuits, and several gentlemen might have slipped away from the city to watch a cock match or backsword:[210]

> To be fought at Mr Rundell's at the George at Phillips Norton, between the Gentlemen of Frome and Warminster and the Gentlemen of Bath to shew and weigh 31 Cocks each side for two guineas each cock and twenty guineas the odd Battle. To weigh Tuesday the 21st instant, and fight the two following days.

> To be Play'd for at Backsword on Monday next, the 8th of this Instant June, at the Full Moon near the Bridge, Bath / A Silver Bowl / He that breaks the first Head to have the Knot; and he that breaks the most Heads, and saves his own to have the Prize. The Gamesters to mount the stage at ten o'clock and to play 'till sun-set.

On a different occasion the prize was a large silver tobacco box, valued at two guineas which, like the bowl, would have been obtained from a local silversmith rather than Bertrand. By this time (1749) tobacco boxes were no longer fashionable and it may well be that those who played at backsword were palmed off with a second-hand box.

In a letter written on 3 September 1716 the Duchess of Marlborough mentions other sport but also reveals the discomforts of Bath even ten years after Nash's arrival, when the city had been attempting to improve its facilities over a period of years:[211]

When Noon approaches, and Church is over, some of the Company appear on the Grand Parade, and other Publick Walks, where a Rotation of Walking is continued for about two Hours …

JOHN WOOD

Key to a painting by William Hogarth showing a performance in 1732 of Dryden's play *The Indian Emperor or, the Conquest of Mexico*, engraving *c*.1800. Several members of the audience visited Bath at some time, including the Duke of Cumberland, Princesses Mary and Louisa, Lady Deloraine, the Duke of Montagu and the Earl of Pomfret. Although this was a private performance with children, the physical proximity of audience and players would have been similar at theatrical performances and puppet shows in Bath.
(BM, 2010,7081.7422)

A Pinch of Snuff, drawing on paper, Marcellus Laroon III, signed and dated 1732.
(BM, 1881,0611.166)

Her Grace of Shrewsbury … plays at Ombre upon the Walks, that she may be sure to have Company enough, and is as well pleased in a great Crowd of Strangers as the common People are with a Bull-baiting or a Mountebank. I have been upon the Walks but twice, and I never saw any Place Abroad that had more Stinks and Dirt in it than Bath; with this Difference only, that we are not starved, for here is great Plenty of Meat, and very good, and as to the Noise, that keeps One almost always awake.

If the weather was good, visitors could take the ferry and picnic in Spring Gardens on the opposite bank of the river, or go out riding to escape the stuffiness of the city — such outings must have been particular favourites among the younger and fitter of Bath's visitors. Lord Chesterfield reported that Mr Herbert 'lies in bed between ten and eleven, where he eats two breakfasts of strong broth; then rides till one or two…'.[212]

Several correspondents reported that they rode out each day: they might have brought their own horses, or hired them once arrived in Bath. Either way, their cost makes yet another interesting comparison with the much criticised price of trinkets. Horse races were held on Claverton Down: the first record in the racing calendar was the meeting on 25 September 1728, but races were mentioned in 1721 and were laid on for the visit of Charles II some decades earlier.

Seal, engraved with a racehorse and jockey, steel, mid-eighteenth century. Height: 3 cm (1¼ in). (Private coll)

Thomas Harrison's assembly room opened in 1708 primarily as a place to gamble, but it served tea, coffee and chocolate, and had private walks beside the river with a summerhouse. It was a venue for meeting friends and making new acquaintances. In 1720 a room was added for balls, to the design of William Killigrew,[213] and Charles Simpson extended the building in 1750. As part of the development of Terrace Walk on the Duke of Kingston's estate in 1728, John Wood built Thayer's rooms in the row of buildings that included Bertrand's shop. It is easily recognisable from the three circular windows set high in the street facade; concerts were given in another room at the rear of the building. Although nominally rivals, the two sets of rooms liaised in organising the programme for the season. They opened on alternate days through the week;

p. 98 illus.

Scrap of an invoice from Paul Bertrand to Lady Jernegan, dated 2 June 1737. (Staffs, D641/3/P/1/3/6)

Shopping for flowers

This scrap off the bottom of an invoice reveals more than is realised at a first glance. It conjures up two possible scenarios. Assuming the invoice was made out to Lady Jernegan, amongst whose papers this fragment now rests, we can imagine her going into the Bertrands' shop, where she bought a group of items for which a bill was made out and totalled. As this was being done, she might have looked round the shop again and added the flowers to her purchases. Or she might have made a second visit and bought the flowers before paying her bill. Either way, it suggests that the flowers were cleverly placed within sight of the shop counter.

The flowers were probably silk and from Italy, but they might have been made of paper. In either material the work would have involved folding, a skill that was also used for napery on the dining table. The flowers were surely three-dimensional and used in the boudoir or to decorate a table for the dessert.

In 1738 the Duke of Gordon bought 'a parcel of flowers' from Judith Willdey in London for one guinea.[214] In 1745 Lewis Coindrieau's stock, sold by Charles Margas, included '50 dozen artificial flowers'.[215] Trade cards list 'fine flowers' (Viet & Mitchell) or 'fine artificial flowers' (Martin, in the Strand). Richard Clarke's linking of 'Italian flowers and watch papers' suggests that his artificial flowers were made of paper. Using paper differently, Mrs Delany in old age turned from needlework to scissorwork and created 'paper mosaick' pictures of flowers: botanically correct collages of astonishing intensity.[216]

balls were held twice a week, once in each of the rooms on different days.²¹⁷

On special occasions there was even closer co-operation. In April 1747, for the Duke of Cumberland's birthday, there was a ball at Mrs Wiltshire's followed by 'an elegant entertainment at Mr Simpsons — at which near 300 Gentlemen and ladies were present. Fine fireworks were play'd off on the Parade by order of Richard Nash'. In November that year, for the King's birthday, the rooms switched roles and a ball was held at Simpson's and 'after that they retir'd to Mr Wiltshire's in order to partake of a great Entertainment which consisted of above 300 dishes; and where upwards of 400 Gentlemen and ladies were present'. While these affairs were 'conducted with the utmost decency and good order' under the supervision of Nash, Bath's Corporation dined and toasted the King at the Guildhall, [▶ p. 67 illus.], where they probably had a rather jollier evening.²¹⁸ At these balls the 2:1 ratio of ladies to gentlemen was overcome by regulating the dancing: the floor was taken by one couple at a time (all eyes focused on a nervous newcomer) and then the man danced the same routine with a second woman before making way for the next couple. It was a practical solution to coping with a crowd of people in a relatively small room. Balls were, of course, what many younger people would have looked forward to most, although the etiquette imposed by Nash intentionally inhibited too much highjinks. Many, of course, passed the hours of a ball in the card room.

Bath's first theatre was built by George Trim in 1705 and paid for by subscriptions from theatregoers among Bath's regular visitors; it was managed by Elizabeth Hayes who, in taking a third of the profits, probably made less money from this enterprise than from the gaming tables at her assembly rooms. The plays and players moved to her rooms some years before the theatre was demolished to make way for the Mineral Water Hospital in 1738.²¹⁹

As to other entertainments, in the early days aristocrats such as the 2nd Duke of Bedford brought their own — in his case Italian musicians. Nash organised regular concerts in the assembly rooms, music in the pump room and visiting performers such as 'the wonderful and surprising Moor... who has the gift of two voices'.²²⁰ Lacon's wax figures were a regular feature. Those with a more serious turn of mind and a guinea to spare could attend a 'Course of Experimental Philosophy by Benjamin Martin' in the mornings at Mrs Wiltshire's.²²¹

Puppet shows were popular at fairs, in booths, and as indoor entertainment. Martin Powell had a puppet show in Bath from at least 1710, and it may have been his entertainment that Gertrude Savile complained of in 1722 when she wrote that 'Pepett Shows

Playing card, early eighteenth century. In August 1743 'Yeates, Warner & Rosoman's Great Theatrical Booth' at Bartholomew Fair, included 'surprising performances of the famous Bath Morris Dancers'. (LMA/WCMPC, 841)

pp. 133 and 288

Richard Percival to Mrs Pendarves, 14 December 1747

I have been in a continual hurry since my first coming hither, & yet have had nothing to do; which might seem a kind of paradox to one unacquainted with Bath, but to you, who so well knows the manners & the busyness of the place, it will be quite clear. I am writing this letter in the Coffee house, where I have this moment heard a Person say, that he would give a good sum of money to any one, that would tell him how he should spend agreeably, or even with a moderate satisfaction, the two hours in a day, from ten to twelve in the forenoon; as to the remainder of the 24 hours, he could destroy them by dressing, eating, drinking & sleeping, & playing at EO, which last he does to as great a perfection as the Wisest Man in the world, if any wise men play at such a foolish game [▶ p. 335, n. 3].

BERTRAND'S SHOP AT BATH

'Verses made ... to laugh people out of their folly and impertinence, of which I think these lines contain a sample.'

To this fam'd shop all loitring people run,
Where with incessant noise themselves they stun –
'Good morrow Sir, what have you new to day? –
'There's nothing new – Who's come to Town? they say
'Only my Lord Drinkwater, who rode post –
'Bertrand, who's that? – Miss Smart the reigning Toast –
'Madam, I hope last night you took no cold,
'Twas a cool evening, cries Sir Simon Bold –
'No Sir I took no cold, nor you I hope –
'But this dull weather cries the pratling Fop,
'Makes me as heavy as a lump of lead –
The sky's grown clear – but heavy still his head!
A senseless Brazen head! always the same,
The weather's not in fault, yet bears the blame.
Sir Simon begs to view that Toy – 'tis sold –
'The Thing is pretty – but the fashion's old.
Here stops the flaunting Belle, here stops the Beau,
The Puppets fly to see a Puppet shew!
Charm'd with the sight, they think such Jewells rare –
But think themselves the finest Jewells there!
Bertrand, expose to sale these curious Toys,
These pretty Rattles, pretty Girls & Boys:
But yet perhaps I give thee wrong advice,
The Toys too many, and too low the price.

RICHARD PERCIVAL, 1747

tyred me past patience'.²²² Powell had a dispute with Sir Richard Steele who, under his pseudonym Isaac Bickerstaff in *The Tatler*, called Powell 'a pragmatical and vain person' who makes his jester puppet Punch 'speak sawcily of his betters'. Powell responded in kind.²²³ Concerts and puppet shows were held in a room adjacent to the lower assembly rooms off Terrace Walk.

Another regular entertainment in Bath and in Tunbridge Wells was Lacon's wax figures. The figures were five feet high 'with the motions and gestures of human life' and were made by three brothers, Anthony, John and Samuel Lacon. Their mother Elizabeth had a house in Bath 'in Barton Ground over against the Chapell' in Walcot.²²⁴ The large payment to Elizabeth Lacon in Bertrand's bank account (for £319 in 1743) possibly relates to fees or ticket money for their shows. The payment was made via Walter Wiltshire and performances most likely took place in his concert room — immediately behind the shop that Leonard Coward took over from Joanna Davis in Terrace Walk.

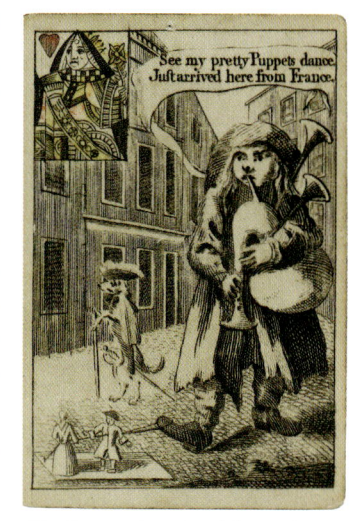

Lacon's over-sized puppet show was also taken to London, where it was put on at the opera house in the Haymarket; tickets were sold at Chenevix's toyshop. In 1732 the ambitious programme included 'Love's Triumph', 'Henry IV With the Humours of Sir John Falstaffe (Intermix'd with Dancing between the Acts)', 'The comical Tragedy of Tom Thumb' and 'The Beggars Opera'.²²⁵ In 1741 they were performing at the old tennis court near the Haymarket. Elizabeth Lacon's will was proved in January 1747/48; her sons had died by December 1760 when the sale of their wax figures 'with a Variety of rich Dresses together with all the Scenes, Machines, and other Theatrical Decorations' was advertised. It was said to have cost £1,000 to make everything. The sale was preceded by the sale of John Lacon's collection of pictures: he was also a painter of miniatures. The Lacons' work in wax was, of course, an entirely different skill (certainly in terms of size) to the creation of small-scale framed wax portraits that were so popular in the middle years of the eighteenth century and sold through toyshops.²²⁶

Most toyshops sold games of every description and at every resort, as at home, many hours were spent playing cards, backgammon, draughts or chess.

Playing card, early eighteenth century. 'See my pretty Puppets dance. Just arrived here from France.' (LMA/WCMPC, 841)

Gaming

A set of dice and a pack of cards — the bread and butter of many a toyshop — were easily carried in a pocket. Games could be played in a coach, on the ground, over a cup of coffee or chocolate, in sessions lasting ten minutes or all night. Boards for backgammon and chess were incorporated into tables or were made to fold and be easily transportable.

Ace of hearts; roly poly, hazard, ombre, quadrille, whist, faro, basset, quinze, evens and odds (EO), roulette, backgammon

Playing card, early eighteenth century. 'A Woodpecker. A Red Wing.' (LMA/WCMPC, 452)

Playing card, early eighteenth century. 'Cat a fidling & Mice a Dancing.' (LMA/WCMPC, 452)

Das Bretspiel, engraving, Johann Esaiss Nilson (1721–88). Board games such as backgammon, chess and draughts, were as popular as cards. (Private coll)

134   PART TWO: BATH AS A RESORT

Bath's notoriety as a centre for gaming was second only to the increasing faith placed in the healing powers of its waters. Gaming brought Richard Nash to the city and his success at the tables persuaded him to remain in Bath for the rest of his exceedingly long life; but it brought about his downfall. Tunbridge Wells and Bath operated in much the same way. Professional gamesters such as Nash mingled with those for whom playing at cards and dice was a social pastime and, on occasion, took advantage of them. Those who had the time and resources to play spent many hours at the tables — more hours in Bath, perhaps, than in London or when at home. Some gambled away jewels, snuffboxes and other intrinsically valuable possessions.

The Duchess of Lauderdale, at Ham in the 1680s, seems to have lost only small and readily affordable amounts. More serious examples of heavy gambling away from Bath were George I's loss of £3,000 in a single night playing ombre with the Duchess of

Record of losses and winnings of the Duchess of Lauderdale. Elizabeth Murray succeeded her father as Countess Dysart in her own right. Her first husband was Sir Lyonel Tollemache, of Helmingham Hall, Suffolk; her second, in 1672, was the Earl (later Duke) of Lauderdale, of Ham House. She died in 1698. Many other women and men kept similar accounts in the early years of the eighteenth century. (Tollemache)

WHAT TO DO: THE DAILY ROUND   135

Monmouth and the Countess of Lincoln.[227] Tales of such losses held a peculiar fascination and fuelled gossipy correspondence. Lady Bristol, in the 1720s, would not have been the only person who reported from Bath 'The news of this day is full of Lord Scarboroughs having lost £13,000' or that Nash had lost £1,400.[228] The interest lay not just in the loss of large sums of money, but also how gamblers reacted to their losses: 'The Countess of Burlington in the absence of her Royal Highness, held a circle at Hayes's, where she lost a favourite snuff-box, but unfortunately kept her temper.'[229]

Whether true or merely false hearsay, it was stories such as these that led to legislation to restrict gaming in the 1730s and '40s. Curiously (some suggest tactlessly) gambling at Court was still permitted under the Acts of Parliament that prohibited it elsewhere, as it was considered to be gaming in a private, not public, place — in January 1744/45 it was reported that 'the Earl of Winchelsea on Monday night at Court won upwards of 1,500 guineas at Hazard'.[230] Periodically there were well-publicised attempts to break up gambling sessions in private houses also.

p. 126

Box of gaming counters, ivory, carved and decorated with staining, penwork and paint, Mariaval le Jeune, French, *c.* 1740–60. Width: 8 cm (3⅛ in). (V&A W.21A/1-1985) In 1730 Richard Hoare exchanged a box of ivory counters for 3s 6d from William Deards. He bought from Paul Bertrand four dozen ivory counters for 4s, in 1747.

136   PART TWO: BATH AS A RESORT

Whist continued to be played and it was in this period of transition for gaming that in 1742 Edmund Hoyle published his guide to whist (so carelessly dropped to the floor in Hogarth's *Marriage à la Mode* II), which by 1748 was in its 9th edition.

The attempt to wipe out gambling was not a total success and there were other ways to win or lose money: Bath was full of lottery shops — indeed most toyshops acted as agents for tickets. And in other places on the social circuit there were further temptations. It was reported in 1718 that 'Mr Herring the great Gamester won in wagers at the horse races at Newmarket the sum of £30,000'.[231] Such free spending was no doubt a reason why the Deards family had a shop in Newmarket.

> In 1738 … the Gaming Act made it an offence to keep any place where games such as ace of hearts, faro, basset and hazard were played. So the gamblers invented new games. In 1739 the government went further and banned all dice games; the gamblers turned to roulette, though this in turn was banned, if not always successfully, in 1745.[232]
>
> One of the new games was EO (evens and odds).

The various Acts of Parliament passed between 1738 and 1745 were a catalyst for social change in Bath and the city was a target for the subsequent drive to suppress gambling. In October 1750 the Bath Journal reported: '… the Sheriffs went to the several Places in this City, where EO Tables were kept, and suppress'd the Playing at any of them.'[233] One biographer of Richard Nash wrote that the 'tightening of the law against gambling throttled Bath in 1745'.[234] It may have stifled the old ways, but Bath did not die: while Selina Countess of Huntingdon and John Wesley encouraged spiritual enlightenment in the city, the entrepreneurial spirit of John Wood and Ralph Allen, financiers and businessmen such as Richard Marchant and James Theobald and numerous shopkeepers, ensured its physical and financial expansion. Most of these people feature in Bertrand's bank account.

p. 285

pp. 292 and 255

Nor, indeed, was gambling stopped. Tales of money lost at the tables later in the century are legion, for example the very substantial losses by the Duchess of Devonshire and her friend the politician Charles James Fox.

To date, ten invoices from Bertrand's shop have been found. A resumé of their contents is given below:

	£	s	d
1. October 1730 (Fairfax) [▶ pp. 42 and 43] receipted by Paul Bertrand			
Four silver salts and two silver sauceboats	23	01	09
2. October 1730 (Fairfax) receipted by Mary Bertrand			
Two silver candlesticks	13	08	11
Tea equipage, silver	5	00	00
Diamond ring	5	05	00
3. November 1736 (Burlington) [▶ p. 160] receipted by Paul Bertrand			
Six hony comb china cups	3	03	00
Four basons	0	07	00
Large bandagio	1	10	00
Sett of stone jump buckles	3	03	00
Box of Indian ink	0	05	00
Snuff box	4	04	00
Smelling bottle	1	15	00
Ditto	1	11	06
Reverbere	2	12	06
Single brilliant ring	1	11	06
Pebble watch	18	18	00
Steel chaine	3	03	00
Silver standish	5	05	00
Powder boxes	4	4	0
4. June 1737 (Jernegan) [▶ p. 130] receipted by Paul Bertrand			
Flowers	0	03	06
5. October 1738 (Prince of Wales) [▶ pp. 148 and 150]			
6. May 1741 (Fairfax) [▶ p. 43] receipted by Paul Bertrand			
Brilliant girdle buckle	113	00	00
Tea kettle & lamp, silver	30	5	0
7. August 1745 (Spencer) [▶ p. 140–41] receipted by John Wiltshire			
Pair of Silver Shoe Buckles	0	10	06
English Ware Cream Jugg	0	10	06
Fine Dresden Honey Comb sugar dish and plate	10	10	00
Role of Pigtail Tobaco	0	01	06
3 Blew and White Old China Jarrs	1	01	00
2 ditto	1	00	00
1 ditto	0	05	00
Pair of Pinchbeck Shoe Buckles	0	4	00
Cash	21	0	0

	£	s	d
8. September 1745 (Spencer) receipted by John Wiltshire			
Role of Tobaco	0	01	06
Silver Studd	0	02	06
6 Dresden Cups and Saucers	6	06	00
9. March 1746 (Hoare) receipted by Thomas Pomfret			
1 lb of French Rappee	0	07	00
4 Dozen of Ivory Counters	0	04	00
Bamboe Cane	0	07	00
Tobaco Stopper	0	08	00
Cork Screw Tobaco Stopper	0	10	06
Polishing a Silver Pencell	0	01	00
10. April 1746 (Spencer) receipted by Thomas Pomfret			
Dresden China	13	13	00

Playing card, *c.* 1720, depicting a shop interior at the time of the South Sea Bubble. (LMA/WCMPC)

WHAT TO DO: THE DAILY ROUND

Sugar dish and plate, porcelain, Meissen, *c.* 1745. Bought by the Hon John Spencer from Paul Bertrand on 9 August 1745. (Althorp)

Milk Jug, porcelain, Chelsea, *c.* 1745.
Bought by the Hon John Spencer from
Paul Bertrand on 9 August 1745.
(Althorp)

WHAT TO DO: THE DAILY ROUND   141

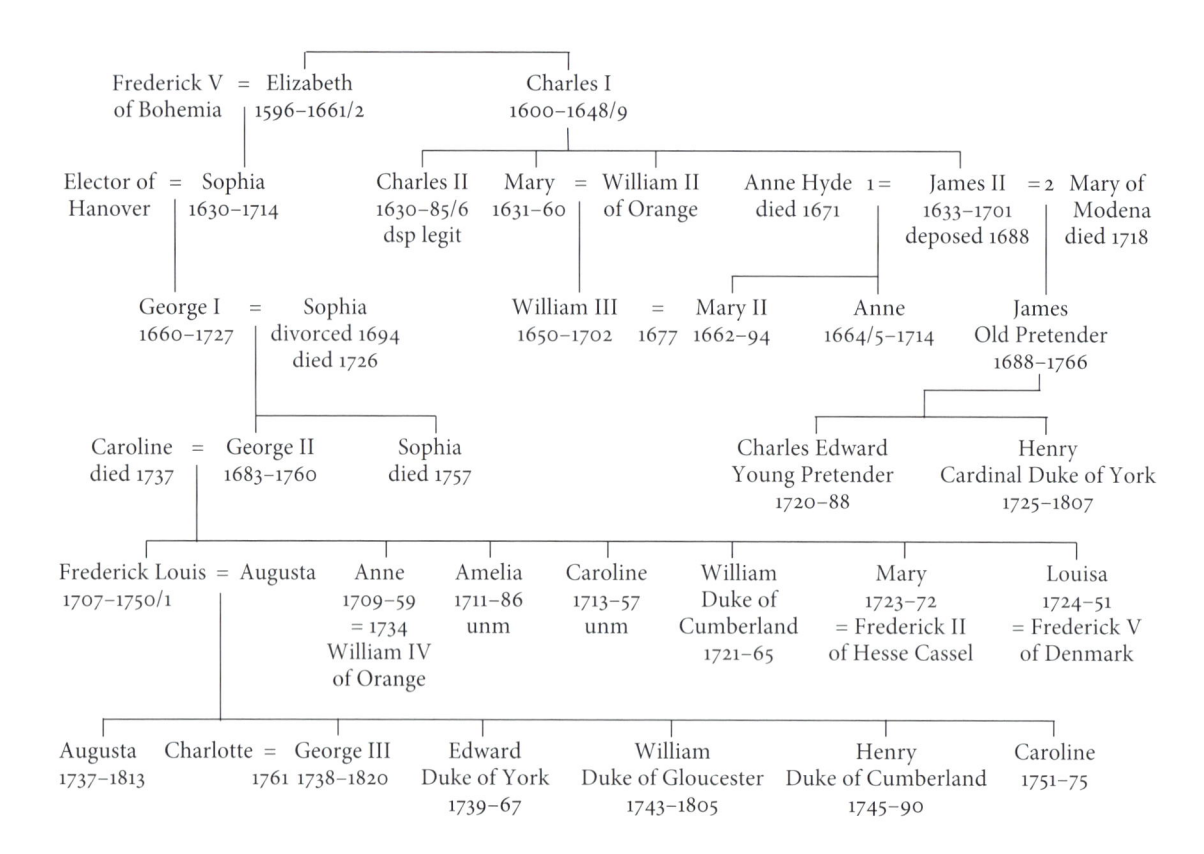

```
                    Frederick V  =  Elizabeth          Charles I
                    of Bohemia  |  1596–1661/2         1600–1648/9

Elector of  =  Sophia        Charles II    Mary   =   William II    Anne Hyde  1=  James II  =2  Mary of
Hanover    |   1630–1714     1630–85/6    1631–60     of Orange     died 1671      1633–1701      Modena
                              dsp legit                                             deposed 1688    died 1718

        George I    =    Sophia            William III   =   Mary II      Anne           James
        1660–1727        divorced 1694     1650–1702    1677  1662–94    1664/5–1714   Old Pretender
                         died 1726                                                      1688–1766

                                                                                Charles Edward         Henry
Caroline   =   George II       Sophia                                           Young Pretender        Cardinal Duke of York
died 1737      1683–1760       died 1757                                        1720–88                1725–1807

Frederick Louis = Augusta    Anne       Amelia     Caroline    William      Mary           Louisa
1707–1750/1                  1709–59    1711–86    1713–57     Duke of      1723–72        1724–51
                             = 1734     unm        unm         Cumberland   = Frederick II  = Frederick V
                             William IV                        1721–65       of Hesse Cassel  of Denmark
                             of Orange

Augusta    Charlotte  =  George III    Edward          William             Henry               Caroline
1737–1813  1761         1738–1820      Duke of York    Duke of Gloucester  Duke of Cumberland  1751–75
                                       1739–67         1743–1805           1745–90
```

The royal lodgings at Abbey House, detail from Joseph Gilmore's map, 1694. Formerly the lodgings of the Abbey's prior, the building and priory grounds were acquired by the Colthurst family in 1543, and demolished by the Duke of Kingston in 1755 in order to build new baths. (Bath in Time, 13805)

The next morning after Eleven o'Clock, the Prince walk'd for some Time in Orange Grove, and was soon followed by the Princess; they visited Mrs. Hays's fine Walks, Mr Bertran's Toy-Shop, Mrs Lovelace's Great Room, and her Royal Highness from thence went to the Abby Church, and several other Places, attended by several of the Nobility, Mr Nash and Crowds of People.

LONDON EVENING POST, 21 OCTOBER 1738.

Royalty and their retinues

Royalty were no strangers to Bath. Queen Elizabeth visited the city in 1574 and Anne of Denmark (wife of James I and VI) came in 1613 and 1615. Charles II brought his wife Catherine of Braganza and James II brought his second wife Mary of Modena (in 1687), both brothers hoping the visits would result in a male heir. The visits secured Bath's position as a place for those seeking a cure, or short-term relief, from a range of maladies, a position that was strengthened by Queen Anne's visits in 1702 and 1703. Although Bath was known as a centre for Jacobites and had a Catholic lodging house, the city supported the Hanoverians and enthusiastically celebrated the king's birthday each year with a ball.

The chance to rub shoulders with royalty was a great lure to all sorts of people, and the visits of the children of George II added to Bath's attractions. All the shopkeepers would have benefitted from the trade these visits brought, in particular the purchasing power of the gentry and 'middling sort' who timed their visits to coincide with the royal family.

Neither Princess Amelia (1711–86) nor Princess Caroline (1713–57) married; their younger sister Mary (1723–72) married the Landgrave of Hesse Cassel in 1740 but spent time with her sisters in Bath, as did the Duke of Cumberland. They brought with them an entourage of servants and members of their households, who would have had their own servants also.

Princess Amelia

Princess Amelia, the second daughter of George II, did not enjoy good health. Her numerous visits to the spas at Tunbridge Wells, Bath and in London were regularly reported in the newspapers. One or other of her siblings sometimes joined her for part of her stay at these resorts. She visited Bath in 1728, when she presented Richard Nash with a silver tureen, and she returned on numerous occasions until her death in 1786. She became something of a

Princess Amelia (1711–86), mezzotint, John Faber jnr after Hans Hysing. (NPG, D7958)

mascot for the city, and her image was widely used on a range of goods sold by many of the shops including, no doubt, Bertrand's.

In April 1728, Mrs Delany noted:

Last week as we were sauntering agreeably in the King's Road to take a little air, we met Princess Amelia in her way to the Bath. She is carried in a chair, not being able to bear the motion of a coach: our coach was very close to her, and she looked smiling and pretty, bowed to us all, and asked who we were. I wish the Bath may do her good, for she has lived hitherto a life of misery, and everybody commends her temper.

In April and June 1733 newspapers reported that the princess visited the New River Head [▶ p. 36/2 map] in Clerkenwell (London) nearly every day, and between April and June 1734 she was in Bath again, shortly after the visit of the Prince of Orange.

Souvenirs were produced and shopkeepers did not hesitate to name-drop. In 1735 Jonathan Pinchbeck advertised a fan depicting the Pump Room at Bath with visitors including Princess Amelia; in December 1754 Deards advertised that the princess and her siblings headed the subscriptions he was taking for an engraving of the Prince of Wales.[235]

The Prince of Orange. January 1733/34

Prince William of Orange fell ill shortly after he arrived in England in 1733 to marry Princess Anne, the Princess Royal, eldest daughter of George II. The ceremony was postponed and arrangements were made for the Prince to go to Bath to recover his health. His extended recuperation there caused immense excitement and set a pattern for future royal visits. Management of the prince's stay in Bath was largely in the hands of Sir Clement Cotterell, the Master of Ceremonies, who attended the prince throughout the time he was in England. The jewelled snuffbox that the prince presented to Richard Nash during his visit might well have been among the 'baubles' he bought from Bertrand; in making the gift the prince set a precedent that Nash exploited for at least the next ten years. To commemorate the prince's visit the area near the Abbey was renamed Orange Grove and an obelisk erected there.

The press kept their readers informed of events, and letters fill out the story.

p. 159

1733

26 December. Preparations are making for the Prince of Orange's going to Bath Monday next, his disorder being no fever, but an indigestion.

29 December. Wednesday or Thursday the Prince of Orange goes to Bath. Dr Tessier attends him, and but three of his own servants, and Sir Clement Cotterel, Master of the Ceremonies.[236]

2 January. The Prince of Orange set out in one of his Majesty's coaches for Bath.

5 January. At 5 in the evening the Prince of Orange arrived at Bath, attended by Sir Clement Cotterell. The whole Town was illuminated on that occasion. [237]

The royal party stopped at Marlborough on their way to Bath:

To Lord Hertford:

Bath, Jan 6th 1733/34. My good Lord, Rather than neglect my Duty in acknowledging the Honour of your Ldps I chuse to trespass upon your Goodness for a pardon for writing to your Ldsp upon this sorry bit of

Sir Clement Cottrell Dormer (1686–1758), oil on canvas, Thomas Hudson. Sir Clement, of Rousham, Oxfordshire, inherited the role of Master of Ceremonies on the death of his father in 1710. (Courtauld)

Gold boxes associated with Frederick, Prince of Wales

Snuffbox, gold, cast and chased, unmarked, *c.* 1745. Width: 6.8 cm (2¾ in). The lid with a medallion of Frederick Prince of Wales. The quality of the box suggests that it might be linked to Jasper Cunst, who is known to have worked with the chaser Augustin Heckel. (Royal Coll, 4047)

Snuffbox, gold, unmarked, *c.* 1749. Length: 9.1 cm (7½ in). Inside the lid is a miniature by Christian Friedrich Zincke of Frederick Prince of Wales, who gave the box to Lord North (1704–90) when he was appointed governor to Prince George, later George III. Zincke was appointed Cabinet Painter to the prince in 1732. (Royal Coll, 3926)

These two gold snuffboxes are associated with Frederick, Prince of Wales (1707–51). They cannot be linked to Paul Bertrand and, being unmarked, the craftsmen who worked on them are unknown.[238]

Snuffboxes were the traditional gift of diplomacy and, like royalty throughout Europe, the prince and other members of his family and their envoys, were the donors and recipients of such gifts. In London gifts were usually ordered through the royal goldsmiths or obtained direct from a craftsman, and not through a retailer such as a toyshop. On his 1738 visit to Bath the prince gave Richard Nash 'a large gold enamelled snuffbox' for his collection and bought eight snuffboxes from Paul Bertrand. The prince was presented with the freedom of the city by Bath Corporation, and this came with a 'fine gold snuff box' supplied by the local goldsmith Philip Masters.

paper all that I can at present come at; the Prince is now writing to your Ldp and will I am sure much better express His service of Yours and my Ladyes Goodness to Him & His followers than I can for Him, only I must beg leave to say had it not been for Lady Hartfords Goodness in storing us so well, wee had literally starv'd for hunger as well as cold, 'twas a most bitter day & every place full at Sandy Lane but wee at last got a dirty room & by my Good Ladys kind care far'd very well, & were enabled to perform our Journey. The Prince is thank God very well, gains ground every day, began at the pump this morning; and if he has not had too much of Quadrille this evening at Lady Blandford's will I doubt not sleep as well as he did last night; I beg leave with my duty to your Ldp & my Lady to subscribe your Ldps most obedient servt C. Cottrell

The Prince wrote the same day and two days later the Princess Royal also wrote:

St James's. 8 Jan 1734. I can't put of thanking you Dear Lady Hartford for all ye trouble you & Ld Hartford have given yourself for ye Prince of Orange. I have had so many proofs of both your attentions & goodness yt I can only reckon yt as one more obligation. Pray be always persuaded of my thankfulness & yt you will always find in me a hearty friend. Anne[239]

26 January.
This morning His Highness bought some baubles of Bertram the Toy Man.[240]

20 February. Mr Nash erected in the new square in the Grove at Bath, now called Orange Square, a Monumental stone with the following inscription:

IN MEMORIAM | SANITATIS |PRINCIPI AURIACO |AQUARUM THERMALIUM POTU |FAVENTE DEO |OVANTE BRITANNIA |FELICITER RESTITUTAE | MDCCXXXIV

27 February. The Prince of Orange arrived at Oxford from Bath ... [He was] met by the Corporation in their Habits ... the Prince, Sir Clement Cotterel and his other attendants were complimented with their freedoms in silver boxes, and with fringed Gloves ... [241]

The marriage of the Princess Royal and Prince William took place on 25 March 1733/34.

The Prince and Princess of Wales. October 1738

The people of Bath must have hoped, but hardly dared to expect, to better this royal visit, and in the autumn of 1738 those hopes were realised when the Prince and Princess of Wales came with a large entourage. Bathonians had enthusiastically celebrated the prince's marriage in 1736[242] and the prince had been generous to the city in donating £100 to the subscription for the Mineral Water Hospital. He arrived on Tuesday, 17 October 1738 to the sound of

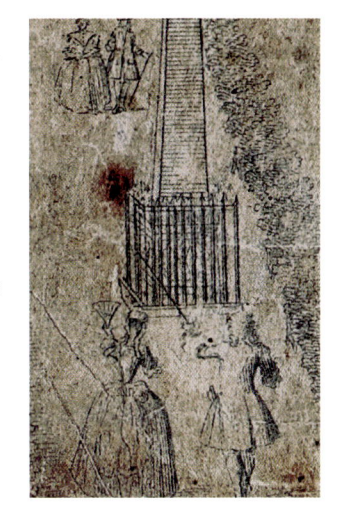

Detail ▶ p. 60. The obelisk in Orange Grove [▶ p. 83 illus.]

p. 90

Their Royal Highnesses are exceedingly well pleased with their Reception, the Prospect, Situation and Nearness of the Place, as are the Inhabitants in an extraordinary Manner with their Royal Guests.

His Royal Highness the Prince of Wales
Oct 24 1738   Bougt of P. Bertrand

a Groupe of China figures	5 : 5 : 0
a pair of Old China Candlesticks	4 : 4 : 0
a Gold Snuff box	26 : 5 : 0
an Enamel'd Snuff box	16 : 16 : 0
a Cornelian Snuff box	7 : 7 : 0
a blood stone pocket case	10 : 10 : 0
a Cameo watch Toy	16 : 16 : 0
a pair of Candlesticks	12 : 12 : 0
Change of ye pocket case for an Inlay'd Estwey	5 : 5 : 0
a Blood stone Estwey	21 : 0 : 0
2 Gold Chaines for Ditto	5 : 15 : 6
Trincketts for Ditto	5 : 15 : 6
a Ring	4 : 4 : 0
a French Clock	30 : 0 : 0
a Snuff box	70 : 0 : 0
a Blood stone Watch, Chaine, &cc	33 : 0 : 0
2 Old white Cups & Silver Gilt Sawcers	10 : 10 : 0
a pair of Sawce boats	17 : 6 : 0
Four Silver Salts	13 : 14 : 0
a Silver Bread Basket	25 : 15 : 0
	342 : 0 : 0

bells (the cost to the Council of the ringers was £2 12s 6d) and, '… immediately after the safe arrival of their Royal Highnesses the Prince and Princess of Wales at Bath, they dressed themselves, and, to prevent Form and Ceremony, went directly to the Ball-Room, without giving the least previous Notice, and were receiv'd with the utmost Joy by the Assembly; where they continued several Hours.'[243] As Lady Mary Wortley Montagu wrote to the Countess of Pomfret that 'All the polite and the gallant are either gone or preparing for the Bath', the assembly must have comprised a good number of the nobility.

The visit had, of course, been planned in advance and a fortnight before his arrival Bath Corporation, at their meeting on 5 October, had unanimously agreed to offer the freedom of the city to the prince and that 'if he agrees … a freedome of this City shall be presented to him in a Gold Box'. The box was supplied by Philip Masters but in all probability was made in London; it weighed 6oz 8dwt (approximately 200 gr) and cost £29 12s. The prince was presented with the freedom at a dinner in the town hall, when further expenses included £1 10s for ringers and nine guineas for music. The prince and princess stayed until early November. Before they left, several members of the prince's entourage were presented with the freedom of the city — this time in silver boxes: Lord Baltimore, Sir Thomas Saunderson, Mr Pitt, Mr Littleton, Mr Douglas, Sir William Irby, Mr Bloodworth, Mr Hamilton, Mr Hammond, Mr Scot, Dr Broxholm, Dr Ayscough. All the boxes, including the prince's gold one, were engraved by Jacob Skinner, in return for which he was made a freeman the following February.[244]

Exactly a week after his arrival, the prince visited Bertrand's shop. The resulting invoice gives by far the best detail of the range of objects he stocked. The prince spent the staggering sum of £745 12s. How many of these things were bought for himself, and how many as gifts, will never be known. One of the prince's biographers, for example, noted that in the twentieth century 'a descendant of Miss Rebecca Pitts, heiress of Hardcott House, Wiltshire, has still in her possession a relic of these days, the fine pair of paste buckles which Prince Frederick presented to Miss Pitts after dancing with her in the Assembly Rooms', although during which of his several visits the prince made the gift appears not to have been recorded.[245] Nash was, of course, amongst the recipients of the prince's generosity in 1738.

The prince would have been expected to distribute presents as mementoes of his visit, and some at least might have been bought locally. Did Bertrand buy stock especially, in anticipation of the royal visit? Or did someone in the prince's entourage, in advance

The first page of Paul Bertrand's bill to Frederick Prince of Wales, dated 24 October 1738. (Cornwall)

p. 172

p. 181

Brought forward	342 : 0 : 0
a Silver hand Candlestick	8 : 8 : 0
a Cornelian Tooth pick case	12 : 12 : 0
a Snuff box	6 : 6 : 0
a Pocket book	6 : 6 : 0
a Ditto	6 : 6 : 0
a Silver Cork Screw	0 : 15 : 0
a double Travelling Case	15 : 15 : 0
a Gold Enamel'd Trunk	57 : 15 : 0
a Smelling bottle	1 : 11 : 6
a pair of Gilt Rose buckles	4 : 4 : 0
a Perfume Pot	6 : 6 : 0
a Silver Sugar dish	21 : 0 : 0
pr Raffle	1 : 1 : 0
a Cornelian Snuff box	8 : 8 : 0
Half of a pair of Brilliant tops	31 : 10 : 0
a Blood Stone Repeater, Chaine, & Seal	48 : 6 : 0
a Gold Smelling bottle	11 : 11 : 0
a Bread Basket	31 : 18 : 6
a Snuff box Ornamented wth brilliants	46 : 0 : 0
an Onix Egg	10 : 10 : 0
a Smelling bottle	4 : 4 : 0
a french Toylet	1 : 11 : 6
Novr 28 a Gold Snuff box	32 : 0 : 0
	716 : 4 : 0

of the trip, visit George Wickes, the prince's goldsmith in London, to stock up on the required gifts. Such items might then have been brought in the royal baggage to Bath.

An annotation to Bertrand's invoice notes that the 'goods' the prince bought were delivered on 9 February 1738/39.

Sir Thomas Saunderson was appointed Treasurer and Receiver General to the Prince of Wales on 27 May 1738 (he became the 3rd Earl of Scarborough in 1739). He was therefore responsible for authorising payment of Bertrand's invoice, which was receipted on 20 February — three months after the transaction. An extra item, 'a Silver dish stand 59 oz £29 8s.' was added to the original purchases and paid for by the Deputy Treasurer, Edward Godfrey.[246] And now Hoare's ledgers turn up trumps: the day after his invoice was paid, on 21 February, the credit page of Bertrand's account shows 'By himself £700'. There he is, depositing at the bank what was surely the payment from the Prince's treasurer.

The 1738 visit was commemorated by the city with the erection of another obelisk, in the centre of Queen Square, and by the Prince of Wales with the gift of a silver-gilt salver and cup and cover in 1739.

The order for the cup was placed with the London silversmith George Wickes, who had held a warrant from the prince since 1735. The design of the cup suggests that it was made in the workshop of Paul de Lamerie, who would have sold it to Wickes, who then supplied it to the prince's office. Wickes would also have acted as agent for the purchase of gold boxes for the prince to distribute as gifts.

The second page of Paul Bertrand's bill to Frederick Prince of Wales, dated 24 October 1738. (Cornwall)

p. 152 illus.

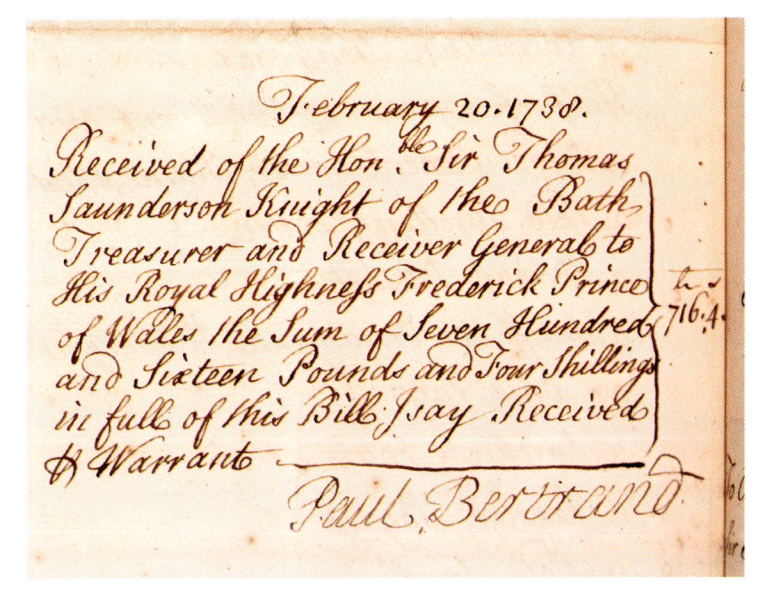

Paul Bertrand's signature on the receipt

Cup and cover, silver-gilt, unmarked, *c*. 1738. Height: 35.5 cm (14 in). Salver, silver-gilt, Lewis Pantin, London 1733/4. With a contemporary fitted case. (Bath)

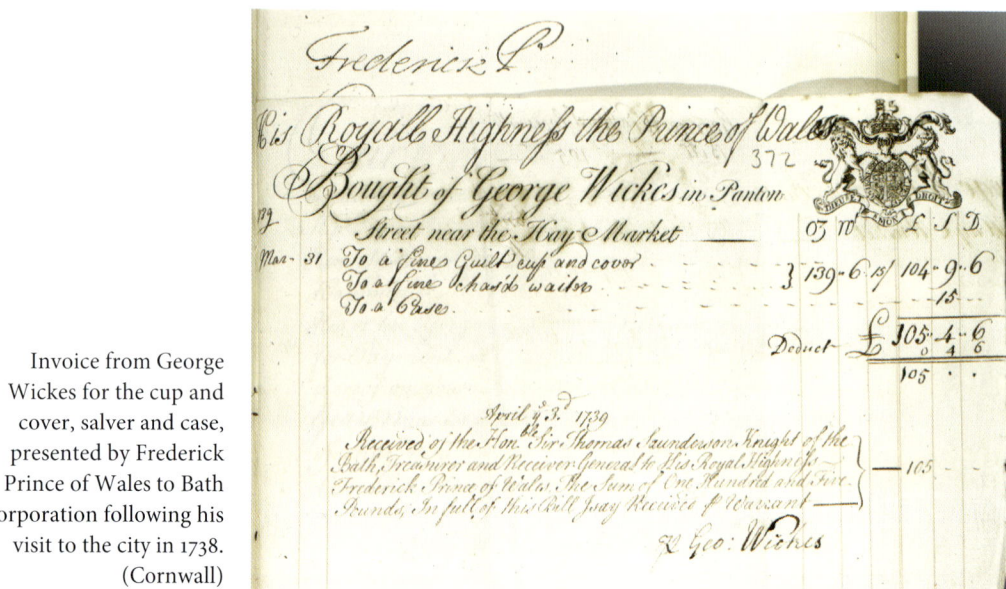

Invoice from George Wickes for the cup and cover, salver and case, presented by Frederick Prince of Wales to Bath Corporation following his visit to the city in 1738. (Cornwall)

Obtaining a royal warrant meant a great deal to a tradesman in terms of prestige and the orders he received from royalty and those who followed in their wake. Whereas Wickes held the Prince of Wales's warrant, all the orders for plate for the royal household and for ambassadors, including New Year gifts and coronation regalia, went through the Jewel Office, which was under the supervision of the Lord Chamberlain's office. From the seventeenth century onwards the post of royal goldsmith was usually awarded to a goldsmith-banker, who subcontracted to working goldsmiths. During the first half of the eighteenth century they were: Samuel Smithin (1702–23), John Tyso (1723–30), Thomas Minors (1730–59) and John Boldero (1759–60), most of whom operated from an office in Lombard Street. Paul de Lamerie was one of several silversmiths who were sub-contracted to supply the Jewel Office.

One of those who followed the prince's lead in going to George Wickes was his private secretary Colonel James Pelham. Silver ordered from Wickes also survives from Pelham's distant cousin the Earl of Lincoln, later 2nd Duke of Newcastle.

p. 157 illus.

Mrs Savil's lodgings [▶ 21/16 illus.], also known as Skrine's lodgings, near the Hot Bath, from Joseph Gilmore's map, 1694. In 1697 Honor Savile married William Skrine, who died in 1725. The lodgings were kept by Rachel Humphries when Princess Caroline stayed here in 1746; she married Ernst von Hetling. (Bath in Time, 13814)

ROYALTY AND THEIR RETINUES 153

Princess Caroline's visit. Extracts from the *Bath Journal*:

31 March. The Princess Caroline is expected here Friday or Saturday next for the Recovery of her Health having been indisposed for some time with Rheumatick Illness. Yesterday some Domesticks belonging to Her Royal Highness arriv'd here in order to provide Lodgings. Saturday several of the Princesses servants with five tumbrils laden with Baggage set out of London for this City. Tis thought we shall have the greatest season that has been for some years. … This morning the Musick will begin at the Pump Room, as will the Balls this week at Mr Simpsons and Mrs Wiltshire's.

7 April. Last Thursday evening between six and seven o'clock her Royal Highness Princess Caroline arriv'd here … escorted by a party of General Hawley's dragoons. … Richard Nash went on Thursday Morning as far as Sandy Lane to meet and pay his Compliments to her Royal Highness. … Yesterday Her Royal Highness carried in her chair to the Pump Room … intends to stay here about two months.

14 April. Last Wednesday morning about ten o'clock a fire broke out in the lodgings belonging to HRH Princess Caroline …which damaged three or four of the upper rooms … attribute it to the airing of linnen by the fire. … When the danger was over Mrs Umphreys, who keeps the Lodgings, waited upon HRH and express'd her Great concern at the event. … HRH spent Wednesday night at Richard Nash's house, returned to the lodgings Thursday.

21 April. Tuesday last … Birthday of HRH Duke of Cumberland … a Ball in the evening at Mrs Wiltshire's and a Grand Entertainment for the Gentlemen and Ladies at Mr Simpson's … the concourse of People was so great for upon a moderate Computation there were upwards of 2000 people here from different parts of the country …

19 May. We hear that Pr Caroline sets out on the 28th.

26 May. Pr Caroline intends to set out Wednesday morning, dine at Sandy Lane and be in London Friday … proposed to return late August/September … her baggage left here.

4 August. The Season will begin much sooner than usual on account of HRH.

11 August. We are informed that HRH the Princess of Hesse is coming over to England to accompany HRH Pr Caroline to this City. Lodgings are already taken for a great many Persons of Quality who are expected here by the end of this month.

15 September. Tomorrow the balls begin for the season.

13 October. Coronation Anniversary, great ball at Mr Simpson's given by Richard Nash, for the Gentlemen and Ladies, at which HRH the Princess of Hesse was present. There was also a great Ball Thursday night at Mrs Wiltshire's.

20 October. [Princess of Hesse leaving, Pr Caroline staying]

27 October. Last Friday HRH Princess of Hesse set out for London with a numerous retinue and propos'd to be at Mr Poyntz's near Newbury the same night, where HRH the Duke of Cumberland intended to meet her.

8 December. Princess Caroline to leave tomorrow sennight, the 16th.

15 December. Pr Caroline left Tuesday 8 o'clock, arrived London between 5 and 6 Thursday evening.

4 May 1747. Pr Caroline is relapsed and lies very ill at her apartments in St James's Palace.

Princess Caroline (1713–57), mezzotint, John Faber jnr after Hans Hysing. (NPG, D9140)

Princess Mary of Hesse (1723–72), mezzotint, John Faber jnr after Arthur Pond. (NPG, D10794)

Princess Caroline. March–December 1746

Princess Caroline's visits in 1746 may have contributed to the increased number of visitors to Bath that year. The newly-founded *Bath Journal* relished the opportunity to give full rein to the reporting skills of its writers, and extracts are transcribed here because they give such a flavour of events unfolding, including several mishaps. The princess did not stay at the royal lodgings near the Abbey but instead went to Skrine's lodgings.

Royal retinues

Colonel James Pelham and Stephen Poyntz [Pointz] were among the entourage in 1746. The large sums of money that appear in Pelham's name in Bertrand's account at Hoare & Co. must represent expenses during the Princess Caroline's visits: in May £451 16s 9d and £500, and in October £300. Pelham had been secretary to Prince Frederick from the time of his arrival in England in 1729 until 1737. Poyntz, who was closely connected to the royal family, was a familiar figure in Bath and had also been present during Prince Frederick's visit. Another member of the royal household whose duties appear to have brought her to Bath was Mary Dering. She was dresser to Princess Amelia and to

p. 157 illus.

p. 209 illus.

p. 162

ROYALTY AND THEIR RETINUES   155

Members of the royal households who feature in Paul Bertrand's bank account:

1736	Viscount Perceval	Lord of the Bedchamber	P of Wales
1738–40	Mary Dering	Dresser to the Princess Royal	George II
1738 & 1741	William Wyndham	Comptroller, Duke of Cumberland's household	George II
1738	Earl of Scarborough	Treasurer	P of Wales
1738–46	Stephen Poyntz	Governor of the household of Duke of Cumberland	George II
1741	Lady Delorane	Governess to princesses Mary and Louisa	George II
1742	Robert Nugent	Comptroller of the household	P of Wales
1743	Viscount Doneraile	Comptroller / Gentleman of the Bedchamber	P of Wales
1745	John Shutz	Steward of the Duchy of Cornwall	P of Wales
1746	James Pelham	Secretary	P of Wales

The return from the chase, oil on canvas, John Wootton, signed and dated 1737. Detail, showing left to right: John Spencer; Colonel Bloodworth; Colonel Schutz (walking towards the Prince); Frederick Prince of Wales; Charles Spencer, 3rd Duke of Marlborough; Henry Brydges, 2nd Duke of Chandos. (Royal Coll, 407814)

Princess Caroline. Her will makes interesting reading and shows not only her familiarity with the ways of court life, but also a liking for toys.

James Pelham (1683–1761), regularly referred to as 'Jemmy Pelham' in correspondence, was Member of Parliament for Newark, then Hastings, between 1722 and 1761. He never married, and was identified within the family's Sussex stronghold as 'of Crowhurst'; his London address was Charles Street in the mid-1730s.[247] Contemporary letters reveal that he was constantly anxious about money, but his bank account with Hoare & Co. from 1726, shows that he was far from impoverished.[248]

Pelham was Secretary to the Lord Chamberlain and was appointed Secretary to Frederick, Prince of Wales at a salary of £800 when the prince arrived in England in 1729.[249] He resigned this post before the vote in the House of Commons on the prince's expenses on 22 February 1736/37. Colonel Pelham was in Bath in April 1746 with Princess Caroline, and with her again, together with the Princess of Hesse, in September the same year. Towards the end of his time as the prince's secretary Pelham ordered a gold cup from George Wickes, to a design by William Kent. He largely paid for this with gold boxes at a melt value of £3 15s 6d per ounce.[250] Gold and silver boxes were regularly given to those of rank and to office holders: Pelham was awarded a silver box when he was made an Honorary Freeman of Bath on 18 October 1752.

The prince's circle also included Johann and Augustus Shutz, who both held appointments within the royal household — the brothers were second cousins of George II. Augustus's daughter Elizabeth is buried in Bath Abbey. Colonel Johann Shutz (d. 1773) was with the prince when he first came to England in 1729. He, too, was a customer of George Wickes between 1738 and 1741, when he lived in Golden Square.[251]

Stephen Poyntz (1685–1750), oil on canvas, Jean-Baptiste van Loo, c. 1740. (Yale, B1985.21)

Colonel James Pelham, wearing blue-coated hunting uniform. Detail of: Frederick Prince of Wales in the hunting field, oil on canvas, John Wootton, the heads by William Hogarth, signed and dated 1734. (Royal Coll, 401000)

ROYALTY AND THEIR RETINUES   157

Snuff box, gold, unmarked, *c.* 1740. Width: 7.1 cm (2¾ in). Set with a portrait miniature inside the lid thought to be Dorothy Boyle, later Lady Euston. (Chatsworth)

Lady Dorothy Boyle, mezzotint, John Faber jnr after a drawing by Dorothy, Countess of Burlington, 1744. (BM, 1902,1011.1242)

158   PART TWO: BATH AS A RESORT

Richard Nash's gold boxes

Following the initiative of the Prince of Orange in 1734, Nash accumulated a collection of snuffboxes. Perhaps visitors saw their gift as a form of payment for the time and energy he spent on their behalf: numerous biographers have written of the extraordinary mix of courtesy and boorishness that he displayed, and his kindnesses to young innocents and elderly infirm. Or a box may have been a tip from a parent or guardian if Nash made introductions for those seeking a suitor. It will never be known exactly how many boxes were in his collection, or who gave them to him.

Did visitors give him boxes that they had tired of, which they brought with them to Bath — or were they purchased specially from Bertrand and the other toyshops during their visit? Possibly a mix of both, and there is no way of judging how much of Bertrand's turnover such gifts represented. When Nash's star had waned and the presents stopped, Bertrand might well have noticed the loss of business.

Through the early 1740s Nash's income was severely reduced as a result of the constraints of the various parliamentary measures against gambling. He needed to raise money: he sold his snuffboxes and other trinkets, but exactly when this happened is unknown. There is no record of whether, when Nash decided to sell his collection, he did so in London or in Bath, or whether he sold the snuffboxes piecemeal or all at once. No large payment to him appears in Bertrand's accounts and Nash probably chose to dispose of the boxes discreetly in the capital, well away from small-town gossip. By the end of his life Nash was virtually penniless.[252]

Goldsmith's description of the possessions remaining to Nash when he died cannot be bettered:

A small library of well-chosen books, some trinkets and pictures were his only inheritance. Among the latter (besides the box given him by the Prince of Wales) were a gold box which was presented to him by the Countess of Burlington, with Lady Euston's picture in the lid. An etui mounted in gold, with a diamond to open it, and ornamented with another diamond at the top, given him by the Princess-Dowager of Wales. He had also a silver teren [tureen], which was given him by the Princess Amelia, and some other things of no great value. The rings, watches and pictures, which he formerly received from others, would have come to a considerable amount; but these his necessities had obliged him to dispose of.

It is understandable that he should have kept something associated with royalty, but why Lady Euston? Nash may have been self-important and lacking in integrity, but he had a soft spot for vulnerable young women and those who were badly treated by

The Prince of Orange had made him a present of a very fine snuff-box. Upon this some of the nobility thought it would be proper to give snuff-boxes too; they were quickly imitated by the middling gentry, and it soon became the fashion to give Mr Nash snuff-boxes, who had in a little time a number sufficient to have furnished a good toy-shop.

OLIVER GOLDSMITH

Lady Burlington's purchases

Three blanc-de-chine reticulated teabowls, porcelain, late seventeenth century. Diameter: 8 cm (3⅛ in.). Bought by the Countess of Burlington from Paul Bertrand for three guineas. His invoice, dated 17 November 1736, describes them as 'Six hony Comb china cups'. (Chatsworth)

Invoice from Paul Bertrand to the Countess of Burlington, dated 17 November 1736. (Chatsworth)

men; he would have met Lady Euston when she visited Bath as a child. The box illustrated contains a miniature of her, possibly taken at about that time. The inscription on the mezzotint portrait illustrated here reads:

p. 158

Once the Comfort, the Joy, the Pride of her Parents The Admiration of all who Saw her The Delight of all who knew her. Born May the 14th 1724. Married, Alas! October the 10th. 1741 & Deliver'd from Extream Misery May the 2d. 1742. This was taken from a Picture drawn seven weeks after her Death from Memory By her most Afflicted Mother Dorothy Burlington

Her mother's namesake, Dorothy Boyle was the daughter of the architect 3rd Earl of Burlington. She was married with a £40,000 fortune at the age of seventeen to Lord Euston, heir of the Duke of Grafton. Both her marriage and her death seven months later shocked society. On the day Dorothy Euston died Lady Pomfret received the news in letters from Lady Archibald Hamilton and Lady Hertford and noted in her diary that she 'had a sweet temper and was unhappily sacrificed to the brutality and ill temper of a man who made no secret of his aversion to her'. Horace Walpole wrote: 'Do you not pity the poor girl, of the softest temper, vast beauty, birth and fortune, to be so sacrificed?'

Nash's box may have been one assembled when Lady Euston was a child, or on her marriage, or as a keepsake after her death. Among the invoices to Lady Burlington that survive there are some for fitting a picture into boxes, from both Bertrand and Chenevix, but no link has been made between the box illustrated and Richard Nash. Until very recently the miniature was thought to be of Dorothy's younger sister Charlotte.

Trans-Atlantic bequests

Mary Dering [Dearing] was linked by blood and friendship to several people named in the ledgers of Hoare & Co.[253]; her own entries in Paul Bertrand's account coincide with her visits to Bath. She was with Princess Caroline in 1746, when Lady Isabella Finch was also in the royal entourage.

Mary Dering was born in 1700, the daughter of Robert Dering and Henrietta de Beaulieu. She was known as 'Moll' to her cousin, the diarist Lord Egmont, who noted on 8 January 1729/30 that she

p. 268

> was made dresser to Princess Royal and kissed her hand, which is looked on as a distinction, none in that place having been allowed that honour before. Her allowance is fifty pounds a year, with all things found her, and the first of the other dressers that dies, she comes into a share of the clothes that are left off.

She must have had a pay rise, as her salary is listed in 1737 at £70.[254] Like other members of the Queen's entourage, she was well placed to keep friends abreast of news; when relating one story to a friend Mrs Delany wrote: 'You may depend on the truth of it, for I had it from Mrs Deering …'.[255]

Mary Dering arrived in Bath on 20 April 1747 and died there shortly afterwards. She had written her will a year before. On 30 May, the day she was buried in St James's, Bath, Lord Egmont recorded:[256]

> I went at cousin Edward le Grand's desire to see the opening of my cousin Mary Dering's scriptore (who died a few days ago at Bath) in search of her will, which being found he sealed up, but being left executor, he conveyed the scriptore to his own house. She has left to his mother 500l and sundry other legacies.

Those sundry legacies included a number of personal treasures or 'triffles' that were typical of the stock of any toyshop. Extracts from the will (which was proved on 13 June 1747) are transcribed here because the bequests are described very precisely, and also because the instructions to her doctor are so revealing of court life.[257]

> I leave to Mr Ranby Sergeant Surgeon to His Majesty Twenty Pounds to cut off my Head after I am dead and that I may not appear Extravagant in this Request it is what I have determined many years as numbers of People can Testify I have from an Infant had the Apprehension of being Buried alive. I have now more reason to fear it than ever as knowing all people are turned out of a Court at their last Gasp and lastly I … appoint Mr Edward Le Grand living now in Spring Garden near Charing Cross to be my Sole Executor …

p. 289

I give and bequeath to the Right Honourable the Lady Isabella Ffinch my Gold Etwee and my Diamond Ring; I leave to the Honourable Mrs Southwell a Saphire ring; I leave to the Right Honourable Mr Southwell a gold Toothpick Case; I leave to the Honourable Mrs Elenora Buckley my Turquois Ring ... I leave to Mrs Robellon [??] a Deer's foot with a Seal at the end of it; I leave to Mr Hamilton our Table keeper five pounds.

I leave to Mrs Stanly Sir Hans Sloanes daughter the largest Madonna for I have two; I leave to the Countess of Egmont daughter to Sir Philipp Parker two venns done in craons; I leave to Mrs Persival wife to Philip Persival Esquire an Emerald ring with little Diamonds; I leave to Lady Ann Montague Six Cups and Sawcers teapot and Bason of Blue and White old China; I leave to the Lady Marchioness of Rockingham my little Indian Cabinet; I leave to Miss Dering daughter to Daniel Dering Esquire my Grandffather Sir Edward Dering's Picture; I leave to the Countess of Portsmouth an Amathist ring with two little Diamonds; I leave to Mrs Ffrancis Dive[??] of St James's a hyacinth ring; all these things ffall in to my Executor if the Persons are not in being at my decease except the two hundred pounds I leave to my Aunt Bullock and her Daughters for they shall be Heirs to one another as witness my hand Mary Dering

I hope these triffles will be accepted of so the People I leave them too only as an acknowledgement of their ffavours having nothing to leave worth their acceptance.[??] I leave to Mr William Southwell a Mother of Pearl patch Box sett in Gold; I leave to Mrs Allen of Cape Ffear in America a little Guilt Smelling Bottle; I leave to Mrs Ragg in Charles Town wife to Mr Joseph Ragg Merchant my fflat silver Candlestick and Snuffers as witness my hand Mary Dering I leave Lady Isabella Ffinch One Hundred pounds for any piece of ffurniture for her house she shall Chuse. I leave Lady Betty Murry my Agate Egg sett in Gold; I leave the Right Honourable Edward Southwell fffifty pounds Mary Dering

The gilt smelling bottle that Mary Dering bequeathed to her childhood friend Sarah Allen in Cape Fear arrived safely: it reappears in Mrs Allen's own will. Both wills highlight the importance of the kinds of object sold in toyshops as things that were valued for practicality and sentiment: in daily use they were a constant reminder of lost friends and relations.

Mary Dering's mother, Henrietta Beaulieu (1674–1729), is recognised as the first professional female portraitist in America. In 1694 she married Sir Robert Dering and they settled in Ireland, where he died. In 1705 she married the Revd Gideon Johnson who, three years later, was appointed Bishop's Commissary in South Carolina and rector of St Philip's Episcopal Church in Charleston. Mary presumably went with her mother, sister and step-father to America, but returned to England later in life. When Mr Johnson's salary failed to reach him from England, his wife was able to support them by painting members of his congregation and their friends. One of her sitters was Colonel William Rhett (Vice Admiral of the province, who repulsed French and Spanish attacks in 1706 but is best remembered for capturing a pirate, Stede Bonnet), whose daughter Sarah married in 1721 Eleazer Allen. Following her husband's death Mrs Allen managed their plantation until her own death in 1763, and her will refers to the 'produce of the Labour of my Negroes, such as tar, turpentine, corn, and the like … and all the plantation stock of cattle, horses and hogs'.[258] She gave much thought to her bequests, all of which might have been acquired from a toyshop or goldsmith, including a gilt smelling bottle which, in all likelihood, was the one bequeathed to her by Mary Dering:[259]

> To my beloved Niece, Mrs Mary Jane Dry, I give and bequeath my Gold Watch, not of modern Taste but an excellent piece of Mechanism, the Gold Chain and all the Trinkets belonging thereto to be worn in remembrance of her affectionate Aunt, who living or dying wishes her happiness. … To my beloved grand Niece, Miss Mary Frankland, I give and bequeath my Silver chased Tea kettle and cream pot and Lamp, as also my walnut tree fineered Tea chest containing three pieces of plate chased as the Tea kettle, in the form of Urns for Tea & Sugar … I give to my Dear Grand Niece, Miss Rebecca Dry, as a small Instance of my Affection, a Dozen tea Spoons and Strainer, in a black Shagreen case, almost new, designed to accompany an eight sided silver coffee pot, put into her possession when I went to England in the year 1756 which I also give to her together with a Shagreen writing stand quite new to encourage her in that part of her Education, in which she seems to be making great progress within these late months. … I give to my beloved grand Niece Miss Susanah Hasell a Mohogony dressing table and a little gilt smelling bottle. … I Give to my loved and long esteemed Friend, Mrs DeRossett, Senr my Silver Etice in a black Shagreen Case as a small Instance of my affection.

Derossett is a name linked to the Huguenot community in Dublin and England: Susanna, daughter of the Bath silversmith Peter Goulet married John Andrew Derussat or de Russat, one of the 'foreign snuffbox makers' researched by Brian Beet.[260]

Mary Dering remembered another childhood friend when she bequeathed to 'Mrs Ragg in Charles Town … my fflat silver candlestick and snuffers'. Judith Dubose married Joseph Wragg in 1717. He and his bother Samuel were merchants and factors in South Carolina; Samuel is also listed in Fenchurch Street, London.[261]

Near Bristol is a place called St Vincent's Rock, where are plenty of hard transparent stones, resembling Diamonds, which some take to be Fluores or Spars: At the bottom thereof is a hot medicinal well.

CHAMBERLAYNE

Summer at Bristol

In the summer months of Bath's quiet season those who needed medical attention went to other spas. Many chose Tunbridge Wells, but some moved between Bath and Bristol, where the season ran from late spring to September. The cities are some fifteen miles apart, a distance easily accomplished — indeed it was possible to go from one to the other and back in a day during the summer months.

When the Hot Wells at Bristol began to be known, from the early seventeenth century, accessibility to the mineral waters was a problem. The water poured from the rock close to the river (near the site of Brunel's later suspension bridge) and some two hundred steep and slippery steps had to be negotiated down to the water's source. By the early eighteenth century the water was pumped to a Pump Room reached via a track, and visitors went by carriage from their lodgings; other attractions were developed nearby such as a Long Room, theatre and shops. The Duchess of Marlborough (who was an early visitor to Scarborough in the 1730s) was at Bristol in 1723 when Richard Nash visited her following near disaster in Bath:[262]

… all ye gamesters are here as usual yet they complain that play goes on very dully; however, bad as it is, poor Nash is almost undone, for tis allowd by all that he has lost £1,400, which I believe made him very indifferent company at Bristol, where he was 2 days to wait upon her Grace of Marlborough …

Bristol was famed for the quality of its water but there were problems when a high tide mingled with the fresh mineral water. The most spectacular contamination was in November 1755 when the water 'became as red as blood and so turbid that it could not be drunk' — it was the day of Lisbon's earthquake. Nonetheless, Bristol developed a reputation for the treatment of diabetes and tuberculosis, in particular.[263] Among those who could not be cured was Mary Delany's much-loved sister Anne Dewes, the recipient of her numerous letters, who died at Bristol in July 1761. In the mid-1750s R. R. Angerstein noted in his diary:[264]

Hotwells Spa or 'St Vincentz Rock' … is located two miles from Bristol, between high hills, on the banks of the River Avon, which all ships to or from Bristol must pass. This Spa is not very old, but nevertheless, a

Bath Metal

In 1749 John Wood wrote that:

... making a peculiar sort of Rings for the Finger, and turning Silver to the Colour of Gold at the Hot Springs continues, to this Day, a small Part of The Trade of Bath.

Now to this Tinging Quality of the Hot Waters we may fairly attribute the Invention of that Metal which, from Times Immemorial, had the Name of Bath prefixed to it; and, like Corinthian Brass, represented the purest Gold: It was a compound Metal; and one Parfit of Wells excelling in the Mixture the Beginning of the present Century, the Metal had then the Name of Wells, instead of Bath, put before it for its proper Appellation: It was probably the very metal the Britons made their most valuable Money of in Caesar's Days; since pieces of Brass, and Iron Rings then pass'd by Weight, as the common Currency of the Britanick Island; and Mendip Hills near Bath have been famous from all Antiquity for producing Lapis Calaminaris, the Ingredient wherewith Copper is made Yellow, and turned into common Brass; to which Arsenick &c being added, the compound produces the Modern Bath Metal.

This Manufacture has been long Extinct in the City; a Loss great, and I fear irreparable: Had it continued, how many Hundreds might have been Employed and Maintained by a Branch of Trade that every Stranger would have Encouraged by way of Curiosity? I once Dined with a Trade at an Ordinary at the White Heart Inn in Bristol, who informed the Company that he supplied the Retailers at Bath, Yearly, with six Dozen double Dozen of Thimbles made with the Metal that bore the Name of the Place: He explained that his Number amounted to Ten Thousand Three Hundred and Sixty Eight; and then assured us that there were other Traders to Bath, besides himself, that vended vast Numbers of Thimbles in the City.

Thimble, copper alloy (enlarged). Height: 1.6 cm (⅝in). (London A3583)

Actual height

number of the houses and lodgings have been built, and their number increases year by year as more and more people go there. The waters of Hotwell are lukewarm and contain dissolved lime or salt as can bee seen when tartaric acid is added, which gives the solution a milky colour that can be clarified again by sulphuric acid. This water is supposed to have the special quality of keeping better in bottles than any other. A large quantity of it is, therefore, sent to America and all over Europe, which gives the glass-houses in Bristol a considerable turnover and advantage. Each dozen bottles filled with Hotwell water costs 1s and that amounts to a large sum of money brought in every year. Those who come here to use the well pay a subscription of 5s in the pump-room, and already, at the beginning of the season, there were 50 subscribers.

The Hotwells were never a serious rival to Bath. During the eighteenth century Bristol's population trebled: it was a thriving city based on its port, second only to London as a maritime centre. Trade was particularly strong to Dublin and across the Atlantic, but its merchants traded worldwide. A small spa perched by the river was but one part of the city's commerce. It is said that those who made their money in Bristol went to Bath to lose it, but Bristol had pewterers, braziers, clockmakers, cabinetmakers, silversmiths, jewellers, potters and glassworks — indeed the full gamut of craftsmen needed to service the burgeoning city. A statute of 1700/01 included Bristol as one of the towns where Mints 'were lately erected for recoining the money of the Kingdom' (others were York, Exeter, Chester and Norwich). The town mark of Bristol, a ship issuing from a castle, is seen on silver c. 1700–40.

None of the silversmiths known to be working in Bristol at this time, including Ralph Good, Stephen Curtis and Edward Jersey, appear in Bertrand's bank account: he preferred to deal with London craftsmen. Among Bristolians whose names do feature are Henry Casamayor, Francis Colston and Dean Creswick; there are a handful of members of parliament who represented Bristol. There is the clockmaker John Walcam and the wine merchant Isaac de Vic [▶ p. 56], who had a branch in Bristol. There is little mention of Bristol goldsmiths setting up shop in Bath during the season other than Mrs Taylor who was 'near the Pump Room' and Charles Delamain [▶ p. 39].

Bristol was also famed for its quartz, known as 'Bristol diamonds', mined in the nearby Mendip hills and close to the spa. The stones were much used by local jewellers and were also sent to

Longcase clock, detail, John Walcam, Bristol, c. 1750. Walcam features in Bertrand's bank account. He was not the only Bristol clockmaker to have links to Bath: Bertrand's assistant, Moses Roubel, was connected with William Bathe in the 1750s. (Smith)

SUMMER AT BRISTOL   167

Elizabeth Taylor, toywoman

In Bath, John Taylor [▶ p. 172], a jeweller and watchmaker, became a freeman in 1730; he took several apprentices. His will was proved in March 1742/43; his shop was advertised two years later and then occupied by Philip Masters in 1748.[265] In the intervening years, Elizabeth Taylor, assumed to be his widow, continued the business until she suffered a serious break-in at her shop in Bristol.

In Bath, Elizabeth Taylor's toy and coffee shop, on the eastern side of the Pump Room forecourt, was notable because the coffee shop was available to female customers — a place where they could read newspapers. When her shop at the Long Room near the Hot Wells in Bristol was broken into, on the night of Saturday 21 July 1744, it must have been expensive and troublesome for her. She lived in Bath, but was in Bristol for the season. As she explained at the subsequent trial, this ran from 15 June to 7 September.

The shop in Bristol had two large folding doors, fastened with a staple and a padlock, which were wrenched open by the thief. On 16 January 1745 Elie Castaing was found guilty of the robbery and sentenced to transportation. At his trial he gave evidence in French, perhaps the reason for two Huguenot toymen, Stephen Triquet and Ferdinand Vigne [▶ p. 319], being on the jury. Castaing came from Bordeaux and several witnesses bore testimony to the standing of his family and his good character — he had moved among good company at Tunbridge Wells the previous season and was well known in Bristol. He may have resorted to robbery after losing money gaming: Mrs Taylor's apprentice, James Berrisford testified that he had seen Castaing 'at the roley poley table' when he was shutting up the shop on the evening of the theft, and had been alerted to the break-in next morning by the maid.

Mrs Taylor acted swiftly. On 23 July she advertised a list of lost items in the *Bath Journal*, offering a 20 guinea reward, increased to 40 guineas on publication of a further list on 24 September (see abbreviated list below), by which time John Kemp, the gold chain maker in Carey Lane, London, was named as acting on her behalf in London – perhaps he was one of her suppliers.[266] Castaing seems to have taken jewellery and a few other small, easily pocketable, items and it is unlikely that this was Elizabeth Taylor's whole stock in Bristol.

On the unproven assumption that Elizabeth Taylor was the widow of the watchmaker John, and that she had a son named John, it seems that at one stage the family had three shops: one in Wade's passage or the churchyard (advertised a month after Castaing was sentenced, in 1744), one near the Pump Room (shown in the post-1751 drawing) and one in Bristol.[267]

	£ s d
Diamond ring of 10 brilliants, set in a cluster	
Ring with 9 rose diamonds set in a cluster, in the shape of a heart	
Ring with four rose diamonds set in a lozenge, a small one in the middle	35 00 00
Ring, single stone rose diamond, the rose diamond fine in colour but not very small	
Fancy ring, with four brilliants and two table diamonds, set showy	
Ring, sapphire large, fine in colour, with two brilliants	
Ditto, sapphire, bad in colour	
Ring, long sapphire, not small	10 00 00
Ring, sapphire, with two rose diamonds	

	£ s d
Ring, fine long narrow amethyst, engrav'd with a Old Man's Head, set long ways; and another	6 03 00
Five rings, cornelian, set in a Roman fashion, engraved with the heads of Pope, Mark Anthony, Alexander, Medusa and Hercules	12 10 00
Two cornelian blank rings, lined with gold	0 14 00
Ring, Alexander's head on a lapis lazuli	3 13 06
Ring, large, pale amethyst, set round with pebbles	1 00 00
Ring, amethyst, six roses set three of a side, in the form of a half lozenge	2 10 00
Ring, cornucopia, set with diamonds, rubies and emeralds, the work very fine	
Two fancy rings, one in the shape of a flower pot, the other like a flower-de-lis, set with rubies, emeralds and small diamonds	7 07 00
Ring, opal, set round with pebbles	1 00 00
Ring, large round opal, and two rose diamonds, large in size	2 10 00
Ring, single ruby, pale	1 10 00
Ring, with a large double stone, amethyst colour	0 10 00
Ring, sapphire deep in colour, set round with pebbles	1 00 00
Ring, single stone, large pebble, and another	0 10 00
Ring, Syrian garnet, deep colour, set with pebbles	1 00 00
Three French paste rings, set in a cluster, mounted high from the finger	2 00 00
Ring, with a single garnet, set with a shell bottom	0 12 00
Ring, with a head engraved on a red onyx, set round with emeralds	1 10 00
Ring, with a blackish onyx, a head engraved thereon, set round with sapphires	1 10 00
Ring, set heart and dart-ways, with one large emerald in it — the ring appears not to be new	2 00 00
Onyx Seal, set in gold, with a back	2 00 00
Seal, engrav'd with Darius's tent, on a white chrystal, set transparent	
Seal with four shells on the bottom	3 00 00
Seven seals engraved, set in gold, one with Otho's head, a star bottom; one with Diana's head, engraved on a white chrystal, set transparent; one with Plato's head; another Socrates's; the other impositions forgot	0 12 00
A shagreen pocket tweezer case, mounted with gold, studded with roses, with an inlaid knife, double-bladed, one blade silver-gilt, Bow scissars, the bows gold, two ivory leaves mark'd, the rest of the instruments mounted with gold	4 00 00
One chas'd silver pocket tweezer-case, not compleat	
Plain silver ditto, not compleat	3 12 00
Plain silver ditto, new, and believ'd to be without scissars	
Gold Watch, well chas'd, with a gold dial plate quite new, a high number, but forgot, the maker's name Tucant	18 18 00

[At the trial John Lewis Damareen [▶ p. 268] said that he had sold the watch to Mrs Taylor about six months before, since when the new dial plate had been added]

merchants in London. One example of trading between London and provincial firms demonstrates how careful shopkeepers and merchants needed to be when doing business with traders who might fail. Henry Coles features in Bertrand's bank account between 1740 and 1747; a few years later the day book of the London jewellers Webb records that on 23 February 1753 they 'Bought of Henry Coles Jeweller' a pair of drops knots and tops 'middling good' for £85, recording 'NB Sold the above Pendants about 18 months ago to Mr Hutchesonn of Bristol for £105, soon after wch he faild'.[268]

p. 263

The Pump Room, pencil drawing copied from an eighteenth-century original. The sign over the shop on the left reads 'Taylor, Jeweller, money for old silver'. The fan shop on the right advertised 'Bathing linen made and sold'. The drawing shows the fifth bay that was added to the Pump Room in 1751. (Bath in Time, 35283)

Artificers in the most Curious Works begin to find such Encouragement in the City, as to induce them to settle in it; for that Bath now boasts of her Painters, Carvers, Engravers, Jewellers, Guilders &c that Branch of Engraving which relates to Seals, is already become no inconsiderable Fibre of the Business of the City

JOHN WOOD

Other shopkeepers and artists in Bath

The comments of two early nineteenth-century writers on Bath might be applied to the city sixty years before, if the word 'inhabitants' is used loosely to embrace 'visitors': 'Half of the inhabitants do nothing, the other half supply them with nothings – a multitude of splendid shops, full of all that wealth and luxury can desire, arranged with all the arts of seduction'. Another wrote that '... the baubles of fashion form at present the most considerable articles of trade'.[269] Bath was famous for its shops and Bertrand faced competition from goldsmiths and jewellers, lacemen, fanmakers and other luxury shopkeepers, several of whom feature in his bank account. In the 1730s and '40s most of these were in Orange Grove and Terrace Walk.[270] It is hard to tell how much of their stock was actually made in Bath, and it is probable that most was sourced elsewhere, increasingly from Birmingham.

Although there were not many goldsmiths, jewellers and watchmakers in Bath, and little is known of them and their work, there were clearly sufficient to meet the needs of a transient population. Bristol was an easy journey from Bath and it had all the skilled craftsmen that Bath lacked, including silversmiths, pewterers, glassmakers and potters. The Reeve family are the best-known seventeenth-century silversmiths, through a brass plaque in Bath Abbey to George Reeve (d. 1664). By 1700 the Corporation were keen to make a new freeman, 'John Sherston the only goldsmith in the city being dead'. They voted that 'Mr Hayes be the freeman'.[271]

p. 96

By the 1720s Bath was better served. Peter Goulet [Gouillet], a jeweller, is known to have been in Bath by 1723 when he was described as 'a stranger' (i.e. a Huguenot) on the birth of his son, Charles. At the age of fourteen, in 1737, Charles was apprenticed to his father and Goulet took another apprentice, William Rogers on 5 March 1737/38. Goulet was made a freeman of Bath but moved to London in 1744.[272] There, his daughter Susanna married John Andrew Derussat, a gold box maker, perhaps one reason why Goulet remained in the capital.[273] Goulet took his son and another

p. 179

p. 164

apprentice, Benjamin Axford with him to London; at some point William Rogers was there also.

By March 1747/48 Benjamin Axford was back in Bath, advertising himself as 'working jeweller from Lombard Street, London.[274] He moved from his mother's house in Orange Court into the Grove itself, and continued at the Ring and Pearl, opposite Morgan's Coffee House in Wade's Passage until the 1770s, described as 'on the left hand from the entrance into Orange Court in the Grove', for a time in partnership with a watchmaker, Richard Laurence.

p. 119

As early as 1708 Philip Masters leased property near Gravel Walks in the name of himself, his son Philip (a freeman in 1718 and known until the mid-1750s) and daughter Elizabeth. Philip jnr's son Benedict was apprenticed to him on 27 October 1735 (free 1744). Benedict would have been in the workshop when his father submitted a bill to Bath Corporation for £62 16s 6d in 1737–38 and also when he leased 'a messuage abutting backwoods on Wades Passage on the south and openeth into the sd street on the north' for 99 years in March 1741.[275] In 1748 'Philip Masters and Son Working goldsmiths and Jewellers' advertised that they had moved from the Market Place 'to the front Shop in Wade's Passage (wherein Mr Taylor, watchmaker, lately liv'd) …'.[276] Masters may have benefitted from the closure of Bertrand's shop, but why Bertrand should have paid him £400 (a large sum) in April 1747, only five months before he began selling off his stock, is a mystery. Benedict Masters was Master Mason of the Royal Cumberland Lodge in Bath, 1755. In 1773 his son, Charles Harcourt Masters, was apprenticed to him.[277]

p. 71

Bertrand would probably have sub-contracted engraving work to Jacob Skinner or to John Wicksteed. Wicksteed's shop in Orange Grove was adjacent to George Speren and Peter Goulet, businesses that continued into the 1750s, by which time Bertrand had retired. Speren is best known for the fans he sold depicting various views of Bath. In order to stay in business shopkeepers needed to be alert to events outside their control that might affect customers' spending patterns, particularly the death of customers' relatives or members of the royal family. Mourning required that drapers had sufficient materials in black to meet a sudden demand, jewellers would have been asked to produce mourning rings at short notice and toymen stocked fans that could be designed to suit many occasions.

pp. 181–83

Bertrand's shop in Terrace Walk was next to Leake's bookshop and lending library. Payment of a subscription to Leake would be one of the first tasks for a newly arrived visitor. Visitors could write letters there and buy stationery and writing materials. Indeed it may have been while he was in the shop that Lord Orrery penned his description of the bookseller. The very large number of entries in Leake's name in Bertrand's bank account suggests business transactions between the neighbouring shops, but it seems odd that Bertrand should have bought books or engravings from Leake to sell in his own shop next door. Perhaps there was an arrangement for visitors to pay their subscriptions to Leake's library through Bertrand's banking facilities.

Round the corner in Orange Grove another bookseller, William Frederick, took a shop near to Peter Goulet in the early 1740s. He appears to have run much the same sort of establishment as Leake, but was perhaps a slightly less colourful character; there is only one transaction with Frederick in Bertrand's account.

Next in importance among Bath's attractions come the milliners, haberdashers, tailors and mantua makers, wigmakers and hatters, but Bertrand seems to have dealt with very few of them. Fame came to the milliner Mary Chandler not through her shop opposite the Pump Room but through a poem that she wrote to Princess Amelia in 1734, published by Leake. Her main competitors were the Walton sisters, whose shop in Orange Grove was between Goulet and Frederick.

Among the most successful shops in Bath were those of the laceman Leonard Coward and his son. Although little ephemera has survived to do with Coward, numerous invoices and account books in private archives relating to the London laceman William Basnet give an idea of expenditure on lace in the early eighteenth century.[278] Lace worn at the throat and wrists was, of course, an important component of male and female dress at this time, but the business of a laceman was not only to sell decorative collars and cuffs of bobbin lace, or edgings for household linen, he also sold gold and silver lace to adorn gentlemen's coats and ladies' dresses and the livery of their servants. It is possible that the numerous entries in Bertrand's bank account for John Graham may relate to another laceman in Green Street (patronised by Lady Luxborough in the 1750s), rather than a member of the London watchmaking family.

We know little of the connections between all these tradesmen but many were related. Formally worded death notices sometimes hint at whether a person was well liked or merely 'esteemed', but there is little that throws light on the Bertrands' fellow tradesmen and the artists who were probably, like Bertrand, members of the Academy of Painting.

FRANCIS BENNET
DRAPER
p. 251
map p. 21/22

The connections between Francis Bennet and the families of Philip Rundell's brothers-in-law, Goldney and Bigge, underpinned the extraordinary success of what became the most famous London luxury retailers in the late eighteenth and early nineteenth century, Rundell & Bridge.[279] There were close financial links, as well as family relationships. Philip Rundell, who was baptized in 1746/7 at Norton St Philip, Somerset, was in partnership in London, from 1788, with John Bridge, who was from Piddletrenthide, Dorset. Both men had been apprenticed to William Rogers. Rundell became a freeman of the Drapers' Company in London in 1771; Bennet, his uncle by marriage, was a mercer or linen draper.[280]

FRANCIS BENNET was painted by Thomas Gainsborough, and so was his brother-in-law Philip Ditcher. As a freemason, Bennet was master of the Bath Lodge in 1745 and later in life was mayor of Bath in 1773 and 1781. He married Jane Ditcher, aunt to Philip Rundell and sister of a Bath apothecary, Philip Ditcher. Bennet died aged 78 in 1790.[281]

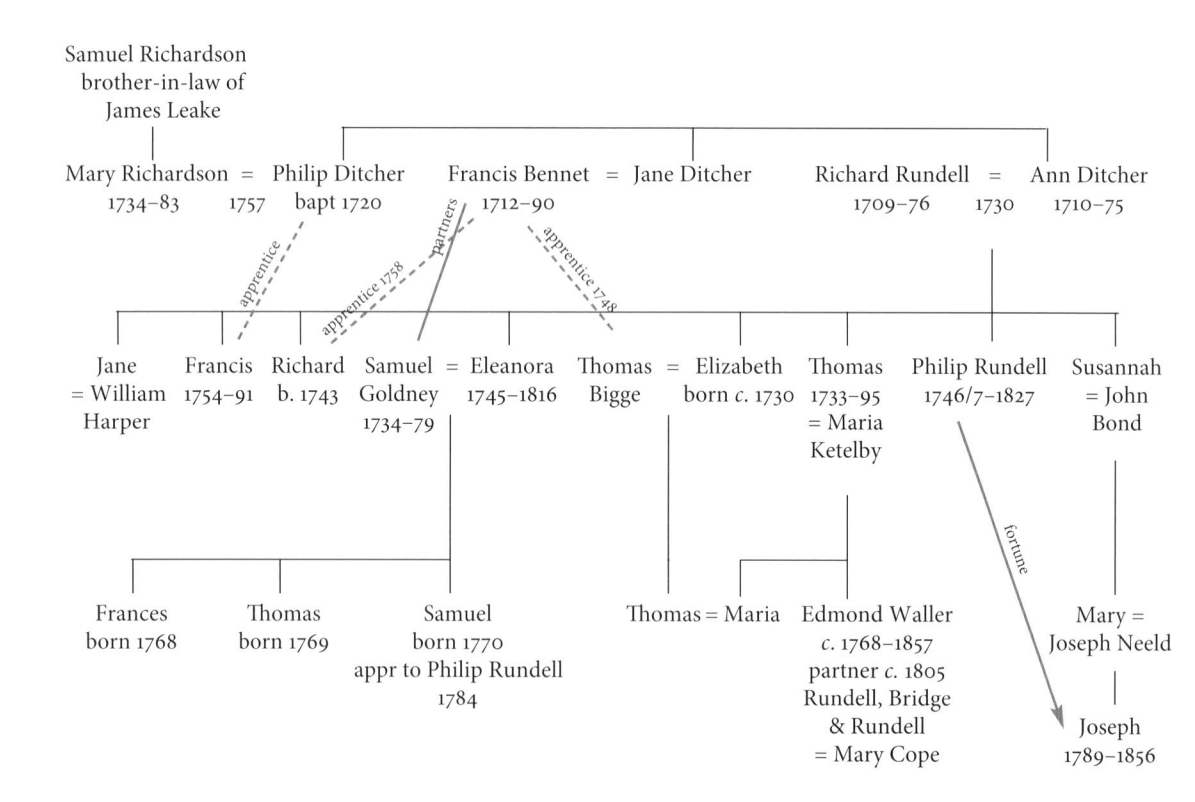

Francis Bennet's connections to Philip Rundell, apprentice of William Rogers

PART TWO: BATH AS A RESORT

Bennet advertised regularly in the Bath Journal: [282]

Remov'd from the Star in the Market Place to the Star in the Churchyard, Bath. Sells all Sorts of Linnen-Drapery, Mercery, and Haberdashery Goods: all sorts of Blanketting Flannels, Swan-Skin and Shags; all Sorts of Teas, Coffee, Chocolate and Sugar; with all other sorts of Grocery Wares; all Sorts of fine Snuffs and Cards: All which are sold as cheap as in London, for Ready-Money.

NB He also furnishes Funerals with a new Pall and Cloaks; and with all other Necessaries, as decent and cheap as in London.

The use of swan (for white) and shag (or cormorant, for black) for mourning is worth noting. Later the same year, he had obviously decided to develop the undertaking side of the business:

Francis Bennet and Comp … at their Ware House at the Star in the Abbey Church Yard and at their several other Ware Houses in Bath /Desire to acquaint the Publick that they have, at Great Expence, lately procured from London, all Sorts of Necessaries for Funerals … Sets of the very best Hangings, Tapers, Branches, Sconces &c. Likewise a full and compleat set of Horse-Hairs, Lead, and State Feathers, and all other things requisite for a Publick or State Funeral.

LEONARD COWARD
LACEMAN

p. 265
map p.21/47

LEONARD COWARD was a lace merchant in Bath. In 1727 he was in Stall Street, the shop for which an invoice in the name of his wife Elizabeth survives dated 1748.[283] His son Leonard went to the shop at the corner of the southern end of Terrace Walk in 1745.[284] At the time of their dealings with Bertrand between 1743 and 1747 the family were running two shops, probably with the help of one or all of Leonard and Elizabeth's four daughters. As Bertrand's account entries begin only in 1743, the expenditure may relate to the assembly rooms rather than the toyshop — but there is no way of knowing this for certain.

Leonard Coward snr 'the best of parents' died in 1764. Leonard jnr became a freeman of Bath in 1739 and died in 1795.[285]

Monument to Leonard and Elizabeth Coward and their son Leonard, in Bath Abbey.

OTHER SHOPKEEPERS AND ARTISTS IN BATH   175

Invoice from Coward's lace shop dated 7 June 1748. Receipted by Leonard Coward, the printed heading is for 'Betty Coward at the two Lappetts & three Cards of Lace in Stall Street'. (Bath in Time, 35269)

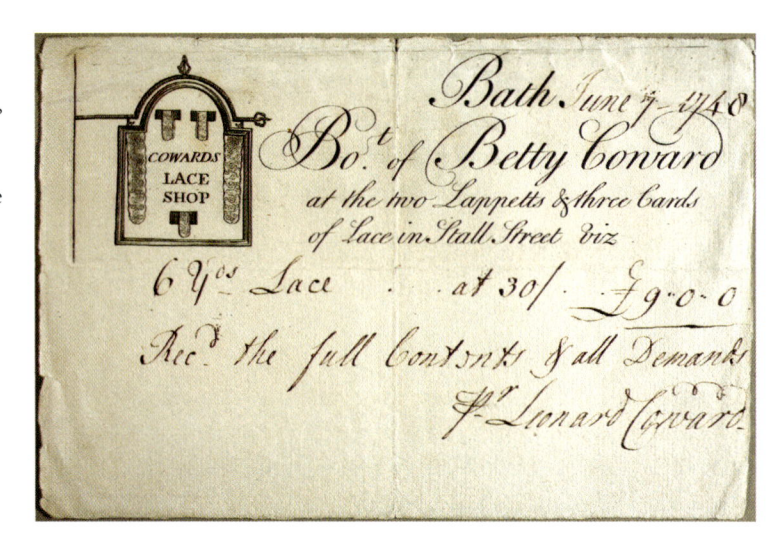

JOHN DAVIS
JEWELLER & INDIA
HOUSE
p. 267

An invoice dated 15 October 1747 for items bought by Lord Hertford is headed 'Bought of Joanna Davis at the India House, Bath' and is receipted by JOHN DAVIS. Their shop in Terrace Walk was taken over by Leonard Coward. In 1748 John Davis's India-House advertised the remaining part of Paul Bertrand's stock. In 1754 John Davis, jeweller and goldsmith was 'on the Lower Walks', he went bankrupt in 1764. One of his shopmen, Lewis Bull, set up on his own, and in 1770 took over the premises of Leake's bookshop.

The invoice to Lord Hertford, like so many others, is frustratingly short on detail, but a pair of Dresden figures (bought for three guineas) possibly survives.[286]

JAMES LEAKE
BOOKSHOP &
LIBRARY
p. 289

JAMES LEAKE (1686–1784) had a bookshop and library at the corner of Orange Grove and Terrace Walk by 1722, next to Paul Bertrand's shop. He probably took over the stock of Henry Hammond, whose daughter he married. According to Defoe, Leake was one of the finest booksellers in Europe. He also published, for example, the work of John Wood the Elder, with whom he went into partnership to develop part of the Kingston estate. Leake was made a freeman of Bath on 9 January 1722/23; he was also a freemason and a governor of the Mineral Water Hospital in 1748.[287] His son was apprenticed to him in 1739, and continued the business.

For a small subscription visitors could visit the shop to read newspapers and write letters, as Count Frederick Kielmansegge recorded in 1761:[288]

There is a fine large bookseller's shop here, where everybody, on arrival, can subscribe five shillings for the whole season, which gives him the

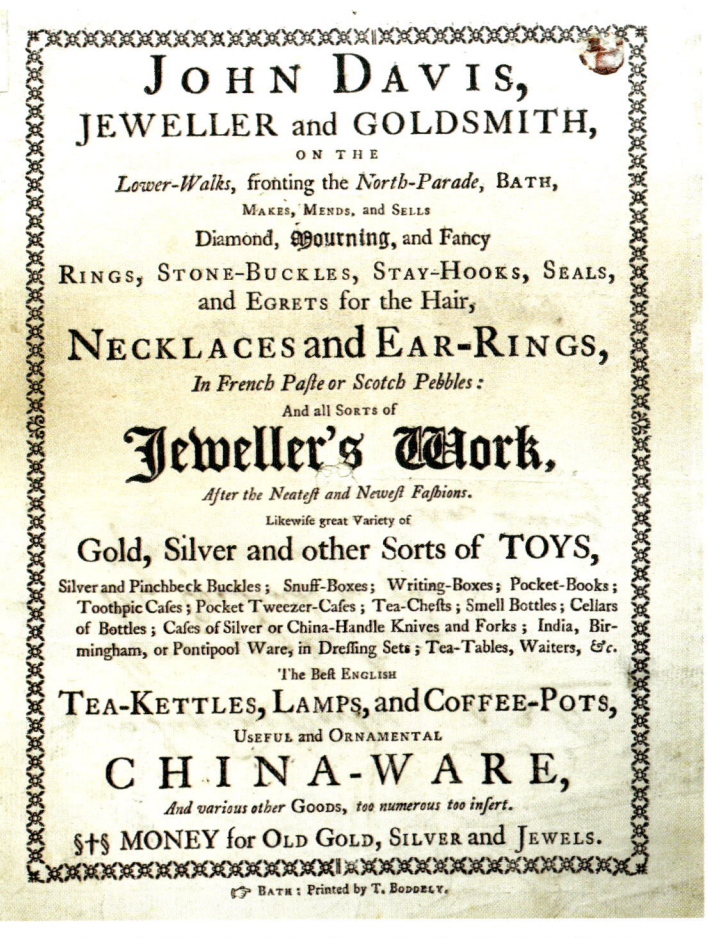

> **JOHN DAVIS,**
> JEWELLER and GOLDSMITH,
> ON THE
> *Lower-Walks,* fronting the *North-Parade,* BATH,
> MAKES, MENDS, and SELLS
> Diamond, Mourning, and Fancy
> RINGS, STONE-BUCKLES, STAY-HOOKS, SEALS,
> and EGRETS for the Hair,
> NECKLACES and EAR-RINGS,
> In French Paste or Scotch Pebbles:
> And all SORTS of
> **Jeweller's Work,**
> *After the Neatest and Newest Fashions.*
> Likewise great Variety of
> Gold, Silver and other Sorts of TOYS,
> Silver and Pinchbeck Buckles; Snuff-Boxes; Writing-Boxes; Pocket-Books; Toothpic Cases; Pocket Tweezer-Cases; Tea-Chests; Smell Bottles; Cellars of Bottles; Cases of Silver or China-Handle Knives and Forks; India, Birmingham, or Pontipool Ware, in Dressing Sets; Tea-Tables, Waiters, &c.
> The Best ENGLISH
> TEA-KETTLES, LAMPS, and COFFEE-POTS,
> USEFUL and ORNAMENTAL
> CHINA-WARE,
> *And various other* GOODS, *too numerous too insert.*
> §†§ MONEY for OLD GOLD, SILVER and JEWELS.
> BATH: Printed by T. BODDELY.

Trade card of John Davis, jeweller and goldsmith, Bath. (Bath in Time, 35270)

privilege of taking home any book he likes to read: this is certainly a great comfort, and brings to the bookseller, Leake, a large profit, as he receives nearly as many five shillings as there are visitors to Bath.

Among the numerous publications Leake advertised in the *Bath Journal* was the sale catalogue for the contents of Ralph Allen's house, Prior Park, in August 1769.

Leake features in numerous contemporary letters: the Earls of Chesterfield and Egmont were among those who lodged with him. His circle included his brother-in-law Samuel Richardson, and Ralph Allen: Mrs Leake and Mrs Allen were friends. By 1757 Mary Delany was writing of meeting the Leake family socially and related how the youngest son was saved from drowning at the Grange, the house of Sir Robert Henley.[289] This suggests that Leake had bridged a social divide and that not all his customers were as critical as the Earl of Orrery:[290]

p. 281

James Leake

This Leake is a most extraordinary Person. He is the Prince of all the coxcomical Fraternity of Booksellers: and, not having any learning himself, He seems resolved to sell it as dear as possible to Others. He looks upon every Man, distinguished by any Title, not only as his Friend, but his companion, and he treats him accordingly; but he disposes of his Favours and Regards, as methodically as Nash takes out the Ladies to dance, and therefore speaks not to a Marquess whilst a Duke is in the Room. As yet he is ignorant that my Earldom lies in Ireland, and to keep him so, I have borrowed the only Book of heraldry He has in his Shop: by this method I shall be served many degrees above my Place, and may have a Squeeze of his Hand in presence of an Earl of Great Britain.

His Shop is a spatious Room, filled from the Cornice to the Skirting. But I could not help observing to him that, The Binding of his Books did not make so glittering a Figure as might be expected from the Library of a Person as illustrious as himself. He owned my observation was right, and added that 'Some Fellows whose Ancestors, he believed, were Snails, had been daily expected from London, to illuminate and glorify his Museum'. I rejoiced at the good News, and told him, 'I doubted not but he would shew the Elasticity of his Genius, and the Nicknackatory of his Understanding by binding Lord Bacon in Hog's Skin, Bishop Sprat in Fish Skin and Cardinal du Bois in Wood'. He seemed highly delighted with my Proposal, and was going to enter it in his Pocket Book, when the Dutchess of Norfolk, snatching him from my Arms, allowed me an Opportunity to assure You that I am, etc. Orrery

The rear of the buildings in Terrace Walk in 2013. The building with the bay was Leake's bookshop. To the right was Paul and Mary Bertrand's toyshop.

James Leake's signature, on a receipt to Lady Ilchester. (Dorset, D/FSI/239)

Detail of ▶ p. 19, with Leake's shop outlined.

178   PART TWO: BATH AS A RESORT

MARY MITCHELL
CHINA SHOP

Invoice from Mary Mitchell to the Duchess of Montrose, dated May 1719. (Montrose NAS, GDL20/6/1339/23)

Whereas MRS MARY MITCHELL, now living in one of the High Streets in Bath and near the King's Bath, in a handsome well accustomed Shop, 30 Foot in Front, with two good Rooms adjoining to it, where for several Years past the said Mrs Mitchell sold all manner of China Wares, Coffee, Tea &c. These are to give Notice that the said shop and rooms are to be lett by lease, or otherwise, she designing to leave that Place and Trade. Enquire of Mr John Caldwall, a toyman, in Bow Lane, or at the said Mrs Mitchell's at Bath.[291]

WILLIAM ROGERS
JEWELLER & GOLDSMITH

map p. 21/34

WILLIAM ROGERS earns a place in any history of the gold and silver trade because of two local boys who were apprenticed to him. Philip Rundell (apprenticed in 1760) and John Bridge (apprenticed in 1769) went on to run London's most successful and world-famous retail silversmiths and jewellers [▶ p. 174].

pp. 168, 172

Rogers was himself apprenticed to Peter Goulet in Bath on 5 March 1737/38; his brother Thomas was apprenticed to the watchmaker John Taylor in 1734. Goulet went to London in 1744 and if he took Rogers with him as well as another apprentice, Benjamin Axford, Rogers may well have remained in the capital for a period to gain experience by working for another business. He later described himself in advertisements as having come from

p. 31 Chadd & Ragsdale, the jewellers and toymen in Bond Street. Rogers obtained his freedom in 1747 and married two years later; he and his wife Mary had three children, born between 1755 and 1759. (His son William was a string, trumpet and horn player in the Pump Room band.[292]) He was listed as a jeweller when Philip Rundell was apprenticed to him on 10 May 1760.[293]

William Rogers' advertisements and trade card promote 'a variety of toys and jeweller's work', including 'Fine French Composition of all Sorts; and Stones for Seals engraved with Coats of Arms, or Antiques copied' and 'All sorts of Plate, Watches, Chains, Equipages, Etwees, Snuff-Boxes, Pontipool tea-boards'. His shop was 'fronting the Abbey Church'.

A theft in 1760 gives a clue to the type of jewellery Rogers stocked: a silver knot, a silver breast buckle, a cornelian stone of a seal, and three stay hooks, none of which sounds particularly exciting.[294]

Notice of Rogers' bankruptcy was published in February 1775,[295] by which time his former apprentice Philip Rundell was a partner of William Pickett in Ludgate Hill and on the way to developing the most important retail business of the period. An unusual feature of Rogers' advertisements was that he published priced lists:[296]

Bath Abbey looking to the east, engraving published by H. George, bookseller in Orange Grove, *c*. 1750. The silversmith William Rogers advertised in 1749 that his shop was 'fronting the Abbey Church'. It was the shop to the left (north) of the Abbey on the corner of Wade's Passage. (Bath in Time, 11500)

> William Rogers, Jeweller and Goldsmith, (From Mr. Chad in New-Bond-Street, London) At the Ring and Pearl in the Church-Yard, Bath, Desires to acquaint the Publick, That he has a Quantity of New Plate to sell, as under.
>
> | | s. | d. |
> |---|---|---|
> | | per ounce | |
> | Tankards at | 6 | 06 |
> | Tables Spoons | 6 | 07 |
> | Coffee-Pots | 7 | 06 |
> | Waiters | 7 | 06 |
> | Pint Cups | 6 | 09 |
> | Candlesticks | 7 | 06 |
> | Sauce Boats | 7 | 09 |
> | Half-Pint Cups | 6 | 10 |
> | Pepper Boxes at | 5s Fashion | |
> | Salts at | 10s a Pair Fashion | |
> | Milk Ewers at | 7 | 00 |
> | Fluted Punch-Ladles at | 5 | 06 |
>
> Great Variety of other Plate, Jewels and all Sorts of Toys, sold in Proportion. Most Money for Old Gold, Silver and Jewels

JACOB SKINNER ENGRAVER

p. 309

It is impossible to judge, now, whether JACOB SKINNER and John Wicksteed were rivals. Skinner appears to have specialised in engraving on metal, whereas Wicksteed engraved stones, but most engravers multi-tasked when accepting work and could cut or carve a variety of materials. The entry for 'Jno Skinner' in Bertrand's bank account probably refers to him.

Jacob Skinner's shop was at the sign of the Grasshopper, in St James's Street, near Abbey Green. As Susan Sloman has pointed out, his shop sign is 'a clever pun on his name, since grasshoppers shed their skins'.[297] As early as 1729 his name appears in the list of those promoting A new book of cyphers by S. Sympson.[298] In 1737 he engraved the City arms and motto on 22-dozen plates and the following year on 5-dozen dishes, for Bath's corporation. He was made a freeman of Bath in 1738 after engraving the gold and silver freedom boxes presented to the Prince of Wales and his party. This prestigious job was followed in 1740 with a fee of two and a half guineas for engraving a seal for the hospital.[299] In 1745 Skinner advertised:[300]

To the CURIOUS A large collection of SHELLS, FOSSILS and a Variety of Natural and Artifical CURIOSITIES, TO BE SEEN At Jacob Skinner's Engraver, At the Sign of the Grasshopper, in St James's Street, near the Abbey-Green, Bath. NB Any Gentleman in the Country may have their Plate engrav'd at their own Houses, on proper Notice.

Detail of John Wiltshire's bookplate, [▶ p. 51], designed by Thomas Ross and engraved by Jacob Skinner, dated 1740. (Bath in Time, 35695)

By going to his customers, Skinner would have saved owners of plate from the need to take it into Bath: in view of its weight and value, it would have been sensible to take advantage of Skinner's initiative. Whereas new silver was engraved at the time of purchase, Skinner probably had in mind the practice of re-engraving armorials following a marriage, death or ennoblement. Skinner also engraved trade cards, notably that of John Pyke in 1755, by which time he was in the Market Place, advertising that he 'Makes and Sells all Sorts of Cutlery Wares and grinds old work every Day &c'.301 He also engraved a bookplate for John Wiltshire.

p. 62 illus.

Paul and Mary Bertrand would undoubtedly have been asked by customers to engrave gold, silver and jewellery with armorials, initials and inscriptions. They might well have sub-contracted this work to Skinner.

GEORGE SPEREN
TOYMAN

pp. 50, 64 and 124 illus

GEORGE SPEREN (1711–96) had a toyshop in Orange Grove, where he seems to have specialised in selling fans. The premises were previously a milliner's. Fans published in 1737 (the design now attributed to Thomas Robins) for example, show the city at a time when the Bertrands' shop was thriving and visitor numbers rising. He also operated as a publisher and appears to have collaborated over a number of years with Robins, who advertised that he was based at Speren's shop.

Fan leaf, published by G. Speren 1737. Orange Grove looking south to the row of shops. Bertrand's former employees set up businesses of their own here following his retirement. (Bath in Time, 12855)

182   PART TWO: BATH AS A RESORT

JOHN WICKSTEED's family had a toyshop in Bath for some years after Bertrand retired; his seal-cutting 'machine' is clearly marked on images of the city, close to Prior Park.[302]

John and Sarah Wicksteed opened a shop in Orange Grove around 1732; he was made a freeman of Bath at the same time as Peter Goulet (both men paid a fee of 10 guineas). His water-powered 'jewelling mill', or cutting machine, was a popular venue for visitors to buy souvenirs and order heraldic intaglio seals. In all probability John mainly worked at the mill while his wife looked after the shop in the Grove, where she stocked porcelain (once it became widely available), and fans. She also sold the work of Thomas Worlidge, who in 1743 married her daughter Mary, and organised commissions for his portraits. When John Wicksteed died in 1754 the business was continued by his son James.[303]

It seems entirely likely that Bertrand stocked some of Wicksteed's seals, but the transactions must have been in cash, for Wicksteed does not feature in Bertrand's bank account. Whether it was Bertrand who took on one of Wicksteed's engravers, or another jeweller or toyman, cannot at this distance of time be known, but it provoked Wicksteed into lowering his prices and publishing the following advertisement in 1741:[304]

JOHN WICKSTEED ENGRAVER & TOYMAN

map p. 21/40

Advertisement of John Wicksteed for engraved stone seals, 1741. (Bath in Time, 26047)

OTHER SHOPKEEPERS AND ARTISTS IN BATH

Artists and exhibitors

In the decades before Thomas Gainsborough arrived in Bath there were numerous artists and engravers who made a living in Bath through portraiture, landscape painting and engraving, of whom William Hoare is the best known today. If there was an Academy of Painting in Bath it is entirely likely that Paul Bertrand was part of its community. He would certainly have known most, if not all, of those mentioned here and been familiar also with the work of the miniaturist Christian Friedrich Zincke (?1684–1767) who worked in London. Bertrand may also have known 'Mr Zurich' — Johann Zurich (c. 1685–1735), a miniaturist who came to England from Dresden.

The work of Lens and Zincke was often mounted into snuffboxes.

MR CORTON

CORTON advertised in 1754 that he could be contacted through the jeweller and toyman Moses Roubel.[305]

BERNARD LENS III
pp. 76, 86 illus.

BERNARD LENS (1681–1740) made several trips to the West Country and after his death topographical drawings of Gloucestershire, Bath, Glastonbury and other Somerset venues were among the items from his workshop sold at auction. He is best known, however, as a limner (painter in watercolours) or miniaturist and for his work on ivory.

His father, Bernard Lens II (1659/60–1725), was an engraver and drawing-master, who also worked in miniature. He was a partner of John Sturt (an engraver and a freeman of the Goldsmiths' Company), to whom Bernard III was apprenticed in 1698, although the latter did not gain his freedom until 1729.[306]

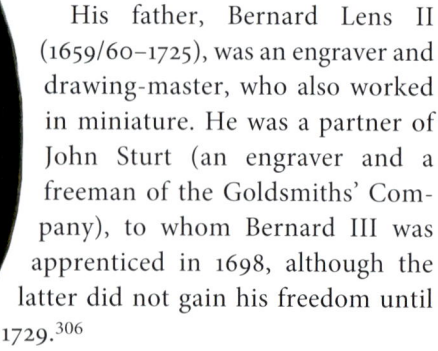

Richard Whitmore aged three, portrait miniature in watercolours on ivory, Bernard Lens III, c. 1718–24. Height: 7.6 cm (3 in). From a group of fifteen miniatures of the family which includes Richard's brother Thomas, whose future mother-in-law, Mary Cope, features in Bertrand's bank account. Most toyshops sold children's playthings: in 1732 Richard Hoare bought two horse toys from William Deards for 4s and 2s 6d. (V&A P.13-1971)

At 4 ft 1 in tall THOMAS LOGGAN (1706–*c.* 1788) was appointed dwarf to the Prince and Princess of Wales. He often depicted himself in the pictures he made of Tunbridge Wells where he regularly worked, dividing his time between there and Bath. Like George Speren, he designed fans.

THOMAS LOGGAN

Advice to the Dwarf in the Rooms, who paints upon Fans

Why little Painter sitst thou unemployd?
Are all the buyers with thy Trifles cloy'd?
Quit the Parad — from me accept a plan,
I'll find fresh matter, & I'll buy a Fan.
Paint N–bles first (since they precedence claim)
To a –nk State a burthen & a sham!
Let Beaus & Belles, who human kind disgrace,
Strive to excel in trifles & in lace.
With hostile glance let rival Beauties fight
Display their scorn, & swell with sullen spite;
As envious Peacocks meet with hateful eyes,
Grown big with plumy pride & varying dyes.
Give Ambition Titles gaind with shame,
Draw the mad frolicks of a young old Dame.
Let —rongs on throngs around EO be seen,
And ladies arms, with stakes thrust in between;
Whilst here, Impatience sits in evry face,
Shew there, Rappito, impatient for his Race.
When you have rightly drawn this various Crew,
They in their actions will seem Dwarfs — to you.

Detail, ▶ p. 64. Loggan depicted himself on the right.

RICHARD PERCIVAL

THOMAS ROBINS (1716–70) was born in Charlton Kings, near Cheltenham and was apprenticed to Jacob Portret, a fan and porcelain painter who bequeathed his house to Robins in 1743. A number of fans dating from 1737 with views of Bath are attributed to Robins, published by George Speren. In a group of sketches of Bath (now in the Victoria and Albert Museum) Robins portrays the city at a particular moment in its development — the rawness of the new stone clearly evident. Before moving with his family to live in Bath in the 1750s, Robins undoubtedly spent long periods there during the season, and he travelled to execute drawings of patrons' houses and gardens, in which his interest in botany is particularly evident. His brilliant watercolour is of Bath from the south — the aspect most popular with artists.[307]

In 1752 Robins advertised in the *Bath Journal*:[308]

THOMAS ROBINS

pp. 98, 124 and 182 illus.

p. 78 illus.

Thomas Robins, Painter, At Mr Sperin's Toy Shop in the Grove, Bath, Teaches Gentlemen and Ladies, at reasonable Rates, the art of Drawing and Painting In Water Colours; Where his Drawings and Paintings may be seen. Likewise Perspects and Perspective Views of Gentlemens Seats in the correctest Manner.

OTHER SHOPKEEPERS AND ARTISTS IN BATH

THOMAS ROSS
PAINTER

JOSHUA ROSS
CARVER & GILDER
pp. 51 and 108 illus.

Active c. 1730–57, THOMAS ROSS has been variously described as 'one of the small number of successful portraitists working in Bath before the arrival of Gainsborough' and 'the most accomplished landscape artist to live and work in Bath before 1750'. He designed a bookplate for John Wiltshire that was engraved by Jacob Skinner. Like Wiltshire and Skinner, Ross was a freemason, and took his turn as master of the lodge in Bath between 1735 and 1740.[309]

Advertisement for Joshua Ross, frame carver and gilder. He came 'from Mr Pascall's in Long-Acre' where Paul Bertrand's cousin, Samuel Gribelin, lived. (Bath in Time, 35274)

JAMES VERTUE
p. 319
p. 67 illus.

JAMES VERTUE (1686–1765) features in Bertrand's bank account. He was the brother of the better-known engraver and antiquary George Vertue.[310] James moved from London to Bath for his health and made his living as a painter, 'an instructor of Ladies and Gentlemen in the Arts of Drawing and painting' and a seller of prints, snuffs and toys. Newspaper advertisements show him opposite Mr Morgan's Coffee House in Wade's Passage 1754; at Mr Page's Pastry Cook in Cheap St 1758; and Westgate House 1760.

The long room at Wiltshire's assembly rooms, pen and ink and wash on paper, James Vertue, *c.* 1750. (Bath in Time, 13432) [▶ p. 98 illus, drawing of the same room by Thomas Robins].

(BOTTOM LEFT) Self portrait, etching, Thomas Worlidge (BM, 1861,0518.133)

(BOTTOM RIGHT) Mary Worlidge, etching, by her husband Thomas Worlidge (Holburne)

THOMAS WORLIDGE

THOMAS WORLIDGE (1700–66) married three times and reputedly had over thirty children; his third wife was Mary Wicksteed, daughter of the Bath toyshop owner and engraver John Wicksteed. Worlidge lived in Bath during the 1740s and '50s but also spent time in London. He worked in several media, executed portrait miniatures, but is best known for his drypoint etchings in the manner of Rembrandt; he made portrait miniatures and also published numerous etchings under the title 'Curious Antique Gems'.[311]

OTHER SHOPKEEPERS AND ARTISTS IN BATH

Featherwork picture of tulips, Nicholas le Normand, signed, *c.* 1720–35. Height: 26 cm (10¼ in); width: 32.4 cm (12¾ in). (Private coll)

NICHOLAS LE NORMAND

NICHOLAS LE NORMAND showed his featherwork in Bertrand's shop:[312]

Bath. Sept 11, 1732

There is likewise here the ingenious Mr Le Normond, Maker of the admired Bed of Feathers, shew'd several Years since to their present Majesties, and afterwards sold to the King of Poland. He exposes now to View, at Mr Bertrand's Toyshop, a Suit of Hangings and some Pictures, all done in Feathers, and which so surprisingly imitate Nature that they give general Satisfaction to all Connoisseurs and Lovers of Art.

Le Normand seems first to have exhibited and advertised his bed in Paris – an account of it was given in *Le Nouveau Mercure* in March 1720. The bed was then erected at Somerset House in London when, according to Bertrand's advertisement, those who came to see it included the Prince of Wales, later George II. It was dismantled in October 1720 and was on show at Exeter Exchange from January 1720/21 to July 1721, when Le Normand[313]

… being willing that some of his Curious Works should be left in England, gives Notice that he will sell several fine Pieces of his feather'd Works, as Skreens and Pictures, by publick Sale to the best Bidder … with several fine Prints and French Plate, and he now leaving England will sell all …

The bed is listed in the 1723 inventory of the Japanisches Palais in Dresden and is now at Schloss Moritzburg.[314]

Le Normand was described as a 'natif de Rouen'. How long he spent abroad, perhaps partly overseeing the installation of the bed in Dresden, is not known. He re-appears in 1732 in Bath and in the intervening years must have been working on the new set of hangings and feather pictures mentioned in Bertrand's advertisement. The ability to display such large items as the featherwork hangings raises questions about the internal arrangement of Bertrand's shop, and how long at least some of Le Normand's work was on show there.

Le Normand died towards the end of 1736:[315]

2 December 1736. Last Week died at Windsor, in the 67th Year of his Age, Mr Le Normand, Native of Rouen in Normandy: He render'd himself famous in England about the Year 1720, when he compleated his twelve Years Labour, that wonderful Bed of State, beautifully described at large in the Freethinker, No.262, Sept 23 1720.

This consummate Piece of Art, undervalued in our own Nation, afterwards became the Purchase and Pride of that true Judge of Merit, the late King of Poland. The Excellence of the said Work, as well as of his other Pieces, consists chiefly in the Draughts of Flowers, Fruits, Animals &c (copy'd from Originals of Baptista and other most eminent Painters, as well as from Nature) wrought in Feathers of suitable Colours, so exquisitely interwoven,

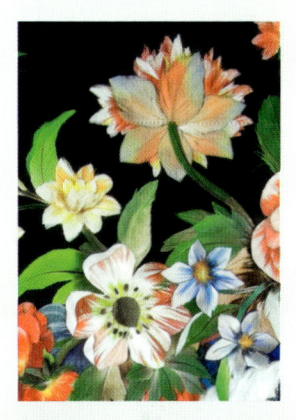

Details, ▶ p. 2

as to exhibit the most natural and lively Representations of Things imaginable. Tis hard to say, whether greater Genius, or Diligence, was requisite to the Accomplishment of each Design; but one may venture to say, that this Gentleman is the only one yet known, to whom an Art of so great Difficulty owed at once its Invention, all its Productions, and its Perfection. To enhance the Difficulty of the Work, it required no less than twenty Years to collect from all Parts of the Globe at a considerable Expence, all the necessary Materials for it.

His sedentary State of Life occasion'd an obstinate Jaundice, which Malady producing reciprocally an Aversion to Motion, and even to Life itself, made him, till he became helpless, decline seeking Help from Medicine.

By his Love of Solitude he seem'd to make these incomparable Performances rather the Amusement than the Business of his Life; so that there are not many of them remaining undispos'd of.

With all the Virtues of a private Life his Courteousness was such, that at his Leisure Hours he was ready to oblige any curious Strangers with a View of his Works, and as he never fail'd of their Applause, so he receiv'd it without discovering the least Degree of that Vanity and Ostention, which detracts so much from the Merit of most Inventers.

According to the 1720 notice in *Le Nouveau Mercure*, Le Normand had a workshop in Putney, and Bosquet & Clerembault were his London agents.[316] Le Normand remembered old friends in his will. He left £100 each to Nicholas Bosquet 'a merchant living in Hackney near London' and to Anthony Clerembault (or Clerimbault) 'a merchant living in New Broad Street, London Wall'. To the latter's son Nicholas Clerenbault [sic] he bequeathed 'the ffeather picture that he shall like best and twenty four volumes of my Books'.[317]

In April 1735, some eighteen months before his death, *Mercure de France* had published a further piece on le Normand which explained that he had a student named Levet, an Englishman, and that the Duke of Leeds had purchased a screen by him after designs by Oudry.[318] The 4th Duke of Leeds (1713–89) was first cousin to Margaret, Duchess of Portland (1714/15–85); their shared grandfather was Robert, 1st Earl of Oxford. The Duchess of Portland's interest in botany and natural phenomena is well known; she had a very large collection of porcelain and was a regular customer of Chenevix and other toyshops. One of the pieces of featherwork described in *Mercure de France* represented 'un Arbre des Indes … Vases bleus et blancs, imitant les plus belles Porcelaines du Japon'.

Several of the duchess's intimates, including Elizabeth Robinson (who married Edward Montagu in 1742), were regular visitors to Bath and to Tunbridge Wells. Elizabeth Robinson was in Bath in 1739–40 and several of her siblings were there in the period 1739–43. Might one of le Normand's feather pictures have been in the toyshop then? There seems to be no first-hand evidence that the Duchess of Portland or Elizabeth Montagu saw the work of either le Normand or of his student Levet in London or Bath. But there is evidence that the ladies were dabbling with featherwork decades before the well-recorded breakfast given by Mrs Montagu in 1791 to show off her feather room in Montagu House, the mansion designed for her by James Stuart. The evidence lies in her correspondence.[319]

As early as 1737 (the year following Le Normand's death) Elizabeth Robinson was asking her brother to bring shells and feathers home from a trip to the East Indies. She made no claims to be creative herself, writing that '… it is an unreasonable thing of people to expect me to be handy', so her request may have been on behalf of the duchess or the artistic and nimble-fingered Mrs Pendarves; but when her feather room was completed in 1791 it was claimed that it was 'executed by Mrs Montagu herself, assisted only by a few female attendants, instructed for that purpose'.[320] There is no way of knowing the scale of her contribution to the feather tapestry, but a screen was created in the late 1740s that also appears to have been a joint effort. It was '… in six panels, one of which was worked by Miss Anstey, in imitation of one of the Duchess of Portland's … it was the Duchess of Portland's original idea'. Miss Anstey's brother Christopher later made his name by publishing in 1766 *The New Bath Guide*.

Elizabeth Montagu's room received a lot of publicity; however three years before its official unveiling one person at least remembered that her idea was not new:[321]

A paragraph in your paper of yesterday says, the idea of fitting up a room with hangings of feather-work first originated with Mrs Montague: I shall not take upon me to determine with whom any idea may have originated, as such a decision seems subject to some difficulty; but I can venture to assert with whom the idea in question did not originate. It did not originate with Mrs Montague: because a Mr Abraham Gosset, of the Island of Jersey, had in his possession, more than twenty years ago, a set of feather-work hangings for a room, the panel in light grey feathers, and the festoon at top in coloured ones. This is a fact — and though a trifle, yet I thought it would be proper to set the feather upon the right bird.

It is worth noting that members of the Gossett family renowned in London for their frames and wax models, came from St Helier. They appear to have been close to the Clerembault family.[322] Matthew and Gideon Gosset feature in the bank account of Paul Bertrand [▶ p. 225].

Augustus the Strong's hangings were exhibited at Somerset House shortly after Elizabeth Montagu was born. His featherwork has survived but hers, which had to be dismantled because of the dust it collected, can only be imagined through the words of William Cowper:[323]

> The birds put off their every hue
> To dress a room for Montagu …

West end of the Abbey photographed from the river, albumen print, *c.* 1855. This very early photograph shows the modified corner building before it was altered again by Charles Edward Davis 1895–97. Bertrand's shop was third (going south, to the left) from the corner. (Bath in Time, 10974)

Part Three

Retirement

Portrait of a man reading, red chalk on paper, William Hoare. The features of the man depicted here are very like Bertrand's monument [▶ p. 26, detail right]. Could this be Paul Bertrand? (Libson)

194 PART THREE: RETIREMENT

Tis a dull farce, an empty show:
Powder, and pocket-glass, and beau

JOHN WESLEY[324]

BERTRAND CLOSED THE SHOP in Terrace Walk early in 1747/48: he would have been about fifty-seven years old. The aim of all members of the middling classes, such as Paul and Mary Bertrand, was a moderately prosperous and early retirement. Shopkeepers and craftsmen and their wives, merchants, doctors, lawyers and civil servants, worked hard from an early age to save and invest wisely for their final years. Many who had spent their working lives in central London retreated to its periphery, to enjoy a rural life in villages near the River Thames (Mary Bertrand's parents had moved to Chelsea) but Paul and Mary Bertrand remained in Bath until he died.

Following retirement, Bertrand's bank account shows that his income largely derived from interest from South Sea and India annuities, in which he had invested considerable sums (they brought him between £108 and £128 annually between 1748 and 1755). He received payments from Walter Wiltshire, and his cousin Samuel Gribelin still featured in both Bertrand's and Wiltshire's financial affairs.

There are few clues as to how Bertrand occupied his time during the eight years of his retirement, other than his continuing involvement with the Mineral Water Hospital.[325] His last duty as house visitor was on 30 July 1755; his general state of health cannot be determined but the fact that he was on the rota for the week following suggests that any final illness may have come upon him quite suddenly. Bertrand died on 23 September 1755; he had made a will on 28 August 1753 and this was proved on 21 October 1755.[326] He was buried in the vault of St Swithin's, Walcot.

p. 68

In his will, Bertrand described William Hoare and Peter Russel as his 'good friends' and appointed them his executors. The three men were linked by Russel's marriages: his first wife was Hoare's sister Hannah, his second Mary Bertrand's sister Elizabeth. As immediate neighbours in Barton Street Hoare and Bertrand must have seen a great deal of one another.

p. 204

A copy of the catalogue of Bertrand's 'Valuable Collection of Pictures, Busts' and other works of art that were sold on 11 and 12 November 1755, does not appear to have survived.[327] As the sale took place only six weeks after Bertrand died, his widow must have decided swiftly what possessions to keep and sell, unless the bulk of the sale represented stock left over from the shop. The only hints

Ealing

Ealing is on one of the main western routes out of London. In the eighteenth century the village of Great Ealing was a cluster of houses around the church, dedicated to St Mary. In 1795, some twenty years after Mary Bertrand's death, there were approximately 700 houses in the parish which 'had a desirable air of retirement and country quiet'.[328]

In the spring of 1774, just months before Mary Bertrand died, John Yeoman described two visits to Ealing on foot. In April he walked between Brentford and Ealing: '… in the course of the walk, about 2 miles, we went by 5 Esquires seats, one Bishop, one Dukes and Princess Amelia House. So I leave the reader to judge the pleasantness of our walk and where there was no Gentleman seat it was gardener's gardens with fruit trees all in full bloom, which makes it like the seat of Paradise.' The following month he '… took a walk up to Ealing to see a grand cricket match, eleven a side Southall and Norwood people against Ealing'.[329]

In the 1750s Fordhook was lived in by Henry Fielding, who knew the Deards family well and whose friend the American writer James Ralph was then at Gunnersbury. There were several properties of substance, including Ealing House, Elm Grove, Pitshanger, Rochester House and Gunnersbury House.[330] There were also good schools, a girls' school founded in 1712 and Great Ealing School founded c. 1698. Mary Bertrand left bequests to the Charity School for girls (£10) and boys (20 guineas), hers being one of thirty donations to the boys' school between 1612 and 1802.

As an aside, Ealing had a tenuous link to two of the most notorious trials of the late eighteenth century resulting from forged signatures on bonds. The twins Robert and Daniel Perreau were hanged following the forgery of the signature of William Adair's father.[331] The 'macaroni parson' William Dodd 'taught a few boys at a house near Pope's Cross' in Ealing in the 1760s, one of whom was Philip Stanhope, who later became the 5th Earl of Chesterfield. Stupidly in 1777 Dodd forged Chesterfield's signature — and he, too, hanged for it.[332]

Admission token to Vauxhall Pleasure Gardens, silver, mid-eighteenth century. Height: 4.5 cm (1¾ in). It is possible that this belonged to the James Smith known to Mary Bertrand during her retirement in Ealing. (Private coll)

196 PART THREE: RETIREMENT

of the Bertrands' possessions lie in the items he bequeathed to William Hoare, 'the five marble bustoes now in my parlour and his own busto now in my study', 'French draws' bequeathed by Mary Bertrand to Mary Wright,[333] and the items she had received from her mother: 'all the furniture in my Lower room, a Marble table that stands in my room, one pair of stairs, a folding Wainscott table'.

At his death, the balance of Bertrand's account at Hoare's was £4,222 11s 7d. He took care to provide for his wife under the terms of his will which confirms, by the absence of any mention of them, that Bertrand's children by his first wife had died.[334] It makes no mention of his wife's family, or the Wiltshire family, or his own relations the Gribelin family. Instead it underlines his friendship with William Hoare and Peter Russel and suggests a closeness to five sisters, Mary, Elizabeth, Ann, Katherine and Jemima Walton, who were shopkeepers in Bath — they were also mentioned in Prince Hoare's will.

p. 201

Mary Bertrand opened an account with Hoare & Co. in her own name on 19 December 1755. Her income from South Sea Company and East India annuities yielded rather less than before her husband's death, at between £70 and £110 — most years it was around £90.[335] Income from the Bath properties mentioned in Bertrand's will amounted to £30; she retained a life interest in the £1,000 loan from her mother dating back to January 1731/32. In addition to the furniture from her mother, she probably also still possessed the silver tankard, brilliant diamond ring and pictures of her parents which she also inherited. Mary Bertrand was buried at Ealing on 19 July 1774 and her will (which she had signed on 18 November 1773)[336] was proved the same day.

The reason why Mary Bertrand moved to Ealing following her husband's death may lie in friendships formed in Fleet Street before her marriage. The name 'Mrs Pinchbeck' is in the Ealing Poor Rate Book for March 1757 — she might be a connection of the family of toymen who had had shops near Mary Bertrand's brother in Fleet Street and her sister in Pall Mall and Tunbridge Wells. 'Mr Isted and his wife', mentioned in the will of Mary Bertrand's mother, might be another link between her family and Ealing.[337] But the closest friendship seems to have been with Ann Shuckburgh, whose husband John was also a publisher in Fleet Street. In April 1761 Mrs Shuckburgh advertised that he '… being lately dead, his business will be carried on by his widow'.[338] Mrs Shuckburgh had a house in Ealing. She died in 1766 and it seems that Mary Bertrand then lived with her daughter-in-law, Diana Shuckburgh.[339] It appears to have been a household of three women, for in her will Mary Bertrand mentions that Mary Winter

p. 51

p. 285

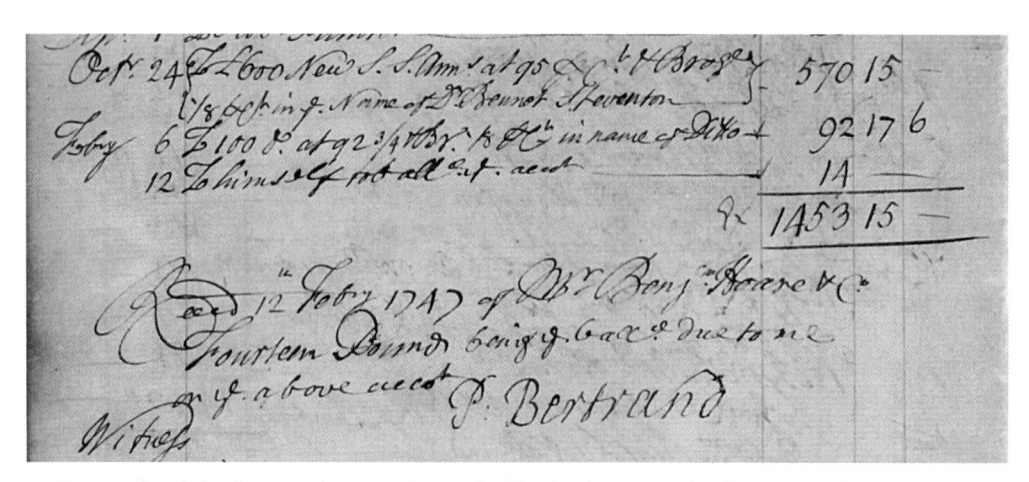

Having closed the shop, Paul Bertrand signed off his bank account, but he remained a customer of Hoare & Co. (Hoare)

A lady writing in a ledger, pencil on paper, William Hoare. The unknown sitter is doing household or business accounts; she is probably Elizabeth Hoare, but her occupation is one that Mary Bertrand would also have undertaken. (Private coll)

was also living with her. Another Ealing resident, James Smyth (a perfumer) may have managed her affairs at this time.[340]

These were the people who comprised Mary Bertrand's circle during her last years.

The intricate network of relationships between the Bertrands' friends and family, and the care taken with their bequests, is a familiar pattern, particularly if a couple had no surviving children. In their wills members of the Hoare and Russel families left bequests to each other and to nieces and nephews; Elias Russel is mentioned in the will of Colonel George Lewis (who married Peter Russel's daughter) and Prince Hoare describes Lewis as 'cousin' in his will — the relationships become ever more complex. The financial bond between Mary Bertrand's mother and husband devolved to her great-neice Rebecca Deards, the grand-daughter of her brother William Deards who had died in 1761. The house in Barton Street went to Mary Lewis, the daughter of Peter and Hannah Russel, which perhaps reflects not just affection between Peter Russel and Paul Bertrand, but also between the two Deards sisters. When Elizabeth Chenevix married Peter Russel in 1750 she and her sister were both in their fifties and Russel's children aged about five and three. Perhaps a further reason for Mary Bertrand's move to Ealing was to be closer to this young family.

p. 202 tree

The wills of Paul and Mary Bertrand, and the people they associated with in London, Bath and Ealing, give a fair indication of their personalities. If the red chalk portrait is indeed our man, he has a kindly face and there is a feeling of great empathy between artist and sitter. Tantalizingly the whereabouts are now unknown of family portraits, passed down through the Lewis family and exhibited in 1905. These were listed as:[341]

p. 194 illus.

… portraits of Wm Hoare's sister, Mrs Hannah Russell, wife of Mr Peter Russell; of his own wife, Mrs William Hoare and of his nephew, the Revd Bertrand Russel, Scholar and Fellow of Trinity College, Cambridge and Rector of Gainford, Durham. Mr Lewis also owns two crayon portraits, or pastels, by William Hoare, one being of Mr Peter Russell, his brother-in-law, and the other of that gentleman's second wife, for after Hannah died Mr Russell consoled himself with a rich and beautiful widow, Mrs Chenevix. The latter pastel is evidently one of his earliest pictures of that particular kind and as a work of art is not the equal of her husband.

William Hoare left numerous sketches of his family, many quietly reading, some sewing. Mary Bertrand is probably among them, unrecognised. This group of tradespeople achieved recognition in their lifetimes. Their portraits are lost to us now, but references in literature keep their names alive; they include verses on Bertrand's shop at Bath, by Richard Percival.[342]

p. 132

A rural retreat

The only description of Mary Bertrand is by Horace Walpole, when she visited Strawberry Hill in 1749. Her sister, Elizabeth Chenevix, sold this rural retreat long before she retired and was negotiating its sale to Walpole:[343]

... I expect but an unpleasant summer; my indolence and inattention are not made to wade through leases and deeds. Mrs Chenevix brought me one yesterday to sign and her sister Bertrand, the toy-woman of Bath for a witness. I showed them my cabinet of enamels, instead of treating them with white wine; the Bertrand said, 'Sir, I hope you don't trust all sorts of ladies with this cabinet'! — What an entertaining assumption of dignity! ...

The sisters probably knew Walpole well — he was certainly a regular customer of Chenevix's shop although he did not like Bath — and there is nothing to suggest that Mary Bertrand, or any of her family, was prudish. No doubt Walpole knew the sisters would appreciate his collection, and perhaps Mary Bertrand thought she could risk a teasing remark, but the episode underlines Walpole's awareness of the niceties of social conventions, and how careful a shopkeeper had to be to avoid over-familiarity.

On 9 August 1785 John Deards, the nephew of Elizabeth Chenevix and Mary Bertrand, is among the list of visitors to Strawberry Hill, in a party with three others.[344] This was a couple of years after he himself retired and handed on the family business in London to Nathaniel Jefferys. Perhaps he had spent time at Strawberry Hill as a child and was curious to see what Walpole had done to his aunt's property.

'Disposition of the Miniatures in the Rosewood Cabinet in the Tribune' at Strawberry Hill, watercolour, John Carter. The cabinet 1743. (Walpole)

Five sisters

Ann, Katherine, Jemima, Mary and Elisabeth Walton were particular favourites of Paul Bertrand: they were each left £100 in his will. They were milliners with a shop in Orange Grove; rate books between 1758 and 1782 show them under various names next to the bookseller, William Frederick.[345] Their trade cards suggest that they each specialised: Elizabeth advertised herself as a mantua and jacque maker, while Ann and Katherine sold lace and millinery wares. Following his retirement they took over Bertrand's shop in Terrace Walk in addition to their premises in the Grove. Their names appear in Walter Wiltshire's bank account with Hoare & Co.;[346] their customers included Lady Caroline Russell and the Duchess of Somerset, who in September 1749 spent £3 11s 6d on 'Dresden ruffs'.[347]

(RIGHT) Trade card of Elizabeth Walton, at the Golden Flower De Lis in Orange Grove, Bath. (Bath in Time, 35277)

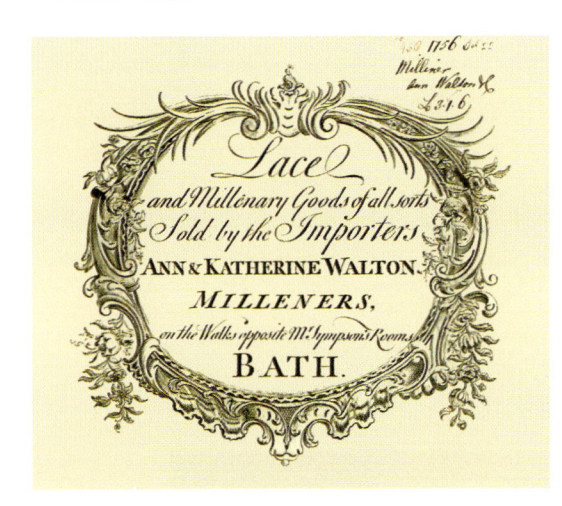

(ABOVE LEFT AND LEFT) Trade card of Ann and Katherine Walton, 'on the Walks opposite Mr Sympson's Rooms'. They took over the premises from Paul Bertrand after his retirement. The reverse used for an invoice dated 1756. Lady Caroline Russel (1742/3–1811) was the daughter of the 4th Duke of Bedford; she married the 4th Duke of Marlborough in 1762. (Bedford)

RETIREMENT 201

Invoice to Lord Arundel dated February 1756, from Peter Russel at Chenevix's Toy Shop. Elizabeth Chenevix opened the shop with her first husband, Paul Daniel Chenevix, in 1729. She married Peter Russel in 1750. (Wilts, Arundel 2667/19/11/5)

```
                                                                    Joseph Barker
                                                              ┌───────────┴───────────┐
 Paul     =    Mary      Elizabeth  =2 Pierre Roussel 1= Hannah    Prince Hoare   William  =  Elizabeth
 Bertrand 1730 Deards    Chenevix   1750 [Peter Russel]  Hoare     1711–69        Hoare       died 1794
                                         1706–73         died 1749 = Mary         1707–92
         ┌──────────────────┬─────────────────┼──────────────────────┬────────────┐
         George Lewis   =   Mary      Revd Bertrand = Susannah   William   Mary =   Anne   Prince
         1735–91        1764 1745–1811  Russel                             Henry
                                        1747–98                            Hoare
    ┌──────┬────────┬────────┬─────────┐
    George Bertrand William Mary Elizabeth
```

Self portrait, pastel, William Hoare, the frame dated 1742. (MWH Bath in Time, 14036)

William Hoare and Peter Russel

Close bonds of marriage and friendship linked the Bertrands to the families of William Hoare and Peter Russel. William's sister Hannah kept house for their brother Prince, a sculptor, in Bath before her marriage to Peter Russel in April 1740. Hannah and Peter Russel's children remained close to their cousins and were favourites of Mary Bertrand.

William Hoare (1707/08–92) is known primarily for his work as a portraitist, working in oil and in pastels. His family moved from Suffolk to Berkshire and William was in London by the 1720s;[348] he followed his brother Prince (1711–69) to Bath in 1739. By the 1760s Prince lived in the Old Post House, Abbey Green; his considerable output included a statue of Richard Nash for the Pump Room.

In 1742 William Hoare married Elizabeth Barker. Her father Joseph, variously described as a silversmith or merchant,[349] would have known the whole Deards family — he was in Bath with them in the 1720s and was bequeathed a clock by Mary Deards snr. The family circle in Bath was extended when he came to live near his daughter. William and Elizabeth Hoare had five children, one of whom died as an infant.[350] Their daughter Mary married Henry Hoare (1744–85), a partner of the bank; their son Prince (d.1824), a godson of John Wiltshire, is buried at Chiselhurst, in Kent, together with his sisters Anne (d. 1821) and Mary (d. 1811).[351] There is a memorial to William Hoare in Bath Abbey and another in St Swithin's church, Bath, near that of his close friend Paul Bertrand.

Hoare's success was founded not just on his work in oils, but on pastel portraits which, being faster to execute, he was able to complete during the time his sitters were in Bath — unlike the later full-length portraits of Thomas Gainsborough. Hoare also left numerous sketches of his family and friends, many probably drawn in Barton Street, but did not name them. The drawings reveal a close-knit and relaxed family: a man asleep in a wing chair, a woman reading, a boy reclining by an open window. They show another aspect of a toyman's life, a life beyond the shop counter.

Peter Russel was not just a close friend of Paul Bertrand: he appears to have been a major supplier to the shop. He was a gold box maker whose marriage to Mary Bertrand's sister, Elizabeth Chenevix — a second marriage for both parties — will, it is hoped, reveal further insights into luxury retailing.

p. 206 illus., and p. 239

Paul Bertrand's Will

I Paul Bertrand of the City of Bath in the County of Somerset make my last Will and Testament in the manner following after my debts are paid and my funeral which I desire may be made with as little expense as decently will permit. I give and bequeath to Mr William Hoare the five marble bustoes now in my parlour and his own busto now in my study, I likewise give to him and his heirs my moiety of the house in Pierpoint Street in this city which we built in partnership provided he pay or cause to be paid twenty pounds per annum to my wife Mary Bertrand during her life. I give to Mr John Maddin, cabinetmaker, his bond and note of hand both amounting to two hundred and fifty pounds provided he settles the house which was bought with that money on his wife Sarah Maddin and her child or children and after their death to return to him and his heirs provided likewise that he pay or cause to be paid ten pounds per annum to my wife Mary Bertrand during her life. I will and permit Mrs Hervey and her sister Mrs Noise remain in the house they now rent of me during their joint or separate lifes rent free provided that they pay the ground rent taxes and keep it good repair and after their death I give the said house to Mr Prince Hoare and his heirs. I give to Mr William Hoare and to Mr Peter Russel the fifteen hundred pounds new South Sea Annuities bought in my name by Messrs Hoare & Co. in trust to be disposed of in the manner following. I desire the said sum be left in the fund it now be or any other government security they shall judge more proper or there to remain until the death of my wife and that she be paid the interst thereon half yearly during her life and after her death to be disposed of in the manner following. To Mr Thomas Pomfret five hundred pounds for which he has my bond, to Mrs Ann Walton one hundred pounds, to Mrs Katherine Walton one hundred pounds, to Mrs Mary Walton one hundred pounds, to Mrs Elisabeth Walton one hundred pounds, to Mrs Jemima Walton one hundred pounds and if either of the said sisters should die before my wife then her share of the said five hundred pounds shall be divided equally among the surviving sisters and lastly I give the remainder of the said fifteen hundred pounds be it more or less to Mr William Hoare and to my godson Bertrand Russel to be shared equally between them. I give to each of my servants living with me at the time of my death one years wages, I will that all my books be sold except twenty volumes which my wife may first chuse and the money to be given to marry an honest young woman at the choice of my executors and if my present servant Jane Jones be not married at the time of my death I recommend her as a fit person. Lastly all the rest of my worldly goods and estate undisposed of I give and bequeath to my dear wife Mary Bertrand. Finally I constitute and appoint my good friends Mr William Hoare and Mr Peter Russel the executors of this my last will and testament and I desire both of them to accept of twenty pounds as an aknowledgement of the trouble I give them. In witness thereof I have hereunto set my hand and seal this twenty eighth day of August 1753 Paul Bertrand. Mr Paul Bertrand declares the above to be his last will and testament in the presence of Edward Brett Richard Gye Esq. *Signed 28 August 1753; proved 21 October 1755.*

William Hoare and Peter Russel, as executors, close Paul Bertrand's bank account on 19 January 1756. (Hoare)

Part Four

Paul Bertrand's bank account

Box, gold, London 1741/2, the mark PR is attributed to Peter Russel. The chasing is signed by George Michael Moser. Width: 11.6 cm (4½ in). The scene on the lid depicts the Roman hero Gaius Mucius Scaevola before the Etruscan king Lars Porsena. (Metropolitan)

Smile at us, pay us, pass us; but do not quite forget;
For we are the people of England, that never have spoken yet

G. K. CHESTERTON, THE SECRET PEOPLE

PAUL AND MARY BERTRAND ran the shop in Bath between 1730 and 1747. The record of Bertrand's bank account in the ledgers of Hoare & Co. begins in May 1736 and continues until his death in 1756, but with relatively few entries during the years of his retirement.

In the majority of entries, names on the debit pages are Bertrand's suppliers (those to whom he was paying money for goods or services). Most credit entries are in rounded figures and must represent transactions in the form of notes or bills of exchange: the names are customers, merchants or bankers whose names were on the note. However in several instances someone who would normally be considered a purchaser appears on the debit pages, and there are a few instances where a tradesman is shown as a creditor.

An attempt has been made to identify close to nine hundred names that feature in the account. It cannot be stated too strongly that while some identifications are made with confidence, most can only be guessed at. Where identities are uncertain, suggestions are put forward to aid researchers — the author will welcome information from readers that may improve, accept or reject these biographical notes.

Even with the extraordinary benefit of having Bertrand's bank account and so many images of Terrace Walk, it is still hard to visualise the interior of the shop filled with stock. Although we can assume that the names of silversmiths, chinamen and watchmakers are in the bank account because they supplied the shop, we lack detail of the type of objects stocked in Bath, in comparison to London shops.

The bank account does not show the name of any porcelain or pottery factory. Although it is safe to say that Bertrand would have bought oriental porcelain and possibly Meissen wholesale through John Cotterell or Thomas Turner, there is nothing in the account to suggest how Bertrand acquired stock from the factories at Bow or Chelsea (Charles Gouyn is a notable absentee from the account) — but English porcelain became available only right at the end of Bertrand's time as a shopkeeper. It is possible to be more specific with precious metals and watches, although relatively few objects appear to have survived made by those in the ledgers.

Names in bold are as transcribed from the ledgers with the amount of each entry, debit or credit, below.

NOTE
Only the items illustrated on pages 140, 141 and 160 can be identified as having been sold from the Bertrands' shop. Items shown in the following pages are the work of craftsmen listed in Bertrand's bank account, to illustrate the kind of goods that may have been in the shop.

pp. 208–09. Examples of the record of Paul Bertrand's bank account in the ledgers of C. Hoare & Co. (Hoare)

1738   Mr Paul Bertrand — Dr

			£ s d
March 28	To Edwd Farcond		100
April 8	To Edwd Feline		49 11 6
	18 To Mary Morin		35
	21 To Jas Leake		20 10 —
	25 To Ja Struder		38 7 —
	29 To Ste: Soame		27 2 —
May 1	To Edwd Ferrond 23 & 35		58
	10 To Edwd Mainwaring		12
	11 To Thos Curtis		18 10
	12 To Jos. Walker		30
	17 To Jas Leake		16 9 10
	19 Do		25 4 —
	25 To Arnd Eliot		14 13
	26 To charges of 64.6 Bill ret. ye 13th May		0 6 9
June 1	To Ann Walton		21
	5 To Beaver		5 5
	To Jas Struder		15
	6 To Mr Nagaveout		19 13
	7 To Edwd Feline		63 —
	9 To One Frogneaux		21 —
	10 To Mr Russell		27 16
	19 To Mary Morin		20
	20 To Mr Aumonier		25
	24 To Mr Mulford		40
	26 To Chas Halfpenny 703.0..t		13 10
	28 To Robt Lee		28
July 21	To Mr Russell		50
	26 To Louis Luce		70 7 —
	To Ste: Desvaux		31 10
	To himself		260 14 5
	28 To		100
Augt 2	To Mr Videy		50
	To himself		100
	3 To Henry Tardott		21 12
	8 To himself		100
	11 To Jos. Barker		14
To be pd	To Greenhill Jones pd 12 augt		53 18
	11 To himself to ball ye acct		194 3 6
	Recd augt 11th 1738 of Mr Benj Hoare &c One Hundred & Ninety four pounds 03 6 being ye ball is due to me on ye acct		£ 1791 3
Witnefs Wm Turner Paul Bertrand			

1746   Contra   312

		£	s	d
	By money due p Cont from folio 228 &c	5757	13	4
Apr 15	By bill on Jn: Hughes	20		
16	By bill on Ben: Fox	25		
	By bill on Ben: Hoare & Co	100		
23	By bill on Sam: Child & Co	60		
24	By bill on H: Osmond	100		
25	By bill on Alex: Wilson	15	15	
26	By bill on Ben: Hoare & Co	30		
May 2	By bill on Jas Collier	100		
3	By bill on Wm Turner	20		
5	By bill on Chauncey Townsend	30		
6	By bill on Jos: Brooke & Co	30		
	By bills on Gosling & Co 100 + 100	200		
9	By bill to Mrs Sarah Archer	30		
10	By bill on Geo: Arnold & Co	196		
13	By bill on Colo: Pelham	451	16	9
19	By bill on Ben: Hoare & Co	50		
	By bill on Honeywood & Co	10	10	
20	By bill on Mr Wakelin	250		
22	By bill on Jn Payne & Co	8		
21	By bill on James Collier	100		
	By bill on Geo Woolley	35		
	By bill on Sam Pechell	84	4	6
23	By bill on Sharp & Dunne	40		
24	By bill on Ben: Hoare & Co	70		
28	By bill on Coll Pelham	500		
	By Robt Faulhaus	200		
31	By bill on Geo: Smith	20		
June 2	By bill on Thos Townsend	30		
3	By bill on Knox & Co	15	12	10
	By bill on James Collier	25		
	By bill on Thos: Fairbank	20		
4	By bill on Wm Walmesley	50		
	By bill on Sam Child & Co	50		
	By bill on Jas Hardinge	100		
6	By bill on Ben: Hoare & Co	70		
7	By bill on Mr Cooper	50		
		8964	12	5

Selected suppliers

A selection of craftsmen and retailers who feature in the bank account are highlighted in pp. 56–57 and 214–45

Pp. 212–13: John Strype's edition, 1720, of John Stow's map of London, numbered to show the locations of the shops of the Deards family, Paul Bertrand's associates, parish churches, theatres and buildings of commerce.

N.B. The positioning of the numbers gives approximate, not exact locations.

Yellow = The Deards family and their associates (also on p. 36)
1. John Deards followed by his son William Deards, in Fleet Street *c.* 1685–1742
2. Clerkenwell: Elizabeth Deards/Chenevix, probable seasonal shop
3. Westminster Hall: John and William Deards, when Parliament in session
4. William Wiltshire's office in Fleet Street 1772
5. Paul Bertrand, unknown locations in the parishes of Savoy, St Clement Danes and St Martin-in-the-Fields, before 1730
6 & 6a. Peter Russel in Villiers Street, *c.* 1740s; moved to Suffolk Street *c.* 1748, then to Chenevix's (below). Sampson Bishop also in Villers Street and Suffolk Street
7. William Deards, corner of Craven Street and the Strand, 1742–57
8. Paul Daniel and Elizabeth Chenevix, Charing Cross, 1729 to his death 1742/3, continued by his widow alone until 1750, then with her second husband Peter Russel until her death in 1765
9. William and Mary Deards, Pall Mall, *c.* 1752–65
10. William Deards followed by his son John Deards, corner of Dover Street and Piccadilly, 1757–83

Interior of Westminster Hall, engraving, *c.* 1750. During periods when Parliament and the Courts were in session, John Deards and then William Deards had a 'shop' here, as did other toymen. The hall is lined with booths. (LMA)

Green = Selected suppliers in Bertrand's bank account
1. Robert Durrance, Windmill Hill, Moorfields
2. John Cotterell and Frederick Stanton, corner of Grocers Alley, Poultry
3. George Greenhill Jones, Foster Lane
4. Peter Deletang, Old Change, Cheapside
5. George Willdey, St Paul's Churchyard
6. Philip Margas, Ludgate Hill
7. Joseph Allen, Golden Lane, Cripplegate
8. John Mulford, Cursitors Alley
9. Thomas Thibault, Fetter Lane
10. Humphrey Pugh, Racquet Court
11. Thomas Wright, Fleet Street
12. Edward Pars, Wych Street
13. James Bernardeau, Russell Court, Drury Lane
14. Edward Feline, King Street
15. Isaac Callard, King Street
16. James Bellis, King Street
17. Christian Hillan, Earl Street
18. John Barbot, Great St Andrew's Street
19. John Jacob Trible, Litchfield Street
20. Samuel Gribelin, Long Acre
21. William Hubert, St Martin's Lane
22. Isaac Fleury, Cecil Court
23. John Jacob, Hemings Row
24. Lewis Pantin, Castle Street
25. Edward Scarlett, Macclesfield Street
26. James Shruder, Wardour Street
27. John Duval, Wardour Street
28. Thomas Turner, St James's Street

Red = Churches, theatres and places of commerce
1. Customs House
2. Africa House
3. East India House
4. South Sea House
5. Bank of England
6. Royal Exchange
7. Exchange Alley & Birchin Lane
8. Goldsmiths' Hall
9. Samuel Cranmer, Fleet Street
10. Hoare & Co., Fleet Street
11. Child & Co., Fleet Street
12. Swan Inn, Holborn
13. St Dunstan-in-the-West
14. St Clement Danes
15. Theatre, Portugal Row
16. St Mary-le-Strand
17. Exeter Exchange
18. Theatre Royal
19. Middleton & Co., Strand
20. Andrew Drummond, Charing Cross
21. Opera House
22. St Martin-in-the-Fields

212 PART FOUR: PAUL BERTRAND'S BANK ACCOUNT

SELECTED SUPPLIERS 213

JOHN BARBOT
ETUI MAKER
p. 249 map, p. 211/18

Necessaire, hardstone, enamel and silver-gilt, attributed to John Barbot, *c.* 1760. (Ashmolean)

The Barbot family featured in the research by Brian Beet that triggered this present work.[352] JOHN BARBOT (1702/3–66) was a tweezer case, or etui, maker — objects that epitomise the stock of a toyshop — and the family were at the heart of the community of craftsmen who supplied toyshops.

Through his wife, Rachel Jourdain, John Barbot was connected with George Willdey, who had a shop in St Paul's Churchyard. Together with James Bellis he acted for John Pyke, Bertrand's former employee, during his bankruptcy in 1759, and John's son Paul was an assignee in the bankruptcy of William Deards jnr in 1764 (the nephew, not the brother, of Mary Bertrand and Elizabeth Chenevix). Barbot's address in 1726, when he entered his mark at Goldsmiths' Hall, was 'att the Blackmoors head a Stuff Shop' (meaning a shop selling fabrics); from 1737 he was in St Andrew Street, Seven Dials. Brian Beet suggested that John and his son Paul were trading as merchants, as had their forebears; John's eldest son was hanged for murder at St Kitts in 1753.

The wider Barbot family encompassed other shopkeepers and merchants whose connections have yet to be researched. For example Mr Barbot of Bond's Court offered a reward in 1729 for the return of another typical toyshop product 'a white dimity pocket without a string' containing money, a knife, a thimble and some keys.

John Barbot is best known for what was described in invoices as a 'trunk toothpick case', usually dated to the early 1760s.[353] The objects he supplied to Bertrand between 1736 and 1746 can only be imagined, but may have been agate or shagreen-mounted cases, considerable numbers of which have survived, mostly unmarked. Paul Barbot diversified into snuff boxes and supplied the retailers Parker & Wakelin during the 1770s.[354]

JAMES BELLIS
p. 251
map p. 211/16

There is only one small entry for JAMES BELLIS in Bertrand's account, in 1746 for £18. Like several of the transactions that went through the bank's ledgers, it seems to show Bertrand buying from a man at the start of his career: Bellis died in 1788, some forty-two years later. He usually described himself as a jeweller and toyman, but he was listed as a goldworker when he registered a mark at Goldsmiths' Hall in 1760. If he had an earlier mark it would have been in the missing smallworkers' book of 1739–58.[355]

On Christmas Eve 1759 a fire entirely destroyed his and forty other houses in King Street, Covent Garden; several people died. Within a week Bellis was advertising the sale of Dresden china through the auctioneer Prestage, as well as appealing for the return of stock looted during the fire. Missing chatelaines included 'one large Onyx Equipage for a Lady's Side, richly ornamented with chased Gold, and opening with three Brilliant Buttons', one in 'china' with a matching watch by Cabrier, a large gold one 'not quite finished', one with chasing in Chinese taste, and so on — each had its own shagreen case.³⁵⁶ He moved temporarily to Villiers Street, off the Strand, and following his return to King Street he advertised in January 1761 a typical range of toyshop stock:

a large Assortment of the newest and most fashionable Toys in Gold, Stone and Jewellers Work; also Garnets in Bunches, elegant Plate and China, Gentlemens walking canes, with all other articles in the Toy Branch

He sold wholesale and retail, adding that 'merchants, shopkeepers &c may be served at the lowest rates'.³⁵⁷

Bellis later had a second shop in Pall Mall, where he fell victim to one of the most notorious and slippery shoplifters of the day, an incident that demonstrates how careful shopkeepers had to be not to upset the gentry, so as to keep up their custom. Even though the thief had been spotted, he was allowed to get away because 'it was a dangerous thing to stop him getting into a coach, as he had the appearance of a gentleman'.³⁵⁸

By 1782 Bellis had decided to retire, advertising to the public that he was selling off his stock 'at such low rates, as to make it worth their attention, the lowest price being marked on each article'. He moved to his property at Woodside, near Hatfield, Hertfordshire, where he died in 1788.

JAMES BERNARDEAU (fl. 1727–53) was a Huguenot and a freemason.³⁵⁹ From March 1726/27 he was at the 'Pistol & L', in Russell Court, Drury Lane, from where he sold 'silver, Chiney, Ivory, Ebony Handled Knives and Forks, etc'. He would have bought in handles and fitted them with steel blades and tines. The shop sign originated with Bernardeau's predecessor at the address, Francis Liege.³⁶⁰

Bernardeau described himself as a razor maker in his will, which was made in 1748 and proved 29 January 1753.³⁶¹ Two sons died young and James's wife Ann continued the business after his death: she is recorded buying Bow porcelain handles in 1756.³⁶² When she died in 1766 their daughter, also named Ann, took over with her second husband and cousin, Stephen Gagnon. Several members of the wider Bernardeau family worked in associated trades.³⁶³

Invoices from James Bernardeau include one to the Earl of Dysart, for a set of six refined steel razors with ivory and silver handles and a pair of scissors, in 'a strong silvr swage white & black case' that cost a total of £15 4s 6d in 1744; another to the Duke of

Snuffbox, gold and enamels, signed on the left flange: *Jas Bellis Londn fecit*, for the retail jeweller and toyman James Bellis. Width: 6 cm (2⅜ in). (CGen, 8.5.1979/122)

JAMES BERNARDEAU
CUTLER
p. 251
map p. 211/13

Gordon in 1745, included 'a double knife silvr blade' and a case inlaid with gold; a further invoice to Richard Hoare shows a 'tweezer case' at £2 12s 6d in 1749. Earl Fitzwalter lists him as 'Signor Bernardo', the spelling used in his mark.[364]

Bernardeau was one of the few tradesmen who contributed small sums to the Bath Mineral Water Hospital through Paul Bertrand: he gave one guinea on several occasions between 1737 and 1743.[365] There may have been a certain amount of self-interest in this: his trade cards advertised lancets and other instruments including those for cupping — perhaps his customers included some of the many medical men in Bath and its new hospital.

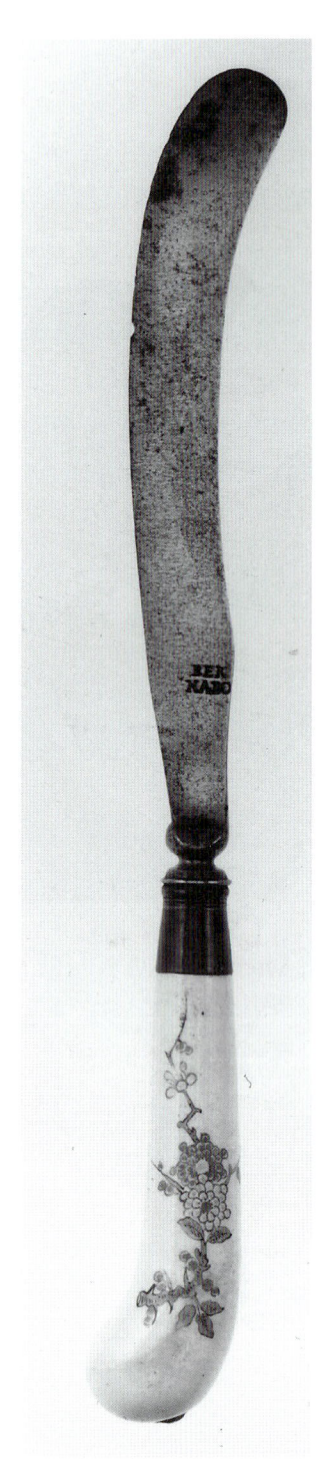

Knife, with soft-paste porcelain handles, Chantilly c. 1725–50, the blade marked *Bernado*. Length: 23.6 cm (8¾ in). (BM, Franks.351)

Invoice from James Bernardeau to Sir Richard Hoare, 1749. (Hoare)

Trade card of James Bernardeau, cutler and razor maker. (BM, Heal.52.11)

216 PART FOUR: PAUL BERTRAND'S BANK ACCOUNT

SAMPSON BISHOP was clearly close to Peter Russel (Elizabeth Chenevix's second husband) who was an executor of his will and described by Bishop as 'my good friend'.[366] No matter how close their working relationship, however, they did not entirely agree when it came to politics: they voted for different candidates in the 1749 by-election in Westminster. At that time, and at his death, Bishop was in Suffolk Street; he had moved there from Villiers Street, York Buildings (off the Strand), which is where Russel lived before he too moved to Suffolk Street.[367]

Sampson Bishop was a jeweller. He was also a freemason, listed at Haymarket Lodge in 1730, together with Alexander Pope and Elias and Peter Russel.[368] Their precise working relationship has not yet been established, but it seems fair to suggest that he might have collaborated with Russel, either working directly for him and Chenevix, or certainly supplying the shop. The signature on Bishop's will (signed in October 1755, proved 26 August 1758) was witnessed by Ann Dupre, who previously worked for Chenevix, and Will Harris, who receipted an invoice on behalf of Peter Russel (to Lord Arundel) in February 1756.

In 1749 Bishop took Augustus le Sage (b. 1736) as an apprentice. His father, the silversmith John Hugh le Sage, had been at the Golden Cup at the corner of Great Suffolk Street since 1720, and Augustus took over the workshop, remaining there until at least 1785. The geographical proximity and social connections between Bishop (a jeweller), Peter and Elias Russel (who made gold boxes), the le Sage family (silversmiths), Chenevix's toyshop and Paul Bertrand, raises many questions about this community of craftsmen and retailers.[369]

There are also entries in Bertrand's account for Samuel Bishop, who appears to have specialised in setting diamonds: the work he carried out for the jeweller Webb is carefully itemised in the latter's daybook — for example on 1 February and 28 August 1753, when the cost of the work totalled £167 15s 6d.[370] Samuel and Sampson may have been brothers, or possibly one and the same person. Sampson's wife was called Charlotte; he had two sons, Edward and Sampson, and two daughters, Elizabeth and Charlotte.

SAMUEL & SAMPSON BISHOP
JEWELLERS

p. 251
map p. 210/6

Toyshops sold a considerable amount of flatware: spoons, forks and knives, especially small items associated with drinking tea. ISAAC CALLARD specialised in making spoons and forks. He entered his mark in February 1726, with an address in King Street, St Giles in the Fields; he was later (1739) at The Crown, Tottenham Court Rd and in 1747 at Earle Street, Seven Dials.[371] The premises in King Street appear to have been retained, however, for in 1755 Isaac's son Paul was the victim of a theft there.[372]

ISAAC CALLARD
SPOONMAKER

p. 256
map p. 211/15

Like so many other petty crimes, the report of this one reveals small details that add to the visual jigsaw of retailing at the time: twelve rings were stolen from a shew-glass by a man called Simpson, from whom Callard had bought goods and who, in the words of Abraham Barrear (Callard's journeyman) Callard had 'trusted … with the drawer in which the rings were to look over them at his pleasure'. The rings, worth 40s, had not been missed immediately because 'There were silver thimbles in the same drawer, and on the nail where he had taken a ring, he had hung up a thimble, so that they were no so easily missed at first sight'. It seems the shew-glass was made as a drawer. Simpson was transported for seven years.

In 1708 Isaac Callard was apprenticed to Paul Hanet, a spoonmaker, and subsequently married one of Hanet's four daughters. Hanet was godfather to Isaac's son Paul in 1724, who was also apprenticed to him (through the Longbowstringmakers' Company) in 1737. Hanet died in 1741; one of his executors was Thomas Callard 'otherwise Coller', a jeweller of the parish of St Anne's. Isaac married a second time, to Susanna Roussel, a widow of Battersea, where they continued to live. Her will, signed on 24 October 1761 in anticipation of that marriage, was witnessed by Paul Callard; she died in 1765.[373] Isaac's will was proved in 1770; his son Paul had died, and he left his 'estate and effects, stock, implements and utensils in trade, plate and china' to Paul's daughter Marguerite.

(ABOVE) Tablespoon, silver, Isaac Callard, London, c. 1740. This is an early example of a spoon made in England with a 'fiddle pattern' terminal, betraying Callard's French origins. (Schredds)

SAMUEL CAWTHORN was apprenticed to the jeweller Thomas Thibault (who also features in Bertrand's bank account) in 1723. He obtained his freedom in 1730 and was elected to the livery of the Goldsmiths' Company in 1746.[374] Bertrand's dealings with him were in 1737 and 1741, at which time he was probably working in some area of the jewellery trade.

It is not known why he took employment at Goldsmiths' Hall, where he was appointed beadle in 1753. John Bodington and Benjamin Pyne, well established silversmiths in their day, were among those who had previously held the position, which seems to have been awarded to those whose business had not prospered. Cawthorn seems to have suffered from ill health, 'afflicted with Body Flux and violent Rheumatic pains' and was 'weakened [in] sight and hearing' when he resigned in 1770. This probably accounts for one of his duties, the circulation of 'warnings' to the trade, being carried out by other almsmen on his behalf.[375]

Cawthorn clearly knew his colleagues well, as evidenced by the following exchange during the trial of William Danborough, acquitted of stealing a soup ladle, butter ladle and tablespoon from the Goldsmiths' Company in 1767:[376]

Samuel Cawthorn. I have the honour of being beadle to the worshipful company of Goldsmiths. Last Lord-Mayor's day I attended at the hall, I saw the prisoner there; there were a great number of people in and about the hall; we asked their business; several of them informed me they were servants waiting for liverymen; I asked the prisoner whose servant he was; he told me he was employed as a whiffler to wait upon the cook; I called to the porter Mr. Wren, and said, pray see this whiffler out of the hall, knowing he had no business there, that is all I know of Mr. Whiffler. I saw him passing and repassing several times between the kitchen and the hall, and I obliged him to go out of the hall.
Q. What was he employed in?
Cawthorn. In carrying dishes, and taking dishes away.
Q. Did you see him at the time of dinner?
Cawthorn. I did.
Q. Were there not many whifflers there?
Cawthorn. There may be many, but they have no business at the hall.
Q. Are not these whifflers employed to attend the cook?
Cawthorn. No, they are not, no farther than to carry dishes to gentlemen's tables.
Q. What is the prisoner?
Cawthorn. He is a lapidary.

By 'whiffler' Cawthorn must have meant an attendant — a person 'employed to keep the way clear for a procession or at some public spectacle', but the word can also mean 'an insignificant or

SAMUEL CAWTHORN
JEWELLER

p. 257

JOHN COTTERELL
CHINA MAN
p. 265
map p. 211/2

Like a bull in a china shop
Yesterday a bullock ran into the shop of Mr Cotterell, a Chinaman, at Stocks market and broke China and glass to a considerable value.[382]

contemptible fellow, a shifty or evasive person'.[377] It seems Danborough may have been moonlighting and trying to earn a little extra at a time when perhaps the jewellery trade was slow.

The entries for JOHN COTTERELL are among the most numerous in Bertrand's account. There was a clockmaker of this name active from the early 1720s but it seems most likely that the entries refer to a chinaman.[378]

John Cotterell and Frederick Stanton were partners at the Indian Queen, at the corner of Grocers Alley in Poultry. The firm advertised that they sold china ware, coffee, tea, chocolate, snuff, India tea tables and fans, double flint glasses, etc. Stanton's name appears in the list of buyers at an East India House sale in 1721, and invoices from them survive in several archives.[379] However the partners may have gone their separate ways: Stanton was in partnership with William Thorne in 1742.[380] Cotterell valued the china in the estate of the toyman George Willdey;[381] in 1753 he advertised that he was selling Worcester china.[383]

(BELOW AND OPPOSITE BELOW) Invoices from Frederick Stanton and John Cotterell to Richard Hoare, dated 1732 and 1734. (Hoare)

(OPPOSITE ABOVE) Invoice from John Cotterell to the Earl of Dysart, 1745. (Tollemache)

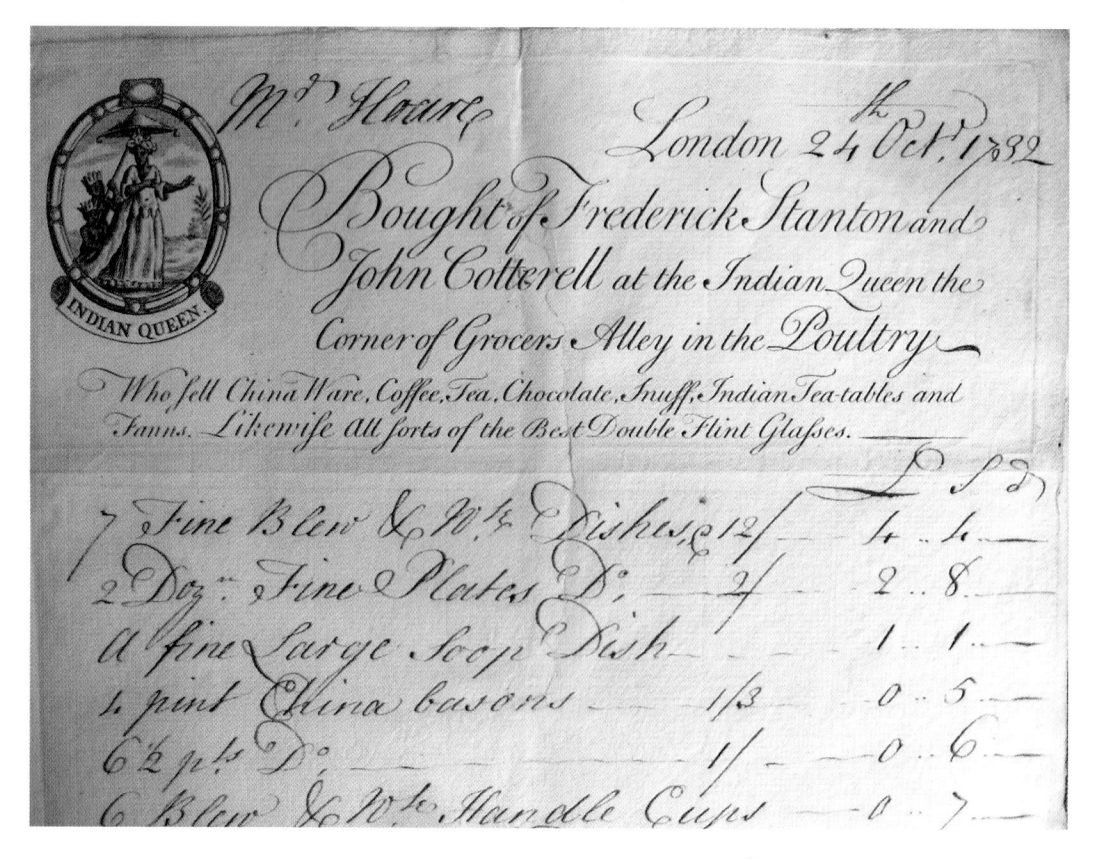

The Right Hon:ble the Earl Dysart

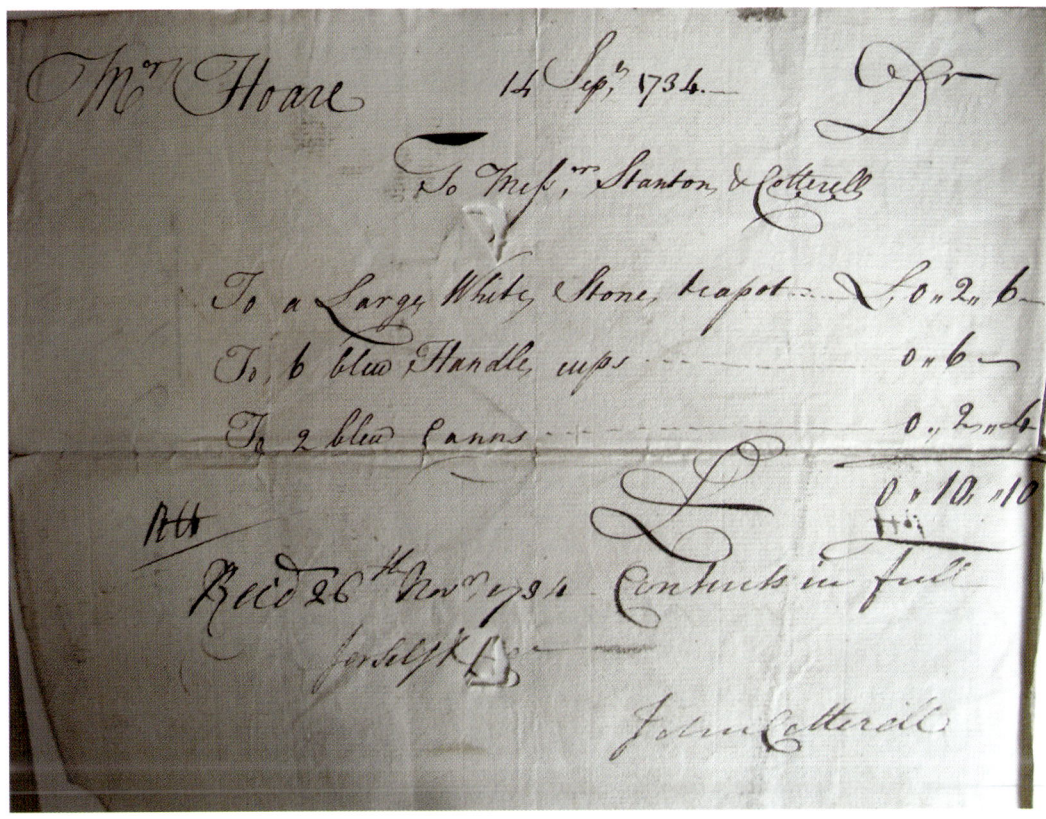

London 5 ap:ll 1745

Bought of John Cotterell

at the Indian Queen and Tea Cannister
against the Mansion House.

Who sells Variety of Old & New China & Lacquer'd Wares, Tea, Coffee,
Chocolate, Snuff, Indian Fanns & Pictures, With all sorts of Flint Glass.
Whole sale & Retail.

JOHN COTTERELL remov'd from ye Indian Queen ye corner of Grocers Alley in ye Poultry.

2 fine Old ... Sallad Dishes 4	0..8..0
1 Large Blew Old Sugar Box	0..6..0
2 ... ... Basons	0..10..0
1 fine Blew Chocolate Cup	......
	1..5..—

Rec'd at same time ye Contents in full
John Cotterell

Mr. Hoare   14 Sep:r 1734   Dr

To Messrs Stanton & Cotterell

To a Large White Stone teapot	£ 0..2..6
To 6 blew Handle cups	0..6
To 2 blew Canns	0..2..4
	0..10..10

Rec'd 26th Nov:r 1734 Contents in full
for self &c
John Cotterell

SELECTED SUPPLIERS: CAWTHORN–COTTERELL

JOHN CRESWELL
p. 266

More research needs to be done on John Creswell, about whom little is known. There is a possibility that the ledger entry at Hoare is incorrect and that it should read Joseph, who had close ties with the Deards family. It seems likely that Joseph and John were somehow related.

John Creswell was a 'haberdasher of small wares' in the Strand in 1716, when he insured his property.[384] He may have been the John Creswell who was baptised in 1680 at St Paul's Covent Garden, who in turn fathered two sons, both baptised John at St Martin in the Fields, in 1716 and 1722.

p. 37

Joseph Creswell, son of a clothworker of the same name, was apprenticed in 1719/20 to John Deards. In 1728 he was married to Jane Addison at St James's Clerkenwell, the same church at which Elizabeth Deards married Daniel Chenevix. They had a son, also Joseph, who was born in 1738. It seems that following his apprenticeship, Creswell moved to work for Elizabeth Chenevix, as he receipted a bill to the Duke of Richmond on her behalf on 7 February 1729/30. Later that year he attended a masonic meeting at the Goat, at the foot of the Haymarket, at which Elias and Peter Russel and Sampson Bishop were also present. He is referred to in a letter to Fanny Carteret from her sister Louisa in 1732: '… 'tis not my fault yr picture is not set by Mr Creswell ….'[385]

It is not yet known when Creswell left the employment of Chenevix, but he set up in business as a toyman at the Unicorn in Suffolk Street, his trade card clearly mentioning his former employer.[386] He was bankrupt in 1746, named as a silversmith of the Strand. In June 1747 he was advertising medals from the Unicorn in New Bond Street,[387] and was listed there in the 1749 poll, but as a jeweller. Between 1774 and 1775, Sir Watkin Williams Wynn acquired an extensive service designed by Robert Adam, that was retailed by Joseph Creswell from his premises in the Adelphi in the Strand.[388] It seems most likely that this was Creswell jnr –listed as a goldworker in 1773.[389]

EDWARD FELINE
SILVERSMITH
p. 273
map p. 211/14

The monetary total for Edward Feline comes second only to John Mulford among those known to be silversmiths on the debit pages of Bertrand's account. The payments are over a five-year period, 1736 to 1741, and are in miscellaneous amounts, suggesting that Bertrand was paying invoices, whereas the rounded figures of £100 or £50 to other craftsmen seem to represent payment by instalments. Today, Feline is far better known than Mulford and, judging from the surviving silver bearing his mark, had a substantial business.

Feline was apprenticed to Augustine Courtauld in 1709 and obtained his freedom in 1721. He was in Rose Street before moving

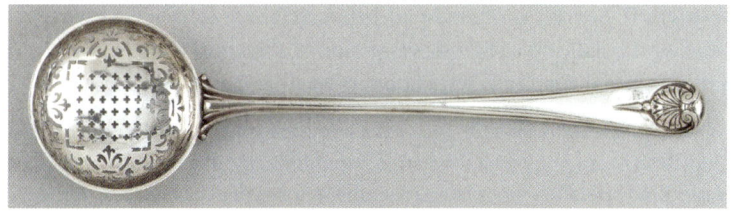

Six candlesticks, silver, Edward Feline, London 1746/7. Height: 16.6 cm (6½ in). (SNY, 9.4.2009/278)

Straining spoon, silver, Edward Feline, London 1737/8, 27.4 cm (10¾ in). (Albert, 762)

Bowl, silver, Edward Feline, London 1744/5. Diameter: 29 cm (11½ in). (SL, 7.5.1953/146)

Inkstand, silver, Edward Feline, London 1744/5. Width: 24 cm (9½ in). (SL)

to King Street, both in Covent Garden.[390] Feline's will was proved in May 1753 on the same day that his widow Magdalen registered her own mark at Goldsmiths' Hall. The witnesses to his signature on the will were Mary Battey and Anthony Jourdan; his wife was the sole executor. Objects bearing her mark are recorded until the 1760s but she had a long retirement, dying in 1792. Nothing is so far known of Henry Feline, for whom there is one debit payment of £105 in 1736 in Bertrand's account.

Other than a few exceptionally large commissions, the bulk of Feline's output was practical, unglamorous, domestic wares made for regular use, and therefore eminently suited to being bought off the shelf in a toyshop. Items in the Ashmolean Museum's collection typify his work: candlesticks, cups, dishes, inkstands, jugs and salvers.[391] Some of his surviving output is recognised today as having irregular marks which would not have complied with the regulations of the Goldsmiths' Company: he may have been evading the 6*d* per ounce tax on plate.

This transaction began on 2 April 1736. It is possible that William Turner, a clerk at the bank, was in Bath to discuss the setting up of an account for Bertrand with Hoare & Co. the following month. Turner wrote an order to the bank for £20 to be paid to Bertrand, who sent it to London countersigned for payment to Edward Feline in London, who acknowledged receipt on 13 April. (Hoare)

Matthew Gossett (1683–1744) was uncle to Gideon (1707–85), and Isaac (1713–99), the sons of his brother John. They were wood carvers and wax modellers, working in Poland Street, London. An example of their output is found in Lord Fitzwalter's accounts: in April 1732 he paid £19 4s 6d for 'a large frame of a table and for two frames for my wife's and my picture at full length'. Gideon was listed as 'carver' in Berwick Street in 1749, the house he and his brother inherited on Matthew's death in 1744. Matthew's frames are inscribed on the reverse 'By Matthew Gossett Esq. Gentleman Pensioner of George II'; as a statuary, he had a yard at St Anne's Westminster. Both Matthew and Gideon were buried in St Marylebone.[392]

Isaac made frames for Thomas Gainsbrough; his models of General Wolfe were advertised for sale by Deards and Peter Russel in 1759. By 1763 James Gossett 'modeller of portraits in wax and carver in wood' was in Berwick St, Soho.[393]

MATTHEW AND GIDEON GOSSET
WAX MODELLERS AND CARVERS
p. 277

Frederick Prince of Wales, wax plaque, Isaac Gosset (1713–99). Height: 14.8 cm (5¾ in). (Royal Coll, 37105)

Although it is a striking design, the cartouche that frames Christian Hillan's trade card gives no hint of the extraordinary nature of some of his work. He modestly claimed that he 'Makes & Sells all sorts of Plate Wrought & Plain of ye Newest Fashion at ye most Reasonable Rates'. Hillan is one of the silversmiths whose work is being re-examined by those studying the output of a mysterious modeller provisionally known as 'the Maynard Master'. The design of a pair of waiters bearing Hillan's mark for 1742/43 has borders showing all the plasticity and inventiveness that is currently attributed to this unknown designer. Other silversmiths who are thought to have used the modeller's designs include Paul de Lamerie.[394]

Bertrand's payments to Hillan are relatively modest: £18 2s; £37; £33 in 1737 and 1738. As so often seems to have happened, Bertrand went to Hillan quite early in his career — less than a year after he entered a mark in April 1736.

It is thought that Hillan came from Scandinavia; he established himself in London first in Bishop's Court, Durham Yard, then in Earl Street, near Seven Dials. By 1741 he was in Compton Street, very close to de Lamerie, Paul Crespin, Nicholas Sprimont and Isaac Callard.[395]

CHRISTIAN HILLAN
SILVERSMITH
p. 282
map p. 211/17

SELECTED SUPPLIERS: FELINE–HILLAN   225

Hot water jug, silver, Christian
Hillan, London 1738/9.
Height: 24.2 cm (9½ in).
(SNY, 6.6.1980/33)

Milk jug, silver, Christian Hillan,
London 1738/9.
Height: 12.7 cm (5 in).
(SL, 3.11.1953/363)

Waiter, silver, Christian Hillan,
London 1742/3. (SL)

226   PART FOUR: PAUL BERTRAND'S BANK ACCOUNT

Trade card of Christian Hillan, goldsmith. (BM, Heal.67.210)

Calendar paircase verge watch, gold, signed James Hubert snr, London, no. 291, *c.* 1715, the case marked *IR*. Diameter: 5.2 cm (2 in). (CGen, 14.11.1995/284)

JAMES HUBERT's name is the first entry on the debit side of Bertrand's account, with a further five entries between 1736 and 1741. A London watchmaker, he was apprenticed to his father (James active to *c.* 1730) in 1721 and was working until *c.* 1760.[396]

WILLIAM HUBERT was one of the most interesting dealers and shopkeepers in London during the early eighteenth century — a man with many interests and a wide circle of contacts, a marchand-mercier. He was based in St Martin's Lane.

There is a possibility that Bertrand and Hubert were connected through Mary le Maitre, Bertrand's first wife. In 1735 Hubert was guardian to two of her sister's step-children (younger siblings of Elias Russel) and was granted administration of her estate. Hubert's own will was proved by Peter Deletang [de l'Etang], a diamond cutter, and Peter Lemaitre, a wine merchant. Due to the similarity of surname, the latter might possibly have been related to Mary le Maitre.

In April 1735 Hubert put his stock up for auction as he was 'leaving off business'. The quality and range of items for sale attracted some of the most knowledgeable collectors of the time whose widespread interests can perhaps be judged by the fact that 'by request of several Noblemen and Gentlemen of the Jockey Club'

JAMES HUBERT
WATCHMAKER
p. 284

WILLIAM HUBERT
p. 284
map p. 211/21

p. 267
p. 289

Ten poultry skewers, silver, John Jacob, London 1749/50. Length: 20 cm (8 in). (CSK, 18.9.2012/361)

Salver, silver, John Jacob, London 1752/3. Diameter: 31 cm (12¼ in). (CNY, 29.1.2010/169)

Cake Basket, silver, John Jacob, London 1741/2. Length: 36.8 cm (14½ in). (SNY, 21.10.2010/198)

228   PART FOUR: PAUL BERTRAND'S BANK ACCOUNT

Mr Cock, the auctioneer, re-scheduled the sale of 'those exceeding beautiful Arabian Horses' to take place immediately after Hubert's paintings by Rubens (bought by Mrs Edwards), by Poussin and Wouwermans, his inlaid Florence and French cabinets, lustres, intaglios and rock crystal. In December 1736 two quite large payments to Hubert went through Bertrand's bank account — for £139 10s and £200. They might well have been for items left over from the previous year's sale.

William Hubert died on 12 April 1740. A month later his widow Marianne Gaudron advertised that she 'carries on the manufacture of rappee snuff, at her house on the pavement in St Martin's Lane',[397] a modest activity that seems at odds with her husband's former business. In March 1741, teamed this time with the stock of the goldsmith and jeweller Peter Pons, Hubert's prints, drawings and books were put up for sale. Then in April 1751, his widow having decided to move to France, a further tranche was advertised:[398]

> a large and capital picture of the judgment of Paris by Rubens and the well-known cartoon of the murder of the innocents by Raphael, both formerly belonging to Mr William Hubert of St Martin's Lane, deceased; and which must now be sold without reserve, his widow being gone to reside in France. … And at the same time will be sold in one lot … His curious cabinet of casts, pastes and impressions, containing upwards of 4000 taken (by particular desire) from the most celebrated and valuable antique gems in the king of France's Collection.

The value of the entries in Bertrand's bank account suggest that they refer to a London silversmith rather than a shagreen case maker of the same name — but it is impossible to be certain.[399]

The silversmith entered his mark as a largeworker in 1734, signing himself as 'JEAN JACOB' at Hemings Row, near St Martin's Lane. He married Ann Courtauld, daughter of the silversmith Augustine Courtauld, whose sister Esther was married to the watch casemaker Stephen Goujon.[400] Jacob moved to Spur Street and was still there in 1773. With Peze Pilleau he valued silver on the death of the toyman George Willdey. Among his clients was William Pitt: Jacob features in Pitt's account with Hoare & Co in 1737.[401]

There are two payments from Bertrand to GEORGE GREENHILL JONES, whose father was an innholder of Highworth, a village near Swindon, through which many visitors might have travelled on a cross-country route to Bath.

Jones's output mainly comprised useful domestic wares such as kitchen peppers, saucepans, sugar bowls, etc. He was in Foster Lane, the same street as Goldsmiths' Hall stands. His Britannia and Sterling marks are of a similar design, with a cinquefoil and crown above his initials.[402]

JOHN JACOB
SILVERSMITH
p. 286
map p. 211/23

GEORGE GREENHILL JONES
SILVERSMITH
p. 287
map p. 211/3

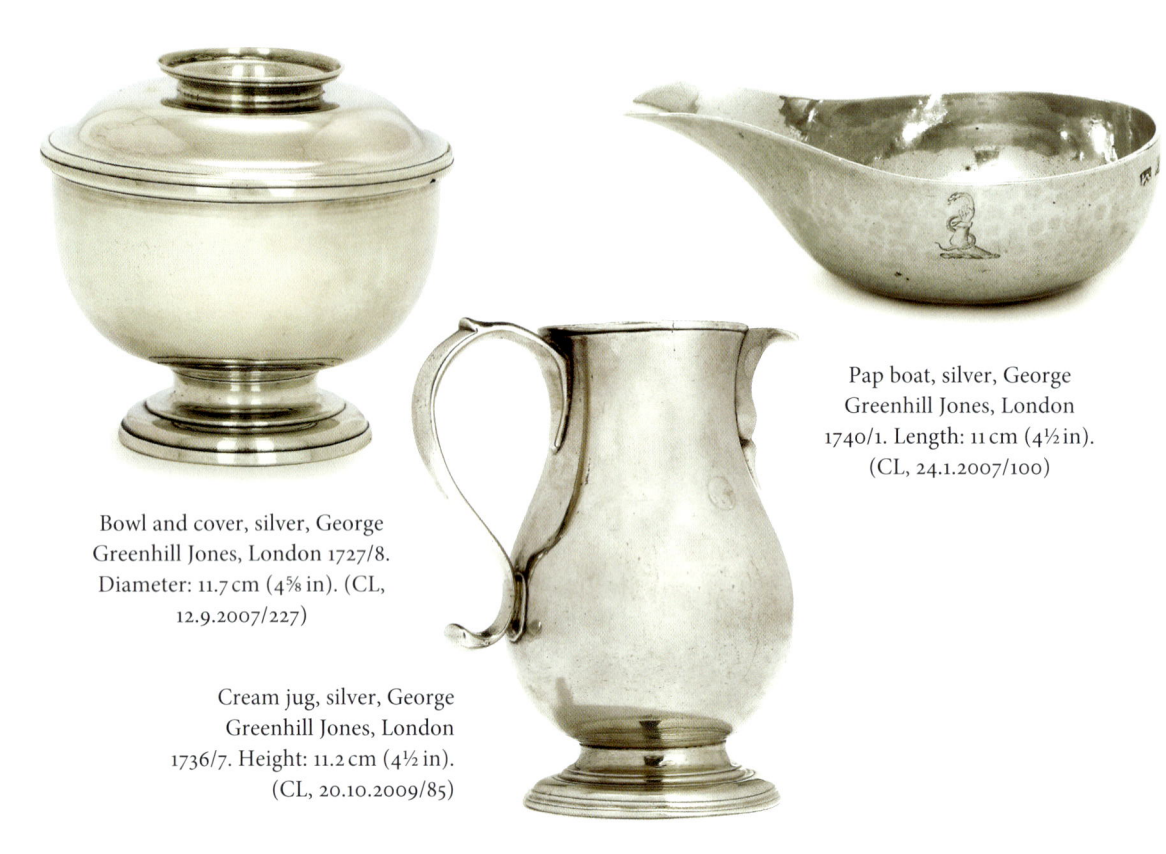

Bowl and cover, silver, George Greenhill Jones, London 1727/8. Diameter: 11.7 cm (4⅝ in). (CL, 12.9.2007/227)

Cream jug, silver, George Greenhill Jones, London 1736/7. Height: 11.2 cm (4½ in). (CL, 20.10.2009/85)

Pap boat, silver, George Greenhill Jones, London 1740/1. Length: 11 cm (4½ in). (CL, 24.1.2007/100)

JOHN LE ROUX
WATCHMAKER

The entries for JOHN LE ROUX (Leroux) in Bertrand's account between 1736 and 1747 suggest that he was a regular source of stock for the shop in Terrace Walk. The known watchmaker of this name (at 8 Charing Cross, Spring Gardens) is recorded from 1744, supplied the toyman George Willdey, and made a gold quarter-repeating watch (now in the British Museum) dating from 1777–8 with a case and chatelaine enamelled by William Hopkins Craft. His will was proved in 1817. Either there were two men of this name, or Leroux lived to be over one hundred, assuming he was not younger than twenty-one in 1736 — unless there was a delay in proving his will.[403] It is worth noting the watch casemaker, Abraham le Roux, of Dowgate Hill.[404]

Cylinder watch with dumb quarter-repeat and en-suite chatelaine, John Leroux, 1777–8. The inner case John Mason, the outer case and chatelaine Mary Reasey, decorated by William Hopkins Craft. Length overall 17.5 cm (6⅞ in). The entries for John Le Roux in Bertrand's bank account are for 1736–47, some thirty to forty years earlier than this watch. The neo-classical style of the case would have been unknown to Bertrand. (BM, 1979,0101)

Philip Margas jnr, a china man, was an important supplier for Bertrand: between 1737 and 1747 there are entries in the accounts totalling £556 12s 6d.

The business spanned two generations. Philip snr bought at East India sales in the 1720s and traded with Holland; the names of 'Margas & Co.', William Margas, and Charles Margas also feature regularly in those sale records.[405] Philip snr had a shop in Ludgate Hill at the sign of the Golden Head; he was a member of the Company of Glass Sellers and became free of the City in 1705.[406] Abraham Giles, son of the glass painter James Giles, was apprenticed to him in 1729.

Philip snr and his wife Anthoinette had a number of children: Charles and Philip were apprenticed to him in 1712 and 1718 respectively; both gained their freedom of the City in September 1733.[407] A third son, Solomon, went to Calcutta.

Early in 1735 the family entered a difficult period. In March 1734/35 the partnership between Philip snr and his sons Philip and Charles was dissolved.[408] Philip snr 'who formerly was a great Dealer in Tea and China Ware' died at Wandsworth the following September aged seventy.[409] In March 1736 bankruptcy proceedings began against Charles Margas 'China-man and Chapman' which continued until 1741, but he continued trading, as he receipted an invoice to the Earl of Dysart in April 1736 for: 1 Red tea pott 16s; 1lb Chocolat 5s; 6 Basons 4s 6d; 1 Punch Jar £3 3s 0d; another invoice, also to Lord Dysart, was receipted by Henry Pyefinch.[410] In June 1737 Charles's effects were sold at auction, but he recovered and afterwards acted as a broker, placing regular advertisements in newspapers promoting sales of china and a range of other wares throughout the 1740s and '50s, including the sale of the effects of the snuffbox maker Jacob Neale in 1743. One advertisement listed 800 tortoiseshell snuffboxes, 900 India fans and 6 cases of Italian artificial flowers.[411]

Meanwhile, Philip jnr moved to the Cheapside end of Bucklersbury 'near Stocks Market' which, when street numbering was introduced, became no. 32. He and his wife Catherine had at least two children; his son Solomon (1743–61) receipted an invoice to the Countess of Burlington in 1755, so must have started in the shop at a young age.[412] In February 1767 the Queen made an evening visit to the shop, now called an India Warehouse, when 'she drank tea; and after seeing the curiosities there, she returned through the City to her Palace'.[413] When Philip jnr died in June 1767 he was said to have kept his India Warehouse 'with great Credit and Reputation near forty years'; he also had a house in Waltham Cross, near Cheshunt, Hertfordshire. A clause in Philip's will specified, rather unusually, that the produce of his estate destined for

PHILIP MARGAS
CHINA MAN

p. 292
map p. 211/6

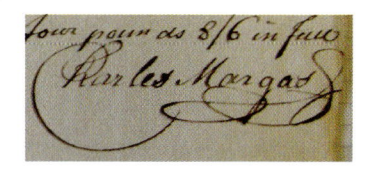

Signature of Charles Margas from an invoice to the Earl of Dysart, dated April 1736. For a total of £4 8s 6d Lord Dysart bought a red teapot, 1lb chocolate, 6 basins and a punch jar. (Tollemache)

p. 130

Invoice headed 'Bot of Philip Margas' and receipted by his son Solomon, dated 2 July 1755. (Chatsworth)

Invoice to the Earl of Dysart, receipted by Henry Pyefinch on behalf of Charles Margas, February 1721. (Tollemache)

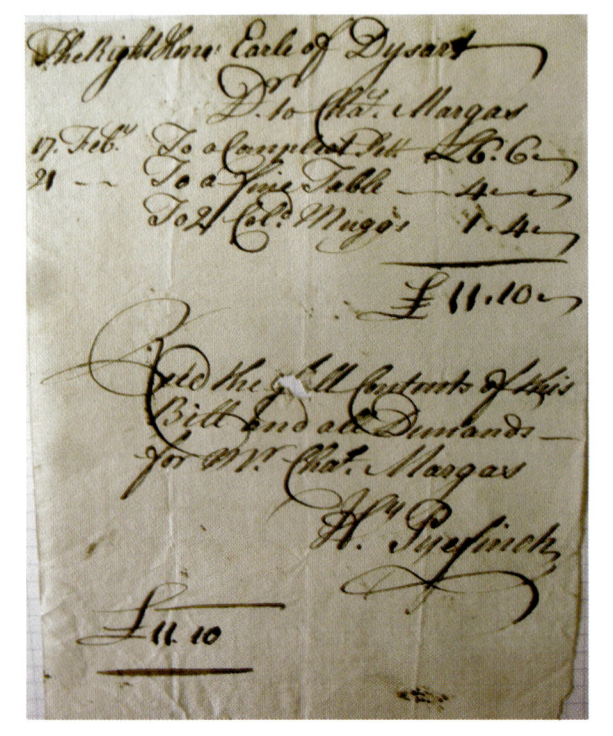

his daughter 'shall not be subject to the controul of her husband in case of her Marriage'; Elizabeth Catherine (b. 1741) married William Desse[r] in September 1767, three months after the death of her father.[414]

Philip's widow Catherine took over management of the shop, and following her death in early 1769 there were auctions in May and June that year of her household effects, fittings and stock. Notices of the sales give a fair indication of what the East India Warehouse sold:[415]

a large parcel of small sea shells, Italian flowers, useful and ornamental China, Muslins, Callicoes, and India Pictures, fine Japan in large and small Cabinets, Boxes, &c lacquered Ware in Chests, Dressing Boxes, Tea-boards, Waiters, &c with great Variety of curious India Goods in carved ivory and Mother of Pearl, Tortoishel, Rice Bronze, Copper &c … Fans, Fan Sticks, and Mounts.

Surviving invoices from the 1750s are further evidence of the wide range of stock held by the Margases, but not of what Paul Bertrand might have bought, as they are after his time. The Duke of Bedford bought handkerchiefs and India silk. Mr Clayton bought: an ice pail £1 5s; 1 sheet pink paper 1s; 1 doz mangoes 5s; a fan 6d; 2 bottle of Hungary water 5s. Between July and September 1755 the Countess of Burlington spent £19 11s on fine Hyson tea and plain green tea.[416]

The Margas family clearly had close business and family ties with the Pyefinch family. Herbert Pyefinch, married to Sarah Margas, was an executor of the wills of Philip and Catherine Margas. Elizabeth Pyefinch was trading at 30 Bucklersury (Margas was at no. 32) with the same sign of the Golden Fan in the 1790s.[417] Solomon Pyefinch 'son of Herbert Pyefinch of Calcutta' is mentioned in the will of another Elizabeth Margas (of Calcutta) signed in 1760. She was Elizabeth de Varenne, who married Solomon Margas 'senior merchant' in Calcutta in 1731. The London and Calcutta branches of the family kept in touch: Elizabeth bequeathed to Solomon Margas (who died the same year as she did, 1761) 'my seal set in Gold being the arms of the ffamily' and to his sister Elizabeth Catherine 'the picture of my brother in law Philip Margas which was lost at the Capture of Calcutta in 1756 ... should it be found and purchased'.[418]

No connection has been made between the Margases who were chinamen and Jacob and Samuel Margas, goldsmiths, but it is worth noting that John Margas (Jacob's son) and Henry Pyefinch were instrument makers and members of the Spectaclemakers' Company in the 1760s.[419]

I Elizabeth Margas of Calcutta in the Kingdom of Bengall, widow ... give to my Slave Girl Peggy her Liberty and all her Toys ...

Invoice from Philip Margas, dated January 1755. In addition to china, his stock included tea, pink paper, mangoes, Hungary water and a fan. (BM, Heal.68.196)

JOHN MULFORD
SILVERSMITH
p. 296
map p. 211/8

Three generations are listed under the name of JOHN MULFORD between 1716 and 1754.[420] When he insured his property in 1717 Mulford snr was in Cursitors Alley, Chancery Lane, described as a clockmaker (i.e. free of the Clockmakers' Company). The following year he moved 'over against the pd [paved] alley, Fish Street, Holborn.[421] The entries in Bertrand's bank account are for the years 1736–47; John Mulford jnr died in 1748. The workshop was clearly a major supplier to Bertrand's shop and Mulford's name also appears in Daniel Chenevix's bank account.

Judging by the relatively few items of silver bearing his mark that have survived today, John Mulford snr specialised in small items of silver such as boxes: objects that were typical of the stock of a toyshop. The mark he entered as a smallworker on 14 November 1718 'for gold' is of unusual design: it has only the initial of his surname beneath a crown. The usual form for this period would have been 'Mu'.

Two powder boxes, silver, John Mulford, c. 1720. Diameter: 4.3 cm (1¾ in). The similarity of the boxes shows the repetitive nature of a silversmith's trade in making what must have been a useful and relatively inexpensive product. (W&W; Cameron)

LEWIS PANTIN
SILVERSMITH
p. 299
map p. 211/24

There is only one debit entry for LEWIS PANTIN in Bertrand's account, for £17 8s on 9 March 1736/37. He is of interest to Bath because his mark is on the salver given by Frederick, Prince of Wales to the City of Bath following his visit in 1738. The salver bears London hallmarks for 1733/34 and would therefore have been one of the earliest pieces Pantin sent for assay: it must have been marked between 21 March (when he entered his mark) and 29 May 1734 (when the year mark changed). The salver would probably have been held in stock either by Pantin or the prince's goldsmith George Wickes until it was sent to Bath five years later. It seems most unlikely that Bertrand had anything to do with the prince's gift.

Pantin was one of the most interesting Huguenot silversmiths working in London during the rococo period; his family had arrived in England from Rouen in the middle of the seventeenth century. He worked from premises at the sign of the Peacock, in Castle Street, near Leicester Fields, where his father Simon had his workshop. After registering his mark he had only about fifteen years of production. Following his death Pantin's entire stock was auctioned in April 1749 by Ford, who interestingly coupled it with a sale of personal effects from Lord Lifford, who had clearly patronised toyshops:[422]

> The rich household furniture of the Rt Hon Frederick William Earl of Lifford dec'd ... a sideboard of plate, several gold repeating and other watches, a rich Gold cased Snuff Box with a Wateo in it and a variety of other snuff Boxes, Jewels and Curiosities ... To which is added The entire Stock of Plate of Mr Lewis Pantin, Goldsmith, Late of Leicester Fields, deceased. Consisting of chased Bread Baskets, Tea Kettles, Cups and Covers, Sauce-Boats, Tureens &c of his own curious Workmanship

One of Pantin's clients was the Jacobite Sir Watkin Williams Wynn, for whom he made some magnificently rococo candlesticks in 1734/35. Another pair of candlesticks dating from 1745/46 has stems in the form of hefty Solomonic columns.[423]

Nearly twenty years later his son, Lewis Pantin jnr, advertised himself variously as goldsmith, jeweller & toyman at the Crown and Scepters, corner of Mitre Court Fleet St; and in 1767 as toymaker and goldsmith, Crewet S, Mitre Court, Fleet St.[424]

Candlestick from a set of four, silver, Lewis Pantin, London 1734/5. Height: 26.6 cm (10½ in). Acquired by Sir Watkin Williams Wynn (1693–1749) of Wynnstay, Denbighshire. One of the wealthiest men of his day, Sir Watkin was a regular visitor to Bath, for example in December 1744, December 1746 and April 1747. (Wales)

Salver, silver-gilt, Lewis Pantin, London c. 1735. Diameter: 44.2 cm (17¼ in). The salver is very similar to the one (marked by Lewis Pantin, 1733/4) given by Frederick Prince of Wales to the Corporation of Bath. (SL, 28.2.1991/199) ▶ p. 152

EDWARD PARS
SNUFFBOX MAKER

p. 299
map p. 211/12

(ABOVE) Bougie box or taper holder, silver, Edward Pars, London c. 1760. (Cameron)

(BOTTOM LEFT) Nutmeg grater, silver, Evert Pars, c. 1760. (Beet)

(BOTTOM RIGHT) Tea caddy, silver, Evert Pars, c. 1760. (Cameron)

Members of the Pars family were box makers, chasers or wax modellers for at least two generations but it is hard to build a coherent story of the family from random pieces of information culled from newspapers and archives.

EVERT PARS — seemingly anglicised to Edward — was baptised in the Dutch province of Groningen in 1698. The four payments in Bertrand's account, in 1736 and 1738, appear to be the earliest known reference to him in England. It is unclear when he and other members of the family came to London, but an Albart Pars (possibly a brother born in Holland in 1702) was bankrupt in 1729 having been in the Strand.[425] He therefore might have worked with, or at any rate close to, Edward Pars, who was in Wych Street, just north-west of St Clement Danes church.

Brian Beet noted that from the evidence of surviving objects Edward Pars specialised in small plain boxes in silver rather than chased gold boxes: he was described as a silversmith when Peter Sherrett was apprenticed to him in 1755, and a snuffbox maker when he took Samuel Bellis as an apprentice in 1744. His first apprentice seems to have been Alexander Bellis in 1740.[426] In 1746 he valued (with Lewis Portal) the snuffboxes in the stock of the jeweller George Braithwaite.[427] The ties to the Bellis family remained close: Alexander Bellis witnessed Edward Pars' signature on his will (proved in 1768), in which Pars left his property to Sara Gatliffe, who was also his executor; he probably lived with her in Wych Street.[428]

JOSEPH (GIUSEPPE) PLURA worked in Bath for a short time; he is listed in Queen Street in 1754, very close to Bertrand's property there.[429] Having arrived in Bath around 1749, he moved to London in 1755 and died the following year.

JOSEPH PLURA
SCULPTOR
p. 302

Diana and Endymion, marble, Joseph Plura, 1752. Width: 54 cm (21¼ in). (Holburne)

HUMPHREY PUGH TOYMAN

p. 304
map p. 211/10

H. Pugh, goldsmith and toyman, 'makes and sells all sorts of Curiosities …',[430] but an entry in the Holkham archives for 1720 suggests that he may also have hired plate: 'Paid to mr Pugh for the use of sconces &c'. The toyman James Cox was apprenticed to him. The type of objects that Cox went on to produce — exotic mechanical toys and clocks — may be an indication of what Pugh's stock might have contained, as well as the everyday silver in the following advertisement:[431]

Burglariously broke open about One this morning the Shop Window of Mr Pugh, at the Corner of Spring Gardens, Charing Cross, and stole thereout, among other things, a silver chased Coffee-Pot, weight 17 oz 14 dwt, a silver bellied Pint Mug 1 oz 5 dwt, a Sauceboat, goodroon Edge, about 12 oz and one Orange Strainer 4 oz 4 dwt, two Pap spoons &c. ….

The address given here, in Spring Gardens, was some distance from Racquet Court, the address on his trade card.

Trade card of Humphrey Pugh, toyman. (BM, D,2.1697)

Trade card of Edward Scarlett, optician. (BM, Heal.105.88)

There is no way of knowing what kind of instruments Bertrand stocked. EDWARD SCARLETT was 'Optician to his Majesty King George the Second, at the Archimedes & Globe near St Ann's Church Soho': his trade card is headed 'The Old Spectacle Shop' and shows a range of goods that might also have been stocked by a toyshop such as magnifying glasses, and drawing and measuring instruments. In 1724 he was at the same sign in Macclesfield Street, Soho.[432]

An invoice to Henry Hoare, dated 3 November 1736 includes 'A 3 foot Mahogany Telescope £1 1s 0d'; another to the Duke of Gordon in 1737 has a camera obscura for 5 guineas.[433]

EDWARD SCARLETT
INSTRUMENT MAKER
p. 308
map p. 211/25

Very little of PETER RUSSEL's work is known to us today. The mark PR in script on the box illustrated is attributed to him — he may have registered it in the now missing register of smallworkers' marks (1739–58). The box is of superb quality and if it is typical of his work and he was a regular supplier to Bertrand, the shop in Bath must have been an extraordinary sight.

PETER RUSSEL
GOLD BOX MAKER
pp. 202–03, 306
map p. 210/6

SELECTED SUPPLIERS: PUGH–RUSSEL

Detail, ▶ p. 206

JAMES SHRUDER
SILVERSMITH
p. 309
map p. 211/26

Trade card of James Shruder, goldsmith and silversmith. (BM, Heal.67.363)

In his 2004 article on foreign gold box makers working in London, Brian Beet published the bare outline of Russel's life as then known, suggesting that Russel (1706–73) began his working life in London around 1740 in Villiers Street, off the Strand. This was the year that he married Hannah Hoare at the Chapel Royal, Whitehall.[434] However Russel features in Bertrand's bank account from 1736 and, as a freemason, Russel was at a lodge meeting near the Haymarket with his cousin Elias in 1730. He moved to Suffolk Street in 1748 (the year before his wife died), premises which were taken over by his cousin on Peter Russel's second marriage to Elizabeth Chenevix in 1750.

Although invoices from the Charing Cross shop are then headed 'Peter Russel at Chenevix's toyshop' it seems likely that Elizabeth Chenevix shared the work of running the shop with her new, and younger, husband. By 1763 retirement beckoned, and the following year the shop was let to Nathaniel Jeffery. Elizabeth Chenevix died in April 1765, after which Peter Russel returned to Suffolk Street, where he lived until his own death in 1773.

Paul Bertrand was buying from JAMES SHRUDER in 1738, the year in which Shruder's journeyman, George Foulkes, was caught after stealing 'about a hundred ounces of unwrought silver. He ... took it by Parcels of 8 or 10 Ounces at a Time, as Opportunity offer'd; but in one Week Mr Shruder lost 36 Ounces'.[435]

The fact that Bertrand was buying from Shruder, one of the most interesting silversmiths working at this time, and from other silversmiths noted for the individuality of their work such as Pantin, Hillan and John Jacob, is an indicator of Bertrand's taste. The cabinets of his shop must have displayed a riot of rococo ornament, tempered no doubt by the more sober output of other craftsmen.

Shruder entered a mark at Goldsmiths' Hall in 1737 with an address in Wardour Street, St Ann's Westminster; he moved to Greek Street, Soho and then to the Golden Ewer on the corner of Spur Street and Hedge Lane, just west of

Pair of tea caddies, silver, James Shruder, maker's mark only, *c.* 1740. Height: 12.7 cm (5 in). (SL, 31.10.1974/191)

Set of casters, silver, James Shruder, London 1737/8. Height: 19.7 cm (7¾ in) and 15.2 cm (6 in). (SL, 24.4.1969/203)

Leicester Fields (now Leicester Square). He was bankrupt in June 1749, but may be the 'Mr Shruder' mentioned in Poland Street in 1763.[436]

In 1746 there are four entries in Bertrand's account totalling £130 for THOMAS TURNER. Presumably these refer to the china man.[437] In March 1741 Turner had to move from the east side of St James's Street:[438]

THOMAS TURNER
CHINA MAN

p. 318
map p. 211/28

To be sold by Hand, This and the following Days ... All the entire Stock in Trade of Mr Thomas Turner, Dealer in China, at his House, opposite Park-Place in St James's Street; consisting of great Variety of rare old Japan, and all other useful and ornamental China, with great Services of Dishes and Plates, with a brown Edge; also a great Sortment of Desert-Glasses, and all other Glass; with Stone and Earthen Ware. The Counter, Shelves, and all Utensils, to be Sold, read fix'd up. The House being oblig'd to be clear'd by lady-Day, all the Furniture will likewise be Sold, and the lowest Price fix'd on each Article. The House to be lett.

SELECTED SUPPLIERS: RUSSEL–TURNER 241

Thomas Turner

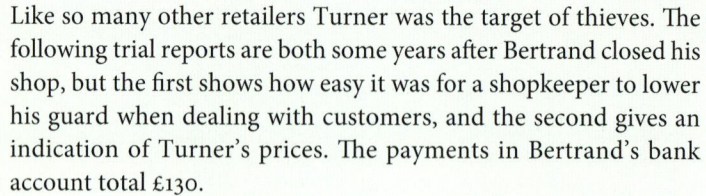

Like so many other retailers Turner was the target of thieves. The following trial reports are both some years after Bertrand closed his shop, but the first shows how easy it was for a shopkeeper to lower his guard when dealing with customers, and the second gives an indication of Turner's prices. The payments in Bertrand's bank account total £130.

1755: After returning from transportation to Maryland before his time, James Bignal committed various offences before[439]

His last attempt was upon Mr. Turner, who keeps a china-shop in St. James's-Street ... Bignal had heard that Mr. Turner generally kept a pretty deal of cash by him, and consequently he thought him a proper subject to exercise his dexterity on; accordingly ... he went to Mr. Turner's shop, under pretence of buying some china toys, and asked for a pair of little pug-dogs, as play-things for his children. Several were produced, none pleased him, except an odd one, which he fixt upon, and gave directions to have a pair made, exactly to that pattern; at the same time saying he would call for them another day. He then desired silver for a guinea; and afterwards begged the favour of Mr. Turner to look him out a king Charles's guinea in exchange for another. Mr. Turner, thoughtlessly turned all his money out of the bag upon the compter, whereby Bignal had the conveniency of tumbling over the whole, under colour of looking for such a guinea as he had asked for. It is not to be presumed our experienced sharper would let slip so fair an opportunity: he managed so dextrously, that he contrived to secrete eighteen guineas, and was marching off with them, when they were missed by Mr. Turner; who immediately went after him, and secured him just as he had got without-side the door. From hence Bignal was conveyed in safe custody to the worshipful John Fielding's house. In his way thither he offered Mr. Turner three guineas to release him, which that gentleman honestly refused.

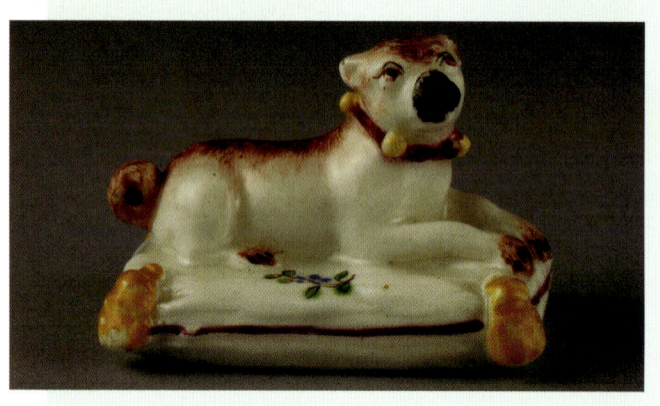

1762: John Davis was acquitted of stealing from Turner:[440] eighteen pieces of fine porcelain ware, called Chelsea china, made for nossels of candlesticks to represent a tulip, value 18s. two other pieces, called Dresden china, made for nossels of candlesticks, value 14s. four other pieces, called Chelsea china, to represent a white lilly, value 2s. two other pieces, called Chelsea china, to represent a rose-bud, value 12d. two other pieces, to represent narcissusses, value 12d. eight doz. of other pieces to represent orange-flowers, value 16s. and sundry other pieces.

Scent bottle in the form of a pug dog, porcelain, Charles Gouyn's factory, c. 1749–54. Height: 4.8 cm (1⅞ in). (V&A, 414:290/&A-1885)

Figure of a pug dog, soft paste porcelain painted with enamels, Bow factory, c. 1755. Height: 4.4 cm (1¾ in). Although made after Bertrand closed his shop, figures of this kind would have been stocked by Thomas Turner and by toyshops. (V&A, C.1323-1924)

He later advertised his shop as 'on the Terras in St James's Street' (i.e. the north-west end) and Horace Walpole, who was in Arlington Street, described him as 'at the corner of next street'. Never one to miss an opportunity, after the London earthquake of 1750 Turner[441] had a jar cracked by the shock: he originally asked ten guineas for the pair: he now asks twenty, 'because it is the only jar in Europe that has been cracked by an earthquake'.

The result of such salesmanship was that when his daughter Betty married a former high sheriff of Radnorshire in 1759, she brought to the marriage a fortune of £10,000.[442]

Turner is regularly mentioned in the account book of William Duesbury 1751–53.[443] Born in Staffordshire in 1725, Duesbury worked in London for about a decade before returning to the Midlands and acquiring an interest in the Derby factory. He went on to acquire the Chelsea and Bow factories, whose output would have been among the items he decorated during his time in London. He is the first 'outside enameller' to be recorded — decorating porcelain for numerous clients who had acquired items 'in the white'; he employed several assistants and also repaired china.

The episode of James Bignal perhaps suggests that Turner had a stock of undecorated pieces that could be enamelled to order. Duesbury's first recorded invoices to Turner are in March and April 1751 for decorating groups of birds and seasons; in September 1752 Duesbury charged 3s for enamelling a pair of large pheasants. The account book goes on to list rabbits, swans, Turkey candlesticks, doctors, marionettes and '12 Bow Seasons 18s.', giving a fair indication of what was in Turner's shop.

Christie's held a six-day sale of Turner's stock in July 1767, which was advertised as including 'some large Lots calculated to suit the trade'.

Vase and cover with chinoiserie decoration, porcelain, Bow, c. 1750–52. Height: 30 cm (11¾ in). (Spero)

Note: The three items illustrated show the type of objects Turner may have stocked; there is no direct connection.

SELECTED SUPPLIERS: TURNER 243

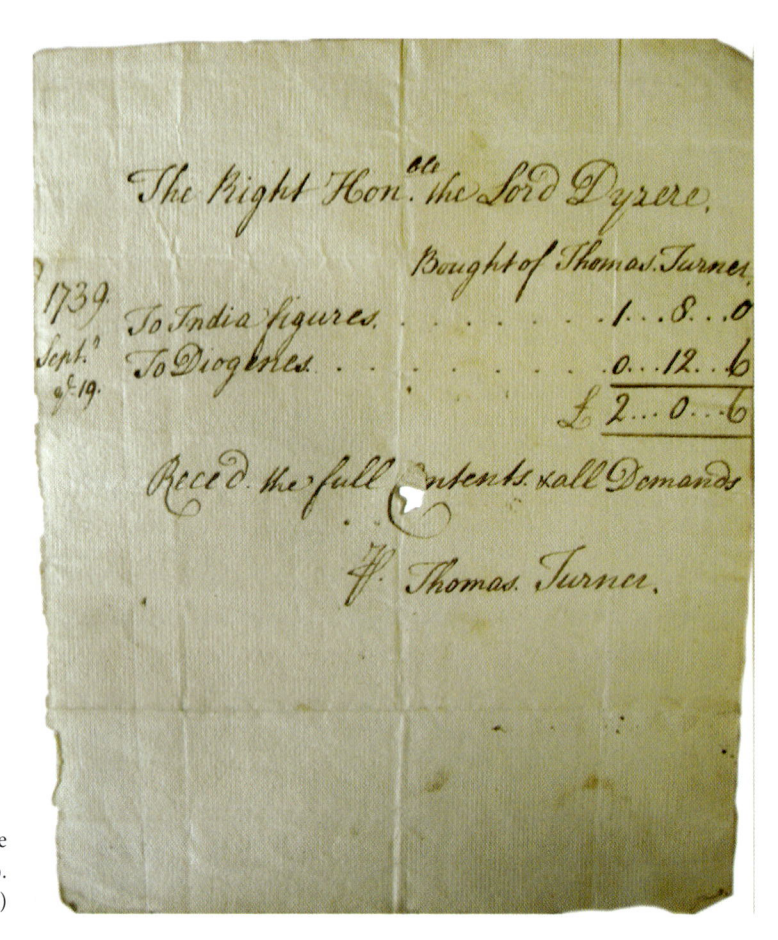

Invoice, Thomas Turner to the Earl of Dysart, 1739. (Tollemache)

THOMAS WRIGHT INSTRUMENT MAKER

p. 322
map p. 211/11

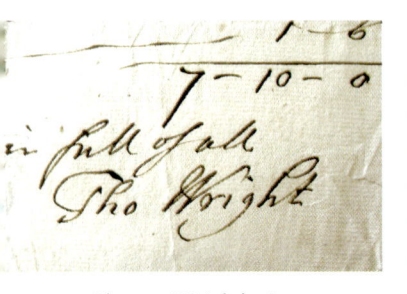

Thomas Wright's signature, from an invoice to the Earl of Dysart, 1735. (Tollemache)

Mathematical instrument maker and toyman (active 1718–47); THOMAS WRIGHT was instrument maker to George II, at the sign of the Orrery & Globe off Fleet Street. Free of the Broderers' Company in 1715, he was the son of a clockmaker. Wright took over the business of John Rowley, and subsequently employed Benjamin Cole, who succeeded him.[444]

There is one payment to Wright in Bertrand's bank account, in 1736, for the small amount of £4 4s 6d. This could represent payment for a pocket sundial (rather than an object like the larger dial illustrated here — William Deards sold a pocket dial in 1748 for £3 13s 6d) or for a set of instruments, a compass or callipers — all of which were typically sold in a toyshop. The figure is close to the £4 16s 6d Lord Fitzwalter paid for a case of mathematical instruments in 1737. In 1734 Lord Dysart bought a pair of globes in mahogany frames from Wright for 8 guineas, and in May 1735 a 'large silver case of mathematical instruments etc' for £21. There is a waywiser by Wright at Longleat.[445]

244 PART FOUR: PAUL BERTRAND'S BANK ACCOUNT

Portrait of Thomas Wright, mezzotint engraving, Thomas Frye, dated 1737. (BM, 1902,1011.2217)

Mechanical equinoctial dial, brass and silvered brass, Thomas Wright, signed, *c.* 1735. Width: 25.5 cm (10 in sq.). (Chatsworth)

SELECTED SUPPLIERS: TURNER–WRIGHT   245

Names from Bertrand's bank account in the Ledgers of Hoare & Co.

A

ADAIR, WM
1745–46: CR £41; £59 6s 1d; £49 10s 2d; £6 7s 4d; £121 19s; £17 1s; £20

Agent, Pall Mall, London.[1] A hint of his activities is given in a notice offering a reward of one guinea per man when twenty-three men deserted from Col. John Cottrell's regiment of Marines in July 1745, mainly men from the west country.[2] Adair was a regimental agent: he acted for about nine regiments, one of them being the Duke of Richmond's. He retired in 1765 and died in 1783, when his lavish funeral cost £195.[3]

Adair had an illegitimate daughter, Jane, who married Edward Brice; his closest male relatives were Alexander and James Adair. When Mary Bertrand was living in Ealing, Adair had recently inherited General Huske's house there; he had bought Flixton Hall, Suffolk, in 1753.[4] His account with the silversmith George Wickes (from 1735) was continued with Wickes's successors, Parker & Wakelin[5] by James Adair. In 1775 the twins Robert and Daniel Perreau were hanged for deception and forgery against him.[6]

1. Kent 1740. 2. *BJ*, 19 August 1745. 3. Lowestoft RO: HA12/A3/1. 4. Ealing rate book; *VCH*, Middlesex vol. VII. 5. Clifford. 6. POB: t17750531–1 & –2; Andrew & McGowen.

AINSLIE, WM
1739: CR £25
1741–46: DR £77 12s 9d; £33; £52 10s

William Ainslie lived at 9 The Circus, Bath. He developed a street named Ainslie's Belvedere, laid out *c.* 1760.[1]

1. Forsyth.

ALCROFT & CO.
1743: CR: £30

ALEX, GIL:
1740: CR: £21

ALINGTON, MAR:
1737: CR £100

Marmaduke Alington (1671–1749) was family lawyer to the Drake family of Shardeloes, with chambers in Lincoln's Inn; MP for Amersham 1728.[1] His name appears on the debit side of Isabella Drake's account with Hoare in 1737. He also features in the account book of Lord Wallingford.[2]

1. Sedgwick; Sun Ins, vol. 9 fo. 95. 2. Hants RO: 1M44/2.

ALLEN, ANTO
1745: CR £20

Possibly a barrister of Middle Temple, d. 1754, of Much Hadham Herts.[1]

1. Venn.

ALLEN, JOS
1747: DR £15; £20

Joseph Allen's trade card reads[1]

> Joseph Allen at the Hand & Snuff Box in Golden Lane near Cripplegate London. Makes all Sorts of Snuff Boxes in Gold, Silver and Metal Gilt, Likewise Ennamelling & Japanning of all kinds.

Notices of his bankruptcy were in the *London Gazette* from 21 April 1752[2] when he is described as 'of Twisters Alley, in the Parish of St Luke, snuff-box maker, lapidary and gilder', but he was in business two years later. He had been apprenticed to Edward Lees 1737;[3] and featured in the trial of Samuel Drybutter in 1757 when a witness said that he 'works for a great many of the trade'.[4]

▶ p.211/7 map.

1. BM: Banks 67.3. 2. (nos. 9160, 9175, 9360). 3. GH: Apprentice Book. 4. Culme 2000.

ALLEN, PHILIP
1743 & 1746: DR £100; £100; £110; £20

A year younger than his brother Ralph (below), Philip Allen became his assistant and closest associate in the postal business. In 1748 he became a governor of the Mineral Water Hospital; in 1752 he was the representative in Bath of the Sun Fire Office.[1] His address is given either as Ralph Allen's town house or The Old Post House, Abbey Green.[2] Allen died in 1765 and is buried with his wife, Jane Bennet, in Bathampton church.

Monument: Bathampton.

1. Young; Boyce; E-Hill, p. 232; Holland. 2. *BJ*, May 1745.

ALLEN, RA
1745: DR £103; £100

One of the three men generally accepted as being the 'creators' of Bath (the others being Richard Nash and John Wood – below).

▶ p. 72.

ALLEN, WM
1742: 1 DR £20

Uncertain identity. Probably the toyman of Bath who was plaintiff in a 1744 action.[1] In March 1745 (when she was in Bath) William Allen charged Lady Jernegan 12s for two dozen bottles of Holt water; he also sold her Alkerton water. He is one of several listed in an advertisement as stocking Duffy's Elixir, when his trade is not mentioned.[2] However in London there was a smallworker of this name who entered a mark in 1724;[3] also a snuffbox maker 'formerly of Featherstone Street, St Luke's' was bankrupt 1755;[4] a watchmaker is listed in Bond Street, 1749;[5] a bucklemaker (possibly the next generation) in Little Bartholomew Close in 1773.[6]

1. TNA: C11/1596/3. 2. Stafford RO: D641/3/P/1/3/6; *BJ*, 7 May 1744. 3. Grimwade. 4. *London Gazette*, 28 June 1755 [9489]. 5. 1749 poll. 6. 1773 Report.

ANDREW & CO.
1741: CR £30

ANDREWS, MR
1745: CR £116 13s 3d

Uncertain identity. The entry could possibly be for Joseph Andrews, listed in the Paymaster General's office[1] or Edward Andrews, governor of the Mineral Water Hospital 1748. A third guess might be a member of the Prince of Wales's Treasury.[2]

1. Chamberlayne, Pt II Bk III, p. 100. 2. *Daily Journal*, 10 December 1734 [4339].

ANNESLEY, MRS
1737: CR £12

Possibly a connection of the Earls of Anglesey, a family in which illegitimacy, dubious marriages, a failed lawsuit and impoverishment cause considerable confusion. Francis Annesley (1663–1750), lawyer to the Earl of Egremont and MP for Westbury 1708–15 and 1722–34, married as his third wife on 31 August 1737 Sarah Sloane, niece of Sir Hans Sloane; the ledger entry is for 11 August. Annesley succeeded to the personal and un-entailed estates of his second cousin once removed, the 5th Earl of Anglesey, in the same year. Following the death of the 5th Earl, the title passed (many suspected wrongly) to another cousin Richard Annesley, 5th Baron Altham. The latter's nephew James had a better claim to the title but his paternity was questioned and Richard Annesley had sent James as a slave to America. James escaped to England in the care of Lord Anson in 1740; Richard Nash raised a subscription for him in 1756. Goldsmith described James Annesley as 'that strange example of the mutability of fortune, and the inefficacy of our Laws'.

APPREECE, SARAH
1739: CR £50

Wife of Robert Appreece, who was a Gentleman of the Privy Chamber;[1] they both banked with Hoare. In 1721 their London address was Dean St, Westminster.[2] Their daughter Rhoda married in 1724 Francis Delaval (1692–1752) who the year before had inherited Seaton Delaval, built by Vanbrugh at an estimated cost of £10,000.[3] Delaval died unexpectedly after breaking a leg.

1. Chamberlayne, Pt II Bk III, p. 708. 2. Sun Ins, vol. 13, fo. 199. 3. Sedgwick.

ARBUTHNOT, ANN
1740: CR £30

Possibly connected to John Arbuthnot (1667–1735), physician, friend of Swift and Pope. His wife was possibly called Margaret;[1] he had a sister whose name has proved elusive. Alexander Pope wrote 'An epistle to Dr Arburthnot' in 1735. A Mrs Arbuthnot is listed in 1766–67 in Cross Bath, next to Ann Cleveland.[2]

1. *DNB*. 2. Bath RO: Rate Books 1 & 4.

ARCHER, ANN & SARAH
1745–46: CR £92; £40; £30

ARDONIN, MICHAEL
1745: CR £25

ARMSTRONG, DANL
1742: CR £40

A Daniel Armstrong matriculated Cambridge 1715.[1]

1. Venn.

ARNOLD, CHR
1743: CR £20

Christopher Arnold began work at Hoare's Bank in 1707 and became a partner in 1725 – uniquely as a non-family member; he died in 1758.[1] There was a governor of Bath's Mineral Water Hospital of this name in 1748.

1. Hutchings.

ARNOLD, GEO & CO.
1742–46: CR: £20; £40; £60; £196

George Arnold (1685–1751) was a linen draper and an alderman of the City of London; a member of the Haberdashers' Company. His signature appears on papers relating to the dukes of Beaufort and Montagu. Arnold was also one of the original five partners in the Bow porcelain factory, founded in 1747.[1]

John Sargent (1714–91), whose mother Mary was Arnold's cousin, was apprenticed to him, became his junior partner and continued the firm. It traded with India and Africa and provisioned Bance Island (Sierra Leone); and became known as Sargent Birch & Co., then Sargent Aufrere & Co.[2] In 1749 John Sargent married Rosamund Chambers; her brother Ephraim published a dictionary in 1728.

Portraits: William Hogarth: George Arnold (Fitzwilliam Museum). Allan Ramsay: John and Rosamond Sargent (Holburne Museum) and by William Hoare.

1. Adams & Redstone. 2. Kent 1740 and *DNB*.

ARTHAND, MR
1736: DR £25 18s

No name with this spelling has been found, but lateral thinking could lead to Stephen Artaud, whose son William (1763–1823) was a portrait and history painter.[1] In the will of Jane Lombard (d. 1790) Stephen Artaud snr of Little Russell Street, jeweller, was bequeathed her interest and shares in Covent Garden Theatre.[2]

1. *DNB*. 2. Wagner.

ASHWORTH, A.S.
1745: CR £1 1s

ASTLEY, SR JNO
1738: CR £20

Sir John Astley, 2nd and last Bt (1687–1771), of Patshull, Co. Stafford and Everley, Wilts, MP for Shrewsbury, a Tory and Jacobite; his only son predeceased him. Of his six daughters Alicia married Charles, 3rd Earl of Tankerville in 1742.[1] The ledgers of the silversmith George Wickes list Sir John Ashley 1736–43; he was also a customer of Paul de Lamerie.[2]

1. GEC, XII p. 634. Burke, *Dormant & Extinct Baronetcies*; Sedgwick. 2. Wickes; de Lamerie salver, arms of Astley impaling Prynce, London 1724–5; Ingamells, p. 32.

ATKINS & CO.
1738–40: CR £30; £50; £50; £50; £60; £21

ATKINS, HONYWOOD & FULLER
1739: CR £25

Atkins, Honeywood & Fuller, Lombard St, London, 1738.[1]

▶ p. 283 Honeywood.

1. H-Price.

ATKINSON, HEN
1736: CR £20

Possibly of Leeds, matriculated Oxford 1715 aged 17.[1]

1. Foster.

ATWOOD, HEN
1746: DR £30

The Atwood family played a prominent part in the civic life of Bath; they were largely in the building trade and bankers. Henry Atwood's portrait is one of eight surviving of Bath council members. He supported General Wade in his election as MP in 1728 and was a councillor also at the 1734 parliamentary election. Thomas Atwood insured property in 1718/19.[1]

Portrait: Johann van Diest, Bath Guildhall.

1. Sun Ins, vol. 9, fo. 41 [13057].

AUMONIER / AMMOONIER, PR/ AUMONDER
1736–40: DR £54; £24; £42; £25; £47; £18 9s

Peter Aumonier is listed as a smallworker, 'Ryders Courte By Lester filds' – his mark, AV oblong, was entered 2 December 1726;[1] of St Anne's Westminster, in 1727.[2] Probably born at Canterbury in 1687,[3] his will was proved January 1754.[4]

1. Grimwade p. 281. 2. Heal LG p. 98. 3. Evans. 4. Wagner.

B

BACON, JAMES
1744: CR £40
1745: DR £30

Uncertain identity. Possibly of the Norfolk family, or perhaps a connection of John Bacon, who made models for the sculptor John Cheere.

BADDELEY, W.
1752: DR £50

Uncertain identity. Possibly a connection of the actor Robert Baddeley, painted by Zoffany.

BAIRD, JAMES
1740: CR £50; £100
1742: DR £30

Uncertain identity: the debit and credit entries could relate to two different people. A John Baird, jeweller and watchmaker, 190 Strand, listed in 1779, is surely too late.[1] Alternatively he might be connected to Sir James Baird, in the Wig Club in 1775.

1. Heal LG.

BAKER, MR
1736: CR £20

BAKER, MRS
1747: CR £105

Uncertain identity. The entries could refer to Philip or William Baker (below) or someone quite different, for example Hercules Baker (1683–1744), MP for Hythe and treasurer of Greenwich Hospital from 1736 to his death.[1]

1. Sedgwick.

BAKER, PHILIP
1739–46: DR £173; £200; £223 3s 6d; £500; £400

Uncertain identity. Given the large payments to Jesser and Neale [▶ pp. 286 and 296], and the size of these payments to Baker, this might be Philip Baker of Bridgwater, who featured in the notice of bankruptcy of Richard Baker, a clothier of Chard, Somerset.[1] Alternatively these entries might refer to a first Clerk in the War Office: see the notice from the *London Gazette* quoted for Henry Pople [▶ p. 302],[2] but he resigned on account of ill health in 1743.

A third option is that he could have been connected to Francis Baker, goldsmith, behind the Royal Exchange in London in 1732, perhaps the same as a silversmith at the Acorn, near the Monument.[3]

1. *London Gazette*, 4 August 1741 [8038]. 2. *London Gazette* [8040 and 8301]; Chamberlayne, Pt II Bk III, p. 100. 3. H-Price; Heal LG.

BAKER, WM
1743–47: CR £50; £50; £100

Sir William Baker, MP and London merchant (1705–70), married in 1742 Mary Tonson. He is described as 'one of the foremost merchants trading with

America, his interests extending over the whole length of the seaboard';[1] connected with the East India Company and the Hudson's Bay Company. He was a partner with Nicholas Linwood [▶ p. 290], and Bryce Fisher (who came from the west country, below) in 'the Hobcaw Barony' in South Carolina.[2] Listed as alderman and merchant, Basinghall-street,[3] the centre of business for Blackwellhall factors (agents in the wool and cloth trade).

Monument: Bath Abbey, by J. F. Moore.

1. Sedgwick. 2. Namier. 3. Kent 1740.

BALDWYN, BS
1739: CR: £20

BALE, CHAS
1741: CR £10 10s; £18 18s

BANCE, JNO & CO.
1744: CR £25

John Bance, bank director & merchant, King's Arms-yard, Coleman Street.[1] A Member of Parliament, he was elected for Westbury 1734–41 and again in 1747; he died in 1755. Bance was a merchant, 'trading to Hamburg … his will shows him to have been a man of considerable wealth'.[2] He was a customer of the silversmith George Wickes in 1738 and 1742.[3]

1. Kent 1740. 2. Sedgwick. 3. Wickes.

BANK SOLA
1744–47: CR £500; £100; £30; £40

BANKS, WM
1744–46: CR £15 10s; £30; £30

Uncertain identity. William Hoare painted Lettice-Mary and Collingwood Banks, William's siblings, in the 1740s (Holburne Museum). Their father was Joseph Banks of Revesby Abbey, who was High Sheriff of Lincs in 1736. William (1719–61) was MP for Grampound 1741–47 but in 1745 'contracted a fever which deprived him of the use of his lower limbs'.[1] He was the father of the famous botanist Joseph Banks (1743–1820). These are credit entries, so it is less likely to be the man who published mezzotints in the 1730s and '40s.

1. Sedgwick.

BARBER, CONSTA
1736: DR £10 10s

Presumably the first name is Constance. The date ties in with a letter from Mrs Delany of 17 August 1736 about Bath's assembly rooms [▶ p. 104]. Alternatively, there was a goldsmith named Barber at the Turk's Head, Lombard St, 1744.[1]

1. Heal LG.

BARBER, JNO
1741: CR £30

Uncertain identity. Possibly John Barber (1675–1741), printer and local politician, friend of Swift and Viscount Bolingbroke.[1] John Barber, alderman and Lord Mayor of London, Queen's Square, Ormond Street.[2]

There is much talk of Alderman Barber's elegant Entertainment last Tuesday at Merchant Taylors Hall where was a Ball led up by the Dutchess of Richmond.
8 April 1730.

1. *DNB*. 2. Kent 1740; Ingamells, p. 48.

BARBOT, JNO
1736–46: DR £33; £30; £23 14s; £25; £220; £63; £63 17s; £41

London silversmith.

▶ p. 214.

BARCLAY, DAVID SNR
1742: CR £130

BARKLEY, JNO
1744–45: CR £25; £20; £50; £21

David Barclay (1682–1769) apprenticed to John Perry 'linen draper of Cheapside at the White Bear'. A Quaker merchant, when David Barclay retired his firm was described as 'the first house in their business', trading German and other linens to New York, Pennsylvania and the West Indies; he was reputedly worth over £100,000 at his death. The business is listed in Cateaton Street. David Barclay was closely linked to the Freame family ▶ p. 275: his second wife was Priscilla Freame, daughter of the Quaker banker John Freame, and his son by his first marriage, James, married in 1733 Sally Freame (sister of Priscilla and his step-aunt).[1] David Barclay had a brother, John, in Dublin, through whom he dealt in Scottish and Irish linens.

1. *DNB*; Kent 1740.

BARHAM, HENRY
1742: DR £262 10s

Possibly a connection of Joseph and Nathaniel Barham, apprenticed in 1718 and 1731.[1] It is a large payment.

1. GH: Apprentice Book.

BARKER, JOS
1736–47: DR £19 10s; £46 10s; £22; £28 12s 6d; £14; £72; £35; £40; £100; £100; £100; £42; £44 14s; £20; £25 11s

London silversmith and merchant who had close connections to the Deards and Hoare families.

▶ pp. 37, 202–03.

BARKER, THOS
1743: CR £30 5s 6d

BARKER & CO.
1740: CR £12

BARLOW, SAML
1744: CR £20

Uncertain identity. An apothecary of this name is listed in Bucklersbury, London.[1] Or, possibly a member of the Barlow family of Pembrokeshire, five members of which were in

Parliament, but none named Samuel.[2]

1. Kent 1740. 2. Sedgwick.

BARNEVELT, ROBT
1742–44: CR £40; £50

A woollen draper, from a large family, Barnevelt features in the account of the silversmith John Curghey with Hoare, also as Ireland & Barnevelt, around 1736–40.[1] Possibly connected with Charles Barnevelt, a freemason, listed with Paul Bertrand at Charing Cross Lodge, London, in 1723.[2] An invoice from his brother Philip for items such as 'sup. Fine black cloth' is dated May 1730.[3]

▶ p. 285 Wm Ireland.

1. Lr. 35 fo.137. 2. Wagner; Songhurst. 3. Hoare: Boxes of Receipts 1730–31.

BARRETT, JOS
1736: CR £35

There was a London goldsmith, Joseph Barrett, at the Three Kings & Spotted Dog, near Old Change, Cheapside (d. 1744),[1] to whom Edward Harrison was apprenticed in 1713.[2] An invoice survives from Jsa Barrett to the Countess of Burlington, dated 1755, for wax lights.[3] Both 'Jos' and 'Jsa' could be abbreviations of Josiah, but this is a credit entry in Bertrand's account and so may not represent a tradesman. Mary Deards mentions in her will (September 1738) 'My sister Barret', but no evidence has been found so far to make any connection.

1. Heal LG, p.102; Kent 1740. 2. Free 1720, GH: Apprentice Book. 3. Chatsworth.

BARRINGTON, JNO
1738: CR £100

Uncertain identity: there seems to be three possibilities, but given the lack of a title in the ledger entry, John Shales Barrington seems the most likely. 'Lady Barrington' visited Bath in March 1745/46.

1. John Shute Barrington, general and colonel of the 8th Regiment of Foot (1719–64), son of 1st Viscount Barrington (who was born John Shute and took the name of Barrington in 1716 (1678–1734).[1]

2. John Shales Barrington, a son of Charles Shales and his wife Anne, sister of Sir Charles Barrington, 5th Bt of Barrington Hall, who inherited her brother's estates in 1717; her sons took the name of Barrington in 1729. There survives a group of silver bearing his finely engraved arms (including two salvers Thomas Farren and Robert Abercromby 1733/4 and a cake basket Thomas Farren 1737/8.[2] John Barrington Esq is listed in Maddox Street, London.[3]

3. Sir John Barrington, 7th Bt (1707–76) MP for Newtown, IoW.[1]

▶ pp. 260, 309 Clarges and Skrine.

1. Sedgwick. 2. Brett 1986, nos 739, 868. 3. 1749 poll.

BATEMAN, JNO LONG
1738: CR £50; £50

The name appears in the account of David Williams with Hoare in 1731.[1]

1. Lr. 33.

BATH, COUNTESS OF
1743: DR £232 3s 6d; £75 15s 8d

Anna Maria Gumley (d. 1758) was described by Lord Hervey as of 'low birth, lower mind, and the lowest manners' and by Sir C. H. Williams as 'Bath's ennobled doxy'.[1] On 27 December 1714 she married William Pulteney (1684–1764) who was created Earl of Bath in 1742. He was Privy Councillor and Cofferer of the Household 1723–25, an opponent of Walpole. A regular visitor to the city he is listed, for example, as arriving on 4 November 1751. The eventual heir to his estates was a cousin, Frances, whose husband afterwards took the name of Sir William Pulteney; their daughter Henrietta Laura was created Countess of Bath in 1803.

1. GEC.

BATHURST, BEN
1745: DR £100

The Hon. Benjamin Bathurst (1693–1767) of Lydney, Glos, Treasurer of Bath's Mineral Water Hospital. The ledger entry, as a debit, might relate to the hospital. He was MP successively for Cirencester, Gloucester and Monmouth. His elder brother, Allen (1684–1775) was one of twelve peers created in five days in 1711/12 (when he was MP for Cirencester) in order to secure a Tory majority; his barony was advanced to an earldom in 1772. No doubt a regular visitor to Bath, Mr Bathurst's arrival is listed 7 January 1744/45.[1] His London house in 1734 was in Conduit Street. Ingamells[2] quotes a letter from him to Burrell Massingberd [▶ p. 293]. By his first wife (m. 1714, d. 1738) he had twenty-two children, and by his second wife (m. 1741) a further fourteen.[3]

1. BJ. 2. Ingamells, p. 60. 3. Sedgwick. Delany, vol.1, p. 465.

BAUGH, ISAAC
1745: DR £50

Baugh was an alderman of Bristol Corporation,[1] and possibly a relation of Edmund Baugh, a Bristol merchant.

1. Bristol 1755.

BAYS, AMOR
1741: DR £20; £20

BEACH, THOS
1744: CR £180

Possibly Thomas Beach of Fittleton, Wilts, who died 1753.[1] Monuments: Steeple Ashton, Wilts.

1. Burke, LG 1850.

BEAUFORT, DUKE OF
1737: CR £50

Henry, 3rd Duke of Beaufort (1707–45) of Badminton House, Glos; a frequent visitor to Bath, he died in the city (having arrived there on 31 December) 'about 5 o'clock in the afternoon' on 24 February 1744/45 and was succeeded as 4th Duke by his brother, Lord Noel Somerset [▶ p. 310]. For his collecting on the Grand Tour see Ingamells.[1] The duke was divorced from his wife Frances Scudamore (who he had married in 1729) in 1743/44.

Portrait: William Hoare, drawing (NPG).

   1. Ingamells, p. 67.

BEEN, DIA
1747: DR £25

Uncertain identity. In London, Daniel Bean, brushmaker, was in Russell Court, London.[1] Or, there might be a link with William Been, chinaman in Panton Street 1758, who sold Chelsea wares.[2] A notice in the *Bath Journal* suggests that 'Mr Been' was a shopkeeper, but does not state his trade.[3]

   1. 1749 poll. 2. Hildyard and 1749 poll. 3. *BJ*, 30 November 1747.

BELK, MICHAEL
1746–47: DR £7 8s 3d; £12; £18 9s; £20 10s; £11

Listed in Broad Street, Bath, in 1731.[1] 'Mrs Belk, Quiet Street, nr Queen Sq, Bath' sold Bristol Toothwater, but the advertisement does not state what kind of shop she kept.[2]

   1. Bath RO: 1776 Schedule of Deeds, p. 213. 2. *BJ*, 17 August 1747.

BELLIS, J
1746: DR £18

London silversmith.

▶ p. 214.

BELLWOOD, MR
1746: CR £60

BENDEN, AUM
1741: CR £10 10s

BENNETT, FRAS
1746: DR £50

BENNETT, MESS
1741: DR £4 6s

▶ p. 174.

BERNARDEAU, JAMES
1736–41: DR £50; £20; £50; £22 18s

London cutler and razor maker.

▶ p. 215.

BERTRAND, MARY
1739: DR £47 11s

The wife of Paul Bertrand, daughter of John Deards snr.

BETHELL, SARAH
1738–47: CR £33; £30; £50; £60; £50; £50

Sarah Bethel was the second wife of Hugh Bethel of Yorks, who died in 1716.[1] Their son Hugh married Anne Cope, who was distantly related to both Sir John Cope and Mary Cope [▶ p. 264]. Anne was possibly the Mrs Bethell living in Queen Square in 1766–67,[2] where her neighbours were Lady Trevor and Lady Cope [▶ p. 317]. Between 1747 and 1751 Hugh Bethel owned Ealing House, just outside London.[3] In 1739 Mrs Bridget Bethell and Mrs Price Bethell contributed £100 and £50 respectively to the Mineral Water Hospital in Bath.[4]

Property: Hot water jug, silver, Jacob Margas *c.* 1710–15, arms of Bethell.

   1. Burke, *Commoners*, vol. 1, p. 452. 2. Bath RO: Rate Book. 3. *VCH* Middlesex vol. VII. 4. *Daily Gazeteer*, 3 February 1739 [1130]; no family link has been found.

BIGGS, ANTO
1745: DR £150; £100; £100

Anthony Biggs had a 99-year lease for 'a piece of ground whereon a stable is built on the east side of the Saw Close or timber yard' from Lady Day 1720.[1] Of the numerous Biggs family, Richard and William Biggs, stonemasons, worked with Ralph Allen on the stone for St Bartholomew's Hospital.[2]

   1. Bath RO: 1776 Schedule of Deeds p. 181. 2. Allen, p. 43.

BINDON, ANN
1742: CR £10 10s

BIRT, SAML
1745: CR: £20

Samuel Birt, printer, publisher and bookseller at the Bible and Ball, Ave Maria Lane, London. His name regularly appears on the title pages of books published in the 1730s and '40s, one example being the poems of Stephen Duck.

BISHOP, SAMPSON
1736–46: DR (3 to 'Mr Bishop') £50; £27 19s; £40; £21; £36 15s; £54; £50; £20; £100; £25; £63

London jeweller

▶ p. 217.

BISHOP, SAMUEL
1739–44: DR £50; £50; £50; £75

London jeweller

▶ p. 217.

BLACKETT, W
1739: CR £42

There are two possible candidates: Walter and William Blackett, second cousins whose grandfathers (who were of course brothers) had different baronetcies.

The most likely candidate is Walter Blackett of Calverley, Yorks and Wallington Hall, Northumberland (1707–77), MP for Newcastle upon Tyne 1734–77.[1] He was a governor of the Mineral Water Hospital in 1748. His uncle William left his fortune to his illegitimate daughter on condition she married his nephew Walter within twelve months of his death – which she did. Sir Walter's grandmother married secondly Sir William Thompson [▶ p. 316]. The ledger entries suggest that they might have been in Bath at the same time. Blackett's entry in the ledgers is for January 1739/40, three month's after Thompson's death in October 1739.

It is possible, however, that the entry might be for William Blackett.

Property: Wallington Hall (National Trust).
Portrait: William Hoare, pastel, (Jeffares p. 239)

1. Sedgwick.

BLACKHEAD
1743: CR £30

BLAIR, WM
1739: CR £19 10s

Possibly the man listed as private secretary to Lord Harrington, Secretary of State for the Northern Province, and as a commissioner for Stamp Duties (at £400 p.a.).[1]

1. Chamberlayne, Bk III, Pt II, pp. 47 & 91.

BLAKE, FRAS
1740: CR £10

Francis Blake of Twisel Castle, Northumberland; went to Oxford in 1725 aged 16, created Bt 1774, d. 1780 of 'the gout in his stomach'.[1]

1. Foster; *Gazette & New Daily Advertiser*, 5 April 1780.

BLAND, LADY
1743–44: CR £100 [see Boroden]; £103 11s

Lady Frances Finch, daughter of Heneage Finch, 1st Earl of Aylesford, married in 1716 Sir John Bland, 5th Bt (1691–1743), he died in Bath. Sir John was MP for Lancashire 1713–27 and in 1715 (the year he inherited the baronetcy) was committed to custody on suspicion of high treason. By this marriage Bland acquired 'vast Lancashire estates including "the whole of Manchester and its environs"'[1] which did not stay in the family for long thereafter. In 1737 the balance of Sir John's bank account stood at a healthy £3,669 0s 6d.

He was succeeded by his son John (6th Bt 1722–55), who 'by his wild dissipation and his unconquerable disposition to play, squandered immense estates … and left little more at his death than the family patrimony at Kippax.' His notorious bet with Lord Mountford in 1755, that Colley Cibber would outlive Richard Nash, is often quoted; in February 1755 Mrs Delany wrote

> Sir John Bland lost to Capt O'Brien, who married Lord Inchiquin's deaf and dumb daughter, £32,000 who honourably gave him his chance of winning it back again …

The 6th baronet committed suicide in France[2] and the baronetcy became extinct when his brother Hungerford, also unmarried, died the year after him, in 1756.

In 1744 Lady Bland was probably in Bath at the same time as her husband's nephew, Hildebrand Jacob [▶ p. 286].

Portrait: Benjamin Ferrers, *Sir Thomas Sebright, Sir John Bland and two others*, c. 1720 (Waterhouse, p. 125).

1. Sedgwick. 2. GEC.

BLOSS & CO.
1746: DR £21 13s

Possibly John Bloss, Stationer, Paternoster Row, St Paul's.[1]

1. Kent 1740.

BLOXMAN
1746: CR £40

Uncertain identity. If the maiden name of Mary Deards snr (Bertrand's mother-in-law) was Bloxom or Bloxham, this could be a relative. A firm of bankers is listed in the 1790s.[1] James Bloxham appears on a note in the Badminton archives.[2]

1. H-Price. 2. FmI 4/14.

BOATE, LUCY
1736–45: CR £20; £13 8s

BODDICOTT, RD
1740: CR £25

Richard Boddicott, merchant and insurer, Savage gardens, Camberwell or Sword-blade coffee house.[1]

1. Kent 1740.

BOISSIER & CO.
1741: CR £80

BOISSIER & SELLON
1745: CR: £70 1s 3d

BOSNER & SELLON
1741: CR £25

Listed as merchants, Austen Friars.[1] In a letter to his son dated 9 May 1749, Lord Chesterfield writes from London

> The Person who will give you this letter, is the nephew of Monsieur Boissier, a rich, and, for all that, a very honest merchant of the city, from whom I have received many civilities. He is a Swiss, and probably you know him by name and reputation.[2]

One branch of the Boissier family was in Genoa,[3] another settled in Bath and Bristol. John Louis Boissier of Bath inherited a tea caddy set acquired from the silversmith Paul de Lamerie on the marriage of his parents, Jean Daniel Boissier and Suzanne Berchere (daughter of a Huguenot banker and jeweller), in 1735.[4]

1. Kent 1740. 2. Mahon, vol. 3 p. 364. 3. Rowe. 4. Lomax, no. 125.

BOLLERK, GERD & CO.
1747: CR £30

Gerrard Bolwerk, merchant, Billiter Square.[1]

1. Kent 1740.

BONTANDON, ELIZ
1744: DR £42

BOOTHBY, MR
1738: CR £66

George Boothby was described as 'silversmith and banker' when he was made bankrupt in 1741. As this is a credit entry, it presumably refers to a banking transaction. He entered his first mark as a largeworker in 1720, at The Parrot, St Clement Danes, Strand. He was still in business in 1745/46 when he marked a cup and cover (Jewish Museum, London). A Mr Boothby is listed arriving in Bath 17 September 1744.[1]

1. BJ.

BORODEN, JNO [LADY BLAND]
1743: CR £100

BOSTOCK, DR RD
1742–45: DR £30; £40; £154; £23 11s 6d; £100

Richard Bostock was a physician and a trustee of the Mineral Water Hospital in Bath in 1737. Catherine Lovelace bequeathed him 'my small pair of square wrought silver waiters' in 1740. When he died in March 1746/47 he asked to be buried in the Abbey between 11 and 12 at night.[1] The sale of his pictures was advertised in the *Bath Journal* 6 April 1747 at his house at the Cross, and his will was proved the next day.[2] His 'famous Purging Cordial Elixir' continued to be sold (at 1s 3d) after his death.

Monument: Bath Abbey.

1. Williams 1976, p. 49. 2. PROB 11/753.

BOUGHTON, RD
1736: CR £40

Possibly the son of William Boughton, Bt, of Warwicks, matriculated from Oxford 1725 aged 17, MA 1736; he died unmarried.[1]

1. Foster.

BOURSIN, DENIS
1736: DR £20

Presumably related to the family of Parisian silversmiths, who emigrated to England. Edmé Boursin, retired goldsmith, and Madeleine Boursin, a jeweller's widow, were living at the French Protestant Hospital in London in 1718.[1] The incuse mark DB a coronet above, entered in 1726, is attributed to Denis Boursin at the Golden Cup, Chandos Street; he is also shown at the Gold (or Golden) Angel, Long Acre, 1723.[2] In that year,

> John Melin, Apprentice to Denis Boursin, Silversmith, at the Golden-Angel in Longacre, ran away from his said Master on Tuesday the 3d of December; if he returns to his Master, he shall be kindly received; or whosoever secures and brings him to his said Master, shall have reasonable Charges, with Thanks. Whosoever entertains him, be it at their Peril. He is about 17 Years of Age, small Stature, short black Hair, a Scar in his Left Cheek, very much freckled.[3]

1. Murdoch & Vigne, p. 12. 2. Grimwade; Heal LG. 3. *London Gazette*, 3 December 1723.

BOWDEN, JNO
1740–44: DR £50; £30; £60; £40

Uncertain identity. The entries probably refer to a haberdasher of Bath, with whom Arthur Collier lodged in 1745 when he met Elizabeth Moseley – a story described as 'Cross-class courtship in the Bath marriage market'.[1] Dorothy Bowden sold gloves in the 1740s.[2]

Or, this might refer to the son of a London toyman who had died by 1738.[1] If Bertrand was dealing with him, it must be hoped that he had improved on his father's trade, for the latter was seemingly prepared to do some rather shady business:[3]

> I had been drinking, and about twelve at Night I met Newman, and asked her to go home with me to my Room in Queen's Head Yard in Tyburn Road. She agreed, and we went to bed. She got up between five and six in the Morning, and took the Buckles out of my Shoes, and carried them away. I was very much in Liquor over Night, and when I saw in the Morning what a Creature I had got, I was glad to get rid of her. She was afterwards taken, and confest that she had pawned one of them to John Bowden for a Quart of Gin and a Shilling …

The shop seems to have been handed to a third generation: John, son of John Bowden dec'd, was apprenticed in 1769 to Thomas Satchwell, jeweller.[4]

1. Stone, p. 68. 2. NAS, GD112/21/269. 3. *London Gazette*, 13 June 1738 [7710]. POB: t17351015-38. 4. GH: Apprentice Book.

BOWEN, HERBERT
1743: CR £50

BOWYER, WM
1746: CR ——

Possibly either William Bowyer (1699–1777), printer to the Society of Antiquaries;[1] or Sir William Bowyer, Bt, of Denham, Bucks, who succeeded his grandfather in 1721/22 when a minor, and d. 1768.[2]

1. *DNB*. 2. Foster; Burke, 1837.

BRADFORD, ANN
1742–43: CR £20; £20; £25 16s; £20

BRADHAM, WM
1742: CR: £4 14s

BRADSHAW, JNO
1745: CR: £20

Uncertain identity. Perhaps a broker, Fenchurch Street, London;[1] there was also a John Bradshaw, watchmaker, in Arundel Street.

1. Kent 1740.

BRAITHWAITE, RD
1738: CR: £30

Related to George Braithwaite, a goldsmith and jeweller in Lombard Street.[1]

1. Brett, 2010.

BRANHAM, MARY
1745: DR £30

BRASSEY & CO.
1743: CR £30; £50

Bankers at the Acorn, Lombard St, founded in the 1690s. John Brassey was in partnership with his son-in-law (the firm named Brassey & Caswell 1700–07); then with his son Nathaniel (c. 1697–1765) as John & Nathaniel Brassey; the firm became Nathaniel Brassey & Lee 1730–40. An advertisement of 1727 gives an insight into money transactions:

> Lost Yesterday, being the 9th of August, a Note of Mr Nath Brassey and Comp. No 501. payable to Dan Ray, 100 l. Whoever bring it to the Bar at Baker's Coffee house in Exchange-Alley shall have Five Guineas Reward. NB Payment is stopt.[1]

Nathaniel Brassey was instrumental in preparing the 1739 bill to prevent fraud and abuses in the sale of silver and gold. A Nathaniel Brassey rented property in Reading in 1721.[2]

1. Jowett. 2. Sun Ins, vol. 13, fo. 316 [23665].

BRIDGES, WM
1744: CR £20

Uncertain identity. Possibly the second cousin of the 1st Duke of Chandos, William Brydges, a lawyer (1681–1764, of Tibberton, Herefordshire) who is known to have visited Bath.[1] Frederick, Prince of Wales, travelled through the park of Col. Bridges of Keynsham, just west of Bath, on his way from Bath to Bristol in November 1738.[2]

Or, William Bridges is listed as a chinaman (or china-ware man) in 1749 and was selling Worcester china in the Strand, London in 1753.[3] His wife was Priscilla Portal.[4]

1. Baker; Mowl; *BJ*. 2. *The Craftsman*, 18 November 1738 [645]. 3. 1749 poll; Hildyard. 4. Wagner, p. 311.

BRIDGES, MR
1741: DR £13

Uncertain identity. Possibly Henry Bridges, 'a natural philosophical showman' who was linked to Benjamin Rackstrow, the figure maker whose anatomical and mechanical museum was close to Temple Bar.[1] He exhibited his 'Microcosm' in Bath in 1747. A Mr Bridges attended a lodge meeting in Bath in November 1737.[2]

Or this may be Wm Bridges (above).

1. Craske 2010, p. 6. 2. Masons Bath; White, quoting *BJ*, 9 November 1747 'of Waltham Abbey'.

BRIFAUT, JNO
1736–40 DR: £25; £16; £30; £15

John Brifaut, or Jean Brifant, appears in a trial in 1742.[1]

'Did you know Jean Brifant?' 'Yes, he was what we call a French-Plate-Worker' … 'Why you talk of a little Brass ting'd over with a Silver Colour!'

1. POB: t17420428.

BRIGSTOCK, OWEN
1740: CR £30

Held an account with Hoare & Co. Brigstock (1679–1746) was MP for Cardigan 1712–22[1] and a fellow of the Royal Society.[2]

1. Sedgwick. 2. Chamberlayne, Pt II, Bk III, p. 127.

BRINSDEN, JNO JUNR
1739: DR £30

BRISCOE, ELIZ
1745: DR £100

Elizabeth Fisher (from Bathampton) married William Briscoe of Bathford in 1733/34; she died on 25 November 1754 aged 54. Four of their children who died young are buried with their parents in Bathford: John (13 days), Elizabeth (2 yrs 4 months), Mary (5 weeks) and John (3 yrs 3 months); another son, William, died at the age of 60 in 1798. There is no reason to suppose any link to the silversmith and jeweller Stafford Briscoe, in London, but this has not been researched.

BROOKE, LORD
1740 & 1742: CR £150; £20
▶ p. 90.

BROOKS, THOS
1745: CR £20

BROWN, H & CO.
1746: CR £100

Henton Brown(e) is described as 'an able watchmaker'.[1] Free of the Clockmakers' Co. 1726, he died in 1775. Listed in Lombard Street, London as watchmaker and goldsmith,[2] he may also have been operating as a banker or broker, as this is a credit entry headed '& Co' – unless this is the wrong identification.

1. Baillie. 2. Kent 1740; Heal LG.

BROWN, JAMES
1738 & 1740: DR £100; £105

Possibly the jeweller, Eagle & Pearl, Church St, Soho, in 1752, but it is a common name.[1]

   1. Heal LG.

BROWNE, CAPT PROSPER
1739: DR £50

Appears to have had close connections with Littleton Pointz Meynell, who ordered the enormous wine cistern of 1734/5 (now in the Hermitage, an electrotype is in the V&A) made by Charles Kandler and ordered through Henry Jernegan. Browne signed a receipt dated 2 December 1736 'Reced of his Grace the Duke of Devonshire seven hundred pounds for the use of Lettleton Ponck Meynell Esq by me Pros: Browne'.[1] Probably the tenant of Horsman's Place, Dartford in 1735, when an inventory of the house was taken.[2]

   1. Chatsworth: 186.16.
   2. www.dartfordarchive.org.uk.

BROWNE, MR
1738: CR £100

Possibly Prosper Browne above?

BROWNE, WM
1746: DR £15 1s 10d

Uncertain identity. This could be William Brown, goldsmith, London 1739-51 (another of the same name is listed in Cheapside in 1773);[1] or more likely William Browne, at the sign of the Fish, who sold fishing tackle.[2]

   1. Heal LG; 1773 Report.
   2. Invoice dated 1736 and advertisement, Buckminster: Box 921-25.

BRUBANK, CHR
1746: DR £50

BRUN, FRAS
1752: DR £30

BRUCE, DAVID
1743: DR £14; £23 12s; £24
1746: CR £90; £40

BRYMER, ALEXR
1744: DR £40

BUKER, PR
1736: DR £17 10s

Uncertain identity. Possibly Peter Bouket, smallworker in Compton Street, Soho in 1773.[1] He may have been the same as Peter Buhet, goldsmith, son of Elias, apprenticed to David Tanqueray 1723, free 1737[2] although it would make for a long working life and mean that he was selling to Bertrand before obtaining his freedom.

   1. 1773 Report.   2. GH: Apprentice Book.

BULL, JNO
1743-46: DR £100; £200; £100

London silversmith and bucklemaker.

BULLOCK, MR
1746: CR £20

Uncertain identity. Mary Dering [▶ p. 163] had an aunt named Mrs Ann Bullock. Possibly Bullock of Falkburn Hall, Essex.

There was a watchmaker in Bath named Thomas Bullock. It seems less likely to be:[1]

> William Bullock, of this City, Victualler, gives this Publick Notice, to forwarn all Persons from trusting Sarah Bullock his wife, for he will not pay any Debts she shall or may contract, after this Publication. The Mark of William + Bullock

   1. *BJ*, 7 October 1745.

BUNBURY, WM
1738-39: CR £10; £50

William Bunbury had an account with Hoare from 1724, with substantial credit balances: in 1732 £5,045 18s and in 1735 £6,445 2s. The 1738 entry in Bertrand's account is for May, the same month that William Bunbury's son-in-law, Edward Mainwaring, is listed [▶ p. 292]. Bunbury was tenuously connected to Lady Hanmer [▶ p. 279]; his great nephew was the caricaturist Charles Bunbury.

Portrait: at Whitmore Hall.

BURCH, MR
1745: CR £60

Possibly the man listed in Barton Street, Bath, in 1736, the properties were later acquired by 'Mr Theobalds',[1] i.e. James Theobald, the timber merchant who acted as an agent for the Duke of Chandos in his dealings with John Wood.[2]

   1. Bath RO: Walcot Rate Book.
   2. Neale, p. 136.

BURDETT, FRAS
1740-41: CR £40; £40

Uncertain identity, there are three possibilities: two are baronetcies who each chose Francis as a name for their sons, but as it is unusual for the bank's clerk not to record a title in the ledgers, a third candidate is suggested.

1. Of Foremark Co. Derby. Sir Robert Burdet visited Bath on 3 November 1744 but as his son, Francis was not born until 1743, the entry is unlikely to be he.[1]

2. Of Burthwaite Co. York. Sir Francis Burdett, 2nd Bt (1675–1747) succeeded his father in 1719; twelve of his fourteen children predeceased him.[2]

3. Francis Burdett, merchant, Cannon Street, nr London Stone.[3]

   1. Burke.   2. Burke.   3. Kent 1740.

BURDSALL, THOS
1745: CR £36 10s

BURGH, B
1743: CR £50

Bertie Burgh inherited from his father John (who died in 1740) the position of steward and receiver general to the 3rd Duke of Beaufort. He mismanaged the Beaufort estates and went bankrupt. Burgh, who had an account with Hoare, lived at Troy House, Monmouthshire, and had an office in Castle Yard, Holborn.[1]

1. Sloman.

BURGOYNE, A:M
1742: CR £60

Anna Maria Burgoyne had an account with Hoare between 1731 and 1734.[1] She was the wife of Capt John Burgoyne (d. 1768, younger son of Sir John Burgoyne, 3rd Bt). Her son John (1723–92, a general, MP for Preston and a playwright) was possibly fathered by Robert Benson, Baron Bingley (d. 1731). Bingley left Anna Maria an independent income and made John Burgoyne his heir, should the issue of his legitimate daughter fail.[2] In 1743 Burgoyne eloped with Lady Charlotte Stanley, daughter of the 11th Earl of Derby]; his illegitimate son (b. 1782), a Field Marshal, died in 1871 – a long span of years for two generations. A Captain Burgoyne gave evidence in the case of Perreau/Adair [▶ pp. 196, 246 Adair]. On 3 November 1744 Sir Roger Burgoigne (6th Bt, MP for Bedfordshire) is listed among arrivals in Bath.[3] He was a nephew of Anna Maria's husband and was married to Lady Frances Montagu, daughter of the Earl of Halifax [▶ p. 294 Barbara Montagu].[4]

Portrait: Allan Ramsay, *Sir John Burgoyne*.

1. Lr.33. 2. *DNB*. 3. *BJ*. 4. For more on this family see Bettany, p.27.

BURNETT, THOS
1738: DR £231; £336

Uncertain identity. Possibly Thomas Burnett, ironmonger and brazier, Leadenhall Street, bankrupt September 1746.[1] Or a connection of Michael Burnett, fan-maker at the Hand & Fan over against Friday St in Cheapside;[2] Or of Robert Burnet who was selling Dresden ware in the 1750s.[3] Alternatively, Bertrand may have been paying out these quite large sums to a gentleman: Bishop Burnet's son Thomas is a possibility.[4]

1. *London Gazette* [8575]. 2. *The Craftsman*, 1732–33 [de Vere Green]. 3. Hoare: tradesmen's bills 1752. 4. Jones, p.20.

BURTON, BAR
1745–47: CR £100; £100; £100

Burton, Bartholomew & Richard, merchants, King's Arms-yard, Coleman St.[1] Bartholomew Burton was receiver general of the excise and his son William, was also given a place on the excise board.[2]

1. Kent 1740. 2. Sedgwick.

BYRON, EDMD
1742: DR £60

C

CALLARD, ISAAC
1736–40 DR £25; £15 5s; £20 7s

London silversmith.

▶ p. 217.

CALVERT, MR
1736: CR £80

Uncertain identity. The ledger entry is for 17 May 1736 – Felix Calvert, one time MP for Reading, died on 28 December that year.[1] His ancester was the first customer entered in the ledgers of Hoare & Co. The family was based in Hertfordshire and had a brewery, William Calvert & Co., in London. His son Felix died in 1755; his brother-in-law was Richard Calvert. They were connected by marriage to the Verney family of Claydon, Bucks, which their descendants inherited.[2]

Alternatively 'Mr Calvert' could be a connection of Charles Calvert, Lord Baltimore (1699–1751), who was Cofferer to the Prince of Wales 1747–51.

1. Sedgwick. 2. Burke, *Commoners*, vol. 3, p. 400. Also mentioned by Clifford as clients of Parker & Wakelin in a later generation.

CAMPBELL & CO.
1747: CR £30

Probably Campbell & Bruce, successors to Middleton & Co. [▶ p. 294]. There is a possibility it refers to Campbell & Currie, merchants, Fenchurch-buildings, who feature in P. D. Chenevix's bank account.[1]

1. Kent 1740.

CANNING, JOSHUA
1743: DR £78

CAREW, JNO
1743: DR £80

A governor of Bath's Mineral Water Hospital 1748, his will was proved 9 May 1751.[1] Although no connection has been made, it is worth noting that Shockerwick, the estate acquired by the Wiltshire family from 1749 on, previously belonged to Antony Carew.

1. PROB 11/787.

CAREW, THOS
1739–40: DR £100; £100

Thomas Carew (1702–66) was first president of the Bath Mineral Water Hospital in 1739. He lived at Crowcombe, near Minehead, Somerset and was MP for Minehead 1739–47. Horace Walpole described Carew as 'a crazy zealot, who believed himself possessed by the devil, till he was cured by his apothecary's assuring him that he had met the devil upon the stairs coming from him'. A Jacobite, he voted in 1744 in favour of the bill to prohibit gaming.[1] Presumably the debit entries in the accounts relate to the Hospital. In London a Thomas Carew 'gent' is listed at Portugal Row, but one would expect a member of parliament to be listed as 'Esq'.[2]

1. Sedgwick. 2. 1749 poll.

CARMICHAEL, MR
1741: CR £50

Uncertain identity. Possibly a son of the 2nd Earl of Hyndford (d. 1737), whose widow died at Bath in 1753. Perhaps James Carmichael, MP for Linlithgow, whose elder brother the 3rd Earl, was in 1741 Envoy to the King of Prussia during the Invasion of Silesia.[1]

1. McCann p. 57.

CARTWRIGHT, CATH
1739–41: DR £20; £29; £10 8s; £21 10s

Uncertain identity. Most probably the wife of Benjamin Cartwright, a London goldsmith and toyman. The broad spread of known dates (1732–74) and addresses in West Smithfield and the Strand, has resulted in some confusion about him. The Benjamin Cartwright at the King's Arms & Snuffers, Strand 1749–56, is undoubtedly the man for whom invoices survive in the archives of Hoare & Co.[1] In 1773 Benjamin Cartwright is listed in both Smithfield and Pall Mall.[2]

There was also a watchmaker named Thomas Cartwright and a scientific instrument maker named John.

1. Grimwade; Heal LG. 2. 1773 Report.

CARY, JNO
1736 & 1746: DR £40; £84

Uncertain identity. Possibly Mr Carey, who had a tavern built by the Duke of Chandos in 1729.[1] Or, there was a tobacco consignment house in London, John & Thomas Cary & Co., with whom George Hartley (uncle and partner of John Norton [▶ p. 297]) was associated.[2]

1. Mowl, p. 29; Jenkins, p. 96.
2. Mason 1968.

CASAMAJOR, HENRY
1741: DR £129 16s 6d

Henry Casamayor, Bristol merchant (c. 1714–75), as was his son Henry (1749–1824).[1]

Portrait: William Hoare, drawing of his daughter (The Art Gallery of Greater Victoria, Canada).

1. DNB.

CASAMAJOR, JNO
1741: DR £150

John Casamayor, merchant, Devonshire St, London, presumably a relative of Henry (above).[1] The Casamajor family had long-lasting links, as merchants, with Madras.[2]

1. Kent 1740. 2. Gill, p. 119.

CASTLEMAINE, LORD
1744: DR £250

Richard Child of Wanstead, Essex (1679/80–1749/50) was created Viscount Castlemaine in 1718 and Earl Tylney in 1731; he took the name of Tylney in 1734. Half-brother of Cassandra, second wife of the Duke of Chandos, his wife died in March 1743/44.

This large debit entry must relate to his son John (1712–82) who was also in Bath on 7 December 1747. John's heir was his nephew, Sir James Long of Draycote Wilts [▶ p. 290]. The great house of Wanstead, designed by Colen Campbell, was sold and subsequently demolished as a result of the debts and dissipation of James Long's son-in-law, later 4th Earl of Mornington, who died in 1857.

Portrait: William Hogarth: *An Assembly at Wanstead House 1728–31* (Philadelphia Museum of Art). Joseph Nollekens, *The Tylney group* (Fairfax House).

CATANACH, DUNCAN
1740: DR £50

CATONACH, GEO
1/38: CR £100

George Catanach, merchant, in Lothbury, London.[1]

1. Kent 1740.

CAWTHORN, SAML
1737 and 1741: DR £25; £50

London silversmith.

▶ p. 219.

CAZALET, STE:
1740: DR £63

Possibly Stephen Cazalet, weaver, Spittal yard, London[1] who was presumably the Huguenot, Stephen Estienne Cazalet (1691–1742) who married Jeanne Rocher in 1716 at L'Eglise de l'Artillerie, Bishopsgate.[2]

1. Kent 1740. 2. www.cazalet.fr

CEESAR, CHAS
1739–40: CR £10 10s; £15 15s; £105

Charles Caesar (1673–1741) of Benington, Herts, MP for Hertford. 'Caesar was trusted as a Jacobite agent until 1729, and the Stuart papers refer to his usefulness and loyalty';[1] Sedgwick quotes extensively from correspondence with the Pretender. Caesar opened an account at Hoare & Co. in 1730 and two years later he gave rise to gossip:[2]

> Heard little news, but the seizing Charles Caesar Esq ... his house and goods in town and country for debt, and the like done by Sir George Oxenden. Mr Caesar was always looked on as a man of sense and fortune ... his estate was 3,500l a year, and he was not noted for extravagance. Sir George Oxenden is a proud, conceited lewd man ...

In March 1739 it was reported that 'Last Tuesday Charles Caesar, Esq, Knight of the Shire for the County of Hertford, was seiz'd with the Palsey in his Head, and yesterday he lay dangerously ill at his House in New Bond Street.'[3]

He is in Bertrand's accounts for

November of that year and September–October of 1740. His wife, Mary Freeman, garden designer, outlived him by only three months. Caesar[4]

> inherited the most part of his father's splendid possessions, in the twenty-first year of his age, in all the pride of youth, health, and ancestry, and died at the age of 67 insolvent and broken-hearted, a melancholy monument of the ruin of a once highly flourishing family. … [on inheriting he] destroyed the venerable mansion of his ancestors at Bennington and built in its stead a palace of modern fashion, which was burnt to ashes immediately after it was completed, and before it had been inhabited.

Alternatively, the entry could be for his son, also Charles (b. 1703/04), whose daughter Jane married Sir Charles Cottrell Dormer of Rousham. He appears to have been involved with Nash in the running of gaming tables [▶ p. 49].

Portrait: Arthur Devis, *Maj-Gen Julius Caesar* (his brother, died unmarried 1762); see: Saumarez-Smith, no. 205.

1. *DNB*. 2. Egmont, vol. 1, p. 213: 7 January 1732/33. 3. *London Evening Post*, 13–15 March 1739. 4. Burke, *Commoners*, vol. 2, p. 21.

CHAMBERS, JONA
1746: DR £5 5s

CHAMBERS & USBORNE
1739: CR £20

▶ p. 277 Gosling.

CHAMPION, SR GEO
1737–38: DR £110; £70
1738: CR £40 10s

Alderman & merchant, Clements Lane, London, MP for Aylesbury (d. 1754).[1] His first wife died in September 1738. Listed 6 April 1747 as arriving in Bath.[2]

1. Kent 1740; Sedgwick. 2. *BJ*.

CHANDLER, DANIEL
1737: DR £6 6s

Uncertain identity. Possibly a relation of Mary or Richard Chandler (below), or of Edward Chandler, a watchmaker.

CHANDLER, MARY
1738–41: DR £50; £30 6s; £100; £100; £80
1744: CR £90

In 1734 Mary Chandler's poem to Princess Amelia, 'A Description of Bath', was published by the bookseller James Leake [▶ p. 176] whose brother-in-law Samuel Richardson printed the 2nd to 7th editions. Born in 1687, a 'spinal deformity precluded marriage and family finances compelled her to set up a milliner's shop in Bath before she was 20'.[1] In February 1717/18 she was in Stall Street but in December 1718 moved 'to her shop at Mr Joseph Palmer's agt the Pump House'.[2] In 1733 she was in 'Stalls Church Yard'.[3] In April 1745 she was described as 'leaving trade' and the *Bath Journal* contained the following advertisement:

> To be Lett or Sold (Furnished or Unfurnished) Two Houses, belonging to Mrs Mary Chandler, one situate in Orange Court in the Grove, Bath, convenient either for a private Family or a Lodging-House; the other opposite the Pump Room, with a well and long accustom'd Millener's Shop – Enquire for further particulars at either of the said Houses.

The report of her death the following September in Orange Court described her as '… of a mild, affable and gentle carriage, courteous in her Behaviour, and ready to do any kind, friendly, and charitable office'.[4]

1. *DNB*. 2. Sun Ins, vol. 7, fo. 299 [10420]. 3. Bath RO: 1776 Schedule of Deeds. 4. *BJ*, 16 September 1745.

CHANDLER, RD
1740: CR £19 5s 3d

Uncertain identity. As it is a credit entry this might be Richard Chandler Esq., listed in New Burlington Street.[1] An alternative identity might be the bookseller (c. 1713–44) who was apprenticed to John Hooke, at the Fleur de Luce, near St Dunstan's, London, and then in partnership with Caesar Ward, at the sign of the Ship between Temple Gates, Fleet St. He 'discharged a pistol to his head as he lay reclined on his bed'.[2]

1. 1749 Poll. 2. *Fog Weekly Journal*; *DNB*.

CHANNING & BRENT
1738: DR £100

Haberdashers, Bread Street, London.[1]

1. Kent 1740.

CHANNON, JNO
1743: DR £40

Possibly the cabinet-maker John Channon (fl. 1733–83), whose family came from Exeter; he settled in London in the mid-1730s.

CHARLTON, MARGT
1745: DR £138

Uncertain identity. Perhaps a connection of Dr Rice Charleton (1710–89), who in 1757 was appointed physician to the Mineral Water Hospital, Bath, and retired in 1781. He had two children, Robert and Susanna and lived in Edgars Buildings, two doors from William Hoare.[1] He had an account with Hoare & Co.

Another possibility is 'M. Charlton' who in 1730 receipted an invoice 'for my master Geo: Graham' to the Duchess of Montrose for mending and cleaning watches.[2]

1. Bath RO: 1766 Rate Book 1 p. 84. 2. NAS: GD220/6/893/56.

Stand Coachman, or the Haughty Lady Well Fitted, engraving detail, J. Wakelin. Behind the coach is Chenevix's toyshop. (Private coll)

CHENEVIX, MR
1736–42: DR £100; £120; £22 6s; £14 8s

CHENEVIX, MRS
1739: CR £100

Paul Daniel Chenevix (1700–43) married Elizabeth Deards in 1726; he was thus Mary Bertrand's brother-in-law. They had London's most fashionable toyshop in Charing Cross, which they opened in 1729/30. They, and the rest of the Deards family, will be the subject of vol. 2 of this research, forthcoming.

▶ p. 38.

CHEYNE, DR
1736–45: DR £47 10s; £125; £105; £25

Dr George Cheyne (1671/72–1743) physician; studied medicine at Edinburgh, settled in London c. 1702 and moved to Bath in 1718 where he was associated with the hospital from its beginning. He was a member of the Royal Society;[1] advocated vegetarianism and published treatises on diet and natural theology. Referred to as 'oracle Cheney' by Helena le Grand[2] [▶ p. 289], he lived in Monmouth Street and was buried in Weston, Bath on 17 April 1743.[3]

His audience was 'the aristocracy and upwardly mobile who frequented Bath and who suffered from diseases of over-indulgence'.[4] He was an advocate of preventative medicine: 'Most men know when they are ill but very few when they are well. And yet it is most certain, that 'tis easier to preserve Health, than to recover it; and to prevent Diseases, than to cure them.'[5] His 'Method to Cure a Cold' was:[6]

> Lye much a-bed; drink plentifully of small, warm Sack-Whey, with a few drops of Spirit of Hart's Horn; Posset-drink; Water-Gruel, or any other warm, small Likquors; … live low upon Spoon-Meats, Pudding, and Chicken, and drink everything warm …

Alexander Pope wrote that 'there lives not an honester man nor a truer philosopher'; Lord Chesterfield corresponded with him about his health.

▶ p. 122 illus.

Portrait: Johan van Diest, engraved by John Faber jnr.

1. Chamberlayne. 2. Chatsworth. 3. PROB 11/727. 4. *DNB*. 5. Eglin p. 200. 6. *Gents Mag*, October 1736.

CHICHESTER, LADY (PR ORDER OF MR GOULD)
1738: CR £30

The second wife of Sir John Chichester of Youlston, MP for Barnstaple, listed as also being in Bath in April 1745.

CHILD & CO.
1736–47: CR £50; £500; £90; £300; £100; £100; £25; £25; £130; £31 10s. £30; £210; £25; £100; £40; £50; £22 10s; £50; £50; £30; £7 17s 6d; £40; £15 1s 9d; £33 15s; £72; £50; £21; £90; £100; £40; £60; £50; £100; £50; £30; £60; £13; £17 12s; £20; £100; £35; £60; £150; £50; £60; £25; £30

Founded in the 1670s, the bank was in the Child family for many generations; sold to Glynn, Mills Bank in 1924. The bank was at the sign of the Marygold, within Temple Bar, later 4 Fleet Street, on the south side. Members of the family visited Bath (for example Lady Dorothy Child arrived on 7 December 1747), but the entries in Bertrand's ledger must relate to customers. The head of the bank when Paul Bertrand began business in Bath was Sir Francis Child (c. 1684–1740), who was Prime Warden of the Goldsmiths' Company 1723–24 and in 1739 supported an Act to prevent fraud in gold and silver wares. He died in 1740 'vastly rich' and was succeeded as head of the bank by his brother, Samuel (1693–1752).[1]

Property: Osterley Park, Middx (National Trust)[▶ p. 211/11 map].

1. *DNB*.

CHORLEY, RD
1740: CR £62 11s

CHURCHILL, GEO
1745: DR £400

Uncertain identity. Possibly the illegitimate son of Admiral George Churchill, younger brother of the 1st Duke of Marlborough, who died in 1710 leaving £24,000 divided between his son George (then under 21) and Francis Godfrey, son of his sister Arabella.[1] His visit to Bath may have been linked to a relative, Lt-Gen Charles Churchill, who is recorded as arriving in Bath on 17 September 1744 and again on 8 April 1745. On 6 May the *Bath Journal* announced:

> The paragraph mentioned in all the Newspapers relating to Gen Churchill's death is a mistake, tho' that Gentleman continues in a very bad state of health here.

The ledger entry is dated 25 March; Charles Churchill died on 14 May, aged 66.[2]

Alternatively, as this is a large debit entry, there was a cabinetmaker of this name near Wild Street, London, in 1717.[3]

Property: Minterne House, near Dorchester.

1. *DNB*; her husband, Col. Charles Godfrey, was Master of the Jewel Office. 2. Stace. 3. Sun Ins, vol. 7 fo. 19 [9028].

CLARGES, MR
1745: CR £60

Uncertain identity. Possibly Thomas Clarges (1721–53) who married Ann, daughter of John, Viscount Barrington in January 1746/47; he predeceased his father, Sir Thomas Clarges. The latter (of Great George St, Hanover Sq)[1] was succeeded in 1759 by his grandson, who married Louisa Skrine in 1777 [▶p. 309].[2]

Or possibly Samuel Clarges, whose death at his aunt's house, near Porlock, Somerset was reported 9 February 1746/47.

Thirdly: George Clarges, listed in King Street, St James's Square.[3]

1. Kent 1740; Sun Ins, vol. 12, p. 250 [1946–7]. 2. Burke, *Extinct Baronetcies*; Foster. Also see Bettany, p. 215, n. 8 regarding this Lady Clarges, friend of Fanny Burney who was painted by Gainsborough in 1778 (Holburne Museum). 3. 1749 poll.

CLARKE, EDWD
1740: CR £21

CLARKE, SAML
1745: CR £167 18s 10d

Samuel and William Clarke, Turkey merchants, Charterhouse Square; Samuel Clarke jnr, merchant, Dowgate Hill.[1] Edward Clarke (above) may be of the same family, so too could the 'Mr Clarke, Garlick Hill', in the ledgers of the silversmith George Wickes.[2] A Samuel Clarke was a fellow of the Royal Society,[3] and Samuel Clarke, at Clarke's Warehouse, Cheapside is listed in 1760.[4] A less likely identification, as it is a credit entry, is S. Clarke designer of printed fans *c*.1740.[5]

1. Kent 1740. 2. Wickes.
3. Chamberlayne. 4. Hildyard.
5. de Vere Green.

CLAXTON, MR
1744: DR £100

CLAYTON, MARY
1736: CR £19 17s 6d

Uncertain identity, but most probably connected to the baronets of Marden Park, Surrey. Henrietta Maria Herring married in February 1736 Kenrick Clayton;[1] the ledger entry is for October that year. Their son Robert, 3rd Bt, married the daughter of F. Standert [▶p. 312]. The first wife of Kenrick's brother William was called Mary; he also had a sister named Mary, who married Jonathan Rashleigh of Menabilly (later made famous by the novelist Daphne du Maurier).

Another possible identification is a relation of Lord Sundon whose wife Charlotte (a Lady of the Bedchamber) was seriously ill in Bath in 1737.[2]

Property: Cup and cover, Paul de Lamerie, London 1742/43 with armorials possibly added by Sir Robert.

1. Sedgwick and Burke, 1837.
2. *DNB*, Charlotte Clayton, Lady Sundon.

CLEMENT, WM
1746–47: DR £32 13s; £100; £99 15s; £50; £160

Most probably William Clement, listed in Wade's Passage, Bath paying rates of 5s 7½d.[1] In December 1745 he placed the following advertisement:[2]

> To be sold Next to the Sign of the Duke of Grafton's Hunter, near Queen's Square, Bath … Fine Old Jamaica Rum (Neat as Imported) In no less Quantity than Two Gallons …

Some years later a Thomas Clement was builder of no. 5 Royal Crescent.[3]

1. Bath RO: 1766 Rate Book, p. 6.
2. *BJ*, 9 December 1745.
3. Yescombe.

CLEUDAR, MRS
1739: 1 DR £26

Uncertain identity. Possibly Elizabeth, widow of J. Cluer, an engraver and printer (including the work of Handel); she continued the business and married secondly Thomas Cobb. Sometimes advertised as 'Cluer's Great Wholesale and Retale Warehouse' in Cheapside.[1]

> To all shop-keepers. At Cluer's Printing office, at the Maidenhead in Bow Church Yard, Shopkeepers Bills and Bills of Parcels are curiously Engraved on Copper Plates: Also Marks for Watchmakers, Tobacconists, Packers, Glovers, Haberdashers of Hats, Peruke

makers, &c are Engraved on Wood or Copper …. Titles for Hungary Water, Directions for Daffey's Elixir and the Spirits of Scurvy Grass …

1. *London Journal*, 1 May 1725 [CCCI].

CLIFFORD, LADY

1743: DR £58 10s

Elizabeth (d. 1778), widow of Hugh, 4th Baron Clifford of Chudleigh (1700–32), was the daughter of Edward Blount of Blagdon, Devon and sister of the Duchess of Norfolk. Her son is listed arriving in Bath in 1745.

CLUTTERBUCK, JAS

1747: CR £150

The Clutterbuck family 'has been for many generations of consideration and fortune'.[1] James Clutterbuck acquired Newark Park and Ozleworth Park, both in the same Gloucestershire valley – he owned land in four counties. Newark was remodelled by James Wyatt and passed to a cousin, the Revd Lewis Clutterbuck, rector of Ozleworth (son of Lewis, ▶ below). James Clutterbuck was given Gainsborough's portrait of Garrick, whose friend he was, and was brother-in-law to the painter's patron John Jacob (1723–76, painted by Francis Hayman).[2] Others in the extended Clutterbuck family included Thomas Clutterbuck, whose daughter married Charles Hotham [▶ p. 283], and Richard Clutterbuck, who owned Frampton Court.[3]

In London, James Clutterbuck, men's mercer, was opposite the church of St Mary le Strand.[4]

1. Burke, *LG* 1848. 2. Sloman. 3. Kingsley. 4. Heal.

CLUTTERBUCK, LEWIS

1742: DR £20

Lewis Clutterbuck 'of Widcome and Claverton'[1] was an attorney in Bath – his name features regularly in advertisements regarding property for sale or to let; one of his brothers, Daniel, was also an attorney, of Bradford-on-Avon. John Wiltshire [▶ p. 46] left £100 in his will to 'Mr Lewis Clutterbuck of Bath Gentleman'; and in the 1760s John Wood jnr borrowed £2,500 from him in connection with the development of Royal Crescent.[2] Clutterbuck witnessed Leonard Coward's will in 1759 [▶ p. 175]. He was made an hon. freeman of Bath 25 October 1742.[3]

1. Burke, *LG* 1937. 2. Neale, p. 161. 3. Bath RO: Council Book 6.

COBB, SR GEO

1746–47: DR £138 9s; £149 7s 6d

Succeeded his brother Edward as 3rd Bt in 1744, married Ann Langton of Newton Park, Somerset, the daughter of Joseph Langton [▶ p. 288] 'and acquired thereby that estate';[1] their daughter Christian married Paul Methuen of Corsham, Wilts. Sir George died aged 90 in 1762 after falling into a moat.

1. Burke, *Extinct Baronetcies.*

COCK, CHRISR

1737: DR £58 19s 6d

Christopher Cock, auctioneer, in Covent Garden from 1731. Henry Fielding includes Cock in his description of a cudgel acquired from Deards:[1]

> He did intend to have painted an auction room, where Mr. Cock would have appeared aloft in his pulpit, trumpeting forth the praises of a china basin, and with astonishment wondering that 'Nobody bids more for that fine, that superb …'.

Cock handled the sale of the Duke of Chandos's estate at Cannons, Edgware in 1747 and restored paintings for Chandos, evidenced by an invoice of 1724 for 'cleaning mending and varnishing two heads on panels by van Dyke';[2] he also had an interest in John Rich's theatre in Covent Garden (now the Royal Opera House). In November 1747 the sale of the silversmith Paul Crespin's stock took place in the former repository of Mr Cocks's waxwork models 'up one pair of stairs at a grocers, the corner of Durham Yard in the Strand'.[3] Cock died in December 1748, when it was reported: 'We hear he has left his House in the Great Piazza, and the whole of his Fortune … to Mr Langford, who succeeds him in his business.'[4] Langford was succeeded by Henry Robins.

1. *The Adventures of Joseph Andrews* (1742), Book III ch 6. 2. Chatsworth. 3. *General Advertiser*, 4 November 1747 [4063]. 4. *General Evening Post*, 10–13 December 1748 [2376].

COCKEE, WM

1746: DR £100

William Cockey: a clockmaker of Yeovil, Somerset. Edward Cockey of Warminster, also a clockmaker, was at a Masonic meeting with Bertrand in Bath in 1737.

COCKS, JAS

1746: DR £180

Uncertain identity. It would be unusual for such a common name to be misspelt in the ledgers, but it is just possible that this is an early reference to James Cox (c. 1723–1800), one of the best-known makers of luxury toys.[1] Apprenticed to Humphry Pugh, free 1745, when his address was Racquet Court, Fleet St (to 1756), he went on to deal in toys and jewellery in partnership with Edward Grace.

If, on the other hand, the entry refers to a customer rather than a supplier, it could be the grandson of Lord Somers; the latter's executors were his sisters, Mary

Cocks (mother of James) and Elizabeth, wife of the Master of the Rolls, Sir Joseph Jekyll.[2]

1. Smith. 2. GEC; Grundy, p. 131.

CODRINGTON, SR WM
1744: DR £150

Sir William Codrington, 2nd Bt (1719–92), MP for Beverley and Tewkesbury; disinherited his son (b. 1739) and bequeathed his estates to his grand-nephew Christopher, of Dodington Park, Glos. His great-grandfather had migrated to Barbados in 1628 where he and his sons 'made great fortunes';[1] some of the estates there were still owned by the 2nd Bt when he died. Mrs Delany wrote of meeting Lady Codrington in Bath in 1760.[2] They were connected to the Bethel family [▶ p. 251] and probably to Mary Codrington, a spinster (d. 1754) who had a house in Barton Street next to Sir Edward Stanley [▶ p. 312] and was therefore a neighbour of Paul Bertrand.[3]

John Codrington, MP for Bath, was of a different family.

1. Sedgwick. 2. Delany, vol. 3, p. 605. 3. Bath RO: Walcot Church Rate 1749 and 1754, PROB 11/808.

COGSWELL, JNO
1745: DR £17 12s

John Cogswell, a vintner, of the Rummer Tavern, Cheap Street, Bath, where trustees of the Mineral Water Hospital held their meetings. On 24 December 1744 he advertised:[1]

> To be Lett, at Lady Day next The Rummer Tavern in Cheap Street, Bath, now in the possession of Mr Alderman John Cogswell, being a very good accustom'd House, in good Repair, extraordinary good Vaults, and every other convenience

He was a councillor at the 1734 election and Mayor of Bath January 1745/46. The death of his wife was noted the same month, she being described rather briefly as 'a good Neighbour'.[2] In 1733 Cogswell had taken a 'messuage and garden, South Gate Street, 42 years from Xmas'.[3] He died in 1751.[4]

1. BJ. 2. BJ 27 January 1745/46. 3. Bath RO: 1776 Schedule of Deeds, p.219. 4. Will 31 October 1751, PROB 11/790.

COKE, GEORGE LEWIS
1743: CR £100; £100

George Coke of Melbourne, co. Derby, matriculated Oxford 1732 aged 17, died unmarried 1750.[1]

1. Foster.

COLCLOUGH, MARGT
1745: CR £20

COLE, HENRY
1741: DR £40

Uncertain identity: perhaps the same as Henry Coles [▶ p. 263]. Heal lists a jeweller named Cole and also a razor maker at the GR & Crown in Old Round Court, in the Strand, from Mr Savigny in Pall Mall.[1]

1. BM: Heal 52.30.

COLE, JNO
1736: DR £250

John Cole gave evidence together with Mr Rollo 'the engraver' in a trial in 1730:[1]

> John Cole, in Fleet-Street, depos'd, That on the 22d or 23d of April last, the Prisoner came to his Shop, and brought a Double-Half-Crown Stamp Paper, and on the 25th of April she came on the same Errant, and brought a Guinea to pay 10s. her Husband ow'd, and paid him the rest of the Money, which was 16s. he taking the Double-Half Crown Stamp at a Crown in part of Payment; that he afterwards looking upon the Stamp, and suspecting it, carried it, and laid it before the Commissioners, who sent for their Engraver, who made Affidavit, that the Stamps were Counterfeit

An invoice presumably relating to the same man is headed 'John Coles, at the Sun and Mitre, against Chancery Lane, Fleet Street'.[2] The signature 'I. Cole Sculp' is on the trade card of Jonathan Sisson, mathematical instrument maker.[3]

1. POB: t17300704-66. 2. BM: Heal, 111.37. 3. WAC: Gardner coll, Box 63, no. 33-I.

COLE, ROT
1738: DR £28

COLEBROOK, JOS & CO. JAS & CO.
1743–47: CR £25; £100; £50; £16 8s 6d

Bankers at 62 Threadneedle St, listed as Jackson & Colebrook, nr the Royal Exchange 1706–20 and 1743–71 as Sir James Colebrooke & Co.[1] Colebrooke & Lightfoot, bankers, are also listed behind the Royal Exchange.[2] James Colebrook, Master of the Mercers Company in 1725, died aged 72 in November 1752 reputedly worth £800,000;[3] his mausoleum by Robert Taylor at Chilham, Kent (now demolished) was completed in 1755 at a cost of £2,000.[4] He had two sons in Parliament, Robert (1718–84) of Chilham, and James (1722–61, created Bt 1759). Robert Colebrook's second wife (married 1756) was the daughter of John Thresher of Bradford-on-Avon, close to Bath. The following advertisement is untypical, because of its detail:[5]

> Whereas the Gold Box under described was advertised in this Paper of Friday and Saturday last to have been stolen, the Proprietor Robert Colebrook, Esq thinking it possible that he might have dropped it in coming from St James's on Thursday last, and that it may

have fallen into the Hands of some honest Person, hereby offers a Reward of Twenty Guineas, to be paid to any such Person on bringing it to Mr. Deard, Toyman, the corner of Dover Street; but if it is offered to Sale or Pawn, it is requested that the Box and the Party may be stopped, and Notice given to Mr. Fielding, Esq; when the like Reward will be paid.

A large square Gold Snuff-Box enamelled with blue, with a Miniature Picture of a Lady sickly, and dressed in a Capuchin and Mob in Water-Colours, on the Inside of the Lid; on the upper Part of the Lid a Shepherd leaning in a Shepherdes's Lap; on the Bottom a Huntsman blowing a French-Horn, with a Hanger by his Side, and several Hounds by him; on the four Sides are Guns, Dogs, Game, and other Figures relative to Game.

The youngest son George, who succeeded his brother James as 2nd Bt in 1761, was associated with Arnold Nesbitt [▶ p. 297] but speculated badly: the bank closed in 1773, the sale of his 'superb pictures' was held at Christie's in April 1775,[5] he was declared bankrupt in 1777 and died in Batheaston in 1809.[6]

Portrait: miniature of Robert (SL 17 November 1975 lot 11). Property: armorial porcelain service c.1737, (Howard, p. 25); silver coffee pot, A. Portal, London 1753/4 (Portal, fig. 2a).

1. Heal; H-Price. 2. Kent 1740. 3. *Gents Mag*, vol. 22, November 1752. 4. Craske, p. 372. 5. *The Public Advertiser*, 9 June 1761 [8295]. 6. Hancock, p. 349.

COLES, HENRY
1740–1747: DR £152; £28; £71 13s 6d

H. Coles, jeweller, at the Eagle & Pearl, Tavistock Street.[1] In 1746 he valued the 'false stone work' in the estate of George Brathwaite.[2]

An entry in the Webb journals for 23 February 1753 shows how carefully jewellers kept records: Webb 'Bought of Henry Coles Jeweller' a pair of drops knots and tops 'middling good' for £85, recording 'NB Sold the above Pendants about 18 months ago to Mr Hutchesonn of Bristol for £105, soon after wch he faild.'[3]

H. Cole, jeweller, Eagle Court, Strand, may be the same man; also a razor maker (above).

Trade card: WAC, Gardner coll.

1. Heal LG and 1749 poll. 2. Brett 2010. 3. TNA: C 108/284.

COLLIER, JAMES
1738–46: CR £100; £100; £25; £30; £100; £100

Uncertain identity. Possibly connected to Mrs Ann Collier, painted by Thomas Hudson,[1] but her husband was Benjamin (d. 1758) of Topsham, Devon.

1. Tate Britain.

COLLINGWOOD, THOS
1747: DR £30

COLLINS, THOS
1746–47: DR £40; £30

Uncertain identity. Freemason, recorded at the first meeting of Royal Cumberland Lodge at 'Brother Robinson's', The Bear in Bath, in 1732.[1]

Possibly connected to Richard Collins, a tailor, and Mary Collins.[2] And/or to George Collins 'of Spittle Fields weaver' to whom Mary Bertrand bequeathed £100.

1. *Masons Bath*, Book 1, 1732–38. 2. NAS: GD112/21/268 & 269, (invoices to Viscount Glenorchy, 1740s).

COLSTON, FRAS
1739: CR £50; £150

The Colston family were closely associated with the development of Bristol and the Society of Merchant Venturers. Francis Colston was made Hon. Freeman of Bristol Merchant Adventurers in 1707. He did not complete his year of office in 1744 as President of the Mineral Water Hospital because of the election of Frederick, Prince of Wales in 1745. Colston gave to the hospital £100 for three years on condition the number of patients was increased to forty-five. Both he and his kinsman Edward Colston (d. 1721) were governors of St Bartholomew's Hospital, in London.

Edward, a merchant, philanthropist and a bachelor, founded schools in Bristol and after his death £71,000 was donated to public charities and £100,000 left to relatives, from his estate.[1] Colston Avenue and Colston Hall in Bristol bear his name. Edward Colston's monument by Michael Rysbrack, designed by James Gibbs, is in All Saints', Bristol.[2]

1. *DNB*. 2. Eustace.

COMPTON, GEO
1746: DR £200

Uncertain identity. Possibly the Hon. George Compton (1692–1758), MP for Northampton and brother of 5th Earl of Northampton. A lord of the Treasury until 1744, he was a follower of Lord Bath and described by Horace Walpole as 'a very silent person'.[1] But it is a debit entry.

1. Sedgwick.

COMYN, VALENS
1744–46: CR £100; £40; £90

Sedgwick describes Comyn as 'having achieved considerable success as a backer of privateering ventures between 1745 and 1747'; he was Accomptant General of Excise 1734–c.1745, and registrar and accountant to the Corporation of the Sons of the Clergy. For the latter charity he 'uncovered the fraudulent activities of one of the treasurers, who had been double listing widows whose pensions he was responsible for paying, and lining his pockets on the proceeds.'[1]

1. Wikipedia

COOK, JOS
1736–39: DR £20; £23; £70

COOKE, JAMES
1743–44: DR £70; £31 10s

Uncertain identity. On 1 December 1746 the *Bath Journal* recorded the death of James Cook, 'an eminent and wealthy Turkey Merchant' of Ashted, nr Epsom; he had died on 19 November. He was a Royal Exchange Assurance Director, Hatton Garden,[1] MP for Tregony 1722–27 and had previously acted as English banker at Constantinople.[2]

1. Kent 1740. 2. Sedgwick.

COOKE, RD
1746: CR £67

COOPER, CHAS
1/40: DR £40

COOPER, CHR
1745 CR £20

COOPER, ELIZA
1740: DR £15

COOPER, GIS:
1736–46: CR £21; £73 10s; £25; £70 19s; £40; £20; £50; £100; £21; £100; £21; £50; £20

Gislingham Cooper, son of the London silversmith Robert Cooper, turned his father's business towards banking, although he continued to deal in silver. There are numerous variants of his name, for example Gillsingham, Gillingham, Gissingham, Greslingham. His address is given variously as 'at the corner of Arundell Street (1716), 'at the corner of Norfolk Street' (1720) and 'over against St Clements Church in the Strand (1723). He is probably the GC recorded in the Beaufort accounts for 1736. Gislingham Cooper died at Phillis Court, nr Henley-on-Thames in 1768.[1]

1. Sun Ins. Heal. Sale.

COOT[E], CATH
1742: DR £20; £30

COPE, JNO
1738–39: CR (one 'Brigr Cope, hands of Hen Popple) £100; £50; £100; £100; £100; £105
1743: DR £52 10s

COPE, JANE
1739: CR £50

Sir John Cope (1690–1760) was disinherited because his grandfather did not approve of the marriage of his parents. He was distantly connected to Sarah Bethel [▶ p. 251]. He married firstly in 1712 Jane Duncombe, sister of Baron Feversham; he was in Parliament between 1722 and 1741, knighted 1743. As a lieutenant general he commanded in Scotland at the outbreak of the 1745 rebellion and was routed by Prince Charles Stuart at Prestonpans. He was cleared at a court martial but not employed again; described as 'a cowardly incompetent; a little, dressy, finical man'.[1] In Bath, the Copes were in Barton Street, and therefore close neighbours of Paul Bertrand. John Wood described the house thus:[2]

> … another House erected by me in the Year 1733 on the East Side of the North End of the same Street for publick Use, but afterwards divided into three Tenements, now the property of Sir John Cope, Sir Edward Stanley and Mrs Codrington, are plain Samples … which by Dress, and an Increase of Magnitude, may be raised from the Rank of Cottages to that of Superb Edifices'.

Sir John's second wife, Elizabeth, is more likely to be the Lady Cope who was living in Queen Square in 1766 than Mary Cope [below].[3]

Possibly the same man who in 1717 was described as 'of Chelsea' when he insured warehouses in the City.[4] With regard to the debit entry, although this is most likely to refer to the same person, it is well to remember that the man who cut the Pitt diamond some twenty-five years previously was also called John Cope.

Portrait: NPG.

1. *DNB* and Sedgwick. 2. Wood 1765. 3. Bath RO: Walcot Church Rate 1749, and 1766 City Rate Book. 4. HinH, vol. 17, fo. 108.

COPE, MARY
1739–40: CR £50; £50; £50; £100; £100; £100; £50; £50; £50

Probably the wife of Sir Jonathan Cope of Brewern (created baronet 1713), a kinsman of Sir John Cope (above). One of her daughters, Anne, married Sir Thomas Whitmore; another daughter was named Mary. Given the date of her husband's death, it is unlikely that the 'Lady Cope' living in Queen Square, Bath, in 1766 was she; it is more likely to have been the second wife of Sir John Cope (above).[1] Mary was, however, a favoured name in the family of the latter: each of the first four baronets had a daughter so called.

Portrait: Bernard Lens, Thomas Whitmore as a child (CL 2 June 2009 lot 225) [▶ p. 184].

1. Bath RO: 1766 Rate Book.

COPSEEL, WM *see* GOPSILL

CORRY, HUGH
1738: DR £40
1740: CR £43

An insurance policy of 1713 lists Corry 'over against the Crooked Billet' in Petty France, Westminster; he took out separate policies for his goods and his dwelling house.[1] Possibly a connection of John Corrie, merchant, George Yard, Lombard Street.[2]

1. Sun Ins, vol. 3, p. 10. 2. Kent 1740.

CORTON, JAS
1737–39: DR £25; £33

COSTER & PERCIVAL
1736: CR £50

Probably Thomas Coster (1684–1739), MP for Bristol 1734–39. The ledgers of the silversmith George Wickes list 'Coster, Esq' Bristol. He inherited copper works in Bristol and mining interests in Cornwall. His first wife was Jane, daughter of Thomas Rous of Gloucestershire [▶ p. 306].[1] For the Percival family, including Joseph Percival [▶ p. 300].

1. Sedgwick.

COTES, (?COATES) HUMPY
1739 and 1741: DR £23 2s 6d; £4 16s

The Coates family of clockmakers do not appear to include a Humphrey.

COTTERELL, JNO
1736–45: DR £21; £20 12s 6d; £47 4s; £20; £28 5s; £9 19s 6d; £20; £6 6s; £20; £20; £40; £50; £27 14s

London chinaman.

▶ p. 220.

COULTHURST, WM
1744: CR 're Walter Wiltshire'

Prince Hoare's wife was 'Miss Coulthurst of Melksham' who he married in 1751; her family were clothiers.[1] The Colthurst family owned Abbey House in Bath from 1543 (demolished 1755) and other property in the city.[2] [▶ p. 142 illus.] An invoice dated London 16 July 1746 for tobacco powder and Hungary water, is signed Will Coulthurst 'for my father Henry'.[3]

1. BJ, 3 June 1751 quoted by Newby, 1986, p. 107. 2. Forsyth p. 105. 3. Hoare.

COURTNY, HENRY
1738: CR £56 16s 6d

At Oxford in 1731 aged 17,[1] MP for Honiton, Devon, died in 1763. Married in 1737 Catherine, daughter of 1st Earl Bathurst; they had two sons and two daughters.[2] His father and elder brother, both William and successively 2nd and 3rd Bts of Powderham, Devon, also sat in the House of Commons. A Capt Courtney who features in Richard Nash's account with Hoare[3] may be of the same family.

Portrait: Thomas Hudson, *The Courtenay Children*, c. 1744–45 (Powderham Castle).

1. Foster. 2. Sedgwick. 3. Lr. 28, fo. 48.

COWARD, LEOD
1743–47: DR £79; £41 10s; £72 5s; £50; £44 19s; £50; £27 5s; £32 6s; £40; £34 5s; £50; £24 3s; £44 5s; £13 13s 6d; £40

Bath laceman.

▶ p. 175.

COWELL & CO.
1742: CR £100

COWPER, JOS
1744: CR £50

Possibly a connection of William, 2nd Earl Cowper (1709–64), a Lord of the Bedchamber 1733–47; he arrived in Bath on 8 April 1745. 'Lady Cowper' came to Bath on 24 September 1744; the ledger entry is for January 1744/45.

COX, JNO
1738: DR £6

Uncertain identity and a common name; three possible candidates are suggested:

John Cox, clothier, of Trowbridge, is mentioned in a property advertisement in 1747.[1] In the Tollemache papers there is a bill for clothes and linen bought from John Cox in August 1731; the Earl of Dysart took four years to pay this bill, by which time Cox had died so an unlikely candidate.[2]

There was a merchant in Bury Street, St Mary-Ax,[3] likely to be the brother of Viscountess Preston [▶ p. 303]; their father was a 'wholesale grocer of Aldersgate'.[4]

In 1717 a goldsmith 'at the Peacock in Cornhill' took out an insurance policy 'for his mill at Bromley near Bow'.[5]

1. BJ, 27 July 1747. 2. Buckminster: Box 921-25. 3. Kent 1740. 4. GEC. 5. Sun Ins, vol. 7 fo. 167 [9781].

COXE, DR WM
1744: CR £35

Physician to the King's household.

COXE, ROBT
1744: DR £118 10s

Uncertain identity. Robert Cox, goldsmith and refiner, was apprenticed to Humphrey Payne in London in 1745 and died in 1790, but his father was Edward Cox of Somerset 'gentleman' not Robert.[1]

1. Grimwade; Fox.

CRABB, WM
1743: DR £20

William Crabb witnessed the will of Walter Wiltshire snr in 1743.

CRACHERODE, JNO
1744: CR £20

Uncertain identity. Possibly John Cracherode, a cabinet maker at the Tea Table, Henrietta Street, London.[1]

Or a relation of Anthony Cracherode of Cholderton, Wilts, an MP, who died unmarried in 1752; or of Col. Mordaunt Cracherod of Queen Square, Westminster.[2]

There are bills from Thomas Cracherode (a draper) to the Duke of Portland in the 1720s.[3]

1. Sun Ins, vol. 14, fo. 406 [26583] £500. 2. 1749 poll. 3. Nottingham Univ Libr, P1 F1/3/2/1-66.

CRAGG, JNO
1736–37 DR £41; £7 15s; £25

CRAGG, JANE
1740: DR £18 7s

Uncertain identities. Probably the London silversmith of New Street, Cloth Fair, who entered a mark in 1730.[1] Or, John Craig who was a partner of George Wickes c. 1730–35, but his widow, who went into partnership with John Neville, was called Anne.

1. Grimwade; Jowett.

CRANE, MICHL
1743: DR £15

CRANMER, JAMES
1737: CR £10 10s

James Cranmer, of Mitcham, died a month after his brother Samuel (below). His son James, also of Mitcham, who was an attorney of Gray's Inn, married Ann Toll (1729-68) in 1750 [▶ p. 316].[1]

1. *London Evening Post*, 14–16 June 1750; *St James's Chronicle*, 10–12 May 1768.

CRANMER, SAM (AND 'MR CRANMER')
1739–45: CR £12 12s; £100; £60; £100; £20; £30; £40; £40; £20; £50; £20; £20

Samuel Cranmer (or Cranmore) nr Serjeants Inn, Fleet St, is listed from 1722 variously described as merchant, goldsmith and banker; his will describes him as goldsmith.[1] He died in 1752 at Mitcham, where James Cranmer (above) also lived. He is presumably the same Samuel Cranmer who signed an invoice in 1729 to Richard Hoare for a 'coat and westcoat buttons and all'[2] and who featured with William Deards as plaintiff in a 1734 chancery case.[3]

1. Heal LG; H-Price. 2. Hoare: Boxes of Receipts. 3. TNA: C/1517

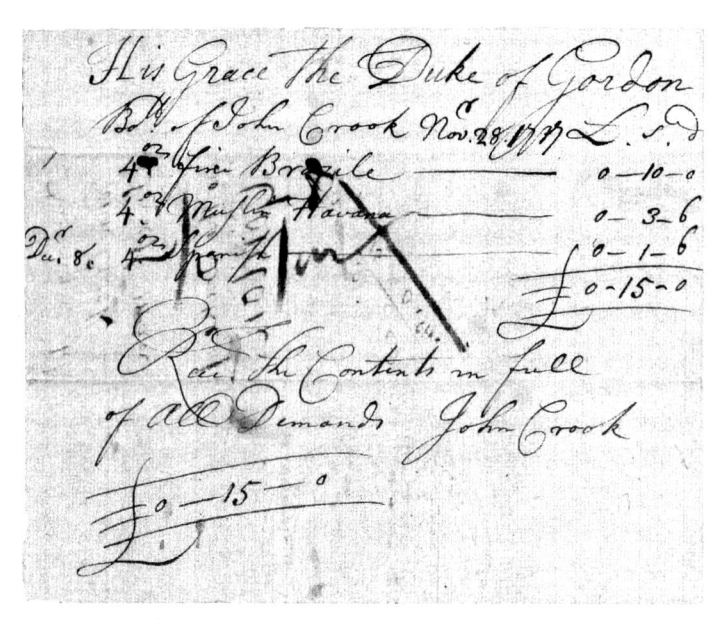

Invoice from John Crook to the Duke of Gordon for tobacco. (Goodwood, NAS44/51/465/3/52)

CRASTER, JNO
1742: CR £40

Probably John Craster, a barrister and MP for Wembley 1754–61. He married Catherine Villiers in 1726 and died in 1763.

CRESSETT, DEAN
1746–47: CR £30; £7 14s 6d; £100

The ledgers of the silversmith George Wickes have Dean Creswick of Bristol, 1737;[1] Bishop of Llandaff 1749, d. 1755.[2] He was prominent in the foundation of the infirmary in Bristol and was a friend and executor of John Elbridge, a sugar merchant who acted as treasurer for the statue of William III in Queen Square, Bristol.[3] The 1st Earl of Egmont commented in November 1735 that 'It appeared by the Dean's writing, which was very bad, that he is a man of no learning, for in six lines he made five notorious false spellings.'[4]

1. Wickes. 2. Foster. 3. Eustace. 4. Egmont, vol. II, 1734–38, p. 204.

CRESWELL, JNO
1743: 1 DR £41

London silversmith.

▶ p. 222.

CREYKER, ELIZ
1746: CR £50

Possibly Creyke, of Devon or of Marton, Yorks.

CRISP, MARY
1746: CR £50

Uncertain identity. Possibly a connection of Thomas Crisp, MP for Ilchester 1727–34,[1] or of Nicholas Crisp, jeweller and pottery manufacturer at Vauxhall.[2]

1. Sedgwick. 2. Edgcumbe p. 109; Scarisbrick.

CROMP, THOS
1737–39: CR £100; £100; £50

Supervisor of the Duke of Kingston's estates.[1]

▶ p. 92.

1. Lincoln RO: MON 28/B/12/4, 1725–27.

CROOK, JNO
1738: DR £26 17s 6d

Uncertain identity, but probably a snuff man.[1]

▶ p. 266 illus.

1. NAS: invoice to Duke of Gordon GD44/51/465.3.52.

CURTIS, THOS
1737–38: DR £16; £10; £18 10s; £17

Uncertain identity. Thomas Curtis, goldsmith, Red Lion Court, Fleet St, insolvent 1723.[1] Or, a Thomas Curtis countersigned a note that took a circuitous route: '17 July 1741 £160; payment of 3 October 1741 to Daniel Adey Esq £200 countersigned Thomas Curtis, [it then went] via Geo Arnold & Co., Bristol 17 October 1741 pr Post to London'.[2]

1. Heal LG. 2. Badminton: FmI 4/14.

CURZON, LADY
1747: CR £150

Mary (d. 1776), daughter of Sir Ralph Assheton, 2nd Bt. Her arrival in Bath is listed on 13 April 1747; and that of her husband Sir Nathaniel Curzon, 4th Bt (1675–1758) on 20 October 1747 and 9 May 1748. He was President of the Mineral Water Hospital, Bath 1753. Their son Nathaniel (1726–1804) of Kedleston, was created 1st Baron Scarsdale in 1761.

Portrait: Jonathan Richardson the Elder: *Sir Nathaniel Curzon with his wife Mary Assheton and their sons John and Nathaniel.*

D

DALTON, JNO
1744: DR £30

John Dalton was apprenticed to John Bailey 1707. He did not register a mark, but probably worked with his father, Andrew, who was in Lombard Street in 1708.[1]

1. GH: Apprentice Book; Grimwade.

DASHWOOD, CHANR
1741: CR £40

Uncertain identity. Chamberlayne Dashwood (d. 1743), eldest son of Sir Robert Dashwood, Bt. Or, Francis Dashwood, 15th Baron le Despencer (1708–81) founder of the Hell-fire Club and Chancellor of the Exchequer 1762–63.

DAVIS, CAREW
1737: CR £25 4s 6d

In 1723/24 Carew Davis paid Bath Corporation £200 'for the two pumps at the Kings Bath' (an annual fee), and a further 5s for an 'incroachment' in Cross Bath Lane.[1]

1. Bath RO: Chamberlain Account Rolls, typescript vol. 2.

DAVIS, GEO
1744: DR £51 11s

Uncertain identity and a common name. Possibly a cabinet maker, will proved 17 February 1759.[1] His business may have spanned several generations: in 1776 there was a cabinet-maker of the same name on the south side of Orange Grove, following Eleanor Davies at the same address.

1. PROB 11/844.

DAVIS, JOHN
1744: DR £200

His India-House sold the remaining stock of Paul Bertrand in 1748.

▶ p. 176.

DAVIS, WM
1736 and 1741: DR £14 14s; £10 11s

Possibly William Devis, watchmaker and goldsmith at the Dial, opposite St Dunstan's Church, Fleet Street.[1]

1. Trade card: BM: Banks 67.46.

DAWNAY, MRS
1739: CR £68 15s

Possibly a member of the family of Viscount Downe.

DEARDS, WM
1737: DR: £47 10s

1737–44: CR £21; £105; £31 10s; £40; £40; £40; £204 14s 6d; £50

William Deards (d. 1761), brother of Mary Bertrand.

DE BEROT, DENIS
1740: CR £20

DEFEURE, LEWIS
1736: DR £10 10s

DEHORNE, A
1745: CR £30

DE LA HYDE, MRS
1737: CR £5

DELETANG, PR
1736–41: DR £75; £45 9s; £33 10s; £20; £35; £39; £10 10s

Peter de L'Etang features in the will of William Hubert [▶ p. 227] described as a diamond cutter in the parish of St Gregory. He is listed as de Leting, jeweller, Crown Court in the Old Change, Cheapside against Distaff Lane, 1744.[1] ▶ p. 211/4 map

1. Heal LG.

DELL, NATH
1739: DR £15

In 1745 Nathan Dell was a witness to the will of James Slater, a merchant taylor.[1] Possibly a relative of Henry Dell, a goldsmith recorded 1706–24.[2]

1. PROB 11/778
2. Grimwade.

DELME, PR
1739: CR £550

Delme's father was a silk merchant, one time Lord Mayor of London and Governor of the Bank of England, who was worth £250,000 on his death in 1728.[1] Peter Delme was in Conduit Street in 1734; he is in the ledgers of the silversmith George Wickes 1735–36.[2] As an MP 1734–54 he represented Ludgershall and Southampton. He is listed as arriving in Bath on 8 October 1744, and was a governor of the

Mineral Water Hospital 1748.³ The Duchess of Northumberland recorded his suicide in 1770:⁴

> Peter Delme Esq having on some pretence or other sent out his wife and daughter, he went into his Garden & shot himself. The world were much at a loss how to account for the Act of Desperation, as Mr Delme was a religious charitable quiet placid Man of Business, of very great riches; of calm unruffled passions; who fill'd up all his Hours by making improvements in his Estate, whereas these catastrophes generally proceed from a Fever, a ruin'd Fortune or violent strong passions.

▶ p. 291 Lupart.

Portrait: James Seymour, *Mr Peter Delme's hounds on the Hampshire Downs*, 1738, (Paul Mellon Collection of Sporting Art). Property: Place House, now Titchfield Abbey, Hants (English Heritage); his family owned Erlestoke, Wilts. among other properties.
Tray, Paul de Lamerie 1735/6 with the arms of Delme's sister Anne, and Sir Henry Liddell 4th Bt, who she married in 1735 (Al Tajir, no. 71).

1. Gwynn; Wagner. 2. Wickes. 3. *BJ*. 4. Alnwick: diary 10 April 1770.

DELOR, MR
1737: DR £6 6s

Uncertain identity. Possibly Francis Lewis Delor, whose son Lewis was apprenticed to the silversmith Peze Pilleau in 1739.

DELORANE, LADY
1741: CR £30

Three women bore this title in 1741. Mary Howard (1703–44) married in 1726, as his second wife, the 1st Earl of Deloraine (who died in 1730). She then became governess to George II's youngest daughters, Mary and Louisa, and the king's mistress. In 1734 she married William Wyndham (d. 1789) [▶ p. 323], but was still referred to as Lady Deloraine. A letter dated 4 December 1736 from Helena Le Grand [▶ p. 289] to Lady Burlington, refers to Lady De La Reyne being in Bath.¹ The ledger entries for Mr Wyndham are also for 1741, so 'Lady Delorane' is less likely to refer to one of the widows of her two step-sons, the 2nd and 3rd earls, who died in May 1739 and January 1739/40, aged 29 and 28 respectively.

▶ p. 128.

Portrait: William Hogarth, *A Portrait of 'The Indian Emperor'* (Hallett, no. 53).

1. Chatsworth.

DELVIN, LORD
1743: DR £26 5s

Presumably Christopher Nugent, Lord Delvin, son of the Earl of Westmeath, who died two months before his father, in 1752 at Bath and was buried in Bath Abbey.

DEMARIN, JNO
1743: DR £20

John Demarine (Demorin) listed as a jeweller, St Martin le Grand, in 1749.¹ He died in 1761.² Presumably the same as John Lewis Damareen [▶ p. 169]. Perhaps connected to James Demarin, a clockmaker.

▶ p. 314 Francis Sutherland.

1. 1749 poll. 2. Wagner.

DENNE, ADAM
1744: CR £40

Adam Denne, silk throwster, Mason's Court, Spittal Fields.¹

1. Kent 1740.

DENNE, COR
1744: CR £39

Uncertain identity. Possibly linked to Snow & Denne [▶ p. 310]; William Denny, broker, was listed in Silver Street, St James.¹ Or a connection of the Revd Dr John Denne, who had an account with Hoare & Co.

1. 1749 poll.

DERBIE, JNO
1743: CR £150

John Derbie's signature, and also that of Ben Derbie, endorses numerous money orders in the papers of the Fox Strangways family.¹

1. Dorset RO: D/FSI Box 239.

DE[A]RING, MARY
1738: DR £20
1738–40: CR £20; £20; £30; £30; £30; £30; £40; £30; £30; £10

▶ p. 162.

DERVAUX, STE
1737: DR £40; £11 15s

DEVAUX / DESVAUX, STE
1736–38 DR £15 18s; £15 15s; £31 10s

S. Devaux, wine merchant, features in the accounts of the 3rd Duke of Bedford, 28 May 1726.¹

1. Woburn: Account Book 1724–33.

DESCA, PAUL
1736–37: DR £20; £12; £15

Tobacco and snuff seller.¹ A 1735 advertisement is illustrated with the use of a tobacco rasp:²

> The oldest Manufacturer of all Sorts of superfine Rappee Snuffs, made after the best French Manner at the Sign of the Spaniard in New Street, Covent Garden. Makes French Rappee, Rappee Clarac, Havannah Rappees, fine Rappee Rolls, best Rappee Brazil, best Scotch Snuffs, fine Havanah, Spanish and italian Snuffs, &c. Wholesale and Retail, at the lowest Price.

1. Heal, 117.38. 2. *London Evening Post*, 8–11 February 1735 [1128].

DESEROTE, JNO
1740: CR £50

Mr Deserote is mentioned as a friend of the Duke of Chandos in

1698. Forty years on this might be the same man, or a relative.[1]

1. Baker.

DESKFORD, LORD
1742: DR £70

James Ogilvy, later 6th Earl of Findlater, styled Lord Deskford from August 1730 on the death of his grandfather. Horace Walpole wrote in 1740 that 'his solemn Scotchery is not a little formidable'. He committed suicide in 1770.

DE VIC, ISAAC (AND JNR)
1742–46: DR £7; £4 3s 7d; £80; £14 14s; £80; £64; £13; £24

DE VIC, ELIZA
1743: DR £40

Isaac De Vic's firm had branches in Southampton, Bristol and Guernsey as well as Bath; they were importers of fine wines. In 1753 (after Bertrand's retirement) he advertised in the *Bath Journal* that he was opening a bank for 'persons who have an occasion to remit money from London to Bath, or from thence to London …', giving his address as near the North Parade, Bath. In 1761 John Viel, de Vic's cooper for over 20 years, set up in business on his own account in St James's Street, Bath.

It is worth noting another, who may have been related: 'Last Saturday died at his House in King Street, St Ann's, Mr de Vic, Watchmaker to his Royal Highness, the Prince of Wales',[1] and also that early in the century Isaac de Vic was described as a druggist or chemist in Southampton.[2]

1. *The London Evening Post*, January 1750. 2. Sun Ins, vol. 4, fo. 184.

DICKER, W
1745: DR £100

Uncertain identity. Possibly William Dicker, who entered a mark as a smallworker in 1720. He is recorded at Ball Alley, Lombard Street until bankruptcy in 1728, but could have continued to work thereafter.[1] In 1749 Earl Fitzwalter paid 'John Hunt of Bath by the hands of Walter Dicker for six Dozen of Mountain Wine £8'.[2]

1. Grimwade; Heal LG.
2. Edwards p. 97.

DICKINSON, VICKI
1743–44: DR £46 17s 3d; £52 10s

Possibly a connection of Joseph Dickinson, goldsmith, St Edmundsbury, who died in 1743.[1]

1. Heal LG.

DICKS, THOS
1743: DR £9

Thomas Dicks was apprenticed to Thomas Wale in 1704.[1] Perhaps related to a Robert Dicks, jeweller, recorded in 1722.[2]

1. GH: Apprentice Book. 2. Heal LG.

DILLON, ROBT & C
1746: CR £24

Theob & Robert Dillon, merchants, Old Broad Street.[1]

1. Kent 1740.

DILLON, WM
1745: DR £36 13s

Uncertain identity. A Mr Dillon had an interest in the playhouse acquired for building the hospital, but there is no reason to suppose a connection.[1]

1. Falconer, p. 18.

DOBSON, WM
1741: DR £8 8s

Uncertain identity. Heal lists Prior Dobson & Williams, plate worker, Paternoster Row 1755 – might the names have been jumbled by the bank's clerk?[1]

Trade cards survive for John Dobson, chinaman, St Martin's Court, and Edward Dobson.[2]

1. Heal LG. 2. V&A; BM.

DODSON, H
1738: 1 CR £10 10s

DOLLPHUS, J. GESS
1745: CR £16

John George Dolfus, merchant, Cloak Lane, College Hill.[1]

1. Kent 1740.

DOMCKE, GEO PR
1742: DR £13

George Peter Domcke published, c.1730, *Philosophiæ Mathematicæ Newtonianæ illustratæ tomi duo*, a discussion of Isaac Newton's *Principia*. He is under 'Persons of other Nations' in the list of the Royal Society.[1]

1. Chamberlayne, Pt II, Bk III, p. 130.

DONERAILE, LORD
1743: DR £137 3s; £11 9s

Arthur St Leger, 3rd Viscount Doneraile (1718–50), MP for Winchilsea 1741–47 and Old Sarum 1747–50 (as an Irish peer without an English title, he could enter the House of Commons). Comptroller, then Gentleman of the Bedchamber to the Prince of Wales 1747–50. He died at Lisbon and was succeeded by his uncle who also died without issue in 1767 when the title became extinct; he was buried Bath Abbey.[1]

> Lord Doneraile has left Miss St Leger (commonly called Sellinger) near an hundred thousand pounds, to confirm the world that their censures were not without foundation. I heard that Lady Doneraile said she would not go into mourning for her Lord, but I hear she has.

Lord Doneraile, and other members of the St Leger family, were customers of the jeweller Arthur Webb; he sold them diamonds to the value of £436 2s in 1745.[2]

Property: Doneraile Park, Co. Cork.

1. Mrs Delany, ser 1 vol. 2, p. 600.
2. TNA. C108/284.

DOUGHTY, JNO
1746–47: CR £60; £40 16s

Uncertain identity. Possibly of Gloucestershire, matriculated Oxford 1729/30 aged 16, MA 1736.[1]

1. Foster.

DOUGHTY, THOS
1743: DR £42

Uncertain identity. Heal has Margaret York alias Doughty, pawnbroker 1725, but it seems an unlikely connection for Bertrand.

DOWNING, JACOB GARRARD
1740: DR £50

Jacob Garrard Downing Bt (c. 1717–64) was cousin and heir to Sir George Downing, 3rd Bt, who died in 1749. Downing Street was built in an earlier generation. Sir George instructed that if the male line failed, the estate should be used to found a college at Cambridge. Without children, Sir Jacob's widow refused to give up the estates and costly legal actions continued until 1800, leaving little money for the college that finally began to be built in 1807.[1] Jacob Downing appears in the ledgers of the silversmith George Wickes, 1740–41; he was MP for Dunwich, Suffolk.

1. DNB; Downing College website.

DRAKE, ISAB:
1741: CR £50

Probably the 'Madam Drake' listed as arriving in Bath on 1 October 1744. Isabella Marshall married Montague Drake of Shardeloes, nr Amersham, Bucks, in 1719.[1] In 1717 Montague Garratt [Garrard] Drake of Bond Street insured goods 'in his chambers up 3 pair of stairs at the Kings Head in Albemarle Street' and his wealth may be gauged by the high sum of £1,000 for which he insured the contents of his house in Portugal Row, Lincoln's Inn in 1720/21.[2] Following his death in 1728 (while his heir was a child), the family lawyer Marmaduke Alington [▶ p. 246] was returned in their interest as MP for Amersham. Isabella Drake had an account with Hoare, listed as 'Guardian to her son'. No connection has yet been made between the Drake families at Shardeloes and at Fernhill, Berks (portrait by William Hoare, now in the Victoria Art Gallery, Bath).

▶ p. 293 Massingberd.

Monument: See Craske, p. 438, n. 163, re the contract between Isabella Drake and Peter Scheemakers for the monument to her husband at Amersham.

1. Burke, *Commoners*, vol. 1, p. 582; Sedgwick. 2. Sun Ins, vol. 7, fo. 11 [8987] and vol. 12, p. 548 [22089].

DRUMMOND, AND
1738–46: CR £100; £25; £210; £20; £100; £30; £40; £180; £31 10s; £100; £50; £50; £132; £100

Andrew Drummond (1688–1769) was banker to the 1st Duke of Chandos among others. He was apprenticed to the goldsmith Colin McKenzie in Edinburgh but was in London by 1712 and started banking in 1717 near to Northumberland House at the Golden Eagle (also called the Golden Faulcon) Charing Cross.[1] Various members of his family subsequently entered the partnership. ▶ p. 211/20 map

Portrait: Johan Joseph Zoffany (Mellon collection), mezzotint by James Watson, in which he holds a snuffbox and cane.
Property: Stanmore House, Middx, which he altered to the designs of John Vardy and Sir William Chambers.

1 Sun Ins, vol. 6, fo. 315 [8712], July 1717.

DUFRESNAY, SAML
1745: CR £49 8s

Samuel Dufresnay & Son, merchants, St Helen's.[1]

1. Kent 1740.

DUNCOMBE, JNO [JNO FRAINE]
1746: CR £93 0s 10d

Uncertain identity. 'Mr Duncombe' is listed on 30 October 1746 as having arrived in Bath (the ledger entry is for February 1746/47) and a Col. Duncombe is listed on 31 August 1747.[1] Col. John Duncombe's granddaughter Susanna married in 1749, as his second wife, Admiral Robert Harland and 'brought him £40,000'.[2]

Anthony Duncombe, created Lord Feversham of Downton in 1747, inherited a considerable fortune from his uncle Sir Charles Duncombe, a goldsmith banker.

▶ p. 264 Cope.

1. *BJ*. 2. Bettany, p. 146.

DUPONT, LEWIS
1738: DR £16 4s; £26 19s; £50

Dupont entered his first mark in 1736 with an address in Wardour Street, Soho; he moved to Compton Street in 1739 when he registered a second mark, and was bankrupt 1747.[1] When his son Stephen was apprenticed to Samuel Courtauld in 1753, he was 'late of St Anne's Westminster but now of the Island of St Domingo, merchant'; another son was apprenticed to Isaac Chartier in 1754. Members of the Dupont family appear in the Royal Bounty Lists between 1691 and 1728, including Etienne, Mary, David.[2]

1. GH: Apprentice Book; Grimwade. 2. Copies in V&A and GH.

DUPPLIN, LORD
1744–46: CR £45; £30

Thomas Hay (1710–87) styled Lord Dupplin 1719–58, later 9th Earl of Kinnoull. He was MP for Cambidge 1741–58; Chancellor of the Duchy of Lancaster 1758–62. According to Horace Walpole he was reckoned among the thirty ablest men in the House of

Commons.[1] 'Far from a fool, he probably owed his reputation of being one to the fact that the word for a bore had yet to be invented.'[2] In 1734 the Duchess of Portland (his cousin) wrote of 'poor Dup's misfortune' [▶ p. 86].[3]

He married in 1741 Constantia, daughter of John Kyrle Ernie of Whetham: the *Bath Journal* printed an advertisement in December 1745 regarding the sale of timber off the estate 'property of Lord Dupplin'. Dupplin was made an honorary freeman of the Bristol Merchant Adventurers in 1750, listed as a 'Lord of Trade'; and was President of the Mineral Water Hospital, Bath, in 1751.

He arrived in Bath on 22 October 1744 and 7 January 1744/45 (one ledger entry is for the latter month), when Lady Dupplin donated 2 guineas to the hospital. The second ledger entry is for 26 March 1746, when his presence in Bath was published on the 31st.[4] In London he is listed in Sackville Street.[5]

▶ p. 35.

Property: Whetham, Wilts.; Brodsworth Yorks. (his younger brother, Archbishop of York).

1. *Peerage*. 2. Sedgwick. 3. Delany, vol. 1, p. 521. 4. *BJ*. 5. 1749 poll.

DURRANCE, ROT
1745: DR £16 19s 6d

Playing card maker and master of his livery company. He held the royal appointment of Frederick, Prince of Wales. He was in Moorfields.

▶ p. 211/1 map

DUVALL, JNO
1738–41: DR £30; £56 10s

John and Peter Duval became royal jewellers and watchmakers. Rundell, Bridge & Rundell acquired the business of John Duval Sons & Co. in 1798. Lord Chesterfield wrote to his son from London, 27 March 1748:

> This little packet will be delivered to you by one Monsieur Duval, who is going to the fair at Leipsig: he is a jeweller, originally of Geneva, but who has been settled here these eight or ten years, and a very sensible fellow. Pray be very civil to him.

This suggests that Bertrand's dealings with Duval were soon after Duval had come to London. In 1749 Peter Duval (Devallee) gent, was listed in Wardour Street.[1] John Duval dealt with the Webb family of jewellers, e.g. an entry in their journal for 14 July 1752.[2] He may been the 'Mr Deval' who briefly featured in the trial of the jeweller Henry Govers.[3] Invoices in the 1750s and '60s are headed 'Fr & John Duval' or 'John & Peter Duval'.[4]

1. 1749 poll. 2. TNA: C108/284. 3. Culme 2000. 4. Woburn: Box NMR 19/23/3.

▶ p. 211/27 map

DUVILLIARD, DL
1745–46: DR £20; £25

Uncertain identity. Could this be Duvivier? Lambert Duvivier was a fan maker.

DYSON, MRS
1746: CR £31 8s 3d

E

EDEY, MARY
1741 and 1743: DR £27 13s; £30

Possibly a connection of Bartholomew Edye, who advertised lessons in shorthand in Bristol.[1]

1. *BJ*, 30 March 1746/47.

EDWARDS, JNO & SON
1745: CR £40

John Edwards, South-Sea Director, Old Jury;[1] and probably the person referred to in a 1731 advertisement:[2]

> Lost in or about Exchange Alley this day, a Draught on the Bank of England, No 5437, N. for 530 l drawn by Mr John Edwards, payable to Mr. Benjamin Mussaphia or Bearer

1. Kent 1740. 2. *London Gazette*, 22–26 June 1731 [6998].

ELKINGTON, SAML
1740: CR £44
1745: DR £40

The Elkingtons were an extensive Bath family. Samuel was a merchant taylor who took numerous apprentices, for example in 1731, 1735, 1736 and 1745.[1] An invoice to Lord Glenorchy is dated 23 October 1740, the entry in Bertrand's account is for the following

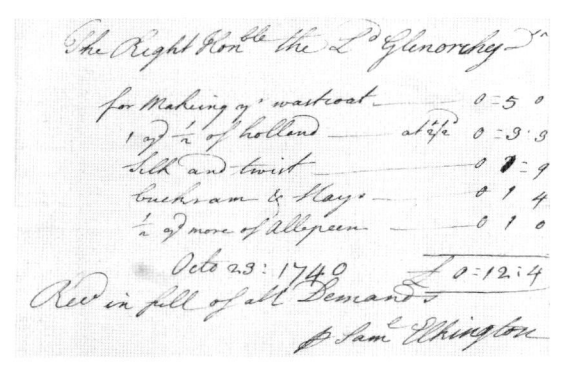

Invoice from Samuel Elkington dated 23 October 1740, for a waistcoat. Lord Glenorchy (1695/6–1782) succeeded his father as 3rd Earl of Breadalbane in 1752. His second wife died at Bath in 1762. (NAS, GD112/21/268/4)

January, 1740/41.² When he died in 1756 the lease of his property was taken over by William Glazby, who took Elkington's son as apprentice.³ Samuel jnr was in Westgate Street in 1767.⁴

▶ p. 271 illus.

1. Bath RO. 2. NAS: GD112/21/268. 3. Neale, p. 673. Bath RO: Rate Book no. 4, p. 14. 4. Bath RO.

ELLIOTT, ARCHD
1738: DR £14 13s

Uncertain identity. Possibly Mr Elliot, gold and silver snuffbox maker, near Carnaby Market, who died of 'a consumption' at Isleworth.¹

1. *Public Advertiser*, 3 April 1753 [5750].

ELLIOTT, JNO
1745: CR £30

Too common a name for positive identification: possibly John Elliott, gent, listed in Curzon Street.¹

1. 1749 poll.

ELLIOTT, RD
1742: CR £100

Uncertain identity. Possibly the husband of Ralph Allen's sister Gertrude, who she married in 1732, of St Austell.¹

Or, Richard Eliot (1694–1748) MP for St Germans and Liskeard between 1733 and 1748; Surveyor General to Frederick, Prince of Wales at £800pa.² When he died he was in financial difficulties caused, his wife believed, by the cost of his Duchy office.³

1. Allen. 2. Chamberlayne, Pt II, Bk III, p. 248. 3. Sedgwick.

ELLIS, SAML
1744: CR £50

EVERELL, MRS
1738 CR £10 10s

Possibly the wife of John Everell, watchmaker, 'at the clock nr the Maypole in the Strand', recorded 1716–43, although this is a credit entry.¹ For a watch signed Everell see SL 13 June 1964 lot 21.

1. Sun Ins, vol. 5, fo. 127 [7795] January 1716/17.

EWER, MR
1745: CR £80

Probably John Ewer, banker in Pall Mall, 1730–54, previously a clerk to George Middleton in the Strand,¹ described as 'an eminent goldsmith in Pall mall'.² There was also a clockmaker of this name, at the Dyal in Plumb Tree St, St Giles, in 1720.³

1. H-Price and Outing. 2. T*he Daily Journal*, 1 July 1735. 3. Sun Ins, vol. 12, p. 221 [19703].

EYLES, JNO
1743: CR £25; DR £36; £63

Sir John Eyles, 2nd Bt (1683–1745). MP for Chippenham, a director of the East India Company and of the Bank of England, and Lord Mayor 1726–27. He married his cousin Mary Haskin Styles [▶ p. 314].¹ George Lillo prefixed his play 'The London Merchant or The History of George Barnwell' with a dedication to Sir John. The play was first staged at Drury Lane in June 1731. Lillo and his father are thought to have been goldsmith/jewellers.²

1. Sedgwick and Burke, *Extinct Baronetage*. 2. DNB

EYNARD, ALEXR
1745: CR £30

F

FAGG, SR ROBT
1737–38: CR £50; £50
FAGG, LADY
1737–38: CR £50; £60
FAGG, ELIZA
1737: CR £50

Sir Robert Fagg, 3rd Bt, of Wiston, nr Steyning, Sussex, opened an account with Hoare in 1724 and was a keen racehorse owner: for example he had a horse running at Epsom on 27 May 1729, a race watched by Frederick, Prince of Wales.¹ He died in 1736, and was succeeded by his son, Robert (1704–40) MP for Steyning, Sussex 1734–40, who had married in 1729 Sarah Ward. Robert 4th Bt had no surviving children and his estates were inherited by his sister Elizabeth who married, as his second wife, Sir Charles Mathew Goring Bt; the title reverted to a cousin. The entries must be for the 4th baronet, his wife and sister.

The account of Christian, Lady Fagg at Hoare & Co. shows a payment to Bertrand of £45 4s 1½d, proving that the record of Bertrand's own account reveals only part of his business dealings.

1. Vivian p. 125.

FAIFAY, FERDO
1746: DR £50

This is probably the 'Ferd: Fairfax Esqr' who had an account with Hoare & Co. In addition to the entry above (for June 1746 in Bertrand's account), Fairfax's own account has Bertrand listed in February 1745/46 and April 1746 – but these transactions do not feature in Bertrand's account.

FAIRFAX, LORD
1741: DR £130

▶ p. 42.

FARNWORTH, WM & CO.
1745–46: CR £100; £60

FARREN, MR
1737: CR £60

Possibly the London silversmith Thomas Farren, but it is unusual that this is a credit entry unless it represents a banking transaction. Farren was presumably dead by 1743 when his wife Ann entered a mark at Goldsmiths' Hall.

FAUQUIER [FAQUIERE], FRA
1738–45: DR £160; £100; £22 17s; £40
1738–45: CR £65; £30; £100; £50; £42 8s 6d

FAUQUIER & OLIVER
1738 and 1740: CR £100; £30; £51 13s; £14 13s 1d

Francis Fauquier (1703–68) was the son of a director of the Bank of England of French birth. He became a director of the South Sea Co., a governor of the Foundling Hospital and a fellow of the Royal Society. He was also a trustee of the Mineral Water Hospital, Bath, and one of its three treasurers, the others being Dr William Oliver and Richard Nash. His name is listed as early as February 1737 when fund-raising began and this is presumably the reason for some of the ledger entries.[1] On 3 June 1745 the *Bath Journal* advertised:

> To be Lett or Sold, One large commodius House, situate in Queen Square lately occupied by Francis Fauquier Esq having four Rooms on a Floor, finished in the Compleatest Manner, suitable for a large Family.

He was a customer of the silversmiths Parker & Wakelin, his address in London given as Argyll St,[2] at which address he was listed as Francis Foquhar/Foquair gent in 1749.[3] In 1758 he went to Virginia as Lt Governor and was there until his death.

Portrait: Benjamin Wilson (Thomas Coram Foundation, the Foundling Museum).

1. Bath RO: vol.0386/1.
2. Clifford. 3. 1749 poll.

FELINE, HENRY
1736: DR £105

FELINE, EDWARD
1736–41: DR £26; £40; £74; £34; £33 10s 11d; £49 11s 6d; £63; £29 10s; £36; £70; £61; £34 15s; £27 12s; £19 15s; £29 16s

London silversmith.
▶ p. 222.

FERRAND, EDWD
1737–38: DR £88 13s; £35; £58

Uncertain identity. Possibly a connection of Elizabeth Ferrand who in 1749 bequeathed 20 gns for a ring to 'my mistress the Duchess of Portland'.[1]

1. Wagner.

FERRETT, GRACE
1741: CR £13 3s

Uncertain identity. Possibly related to Richard, below – possibly from a Devon family, but they have not been traced. A John Ferrett 'late of Kingmore, Ireland' died in Bath in 1738.[1]

1. *London Evening Post*, 23 December 1738.

FERRET, RD
1743: CR £330

FIGES, JOHN
1744: DR £15 16s

Listed as a freemason, King's Arms, Cateton St, London in 1730.[1]

1. Songhurst.

FILSON, HENRY
1737: CR £100

FINES, MR
1738: CR £300

Uncertain identity. Probably Kendall Fines [Fynes], jeweller, at the Golden Ring in Villars (Villiers) Street, York Buildings.[1] Heal records him as insolvent in 1723, but he was trading in 1727 when a lost seal was advertised.[2]

Or a member of the Fynes family, painted by Thomas Hudson.[3]

1. Sun Ins, vol. 9, fo. 72, January 1718/19 7s 6d. 2. *Daily Post*, 13 January 1727 [2280].
3. Kenwood, no. 55, sold at auction in 1945.

FISH, JOS
1746: CR £100

FISHER, BRICE
1753–55: DR £35 15s 6d; £15 11s; £7 7s

MP and partner of William Baker [▶ p. 248]; see also Benjamin Griffin [▶ p. 278]. His printed signature appears on a 1758 Sun Fire Office receipt;[1] his close friend William Braund was a manager of that company 1751–74. Braund was also a director of the East India Company 1745–53 and traded extensively with Portugal: Fisher supplied him with cloth for that market. In 1754 Fisher was accused of fraudulent sales to the East India Company involving a group of Wiltshire clothiers.[2]

1. Hants RO: 44M69/E10/26 to Richard Jervoise. 2. Sutherland.

FISHER, THOS
1746: CR £21; £25 8s

Possibly of Freshford, Somerset; matriculated Oxford 1731/32 aged 18.[1] In London, a Thomas Fisher was listed in Wardour Street.[2]

1. Foster. 2. 1749 poll.

FITCH, GRACE
1743: CR £40

FITZGERALD, GEO: & CO.
1737: DR £40
1741–43: CR £50; £150; £100; £50

FITZHERBERT, RACHEL
1744: CR £50

FLEURY, ISAAC
1736: DR £17 5s 6d

Silversmith in Cecil Court, St Martin's Lane in 1721; married to Mary Buhet.[1] Ford sold Fleury's effects in 1739:[2]

> To be sold by Auction / Tomorrow and Wednesday next / All the Houshold Furniture and other Effects of Mr Isaac Fleury, Snuff-Box Maker, deceased, at his late Dwelling house next the Pine-

Apple in Castle Street, near Leicester Fields. Consisting of Crimson Mohair, Damask, and other Furniture, Glass Sconces, Wallnut-tree Book-cases and Buroes, Mahogany Tables, French Carpets, China, Linen and Wearing Apparel, several curious Snuff-boxes, Plate, Watches, Rings, and other curiosities, and his Working Tools. …

Possibly connected to Oliver Fleury who had a watch stolen out of the cabin of a French sloop at Brown's Wharf in 1740.[3]

In the unlikely event that Fleury is confused with Fleureau, it is worth noting the sword cutler Isaac Fleureau, who sold knee and other kinds of buckles;[4] and Francis Fleureau, a jeweller in Pall Mall in 1749.[5]

1. Sun Ins, vol. 13, p. 48, 1 April 1721; Wagner, p. 48. 2. *London Daily Post and General Advertiser*, 21 May 1739 [1423]. 3. POB: 17401015-48. 4. BM: Banks 52.27 (see Southwick), listed as attending a Masonic lodge in Southwark (Songhurst). 5. 1749 poll.

▶ p. 211/22 map

FLOYD, MISS
1743: CR £10

FLOYER, JANE
1736–43: CR £20; £20; £20; £20; £20; £20; £20; £20 [and 1 re Wm Turner]

Jane Turner married Charles Floyer in 1714; his father (Sir Peter) died in 1702; her brothers William and Nathaniel are listed below [▶ p. 318]. Charles and Jane's daughter, also Jane, married Norton Nicholls in 1741 – the correspondence of their son Norton (b. 1742 he later lived at Blundeston, Suffolk) is published.[1] Mrs Floyer is listed as arriving in Bath also in October 1747, when Bertrand was in the process of closing his shop. She and her son were buried in Richmond.

Charles and Jane Floyer both held accounts with Hoare.

It is worth noting here Peter Floyer, the refiner of Foster Lane, who had dealings with the silversmith Paul de Lamerie.[2]

1. Bettany. 2. POB: t17480224-40; Culme 2000, p. 108, etc. His widow died in 1732, *London Evening Post*, 13–15 April 13 1732 [683].

FOLET, JNO
1739: CR £14
1741: DR £105

FOLEY, PAUL
1736–37: CR £20

Paul Foley (d. 1739) of Newport, Herefordshire, married firstly Susannah, sister of Sir William Massingberd, 3rd Bt [▶ p. 293] and secondly, in 1722, Susannah, daughter of Henry Hoare.[1]

1. Sedgwick.

FOLL, MRS
1739: CR £20

FONNEREAU, PHIL
1739–41: CR £25; £10; £25
1739: DR £750

Zachary, Philip and Peter Fonnereau were merchants specialising in linen in 'Sise-lane', London.[1] In the seventeenth century the family had been watchmakers in La Rochelle. In 1735 their father, Claude Fonnereau, a Hamburg merchant who died in 1740, purchased Christchurch Mansion, Ipswich; he was an early patron of Francis Hayman.[2] Philip Fonnereau (1706–78) was MP for Aldeburgh 1747–74; his elder brother, Thomas, was also in parliament, for Sudbury and Aldeburgh.[3]

1. Kent 1740. 2. Allen 1983. 3. Sedgwick.

FORD, JNO
1747: DR £14 10s

John Ford, mason, one of those who built New King Street in Bath 1764–70.[1] The rate books list him near to Bertrand in Queen Street.

1. Forsyth, p. 252.

FORSTER, ELIZ
1745: DR £11

Uncertain identity. Possibly connected to Forster & Johnson, 'Jewellers & Goldsmiths at the Pearl in Wood Street, Cheapside … makes and sells and keeps constantly ready made great variety of Work at a reasonable Profit'.[1]

1. Trade card: Heal 67.147.

FORTH, ELIZA
1737: DR £40

FOSSICK, THOMAS
1746: CR £20; £30

FOTHERBY, FRANCES
1741: CR £21; £10 10s

Uncertain identity. Perhaps connected to John Fotherby Esq, of George St, York Buildings, London,[1] and/or to Mary Fotherby, the second wife of Sir Edward Dering, 5th Bt.

1. 1749 poll.

FOUBERT, THOS
1741: DR £15 15s

Thomas Foubert, goldsmith and jeweller, Crown & Pearl, Frith St Soho.[1] He had a 'Mathematical Machine' that he used to raffle objects: in 1735 he advertised plate and jewels, in 1737 William Deane's grand orrery and in 1738 a ' fine Table of Most exquisite Workmanship, inlaid with choice Collections of English Pebbles'. Chenevix's toyshop was one of the venues where 'particulars' of the raffles could be obtained.[2]

1. Heal LG. 2. *London Evening Post*, 31 May 1735 [1176] with illustration of the machine, 28 April 1737 [1475], and 23 February 1738 [1604].

FOWLER, ABM/AL
1746: CR £30; £30

Goldsmith banker at Three Squirrels, Fleet St; 1723–28 known as Abraham Fowler & Rocke; by the 1740s Gosling was in the partnership [▶ p. 277]. The firm is listed as Goslings & Sharpe until 1896.[1] Eli Fowler and his wife were left mourning rings in the will of Mary Deards, who died in 1739; they had been neighbours for many years, as Abraham Fowler is listed in Johnson's Court, in the property next to John Deards, between 1715 and 1720, having had insurance there in 1710.[2]

    1. Outing. 2. LMA: micr. 11,316. Sun Ins, vol. 1, p. 99.

FOX, HENRY
1736 and 1739: DR £178 10s; £252
1744–47 CR £25; £60 10s; £78 19s 6d; £53 3s; £100; £25; £25; £38 5s 6d; £25; £25

Henry Fox (1705–74) was an MP from 1735 until created 1st Baron Holland in 1763;[1] he acquired Holland House, London in 1767, before which he is listed in Conduit Street. He married Lady Caroline Lennox in 1744; she visited Bath on several occasions.[2] His brother Stephen Fox became Lord Ilchester.

The ledger entries are unusual for the substantial debit payments to a customer.

Portrait: William Hogarth: *The Holland House group*, 1738

    1. *DNB*. 2. *DNB*; Tillyard.

FRAINE, JNO
1746: CR [Jno Duncombe]

FRANKS, NAPHS
1737: CR £100

Naphtali Franks was a third generation member of one of the most successful Jewish merchant houses in London; they specialised in the coral-diamond trade. His grandfather, Abraham, was 'one of the earliest Jewish brokers in London', who had three sons, Isaac, Aaron (listed in Billiter Square in 1740)[1] and Jacob, who established a house in Philadelphia. Jacob had two sons, Naphtali and Moses, who returned to London and married their cousins, the daughters of Isaac and Aaron. From at least 1740 Naphtali and Moses had government contracts to supply British Forces in Jamaica.[2]

    1. Kent 1740. 2. Yogev, pp. 65–66

FREAME & CO.
1743 and 1744: 2CR £20; £42

FREAME & BARCLAY
1746: CR £47 18s 11d

John Freame and his partner Thomas Gould [▶ p. 277] founded a bank in Lombard St in 1690. James Barclay [▶ p. 249] became a partner in 1736 and the new bank was named Barclay and Company; because of its network of family and business relationships it became known as the 'Quaker bank'. Listed at the Black Spread Eagle, Lombard Street.[1] John Freame was one of the deputation of Quakers who paid respects to Frederick, Prince of Wales in 1729, soon after his arrival in England.[2]

    1. *DNB*; Kent 1740; H-Price; Outing. 2. Vivian p. 113.

FREDERICKE, WM
1742: DR £23

Bath bookseller and printer. In 1748 James Tilly [▶ p. 62] was at King's Arms next to 'Frederick, bookseller'. His shop in Orange Grove is frequently referred to in the *Bath Journal*.

FREEMAN & CO.
1745: CR £50

FREEMANTLE, JNO
1741: CR £100

Possibly a Lisbon merchant, ancestor of the Barons Cottesloe.

FRENCH, THOMAS
1746 : DR £303 7s
1748: CR £24

The debit entry is for 300 South Sea Annuities 'In Thos French's name'. An apothecary in Bath; he took several apprentices[1] and is mentioned in an advertisement for a property for sale.[2] He was the brother-in-law, executor and guardian of the children of John Harvey, who had the Pump Room in Bath (d. in 1742).[3]

▶ p. 280.

    1. Bath RO: Apprentice Book p. 38. 2. *BJ*, 23 February 1746/47. 3. PROB 11/721.

FULLER, JNO
1736–41 DR £20; £30; £35; CR £45; £100; £80; £60

FURLY, MR
1744: CR £100

Possibly John Furley, snr and jnr, merchants, Great St Helens.[1]

    1. Kent 1740.

FURSTENAU & SCHRODER
1745: CR £50

Furstenau & Schroeder & Co., merchants, Scot's Yard, Bush Lane.[1] The German firm later became Langkopf, Molling & Rasch.[2]

    1. Kent 1740. 2. Price.

G

GALLINGTON, JNO
1736: DR £7

GALLOWAY, WM
1743: DR £7 10s

William Galloway was an apothecary in Bath, apprenticed on 30 August 1734 to William Seager for seven years.[1] North Parade Buildings (off North Parade Passage) was formerly Gallaway's Buildings, which name is carved at the corner. He bought the site from the Duke of Kingston and building was completed in 1750.[2] The leases specified that he would 'not permit or suffer any horses, coaches, chariots or other wheel carriages whatsoever to come into or upon the said street called Galloway Buildings'.[3] He appears to have traded in Bath water as a sideline: he charged Lady Jernegan 3s 6d per dozen bottles in the 1740s.[4]

There was also Galloway's coffee house.

1. Bath RO: Apprentice Book p.18. 2. Forsyth; Holland. 3. Neale p. 205. 4. Stafford RO: D641/3/P/1/3/4.

GARNHAM, THOS
1745: CR £20 [Thos Hunt]

GARNIER, GEO
1746: DR £394

Probably the London apothecary George Garnier, who succeeded to the practice of his uncle Isaac Garnier. He was Apothecary General to HM Establishment of Guards, Garrisons and Land Forces in Great Britain,[1] and one of the doctors consulted by Earl Fitzwalter in London.[2] The substantial sum in the ledgers was paid in January 1746/47; it seems too large to represent medical bills for Bertrand, who retired a year later.

Garnier may have been a connection of the London silversmith Daniel Garnier, working in London from the 1690s.

1. Chamberlayne, Pt II, Bk III, p.101. 2. Edwards, p. 147.

GAUSSEN, PETER
1746: CR £100

Peter (d. 1759) and Francis (d. 1744) Gaussen were Huguenot merchants in Great St Helens, London.[1] Peter's son, also Peter (d. 1788), was a director of the Bank of England.[2]

▶ p. 86 illus.

Property: Brookmans Park, Herts, acquired 1786.

1. Wagner. 2. Kent 1740.

MAJOR GEARY / GERY, THOS
1745–46: CR £70; £200; £100 through Jno Jackson

It is unclear how many people the following relates to: a Thomas Gery is listed in Johnson's Court in 1703, the year before John Deards is listed in another house there. Sir Thomas Gery was a master in Chancery; he was a governor of the Mineral Water Hospital in Bath in 1744 and 1748.[1] Several of those who owned Ealing House after Gery feature in Bertrand's accounts,[2] and he appears to have been a customer of another Ealing resident, John Jackson [▶ p. 285]. 'Major Geary' is presumably the Thomas Gery who was a major in the dragoons.[3]

1. *BJ*, 7 May 1744. 2. *VCH*, Middlesex vol. VII: Sir Thomas Gery had Ealing House in 1724; his widow sold it to Nathaniel Oldham of Holborn, who conveyed it in 1735 to Thomas Bale, who sold it in 1747 to Hugh Bethel. His brother Slingsby sold it in 1751 to Richard Coope, who surrendered it in 1753 to Lt.-Gen. John Huske (who died there in 1761), it then went to William Adair. 3. Chamberlayne, Pt II, Bk III, p. 99.

GEEKIE, JOSA
1745: CR £25

Joshua Geekie (1697–1761) was baptised at St Bride's Fleet Street, a lawyer in Middle Temple. An invoice from him to the executors of the 2nd Duke of Montagu dated 1750 itemises for 'taking instructions for Bill', 'Drawing the Bill' etc.[1] His father, Alexander, was a surgeon and collector, who joined the Great Queen Street Academy in 1711.

1. Buccleuch: Duke John exec bills 1750.

GIBBONS, SARAH
1737: CR £15

Uncertain identity. A Walter Gibbons had an account with Hoare.[1]

1. Hoare: Lr. 37, fo. 174.

GIBSON, CHR / GIBSON & CO. / MR GIBSON
1739–44: CR £60; £20; £21; £52 10s

Uncertain identity; it is impossible to know whether these entries relate to the same person or firm. Christopher Gibson, upholder, St Paul's Churchyard, is a possibility.[1] Some entries may refer to Thomas Gibson (1667–1744) MP for Marlborough 1722–34, Cashier to the Pay Office until July 1744.[2] Thomas Gibson is described as one of the Duke of Chandos' brokers.[3]

1. Kent 1740. 2. McCann. 3. Neale, p. 140.

GILBERT, THOS
1745: CR £40

Uncertain identity, possiblities include: Thomas Gilbert, salter, Thames Street, London.[1] A Thomas Gilbert was an associate of the Duke of Chandos, investing nearly £2,000 in lead mining in Staffordshire in 1732–33.[2] The ledgers of the silversmith George Wickes have Thomas Gilbart, Hollis St 1735–43.[3] Another candidate may be the satirist (1713–66) whose 'first verse satire, *View of the Town* (1735) attacks such targets as epicurean clergy, fops and sodomites'.[4]

1. Kent 1740. 2. Neale, p. 131. 3. Wickes. 4. *DNB*.

GLANFIELD, JAS
1740: DR £14

GLANVILLE, FRAS
1746: CR £31 9s

Uncertain identity. William Glanville, MP for Hythe, whose first wife, Frances, died in 1719 had a daughter, who may have been named after her mother.

Glanville is often mentioned in the Egmont diaries.

GODOLPHIN, ELLEN
1740: DR £26 17s 6d

GODOLPHIN, FRAS
1739: CR £50

Probably Francis Godolphin (c. 1706–85), first cousin of the 2nd Earl of Godolphin of Baylis, co. Bucks, and son of the provost of Eton College and Dean of St Paul's Cathedral. MP for Helston 1741–66; he inherited the barony of Godolphin from the earl in 1766. He married firstly Lady Barbara Bentinck, and secondly Lady Anne Fitz-William, but died without issue.[1] In 1749 his address was Pall Mall.[2]

    1. Sedgwick. 2. 1749 poll.

GODSKRALL, SR ROT
1739: CR £52 10s

Sir Robert Godschall (c. 1692–1742) was a Royal Exchange Assurance Director, of College Hill, London;[1] also described as a Portugal merchant. He was president of St Bartholomew's Hospital from 1741;[2] died in June 1742 aged 50, in the year he was Lord Mayor, and is buried in Albury, Surrey.

    1. Kent 1740. 2. Sedgwick.

GOODWIN, JNO
1743: CR £31 10s; £25

GOPSILL, WM /GOPSALL/GOSPILL/GOSPITT
1736–41: DR £11 4s; £5 16s; £26; £26 12s; £16 9s; £15 16s; £20 15s

COPSEEL, WM
1742: DR £9 10s

Probably a connection of Thomas Gopsill, although the trial quoted is some 20 years after the ledger entry:[1]

    The prosecutor is a cutler in Christopher-court, St. Martin's-le-Grand; the prisoner was his Journeyman: the prisoner confess'd he stole the hafts; but as that confession was not voluntary, but drawn out of him under a promise of favour, he was acquitted.

    1. POB: t17640912-25.

GORE, HR
1744: DR £30

Katherine, daughter of Henry Gore of Leatherhead, married William Wade in 1760,[1] master of ceremonies in Bath 1769–77 and a great-nephew of General George Wade.

    1. DNB.

GORHAM, JNO
1747: CR £50

GOSLING & CO.
1746: CR £200; £25

Robert Gosling, bookseller, was at the Mitre & Crown over against St Dunstan in the West, 1712, described as 'next the Inner Temple Gate' in 1723; he had a warehouse in Hercules Alley.[1]

Richard Gosling was a goldsmith and bookseller in Fleet St at the sign of the Three Squirrels, opposite St Dunstan's Church in Fleet Street; he was free of the Goldsmiths' Company in 1719 and his son Matthew was apprenticed to him 1737.[2] He is listed from 1742 at the bank that was founded by Chambers c. 1684 and continued until 1896. The firm saw numerous partnerships, including several that appear in Bertrand's accounts: Chambers & Usborne; Fowler & Rocke; Simpson & Ward.[3]

    1. Sun Ins, vol. 2, p. 207 and vol. 15, fo. 225. 2. GH: Apprentice Book. 3. Outing; H-Price.

GOSSETT, MATTHEW
1736: DR £10 10s

GOSSETT, GIDEON
1742: DR £40

▶ p. 225.

GOULD & NESBITT
GOULD, KING
1745: DR £10
1738 and 1744: CR £30

King Gould (c. 1688–1756) was an army agent; his name appears in a 1737 listing of 'Agents for the Plantations' for Nova Scotia.[1] In 1749 he was in Sackville Street, he died in 1756.[2] His son Charles was presented with a gold cup, with the mark of Gabriel Wirgman.[3]

▶ p. 297 Nesbitt.

Property: Pitshanger, Ealing.

    1. Chamberlayne, Pt II, Bk III, p. 54. 2. 1749 poll; VCH Middlesex vol. VII. 3. CL, 17 November 2009, lot 278.

GRAHAM, DAVID
1741: CR £30

Uncertain identity. David Graham, merchant, Black Swan Court, Bartholomew Lane.[1] Or, an army contractor, David Graeme.[2]

    1. Kent 1740. 2. Hancock.

GRAHAM, JANE
1744: DR £40; £80; £40; £40; £40

GRAHAM, JNO
1740–46: DR £40; £20; £40; £30; £20; £26; £40; £50; £27; £10.10s; £20; £30; £100; £30; £25; £25; £50; £40; £30; £30; £30; £60; £30; £20; £25; £30; £10; £19; £30; £30; £60; £20; £40; £40; £29 10s; £40; £20

Uncertain identity. It is not known that the celebrated watchmaker, George Graham (d. 1751) had a relative working with him named John. An alternative candidate for this large number of entries may, therefore, be a laceman of Green St Bath.[1]

    1. Williams 1945, p. 31.

GRANVILLE, BERD
1737: CR £25

Bernard Granville, purchased the estate of Calwich Abbey, Staffs and died unmarried in 1775.[1] He was Mary Delany's brother.

    1. Burke, LG 1848.

GREAVES, JOS
1741–43: CR £40; £50; £60; £40

Possibly of Ingleby, Derbys, whose son (also Joseph) matriculated Oxford 1749.

GREEN, HENRY
1751: DR £27 6s

GREEN & AMBER / GREEN & CO.
1743–45: CR £30; £60; £17

Goldsmith bankers in the Strand, near Durham Yard.[1] Richard Green and Norton Amber were bankrupt 1745; they were for a short time involved in the Covent Garden theatre.

 1. Outing; Kent 1740.

GREGORY, ANN
1743: DR £38 8s

GRIBELIN, SAML (GRIBBELIN, GRIBLIN)
1738–46: DR, £14; £30; £50; £90; £50; £50; £49 12s; £87 5s 6d; £20; £40; £200; £40; £50; £300; £50; £100; £100; £20; £50; £50; £500; £50; £200; £100; £40; £66; £29; £50; £100; £100; £50; £50; £21
1742–52: CR £250; £81 15s 3d; £41 16s; £40 5s

▶ p. 33.

GRIBELIN, SIMON
1739: DR £30

▶ p. 33.

GRIFFIN, BEN
1739: CR £40; £50

Uncertain identity: it is possible that there was more than one person of this name.

Gunsmith in Bond Street: Earl Fitzwalter bought 'a small pair of pistols' from him in 1742;[1] an invoice survives to Lord John Sackville for guns, gunpowder and pistols, dated 1745;[2] Joseph Griffin, his son, gave evidence at the Old Bailey in 1753.[3]

Griffin had an account with Hoare & Co., which has entries relating to Paul Bertrand and also Mrs Dering and Mr Guerin; his name also features in William Pitt's account with the bank and Walter Wiltshire's [▶ pp. 48] .[4] Perhaps a connection of Susanna Griffin of Bath, who was the sister of Bryce Fisher [▶ p. 273] and William Baker [▶ p. 248]; their father was a Wiltshire clothier.[5]

 1. Essex RO: D/DM/A7.
 2. Maidstone RO: V269 A233/5.
 3. POB: t17530221-23. 4. Ledgers: 37; 38 fo. 11; 38 fo. 182; 40 fo. 70; 40 fo. 188. 5. Namier.

GROBE, OM. SA
1742: DR £150

GROVE, SAML
1747: CR £420

Uncertain identity. 'Mr Grove and lady' are listed as arriving in Bath, 31 August 1747.[1] His ledger entry is the last for an individual in Bertrand's account with Hoare, on 21 October 1747. He may be of the Grove family of Ferne House, Wiltshire.

He seems less likely to be the Samuel Grove 'minister' listed in Blenheim Street, London, in 1749.[2]

A portrait of 'A grandmother with her granddaughter' by George Beare, 1747, is said to be of members of the Grove family of Taunton.[3]

 1. BJ. 2. 1749 poll.
 3. Waterhouse, p. 45.

GUERIN, MAYD
1738–46: CR £75; £42; £75; £100; £100; £71; £241 8s 6d; £10; £101 0s 4d; £20; £30; £34 8s 3d; £70; £50 10s

Maynard Guerin, Esq is listed under 'Agents for Plantations' with Mr Pacheco, as agent for New York.[1] He was agent to the 2nd Duke of Montagu's regiment in the 1740s.[2] Guerin was a customer of Hoare and his name features (presumably in respect of banking transactions) in the accounts of Richard Nash (November 1732) and B. Griffin in November 1737. Mr and Mrs Guerin contributed one guinea each to a fund set up for Samuel Emes following a fire at his house in Bath in May 1747.[3]

Guerin may have been distantly connected to the Harrache family of silversmiths: Isabeau Guerin was married to Pierre Harrache (d. Rouen 1679).

 1. Chamberlayne, Pt II, Bk III, p. 54. 2. Buccleuch: Duke John exec bills 1750-52. 3. BJ.

GUINARD, MESSRS
1739: CR £50; £10 10s

Henry and Joseph Guinand, merchants, Little St Helens, Bishopsgate street.[1] John Henry Guinand (1686–1755) and his son Henry Guinand (1722–85), were both involved with the French Hospital.

 1. Kent 1740.

GUNMAN, CAPTN JNO
1739: CR £52 10s

GUPWELL, JANE
1746: DR £35

Unidentified. Her name features on the debit side of Benjamin Griffin's account at Hoare.[1]

 1. Lr. 40 fo. 70.

GUY, THOS
1745: CR £100 [Jno Jackson]

This cannot be the founder of Guy's Hospital in London, who died in 1724.

GWATKIN, EDWD
1740: DR £170

Listed as a 'sopeboiler' in Bristol in 1754;[1] also a merchant in London and with property in Cornwall.

 1. Bristol 1755.

GWYNN, HOWELL
1742: DR £100; £44

'A gentleman of fortune residing in Bath'. He was master of the Lodge in 1742 (followed by Lord

Ann Hamilton [▶ below]) and in that year presented the lodge with a silver trowel.[1] Possibly the Gwynn of Garth, Brecon (now Powys) who stood against Thomas Morgan of Tredegar [▶ p. 295] for a parliamentary seat in the 1750s and was sheriff of Brecon in 1761.

▶ p. 71

1. Masons.

GYLES, SARAH
1744: DR £36

Uncertain identity. She may have been connected with one of the following: John Gyles, a bookseller and publisher in Fleet Street; Laurence Gyles, free of the Turners' Company 7 August 1723; or Isaac Gyles, bookkeeper to the silversmith Paul de Lamerie.

H

HADDOCK, NICS
1743: CR £25

Haddock (1686–1746) was MP for Rochester 1734–46; Rear Admiral of the Red 1737; Commander in Chief of the Mediterranean 1738–42; Admiral of the Blue 1744.[1]

1. McCann.

HALE, GEORGE
1745: CR £55 15s

HALFPENNY, CHAS
1738: DR £13 10s

Most probably the steward of the Duke of Beaufort's estates in Monmouth, and town clerk.

He is less likely to be a connection of William and John Halfpenny, architects who published *The Modern Builder's Assistant*, 1742, and chinoiserie designs in the 1750s.

HALL, EZE
1736: CR £10 Jas Leake

HAMILTON, LORD ANN
1741 and 1742: CR £80; £63

Lord Anne (1709–48), son of the 4th Duke of Hamilton, was named after his godmother Queen Anne. His father died in a duel with Lord Mohun in Hyde Park in 1712; the duke killed Mohun but was himself killed by Mohun's second, General Macartney, who was later convicted of manslaughter. In 1731 Lord Anne married clandestinely Mary Edwards, who inherited a fortune in 1728 from her father that reputedly gave her an annual income of some £50–60,000. The marriage was a disaster (Lord Anne, five years her junior, has been described as 'profligate and unreliable') and she extricated herself from him, expunged all records of the marriage and regained control of her fortune. She died in 1743, having been a major patron of William Hogarth.

In Bath, Lord Anne lived in Queen Square. A freemason, he was Master Mason of the Lodge there in 1742, in which year he married Anna Powell (his previous marriage is not recorded in Burke's *Peerage*). His movements were often reported in the *Bath Journal*.

Portrait: William Hogarth, *Mary Edwards*, 1742 (Frick Collection).

HAMILTON, RD
1739: CR £20

Listed in the Upper Water Rent Roll for 1748, with a dwelling house in Cheap Street, Bath.[1] Uncertain identity and a common name.

1. Bath RO.

HAMILTON, WM
1739: CR £50; £100

Possibly Mr Hamilton (indexed by McCann as William Hamilton) of Binderton 'a man of great property … in very high ranke at the barr … a very gentleman like man'.[1]

1. McCann, p. 219 (Duke of Richmond to Stone May 1746).

HANKEY, SR JOS & CO.
1745–47: CR £20; £20; £30; £25; £30; £30; £30; £31 10s; £26

Sir Joseph Hankey & Co. at the Gold Ball, Fleet Street, 1739–69;[1] Sir Joseph Hankey, alderman, Fenchurch street; Sir Joseph & Thomas Hankey, banker, Fenchurch St.[2]

1. Outing. 2. Kent 1740.

HANMER, LADY
1736: CR £100

Elizabeth, daughter of Thomas Folkes of Barton, Suffolk, second wife of Sir Thomas Hanmer (1676–1746), Speaker of the House of Commons from 1714 and a supporter of Frederick, Prince of Wales. He died without issue, when the baronetcy became extinct and his estate at Mildenhall devolved upon his cousin the Revd Sir William Bunbury, nephew of the William Bunbury listed above [▶ p. 255]. Lady Hanmer was much younger than Sir Thomas and 'ran off with the son of one of [her husband's] friends and again made him appear ridiculous';[1] the man involved was Thomas Hervey, one of the 1st Earl of Bristol's twelve sons. She died in 1741.

A possible alternative identification is Lady Catherine Perceval, daughter of 1st Earl of Egmont, who married Thomas Hanmer MP (1702–37) who was due to inherit from Sir Thomas Hanmer (above) but predeceased him.[2] She was painted by Allan Ramsay.[3]

1. *DNB*. 2. Sedgwick. 3. CL, 6 July 2011 lot 158.

HAQUE, JOS
1745: CR £39

HARDINGE, JAS
1745 & 1746: CR £39; £100

Possibly a member of the Harding family who bought Newark Park, Glos, in 1722; the house was later acquired by the Clutterbucks.

▶ p. 261.

HARFORD, CHAS
1745–47: DR £20; £32; £20; £26; £15; £79; £28; £22; £30; £29; £78; £130; £7 13s; £60; £31

HARFORD, RD
1751: DR £25

Charles Harford was apprenticed to his father, a linen draper, for seven years on 4 December 1739.[1] An advertisement for a property that requests readers to 'enquire of Charles Harford, Market Place, Bath',[2] is one of several similar. Surviving receipts[3] suggest a family business:

> I this day sent by Mr Walter Wiltshire Waggon carraidge paid ye fine knapt rugg you sent for … Rd Harford, Bath March 26: 1749/50. Recd ye Above by ye Hands of Mr J Wilshire.

Richard Harford is recorded as a woollen draper in 1720, and as a mercer: a John Wiltshire was apprenticed to him in 1709.[4] In the 1750s Earl Fitzwalter bought cloth for his servants' liveries from Harford on several occasions [▶ p. 113–14].[5]

1. Bath RO: Apprentice Book p. 26. 2. *BJ*, 10 November 1746, 19 August 1745, 23 February 1746/47 and others. 3. Hoare: Boxes of receipts (1750) HFM/7/9. 4. Neale; Bath RO: Council Book 5, Wiltshire made a freeman 24 January 1728. 5. Essex RO: D/DM/A8 etc.

HARRINGTON, JNO
1736: DR £11 11s

John Harrington was a JP in Somerset.[1] One of his sons, Dr E. Harrington (1696–1757), was one of the first three physicians to the Mineral Water Hospital in 1739 [▶ p. 298 William Oliver]; he gave £50 to the hospital in 1738. In 1744 he placed a notice in the *Bath Journal*:

> A Gentleman … made an enquiry at Kelson, near Bath, if Benjamin Harrington … was then alive, or if he left a son who lived thereabouts, and hinted, if there was, that he could inform him of something that might be to his advantage. This is to give Notice that John Harrington, eldest son of the said Benjamin Harrington, lives at Corston, near Bath …

The following January he was selling a farm;[2] Kelston Hall was sold in 1759. Harrington was a descendent of his celebrated sixteenth-century namesake, who invented the water closet.[3]

1. Falconer, p. 25. 2. *BJ*, 15 October 1744, and 7 January 1744/45. 3. Rolls, p. 157.

HARROLD, JOHN
1736: DR £13

Uncertain identity. Possibly connected to Edmund Harrold, to whom Peter Webb sold diamond jewellery in December 1740.[1]

1. TNA: C 108/284.

HART, ARTHUR
1746: DR £300

Possibly linked to the goldsmith William Hart, who was apprenticed in 1712 and free 1719.[1] No receipts survive but 'Mr Hart' appears in Richard Hoare's private account book in 1732 (an entry of £55), in 1739 for a 'sett of silver tea canister & case £25 19s 0d', and in 1740: 'Wm Hart, silversmith, a sett of teaspoons, tongs &c £6 12s 0d'. According to Heal he was 'goldsmith & banker' at the sign of the Grasshopper, Fleet Street, 1738–47 and he is also recorded 'at a Fan Shop' on the south side of Fleet Street near Salisbury Court.[2] Hart is a common surname, however, and Arthur and William may not have been related.

1. GH: Apprentice Book. 2. Jowett.

HARVEY, WM
1740: CR £50

HARVEY, MR
1742: CR £10 10s

Uncertain identity. Possibly connected to the Mrs Harvey mentioned in Bertrand's will: 'I will and permit Mrs Hervey and her sister Mrs Noise remain in the house they now rent of me during their joint or separate lives rent free'. [▶ p. 297 Noyes]

Or, the entries may relate to William Harvey (1714–63) MP for Essex.[1]

If Mr Harvey and William Harvey were two people rather than the same, the 'Mr Harvey' might be John Harvey jnr, who designed St Michael's church 1734–42, and was probably the son of the stonemason who built the Pump Room 1704–06.[2]

Another option could be Mr Felton Harvy, referred to in a letter from Helena le Grand [▶ p. 289] 'who I fear is now in a dying condition with cough astma and lowness of spirits'.[3]

1. Sedgwick. 2. Forsyth, p. 130 and see Bath RO: Council minutes for 1 July 1706 (he carved the capitals at the Pump Room); John Harvey, carver of Bath, will 13 November 1742, PROB 11/721. 3. Chatsworth: 240.2.

HAUKINS, RD
1745: CR £50

HAWKES & CO.
1739: CR £52 10s

HAWKINS, JNO
1744: DR £200

Uncertain identity, and a common name. Possibly a Bath man named in an indenture of 1739.[1] The will of a John Hawkins of St Michael, Bath was proved 22

September 1747[2] when he appears to have been in Green Street:[3]

> To be Lett at Christmas next, a very good and convenient house, situate in Green St Bath, late in the possession of John Hawkins Esq. Enquire of Samuel Emes

Or, as it is a debit entry, it might refer to John Hawkins, apprenticed to Timbrell & Bell 1706, free 1716.[4]

1. Hants RO: 13M63/356. 2. PROB 11/756. 3. *BJ*, 26 October 1747. 4. GH: Apprentice Book.

HAWLEY, LADY
1739 and 1743 DR: £40; £40

HAWLEY, SAMUEL
1739 and 1745: DR £21; £500; £252 3s 6d

HAYES, ELIZA
1738: DR £40 8s 6d

▶ p. 95.

HAY, JNO
1740: CR £28 12s

Uncertain identity. Possibly Col. John Hay, youngest son of 6th Earl of Kinnoull, who died childless in 1740; he took an active part in the Jacobite uprising of 1715.[1] Or John, 3rd son of the 7th Earl, matriculated Oxford 1737 aged 18, later rector of Epworth, Lincs, who died in 1751.[2] Capt John Hay, Privy Garden Whitehall, is listed in 1749.[3]

1. Burke. 2. Foster. 3. 1749 poll.

HAY[N]ES, JOS
1739: CR £21; £20

Uncertain identity: written as Hayes and Haynes. Possibly the cashier of the Haymarket Theatre: his name appears on a receipt for a silver ticket for opera at the theatre dated 1734 (which cost 20 guineas).[1] In 1733 and 1736 Thomas Coke paid 'Jos Haynes' 10gns and £50 for opera subscriptions, and in February 1737/38 'Mrs Haynes' £71.[2] He may have been connected to the 'low comedian' with the same name.

Hayes and Haynes are common surnames, and there are the possibilities that he might have been related to Elizabeth Hayes [▶ p. 95], or had other connections in Bath. The Haynes family owned the Barton Farm estate there; Daniel Haynes acquired Ladymead in the seventeenth century and Charles Haynes leased property in Walcot Street 'for lives of self Samuel Rundell and John Rundell'.[3]

1. Woburn: 2/34/1. Hume, pp. 357–58. 2. Holkham: A25 House Stewards account. 3. Dorset RO: D/HAB; Bath RO: Council Book 5, 28 March 1736 and on Ladymead House.

HAYTER, MRS
1745: CR £30

Uncertain identity, and a common surname. Possibly the wife of George Hayter, a banker of Pancras Lane, London (b. 1707) who was the second son of the Revd George Hayter, rector of Chagford, in Devon.

Or, William Hayter, a merchant connected with the work of the painter Bellotto, had a wife named Elizabeth.

HEAD, JANE
1740: CR £143 5s

HEATH, GEO
1739–40: DR £20; £20

HELLETT, JNO
1740: DR £10 2s 6d

HELST, JNO
1739: DR £16 15s 6d

Possibly John Helot, watchmaker, who was connected to Bertrand through his first wife.

HEMING, SAML
1743: DR £65; £50

Samuel Hemming witnessed the will of Lady Hawley [▶ p. 97] together with Paul Bertrand and Thomas Pomfret.

HENLEY, ANTO
1736: DR £260

Anthony Henley, of the Grange, Hants (?1704–46 or 1748), MP for Southampton 1727–34. In 1740 William Friend wrote to his cousin Elizabeth Montagu 'Anthony Henley is here, and become Sir Anthony. He is actually now at law with the Mayor for having sent a Lady of Pleasure he keeps to Bridewell.'[1] Lord Wharncliffe wrote of him 'He was said to have very good parts, but was a man of the most profligate and dissipated habits.'[2] Mrs Delany wrote of his marriage in January 1727/28:[3]

> Lady Betty Berkeley, daughter to the Earl of that name, being almost fifteen, has thought it time to be married, and ran away last week with Mr Henley, a man noted for his imprudence and immorality, but a good estate and a beau – irresistible charms in these days.

He was succeeded by his brother Robert (below). It was possibly their father who was referred to in a letter to the Duke of Kent 'because the basset bank, kept by a Mr Henley, was inadequate to the demands placed on it, "Lady Basset … will no longer appear in public at Mr Harrison's …".'[4]

Property: The Grange, Hants.

1. Neale p. 20. 2. Wharncliffe, vol. 2, p. 35. 3. Delany, vol. 1, pp. 156–57. 4. Eglin, p. 120.

HENLEY, RT
1740 and 1743: DR £160; CR £21; £100

Robert Henley (c. 1708–72), MP for Bath 1747–57, Recorder of Bath; made a freeman of Bath with his brother (above) in 1740.[1] Attorney General, created Earl of Northington in 1764. He 'liked

Bath and courted a wife there in 1742'.[2] Known to his friends and others as 'surly Bob'. His cousin Mary Janssen married Charles Calvert, Lord Baltimore.

Portrait: Thomas Hudson (All Souls College, Oxford).

1. Bath RO: Council Book 6.
2. Allen.

HENSHAW, ROBT

1746: CR £200

Uncertain identity. Possibly Robert Henshaw, attorney, Cook's Hill, Aldergate Street.[1] He may have been related to Elizabeth Henshaw, the first wife of Sir Edward Dering 5th Bt.

In the north aisle of Bath Abbey there is a monument to Jonathan Henshaw, alderman of Bath, who died 1764; probably the man who sold Elizabeth Walpole 'two dozen of Bath waters 9s' in 1755.[2] He was married to Mary Chapman, whose brother John married Mary Coward.[3]

1. Kent 1740. 2. Wolterton: 18/9/1-3, Box 70(A)L.
3. Information from Elizabeth Holland.

HERN, AND

1743: DR £25 6s

Uncertain identity. In the handwritten lists recording goods for sale at the East India House[1] there is: 'Thomas Smith & Co. 1714 / Fans, pr Herne £199 8s 6d.' There is no evidence to link this with Andrew Hern.

1. BL, H/14.

HICKEY, JOS

1746: CR £100

Father of the diarist William Hickey, who was his eighth child; he was an attorney of St Albans Street, Pall Mall.[1]

> In or about 1752 Mr Nash employed the said Hickey in the EO cause, who promised to serve his client faithfully against the Masters of the Rooms at Bath and Tunbridge: but soon after, Mr Nash received a letter (dictated by Hickey) from Metcalfe Ashe at Tunbridge, denying that Mr Nash had any share in EO and upon reading the Honble Thomas Hervey's Pamphlet against Hickey, Mr Nash dismissed him, and then he became solicitor for the Defendants at Bath and Tunbridge.[2]

Portrait: A.W. Devis, *William Hickey and an Indian Servant* (Paul Mellon Collection, Yale)

1. 1749 poll. 2. Bath RO: Acc.662.37.

HIGGENSON, WM

1740 and 1741: CR £50; £30

HIGGONS, JNO

1740: DR £26

Uncertain identity. John Higgons, turner, is listed in Chandos Street.[1]

1. 1749 poll.

HILL, GRACE

1744: 1 CR £100

In 1767 Mrs Grace Hill in Chappell Rowe paid rates of 3s 4d.[1]

1. Bath RO: Rate Book 4, p. 90.

HILL, RD

1737–40: DR £170; £100; £200; £105; £113 5s

Uncertain identity. Richard Hill, cordwainer, is listed in St James's Street, London.[1] It is a common name, but if the entry was for this man, it suggests that Bertrand might have stocked footwear.

Or Hill might have belonged to a family of watch casemakers.

1. 1749 poll.

HILLAN, CHRISTIAN

1737 and 1738: DR £18 2s; £37; £33

London silversmith.

▶ p. 225.

HINCHLIFF, JNO

1743: DR £26 10s

Probably a connection of the mercers Thomas & William Hinchliff & Co. Their billhead has the name Hinchliffs & Harris 'at ye Hen & Chickens in Henrietta Street Covent Garden Londo'.[1]

1. Lowestoft RO: HA12/A3/1.

HITCH, MR

1742: CR £14 14s

HOARE
BEN HOARE & CO., RD HOARE, HENRY HOARE & CO.

1739–54 CR £50; £80; £50; £40; £40 19s; £15; £15 15s; £10; £20; £30; £30; £50; £50; £188; £50; £40; £50; £120; £50; £100; £70; £68 10s; £160 10s; £50; £50; £50; £20; £10 10s; £100; £100; £60; £40; £60; £100; £100; £50; £30; £20; £40; £100; £20; £100; £30; £80; £320; £73 10s; £177; £40; £100; £25; £100; £30; £25; £50; £30; £20; £40; £50; £105; £84; £50; £56; £305; £40; £30; £14; £30; £50; £60; £140; £50; £814 10s; £25; £30; £50; £50; £25; £30; £100; £50; £45; £30; £260; £100; £50; £30; £76; £20; £30; £17; £128 13s; £20; £150; £30; £5 17s 10d; £80; £30; £31 10s; £20; £17; £10; £40; £50; £50; £43 7s 6d; £20; £30; £176 6s 7d; £25; £21; £66 15s; £392; £50; £40; £100; £30; £50; £70; £70; £105; £42; £100; £50; £32 18s; £25; £105; £90; £60; £71; £300; £50; £90; £100; £100; £50; £13 13s; £19; £100; £10 10s; £75; £100; £161 8s; (shop closes) £1,000; £1,040; £139 17s

Goldsmith banker, at the Golden Bottle, 37 Fleet St, with whom Paul Bertrand had an account.

▶ p. 53.

HOARE, ELLEN

1740: CR £50

Sister of Prince, William and Hannah Hoare.

HOARE, HANAH

1738: DR £157 10s; £100

Sister of William and Prince Hoare and first wife of Peter Russel [▶ p. 202].

HOARE, MARY
1740: CR £30

Sister of William, Prince and Hannah.

HOARE, PRINCE
1736: DR £12 12s

Sculptor (1711–69), brother of William and Hannah.

▶ p. 202.

HOARE, WM
1743: CR £50

1740–55: DR £200; £83; £63; £24 13s; £24 5s; £94; £21

William Hoare (1707/08–92), painter.

▶ p. 202–03.

HODGKIN, ANN
1745: CR £20

Sister-in-law to Thomas Harrison, owner of one of the Bath assembly rooms; she is mentioned in his will.

HODGSON, JNO
1746: DR £75 16s

HOG, ALEXR
1736: DR £24 15s

HOGG, ROGER
1737 and 1741: DR £13 15s; £30

There are several individuals with the surname Hog or Hogg who had connections with the Deards family and who worked in a variety of specialties linked to the luxury goods market.

HOLLAND, DOROTHY
1744: DR £170

Uncertain identity. Possibly connected to John Holland, plateworker, Queen's Head, Foster Lane, 1711–12; Bishopsgate St 1711–39;[1] or Joshua or Thomas, also working at this time.

1. Heal LG.

HOLLOWAY, EDWARDS
1744: CR £30
1/4/: DR £180

HOLLOWAY, GEO
1742: DR £60

Unknown identity. Perhaps connected to a builder, Benjamin Holloway, who worked for the Duke of Chandos in Bridgwater, or his brother Stephen.[1]

1. Baker. Neale p. 114.

HOLMES, THOS
1741: DR £10

Uncertain identity. A Thomas Holmes was apprenticed to Edward Dowdeswell 1694.[1] Thomas Holmes (1699–1764) was MP for Newton and Yarmouth and Governor of the Isle of Wight 1763–64.

1. GH: Apprentice Book 4/42.
2. McCann, p. 157; Sedgwick.

HOLTON, JOS
1745: DR £64

HONEYWOOD & CO.
1746: CR £10 10s

▶ p. 248 Atkins.

HOOPER, MARGT
1742: DR £20

Uncertain identity. Possibly connected to Nicholas Hooper of Walcot,[1] but it is a common name.

1. Neale p. 103.

HOPKINS, JNO
1742: DR £50

Silversmith based at the eastern end of Fleet Street, in or near St Bride's Lane. He seems to have moved several times during the 1720s and '30s, working at premises with a variety of shop signs. He obtained his freedom in 1723. In the 1730s he placed advertisements warning of the 'decoys and impositions … from publick sales, auctions, etc sold by brasiers'.[1] He was targeting French Plate. He advertised that it was 'his principal and Chief Business to deal in Second-Hand Plate, Watches, Jewels &c.' To which he added the interesting note:[2]

Nothing engrav'd with Coats of Arms &c will at any Time be exposed to Sale before the Engraving be entirely taken out, so that it shall not be known the same ever was engrav'd, which is presum'd will be most pleasing to Buyer and Seller ….

1. *London Evening Post*, 14 February 1745 [2696]. 2. *Country Journal or The Craftsman*, 3 July 1736 [522] and others.

HOPKINS, WM
1736–39: DR £40; £18 12s; £150

Possibly no relation to John (above), William entered his mark only two months before him (with no record of his apprenticeship), giving his address as 'Great Kerby Street', Hatton Garden, London. Heal records him as a plateworker, which seems to conflict with Grimwade's description of the (second) mark he entered in 1739 as being 'very small'.[1] In 1712 a Lorriner of the same name took out an insurance policy.[2]

1. Grimwade; Heal LG. 2. Sun Ins, vol. 2, p. 44.

HORNE & TEMPLE
1737 and 1738: CR £40; £50; £50; £60 15s; £50

Bankers, at the Angel & crown, 'over against New Exchange' Strand, established as Horne & Killmaine, *c.* 1716.[1]

▶ p. 278 Green & Amber.

1. Outing; H-Price.

HOTHAM, LADY
1739: CR £100

Lady Gertrude Hotham, half-sister to Lord Chesterfield and Sir William Stanhope. She had a house in Queen Square, Bath. Her husband Sir Charles Hotham died in 1738, the year before the ledger entry. He had been MP for Beverley, and a groom of the bedchamber to George II at £500 p.a. He opened an account with

Hoare in 1724. In 1730 he was sent on a mission to Berlin, which gave rise to differing reports: he 'acquitted himself to the satisfaction of George II'[1] but the visit ended in his recall following a disagreement with Friedrich William of Prussia.[2] Bath was not the only spa town Lady Hotham visited: she and Lord Chesterfield were at Scarborough in the summer of 1732, at the same time as the Duchess of Marlborough.

Lady Hotham's brothers were regular visitors to Bath. 'The Hon. John Stanhope, brother to the Earl of Chesterfield, who lay here lately at the point of Death, is so well recovered as seemingly to be out of Danger'. John, also an MP, died unmarried in 1748.[3] Sir William Stanhope was married three times; his first wife died in 1740; he was in Bath with his second wife, Elizabeth, in January 1744/45; she died a year later.[4] His third marriage to Anne Delaval was unsuccessful: they separated in 1763. Lord Chesterfield wrote to his son (30 September 1763):

> If my brother had had some of those self conversations, which I recommend, he would not, I believe, at past sixty, with a crazy battered constitution, and deaf into the bargain, have married a young girl, just turned twenty, full of health and consequently of desires.

1. Sedgwick. 2. Vivian, p. 186. 3. *BJ*, 3 November 1746; Sedgwick. 4. Sedgwick.

HOUGHTON, WILLM
1744: CR £73 10s

Had an account with Hoare.

HOWE, WM
1745: DR £54

Uncertain identity. 'Madam Howe' is listed as arriving in Bath 1 October 1744; 'Mr Howe' on 8 April 1745, and in March 1746/47 'Died Wm How, a JP'.[1]

This is a debit entry however, and it is possible that the entry should read Howse. A toyman of St Dunstan in the West was witness to the will of William Deards snr in 1761. He was a goldsmith and clock-maker 'between the two Temple Gates, Fleet St' c. 1730–80.[2]

Or, a bill survives from William Howse, tailor, 1739 to the Duchess of Montrose, signed Margaret Howse.[3]

1. *BJ*, 9 March 1746/47. 2. Heal LG; Baillie. 3. NAS: GD220/6/896

HOWSE, SAMUEL
1746–52: DR £100; £60; £20

'On Saturday died Mr Samuel Howse, Linnen Draper of this City, who carried on Great Business with a fair Character.' Also described as 'mercer', his sons Samuel and John had the 'Nag's Head' in Northgate Street since at least 1725.[1] The ledger entry presumably refers to Samuel jnr, who was in Market Place, Bath (his house had a water supply) in the 1740s, with John, and advertised:[2]

> Blanks and Prizes In the Present Lottery are bought By Samuel Howse and Comp in the Market Place, Bath

There are numerous references in the *Bath Journal* to people with this surname: an apothecary in Abbey Church Yard, Bath, and a trustee of the hospital.[3] Elizabeth Howse, wife of Samuel died 8 October 1787 aged 31.

Monument: Elizabeth Howse, North Aisle, Bath Abbey.

1. *BJ*, 26 November 1744. Bath RO: 1776 Schedule of Deeds, p. 195; Council Book 5, 2 October 1732. PROB 11/749 28 August 1746. 2. *BJ*, 21 December 1747. Bath RO: 1748 Roll; 1766 Rate Book 1. 3. Holland KE1750 n023.

HUBERT, JAMES
1736–41: DR £105; £52 10s; £40; £9 9s; £30; £42

London watchmaker.

▶ p. 227.

HUBERT, MICHL (STEPN GARDES)
1737: CR £84; £105

HUBERT, WM
1736–38: DR £139 10s; £200; £25; £25

▶ p. 227.

HUGHES, HUGH
1740: DR £20 16s

Uncertain identity. Possibly Huges/Hughes, a jeweller, listed at the Ring & Pearl, over against the Five Bells tavern in the Strand, 1722.[1]

1. Heal LG.

HUGHES, JNO
1745 and 1746: CR £20; £20

HULL, RD
1745: CR £60

HUMBLE, WM
1740: CR £50

Sir William Humble, 5th Bt, succeeded his father in 1723, died 1742. The baronetcy became extinct on the death of his son, aged six, when at school in 1745.[1]

1. Burke, *Extinct Bt*.

HUMMERHAYS, THOS
1740: DR £22 10s

HUMPHREYS, AMBROSE
1736–44: DR £26 5s; £35; £100

Uncertain identity. The owner of the lodging house where Princess Caroline stayed in Bath in 1746 was Mrs Humphreys [▶ p. 153].

HUNT, JOS
1744: CR £50

HUNT, STEPHEN
1746: DR £200

HUNTER, AND
1754: DR £10 10s

Joseph Barker's partner [▶ p. 249].

HUNTINGDON, COUNTESS OF
1741–44: CR £50; £60; £12 12s

Selina Hastings, Countess of Huntingdon (1707–91), an early convert to the teachings of John Wesley and a prominent evangelist. The chapel she built in Bath 'to protect the residents from the evils of Bath society' is in Gothic style.[1] She was a regular visitor to Bath; her husband, the 9th earl, died in 1746.

▶ p. 112.

1. Forsyth.

HURD, MESS
1746 & 1747: CR £30; £20; £50

Uncertain identity: possibly Francis Hurd, merchant, Love Lane, Wood St, London.[1]

1. Kent 1740

HUTCHINSON, GEO
1736: DR £10 10s

Possibly a turner, listed as supplier to the toyman George Willdey, 1737.[1]

1. Clifford 1999.

HUTTON, THOS
1740: CR £40

HYDE, SAML
1738: CR £100

Samuel Hyde, East India Director and merchant, Rood Lane, London,[1] dealt in tobacco, evidenced by three court cases in 1723, 1724 and 1737,[2] one involving 5 dwt of tobacco, another six lb and in the third, referring to the property of John and Samuel Hyde:

> The Prisoners were Ticket-Porters, who were employ'd to land Tobacco out of a Lighter and that they were seen several Times to carry away Tobacco … in the Knees of their Breeches, &c.

A Samuel Hyde appears in the ledger of the silversmith George Wickes for 1738.[3]

1. Kent 1740. 2. POB: t17230828-28, t17240117-23, t17370216-2. 3. Wickes.

I

INGRAM, MARY
1737: CR £40; £50

Uncertain identity. Possibly a connection of Arthur Ingram of Bath, will proved 13 June 1749.[1] Wm Ingram was a witness to Mary Lindsey's will in 1732.

1. PROB 11/771.

INNOCENT, JNO
1737: DR £32 18s

John Innocent had the Mitre Tavern[1] in the same block of houses on the south side of Fleet Street as Humphrey Pugh, John Deards, Richard Hoare and the silversmith George Houstoun. In the next generation, a London spoonmaker of the same name is recorded c. 1764–93 in Little Newport St, London; in 1767 he was discharged after a 'false and malicious' accusation of forging marks.[2] No connection between the two men has been made.

1. Sun Ins, 1715. 2. *Public Advertiser*, 5 March 1767; Heal LG.

IRELAND, WM
1738: CR £10

William Ireland was Chief Clerk in the Auditor's Office of the Exchequer in 1737, when George, Earl of Halifax was Auditor.[1] Ireland & Co. and Ireland & Barnevelt [▶ p. 250] feature in the account of the silversmith John Curghey, in Fleet Street.[2]

1. Chamberlayne, Pt II, Bk III, p. 58. 2. Hoare: Lr. 35 fo. 137.

IRONSIDE, ED & CO.
1746: CR £20

Ironside & Belchier, goldsmiths and bankers, Black Lion, 65 Lombard St, 1729–56. Edward Ironside was a member of the Benn Club, a group of City aldermen with Jacobite sympathies. His sister was married to his partner, Belchier.[1]

▶ p. 84 illus.

Portrait: Benn's Club of Aldermen (GH).

1. *London Evening Post*, 10–12 October 1738 [1702].

ISTED, AMB:
1737 and 1739: CR £20; £50

Ambrose Isted of Ecton Hall, Northamptonshire (1717–81). His mother's second husband was Sir Hans Sloane. Ambrose married Anne, daughter of Sir Charles Buck, 3rd Bt, in 1746. It seems probable that there was a long-standing connection between the Isted family and the Deards, but no direct link has been found between Ambrose and John Isted, a publisher and bookseller in Fleet Street, who was probably the 'Mr Isteard' who, with his wife, was left mourning rings in the will of Mary Deards in 1738. John Isted's shop was at the Golden Ball, between St Dunstan's Church and Chancery Lane.[1]

Portrait: Enoch Seeman, *Ambrose Isted* (Bonhams London, 27 October 2010 lot 49); George Romney (his wife); Thomas Hudson (his daughter Anne) and others by William Hoare.

1. Sun Ins, vol. 13, fo. 523.

IVORY TALBOTT, JNO see TALBOTT

J

JACKSON, JNO
1745 and 1746: CR see [Major Geary]

Uncertain identity. Mary Bertrand made regular payments in the late 1750s and 1760s to John Jackson, and also Richard Jackson. There were various partnerships that included a 'Jackson'. Adair & Jackson, merchants, Milk Street [▶ p. 246 Adair]. Also John Jackson, the

Angel, Fleet Street, 1684–1715; Knight & Jackson, bankers, Lombard Street.[1]

It seems unlikely to be the John Jackson recorded at the London freemason's lodge at the Horn & Feathers, Wood Street in 1730, or a toyman whose trade card is dated 1699.[2] Nor is it likely, as they are credit entries relating to Geary, to be a bookseller and stationer of this name.[3]

1. H-Price; Kent 1740.
2. Songhurst. BM: Heal 119.17.
3. BL, Add Ms 22258, fo. 545, invoice to Countess of Strafford.

JACOB, JNO
1736–43: DR; £21; £40; £27; £23 10s

London silversmith.

There is no 's' written at the end of Jacob, so the entries are unlikely to be a builder and plasterer of Bath. There was also a shagreen case maker called John Jacobs.[1]

▶ p. 229.

1. Culme 2000, p. 106.

JACOB, SR HILD:
1738: CR £38
1741 and 1744: CR £25; £20

The ledgers accurately record when Sir Hildebrand Jacob (d.s.p. 1790) succeeded his grandfather to the baronetcy in March 1740, his father (also Hildebrand and married to Muriel Bland [▶ p. 252]) having died in 1739. His father (b. 1693) published his collected writings, including poetry and plays, in 1735.

Portraits: CSK, 17 & 19 February 2008 lots 6 & 7.

JANEWAY, THOS
1741: DR £13 10s

Probably a connection of John Janaway (son of Joshua), goldsmith, St Paul's Churchyard; and later Wetherell & Janaway, 'jewellers, goldsmiths and toymen to the royal Family', 114 Cheapside 1785–96.[1] Janeway's Coffee House was near the Royal Exchange in London.

1. Grimwade; Heal LG.

JARVIS, SAML
1741 and 1747: DR £32 4s; £54

Uncertain identity. Possibly Samuel Jarvis, watchmaker, Birmingham c. 1710.[1] Or, there was a turner of the same name.[2]

1. Baillie. 2. BM: trade card Heal, 122.25.

JASPER, EDWD
1738 and 1739: CR £50; £50; £20

'Edward Japer Esq', Tower Hill, London.[1]

1. Kent 1740.

JEFFREY, NICS
1736: CR £20; £21; £31 10s; £10 10s

When he married Frances Eyles, Nicholas Jeffreys was at Inner Temple.[1]

1. PROB 11/756

JEFFREYS & DIXON
1742: DR £77

JENNING[S], DEBR
1738: CR £25; £25

The entry is for April 1738, the month before Samuel Masham's [▶ p.293]. It is possible they were related, as Sarah Jennings (Duchess of Marlborough) came from a large family.

JENNINGS, GEO
1744: DR £51 10s
1745: CR £50

Uncertain identity: the debit and credit entries may be for different people. George Jennings, laceman, is listed in Dukes Court, London;[1] he was very likely the Mr Jenning, lace merchant, who advertised in Pierrepont Street, Bath.[2]

The credit entry might be for a son of Admiral Sir John Jennings (MP for Whitchurch), who married Mary, daughter of 10th Earl of Clanricarde in 1741, d. 1790.[3]

1. 1749 poll. 2. BJ, 1 October 1744 advertisement. PROB 11/776, proved 31 January 1750. 3. Venn.

JENNING[S], PHIL
1739: CR £50; £50

Philip Jennings (?1679–1740), MP for Queenborough 1715–22, a lawyer who died in 1742.[1] His son, also Philip, matriculated, Oxford, in 1739 aged 17, created a baronet in 1774.[2]

1. Sedgwick. 2. Foster.

JESSER/JESSOR, JNO
1739–46: DR £105; £27; £147; £199 10s; £50; £105; £105; £90 13s; £31 10s; £50; £73 10s; £52 10s; £178 10s; £262 10s; £400; £104; £147 10s; £150; £105; £60; £315

JESSER, JOS
1739–45: DR £105; £50; £200; £95 12s

John Jesser (d. 1756) was a clothier in Frome, Somerset; his wife Elizabeth died in 1753. The very large sums paid to someone who apparently had no connections to the toy or jewellery trade, are hard to explain unless they were to do with the assembly rooms.

Portrait: William Hoare, Bristol Art Gallery.

JESSOP, BETHIA
1738: CR £35; £25; £30; £30; £25

Bethia Jessop had an account with Hoare and, very unusually, ledger entries show payments that match payments in Bertrand's account. They also show a payment to the silversmith Benjamin Godfrey in 1741.

JOHNSON, ELIZ
1739: CR £60; £20

JOHNSON, GEFFRY/JEFF
1739: CR £30; £40

JOHNSON, SAML
1744: CR £50; £50

Uncertain identity. Possibly Samuel Johnson (1709–84), the writer and lexicographer – but he is not recorded as having visited Bath this early, although his brother at one time lived in Frome (d. 1737). Or this might refer to Samuel Johnson, dancing master and playwright (1690/1–1773), who spent much of his life in Manchester and Cheshire.[1]

1. DNB.

JOHNSON, THOS
1745: CR £25

Uncertain identity. If this entry, which is a common name, refers to a Maryland planter, it could mean that Bertrand retained links to his parents' failed attempt to start a new life in Calvert County [▶ p. 30]. Thomas Johnson (1702–77) was the father of the merchant Joshua Johnson, whose letter books detail his correspondence between London and Maryland.[1]

Although it is a credit entry, it could alternatively refer to the London carver.

1. Price.

JOHNSTON & ELLIOTT
1740: DR £50

Possibly Johnston & Eliot, oilmen, without Bishopsgate.[1]

1. Kent 1740.

JOHNSTON, WM
1744: CR £40; 1745: CR [Jno Hardinge] £50

Uncertain identity. Possibly the nephew of Alexander Johnston, merchant.[1]

1. Hancock.

JONES, EDMD
1743 and 1744: CR £27 15s; £35 10s

JONES, GEO GREENHILL
1738 and 1739: DR £53 18s; £76 10s

London silversmith.

▶ p. 229.

JONES, GILES
1739: DR £30

'Saturday morning was married Mr Giles Jones, a surgeon of this City to Mrs Vaughan, Daughter of Thursby Robinson Esq Mayor, a very agreeable young Lady'.[1] He is later listed at premises in Orange Grove, and in Edgars Buildings (next to William Hoare).[2]

1. BJ, 7 December 1747. 2. Bath RO: 1766 Rate Book 1.

JONES, HENRIETTA
1739: DR £10 10s; £21

JONES, RICHD
1742 and 1743: DR £120; £50

Surveyor, and clerk of works to Ralph Allen 1731–64, whose 'Life' he wrote.

▶ p. 73.

JORDEN, ABRM
1740: DR £40

In 1708 Bath Council 'agreed … to a certificate of Mr Abraham Jordan which sets forth that he has perfected the organ in St Peter & St Paul's Church' [Bath Abbey]. It is just possible that thirty-two years on, this is the same man.[1]

1. Bath RO: Council Book 3, fo. 511.

JOURDON, JNO
1746: 1 DR £40

This could be Jourdain rather than Jourdon. There was a Nicholas Jourdain, silkweaver in Spitafields. The personal account books of Richard Hoare reveal that 'John Jourdain' was a tailor; Hoare spent £75 with him on 1 February 1737/38. If spelling is not reliable, this may be the same person. It is thus possible that he was connected to William Jourdain, clockmaker, and also, perhaps, to Anthony Jordan, who witnessed the will of the silversmith Edward Feline.

JOWELL, MARTHA
1738: CR £30

Possibly a connection of George Jowell. He witnessed the document between Richard Nash and the Duke of Bedford in 1731.

▶ p. 75 illus.

JOYE, THOS
1740: DR £20

Thomas Joye was heavily involved in the running of gaming tables in Bath and Tunbridge Wells. In 1730 a Mr Joy 'son to a late director of the South Sea, but one who reads much and had University education' was part of Lord Egmont's circle in Bath, who met regularly in a coffee shop to converse in the evening.[1] Invoices survive from Thomas Joye for wine and tobacco and on 19 February 1736/37 he wrote to Lady Burlington (who had been in Bath in November 1736):[2]

> Madam: I took the Liberty to send your Ladyship Halfe a doz potts of Lampreys by the bath carrier that set out yesterday and hope they will prove good.

It may be that there was more than one person of the same name. On 22 May 1762 George Scott wrote of 'Nash and his Gambling Friends, one of whom (Joye) is now starving at this Place'.[3]

1. Egmont, vol. 1, p. 117.
2. Chatsworth: 239.0 and invoices. 3. Ferguson.

K

KELSALL, JNO
1745: DR £100

Possibly connected to Daniell Kelsall, jeweller.[1] J. Kelsall signed an invoice dated 1732, but it does not specify his trade.[2]

1. *London Gazette* [9479].
2. Hoare.

KENDALL, JAMES

1737–40: CR £42; £42; £42; £42; £31; £46; £42; £31 10s; £31 10s; £37

In 1766 James Kendall was listed in South Parade, Bath.[1] His account with Hoare is a rare instance of entries for payments to Bertrand tallying with those in Bertrand's account, in October–December 1739 and November–December 1740.

1. Bath RO: Rate Book 1, p. 30.

KENDALL, JOHN

1746: DR £9 10s

Uncertain identity. John Kendall is shown in Westgate Street, Bath, in a property advertisement in 1745;[1] he is presumably the same man listed in the 1760s at the Golden Cannister, Pierrepont St, Bath, selling china.[2] In 1750 Luke Kendall, son of John dec'd was apprenticed in London to Lewis Benoimont, so there were at least two men with this name and no doubt more.

1. *BJ*, 30 September 1745.
2. Hildyard.

KENDRICK, THOS

1736: DR £10

Thomas Kendrick is listed as a freemason at the lodge at the Queen's Arms, Newgate Street, London in 1730, with Benjamin Cole.[1] He was probably the silversmith listed from 1731 in Water Lane, Fleet Street, over against ye Black Lion.[2] There was also a jeweller named Kendrick, in Hog Lane, St Giles in the Fields, who died in 1764: 'being out on an airing at Islington, was seized with a fit of apoplexy and notwithstanding the assistance of a surgeon, who immediately bled him, he expired in a few minutes'.[3]

1. Songhurst. 2. Grimwade [2822], p. 569. 3. *Lloyd's Evening Post*, 11 July 1764.

KENNEDY, HUGH

1746: DR £5 10s

Master Mason of Royal Cumberland Lodge, Bath, 1732–34 and 1738. It seems unlikely, but possible, that he is the same man listed as 'gent' in York Buildings, London.

KING, JNO

1737–39: DR £15 15s; £20; £30; £30; £8 8s

Uncertain identity and a common name. The Kings were a family of watchmakers; this is probably John King apprenticed 1726.[1]

In 1754 there was a merchant of this name in Bristol.[2]

1. Baillie. 2. Bristol 1755.

KINGMAN, JNO

1745: DR £5 5s

Apprenticed to John Deards snr. 12 November 1711; free 29 October 1743. The rate books show a John Kingman in Queens Head Court 1741–49 and another in Bishops Court 1742.

KIRK, GEO

1739: DR £20

Most probably a member of the London family of engravers; they had a toyshop in St Paul's Churchyard.

KIRKPATRICK, WILLIAM

1744–47: DR £10 10s; £12 10s; £10; £7 13s; £20; £10; £10; £13 13s; £20 5s 6d; £12 13s; £10; £10; £10; £10 10s; £20; £10

William Kirkpatrick was Master Mason at the Royal Cumberland Lodge in Bath in 1753. When the Earl and Countess of Findlater visited Bath in September to November 1742, Kirkpatrick's bill for '8 weeks powdering and Buckelling at 1s 6d pr week' came to 12s (he received 11s in payment).[1]

1. NAS: GD248/905/1.

KNIGHT, JOSIAH

1744: DR £16

KNIGHT, ROBINSON

1739–43: CR £80; £30; £100

KNOX & CO. / KNOX & CRAGHEAD

1736–46: CR £100; £40; £100; £100; £27 8s; £21; £180 10s; £22 14s 6d; £15 12s 10d; £46 3s 9d; £41 6s 6d; £50; £70; £14; £100

Knox & Kraghead, merchants, Crosby Square.[1]

1. Kent 1740.

KORTEN & CO.

1742: CR £70

John-Abraham Korten & Co., merchants, Mincing Lane.[1]

1. Kent 1740

L

LACON, ELIZ

1743: DR [see W.Wiltshire] £319 3s

Puppeteer.

▶ p. 133.

LACOUY, MR

1742: DR £10 10s

Possibly Lacon, above.

LAMB, MATH

1744 and 1745: CR £50; £100; £100; £50

Of Brocket Hall, co. Herts and Melbourne Hall, co. Derbys, an MP 1741–68. Lamb was a lawyer whose uncle left him an estimated £100,000 and chambers in Lincoln's Inn; his fortune on his death was estimated at over £1,000,000. He advised and acted as agent to several members of the aristocracy. His son was created Viscount Melbourne; his grandson became Prime Minister.

LANGTON, JOS

1744 and 1745: DR £136 10s; £60

MRS LANGTON

1745: CR £100

Probably Joseph (Joshua) Langton of Newton St Loe, co. Somerset. Newton Park (c.1762–65) is described by

Nikolaus Pevsner as 'one of the finest country mansions of the 18th century'; the family also owned coalmines near Midsomer Norton in the same county. His wife, Charlotte Bathurst (of Clarendon Park), died in 1757 in the same year as her sister, Lady Feversham; their daughter Anne married Sir George Cobb [▶ p. 261]. Langton stood in the 1747 election for Bath, when George Wade and Robert Henley were voted in.

LANT/LAUT, ROBT
1741 & 1742: CR £50; £50; £50

Possibly Robert Lant, Hop Merchant, Three Crown-court, Borough, Southwark.[1]

1. Kent 1740.

LAPOTTRE, HEN [SEE RD NASH]
1740: CR £10 10s

Henry Lapostre, Georgia Trustee, Soho Square.[1] He is referred to in Lord Egmont's diaries as Mr Lapautre, Lapauter, La Potre, common councilman of the Georgia Society.

1. Kent 1740.

LAUGHTON, B [ELIZ TURNER]
1745: CR £100

LAWRENCE, THOS
1741: DR £63 12s

Uncertain identity. There was a physician (1711–83), who qualified in 1740 and became known for his anatomical lectures. He was friend and doctor to Samuel Johnson. His grandfather was a physician to Queen Anne. But there was also a plateworker, in Golden Lane, 1742.[1]

1. Heal, LG.

LEAKE, JAS
1736–37: CR £50; £10; £100; £100; £80
1736–54 DR £22; £60; £80; £20 10s; £16 9s 10d; £39 8s; £16 10s; £25; £25; £25; £23 10s; £24 5s; £97 7s 6d; £10; £21; £44 14s; £50; £50; £100; £70; £80; £54 3s 6d; £97 10s; £26; £25; £16; £75; £25; £25

Bookshop owner, Bath
▶ p. 176.

LEAVER, GA:
1741 and 1744: CR £105; £40

A Mr Leaver is listed at the Cross Bath in 1748.[1]

1. Bath RO: 1748 Water Roll.

LEGGE, HENEAGE
1745 and 1746: CR £200; £50

Heneage Legge, second son of the 1st Earl of Dartmouth; was one of the Barons of the Exchequer from 1749. He married Catherine Fogg in 1740 and died in 1759.

LE GRAND, MRS
1736: CR £30

In October 1705 Helena Southwell married William Lewis le Grand by special licence; he was a Gentleman of the Bedchamber. From 1709 they lived at Maiden Earley, Berks; he died in January 1733. Mrs le Grand and her daughter received legacies in the will of Mary Dering (her first cousin [▶ p. 268]), of which her son, Edward le Grand, was executor.[1] She corresponded with Lady Burlington from Bath during this visit (letter dated 4 December 1736; [▶ p. 268 Delorane]).[2]

Another son, William Southwell Legrand, was a page in the Prince of Wales's household 1729–38. Her daughter Helena (1712–91) specified in her will that she be buried 'without Lights or Iscutions'; Wagner notes legacies of £2000 'to swells'.[3]

1. PROB 11/755. 2. Chatsworth: 246.0. 3. Wagner.

LEHOOK, MESSRS
1744: CR £80 [re W. Wiltshire]

Benjamin & Samuel Lehook, Blackwelhall-factors, Cateaton-street.[1] Blackwell Hall, Basinghall Street, was the centre of the cloth trade in London.

1. Kent 1740.

LE MAISTRE, PETER /MESS LE MAITRE
1736 and 1741: DR £375 14s 6d; £9 13s

Peter & Cesar Lemaitre were merchants, St Martin's Lane, Strand.[1] A note of exchange countersigned P&C Lemaitre, is dated 1742.[2] The name LeMaitre, as wine merchants, features in several archives, for example Stanhope, Gordon Castle and Verney.[3] Cesar Lemaitre is also listed in Leicester Square or in Frith Street; Peter was of St Paul's Covent Garden when he died in 1758.[4] In 1740, with Peter Deletang [▶ p. 267] Peter Le Maitre proved the will of William Hubert [▶ p. 227]. Peter and Cesar married sisters, Laetitia and Susanna de la Creuze (daughters of Stephen and Susanna), in 1736. He enjoined his son 'not to marry a woman above 3 years older then himself, or any woman of low mechanical birth'.[5]

It is not yet known if there was a connection between Peter Lemaitre and the family of Paul Bertrand's first wife: William Hubert might provide a link.

1. Kent 1740. 2. Badminton: FmI 4/14. 3. Maidstone RO: U1590/A98, a/c book, 7 August 1738; NAS: GD44/51/202/44; Claydon. 4. Evans; 1749 poll; PROB 11/836. 5. Wagner.

LE ROUX, JNO
1736–47: DR £14 7s; £50; £47; £23; £40; £10 11s; £100

London watchmaker
▶ p. 230.

LE SEUR, DANL
1739–41: DR £25 12s 6d; £5 14s

LECHIEUR, DANL
1739: DR £28

Listed as a Portugal Merchant, Lime Street Square, in 1763.[1] His name appears (with Frederick

Standert [▶ p. 312] and others) in a 1756 list of traders to Portugal who complained of duties imposed by Portugal after the Lisbon earthquake in order to rebuild the Custom House there.[2]

Wagner lists two men of this name in London.[3] Alternatively, le Seur might be a connection of a French enameller.[4]

> 1. Mortimer. 2. Sutherland.
> 3. Wagner. 4. Truman 2013, p. 76.

LEVETT, CAPT
1743–45: CR £100; £30; £25

Most probably Thomas, son of Theophilus Levett (d. 1746) of Wichnor Park, Staffs. Capt Levett was in the Royal Regiment of Horse Guards; accounts he submitted to the Earl of Hertford in 1738 (£118 14s 6d), 1744 (£4,292 12s 7½d) and 1746 (£5,496 12s 5½d) survive [▶ p. 89]. The 1744 invoice for equipment includes uniforms, saddles, etc including 128 gross & ½ of coat buttons at 11 £76 2s 6d; 70 do of small do at 6 £21; 684 yds of Hat Lace 416 oz 12 dw £166 12s 10d, etc.[1] In 1749 Thomas Levett Esq is listed in Warwick St, Golden Square;[2] in 1762 he married Catherine, daughter of Charles Floyer [▶ p. 274].

He might have been connected to John Levett, alderman, Temple,[3] an India merchant, whose brother Francis was a merchant with the Levant Company in Leghorn, then Florida [▶ p. 344, n. 318].[4]

> 1. Alnwick: U.I.23j.2. 2. 1749 poll.
> 3. Kent 1740. 4. Hancock.

LILLIE, EDWARD
1746: DR £100

Unknown identity. Possibly a connection of Charles Lillie, London perfumer.

LINWOOD, NCS
1741: CR £50

Nicholas Linwood was a partner with William Baker and Brice Fisher (▶ p. 273) in a property in South Carolina known as the Hobcaw Barony. He was a London merchant and army contractor, MP for Stockbridge, Hants in 1761 and financial adviser and agent to Henry Fox.[1] In 1763 he was listed as 'South Sea Director and Wine Merchant, St Mary Axe'.[2]

> 1. Namier. 2. Mortimer.

LLOYD, EDWARD
1741–45: CR £20; £40; £81; £50; £150

Uncertain identity. An Edward Lloyd was witness to the will of Catherine Hayes [▶ p. 95]; two men of this name are listed in 1749, in Brook Street (St George, Hanover Sq.) and in Duke Street (St Martin-in-the-Fields).[1]

> 1. 1749 poll.

LOCKWOOD, RD & CO.
1739 and 1745: CR £160; £20

Richard Lockwood (1676–1756), Turkey merchant and deputy governor of the Royal Exchange Assurance.[1] He represented three different constituencies in the House of Commons between 1713 and 1741; through the African Company he was associated with the Duke of Chandos (to whom he was banker), and with whom he played whist at Bath in 1726.[2]

> 1. Kent 1740. 2. Sedgwick. Baker p. 298.

LONDONDERRY, LORD
1744: CR £50; £117 0s 6d

Ridgeway Pitt, 3rd Earl of Londonderry (1722–65), MP for Camelford 1747–54, inherited the title from his brother in 1734 and died unmarried, when the title became extinct. His arrival in Bath was listed for 15 October 1744; he banked with Hoare where the ledgers accurately record both sides of these transactions. His mother also visited Bath often, for example in September 1732, in which year she married Robert Graham, 'the son of William III's tailor'. In her will she specified:[1]

> The coffins of her late husband Robert Graham, and dear friend Thomas Newland esq., to be laid side by side with hers, the latter and hers open. To be buried in waistcoat and nightcap, wedding ring and hoop ring, and white cotton stockings; with bible open at St. John chap. xx.

> 1. Annual Register.

LONG, DRAKE
1744: CR £50

Drake Pennant & Long, merchants, Crutched-friers.[1]

> 1. Kent 1740.

LONG, WALTER
1744 and 1746: DR £80 10s; £100; £20; £20

Although debit entries, this must refer to Walter Long of Bath (1712–1807), whose family owned estates at Whaddon, Rood Ashton and South Wraxall, in Wiltshire. He was a kinsman of Catherine Tylney-Long [▶ p. 257 Castlemaine]. In middle age he fell in love with the singer Eliza Linley, but he was 40 years her senior and didn't stand a chance when Richard Brinsley Sheridan came to Bath in 1770: Linley was 17, Sheridan 18, and Long then aged 57.

LOOKUP, GEO:
1741 and 1746: CR £21; £411 7s
1743–46 DR £11 9s 6d; £10; £14 10s; £71; £14; £30 10s

The will of a George Lookup of Covent Garden, London, who died in 1771, gives no hint of what these payments might represent, but makes provision for a natural daughter.[1] His name appears also in the account of Walter Wiltshire with Hoare, e.g. in 1737.[2] His loss of a gold watch during the procession on Lord Mayor's Day, is a good example of the 'warnings' issued to goldsmiths and pawnbrokers about thefts; it suggests that Lookup might have been a gambler:

> and the gentleman came the next morning to see the chain; he saw it, and said he did not chuse to swear to it, but he could lay an hundred pounds to one it was his chain.[3]

His death in Amsterdam was reported thus:

> George Lookup, Esq. who came here about twelve months ago, to demand and settle the payment due to the representatives of the late Jerenomy Clifford, merchant, died here …

followed by the sale of the contents of his house.[4]

1. PROB 11/972. 2. Lr.38 fo.199. 3. POB:, t17661217-58. 4. *Bingley's Journal*, 2 November 1771; *Daily Advertiser*, 24 April 1772.

LOUBIER & CO.
1740 and 1741: CR £50; £21; £30

Individual members of the Loubier family were usually described in the press as 'an eminent French Merchant', based in and around Basinghall Street. They were directors of the London Assurance Company and supporters of the London Hospital. The family included: Anthony Loubier (d. 1734), John Lewis snr (d. 1739), John Anthony (d. 1744), Henry (d. 1755), Charles (d. 1765), John Lewis jnr (d. 1767). The marriages and deaths of daughters and nieces were regularly reported in the press. At one time they were in partnership with the Tessier family: one of Anthony's daughters married James Tessier. Henry Loubier is listed at Devil Tavern Lodge within Temple Bar in 1730, with William Deards and George Moody.[1]

Although it is important to consider mis-spellings and mispronunciation, it seems unlikely they were connected with Louis Loubie, who was apprenticed to Thomas Thibault 1727, free 1746 [▶ p. 315].[2] Lewis Laubie, jeweller, is listed in Archer St, Windmill Street in 1749.[3]

1. Wagner; Songhurst. 2. GH: Apprentice Book 6/88. 3. 1749 poll.

LOWTHER, THOS
1740 and 1741: CR £63 15s 6d; £20; £30; £59 8s

Sir Thomas Lowther, Bt (c.1699–1745) of Marske, Yorks is listed as arriving in Bath in September 1744; he died in March 1745. MP for Lancaster 1722–45, he married Lady Elizabeth Cavendish daughter of the 2nd Duke of Devonshire. A donation of £100 towards the Mineral Water Hospital in Bath 'Governor Lowther by hand of Sir Thomas Lowther' was made during his 1744 visit.[1]

1. *BJ*, 7 January 1744/45.

LUCE, LEWIS/LOUIS
1738 and 1739: DR £46 10s; £70 7s

It seems likely that this is Louis-René Luce (1695–1774), type founder of the Royal Printing House of Paris. He produced miniature books that might well have been sold in a toyshop and, unbound, for mounting into cases of gold, silver, mother-of-pearl or leather usually known today as almanac cases. His diamond-size type was approximately seventeen lines to the inch. An example of 1740 is *Épreuve du premier Alphabeth droit et penché, ornée de quadres et cartouches, gravés par ordre du Roi pour l'Imprimerie Royale*; the cover measures approximately 11 × 7.5 cm (4⅜ × 3 in), the border to the printed area approx 6.2 × 3 cm (2½ × 1⅜ in). Into this small space he fits, for example, extracts from Fontaine's *Fables* and Pope's *Imitation d'Horace*.[1] In the 1740s Luce completed the work of Philippe Grandjean and Jean Alexandre on the font known as Romain du Roi. He replicated in cast metal earlier wood-engraved designs of fleurons and emblems for tail-pieces.[2] The entry raises interesting questions as to whether Luce was in England in the late 1730s, and/or which agent he used in dealings with Bertrand. The sums of money are large, if they represent only books.

A less probable identity might be a dancer from Paris, Mr St Luce, who performed in London 1729–30.

1. BL: shelfmark 51.a.26. 2. *Essai d'une nouvelle typographie, ornée de vignettes, fleurons, trophées, filets, cadres & cartels*, 1771. BL: shelfmark C.97.d.10.

LUPART, MR
1736 and 1739: CR £60; £120

Uncertain identity. Possibly William Lupart, steward to Peter Delme [▶ p. 267]. Delme is regularly mentioned in the Earl of Burlington's account books.[1] Peter Lupart is listed as a goldsmith in 1696 at the Golden Lion, Lombard St; his name appears, for example, in the Verney papers 1702.[2]

1. Chatsworth. 2. H-Price; Claydon.

LYTTON, BARBR
1740: CR £50

Probably Barbara Lytton, b. 1710, who married William Warburton [▶ p. 319 Barbara Warburton]. Her father was William Robinson [▶ p. 305]. The barony of Lytton was not created until the early nineteenth century.

M

MACHUNE, DANIEL
1736–41: DR £21 15s

MACHUNE, PRIS
1741: DR £31

MACKVILL, THOS & SON
1745: CR £25

Possibly Thomas Mackrell, wool stapler, Barnaby Street.[1]

1. Kent 1740.

MADDEN, JOHN
1754: DR £24

Cabinetmaker who features in Paul Bertrand's will; Mary Bertrand bequeathed £500 to his wife Sarah.

MADDOCKES, THOS
1736: CR £30

Unknown identity. A man of this name was in Bristol in 1754.[1]

1. Bristol 1755.

MAINWARING, EDWD
1738: DR £12

In spite of this being a debit entry, this appears to be for Edward Mainwaring (6th of that name), of Whitmore Hall, Staffs, who married in 1735 Sarah, daughter of William Bunbury [▶ p. 255]. They might have been in Bath for Sarah's health: having married in 1735 she gave birth to sons in 1736 and in 1737. The ledger entry is for May 1738, when her father's name is also listed. Mainwaring 'signalised himself by his great zeal in repelling the invasion of Charles Edward in 1745 against whom he marched to Derby at the head of his tenantry'.[1]

It is worth noting, however, that in the 1760s the premises next to those that had been Bertrand's shop, are listed in the name of Ambrose Mainwaring.[2]

Portraits: at Whitmore Hall.

1. Burke, *Commoners*, vol. 3, p. 590. 2. Bath RO: City Rate Book 1766.

MALTBY, THOS
1741: CR £50

MANN, ROBT
1739: DR £15; £25
1739: CR £41

Possibly Robert Mann jnr, African Director, Great Tower-hill. Robert Mann listed as an officer in the Customs House at the Port of London, collector of Inwards business, at a salary of £446 p.a.[2] Possibly connected to Galfridus Mann, a woollen draper who supplied military uniforms.

1. Kent 1740. 2. Chamberlayne, Pt II, Bk III, p. 64.

MARBUTT, MRS
1737: DR £20

MARCH, THOS
1744: CR £50

Uncertain identity, perhaps: Henry, John & Thomas March, Turkey Merchants, Devonshire-Square.[1]

1. Kent 1740.

MARCHANT, EDWD
1740 and 1746: DR £100; £225; £46 14s

The Marchants were a large Bath family. On 14 January 1742 George Marchant was apprenticed to his father Edward Marchant, a distiller.[1] In 1745 there was advertised:[2]

> To be Lett at Midsummer next. The House, Cellars, Warehouse &c that Edward Marchant, Distiller and Hop-Dealer, lately went out of, having very good Conveniences for that Trade, or any other that may offer, situate in the Market Place. Enquire of Richard Marchant.

The following month, July 1745, Mrs Elizabeth Marchant, widow, is mentioned in a similar advertisement. Two years later Edward Marchant, victualler, is listed in the water rates for 1747–48.

Other members of this extended family included another Edward, chief mason and contractor for the Avon Navigation scheme,[3] and Richard Marchant, Quaker timber merchant, land speculator, developer and banker, who acted as agent for the Duke of Chandos.[4]

There was also a jeweller and silversmith named Peter Marchant in St Helen's, London.[5]

1. Bath RO: Apprentice Book p. 32. 2. *BJ*, 3 June 1745. 3. Bath RO Apprentice Book, p. 16, 1731; will proved 14 January 1746, PROB 11/744. 4. Eglin; Baker, p. 299; Neale. 5. Wagner pp. 50 and 280.

MARGAS, PHILIP
1737–47: DR £60 10s 6d; £50; £25; £75; £50; £34 17s; £50; £29 10s; £37 14s; £52 10s; £91 11s

London chinaman

▶ p. 231.

MARRIOTT, CAPTN
1738: CR £60

Possibly a connection of the Revd Mr Marriot who contributed five guineas to the Mineral Water Hospital in 1738, the year of this credit entry.

MARSH, JNO
1740: CR £30

Uncertain identity and a common name. Possibly John Marsh of Air Street, London, gent.[1]

1. 1749 poll.

MARSHALL, HENRY
1747: CR £10

Henry Marshall (1688–1754) alderman and grocer, St Mary Hill.[1] He was Master of the Drapers Company 1738, president of St Bartholomew's Hospital 1745 to his death, MP for Amersham 1734–54.

Portrait: Thomas Hudson, *The Benn Club* (GC) [▶ p. 84].

1. Kent 1740.

MARTIN & CO.
1737–47: CR £60; £80; £100; £40; £30; £100; £30; £50; £201.10s; £100; £52 10s; £40; £20; £50; £30; £50; £50; £157 10s; £20; £50

Goldsmith and banker, at The Grasshopper, 68 Lombard St, the entries are also given as James Martin & Co. (1743) and John Martin & Co. (1746).

1. Outing; Kent 1740.

MARTIN, MMC
1738: DR £126

Uncertain identity. Possibilities include: Martin, toyman at the Three Rabbits, near Durham Yard, Strand;[1] Charles Martin, silversmith, at the Rose and Crown, Brides Lane, Fleet St; M. Martin, just without West Gate Printer, Bath.[2]

1. Heal signs. 2. Benjamin Layton's trade card, Bath CL.

MARTYN, ANN
1744: CR £65 8s [Jno Noyes]

'Widow of Bath' whose will was proved 8 September 1755.[1]

1. PROB 11/818.

MASHAM, SAML
1738: CR £50

The Hon. Samuel Masham, Cork Street.[1] His father, 4th Bt (who d. 1758 and whose seven elder brothers predeceased him), was created Baron Masham in 1712 largely due to the influence of his wife Abigail, the favourite of Queen Anne; his was one of twelve peerages created in five days to secure a Tory majority. Abigail Masham's first cousin was Sarah, Duchess of Marlborough [▶ p. 286 Jennings]. Samuel's sister Anne was the first wife of Henry Hoare (nicknamed 'the magnificent') of Stourhead, whose daughter, also Anne, married her cousin Richard Hoare. Samuel Masham was a fellow of the Royal Society; he died in 1776, without children.[2]

1. 1749 poll. 2. Burke, *Extinct Peerage*; GEC; Foster.

MASON, EDMD
1746: CR £50

MASS[E]Y, FRAS
1746 and 1747: DR £10 10s; £30

Francis Massey I of Eccleshall, Staffs, watchmaker, pre-1750.[1]

1. Loomes.

MASSINGBERD, MR
1736: CR £840

£840 was a substantial sum, and seems all the more extraordinary because of Massingberd's youth: William Burrell Massingberd was only about 17 at the time of the entry. His monument in South Ormsby Church records he was 83 when he died in 1802. Were it not for the evidence of Massingberd's account with Hoare, it would be tempting to think that the entry referred to William Meux, who assumed the surname Massingberd when he inherited Gunby in Lincolnshire (National Trust) through his mother; his second wife was Miss Drake. Unusually, however, the transaction can be traced through Massingberd's account:[1] £900 was paid into Massingberd's account by three bills in December 1736 (7th: £200 on Dyor & Antrim, 13th: £400 on Geo Vincent, £300 on Dyor & Antrim). On 17 December £900 was taken out of the account ('To mony recd pr 3 bills') and on the same day £840 was credited to Bertrand's account. The sums bear no comparison with records kept by his mother, Philippa (née Mundy), who noted that she used a snuffbox for keeping cash:[2]

26 September 1723: Taken out of ye snuff box £2-2-0
27 September: Rec'd of Mr M £10-10-0 out of wh I am to put 2-2-0 into ye snuff box, remains 8.8.0
17 Oct: out of ye snuff box 8-8-0

1. Lr. 37 fo. 133. Burke, *LG*, listed under Massingberd-Mundby of Ormsby. 2. Lincoln RO: MM/10/7.

MASTER, THOS
1746: DR £13

A governor of the Mineral Water Hospital, Bath, in 1748.

MASTERS, DECA
1747: DR £400
1747: CR £103 7s [Capt Shadwell]

Benedict Masters, Bath silversmith.
▶ p. 172.

MASTERS, HENRY
1739: DR £21

Henry was probably related to Philip and Benedict (above). The Masters family was large: Richard Masters had Hart Lodgings in Stall Street early in the century and was Mayor of Bath 1701–02.[1]

1. Fawcett 1994.

MATHEW, MR
1746: CR £50

MATHIAS, VINCENT
1745 and 1746: CR £40 18s 6d; £30

John Cope's account with Hoare has credit payments 'By Vincent Mathias' in 1741. He married Marianne (1724–99), daughter of Alured Popple [▶ p. 302 Henry Popple]. She inherited from her aunt Sophia William Hogarth's painting of the Popple family, now in the Royal Collection.[1]

1. Shaw-Taylor.

MAXWELL, CAPT GEO
1743: DR £42

MAXWELL, SAML
1745: CR £100

MAY, CHRISR
1736: CR £150

MAY, RD
1741: CR £50

Possibly members of a family local to Bath: see monuments in Melksham church.

MCCONNELL, DR
1746: CR £105

MCFARLAN, MRS
1736: DR £11

Possibly Jessie McFarlan, the widow of John Mackfarlan, London silversmith, who registered her own mark in October 1739 with an address in New Street, Cloth Fair.[1]

1. Grimwade.

MEDCALFE, ANN
1742 and 1743: CR £30; £15

MENIER, MR
1736: DR £20

Heal lists Guillaume Menier, goldsmith, in St Andrew's Street, 1706–07.

MEREDITH, FR HUMP
1745: CR £34 0s 6d

Uncertain identity: It was unusual for a Catholic priest to be termed 'Father' in the eighteenth century, so 'Fr' may mean Francis. Possibly a Welsh family: Humpfrey Meredydd was High Sheriff of Carnarvonshire in 1738; his father had the same name. Or, there was a Humphrey Meredith of Ufton Court, near Reading, described as 'gardener' and a non-juror.

MERLE, MR
1745: CR £36

John Anthony Merle (d. 1776), African Director & Merchant, Spittal Square. His name features in the Hoare account of Wm Peere Williams [▶ p. 321]. With Susannah Passavant [▶ p. 299], he testified to the signature of George Willdey on the latter's will.[1]

1. PROB 11/686, Wagner.

MICHELL, JNO
1738: CR £100

Uncertain identity. Possibly John Michell of Kingston Russell, Dorset, who died in 1739;[1] or John Michell (1710–66) MP for Boston, Lincs.[2]

1. Burke, *LG* 1848.   2. Sedgwick.

MICHELL, RICHARD
1736: CR £73 10s

MIDDLEMORE, JNO
1739 and 1740: CR £30; £52 10s

MIDDLETON & CO.
1736–46: £25; £21; £52 10s; £20; £30; £100; £50; £26 5s; £34 5s; £100; £81 18s.
1738–45: DR £105; £28; £28

The bank (now Coutts & Co.) was founded in 1692 by John Campbell (d. 1712) at the Three Crowns in the Strand.[1] In 1708 he took George Middleton as partner, who married Campbell's daughter. John Campbell's brother George joined Middleton in 1727. An 'eminent banker in the Strand' Middleton died in Bath in 1747; his sister was married to Dr George Cheyne [▶ p. 259].[2] In 1744 David Bruce joined the partnership (probably the Campbell & Co. listed on p. 256) and James Coutts entered the firm in 1755 [▶ p. 211/19 map].

P.D. Chenevix had an account with Middleton & Campbell 1735–38.

1. Outing; H-Price; Coutts website.   2. *BJ*, 26 January 1746/47.

MILLES, E
1745: CR £30

MILLS, MR
1736: DR £5 5s

MINORS, THOS; MINORS & CO.; MINORS & BOLDERO
1738–46: CR £10 10s; £40; £52 10s; £70; £56; £21; £20; £50; £50; £144; £20; £146 6s

Thomas Minors, banker, The Vine, Lombard Street, established 1738.[1]

1. Outing; Kent 1740; H-Price.

MOLLOY, FELIX
1738: DR £23; £27

MONTAGU, LADY BARBA
1744 and 1746: CR £50; £70

'Lady Bab' (*c.*1722–65), daughter of the Earl of Halifax; from 1748 she lived with Sara Robinson [▶ p. 305] with whom she 'formed a very intimate friendship'.[1] During the latter's ill-fated marriage to George Scott in 1751, which lasted less than a year, Lady Barbara lived with the couple in London. Following the break-up of the marriage, the two women returned to Bath, where Lady Barbara had a house in Beaufort Square, for a period spending summers in nearby Bath Easton, 'for a life of domesticity and practical piety' which included running a school. Lady Barbara's cousin George Montagu, friend of Horace Walpole, wrote that:[2]

> She was the one I always loved and passed all my youth with in daily gaiety and joy, for she had all the wit and humours of the family, generous and beneficient; her constitution was so delicate that her life has been a sufferance for many years.

1. Delany, vol. 3, p. 115.   2. Scott; Hurley.

MOODY, GEORGE
1746: CR £25

Listed as a smallworker and 'free Haberdasher'.[1] He was a freemason and master of Temple Bar Lodge in 1730, listed with William Deards. On 29 January 1731:[2]

> Br Moody, Master of the Lodge at the Devil Tavern within Temple Bar and Sword Cutler to their Majesty's household was ordered by the Deputy Grand Master to produce the Sword of State by him finished and the Brethren present acknowledged that it was not only finely designed but executed in the best manner and owned to be a curious piece of workmanship.

Moody was first Grand Sword Bearer of Grand Lodge; the sword can be seen at Freemasons' Hall in London, signed on scabbard 'G. Moody fecit'. He was cutler to Frederick Prince of Wales; his name features regularly in the prince's household accounts.[3] Moody's account with Hoare shows payments to Bertrand in 1746 and an invoice of 1731 reveals that he dealt in snuff.[4] In 1713 he was 'next the Queens Armes Tavern near Temple Barr'.[5]

1. Grimwade. 2. Songhurst. 3. Chamberlayne. 4. Lr. 45 fo. 412. 5. Sun Ins, vol. 3, p. 118. For more on Moody, see Southwick 2011.

MOODY, HATCH
1746: CR £25; £32

Hatch Moody was in the office of the Paymaster General of the Land Forces (Henry Pelham was Paymaster General).[1] Payments from Moody to Sir Francis Poole for 1737–40, shown in the latter's account with Hoare, amount to the considerable sum of £2,060 1s 7d.[2] Poole was Receiver General for Stamp Duties at the Excise Office.[3]

1. Chamberlayne, Pt II, Bk III, p. 100. 2. Lr. 37 fo. 259. 3. Chamberlayne, Pt II, Bk III, p. 91.

MOORE, JAS
1739: CR £27; £25

Uncertain identity. Possibly of Fetcham, Surrey, matriculated 1717 aged 17[1] – but it is a common name.

1. Foster.

MOORE, MR
1745: CR £35

MOORE, JNO
1745: DR £450

Uncertain identity: this is a large payment. In London there was a silver spur maker, at the Hand & Spur, nr Exeter Exchange, Strand;[1] and also a watch casemaker.[2] It is more likely to refer to a Bath apothecary who in 1744 bought 'The Tennis Court … Mr Mores lodgings in the Abby Church Yard' and who built a large house in Orange Grove fronted with railings, clearly seen in contemporary illustrations. His will was proved in 1753.[3]

1. Grimwade; 1749 poll. 2. Priestley 2000. 3. Holland; PROB 11/800.

MOORE, WM
1744: DR £530; £40; £40

Probably William Moore, mathematical instrument maker, of Old Boswell Court, St Clement Danes.[1] Possibly the William Moore II listed by Clifton, but dates do not match; or an apprentice to George Bass. One debit entry is for a very large sum.

1. 1749 poll.

MORELL, MARK
1739: DR £50

Possibly connected to Thomas Morell, orris weaver, of Denmark Court, London.[1]

1. 1749 poll.

MORGAN, FRAS
1740: DR £20

MORGAN, JAS
1745: CR £45

MORGAN, JNO
1736: DR £10

Uncertain identity. Perhaps John Morgan apprenticed to Thomas Thibault [▶ p. 315] in 1730, free 1738.[1]

1. GH: Apprentice Book 6/133.

MORGAN, THOS
1747: CR £31 15s

1702–69 of Tredegar; MP and Lord Lieutenant for Monmouth and Brecon.[1] In London his address was given as King Street, St James's, then Privy Gardens, Whitehall.[2] His daughter Jane married Charles Gould, son of King Gould [▶ p. 277]; another son-in-law, Charles Vanne, was painted by William Hoare.

There was a china dealer of the same name in St James's Street, but this is a credit entry.[3]

1. Sedgwick. 2. 1749 poll. 3. *Whitehall Evening Post or London Intelligencer*, 2–4 July 1747 [217].

MORGAN, MR
1738: CR £30

MORICE, HUMPHREY
1746: CR £54

1723–85, of Werrington, Devon, MP for Launceston 1750–80; he was unmarried.[1] His London address was listed as Berkeley Square.[2]

1. Sedgwick. 2. 1749 poll.

MORIN, MARY
1738 and 1741: DR £35; £20; £10

This is presumably Bertrand's godmother, Mary Marin, but records are confusing and it is possible that Mary Marin and Mary Morin were two different people. Mary Marin died in 1744.

MORRIS, JNO
1741–51: DR £10 10s; £14; £25; £18 15s; £52 15s; £6 2s 6d; £10 4s; £33 13s

Morris was the first apothecary at the Mineral Water Hospital, 1741–57, and according to Sloman, the 'highest paid member of the resident staff at the hospital'. The role of apothecary combined that of doctor, pharmacist and general manager; his salary was £60 per year, together with board and lodging.[1] He was listed as 'visitor' at the hospital with Bertrand. Master Mason of the Royal Cumberland Lodge in 1737, listed at the Bear Inn meeting. The payments in Bertrand's accounts may relate to the hospital or could be personal medical bills. Morris's will was proved in 1759 [▶ p. 122 illus.].[2]

1. Rolls, p. 145. 2. PROB 11/846.

MORRIS, MATH: ROBINSON
see **ROBINSON**
▶ p. 305

MORRIS, VAL
1746: CR £10

Valentine Morris (1727–89) inherited Piercefield Park, Chepstow from his father, also Valentine (d. 1743), who had been born in Antigua, and who had bought the property in 1740 from Thomas Rous of Wotton under Edge [▶ p. 306]. Morris was bankrupted in the 1770s through gambling, business dealings and the cost of being Governor of St Vincent.[1] Piercefield Park was later re-built to designs of John Soane and is now a ruin.

Portrait miniature: Richard Smart, *Col. Valentine Morris* (1765), SL 31 July 1952 lot 109; CL 2 June 2009 lots 233 & 234.

   1. Piercefield Park website.

MOUNTFORD, MARY
1736: CR £80; £85

MULFORD, JNO
1736–47: DR £31; £57; £25 6s; £40; £105; £52 10s; £137; £30; £38 14s; £50; £46 19s; £32 4s; £100; £68; £120; £38; £28 9s; £37

London silversmith
▶ p. 234.

MUNDY, E
1740: CR £28 9s; £37

Possibly the Mr and Mrs Mundy listed as arriving in Bath September 1746.

MURRY, MR
1745: CR £50

MUSGRAVE, B
1742: CR £100

Barbara was a relatively common name in the Musgrave family, but this appears to be one of the six daughters of Sir Christopher Musgrave, 4th Bt, by his second wife. Although her father died in 1704, three of her brothers were alive in the 1750s, so she was presumably the spinster whose will was proved 15 January 1747.[1] She was the great-aunt of Sir Philip (below).

   1. PROB/1/752.

MUSGRAVE, SR PHILIP
1742: CR £50

Sir Philip Musgrave, 6th Bt (?1712–95), one of eleven children, married in 1742 (the year of the ledger entry) Jane Turton; he was MP for Westmoreland 1741–47. He succeeded his father Christopher in January 1735/36; which suggests an error in the *Bath Journal* when reporting the arrival of a Sir Christopher Musgrove in Bath 14 April 1746. In 1746 he inherited Kempton Park from his uncle, Sir John Chardin; Matthew Craske has researched the connections between the Musgrave and Chardin families, and their association with Henry Cheere.

N

NASH & OLIVER
1739 CR £100
1740: CR £10 10s [cf Hen: Lopottre]

RICHARD NASH
1745: CR £50

The entries for Nash and Dr Oliver [▶ p. 298] no doubt relate to the hospital in Bath, of which Nash was a major supporter, raising its profile and obtaining funds for its building; in 1738 he is listed as personally giving £100.
▶ pp. 49, 73.

Portrait: Thomas Worlidge, William Hoare, Prince Hoare, etc.

NASH, THOS
1747: DR £10 10s

A Bath attorney; Master Mason in 1747. He advertised a chariot for sale at Cornwell House in 1745.[1]

   1. Yescombe. *BJ*, 3 June 1745.

NAYLOR, JOS
1737: CR £15

Possibly Joshua Naylor, a jeweller listed in King Street, Covent Garden; but this is a credit entry.[1]

   1. 1749 poll.

NEALE, ROBT
1737–46: DR £100; £79 1s; £15; £127; £150; £105; £5; £140; £25; £100; £320; £185; £60; £64; £135; £120; £10; £350; £150; £390; £95; £100; £270; £60

Of all the entries that remain unidentified, this is the most disappointing. Because of the number and value of entries, possible candidates are given here to aid future attempts at identification. The first candidate, like the entries for Jesser [▶ p. 286], might suggest that Bertrand was dealing in cloth.

1. Robert Neale (1706–76) of Corsham, Wilts, MP for Wootton Bassett 1741–54, whose father was a wealthy clothier (woolstapler, will proved 1734). He married Elizabeth, daughter of Thomas Smith of Shaw House, Melksham, in 1735 [▶ p. 310]. Possibly Mr Neale who paid rates in Kings Meade St, Bath 1736–38.

2. Robert Neale of Middle Temple, London, regularly features in notices regarding the sale of properties and other business or legal affairs, for example for a property in Mothecombe, Devon:[1]

   Surveys, and particulars of the Premisses, may be had from Mr. Robert Neale, at his House in Fetter-Lane near Clifford's Inn, London.

3. There are several craftsmen with the surname Neale, who might have had a Robert within the family. These include: [a] Francis Neale, son of a turner of the same name, who was apprenticed to Bertrand in 1712 [▶ p. 31]; [b] Abraham Neal, son of Francis, apprenticed in 1730, as a chaser.[2] [c] Jacob Neale, snuffbox maker, bankrupt 1730;[3]

[d] Mr Neal at a toyshop, the Blue Last and Comb, against the White Hart Inn in the Borough, Southwark.

4. A further possibility is if Robert Neale was connected to John Neale of Chandos St (victualler) or Daniel Neal of Stafford St (vintner) in London. Lord Fitzwalter's accounts include, on 11 November 1724, a payment of £14 to 'Mr Neale for a HHd of red port'.[4]

1. *London Evening Post*, 28 June 1750 [3539]. 2. Edgcumbe. 3. *London Gazette* [6946]; CL, 27 March 1973 lot 207. 4. 1747 poll. Essex RO, D/DMA4.

NEEVE, GABRIEL
1741 & 1743: CR £52 10s; £30; £52 10s; £60

'Of London, Gent' insured a house on the east side of Freeman's Court on the north side of Cornhill, in 1716.[1] In the 1770s 'Richard Neave & Son' was a merchant house trading between London and Philadelphia – there might be a connection.[2]

1 HinH. 2. Price.

NESBITT, AL; MESSRS NESBITT
1739–47: CR £100; £100; £50; £50; £52 10s; £21; £125; £40; £80; £151 10s; £50; £81 10s

GOULD & NESBITT
1736: CR £100 [re Leake]

Nathaniel Gould (1661–1728) director of the Bank of England, was a Baltic merchant and involved in the East India trade, and in the export of tobacco from England to Russia; the firm also diversified into the import of wine. Sedgwick describes him as 'a leading figure in the City, belonged to a wealthy nonconformist family of London merchants, engaged in the cloth export trade to Turkey and the East'. Following Gould's death, the firm was run by his nephews in partnership with Albert Nesbitt. At one time Nesbitt also had a partnership with James Colebrook [▶ p. 262].

The Nesbitt family were merchants and bankers c. 1717–1900, in Coleman Street until the 1750s. Albert Nesbitt married Elizabeth Gould, the sister of his partners Nathaniel (d. in Bath 1738) and John (d. 1740).[1] John Gould, Nesbitt and James Colebrook each contributed to Bath's Mineral Water Hospital in 1738. Nesbitt was a freemason, listed at the lodge at The Ship, behind the Royal Exchange, in 1723.[2] In 1736 he was the victim of a burglary:[3]

> I serve Mr. Nesbit, and had laid the Cloath in the Parlour according to Custom. There were on the Table 4 Salts, four/Salt-Shovels and four Spoons. I shut the Parlour Door, and went down to dress myself … We sent for the Silversmith who made the Plate, and advertised it; but before the Advertisement came to his Hands, the Spoon mentioned in the Indictment, was brought to his Shop, and he stopt it. … Archibald Gilchrist: After Mr. Nesbit had lost the Things, he sent for me, and I caused Advertisements to be printed, and left at the Goldsmith's. I offered two Guineas Reward and no Questions ask'd: About 7 o'Clock as the Man who gave out the Bills, was putting one into my Hand, Mr. Newsome came, and told me, he had stopt one of the Spoons, and said he believed he could help us to take the Person that brought it to him.

The Earl of Burlington was a customer: his 'Book of Accounts with Nath Gould & Robert Nesbitt Esqr begun 29th March 1732', with embossed title, is bound in brown suede.[4]

1. *DNB*. 2. Songhurst. 3. POB: t17360225-33. 4. Chatsworth.

NEWBERRY, NATH
1746: CR £60

Nathaniel Newberry, Warehouseman, Walbrook.[1] He features in the accounts of Richard Braithwaite.[2]

1. Kent 1740. 2. TNA: C/105/5; Brett.

NEWCOMEN, RT
1740: CR £104

Rector of Caldecote, Hants, d. 1745.[1]

1. Venn.

NOBLE, GEO
1744: DR £27 6s

NORRIS, JNO
1742 and 1743: DR £150; £300

Uncertain identity. A John Norris registered a mark as a smallworker in 1735, at King's Head Court, Gutter Lane;[1] the sums in Bertrand's account are large. They are debit entries, so less likely to refer to John Norris (1702–67), MP for Rye 1727–32, who later held 'a customs post which disqualified its holder from sitting in Parliament'.[2]

1. Grimwade. 2. Sedgwick.

NORTON, CATH:
1742: CR £20

Uncertain identity. Possibly a connection of the tobacco merchants John Norton & Sons, based in London and Yorktown, Virginia, [▶ p. 257 Cary].

NOTTINGHAM, J
1741–44: CR £100; £200; £250; £300; £280; one referenced 'see Saml Strowde'

NOYES, JNO
1744: CR [Ann Martyn]

Uncertain identity. Possibly connected to a lady mentioned in Bertrand's will:

> I will and permit Mrs Hervey and her sister Mrs Noise

remain in the house the now rent of me during their joint or separate lifes rent free.

And/or Anne Noyes, a maltster in Beckington, nr Frome.[1]

1. Sun Ins, vol. 17, fo. 47.

NUGENT, ROT
1740: CR £63 [Mrs Nugent]
1742: CR £100

Robert Craggs Nugent (1709–88), MP for either St Mawes or Bristol 1741–84. He came from co. Meath and lived at Gosfield, nr Braintree, Essex. He was created Viscount Clare, then Earl Nugent in 1776. He followed Lord Doneraile [▶ p. 269] as Comptroller of the Prince of Wales's household 1747–51. In September 1739 Lord Chesterfield wrote to him:[1]

> Though I can't accept at present your invitation to Ireland, yet I confess there are two circumstances in it very tempting; the first, without a compliment, is being with you, with whom I would as willingly be upon the top of an Irish mountain as with any man in Europe …

His second wife, Anne Craggs, brought him £50,000, but 'she was fat and ugly and he was notoriously unfaithful to her'.

Portrait: Thomas Gainsborough, (The Holburne Museum, Bath) [▶ p. 84].

1. Sedgwick.

O

O'HARA, CHAS
1737: DR £11; £100

OAKE, CATH
OAKE, DR
1737: CR £73 10s; £31 10s

OAKES, ABRM
1737 and 1738: CR £52 10s; £21; £10

OGILVY, CAPT DAVD
1742: DR £50

OLIVER, DR
1739: see Nash & Oliver
1742: DR £103 11s; £100

Dr William Oliver (1695–1764) was chief physician of the Mineral Water Hospital in Bath for twenty-one years and was a trustee from 1737. He is remembered today through the Bath Oliver biscuit, still in production, which he devised for overweight patients. He was made an Honorary Freeman of Bath, 7 August 1730. In 1739 Viscount Weymouth purchased for £2,350 'Dr Wm Oliver's estate' comprising Bull Garden and large premises subsequently known as Weymouth House. The Water Roll of 1748 lists Oliver's 'dwelling house' in Westgate Street. Portrait: MWH, Bath [▶ p. 122].

ORANGE, ANN
1746: DR £12 10s

ORKNEY, COUNTESS OF
1746: CR £25

Anne, Countess of Orkney (d. 1756), was the daughter of Elizabeth Villiers, mistress of William III, whose husband Lord George Hamilton was created Earl of Orkney in 1695, the year the king bestowed on her 'nearly all the Irish estates of James II'. The Earl of Orkney owned Cliveden, Bucks, visited in 1729 by Frederick, Prince of Wales, who later rented the house. Anne inherited the title in 1737 and married her first cousin William, 4th Earl of Inchiquin (their mothers were sisters). Six of their eight children, including four sons, predeceased her; her daughter Mary therefore succeeded Anne as Countess of Orkney. Mary married her cousin Murrough who succeeded his uncle and father-in-law as 5th Earl of Inchiquin.[1] Lord Inchiquin is listed in the ledgers of the silversmith George Wickes, 1739–44.[2] Anne was probably in Bath in 1746 to visit her mother-in-law Mary, dowager Countess of Inchiquin, whose name people understandably found hard to spell. Lady Bristol wrote it as Inshequeen, whereas Council officers listed her property in Quiet Street (which she had between 1736 and her death in 1753) as 'Lady Ingee Qeens Garden' or 'Lady Ingeequeens Garden'; it was subsequently in the name of Richard Nash.[3]

1. GEC. 2. Wickes. 3. Bath RO: Walcot Church Rate Book.

OSBALDESTON, MR
1740: CR £35 9s

Most probably William Osbaldeston (1688–1766) MP for Scarborough, who is listed in 1747/48 for water rates in Bath. One of his brothers was the Revd Richard Osbaldeston, Bishop of London, but this Yorkshire family is best known through the sportsman George 'Squire Osbaldeston' (1787–1866). A set of robustly plain silver mugs, Paul de Lamerie 1746–47, bears the family coat of arms.[1]

1. SL, 16 July 1970 lot 93 (Plohn).

OTWAY, THOS
1740: CR £25

Probably an apothecary; he insured property in Panton Street, London, 1718/19.[1]

1. Sun Ins, vol. 9, fo. 45.

OWEN, WM
1743: DR £20

Uncertain identity. Possibly a London goldsmith whose business was continued by his widow Mary in 1739: she would have had to work with a son for this identification to be correct. She is recorded at the Wheatsheaf, upper end of Cheapside in 1745.[1]

Trade card: BM: Heal 67.305.

1. Grimwade; H-Price.

P

PAINTER, ROBT
1747: DR £20

Warden of Bath Merchant Taylors, 1734.

PALMER, ELIZT
1736: CR £25

Probably the widow of Thomas Palmer of Fairfield, Somerset, MP for Bridgwater (d. 1735). He was the brother of Peregrine (below). She died in 1737.

PALMER, PERE
1741 and 1745: DR £20; £30; £60

Peregrine Palmer (?1703–62) of Fairfield, Somerset,[1] was MP for Oxford University 1745–62. He was described by Lord Egmont as 'an honest plain man, much affected with the gout …'.[2]

1. Foster.   2. Sedgwick.

PANTIN, LEWIS
1736: DR £17 18s

London silversmith

▶ p. 234.

PARISH, EDWD CLARKE
1743: CR £64 13s 6d

Possibly misleadingly written in the bank's ledgers, this may be Edward Brett, parish clerk in Bath and register [registrar] of the Mineral Water Hospital.

PARKER, CHRISR
1739: DR £15

PARKER, HENRY
1738: CR £21 1s 6d

PARS, EDWD/ MR
1736 and 1738: DR £26; £11 16s; £21; £34

London silversmith

▶ p. 236.

PARSONS, THOS
1745: CR £20

PASSAVANT, JNO/ MR
1738–41: DR £19 13s; £24; £31 17s; £25; £22; £19 15s

John Passavant is listed as a goldsmith, Craven Buildings, St Clement Danes.[1] Most probably connected to Susanna Passavant, toywoman and jeweller, at the Plume of Feathers, in Ludgate Hill, opposite the Old Bailey.

1. 1749 poll.

PATEALL, JAMES
1736: DR £10

PATERSON, THOS
1744: CR £50

H-Price lists a banker at the foot of Haymarket, London, 1714.

PAWSON, CATH
1736: CR £10 10s

Possibly the widow of Henry Pawson, Lord Mayor of York (d. 1735); she d. 1767.[1]

1. Burke, *Commoners*.

PAYNE, JAS & CO.
1746: CR £8

Bankers at the King's Arms, Lombard Street from *c.* 1710.[1]

1. Outing; H-Price.

PEACHEY, MR
1736: CR £10

Presumably one of several sons of William Peachey, a London merchant, several of whom were Members of Parliament: Bulstrode (d. 1736) of West Dean, Sussex; Henry (d. 1737); James (d. 1771); or John (d. 1744).[1] The 1749 by-election poll lists two men named James Peachey, living in George St and St James's Street.[2]

1. Sedgwick.   2. 1749 poll.

PEARSE, JAMES
1737 and 1740: CR £31 10s; £31 10s; £31 10s

Uncertain identity. Possibly either Capt James Pearce, London Assurance Director, College Hill, or James Peirce, merchant, College Hill.[1] Sedgwick suggests that Thomas Pearse (MP of Tower Hill, d. 1743) was the son of James Pearse of Weymouth.

1. Kent 1740.

PEARSE, MARY
1744: CR £21

PEARSON, MR
1742: CR £31 10s

PECHELL, SAML
1746: CR £84 4s 6d

Listed in Boswell Court, St Clement Danes, d. 1782.[1] He is probably the man mentioned in an Irish mortgage in the 1760s that involved Bishop Chenevix and his nephew Daniel (thus also a nephew of the toyman Paul Daniel Chenevix).[2] As a notary, his name features in several Huguenot wills, e.g. as co-executor with Elizabeth Peere Williams [▶ p. 321] of Marianne Gaultier and of John Schutz's estate.[3]

1. 1749 poll.   2. www.bomford.net.
3. Wagner.

PEDLEY, ESSEX
1739: CR £50

Essex Pedley, widow, of Tetworth, Hunts.[1] John Pedley was MP for Huntingdon 1706–08.[2]

1. A2A website.   2. Venn.

PEIRCE, JNO
1745: CR £70

Uncertain identity. Might it be a mis-spelling for John Pearce, London distiller, who lived at Little Ealing; his son Zachary became Bishop of Rochester. Alternatively if Jno was written in error, it could be Dr Jeremy Pierce, surgeon at the Mineral Water Hospital, Bath.

PELHAM, COL.
1746: CR £451 16s 9d; £500; £300

James Pelham was in the Prince of Wales's household.

▶ p. 155.

PEMBERTON, JERE:
1737: CR £50

Jeremiah Pemberton of Much Hadham, Herts, admitted Inner Temple 1700, d. 1741.[1]

    1. Venn.

PENNY, THOS/MR
1736–40: DR £100; £8 12s; £40; £30

Uncertain identity. Thomas Penny, linen draper, took an apprentice in 1735.[1] Thomas Penny of Bath, maltster, brewer and chapman, was reported bankrupt in 1745, when his properties in Bath and Bradford-on-Avon were to be sold; they were subsequently advertised as a messuage in South Parade and an inn, The Christopher, in the Market Place.[2] His name appears on the water roll for this last address in 1748, however. One or other of these men was made a freeman of Bath in April 1728.[3] In London there was a pawnbroker of this name in Long Acre, 1712 and a pattenmaker in Aldgate 1721.[4]

    1. Bath RO: Apprentice Book p. 20. 2. *BJ*, 20 May 1745; 12 August 1745. 3. Bath RO: Council Book 4. 4. Sun Ins, vol. 2, fo. 37, vol. 10, fo. 156 (1719), vol. 13, fo. 148 (1721).

PENTON, ELIZ
1747: CR £12 10s

Possibly connected to Henry Penton, MP for Winchester in 1747, who is listed in the silversmith George Wickes' accounts 1740/41,[1] and in Arlington Street 1749; he died 1762.[2]

    1. Wickes. 2. 1749 poll; Foster.

PEPYS, MR
1736: CR £52 10s; £52 10s

William Pepys (1698–1743) is listed as establishing a bank in 1729 that became Pepys & Hollingsworth, in Lombard Street, London.[1] He appears to have been operating earlier than this, however, as the Duke of Portland was a customer in the 1720s.[2] His father, John Pepys, was master of the Clockmakers' Company; his grandson became 1st Earl of Cottenham.

It is worth noting Steventon Pepys, stationer at the Golden Falcon & 3 Flower de Lis, Fleet Street, in 1717/18.[3]

Property: Tray, silver, John Edwards 1738–9, Manchester Art Gallery [1957.537].

    1. Kent 1740; H-Price.
    2. Nottingham. 3. Sun Ins, vol. 7, fo. 335, [10612].

PERCIVAL, JOS
1741: DR £150

Possibly of the same family as Richard Percival [▶ pp. 132, 185]. A poem on 'Bertrand's Shop at Bath' and 'Advice to the dwarf in the rooms, who paints upon fans'.[1]

▶ p. 265 Coster & Percival.

    1. Samuel Gedge catalogue xv, no. 92.

PERCIVAL, LORD
1736: CR £20

John, later 2nd Earl Egmont (1711–70) was styled Viscount Perceval 1733–48. He was a Lord of the Bedchamber to the Prince of Wales 1748–51. His father, author of the *Egmont Diary*, was created Earl Egmont in 1733.[1] The 1st Earl visited Bath on several occasions, as recorded in his diary [▶ p. 301 Phillips] which also shows how close he was to his wider family, including Mary Dering, Edward Southwell and the le Grands, who all feature in Bertrand's account.[2] The family had close connections with Ireland and their Irish title was some compensation for financial losses during the troubles there, estimated at £40,000.

Portrait: Francis Hayman, National Gallery of Ireland.

    1. Sedgwick. 2. Egmont.

PERRY, CAPT CHAS
1741: DR £52 10s

PERRY, MICAJAH
1736: CR £25

Micajah Perry was a third generation merchant whose firm is described as 'this major house, with commitments all over the Atlantic trading world'; his grandfather was 'the greatest tobacco merchant in England'

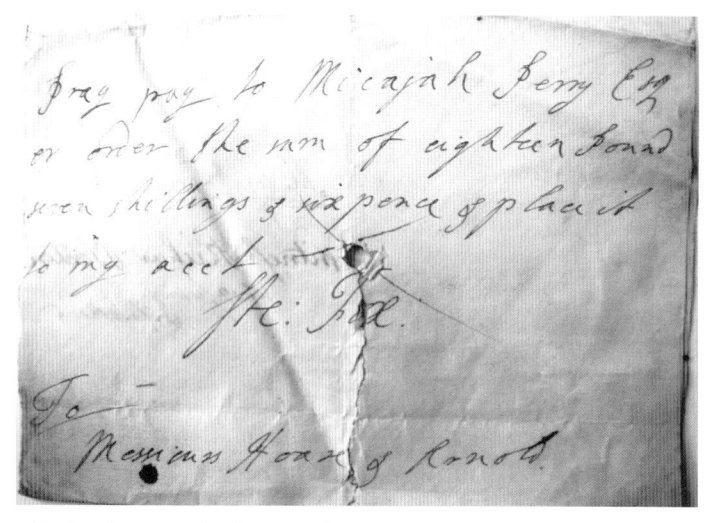

Bill of exchange: order from Stephen Fox, later Lord Ilchester, instructing Hoare & Co. to make a payment to Micajah Perry. (Dorset, D/FSI/239)

300   PART FOUR: PAUL BERTRAND'S BANK ACCOUNT

and agent for Virginia; his father, who had 'extensive dealings' with Virginia, died in 1721. Micajah (1694–1753) was born in New England and was agent for Pennsylvania in the 1720s. His business was based in Jeffery's Court, St Mary-Axe. He was an alderman and Lord Mayor of London 1738–39, and MP 1727–41. He 'focussed on politics to the detriment of his business', and spent time in Bath in 1743 avoiding bankruptcy and 'in a condition which made his friends despair for his life', suffering from dropsy.[1] Described as 'rather slippery' and 'despised' by Virginian planters, he was active during Walpole's problems over Colonial debt in 1732–33.[2] In 1716 he insured for £1,000 a brick building of four stories of warehouses on the north side of the River Thames.[3]

1. Kent 1740; *DNB*. 2. Ashworth. 3. HinH.

PETER, GEO
1742: DR £80

PETRE, MR
1736: CR £30

To be Lett, At the Corner of Trim Street, Bath. A House completely furnish'd with all Conveniences, from the First of March to the first of September following, 1745, in the present Occupation of William Petre, Esq. Enquire at the said House.[1]

Later advertisements give the name as the Hon. William Petre, who seems not to feature in the Catholic family of Baron Petre, of Essex.[2] Robert, 8th Lord Petre (b. 1713) was a fellow of the Royal Society and is remembered for introducing cammelias to England in 1739; his mother, Catherine Walmersley, may have been related to William Walmersley [▶ p.319].

1. *BJ*, 7 January 1744/45; June 1745. 2. Burke.

PHILLIPS, ANN
1741: 1 CR £20

Lodging house keeper in Bath. She was a tenant of properties the Duke of Chandos developed around the Hospital of St John the Baptist in 1726–27, now known as John Wood House. The duke came to respect Ann Phillips for running a good business. The completed house consisted of 'seven kitchens and pantries, seven rooms on the first floor, sixteen on the second, seventeen in the attic and seventeen garrets'.[1] Her sister Joanna (below) also ran lodgings. It is impossible to tell to which of the sisters the following entry in the diary of Viscount Perceval (later Lord Egmont) refers, in 1730:[2]

> August 26: After Court was over, which was near four o'clock, we went to dinner with Augustus Schultz, and at night took coach and proceeded to Maidenhead Bridge, where we lay. Thursday 27: Dined at Theal and lay at Spinham Land. Friday 28: Dined near Marlborough, and lay at Sandy Lane. Saturday 29: Dined at Bath and lay at the Greyhound Inn in the Market place. We took very good lodgings at Mrs Phillips at four pounds a week, and went into them next morning.

1. Eglin, p. 152. 2. Egmont, vol. 1, p. 102.

PHILLIPS, GEN
1745: CR £20

PHIP[PS], RD
1744: CR £39; £40 [Denne, Adam]
1745: CR £20

Probably Brigadier General Richard Philips.[1]

1. Chamberlayne, Pt II, Bk III, p. 98.

PHILLIPS, JOANA
1739: (mony recd at Bath) DR £48

Sister of Ann Phillips (above) and like her, a lodging house keeper in properties completed for the Duke of Chandos in 1728. She married one of his agents, John Ferguson.[1] In December 1735 the duke paid part of his account with the silversmith George Wickes 'by a note on Mrs Joannah Phillips of Bath £75' [▶ p. 117].[2]

1. Eglin. 2. Wickes.

PHILLIPS, MARY
1741: DR £20

Mary Phillips / Necklace Maker, Successor to the late Mrs Wheatley / No20 Green Street, Leicester Fields / Pearls Strung in the Newest Taste.[1]

1. Trade card: BM: Banks 67.155.

PICKERING, JAS
1737: DR £18 5s

Uncertain identity. Possibly the husband of Mary Deards' cousin, Elizabeth; they were mentioned in her will, proved in April 1739.

PITT, WM
1737: CR £152 [Turner]

William Pitt (1708–78), statesman, later 1st Earl of Chatham. MP for Bath 1757–66, he represented other constituencies from 1735. 'A martyr to gout' from a teenager, he was a regular visitor to Bath: he bought no. 7 The Circus in 1755 and maintained it for about ten years.[1] In 1749 his London address was listed as 'next the Admiralty Office, Whitehall'.[2] The Duchess of Marlborough left him £10,000 in her will 'upon account of his merit in the noble defence he has made for the support of the Laws of England and to prevent the Ruin of his Country'.[3] Copies of the famous Pitt diamond, brought to England by William's father in 1702, were sold by Bertrand's brother-in-law in London. Pitt's account with Hoare reveals transactions with the silversmiths John Jacob and John White [▶ pp. 286 and 320]. In 1754, at the age of forty-six, he married Lady Hester Grenville, twelve years his junior.

Portrait: William Hoare, Guildhall, Bath.

> 1. Sedgwick; Lowndes. 2. 1749 poll. 3. *BJ*, 12 November 1744.

PLURA, JOS

1751: DR £15; £15

Sculptor

▶ p. 237.

POINTER, HEN

1744: CR £50

Uncertain identity. Possibly Henry Pointer, Blackwelhall factor, Coleman Street;[1] or Mr Pointer at Kelsey Hall, Hants.[2]

> 1. Kent 1740. 2. Chamberlayne, p. 13.

POINTZ/POYNTZ, STE:

1738: CR £50; £42; £71 (one for Mrs Poyntz 1746: £16)
1744–46: DR £25; £31 10s; £40; £28; £45

Stephen Poyntz (1685–1750), envoy to Sweden 1724; privy councillor, then governor of the household of the Duke of Cumberland, Princess Mary and Princess Louisa.[1] In 1717 he lived in Battersea.[2] He was 'a frequent visitor to Bath on account of his own bad health and his wife's recurrent bouts of the stone'. He arrived in Bath on 7 April 1746 with Col. Pelham for Princess Caroline's visit. In October that year the Princess of Hesse broke her return journey to London at his house at Midgham (between Newbury and Reading). Walpole wrote of Poyntz that he was 'ruined in his circumstances by a devout brother, whom he trusted, and by a simple wife …'.[3] When Stephen Poyntz died, Mrs Delany wrote:[4]

> Poor Mrs Pointz! she has had a great loss; and though not a woman of bright parts, had discernment enough to know her happiness in having such a worthy guide, companion and friend, and will be much afflicted.

His daughter married in 1755 John, later 1st Earl Spencer (their daughter Georgiana married 5th Duke of Devonshire).

Portrait: Jean-Baptiste van Loo, (Yale) [▶ p. 157].
Property: Set of 12 silver candlesticks, Thomas Farren 1728–29, probably part of Poyntz's official plate when commissioner to the Congress of Soissons.[5]

> 1. Chamberlayne, Pt II, Bk III, p. 257. 2. Sun Ins, vol. 6, fo. 290 [8592]. 3. *DNB*. 4. Delany, ser 1, vol. 2, p. 635, where Pointz's role was described as 'preceptor' to the Duke of Cumberland, then steward of his household. 5. Schroder no. 177.

POYNTZ, WM

1743 and 1746: DR £60; £80
1747: CR £50; £80

William Poyntz (1682–1748) was the elder brother of Stephen (above). Consul General in Lisbon; Treasurer (or Receiver General) of Excise, for which he received (for himself and his clerks) £1980 p.a.[1] 'Capt Poyntz' arrived in Bath on 31 March 1746 with Princess Caroline. His second wife, Mary Moncrief, was buried in Bathampton.

> 1. Chamberlayne, Pt II, Bk III, p. 84.

POLE, CHAS

1744: CR £40

Probably Charles Poole, jeweller of St Clement Danes, who witnessed William Deards snr's will in 1758. His signature, with Paul Barbot, is on an invoice to Lady Monson dated 1764 'for a debt due to the Estate of Willm Deards a Bankrupt to whom wee are Assignees'. This was William jnr, Mary Bertrand's nephew.

The family of William Poole (Grace Poole, below) does not appear to include anyone named Charles.

POMFRET, THOS

1741 and 1745: DR £100; £13 13s; £100

Uncertain identity. Pomfret is mentioned in Bertrand's will and witnessed Elizabeth Hawley's will. There was a wine merchant of this name in St Martin-in-the-Fields;[1] a hosier, whose stock was sold in 1749 '250 dozen of stockings, caps, gloves etc';[2] and a waiter at Wiltshire's assembly rooms.[3]

> 1. West Sussex RO: Mitford archives. 2. *The General Advertiser*, 15 August 1749 [4622]. 3. Bath RO: Acc.662.18.

▶ p. 48 illus.

POOLE, GRACE

1736 and 1737: CR £20; £34; £20; £40

Grace, daughter of Henry Pelham (younger brother of 1st Lord Pelham), married William Poole, an alderman of Bishopsgate Ward[1] and nephew of Sir James Poole, 1st Bt. Her brother-in-law, Francis Poole, was Receiver-General for Stamp Duties and first cousin to her husband.[2]

▶ p. 295 Hatch Moody.

> 1. *London Evening Post*, 6 February 1728 [26]. 2. At a salary of £500 p.a.; Chamberlayne, Pt II, Bk III, p. 91.

POPE, ALEXR

1741: CR £100

Alexander Pope (1688–1744), poet and writer, made numerous visits to Bath from 1714 onwards and became close to Ralph Allen, with whom he stayed until they quarrelled 1743 over Martha Blunt. His *Epistle to Lady Shirley* mentions Bertrand [▶ p. 59].

POPPLE, HEN:

1738: CR £50 and see Brigr Cope

Henry Popple and his brothers were from a mercantile family with close links to the colonies. Henry was Clerk and his brother Alured was Secretary at the Board of Trade & Plantations, and

'Agent to the six new raised Independent Companies' in Jamaica.[1] In 1737 Henry is listed as Clerk in the Queen's Household at £130 p.a., with an extra £10 'for Paper and Books'. In 1733 he published a map of the British North American colonies, which was still advertised six years later.[2] His brother Alured (1699–1744) was Governor of Bermuda 1733–44.

Portrait: William Hogarth 1730, conversation piece depicting Henry, Alured (whose daughter married Vincent Mathias [▶ p. 293], William (Governor of Bermuda 1747–63) and their sister Sophia. Royal Collection [400048].

> 1. *London Gazette*, 11 August 1741 [8040]. 2. *London Daily Post and General Advertiser*, 16 March 1739. Chamberlayne, Pt II, Bk III, pp. 55 and 243.

POPSKILL, WM
1738: DR £7 16s

PORTER, MESS
1745: CR £8 8s

John and James Porter, merchants, Tokenhouse Yard; Joseph Porter, merchant, Trump-street, Guildhall.[1] A trial of 1725 may refer to the same firm: 'Eight Pair of Silk Stockings val. 40s and three Pair of Worsted Stocking val. 10s. the Goods of John Porter'.[2]

> 1. Kent 1740. 2. POB: t17250407-2.

POTTS, HEN
1744 and 1745: CR £30; £25; £40

Henry Potts was Secretary to the Post Office and therefore regularly in touch with Ralph Allen at Bath.[1]

> 1. E-Hill, p. 206.

POUKLINGTON, ROT
1743: CR £25

POWELL, ANTO
1740: DR £105

Uncertain identity. He may have been associated with the puppeteer Martin Powell, whose sons are known to have worked with Yeates, another puppeteer. The entry for 'Mr Yeat' [▶ p. 323] is also for 1740.

POWELL, JNO
1740: 1 DR £70
See the above entry.

POWELL, MARTHA
1738: CR £40; £20

Martha, daughter of Henry Hoare of Stourhead, married in 1734 Mansel Powell, a Hereford attorney (1696–1775). In 1738, the year of this ledger entry, he acquired Eardisley Park 'the property of a client, William Barnsley, by a forged will disinheriting Barnsley's only son, a lunatic'; when this was discovered in 1749 'Powell and his co-defendants had to pay costs and refund all the rents and other money they had received from the estate'.[1]

> 1. Sedgwick.

POWIS, DUKE OF
1738: CR £5

William Herbert, Marquess of Powis, titular Duke of Powis (c. 1665–1745). A Jacobite, he spent time in both Newgate and the Tower of London, but was restored to his estates in 1722. In London he had a house in Lincoln's Inn Fields, later in Great Ormond St. An auction of his property was held by Cock on 12 February 1727/28[1] and in 1728/29 'he was said to be in low circumstances, all his real estate greatly encumbered, and he had sold or disposed of all his personal estate'. This may explain the very small sum in Bertrand's account. When his father was outlawed for high treason in 1689/90 his forfeited estates were valued at above £10,000 p.a.[2]

Property: Powis Castle.

> 1. Lugt. 2. GEC.

POYNTZ: see POINTZ

PRESTON, LORD
1738: CR £100; £100; £100; £100; £100

Charles Graham, 3rd Viscount Preston. The account entries are for October 1738 to February 1738/39 when he died without issue aged 32 at Bath, when the peerage became extinct. He married Anne Cox, whose brother John [▶ p. 265] proved her will February 1744/45.
Property: Nunnington Hall, Yorks, (National Trust).

PRESTON, THOS
1745: CR £40

PRICE, SAML
1740: DR £21

PRITCHARD, MR
1738: DR £100

Uncertain identity. No first name is given and Pritchard is a common name. The following may refer to one or more persons. Thomas Skrine Pritchard, apothecary, in Cheap Street, Bath 1745–48.[1] A Thomas Pritchard had an account with Hoare from 1728, where there is a South Sea Stock receipt in his name dated 1731, and an unrelated entry 'To Thomas Pritchard for insuring the Duke of Newcastle's life for £500: £30'.[2] Sir Robert Long and John Cox were executors of his will. Cox and Pritchard were both in Bath in 1738 [▶ p. 265]. Thomas Pritchard Esq. is listed in Gt Marlborough Street, London.[3]

There is a trade card for John Pritchard, weaver and mercer in the Grove, Bath, stylistically rather later than this bank account entry.[4]

> 1. Bath RO: Apprentice Book p. 16, 1731; 1776 Schedule of Deeds; 1748 water roll. *BJ*, 23 February 1746/47. 2. Hoare: PL payments 1734–42 (27 January 1735 and years following). 3. 1749 poll. 4. Bath CL.

PUGH, HUMPY
1736 and 1738: DR £10 10s; £41

Humphrey Pugh, goldsmith & toyman.

▶ p. 238.

PULESTON, JNO
1737: CR £20

Probably John Puleston of Bangor, matriculated Oxford 1723 aged 16, BA 1736.[1]

1. Foster.

PURDEY, JNO
1738: DR £14 16s

Uncertain identity. Possibly a connection of William Purdie, a wine merchant, who was an executor of the will of Moses Roubel in 1777, together with Robert Salmon (a cabinet maker in Bristol). There is an outside chance that it could be the grandfather of James Purdey, founder of the gunmakers.

PURLEWENT, SAML
1743–46: DR £59 15s 6d; £137; £100

Samuel Purlewent, described as 'attorney and steward' to Ralph Allen; he took minutes at meetings of the Mineral Water Hospital and was a governor 1748.[1] His name occurs frequently in advertisements in the *Bath Journal* for property to let or for sale: 'Enquire of Mr Samuel Purlewent, attorney at law'. His acquisition of property from the Duke of Kingston's estate is recorded by Holland. He became a freeman of Bath in July 1733, paying 10 guineas. There are numerous payments to him in the Bath Corporation records.[2] His will was proved May 1759.[3] A Samuel Purlewent was also rector of Stanton Prior, Somerset c. 1739–75.

1. Allen p.154. 2. Bath RO: Chamberlain's Accounts 1733–71. 3. PROB 11/846.

Q

QUIN, GEO
1745: DR £21

Uncertain identity. Although a debit entry, this may be George Quin of Quinborough, Co. Clare, uncle of the 1st Earl of Dunraven. There are references to 'Mr Quinn' in the freemasons' archives[1] and at Hoare,[2] but these are probably for the actor James Quin, who became a resident of Bath. A Mrs Quinn was a customer of Webb, the jeweller, in August 1753. The entry seems unlikely to be connected to 'Le Quin marchand orfevre jouaillier' in Paris.[3]

1. Songhurst. 2. Lr.41 fo. 349 Sir John Cope's a/c. 3. Trade card, BM: Banks 133.111.

R

RAGDALE, THOS
1738: CR £8 8s

Partner of Richard Chadd in London. The firm of Chadd & Ragsdale were 'almost opposite Conduit Street' and advertised at various times as toyman, silversmith and jeweller. In the 1720s 'Ragdale' and Robert Chadd were in Exeter Market when William Allen (▶ p. 246) is listed in the rate books next to Chadd.[1] A John Allen was connected to Chadd & Ragsdale in the 1760s. Among their later employees was William Rogers.

1. LMA: Poor Rate 1725–26, micr. box 182.

RAMSDEN, MESS/MR
1737–40: CR £120; £100; £120; £52 10s; £52 10s

Henry Ramsden, merchant, listed Duke Street, York Buildings.[1]

1. 1749 poll.

RANSFORD, GEO
1745: DR £34 14s

A freemason, George Rainsford was present at the first meeting of the lodge at the Bear Inn, Bath, in December 1732.[1] Possibly of a watchmaking family.[2]

1. Masons Bath, Book 1 1732–38. 2. Loomes.

RAVAND, MR
1745: CR £50

Possibly David Ravaud, FRS 1747, d. 1776.[1] Margaret Mary Ravaud, a spinster (d. 1800), was in Barton Court, Bath in 1767.[2]

1. Venn. 2. Bath RO: Rate Book 4; Wagner.

RAVENHILL & CO.
1740: CR £30

RAWLINS, JOS
1744: CR £100

Possibly connected to Thomas Rawlins, a member of the Benn Club (▶ p. 285 Ironside).

READ/REED, JAMES
1744: CR £30; £25

Uncertain identity. Possibly James Read of Farmborough, Somerset, matriculated 1724 aged 18, MA 1731.[1]

1. Foster.

RENON, ANDREW
1736: DR £36

Possibly Renou. Philip Renou was apprenticed to the silversmith Paul Crespin 1720; Edward and John Renou and Timothy Renon are also listed, but no Andrew.[1]

1. Grimwade, pp. 294, 306, 322.

REVELL, THOS
1745: CR £50

Thomas Revell Esq., Cleveland Row[1] is listed as arriving in Bath 13 October 1746, and 'Mr Revell' in the same month the next year. MP for Dover, victualler of the forces at Minorca &c, he died 'very rich, leaving an only daughter under age' in 1752.[2] His third wife was a niece of the 1st Duke of Bridgwater.[3]

1. 1749 poll. 2. *Gents Mag*, vol. 22, p. 44. 3. Sedgwick.

REYNOLDS, FRAS
1746: CR £50

Uncertain identity. Francis Reynolds Esq., Clifford Street, listed in 1749.[1] There was a clockmaker of this name, but this is a credit entry.[2] A third possibility is that the 1725 map of the Kingston Estate was drawn by a Mr Reynolds, but his first name is not known.

> 1. 1749 poll. 2. Loomes; Chatsworth.

RICHARD, SAML
1745: CR £22

Possibly Samuel Richardson, novelist and publisher (1689–1761), who lived in Salisbury Court, London. He was married to Elizabeth, sister of James Leake, the Bath bookseller. Richardson's novel *Clarissa* was advertised in Bath in 1747.[1]

> 1. *BJ*, 30 November 1747.

RICHARDS, ELIZA
1742: DR £215

RICHARDS, MRS
1744: DR £10

RICHARDSON, MICHAEL
1746: DR £300

ROBINSON, BARB:
1741: CR £34 17s 6d

This might be Barbara Lytton, wife of William Warburton [▶ pp. 291 and 319]. However the account entry is only two days after one for Mathew Robinson [▶ below] so she is more likely to be a connection of his.

ROBINSON, ELIZA
1741: CR £50

Elizabeth Robinson (1720–1800) was brought up in Yorkshire, Kent and in Cambridge. She married Edward Montagu in 1742; they lived at Sandleford Priory, Berks and 23 (now 31) Hill Street in London. Following her husband's death in 1775 she built Montagu House, 22 Portman Square, to designs of James Stuart. As a leading member of the 'Bluestocking Circle' she is renowned for her abilities as a letter writer and hostess. A regular visitor to Bath and Tunbridge Wells, the daily routines and people she met there feature in correspondence between her and her sister Sarah [below]. Her heir was her nephew Matthew (1762–1831), son of her brother Morris, who she adopted.

Portrait: Edward Haytley, *The Montagu Family at Sandleford Priory*, 1744 (Waterhouse, p. 156).

ROBINSON, MATH
1739 and 1741: CR £80; £83 4s; £20

Matthew Robinson (1694–78), father of Elizabeth, Sarah and Matthew and nine other children. His wife Elizabeth Drake inherited property, including their house 'Mount Morris', through her mother Sarah Morris. They were in Bath at the same time as Isabella Drake [▶ p. 270].

Portrait: Gawen Hamilton, *A Conversation of Virtuosi* (NPG).

ROBINSON, MORRIS, MATH:
1741 & 1742: CR £25; £40; £30

Matthew Robinson (1713–1800), son of the above and brother of Elizabeth Montagu, took the additional surname of Morris when he inherited property from his mother in 1746. He was MP for Canterbury 1747–61 and succeeded a cousin as 2nd Baron Rokeby in 1794; he died unmarried. Confusingly one of his brothers was christened Morris, whose son Matthew was heir to Elizabeth Montagu (née Robinson, above).

ROBINSON, SARAH
1743: CR £22; £13

Sarah (1720–95) was the sister of Elizabeth and Matthew (above). One of twelve children, she contracted smallpox in 1741 and lived in Kent until 1746. In 1747 she met Barbara Montagu [▶ p. 294] in Bath, who was younger, and lived in her house from 1748. In 1751 Sarah married George Lewis Scott: the marriage ended nine months later when her father removed her from Scott's house in Leicester Fields.[1] She returned to Bath, where she had a house at Batheaston. A writer, she is best known for the *History of Mecklenburgh* and *Millenium Hall*. In 1744 her sister Elizabeth requested Sarah to 'Buy me a pink paste cross and earings, the best you can get at Chenevix'. Neale quotes extensively from the correspondence between the sisters.[2]

Portrait: Edward Haytley, 1744 (Saumerez Smith no. 164).

> 1. Referred to by Delany, vol. 3, p. 115. 2. *DNB*. Montagu 1813, p. 187. Neale, pp. 15–22. Yescombe.

ROBINSON, WM
1744 & 1746: DR £36 3s; £12 3s

Uncertain identity. Possibly the brother (1726–1803) of Elizabeth Montagu and Sarah Scott but these are debit entries. A William Robinson bought a property from the Duke of Kingston in 1743, (now known as Sally Lunn's, a rare example of a surviving early Stuart house in Bath). An advertisement refers to Mr Robinson, Bear Inn Bath;[1] a deed of 1766 refers to William Robinson's property: 'the Crown, now let to Peter Berwick, peruke-maker and hairdresser'; and again, 'Mr Alderman Robinson' selling the Queens Head Tavern in Queen Street.[2] He was possibly the man who proved Catherine Lovelace's will [▶ p. 104].

> 1. *BJ*, 19 November 1744. 2. Holland.

ROBLEY, N
1746: CR £30

ROFFREY & CO.

1744: CR £150

Merchants and bankers in London: Roffey & Wood, Philpot Lane;[1] Roffey is also listed with James Neale.[2] In Bath a James Roffey Esq., Gallaway Street, is listed in 1766.[3]

1. Kent 1740. 2. H-Price. 3. Bath Rate Book.

ROOKE, LADY CATH

1737: CR £60; £25

'Lady Rooke' is referred to in a letter from Helena le Grand [▶ p. 289], dated January 1736/37,[1] the ledger entries are for May 1737.

1. Chatsworth: 240.2.

ROSS, THOS

1739 and 1744: DR £12; £12 12s; £23 12s
1741: CR £3 11s

Artist, active *c*. 1730–57.

▶ p. 186.

ROUFE, JAS

1739: DR £100

ROUS, JAMES

1740: DR £230; £100

James Rous, chapman, of Wotton under Edge, Glos and Old Jewry, London, was bankrupt in 1744; he was in partnership with Peter Laprimandaye until 1759.[1] The latter was in Angel Court, Throgmorton Street, when he described Samuel Courtauld as his silversmith. He was a director of the London Assurance office 1774–89.[2] It is not known what Bertrand's payments to Rous represent.

Thomas Rous, ▶ below.

1. *London Gazette*, 3 July 1744 and 3 November 1759. 2. POB: t17630114-23.

ROUS, ROBT

1740: CR £50

Robert Rous had an account with Hoare; his name also appears in the account of Wm Peere Williams [▶ p. 321].[1] He was described as a 'proctor in Doctors Commons very much esteemed by all that knew him' when he died in November 1744.[2] His insurance policy of 1713 says he was at 'the 3rd door on the left hand in Crane Court in Fleet Street'.[3]

1. Lr. 30 (1728); Lr. 40, fo. 182 (1739). 2. *London Evening Post*, 3 November 1744. 3. Sun Ins, vol. 3, fo. 79.

ROUS, THOS

1740: DR £400

Thomas Rous, merchant of College Hill;[1] was a director of the London Assurance Co. in 1741 and the East India Co. in 1751. His name appears on a note of exchange dated 10 October 1740.[2] He is presumably the man who sold, in the same year, Piercefield House, co. Mon, to Col. Valentine Morris (d. 1743, ▶ p. 296) for £8,250. This was nearly £5,000 more than his father (of Wotton-under-Edge) had paid for the property in 1727.[3] It is worth noting that the name Rouse is listed in East India Co. sales in 1715 as a purchaser of blue and white cups.[4] As this is a debit entry, it might suggest that Rous dealt in oriental wares.

▶ p.265 Coster & Percival.

1. Kent 1740. 2. Badminton: FmI 4/14. 3. www.welshicons.org.uk. 4. BL, H/1/L fo. 359.

ROWE, HENRY

1740: CR £50; £40; £5 6s

Probably connected to Thomas Green, a banker in Lombard Street in 1677.[1]

1. Directory 1677.

RUDDOCK, MARY

1753: DR £20

RUSHWORTH, EDWD

1740: DR £40

RUSSELL, PR

1736–45: DR £30; £20; £30; £100; £35; £20; £40; £27 16s; £50; £22 10s; £80; £50; £80; £180; £55; £100; £50; £61 12s; £50; £50; £6 6s; £10; £10 10s; £9; £12 5s; £35; £31 3s; £22 14s; £25; £25; £26; £46 14s 6d

▶ p. 56 table

London goldsmith (d. 1773) who became Elizabeth Chenevix's second husband in 1750; his first wife was Hannah Hoare.

▶ pp. 202–03, 239.

S

SALE, EDWD

1743: DR £20

Sale cleaned pistols for Viscount Glenorchy during his visit to Bath in 1740 [▶ below illus.].[1]

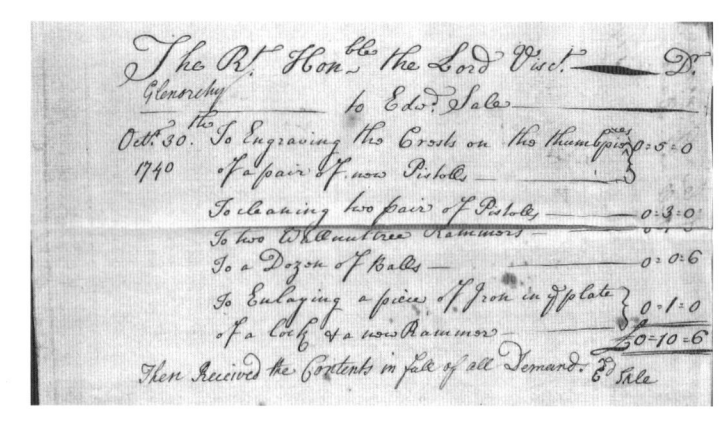

Invoice from Edward Sale to Lord Glenorchy, dated 30 October 1740. For engraving crests on a pair of pistols, cleaning, repairing, and for 'a dozen of balls 6d'. (NAS, GD112/21/268/3)

'Mr Sale' an appraiser of Golden Square, is mentioned in papers following the Duke of Kingston's death in 1726.[2]

1. NAS: invoice October 1740, GD112/21/268. 2. Lincoln RO: Monson 28B/12/4.

SALMON, LZA:

1742: DR £64

Lazarus Salmon, a tailor, is listed near the Cross Bath and Bell Lane, in Bath and later in Burough Walls.[1] He was warden of the Merchant Taylors in Bath 1731–33. An invoice to Lord Glenorchy survives, for October 1740.[2]

▶ right, illus.

1. Bath RO: Water Rent 1747/48; 1766 Rate Book 1. 2. NAS: GD112/21/268.

SALOMONS, DAVID

1744: CR £52 10s

Diamond merchant, French Ordinary Court, Crutched Friers, bankrupt 1762. One of five brothers who through their mother Abigail were related to Naphtali Franks [▶ p. 275].[1] The jeweller Webb purchased 'Dutch cut brilliants' in September 1753 from Rheuben Salomons & Co.[2]

1. Kent 1740; Yogev p. 157.
2. TNA: C 108/284.

SAMBROKE, LADY

1744: CR £50

Judith Sambroke died in 1744, her husband, Sir Jeremy, having predeceased her in 1705. Her second son, Jeremy, is remembered for the house he built in Hertfordshire to designs of James Gibbs called 'Gubbins'; the King and Queen visited and 'view'd his fine Gardens, Waterworks and his Collection of Curiosities'.[1] He succeeded his nephew, a Gentleman of the Privy Chamber, to the baronetcy.[2] The third son, John, was a Turkey merchant and MP whose daughter Diana married Lord George Sackville (who changed his name to Germain on inheriting Drayton from Lady Elizabeth Germain in 1769). In February 1714/15 Jeremiah Sambrooke Esq. insured property at the Blue Balcony in Cecil Street, Strand.[3]

1. *Gents Mag*, July 1732, p. 874.
2. Chamberlayne, Pt II, Bk III, p. 207. 3. Sun Ins, vol. 4, fo. 168 [5029].

SANDYS, MRS

1740: DR £21 12s

This is a debit entry, but could possibly refer to Letitia, the wife of Samuel Sandys, MP for Worcester, who was created Lord Sandys in 1743.

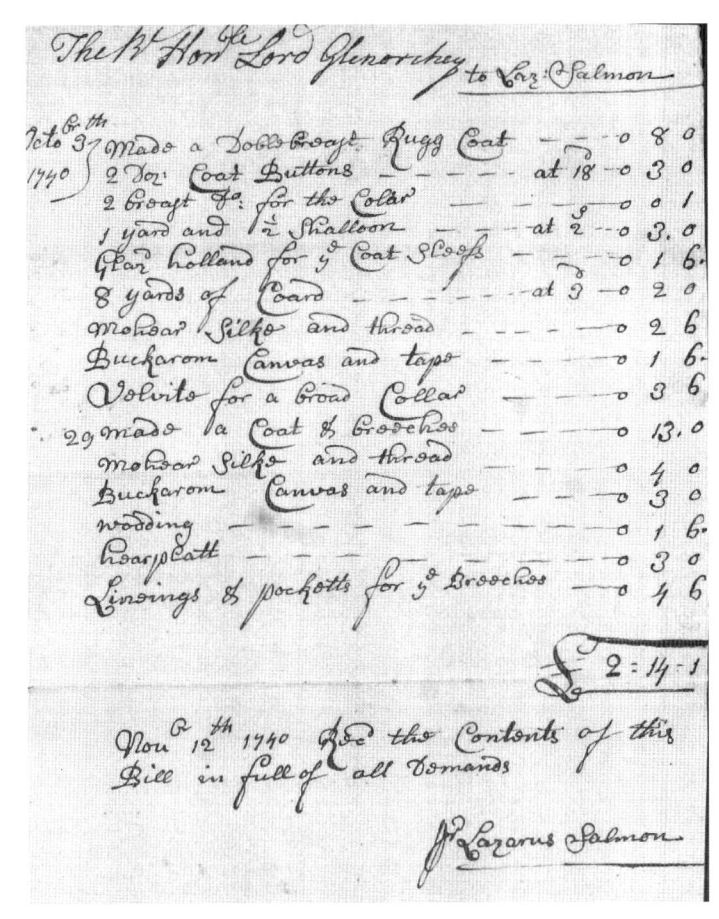

Invoice from Lazarus Salmon to Lord Glenorchy receipted 12 November 1740. (NAS, GD112/21/268/1)

SARDETT, HENRY

1738: DR £21 12s

Possibly the father of Henry Sardet, High Holborn, nr the Coal Yard, who entered a mark in 1765.[1] Heal lists him as plateworker 1773–77.

1. Grimwade.

SAWBRIDG & CO.

1739: CR £20

Jacob Sawbridge took over Sword Blade Bank, with George Caswall and Elias Turner.[1]

1. E-Hill, p. 171.

SAWYER, GEO

1747: CR £18 12s

Possibly George Sawyer, the son of John Sawyer of Heywood,

Berks, who was b. 1722.[1] A Major Sawyer is listed as arriving in Bath 8 October 1744; Major Sawyer is listed in Brewer Street, London.[2]

1. Burke LG 1848. 2. 1749 poll.

SAYER, JOS
1736: DR £6 18s 6d

Uncertain identity. He could be associated with Robert Sayer, engraver and printseller; or Mary Sayer, milliner in New Round Court, who advertised that she made, mended and mounted fans.[1]

1. WAC: Gardner coll, Box 63, 24D.

SCARBROUGH, LORD
1738: CR £105

Richard, 2nd Earl of Scarborough, whose brother was Treasurer to the Prince of Wales: the latter's name features on Paul Bertrand's invoice of 1738. He was 'at Spa, presumably for his health'[1] in August 1738, which would usually refer to Spa (now in Belgium) rather than Bath; however the ledger entry is for the following month and the Prince arrived at Bath in mid-October. He contributed 20 guineas to the hospital fund in 1738. Lord Scarborough was 'amiable and beloved' but he committed suicide at his house in Grosvenor Square in January 1739/40 – he had been unwell since 1737 following a blow to the head when his coach overturned. *The Bath Journal* lists Lady Scarborough arriving in the city on 14 April 1748, which would refer to his sister-in-law.

1. GEC, vol. XI, p. 511, which refers to a portrait.

SCARLETT, EDWD
1736–41: DR £43 10s; £15 14s; £12 18s; £15

London optician.

▶ p. 239.

SCARLEY, NICS
1738: DR £20

SCATTERGOOD, FRAS
1740 CR £50

SCATTERGOOD, MARIA
1740 CR £50

SCOTT, MARK
1744: CR £20

Uncertain identity. Possibly Scott & De Burdt, Blackwelhall factors, Artillery Court, Chiswell Street.[1]

1. Kent 1740.

SCRASE, CHAS
1745: CR £20

Possibly Charles Scrase of Inner Temple, St Clement Danes, recorded in 1750s.[1]

1. East Sussex RO: Pelham papers.

SCRIVENER, JNO
1741: DR £40

Possibly a connection of George Scrivener, cutler.[1]

1. Southwick, p. 219

SEAGRAVE, AML
1740: DR £31 10s

SHADWELL, CAPT
1747: CR [Deca Masters]

Possibly Lancelot Shadwell, d. 1755, whose name appears on a tontine snuffbox.[1] Capt Shadwell is listed as arriving in Bath 8 October 1744 (with Sir John Shadwell Bt) and 31 March 1746. The death of Sir John Shadwell, Kt, physician to Queen Anne, was announced 12 January 1746/47.[2] The ledger entry is for June 1747 via Benedict Masters.

1. Glynn. 2. *BJ*.

SHARPE, THOS
1744: CR £20

SHELOOCKE, GEO:
1742–46: CR £100; £39 1s; £100

Both George Shelvocke (c. 1702–60) and his father, a privateer, are buried in St Nicholas, Deptford. He was Secretary to the General Post Office and thus knew Ralph Allen well; Allen 'used him as a kind of banker'.[1] A freemason, listed at the lodge at the Horn at Westminster, 1723 and 1725.[2] He was associated with the Duke of Chandos.[3]

1. Allen p. 170. 2. Songhurst. 3. Baker.

SHEPH[E]ARD, SAMUEL
1739: DR £8 10s; £7 10s

Although these are debit entries, they probably relate to 'Samuel Shepherd Esq.' who is listed as being in Bath on 1 October 1744, 2 September 1745 and 29 September 1746.

To be Lett, Ready Furnish'd or Unfurnish'd, At Bottisham, within five Miles of Cambridge, and five of Newmarket. A Large Capital Mansion House, called Bendish Hall, late in the Possession of Samuel Shepheard, Esq; and now of Watson Powell Esq, with Stabling for twenty Horses, a good Dove-House, and Canals round the Gardens well stock'd with Fish; there are likewise twenty Acres of Pasture-Ground adjoining to the same. For further Particulars enquire of W. Powell, at the House, aforesaid; of Mr Deard, in Fleet Street; or of Mr Cutler, Coachmaker in Cow-Lane, near Smithfield.[1]

1. *London Evening Post*, 16 May 1747 [3048].

SHERRARD, SR B
1736: CR £50

On 29 January 1736 died:[1]

Sir Brownlowe Sherard, Bt in Burlington Gardens. He was of a human Disposition, kind to his Servants, dislik'd all extravagant Expence, but very liberal of his Fortune, as well to his Relations and Friends as to Numbers of distressed Objects; and in particular, to St George's

Hospital, near Hyde-Park Corner.

A freemason, he was listed in 1730 at the Rose Tavern without Temple Bar.[2] The ledgers of the silversmith George Wickes for 1735/36 reveal purchases in the name of his executors: 'Feb 5 – 20 motto rings £20; Feb 8 – 10 motto rings £10; Feb 28 – 16 motto rings £16 …. total £46'. He was a customer of Hoare, where his account reveals payments in 1737 to Daniel Chenevix (£24) and the jeweller, Lacam (£65). Pulls of his coat-of-arms engraved on silver are in the V&A.[3]

1. *Gents Mag*, February 1736.
2. Songhurst. 3. Wickes; V&A: album of engravings, P&D drawer EP/3.564; E.905.1954.dd (1731).

SHRUDER/STRUDER, JAS
1738: DR £15; £60; £38 7s

London silversmith

▶ p. 240.

SHURMER, JNO
1740: DR £100

John Shurmer, mealman and chapman of Bath, was listed as bankrupt in the *Bath Journal* on 15 April 1745. In August was advertised:

> Monks Mill on the River Avon, Bath, in good Repair with all the necessaries for a Meal Man, late in the possession of Mr John Shurmer – enquire of Mr Moore, Apothecary in Bath.

Dividends were paid out to creditors in December 1745 and again in December 1747. His name appears in Walter Wiltshire's account with Hoare.[1]

1. Lr. 38, fo. 408.

SHUTZ, COLO
1745: CR £44 11s

Cousin to George II; in Prince Frederick's household.

▶pp. 156–57, 299

SIDDALL, SAML
1736: CR £30

Possibly a connection of John Siddall, cutler, at the Unicorn and 2 Daggers, London Bridge in 1720.[1]

1. Sun Ins, vol. 12, p. 203 [19634].

SIMPSON & WARD
1738 and 1739: CR £105; £37

> Whereas the Shop of Mess Simpson and Ward, Bankers in Fleet Street, was attempted to be robb'd on Saturday last; and whereas Information has been made before a Justice of the Peace that Robert Lucas, a Fan stick Maker in Britain's Court in Water Lane, Fleet Street, and Edward Lloyd, late Tallow Chandler, and Prisoner in the Fleet, who lately lodged in Black-and-White Court in the old Baily, were concern'd in the same; whoever apprehends either of them shall receive Ten Guineas reward, or Twenty for both, on Conviction, to be paid the said Mess Simpson and Ward.[1]

▶ p. 277 Gosling.

1. *Daily Advertiser*, 13 January 1742.

SKIMER, NICS
1739: CR £21

Nicholas Skinner, merchant, Aldermanbury.[1]

1. Kent 1740.

SKINNER, JNO
1739: DR £100

The ledger entry appears to read Skumer, but is most probably for Jacob Skinner, the Bath engraver.

▶ p. 181.

SKRINE, ELIZ
1746: DR £65; £90

'Mr Skrine' is listed as arriving in the city 29 September 1746, the month of the first ledger entry. The Skrines were a large family local to Bath. There were four consecutive generations of women called Elizabeth Skrine. This could be the mother or wife of Richard Dickson Skrine (d. 1791) of Warleigh, just south of Bathford.[1] In 1766 Richard Skrine had a house in Edgar Buildings, next to William Hoare.[2] Monuments to the Skrine family in Batheaston (dating to the mid-twentieth century) describe them as 'of Claverton and Warleigh'.

Claverton was bought in 1714 by William Skrine, an apothecary of Bath (d. 1725) who in 1697 married Mrs Savil, the owner of the lodging house in which the princesses stayed in 1746 [▶ p. 153], described as:[3]

> A Commodious Dwelling House at the Cross Bath. Well Known by the name of Skrine's Lodging-House, Part new-built, and the other Part in good repair …

His son William (1722–83) sold Claverton to Ralph Allen in 1758. William Skrine jnr married Jane Sumner (d. 1766), whose probably illegitimate daughter Louisa (1760–1809) may have been fathered by John, 4th Earl of Sandwich. Louisa married Sir Thomas Clarges [▶ p. 260] and was painted by Gainsborough.[4] Anne, daughter of Richard Skrine 'with £30,000' married Hugh Barlow MP in 1733.[5]

1. Landscape by William Delamotte (1775–1862), Bearne's Exeter 3–4 July 2007 lot 473.
2. Bath RO: Rate Book 1.
3. Wood p. 85; Holland, 1998. *BJ*, 15 July 1745. 4. Ingamells; Sumner; SNY, 6 April 2006 lot 92, ex Virginia Museum of Fine Arts. 5. Sedgwick.

SMART, BEN
1736: CR £20

SMITH, ELEANOR
1739: DR £20

SMITH, GEO
1745 and 1746: CR £20; £40; £50; £20

A common name. George Smith, gentleman, is listed in Curzon Street in 1749.[1] His name (written as Smyth), and that of James Smyth, appear in Mary Bertrand's account with Hoare in the early 1770s, suggesting he was a banker.

1. 1749 poll.

SMITH, JAS
1738: DR £23
1746: CR £30

Presumably a connection of George (above), his name also features in Mary Bertrand's account. There was a goldsmith in Fleet Street, but it seems likely that the entries refer to a perfumer, at the sign of the Civet Cat in New Bond Street.

▶ p. 196 illus. and p. 199.

SMITH, JNO
1741: DR £10 4s

Uncertain identity. He may be John Smith, the son-in-law and successor of John Marshall, who sold scientific instruments. Other possibilities are: John Smith of Bristol, merchant, bankrupt 1747.[1] John Smith of Shaw House, Melksham, whose sister Elizabeth married Robert Neale [▶ p. 296 Neale and, below, Thomas Smith]. John Smith, earthenware man, Clements Inn Passage.[2]

1. BJ, 27 July 1747. 2. 1749 poll.

SMITH, SAML
1736–45: CR £42; £20; £60; £15; £30; £43 5s; £14; £30; £60

Probably Samuel Smith, Georgia Trustee and South Sea director, Love Lane, Aldermanbury.[1]

1. Kelly 1740.

SMITH, SR WM & CO.
1745: CR £143

William Smith, merchant, Fenchurch Street.[1]

1. Kelly 1740.

SMITH, THOS
1740–43: CR £16 16s; £31 10s; £15 15s

Uncertain identity, candidates include:

1. Thomas Smith of Shaw House, Melksham, whose daughter Elizabeth married Robert Neale of Corsham [▶ p. 296].[1]

2. The pumper at Bath:[2]

… the True and Genuine BATH WATERS are now sold at Wiltshire's (the Bath and Bristol Carrier) Warehouses at the White Bear Inn in Piccadilly and the White Swan, Holborn Bridge, and at no other Place in London Whatsoever – And where the Publick may depend on having it fresh three times a week. Thomas Smith, Pumper.

3. Thomas Smith, accountant for duties on candles, soap, gold and silver wire, starch etc. in the Excise office.[3]

4. Portrait: Robert West, *Thomas Smith and his Family* 1733.[4]

5. Thomas Smith & Co. purchased Fans ('pr Herne') for £199 8s 6d. in the East India Co. sale 1714, at which sale Phillip Margas [▶ p. 231] was buying fans and chinawares.[5]

6. Thomas Smith jeweller, Drury Lane, 1714.[6]

7. An attorney of York Buildings, who witnessed the will of Henry Fielding's mother-in-law.[7]

1. Sedgwick. 2. BJ, 13 January 1745/46. 3. Chamberlayne, Pt II, Bk III, p. 82. 4. Saumerez-Smith no. 90 (Bearsted coll, Upton House, Warwicks (National Trust)). 5. BL, H/1/L. 6. Sun Ins, vol. 4, fo. 65 [4430]. 7. PROB 11/669.

SNOW & CO.
1737–46: CR £25; £40; £105; £50; £100; £55; £52 10s; £73 10s; £50; £30; £52 10s; £50; £30; £50; £10; £50

SNOW & DENNE
1746: CR £20; £40

SNOW, THOS
1740–44: CR £25; £100; £100

Bankers at the Golden Anchor, Strand, London, 'without Temple Bar'.[1] Thomas Snow & Co. 1736–54; Snow & Denne 1754–68

1. Kent 1740; Outing; H-Price. Badminton: FmI 4/14, receipt February 1741/2 witnessed for Thos Snow & Co. by Alexr Ross.

SNOWDEN, JAS
1737: DR £20; CR £20

SOAME, STE:
1738: DR £27 2s
1739: CR £50; £16 16s

Stephen Soame was a governor of Bath's Mineral Water Hospital and contributed £20 to its initial fund-raising in 1738.

SOMERSET, LORD NOEL
1739: CR £21

Charles Noel, later 4th Duke of Beaufort (1709–56), younger brother of Henry, 3rd Duke (d. 1744/45, ▶ p. 251). On 25 January 1739/40 Elizabeth Robinson wrote from Bath that 'Except Lord Noel Somerset's match with Miss Berkley, we have had no transactions of any consequence'. A regular visitor to Bath he is often listed as arriving there, for example on 24 December 1744 and again on 4 March 1744/45, his brother having died in February. In 1748, as Duke of Beaufort, he followed the Prince of Wales as president of the Mineral Water Hospital. He and his brother bought jewellery from Andrew Mayaffre on a regular basis, the largest sum spent was in May 1740 when Lord Noel married Elizabeth Berkeley; the wedding was on 1 May and on 22 May the Beaufort accounts show a payment to Mayaffre of £1,247.[1]

1. Badminton: FmJ 3/7.

SOUTHWELL, EDWD
1738: DR £8

1705–55, MP for Bristol 1739–54. His house, King's Weston, was one of the 'chief seats' of Gloucestershire.[1] He was a great favourite of Mrs Pendarves, Elizabeth Robinson, and their circle, and a regular visitor to Bath: his name features in Eliza Hayes' account with Hoare.[2] He and 'his Lady' (he married Catherine Watson in 1729, ▶ p. 110, Rockingham) gave £50 each to the Mineral Water Hospital in 1738 of which he was a governor 1748.[3] His London house was in Spring Gardens, close to Chenevix's shop:[4]

> I am porter to Edward Southwell, Esq; at Spring-Garden, by Charing-Cross. Last Saturday morning there was an iron rail lost from his chapel, which was fixed to the stone-work; the stone was broke, and the iron rail was taken out.

▶ pp. 163, 300.

1. Chamberlayne, Pt I, Bk I, p. 12. 2. Lr. 30, fo. 71 (1728). 3. *Daily Gazetteer*, 8 Apri 1738 [862]. 4. POB: t17441205-4.

SPARKE, RD
1739: CR £40 4s

SPENCE, AMA
1739: CR £80

SPENCE, ELIZA
1741: CR £29 2s 6d

SPENCE, ROT
1741: CR £30

SPENCE, RUTH
1740–47: CR £80; £36; £45 18s 3d; £31; £16; £66 8s 6d; £50; £157 12s; £50; £100; £30; £100; £171 16s 6d; £36 6s; £55; £118 18s; £52; £60; £25 16s 9d; £70; £63 13s; £40; £50; £32 18s; £38 18s; £39 3s 6d; £40; £40; £63 12s 6d

Ruth Spence died in 1767, thereafter her house in Barton Street, Bath is listed in the name of Thomas Rundell. If the three persons above were her relatives they might have been disappointed in her will, by which she left 'her freehold estates and lands … watches, rings, jewels and paraphernalia, plate, linen, china, household goods …' to 'Robert Hamden Trevor, Lord Trevor and his brother Richard, Lord Bishop of Durham and to their heirs…' [▶ p. 317]. She also left money annually to her servant Philadelphia and to the wife of a Bath tobacconist whose husband '… is not to intermeddle or have any thing to do therewith nor is the same or any part thereof to be subject or liable to his debts, control or management…'.[1]

1. PROB 11/932.

SPENCER, MR
1744: CR £157 10s

Probably the Hon. John Spencer (1708–46), a regular visitor to Bath (for example in October and December 1744, August 1745 and January 1745/46), MP for Woodstock 1732–46. He was the youngest son of 3rd Earl of Sunderland and Anne, daughter of the Duke of Marlborough. Through the will of his grandmother, Sarah, Duchess of Marlborough he inherited a substantial fortune in 1744, reported as producing an income of £35,500 p.a., together with 'all her gold and silver plate … and all her seals and trinkets and small pieces of Japan'.[1] Properties included Althorp, Spencer House and Wimbledon Park. His son John was created 1st Earl Spencer in 1765 and married Margaret, daughter of Stephen Poyntz [▶ p. 302].

▶ pp. 138–41, 156.

1. *BJ*, 5 and 12 November 1744.

SPICER, THOS
1745: CR £50

Uncertain identity. Thomas Spicer was a cutler at the sign of the Tobacco Pipe 'Cranburn Ally near Leicester Fields' from at least 1713.[1] He advertised that he sold 'Fishskin and White Skin Cases fitted with Silver or Plain … New Blades fitted in Silver Agate or China hafts after the newest Fashion'. But as this is a credit entry, it may refer to another, and it is a common name. A Thomas Spicer was listed in Johnson's Court, 1746.[2]

Trade card: Lincoln RO: Asw 2/104/15.

1. Sun Ins, vol. 3, p. 8. 2. LMA: 692–5 copy of St Dunstan's rents.

SPILSBURY, FRAS
1736: DR £8 18s

London silversmith, who gained his freedom in 1717 but did not enter a mark until 1729. Heal records him as plateworker, Spread Eagle, Foster Lane, 1729–39. When he was a journeyman he signed the petition against the assaying of work by foreigners who had not served seven years apprenticeship.

SPURRIER, ISAAC
1737–43: DR £21 17s; £11 18s; £40; £30; £20; £28; £30; £30; £20; £30

SPURRIER, JS
1736: DR £12 12s

Probably connected to Jonathan Spurrier, 'late of Salisbury Court Fleet Street, snuff box maker and lapidary' who was bankrupt August 1748.[1] Five years previously Isaac had had trouble with an apprentice:[2]

> Whereas William Penny, Apprentice to Isaac Spurrier, Snuff Box Maker, in Salisbury Court, Fleet Street, did absent himself from his said Master's Service on Friday Night … It is apprehended that he was entic'd away by some ill-principled Person or Persons … if he will return … he shall be kindly receiv'd … He is a tall thin Lad, about five Feet seven Inches, high, eighteen or

nineteen years of age, a little battle-hamm'd … remarkable for having a bald Place on one side of his Head.

1. *London Gazette* [8775].
2. *Daily Advertiser*, 19 August 1743 [3927].

STAINBANK, THOS
1746: CR £20

STANDERT, MR
1745: CR £50; £20; £20; £40

William and Frederick Standert were wine merchants, Martin's Lane, Cannon Street.[1] Frederick Standert's name appears (with Daniel le Sueur, ▶ p. 289) in a list of traders to Portugal who complained in 1756 of duties imposed there after the Lisbon earthquake, in order to rebuild the Custom House.[2] A Vauxhall Gardens ticket in the BM is engraved with his name.

1. Kent 1740; Hoare: invoice dated 1732. 2. Sutherland.

STANHOPE, LADY JANE
1746 and 1747: CR £55 9s 6d; £25

STANHOPE, LADY LUCY
1747: CR £85 16s 2d

Lucy (b. 1714) and Jane (b. 1719) Stanhope were sisters of the 2nd Earl of Stanhope: Lucy was his twin.[1] The dates of their ledger entries (February 1746/47 and May 1747), overlap Sir William Stanhope's arrival in Bath on 24 March 1746/47.[2] Although they were only distant cousins to Sir William and his siblings [▶ p. 283 Hotham], they must have known each other. Sir William purchased Pope's villa at Twickenham after his death. In 1760 Mrs Delany wrote of her god-daughter visiting 'her old acquaintances Lady Lucy Stanhope and Mrs Trevor'.[3] The sisters feature in an inventory of silver and jewels from Chevening, in which Lady Lucy is listed as receiving a set of dressing plate (£123 6s 8d) and Lady Jane jewels valued at £157.[4]

1. Brydges, vol. IV, p. 178. 2. *BJ*.
3. Delany, vol. 3, p. 605.
4. Maidstone RO: U1590, A104.913.

STANLEY, ED
1736: CR £50

Sir Edward Stanley, 5th Bt, died in 1755.[1] He had a house in Barton Street in Bath, next to Sir John Cope, at which his widow and then their son, Sir John, were listed into the 1770s; he was therefore a neighbour of Bertrand [▶ p. 264].[2] In 1746 he inherited the baronetcy from his brother John, whose wife was Mary Delany's aunt. Mrs Delany lived with Sir John Stanley for long periods of her life, and liked Edward Stanley, who she described as 'my pert lawyer' and 'an honest man, and not likely to increase his fortune by the common tricks of the law.'[3] At the coronation of George II (when she was Mrs Pendarves) she wrote of being 'rescued' by Stanley. He married Miss Ward, daughter of a 'rich bookseller'.

1. Burke, *Peerage*, 1837. 2. Bath RO: Rate Book. 3. Delany, vol. 1, pp. 207 and 260.

STANTON, WM
1743: DR £25

Uncertain identity. Possibly a witness in a trial: 'I have the honour of being one of the Ward Beadles to Alderman Hoare; it was my night to set the watch'.[1] A William Stanton is listed as a freemason in London, at the lodge at the Queens Arms, Newgate St, 1730; Thomas Kendrick and Benjamin Cole [▶ p. 288] were in the same lodge.[2] Alternatively he may have been a connection of Frederick Stanton (who was a partner of John Cotterell, ▶ p. 220); or of Edward Stanton, lancet maker.[3]

1. POB: t17441205-23.
2. Songhurst. 3. Trade card: BM: Banks 105.52.

STEPHENS/STEVENS JAS
1738 and 1739: CR £52 10s; £105; £52 10s; £52 10s; £52 10s

Most probably the man referred to in the following letter from Littleton Pointz Meynell [▶ p. 255 Prosper Browne] to the Duke of Devonshire:[1]

> My Lord. As your Grace was pleased to give me permission I have drawn for 800 Guineas, payable to Ja: Stephens, my servant in London, who will wait on your Grace. … since I came hither I have been reconing up the number of my voters; & I believe I shall be able to command at least an hundred to give double or single votes as you shall direct. Bradley, Oct 30th 1738.

As these are credit entries, it seems far less likely to be the J. Stephens who advertised an auction of china 'at Mr Strange's dining room' in Cheap Street, Bath.[2]

1. Chatsworth: 186.17. 2. Bath CL: trade cards.

STEVENSON, B
1746 and 1748: CR £8; £22
1748: DR £602 5s

The Revd Bennet Stevenson was Minister of the Presbyterian congregation in Frog Lane, Bath from 1719, taking over from Mary Chandler's father [▶ p. 258]. He was a Governor of the Mineral Water Hospital but resigned after the Cleland affair. However the large payments to him and Henry Wright [▶ p. 322] for South Sea Annuities during Bertrand's retirement, may relate to the Hospital. He is presumably the 'Stevenson' listed near Bertrand in Barton Street; from Michaelmas 1747 he had a 99-year lease on property in Orange Court.[1]

1. Bath RO: Walcot Church Rate Book and 1776 Schedule of Deeds p. 255.

STIBBS, EDWD
1739: DR £100
STIBBS, JNO
1747: DR £12

Probably members of a Bath family; George Stibbs was at the Royal Oak in Broad Street,[1] 'Stibbs & Hickes' are listed on the Water Roll 1748; Gilmore's map of Bath (1690) illustrates 'Alderman Stibbs's Lodging in West Gate Street'.

1. Bath RO: 1776 Schedule of Deeds p. 249.

STILLINGFLEET, JNO
1744: DR £105

Uncertain identity, but he attended a Masonic meeting in Bath, at which Bertrand was also present, in Novmber 1737, and on other occasions.[1] A John Stillingfleet had an account with Hoare with a balance in 1724 of £1,293 4s 6d.

There were several men with the surname of Stillingfleet worth noting, for example Benjamin (1702–71), source of the term 'bluestocking'; his father Edward;[2] and Thomas Stillingfleet, Yeoman of the Cellar to the Prince of Wales. The Revd Mr Stillingfleet gave 5gns to the Hospital in 1739.[3] Edward and James Stillingfleet were Methodist preachers and theologians.

1. Masons Bath: Book 1, 1732–38. 2. Vivian. p. 473; Ingamells. 3. *Daily Gazetteer*, 3 February 1739.

STODDART, RD CHAS / REVD
1741: CR £6 14s; £20; £15

Charles Stoddart (d. 1790), from Bamburgh, Northumberland;[1] but more likely to be his father, also a clergyman and also named Charles.

1. Venn.

STONER & CO.
1740: CR £88 17s 9d; £50
STONER & BELASYSE
1741: CR £41 1s 8d

Stoner & Belasyse, merchants, Coleman Street.[1]

1. Kent 1740.

STRAHAN, JNO
1739: DR £10

John Strahan, architect in Bath and Bristol. He built Kingsmead Square, Beaufort Square and Kingsmead, Monmouth and Avon Streets, at the same time that Wood was building Queen Square. The Duke of Chandos turned down his designs for the St John's Hospital site in favour of Wood.

STRATTON, OSBORN
1736: DR £30

STREET, MR
1746: DR £32 17s

Possibly James Street, apothecary, who took an apprentice in 1731; his son, William was also apprenticed to him in 1743.[1] William was master of the freemasons' lodge in 1753.[2] Mr Street is listed in the Water Roll 1748, for a tenement in Broad Street, Bath. Described by Roland Leffever as 'apothecary and Chymist nr St Michael's Church'.[3]

1. Bath RO: Apprentice Book, pp. 16 and 34. 2. Songhurst. 3. Bath RO: Acc.662.

STRIDE, GRACE/GRATIOUS
1741 & 1742: DR £50; £30

Gracious Stride was a carpenter and maltster in Bath:[1]

> To be sold, very reasonable … three tenements adjoining to the said Malt-House, lett for 4 l a Year each; and one House backward, with a pleasant Garden before it, very agreeable for a small Family, having Plenty of good Water and all other Conveniences, all in good Repair … being late the Estate of Gracious Stride, Carpenter.

He had property in Barton Street,[2] close to Paul Bertrand and William Hoare. He also built an alley containing fifteen houses, named Gratious Street, between Walcot Street and Broad Street.[3]

1. *BJ*, 16 September 1745 and 23 February 1746/47. 2. Bath RO: First Church Rate Book 1738. 3. Wood, p. 334.

STRODE, JAS
1746: DR £165 7s 6d

STRODE, SAML / MRS
1742 and 1745: CR £210; £100; £200; £200; £15 15s; £42 [last pr hand of Jno Nottingham]

Col. Samuel Strode was appointed a Governor of the Mineral Water Hospital in May 1744 and was a regular visitor to Bath. In March 1746/47 he was described as 'Counsellor Strode'.[1]

> On Thursday last the Bath Company of Comedians perform'd the Comedy of the Conscious Lover for the Benefit of the Sufferers by Fire at Crediton in Devonshire. Sir Bourchier Wray Bart and Samuel Strode Esq collected the Money at the Doors, which amounted to near 60 l.[2]

Samuel's brother William was 'a wealthy city magnate', who lived in Duke Street, London.[3]

Portrait: William Hogarth, *The Strode Family*, c.1738, (Tate Britain; Hallett no. 54 and Saumarez Smith, no. 105).

1. *BJ*, 16 March 1746/47 and 5 May 1746. 2. *BJ*, 14 May 1744. 3. Sedgwick; Ingamells.

STURT, CATH
1742: CR £33 6s 8d
1744: DR £21 7s

Uncertain identity. Possibly Catharine Sturt, daughter of Humphrey Sturt (d. 1740) of Horton, listed as a Gentleman of the Privy Chamber;[1] he had an account with Hoare. Alternatively, as there are both credit and debit entries, Catherine may have been a connection of John Sturt,

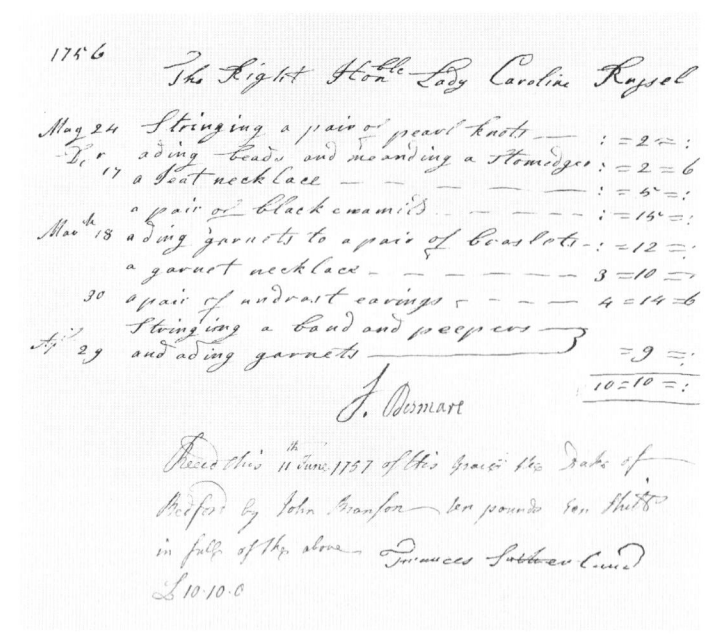

Invoice for stringing necklaces from Frances Sutherland to Lady Caroline Russel, dated 1756. (Bedford)

engraver, who in 1729 subscribed to S. Sympson's *New Book of Cyphers*.[2]

1. Burke, *LG* 1848; Chamberlayne, Pt II, Bk III, p. 208. 2. V&A P&D.

STYLES [STILES], FRAS H EYLES
1737: CR £80
1746: DR £60

Francis Haskin Styles, matriculated Camb 1728, FRS 1742,[1] succeeded his father, John Eyles (▶ p. 272) as 3rd Bt in 1745, died in Napes 1762.[2] He assumed the additional surname of Haskin-Styles when he inherited the estate of his uncle, Benjamin.

1. Venn. 2. Burke, *Extinct Bt*.

SUTHERLAND, FRAS
1737 and 1740: DR £13 15s; £10

An invoice receipted by Frances Sutherland to Lady Caroline Russell, dated 1756, is for stringing pearls and garnets. Another signature on the invoice might read Desmare, possibly a link to Demarin [▶ p. 268]. She may have been connected to John Sutherland, a toyman who died in 1740.

▶ above, illus.

1. Woburn: Box 19/23/3.

SWAN, MARY
1746: CR £20

T

TAAFF, JNO
1738: DR £25; £21

Uncertain identity; these are debit entries, but possibly a connection of Viscount Taafe and the Earls of Carlingford (the latter extinct 1738); a branch of the family was strongly Catholic. Theobald Taaffe, a notorious gambler, was MP for Arundel 1747–54;[1] 'Mr Taff' is listed as arriving in Bath 30 October 1746. The family had close links with Ireland and also Vienna.

1. See Sedgwick for Taaffe's involvement with Sir John Bland, the Duke of Bedford and Edward Wortley Montagu [▶ p. 252].

TABART, DANIEL
1739–42: DR £26; £31 10s; £20

Jeweller, of St Anne's Westminster, d. 1775. In August 1733 Daniel Tabart sold the Earl of Dysart a 'triangle gold seal with a topas' for £35 10s and a shagreen watch case studded in gold with a coronet (£4 10s). By the time the Earl paid for his purchases in December 1735, Tabart was bankrupt.[1] Probably related to James Tabart, a lace merchant [▶ p. 317 John Trible].

▶ p. 323 illus.

1. Buckminster: Box 921–925pt.

TALBOTT, JNO IVORY
1738: CR £49

John Ivory Talbot of Lacock Abbey, Wilts (?1691–1772), MP for Ludgershall 1715–22 and Wiltshire 1727–41. John Ivory assumed the name of Talbot when he inherited the Wiltshire estates of his grandfather in 1714. He rebuilt much of Lacock Abbey in Gothic taste; his great-grandson was the photographer William Fox-Talbot.

Portrait: Michael Dahl, Lacock Abbey.

TEMPLE, MR
1739: CR £6 6s; £60; £21

Probably a connection of John Temple, a banker at the Three Tunns, Lombard Street, in 1677.[1]

1. Directory 1677.

TERRY, WM
1738: CR £60

William Terry, merchant, at Mr Cuzack's in Coleman Street;[1] in Bond St 'gent', 1749.[2]

1. Kent 1740. 2. 1749 poll.

THELKELD, PR
1739: DR £200

An unusual surname, so probably a connection of one of the following: William Threlkeld, a watchmaker of St Martin-in-the-Fields; Mary, a goldsmith, at the

Ring & Ball, Minories;[1] or William, a toyman in Russell Court.[2]

1. BM: Heal 67.399. 2. Sun Ins, 16 August 1714 [4407].

THIBAULT, THOS
1738 and 1739: DR £40; £25

Thomas Thibault, jeweller, also spelt Tibbault, Tibboe or Teboe. Heal lists Thomas snr in Soho, but the ledger entry must refer to Thomas jnr. His apprentices included Samuel Cawthorne 1723 [▶ p. 219]; Peter Tibboe (his son) 1725; Louis Loubie 1727 [▶ p. 291]; John Morgan 1730 [▶ p. 295]. Thibault was himself apprenticed in 1699 to Daniel Antrobus (amongst whose other apprentices was Stafford Briscoe, later a retailer in Cheapside), free 1712, livery 1731.[1] On 25 March 1711 the insurance policy of Thibault (snr?) has the address 'corner of Beauford Buildings in the Strand in the Duchy of Lancaster'; by July 1723 Thibault (jnr?) was in Red Lyon Court, and he moved to Hind Court a year later; Heal lists him in Fetter Lane.[2]

1. GH: Apprentice Book. 2. Sun Ins, vol. 1, p. 135; vol. 15, p. 531, £500; Heal LG; Jowett.

▶ p. 211/9 map.

THOMAS, EVANS
1739–46: DR £27 10s; £30; £100; £100; £100; £100; £100; £100; £200; £100; £100; £200; £100; £15; £6 6s

Evans Thomas was a wine merchant in Orange Court, Bath.[1] He was a governor of the Mineral Water Hospital in 1748. His will was proved September 1752:[2]

All Persons indebted to the Estate of the late Mr Evans Thomas, Wine Merchant, at Bath, deceas'd, are desir'd forthwith to pay their Debts to Brice Fisher, Esq; of London, Michael Atkins, Esq; of Bristol, and Mr. P. Bertrand of Bath, or they will be immediately sued for the same: …

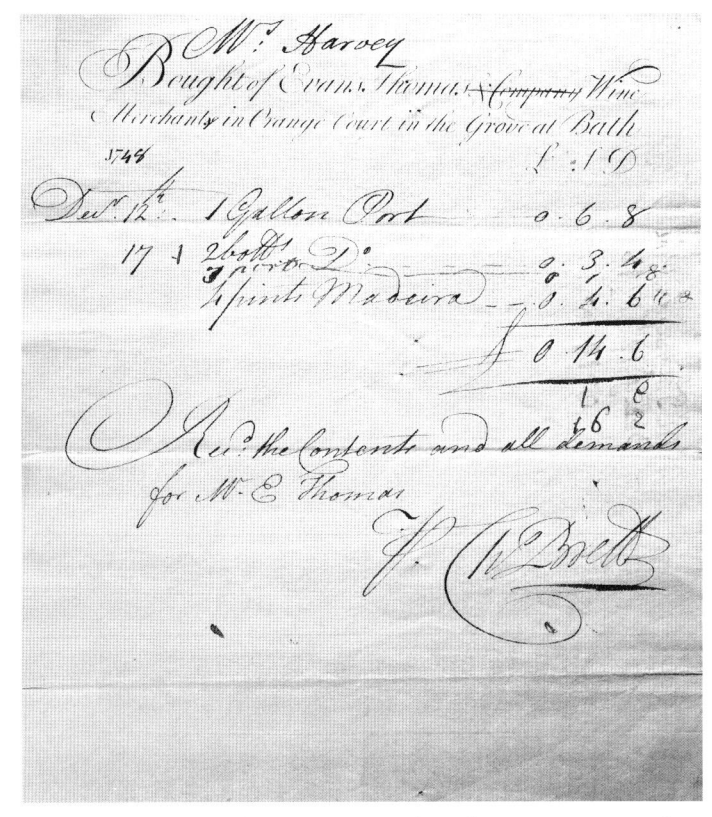

Invoice from Evans Thomas, wine merchant, 'in Orange Court in the Grove', dated 12 December 1748. (Bath in Time, 35275)

The ledger entries probably refer to the assembly rooms rather than the toyshop.

1. Bath CL: invoice. 2. PROB 11/797. *London Evening Post*, 20 January 1753 [3937].

THOMAS, SR ED
1747: CR £100

Sir Edmond Thomas, 3rd Bt (1712–67), MP for Chippenham 1741–54. In 1765 he sold Wenvoe Castle to Peter Birt, by which time the Thomas family had been there for 200 years. He married in 1740 Abigail, daughter of Sir Thomas Webster of Battle Abbey and widow of William Northey. His mother's house in Kings Mead Street, Bath, was advertised to be let in February 1745/46[1] and her death announced three months later.[2] He was a groom of the bedchamber to the Prince of Wales and treasurer to the Princess Dowager 1757–61.

1. *BJ*, February 1745/46. 2. *BJ*, 5 May 1746.

THOMOND, LORD
1738: CR £5 5s

Henry O'Brien, 8th Earl of Thomond (1691–1741), married in 1707 Elizabeth, daughter of the 6th Duke of Somerset (1685–1734). The ledger entry is for June 1738; nine months later he gave £50 to the Mineral Water Hospital in Bath.[1] His family seat was at Shortgrove, Essex,[2] but he also owned a house in Kew, next to the property acquired by Frederick, Prince of Wales, in 1738.[3] He died without issue and his estates were inherited by his wife's nephew, who visited Bath in 1745:[4]

Thursday arrived here Piercy Windham O'Brien, Esq, Brother to Charles Windham Bt and who, by the Death of Lord O'Brien, son to the Earl of Inchiquin, hath got the Thomond Estates.

The sale of Thomond's 'Houshold Furniture, Pictures, Plate, jewels, Linnen, Fine Old China and Japan, and Valuable Library of Books (most of which are the best editions and large Papers)' at his house in Dover Street was advertised in January 1742.[5]

> 1. *Daily Gazetteer*, 3 February 1739. 2. Chamberlayne, Pt 1, Bk 1, p. 11; Sun Ins, vol. 14, fo. 158. 3. Vivian. 4. *BJ*, 5 August 1745 printing a report from Dublin dated 20 July. 5. *The Daily Advertiser*, 13 January 1742.

THOMSON, SR WM
1739: CR £50

William Thompson (?1676–1739), MP for Orford and Ipswich; knighted in 1715; his second wife was the widow of Sir William Blackett, 1st Bt, Her grandson, Walter Blackett [▶ p. 251] appears in the ledgers in January 1739/40; the entry for Sir William is eight months previously, in May 1739 and he died in October of that year.[1] Sir William lost his seat at Orford following his part in the impeachment of Henry Sacheverell 1709–10; he was also involved in the impeachment of the Jacobite 5th Earl of Winton (who was sentenced to death but escaped from the Tower of London and died in exile). Sir William introduced the Transportation Act (1718), which formalised the transportation of British criminals (excluding Scots) to the Americas and later to Australia, a policy that ended in 1867. John Wood related that Thompson was at a meeting in January 1737/38 about structural improvements to the Baths and that he complained that he 'by a line of wind from a low corner of the walls surrounding the King's Bath, had catched such a cold, as had like to have caused his death'.[2]

> 1. PROB 11/699. 2. Wood, p. 266.

THORNBURY, NICS
1741: DR £15

THORNTON, BARON
1736: CR £12 4s

THOROLD, JNO
1745: DR £14 14s

This is a debit entry, but may refer to John Thorold of Harmeston whose son Nathaniel inherited a baronetcy in 1738 from a kinsman.[1] Sir John Thorold's account at Hoare & Co. has payments to John Thorold, Esq.

Portrait miniature: Lady Thorold (d. 1733) Royal Collection.

> 1. Burke, *Extinct Bt*.

THURETT, ISAAC
1746: DR £10

A freemason – present at a meeting of the Bath Lodge in 1735, for example.[1] An Isaac Thuret is in the denization list for 2 March 1681, the same day as Jacob Trigau. Possibly linked to the Gaultier family and a connection of Jacques T(h)uret, clockmaker to Louis XIV (fl. 1694–1712) [▶ p. 318].[2]

> 1. Masons Bath, Book 1 1732–38. 2. Baillie.

TILLY, JAMES
1739: DR £20

TILLY, MGT
1742: DR £10

Described as a 'French jeweller' James Tilly was chief workman to Bertrand in Bath. When Bertrand retired he set up in business on his own, advertising that 'He mends all Things in the Jewelling, Gold and Silversmiths Way'. Margaret Tilly was presumably his wife [▶ p. 62].

TILSON, JAMES
1736: DR £136 10s

This is a debit entry, but very likely refers to James Tilson of Bolesworth Castle, Cheshire (1709–64), son of Thomas Tilson of Dublin. An entry in the journal of the Webb family of jewellers probably refers to his first wife, Jane: on 18 February 1742/43 they sold 'Mrs James Tilson Pendants' to the value of £930, paid by a draft on Messrs Nesbitt;[1] they had married the previous December. He married again in July 1750 on which occasion Mrs Delany reported that: 'The present talk of Dublin is of Mr Tilson's marriage with Lady Kerry last Thursday – nobody suspected it; he is a very lively gay man, and she rather of the insipid strain.'[2] Two miniatures in the Gilbert Collection are possibly Thomas Tilson and his wife.

> 1. TNA: C108/284, Journal 2, 1735–50. 2. Delany, series 1 vol. 2, p. 570. 3. Coffin, nos. 53 and 71.

TINSLEY, GEO
1746: CR £14 14s; £10 10s

TOLE/TOLL, ANN
1738 and 1739: CR £20; £35; £3

Uncertain identity. Possibly Anne, wife of Ashburnham Toll of Grewell, co. Hants,[1] or the wife of the Revd Fifield Allen (married Bridewell 16 October 1738 by licence). Another possibility is the wife of James Cranmer (above), who was the daughter of Richard and Esther Toll of Tottenham, b. 1729.

> 1. Burke, *LG* 1848.

TORIANS, SAML
1743: DR £17 8s

TORVANO, SAML
1744: DR £26 16s

It is unclear whether the entries relate to Samuel Torin or Samuel Torriano, both their wills are summarised by Wagner.

The Torin family, had links to Madras for many years through the East India Company. Samuel Torin, broker, is listed in Nicholas Lane, Lombard Street.[1] He regularly advertised sales of a wide range of goods from the East. In the months of the ledger entries these included, for example, 924 canes, bundles of rattans and boxes of borax (1743), chinaware and taffaties (1744) but there were also consignments of fans, lacquer chinaware and bags of cowries.[2] Bertrand might have purchased any one of these. An association between Torin and Philip Margas [▶ p. 231] is revealed in a notification regarding partnerships within the Margas family in 1735, when Torin was in Budge Row.[3] It is worth noting, also, a James Lewis Torin, jeweller, Throgmorton Street.[4]

Allan Ramsay painted a portrait of Samuel Torriano in 1738.[5]

> 1. Gill, p. 119; Kent 1740.
> 2. *General Advertiser*, 25 July 1748 [2489]. 3. *London Gazette*, 4 March 1735 [7382]. 4. Kent 1740; *London Evening Post*, 12 February 1736 [1286]. 5. Strong & Allan, pl. 152.

TOWERY, PENE
1742: CR £40

TOWNSEND, CHAUNCEY
1746: CR £50

Chauncey Townsend (1708–70) was a linen draper and merchant, who held government contracts for provisioning troops in Nova Scotia. He also had coalmining interests in Wales. In 1730 he married Bridget Phipps of Westbury and represented Westbury as MP 1747/48–68.

TOWNSEND, HORATO
1745: CR £45

Horatio, 3rd son of 1st Viscount Townshend (d. 1751), was MP for Yarmouth, then Heytesbury. His London address in 1734 was Berkeley Street and in 1749 Blicks Row, Bolton St. His only daughter Letitia married in 1749 Brownlow, 9th Earl of Exeter.[1] He was a Commissioner of Excise, from 1735 until his death at a salary of £1000 p.a.,[2] and described as 'a wealthy London merchant'.[3]

> 1. Burke. 2. Kent 1740; Chamberlayne. 3. Sedgwick.

TOWNSEND, THOS
1746: CR £30

The Hon. Thomas Townsend (1701–80), second son of the 2nd Viscount Townshend and nephew of Horatio (above); one of the Tellers of the Exchequer and MP for Cambridge University 1727–74. He is listed in Cleveland Row, London.[1]

> 1. 1749 poll.

TRACEY, MARY
1742: DR £15

TRAVERS, WM
1737–46: CR £10 10s; £50; £10; £15 15s; £150; £30; £45

TREVOR, ARA
1737–47: CR £25; £25; £50

TREVOR, GER
1737 & 1740: CR £25; £50; £100

TREVOR, GRACE
1747: CR £100; £22 11s; £50

TREVOR, JNO
1740: CR £50

TREVOR, RUTH
1740: CR £100

John, Arabella, Gertrude, Grace and Ruth Trevor were from a family of three boys and nine girls, the children of John Morley Trevor of Glynde, Sussex. John (?1717–43) was MP for Lewis 1738–43 and commissioner for the Admiralty; his two elder brothers and youngest sister died as infants. Four of his sisters feature in the ledgers: Gertrude married the Hon. Charles Roper and died in 1780 (hence the family of Trevor-Roper); Grace, Ruth (1712–64) and Arabella (b. 1714) were unmarried. On the death of John Trevor in 1743 the male line came to an end and his eight sisters became co-heiresses. Glynde devolved to his cousin Richard (Bishop of Durham from 1752, d. 1771); he and his brother Robert (1701–83, 4th Baron Trevor, cr Viscount Hampden 1776) were the executors and beneficiaries of the will of Ruth Spence [▶ p. 311]. One of the witnesses to her will in 1764 was Eliza Trevor, but as the 1st, 2nd and 3rd Lord Trevor each married an Elizabeth it is difficult to determine who was the witness.[1] 'Lady Trevor' was listed 7 December 1747 arriving in Bath.

Members of the family banked with Hoare & Co.; the ledgers show Gertrude Trevor's account credited with the very large sum of £4,000 by notes on several occasions.

> 1. Burke, *Dormant and Extinct Peerage*; Sedgwick.

TRIBLE, JNO
1737–46: DR £21; £25; £38; £50; £105

Listed as jeweller of Litchfield Street;[1] he valued the estate of the toyman George Willdey in 1737.[2] John might be the same as (or a connection of) Jacob Trible, who was apprenticed to James Tabart [▶ p. 314].[3] The correspondence of Lady Mary Wortley Montagu reveals that he offered facilities for her to draw money from him 'of whose discretion she had a good opinion, though she had never put it to any test', when he was 'off Soho Square'.[4] He is mentioned in a court action involving the creditors of Peter Pons, jeweller, in 1747,[5] and was executor of the jeweller Francis Creuze.[6] The list of customers at Meissen includes Jacob Trible of Amsterdam [▶ p. 211/19 map].[7]

> 1. 1749 poll. 2. Clifford 1999.
> 3. Edgcumbe. 4. Montagu 1956.
> 5. TNA: C11/338/46. 6. Wagner.
> 7. Weber.

TROGNAUX/TRIGNEAU, JNO
1736–41: DR £40; £12 14s; £50; £27 14s 6d; £10 10s; £14 5s; £10; £25; £21; £10; £10; £20; £10; £10; £35; £22; £10; £20

Uncertain identity. Whoever he was, this man seems to have been a regular supplier to Bertrand. Reading the name(s) phonetically might lead to Trigau, but the majority of entries are Trogn[i]aux.[1] Another guess is Trinquand (possibly a brazier, d. 1769, or a peruke maker in Flying Horse Court).[2]

▶ p. 316 Thurett.

1. Wagner. 2. LMA, rate books and newspaper advertisements c. 1707–35.

TRUMAN, THOS/ & CO.
1739–45: CR £23 18s 6d; £30; £24 5s 6d; £25; £30; £50; £35

Thomas Truman, merchant, Broad Street.[1]

1. Kent 1740.

TUITE, NICHS
1746: CR £50

Nicholas Tuite (1705–72), an Irishman, had houses in London and Bath and also the island of St Croix in the Leeward Islands.[1]

1. Hoffman, p. 176.

TURMEAU, ALLAIN
1737: DR £31

Heal lists Allain Turmeau, goldsmith, at the Golden Key, Grafton Street and then Litchfield Street from 1748;[1] Bertrand was dealing with him eleven years previously. He made a will in 1750 proved in 1762, in which he left his effects to his wife Jane 'understanding thereby all Silver Moveables Merchandizes of whatsoever nature they be'. His widow continued the business and later advertised as a linen draper.[2] Members of the wider family were watchmakers and jewellers; Isaac Turmeau was in the Fleet Prison in 1765.[3]

1. Heal LG. 2. PROB 11/874. V&A: trade card 12853.8. 3. *London Gazette* [10526].

TURNER, ELIZ
1739: CR £30; £30; £6 10s
1745: CR [B.Laughton]
1746: Mrs Turner: CR £20

TURNER, JNO
1737 and 1739: CR £20; £40; £12
1737: CR [Wm Pitt]

TURNER, NATH
1737: CR £52

Five siblings in the Turner family banked with Hoare: William, Nathaniel (d. 1737, whose wife was Elizabeth), John, Whichcote and Jane (married in 1714 Charles Floyer, ▶ p. 274). Nathaniel was a merchant of Fort St George, with the East India Company, as was his son Charles. The family should not be confused with Turnour (Earls of Winterton) for whom invoices survive at Hoare & Co. and in the British Museum.

TURNER, WM
1740–46: CR £10; £20; £20; £10; £21; £20; £20; £20; £20 [for Jane Floyer]

Possibly the brother of those listed above. There was also a clerk at Hoare & Co. of this name, whose name appears as witness to many signatures in the ledgers. He appears to have been taken on following the death of Henry Hoare in 1725 [▶ pp. 52 and 224].

TURNER, THOS
1746: DR £65; £20; £20; £25

London chinaman.

▶ p. 241.

TURNPENNY, JNO
1745: CR £17 13s

TYNDALL, THOS
1743: DR £23 19s

In 1746 there was advertised to let, a 'Coach House and a Stable for three Horses, without West Gate Bath, the Back of the House now Mr Tyndale's'.[1] Tyndall died the following year:[2]

> On Sunday 18 October died Thomas Tyndale Esq of Bathford, whose charity was extensive and whose Death is greatly lamented by the Poor.

There is a monument to his daughter in Bathford church.

1. *BJ*, 7 April 1746. 2. 2 November 1747.

U

UDNEY, GEO
1741: CR £100

George Udny, merchant, Angel Court, Throgmorton Street,[1] had widespread interests: 'Among those securing Florida lands in June 1766 were … George Udney.'[2] The papers of the Duke of Gordon in the 1740s have bills drawn on him.[3]

1. Kent 1740. 2. Laurens, vol. 5. 3. NAS: GD44/51/299/1/26.

UNDERWOOD, JAMES
1737: CR £50

V

VALENTINE, ELIZ
1745: CR £27

VANE, MORGAN
1739 and 1740: CR £30; £20; £20; £71 10s

Morgan Vane (1706–79) of Bilby Hall, Notts, second son of Gilbert Vane, 2nd Baron Barnard, was married three times; his first wife, Miss Knight, who he married in January 1732, died in 1739. Writing to Lady Hertford, Mrs Knight reported that 'Mrs Morgan Vane lies in in Hampshire her son liv'd but 12 hours & he is as afflicted for ye loss as if it had been 12 years old.'[1] In January 1740 Elizabeth Robinson reported that 'Mr Morgan Vane has lately admitted himself of the dismall coffee-house'.[2] He was

Comptroller, Stamp Office in 1729, and in 1737 was listed with Francis Poole [▶ p. 302 Grace Poole] at a salary of £400 p.a.[3]

1. *Gents Mag*, January 1732, p. 588; Alnwick: DNP MS 25, Percy letters, *c*. 1734. 2. Montagu (1809), vol. 1, p. 92. 3. Chamberlayne, Pt II, Bk III, p. 91.

VERNON, JANE
1739: 1 CR £60

Uncertain identity. Two members of parliament had wives named Jane: Bowater Vernon (d. 1735) of Hanbury Hall, Worcs. (National Trust); and Thomas Vernon (d. 1726)[1] whose business as a Turkey merchant was continued by James and Thomas Vernon in King's Arms Yard, Coleman Street.[2] James Vernon was a Commissioner of Excise at a salary of £1,000 p.a.[3]

1. Sedgwick. 2. Kent 1740. 3. Chamberlayne, Pt II, Bk III, p. 81.

VERTUE, JAMES
1743: DR £21

▶ p. 186.

VIGNE, THOS
1738: DR £30

Probably one of the family of watchmakers, who were connected by marriage to the Triquet family of London toyshop owners. A Ferdinand Vigne sold 'a Blood Stone in a Gold Watch' to the Webbs (jewellers) in 1752 for £16, paid for with a draft on Minors & Co.,[1] and was a jury member at the trial of Elie Castaing [▶ p. 168].

1. TNA: C108/284.

VIZIN, MARY
1739: DR £21

Probably Voizin, a Huguenot family, recipients of financial relief in the early eighteenth century.[1]

1. PAS Phillips MSS, V&A metalwork dept.

W

WAKELIN, JNO / CHARLOTTE
1743–46: CR: £50; £20; £250; £50; £20

Uncertain identity. Possibly the publisher of the engraving 'Stand Coachman …' (1750) which depicts Chenevix's shop [▶ p. 259 illus.], but as these are credit entries it might be the John Wakelin who had an account with Hoare in the early 1730s. A John Wakelin was rector of Fletton, Huntingdonshire 1730–60, but these are substantial sums for a clergyman.[1]

1. Venn.

WALCAM, JNO
1740: DR £75; £182 14s

Bristol clockmaker, who married Anne Williams in 1753.[1] The following year a broker and teaman of the same name was in Castle Precinct. Records of a further marriage, in 1766, appear to conflict.[2]

▶ p. 167 illus.

1. Loomes. 2. *Public Advertiser*, 1 July 1 1766 [9877]; www.findmypast

WALKER, JOS
1736–38: DR £13; £27 13s 6d; £14 14s; £30

Uncertain identity and a common name. Possibly the inventor of Walker's original new invented clock lamp, advertised in 1731.[1]

1. *Daily Post*, 25 March 1731 [3593].

WALLIS, JNO
1745: CR £55 15s 7d

Possibly the Capt Wallis, listed as arriving in Bath 1 October 1744, but the ledger entry is for November 1745. Or a descendant of John Wallis who was a banker in Lombard Street in 1677.[1]

1. Directory 1677.

WALME[R]SLEY, WM
1737 and 1746: CR £50; £60

William Walmesley, Esq., listed in Whitehall.[1] In August 1734 he signed off payment (of £246 15s) for a painting by Wootton and Hogarth, *Frederick, Prince of Wales in the Hunting Field* [▶ p. 157].[2]

1. 1749 poll. 2. The Royal Collection [401000].

WALTON, ANN
1737: CR £10
1738: DR £10 10s; £10 10s; £21

WALTON, MESSR
1739–45: CR £150; £50; £52 10s; £63; £100

Milliners in Bath who took on PB's shop when he retired.

▶ p. 201.

WARBURTON, BARBA
1741: CR £75

Barbara Lytton, of Knebworth, b. 1710, the younger sister of John Robinson Lytton [▶ p. 291], married William Warburton of Yarrow, Queen's Co. Her son Richard (b. 1745) assumed the name of Lytton in lieu of Warburton in 1762.

WATSON, JONA
1742: CR £50; £50; £50

Uncertain identity. Possibly Thornton & Watson, merchants, Leadenhall Street; but Joel Watson & Co., merchants, Leadenhall Street, is also listed.[1] Alternatively the entry might be for a member of the Rockingham family.

1. Kent 1740.

WEBB, DANIEL
1745: CR £48;

Uncertain identity. He may be a connection of Richard (below): Daniel's entry is for July 1745, Richard's for October. Possibly Daniel Webb (1719?–98) author of *An Inquiry into the Beauties of Painting*, published by Robert Dodsley in 1760. He lived in Bath in the 1760s and '70s.[1]

Or this may be Daniel Webb of Monkton Farleigh, Wilts whose

daughter Mary married in 1716/17 the future 8th Duke of Somerset, of Maiden Bradley, Wilts. (A distant cousin of the 'proud' 6th duke, his claim to the title was accepted in 1750.)

1. Sloman; Foster.

WEBB, RD
1745: CR £5 10s

WENHAM, MR
1743: CR £70

Uncertain identity. A John Wenham appears in the ledgers of the silversmith George Wickes, 1740–44.[1] A merchant in Walbrook is listed 1740.[2]

1. Wickes. 2. Kent 1740.

WEST, THOS
1744: CR £31 4s

Uncertain identity. 'Mr West, Attorney' features in a Bath advertisement:[1] Samuel, son of Thomas West, was apprenticed to Samuel Emes, mason, 1743.[2]

1. *BJ*, 7 October 1745. 2. Bath RO: Apprentice Book p. 35.

WHEATLEY, GEO
1746: CR £42

'Gentleman of Bath', will proved 2 October 1750.[1] According to Roland Leffever's papers (which also mention his wife Diana Wheatley), he was one of the partners in a gaming table at Morgan's Coffee House in Bath, and he had a tenth share at Ashe's rooms in Tunbridge Wells [▶ p. 50].

1. PROB 11/783.

WHITCHURCH, JAMES
1744 and 1745: CR £100; £50

Uncertain identity. Possibly linked to Whitchurch & Newland, merchants, Copthal Court, Throgmorton Street.[1] Ledgers of the silversmith George Wickes list a Miss Whitchurch in 1735/36.[2]

1. Kent 1740. 2. Wickes.

WHITE, JNO
1743: DR £42

London silversmith who was apprenticed to Robert Cooper [▶ p. 264 Gislingham Cooper]; he entered his first mark in 1719. He was first at the Golden Cup, corner of Arundel Street, Strand, then the corner of Green Street near Leicester Fields. He was bankrupt towards the end of 1740. The Duke of Beaufort and Lord Noel Somerset [▶ pp. 251, 310] were among his clients.[1]

1. Sale.

WHITE, MR
1747: CR £10 10s

WHITE, ROBERT
1740: DR £20

There was an engraver of this name, but it is too common to identify.

WHITEHEAD, F.W.
1744: CR [re Walter Wiltshire]

WHITEHEAD, THOS
1744–47: CR [re Walter Wiltshire] DR: £140 11s; £38 16s; £42; £97; £25

Whitehead appears to have had some business association with the Wiltshire family, but his identity is unknown. There is a payment of £1,500 to Whitehead in the account of Walter Wiltshire jnr following Bertrand's closure of the shop. A William Whitehead is named in papers of the executors of the 2nd Duke of Montagu 1752.

WHITWORTH, JAS
1745: CR £10

WILBRAHAM, RAND:
1740: CR £100

Based in Cheshire since the thirteenth century, Roger Wilbraham purchased the Rode estate in 1669. His son, Randle, built a new house on the site *c.* 1705. The entry must refer to the latter's son, also Randle, who inherited in 1732. He was a lawyer and MP for Oxford University; MP for Appleby 1747. Portrait: Thomas Hudson

WILCOX, THOS
1738: CR £30

WILLCOX, JNO
1738: CR £20

Possibly vicar of St Mary Abbots, London; Prebend of St Paul's from 1731 and master of Clare College, Cambridge from 1736 until his death in 1762. He 'left his fortune for the building of the college chapel'.[1]

1. Venn.

WILDEY, MRS
1738: 1 DR £50

Mrs Willdey 'kept the great toyshop in St Paul's Churyard … died very rich' in 1740. The shop was started by her husband George in about 1707 and was continued by his brother Thomas, who died in 1748 [▶ p. 211/5 map].[1]

1. Clifford, 1999.

WILKINSON, THOS
1745: DR £20 2s

WILL, RD
1741: CR £21

WILLIAM[S], DAVID
1736–40: CR £40; £30; £20; £25; £30; £5 5s

Uncertain identity. It is possible, but unlikely, that this refers to the Huguenot silversmith/banker David Willaume (died 1741), whose name was sometimes anglicised.

The will of Mary Deards (mother of Paul Bertrand's second wife) mentions 'aunt Williams': there is no clue as to who she was. A David Williams had an account with Hoare, continued in 1739 by his wife Martha as executor.

Early in the century there was a cardmaker of this name, but these are credit entries.[1]

1. Sun Ins, vol. 1, p. 146.

WILLIAMS, JNO
1746: DR £25

Uncertain identity. Possibly the John Williams from whom Lady Jernegan hired a 'sett of Cheny' for 18 weeks for her visit to Bath 1745–46, at a cost of 6*d* per week. A chocolate pot was charged at 5*s* 9*d* for 15 weeks.[1] He might be connected with James Williams who advertised himself as 'watchmaker, silversmith and jeweller, successor to Mr Roubel'.

Or, as with David Williams (above), he may have been related to Mary Deards; a John Williams was in Boult Court, Fleet Street, in 1717.[2]

1. Stafford RO: D641/3/P/1/3/6.
2. Sun Ins, vol. 6, fo. 177.

WILLIAMS, WM PEER
1741: CR £30

William Peere Williams was killed in Bellisle in 1761, unmarried. He was the elder son of Sir Hutchins Williams (d. 1758) and his wife Judith (related to George Booth of Dunham Massey). His brother and sister both married into the Fonnereau family [▶ p. 274]. He was a customer of the silversmith Paul de Lamerie.[1]

1. Hoare: Lr. 40, fo. 182.

WILLIAMS, WM
1747: DR £16 3*s*

Uncertain identity. Possibly the silversmith who was in partnership with Thomas Whipham.[1] Roger Williams, owner of a London coffee house who was also Clerk of the Course at Newmarket (d. 1747) had a son, William. It is a common name.

1. Whipham. PROB 11/758, December 1747.

WILLIS, JNO
1741: CR £30; £50

Possibly John Willes (1685–1761), MP for West Looe 1727–37, knighted 1733/34.[1] He was a governor of the Mineral Water Hospital, Bath, 1748.

1. Venn.

WILSON, AARON
1745: DR £14 10*s*

WIL[L]SON, ALEXR/CAPT
1743–46: CR £25; £50; £15 15*s*; £30; £52; £25; £25; £150; £50; £21

Capt. Alexander Wilson, Queen's Street, Westminster.[1]

1. Kent 1740.

WILLSON, WM
1743: CR £52 10*s*

WILMOTT, JNO EARLEY
1744: CR £42

A barrister (1710–92) who became a High Court Judge in 1766 and Chief Justice of the Common Pleas; of Osmaston, co. Derby.[1]

1. Foster.

WILTSHIRE, ANN
1739–47: DR £300; £200; £200; £100; £200; £100; £19 15*s*; £19 4*s* 9*d*; £29; £55 7*s* 6*d*; £14; £29 9*s*; £14; £27 11*s*; £39; £140; £368 15*s* 6*d*; £24; £150; £62
CR: £70

The mother of Bertrand's partner, John Wiltshire.
Monument: Bath Abbey [▶ p. 46].

WILTSHIRE, JNO
1739–54: DR £100; £100; £100; £100; £100; £60; £89; £50; £36 2*s* 8*d*; £58 5*s* 6*d*; £504; £24 7*s* 6*d*; £39 13*s*; £446; £354; £481 13*s*; £24 2*s*; £352; £886; £500; £378 10*s*; £141; £7; £604; £111 14*s*; £14 6*s*; £91 12*s* 6*d*; £354 10*s*; £17 10*s*; £150; £9; £515 5*s*; £35; £50; £30; £25
1737: CR £59 1*s* 6*d*

Apprenticed to Paul Bertrand and then his partner [▶ p. 45].

WILTSHIRE, W
DR: £125; £100; £30
CR: £100; £80; £156; £20

The ledgers are unclear as to which family member these entries refer to.

WILTSHIRE, WALTER
1737–52: DR £100; £100; £100; £60; £148; £22; £100; £417; £100; £60; £310; £319 3*s*; £70; £32 10*s*; £24 15*s*; £40; £20; £100; £60; £150
CR: £300; £150; £30; £4; £112 3*s*; £300; £315; £60; £420; £89 3*s* 6*d*

Some entries refer to Walter 'junior', who was in Broad Street, Bath [▶ p. 46].

WILTSHIRE, WILLIAM
1744: DR £20; £46 7*s*

The 1748 Water roll for Bath lists William at Green Street and Sadlers Arms, Stall Street [▶ p. 46].

WINCH, JNO
1737: DR £280

WINDSOR, LORD
1738: CR £105; £50
1746: DR £210 17*s*

Herbert, 2nd Viscount Windsor (1707–58), was MP for Cardiff 1734 until he inherited the viscountcy on the death of his father in June 1738; the credit entries in the ledgers are for December 1738 and January 1738/39; his account with Hoare is headed 'Hon. Herbt Windsor Esq. since Lord Windsor'.[1] He was a governor of the Mineral Water Hospital 1748 and died at Bath in 1758. In 1735 he married Alice Clavering 'worth £60,000', sister of Sir James Clavering, 4th Bt.[2] He was also a customer of the jeweller Arthur Webb, for example purchasing diamonds from him costing £230 on 14 May 1740 and a 'solitaire' on 17 March 1742 at £320, which he later had turned into a cross; he bought from them on 8 June 1753 '2 Brilliant Drops very much spread fine Water (formerly cost £700) for £483, which was paid for partly in cash through Hoare and partly by trading in old stones.[3]

1. Lr. 38, fo. 242. 2. GEC. 3. TNA: C/108/284.

WINTER, DR
1739: DR £6 6s

Lady Russell to Mrs Clayton, Bath, 18 October 1731:[1]

> I cannot say I have found any benefit by the waters ... I immediately sent for Dr Winter; your having once named him was sufficient to prejudice me in his favour. Dr Bave is the man in fashion here; but from seeing him in black velvet, strangely powdered, and terribly perfumed, I never would have any opinion of his judgment; and indeed, Madam, everybody agrees that Dr Winter is a very ingenious man ...

1. Sundon, vol. II, p. 67.

WITTS, EDWD
1755: DR £25

Might possibly be a connection of Thomas Witt, who in 1746 signed on behalf of W. Wiltshire for a box belonging to Lady Jernegan.[1] The entry, in the year of Bertrand's death, does not fit the dates of any of three members of the Witts family named Edward in three generations (1676–1736; 1701–54; 1746–1816). The wife of the last, Agnes Travell, was painted by Joseph Wright.[2]

1. Stafford RO: D641/3/P/3/5
2. Sutton, 2008

WOGAN, NICS
1745: CR £50

Possibly Wogan & Co., agents, Spring Gardens.[1]

1. Kent 1740.

WOLLESTONECRAFT
1745: DR £54

Possibly Edward Woollstonecraft (1688–1765), silk weaver of Spitalfields.

WOOD, JNO
1736: CR £25

WOOD, JNO JNR
1746: DR £30

Architects of Bath.

▶ p. 72.

WOOD, THOS
1737: DR £20

WOOLMOR, MABELL
1736: CR £30

In 1717 Edward Woolmer, a Bath apothecary, took out an insurance policy which was paid on his behalf by Henry Woolmer in London.[1] Five years later there is: 'Mary Woolmar in Stall Street, Bath, Apothecary, for his dwelling house £500, for goods &c in the same place £500, pr Mr Woolmer in Smithfield.'[2] This is confusing. Henry Woolmer is mentioned in the will of the Bath toyman John Hayward [▶ p. 39]. He had a business in London as a distiller, at the Green Man & Still in West Smithfield (1720), and in Bath had a brewhouse and malthouse at the Golden Lyon, Stall Street, Bath 1725.[3] Edward, Henry and Mabell were presumably related to Susannah Woolmer, widow of Bath, whose will proved in 1752.[4]

Mabell and Mary were possibly the same person.

1. Sun Ins, vol. 6, fo. 192 [8124].
2. Sun Ins, vol. 14, fo. 172 [25506] 26 May 1722.
3. Bath RO: 1776 Schedule of Deeds. Sun Ins, vol. 10, fo. 379 [18184] and vol. 13, fo. 411.
4. PROB 11/797.

WOOLLEY, GEO
1746: CR £35

Probably connected with a hamlet near Bradford-on-Avon. A Joseph Wooley was a freemason in Bath.

WOOTTON, WM
1737: CR £100

The name of William Wotton appears in the papers of Judith Willdey [▶ p. 320], when he paid her for Lord Kingsale's account.[1]

1. PRO C104/21.

WORLEAN, JNO
1740: DR £100

WRAY, CHAS
1738: CR £10

Charles Wray started work at Hoare's Bank in 1737 and was head clerk 1766–91.

▶ p. 52 illus.

WRIGHT, ANTO
1737–46: CR £100; £82; £16 15s; £100; £125; £59; £200; £41; £30; £50; £60; £200; £50; £100; £50; £125; £20; £30; £60.10s; £30; £20; £30; £35; £25; £100; £100; £100; £17 10s; £60; £50; £40

Anthony Wright, goldsmith banker, Great Russell Street, Covent Garden, from 1729.[1] Many of his customers were Catholic gentry.

1. Outing. Joslin.

WRIGHT, HENRY
1751: DR re SS Anns £1,060

Henry Wright was surgeon to the Mineral Water Hospital in Bath 1742–94. This large payment probably relates to hospital finances.

▶ pp. 69, 122 illus.

WRIGHT, THS
1736: DR £4 4s 6d

Mathematical instrument maker and toyman; he was instrument maker to George II.[1]

▶ p. 244.

WYKE, PR/ MR
1738–45: CR £100; £36 5s; £30; £49 14s; £34 8s

WYKES, HENRY
1738 and 1741: CR £23 15s; £46

WYNDHAM, JNO
1747: CR £100

Possibly John Wyndham of Norrington, Wilts.[1] His monument by Rysbrack is at Alvediston, Dorset.

1. Burke, LG 1848.

WYNDHAM WM/MR/WINDHAM

1738 and 1741: CR £50; £105; £50; £50

It is unclear whether these entries are for the same person or two individuals. The entry for 1738 'Wm Windham' could be for Sir William Wyndham, 3rd Bt (1688–1740, MP for Somerset), whose first wife was a daughter of the 6th Duke of Somerset. Sir William suffered from gout and was in Bath in January 1729/30 when his wife wrote to her sister-in-law (the Countess of Hertford, ▶ p. 89) saying that 'he has had such a pain in his heall for this four days that he cannot get up or down stairs without the help of a servant and a stick').[1]

The other candidate is William Windham (c. 1706–89), MP for Aldeburgh, who in 1734 married as her second husband the widow of 1st Earl of Deloraine [▶ p. 268]. She was a mistress of George II. Windham was sub-governor to the Duke of Cumberland from 1731 and then comptroller of his household. His wife continued to be called Lady Deloraine and was in Bath also in 1741.

1. Alnwick: DNP MS25.

Y

YEAT, MR
1740: CR £70

Uncertain identity. This might refer to the puppeteer Richard Yeates, but there were others of the same name. Rosenfeld mentions John Yates (showman), Richard Yates (actor), Yeates jnr (showman and conjuror), Thomas Yeates (showman).[1]

Other possibilities include: William Yeat, merchant, Lombard Street.[2] The ledger of the silversmith George Wickes has Mrs Yeats, Dover Street, 1735–36.[3] In 1721 an advertisement refers to Yeats 'at the Iron Railings in Richmond Street, near St Ann's Church'.[4]

▶ p. 303 Powell.

1. *Daily Advertiser*, 26 August 1743 [3933]. Rosenfeld. 2. Kent 1740. 3. Wickes. 4. *London Journal*, 1 April 1721 [LXXXVIII].

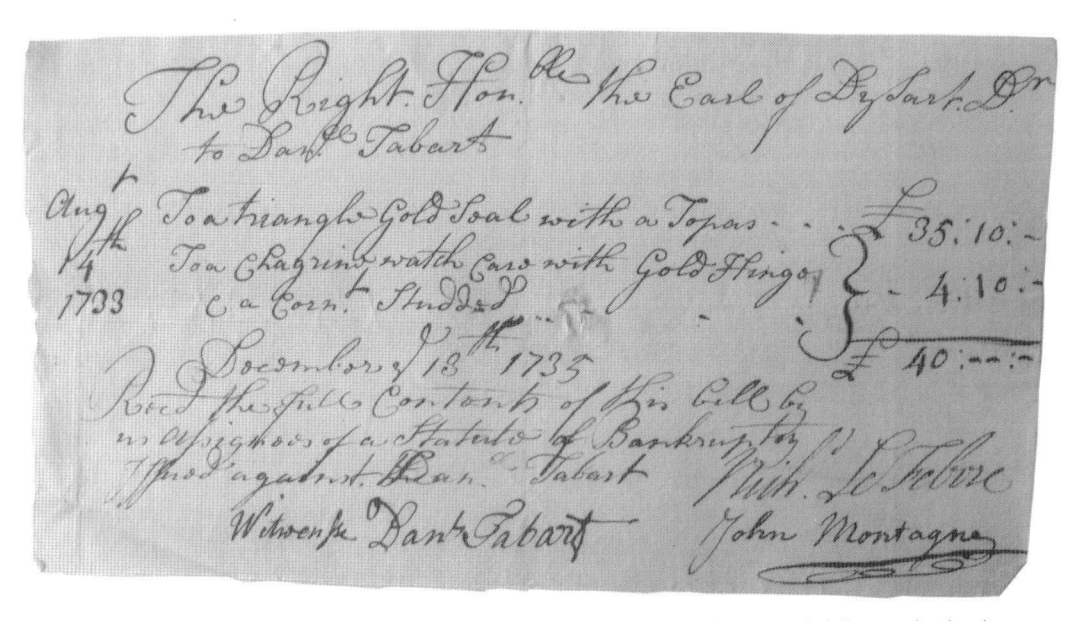

Invoice from Daniel Tabart to the Earl of Dysart dated 4 August 1733 and receipted, following his bankruptcy, on 13 December 1735. (Tollemache)[▶ p. 314]

Bibliography

Alnwick	The archives of the Duke of Northumberland at Alnwick Castle
Badminton	By kind permision of His Grace the Duke of Beaufort
Bath CL	Bath Central Library
Bath RO	Bath Record office, Guildhall, Bath
BL	British Library; www.bl.uk
BM	British Museum, London
Boughton	The Buccleuch Archives, Boughton House; by kind permission of The Duke of Buccleuch, KBE,
Buckminster	Sir Lyonel Tollemache
Chatsworth	The Devonshire Collection, by permission of the Duke of Devonshire and the Chatsworth House Trust
Claydon	Claydon House Trust archive
Collage	City of London Library & Art Gallery (LMA); http://collage.cityoflondon.gov.uk
Cornwall	Duchy of Cornwall archives, on microfilm at the British Library
Dorset RO	Dorset History Centre
Ealing	Ealing Central Library
East Sussex RO	East Sussex Record Office, Lewes
Essex RO	Essex Record Office, Chelmsford
Guildhall	Guildhall Library, London
GH	The Worshipful Company of Goldsmiths, Goldsmiths' Hall, London
Hants RO	Hampshire Record Office, Winchester
Hist.MSS	Historical Manuscripts Commission, BL
Hoare	C. Hoare & Co., London
Holkham	Holkham Archives, Viscount Coke and the Trustees of the Holkham Estate
Hug.Soc	Huguenot Society of London
IHR	Institute of Historical Research, London, www.history.ac.uk
Lincoln RO	Lincolnshire Archives, Lincoln
LMA	London Metropolitan Archives
Longleat	The Marquess of Bath, the Trustees of the Longleat Estate
Lowestoft RO	Lowestoft Record Office, Lowestoft, Suffolk
Maidstone RO	Kent History and Library Centre, Maidstone
Masons	United Grand Lodge of England, London
Masons Bath	Royal Cumberland Lodge no. 41
MWH/RNHRD	The hospital in Bath was called Bath General Hospital, then the Royal Mineral Water Hospital. Archives are catalogued under its title since 1935, The Royal National Hospital for Rheumatic Diseases, at Bath Record Office.
NAL	National Art Library, Victoria and Albert Museum, London
NAS	National Archives of Scotland, Edinburgh
NPG	National Portrait Gallery, London
Northallerton	North Yorkshire RO
Nottingham	Nottingham University Library
Somerset RO	Somerset Heritage Centre, Taunton
Stafford RO	Staffordshire Record Office, Stafford
TNA	The National Archives, Kew
V&A	Victoria and Albert Museum, London
WAC	Westminster Archive Centre
West Sussex RO	West Sussex Record Office, Chichester
Wilts RO	Wiltshire and Swindon archives
Woburn	The Duke of Bedford and the Trustees of the Bedford Estates
Wolterton	Lord and Lady Walpole
Ancestry	Ancestry.co.uk.
Banks	Trade cards from the collection of Sophia Banks [BM].
HinH:	Hand in Hand Fire and Life Insurance Co. register, MS 8674 unless stated otherwise [LMA].
Heal	Trade cards from the collection of Sir Ambrose Heal [BM].
IGI	www.familysearch.org
POB	Proceedings of the Old Bailey, www.oldbaileyonline.org
PROB	Wills at the National Archives Kew [TNA], http://discovery.nationalarchives.gov.uk
SoG	[Society of Genealogists] www.findmypast.co.uk
Sun Ins	Sun Insurance policies, MS 11936 unless stated otherwise [LMA].
TNA	The National Archives
VGM	Vicar General marriage licence allegation / Boyd's Marriage Index.

With the exception of the *Bath Journal* and *Gentleman's Magazine*, unless stated otherwise all newspaper extracts are from the Burney Collection of eighteenth-century newspapers, held at the British Library [BL] available at http://infotrac.galegroup.com

The survival rate of parish and corporate records, particularly rate books, is uneven. In Bath the earliest city rate book is 1766; the earliest records for St James's (the parish for the Bertrands' shop) is 1763; for Walcot (where they lived) 1734; for the Abbey 1784 and for St Michael's (the other city centre parish) 1741.

Insurance records at LMA have not yet been fully searched by the author. Information found in the future that is relevant to the present book will be incorporated into a later volume of this research.

Peerages

Various editions of dictionaries of the peerage, baronetage, knightage, commoners, landed gentry, extinct or dormant peerages and baronetages, have been referred to, in particular:

1734	*An Exact List of the Lords Spiritual and Temporal*, facsimile reprint of *The First Peerage Directory for 1734*, Elliot Stock, London 1902.
Burke, John	*Peerage, Baronetage*, 1837, 1913
	Dormant & Extinct Peerages, 1883, reprinted 1978
	Extinct & Dormant Baronetcies, 1841
	History of the Commoners of Great Britain and Ireland, 4 vols, 1836–38
	Landed Gentry, 1848, 1850.
Brydges	Sir Egerton Brydges, *Collins Peerage of England*, 1812.
Debrett	*Complete Peerage*, 1834
GEC	Vicary Gibbs (ed), *The Complete Peerage, by G.E.C.* [George Edward Cockayne], 13 vols., London 1910.
GEC 1983	George Edward Cockayne (ed), *The Complete Baronetage*, 6 vols, 1900–09, reprinted in one volume, Alan Sutton Publishing, Gloucester, 1983.
Lodge	*Peerage*, 1859.
Wotton	*The English Baronetage*, 5 vols, Thomas Wotton, 1741.

Books, articles and exhibition catalogues

1749 Poll	G. F. Osborne, *Alphabetical Index of those who went to the Poll in the Westminster By-Election of 1749*, compiled 1979, at WAC.
1773 Report	A Report from the Committee appointed to enquire into the Manner of conducting the several Assay Offices, reported by Thomas Gilbert Esq., 29th April 1773; at GH.
Adams & Redstone	E. Adams & D. Redstone, *Bow Porcelain*, Faber & Faber, London 1991.
Alcorn – Lamerie	Ellenor Alcorn, *Beyond the Maker's Mark, Paul de Lamerie Silver in the Cahn Collection*, John Adamson, Cambridge 2006.
Alcorn	Ellenor Alcorn et al., 'Rococo silver in England and its colonies', *Silver Studies, the Journal of the Silver Society*, no. 20 2006.
Allen 1983	Brian Allen, 'Joseph Wilton, Francis Hayman and the Chimney-Pieces from Northumberland House', *The Burlington Magazine*, April 1983.
Allen 1987	Brian Allen, *Francis Hayman*, Yale University Press, 1987.
Al Tajir	*The Glory of the Goldsmith, Magnificent Gold and Silver from the Al-Tajir Collection*, Christie's, 1989.
Andrew & McGowen	Donna T. Andrew & Randall McGowen, *The Perreaus & Mrs Rudd*, University of California Press, 2001.
Andrew	Donna T. Andrew, *Aristocratic Vice*, Yale University Press, 2013.
Angerstein	Torsten & Berg, *R. R. Angerstein's illustrated travel diary, 1753–55*, The Science Museum, London 2001.
Ashley	Thomas Payne Ashley, *An abridged history of the Royal Cumberland Lodge no. 41*, Bath 1873.
Ashworth	William J. Ashworth, *Customs and Excise*, Oxford University Press, reprint 2006.
Baker	C. H. Collins Baker & Muriel I. Baker, *The Life and Circumstances of James Brydges First Duke of Chandos*, Clarendon Press, Oxford 1949.
Barbeau	A. Barbeau, *Life & Letters at Bath in the Eighteenth Century*, Heinemann, London 1904.
Barr	Elaine Barr, *George Wickes 1698–1761, Royal Goldsmith*, Studio Vista/Christie's, London 1980.

Beet	Brian Beet, 'Foreign snuffbox makers in eighteenth-century London', *The Silver Society Journal*, no. 14, 2002.		Palais in Dresden', *Furniture History*, vol. XXXIV, 1998.
Benjamin	Susan Benjamin, *English Enamel Boxes*, Orbis, London 1978.	Chamberlayne	John Chamberlayne, *Magnae Britanniae Notitia: or the Present State of Great Britain*, London 1737.
Bettany	Lewis Bettany, *Edward Jerningham and his friends*, New York 1919.	Clifford	Helen Clifford, *Silver in London, The Parker and Wakelin Partnership 1760–1776*, Yale University Press, 2004.
Bird	N. du Quesne Bird, 'The Goldsmiths and Allied Craftsmen of Bath 1620–1750', *Somerset and Dorset Notes and Queries*, vol. 33, 1996.	Clifford, 1999	Helen Clifford, 'In defence of the toyshop: the intriguing case of George Willdey and the Huguenots', *Proceedings of the Huguenot Society*, vol. XXVII.2, 1999.
BJ	*Bath Journal*, published from 1744, on microfilm at Bath Central Library.	Clifton	Gloria Clifton, *Directory of British Scientific Instrument Makers 1550–1851*, Zwemmer, London reprinted 1996.
Black	Jeremy Black, *The Hanoverians*, Hambledon & London, London 2004.		
Boyce	Benjamin Boyce, *The Benevolent Man, a life of Ralph Allen of Bath*, Harvard University Press, 1967.	Coffin	Sarah Coffin & Bodo Hofstetter, *The Gilbert Collection. Portrait Miniatures in Enamel*, Philip Wilson Publishers, London 2000.
Brett 1986	Vanessa Brett, *The Sotheby's Directory of Silver 1600–1940*, Philip Wilson Publishers, London 1986.	Connely	Willard Connely, *Beau Nash*, Werner Laurie, London 1955.
Brett 2007	Vanessa Brett, 'Chains of office and a "Jews Cup". Richard Hoare's purchases from John Curghey and John Kemp in his mayoral year', *Silver Studies, the Journal of the Silver Society*, no. 22, 2007.	Coombs	Katherine Coombs, *The Portrait Miniature in England*, V&A, London 1998.
		Craske	Matthew Craske, *The Silent Rhetoric of the Body*, Yale University Press, 2007.
Brett 2010	Vanessa Brett, 'The paper trail of eighteenth-century retailers', *Silver Studies, the Journal of the Silver Society*, no. 26, 2010.	Craske 2010	Matthew Craske, '"Unwholesome" and "pornographic"', *Journal of the History of Collections*, 2010.
Brett 2014	Vanessa Brett, 'Nicholas Le Norman's Featherwork', *Furniture History Society Newsletter*, no. 193, February 2014.	Culme 1991	John Culme, 'A devoted attention to business: an obituary of Philip Rundell', *The Silver Society Journal*, no.2 1991.
Bristol 1755	*A Genuine List of the Freeholders and Freemen who voted at the General Election … Bristol … April 1754*, publ. 1755	Culme 1998	John Culme, 'The embarrassed goldsmith, 1729–1831', *The Silver Society Journal*, no. 10, 1998.
Britten	G. H. Baillie et al. (eds), *Britten's Old Clocks and Watches*, Bloomsbury Books, London 1982.	Culme 2000	John Culme, 'Trade of fancy: new findings from eighteenth-century London', *The Silver Society Journal*, no. 12, 2000.
Brydges	see above, Peerages.		
Burke	see above, Peerages.	Dack	Charles Dack, *Sketch of the Life of Thomas Worlidge, Etcher and Painter, with a Catalogue of his Works*, Peterborough 1907.
Butler	Robin Butler, *The Albert Collection*, Broadway Publishing, London 2004.		
CL/CSK/CNY	Christie's auction catalogues: CL (King Street, London), CSK (South Kensington, London) CNY (New York).	Davis & Bonsall	Graham Davis & Penny Bonsall, *Bath, a new history*, Keele University Press, 1996.
Cannon	John Cannon, *Aristocratic Century*, Cambridge University Press 1984.	Defoe	Daniel Defoe, *A Tour Through the Whole Island of Great Britain* (1724), Everyman edition in 2 vols, reprinted 1966.
Cassidy-Geiger	Maureen Cassidy-Geiger, 'The Federzimmer from the Japanisches		

Delany	Lady Llanover (ed.), *The Autobiography and Correspondence of Mary Granville, Mrs Delany*, London 1861.		*Association)*, vol. 80.4, September 1965.
		Fiennes	Celia Fiennes, edited by Christopher Morris, *The illustrated journeys of Celia Fiennes, c. 1682–1712*, Exeter 1988.
Directory 1677	*The Little London Directory of 1677*, reprinted J. C. Hotten, London 1863.		
DNB	*Oxford Dictionary of National Biography*; www.oxforddnb.com	Fleming	Francis Fleming, *The Life and Extraordinary Adventures of Timothy Ginnadrake*, Bath 1771.
Edgcumbe	Richard Edgcumbe, *The Art of the Gold Chaser in Eighteenth-Century London*, Oxford University Press, 2000.		
		Forbes	John Forbes, 'Change of date letter at the London Assay Office', *The Silver Society Journal*, no. 12, 2000.
Edwards, A. C.	A. C. Edwards, *The Account Books of Benjamin Mildmay, Earl Fitzwalter*, Regency Press, London 1977.		
		Forsyth	Michael Forsyth, *Bath*, Pevsner Architectural Guides, Yale University Press, 2003.
Edwards	Averyl Edwards, *Frederick Louis, Prince of Wales*, Staples Press, New York & London 1947.		
		Foster	Joseph Foster, *Alumni Oxonienses, The Members of the University of Oxford 1715–1886*, Kraus reprint 1968.
E-Hill	Howard Erskine-Hill, *The Social Milieu of Alexander Pope*, Yale University Press, 1975.		
		Fox	Ross Fox, 'Robert Albion Cox', *Silver Studies, the Journal of the Silver Society*, no. 23, 2008.
Eglin	John Eglin, *The Imaginary Autocrat, Beau Nash and the Invention of Bath*, Profile Books, London 2005.		
		GEC	See Peerages, above.
		Gents Mag	*The Gentleman's Magazine*.
Egmont	Hist.MSS, *Diary of the First Earl of Egmont (Viscount Perceval)*, 3 vols, London 1923.	Giermann	Ralf Giermann & Jürgen Karpinski, *Das Federzimmer im Schloss Moritzburg*, Dresden 2003.
Eustace	Katherine Eustace, *Michael Rysbrack*, exhibition catalogue, City of Bristol Museum & Art Gallery, 1982.	Gill	Conrad Gill, *Merchants and Mariners of the Eighteenth Century*, Edward Arnold, London 1961.
Evans	Joan Evans, 'Huguenot Goldsmiths in England and Ireland', *Proceedings of the Huguenot Society*, vol. XIV.4.	Glynn	Gale Glynn, 'Some tontines commemorated on English plate', *The Silver Society Journal*, no. 8, 1996.
Falconer	R. W. Falconer, *History of the Royal Mineral Water Hospital, Bath*, Charles Hallett, Bath 1888.	Godden	Geoffrey Godden, *Oriental export market porcelain and its influence on European wares*, Granada, London 1979.
Faulkner	Thomas Faulkner, *The History and Antiquities of Brentford, Ealing & Chiswick*, London 1845.	Goldsmith	Oliver Goldsmith, *Life of 'Beau' Nash*, Sisley, reprinted c. 1905.
Fawcett 1990	Trevor Fawcett, 'Eigtheenth-century shops and the luxury trade', *Bath History*, vol. III, 1990.	Graf	Holger Th. Gräf, 'Sarah Scott: Female Historian in mid-eighteenth-century Bath', *Bath History*, vol. X, 2005.
Fawcett 1995	Trevor Fawcett, *Voices of eighteenth-century Bath*, Ruton, Bath 1995.	Grimwade	Arthur Grimwade, *London Goldsmiths 1697–1837*, Faber & Faber, 2nd edition, London 1982.
Fawcett 1998	Trevor Fawcett, *Bath Entertain'd*, Ruton, Bath 1998.	Grist	Elizabeth Grist, 'Peter Motteux (1663–1718) Writer, Translator, Entrepreneur', *Proceedings of the Huguenot Society*, vol. XXVIII.3, 2005.
Fawcett 2002	Trevor Fawcett, *Bath Commercialis'd*, Ruton, Bath 2002.		
Fawcett & Inskip	Trevor Fawcett and Marta Inskip 'The Making of Orange Grove', *Bath History*, vol. V, 1994.	Grundy	Isobel Grundy (ed.), *Selected letters of Lady Mary Wortley Montagu*, Penguin, London 1997.
Ferguson	Oliver W. Ferguson, 'The Materials of History: Goldsmith's Life of Nash', *PMLA (Modern Language*	Gunnis	Rupert Gunnis, *Dictionary of British Sculptors 1660–1851*, Abbey Library, new revised edition, 1968.

Gwynn	Robin D. Gwynn, *Huguenot Heritage*, Routledge & Kegan Paul, London 1985.	Hounsell	Peter Hounsell, *Ealing and Hanwell Past*, Historical Publications, London 1991.
Hallett	Mark Hallett & Christine Riding, *Hogarth*, exhibition catalogue, Tate 2006.	Howard	David Howard, *The choice of the private trader*, Minneapolis. Institute of Art, London 1994.
Hancock	David Hancock, *Citizens of the World*, Cambridge University Press, 1995.	Hudson	*Thomas Hudson 1701–79*, exhibition at The Iveagh Bequest, Kenwood, GLC, London 1979.
Hartop 2005	Christopher Hartop, *Royal Goldsmiths: The Art of Rundell & Bridge 1797–1843*, John Adamson for Koopman Rare Art, 2005.	Hughes	Helen Sard Hughes, *The Gentle Hertford, her life and letters*, Macmillan, New York 1940.
Hartop 2010	Christopher Hartop, *The Classical Ideal, English Silver 1760–1840*, Koopman Rare Art, 2010.	Hume	Robert D. Hume, 'Handel and opera management in London in the 1730s', *Music & Letters*, vol. 67.4, October 1986.
Heal LG	Ambrose Heal, *The London Goldsmiths 1200–1800*, David & Charles reprint, Newton Abbott 1972.	Hume 1985	Judith Milhous & Robert D. Hume, in *Theatre Notebook*, vol. 39, 1985.
Heal Signs	Ambrose Heal, *The Signboards of Old London Shops*, Batsford, London 1947.	Hurley	Alison Hurley, 'A Conversation of their own: Watering-Place Correspondence amonth the Bluestockings', *18th century studies*, vol. 40.1, 2006.
Hervey	*Letter Books of John Hervey, 1st Earl of Bristol 1651–1750*, 3 vols, E. Jackson, Wells 1894.	Hutchings	Victoria Hutchings, *A History of the Hoare Banking Dynasty*, Constable, London 2005.
Hildyard	Robin Hildyard, 'London Chinamen', *English Ceramic Circle Transactions*, vol. 18.33, 2004.	Hyman	Robert Hyman & Nicola Hyman, *The Pump Room Orchestra Bath*, Hobnob Press, Salisbury 2011.
Hoffman	Ronald Hoffman, *Princes of Ireland, Planters of Maryland*, University of North Carolina Press, Chapel Hill & London 2000.	Ingamells	John Ingamells, *A Dictionary of British and Irish Travellers in Italy 1701–1800*, compiled from the Brinsley Ford Archive, Yale University Press, 1997.
Holbrook	Mary Holbrook, *Science preserved: a directory of scientific instruments in collections in the United Kingdom and Eire*, HMSO, London 1992.	Jacobsen	Helen Jacobsen, *Luxury and Power; the material world of the Stuart diplomat 1660–1714*, Oxford University Press, 2012.
Holburne 2002	*Pickpocketing the Rich*, exhibition catalogue, Holburne Museum of Art, Bath 2002.	Jeffares	Neil Jeffares, *Dictionary of pastellists before 1800*, Unicorn Press, London c. 2006.
Holland	Elizabeth Holland and Mike Chapman, *The Kingston Estate within the walled city of Bath*, The Survey of Old Bath, 1992. [A copy of the 1720s map of the Kingston estate is at Bath RO; there is a 19th-century version at Bath CL. Rentals lists are at Nottingham University; deeds are at TNA.]	Jenkins	Susan Jenkins, *Portrait of a patron: the patronage and collecting of James Brydges, 1st Duke of Chandos*, Ashgate, Aldershot, c. 2007.
		Joslin	D. M. Joslin, 'Private Bankers 1720–85', *Economic History Review*, 2nd series.7, 1954.
Holland 1998	Elizabeth Holland, 'Families and Heraldry of Abbey Church House', *The Survey of Bath and District*, no. 10, October 1998.	Jowett	Judy Jowett, *The Warning Carriers*, special issue of *Silver Studies, the Journal of the Silver Society*, no. 18, 2005.
H-Price	F. G. Hilton Price, *A handbook of London Bankers*, Leadenhall Press, London 1890.	Jowett 2012	Judy Jowett, 'The Le Sage family of Goldsmiths', *Silver Studies, the*

	Journal of the Silver Society, no. 28, 2012.	Meroney	Geraldine Meroney, 'The London Entrepôt Merchants and the Georgia Colony', *The William and Mary Quarterly*, 3rd series, vol. 25, no. 2.
Jones	Louis C. Jones, *The Clubs of the Georgian Rakes*, Columbia University Press, 1942.		
Kent 1740	*Kent's Directory*; http://freepages.history.rootsweb.ancestry.com	Montagu 1813	*The letters of Mrs Elizabeth Montagu*, 4 volumes, printed for T. Cadell & W. Davies, 1809–13.
Kielmansegge	Count Frederick Kielmansegge, *Diary of a journey to England in 1761–61*, London 1902.	Montagu 1906	Emily J. Climenson, *Elizabeth Montagu the queen of the blue-stockings; her correspondence from 1720 to 1761*, John Murray, London 1906.
Kingsley	Nicholas Kingsley, *The country houses of Gloucestershire*, Phillimore, Chichester 1992.	Montagu 1923	Reginald Blunt, *Mrs Montagu, 'Queen of the blues', her letters and friendships from 1762 to 1800*, Constable, London 1923.
Laird	Mark Laird & Alicia Weisberg-Roberts (eds), *Mrs Delany & her circle*, Yale University Press, 2009.		
Laurens	Henry Laurens, *The Papers of Henry Laurens*, vol. 5, University of South Carolina Press, 1989.	Montagu 1956	Robert Halsband, *The life of Lady Mary Wortley Montagu*, Clarendon Press, Oxford 1956.
Lewis	Wilmar S. Lewis, *The Yale edition of Horace Walpole's Correspondence*, Yale University Press, 48 vols, 1937–83.	Moore	Dennis Moore, *British Clockmakers & Watchmakers apprentice records 1710–1810*, Ashbourne 2003.
		Mortimer	Thomas Mortimer, *The Universal Director, 1763*; reprint Gale Ecco.
Lippincott	Louise Lippincott, 'Arthur Pond's Journal of Receipts and expenses 1734–50', *The Walpole Society*, vol. 54, 1988.	Mowl	Tim Mowl & Brian Earnshaw, *John Wood Architect of Obsession*, Millstream Books, 1988.
Lomax	James Lomax, *British Silver at Temple Newsam and Lotherton Hall*, Leeds Art Collections Fund, 1992.	Munting	Roger Munting, *An economic and social history of gambling in Britain and the USA*, Manchester University Press, 1996.
Loomes	Brian Loomes, *Watchmakers and Clockmakers of the World*, NAG Press, London 2006.	Murdoch	Tessa Murdoch, *The Quiet Conquest*, exhibition catalogue, Museum of London, 1985.
Lopato	Marina Lopato, 'Notes on some celebrated pieces of English Silver in the Hermitage Collection', *Silver Studies, the Journal of the Silver Society*, no. 28, 2012.	Murdoch & Vigne	Tessa Murdoch & Randolph Vigne, *The French Hospital in England*, John Adamson, Cambridge 2009.
		Namier	L. B. Namier, 'Brice Fisher, MP A mid-18th century merchant and his connections', *English Historical Review*, vol. 42.168, 1927.
Lowndes	William Lowndes, *They Came to Bath*, and *The Theatre Royal at Bath*, both Redcliffe, Bristol, 1982.		
Lugt	Fritz Lugt, *Répertoire des catalogues de ventes publiques …*, 1936.	Neale	R. S. Neale, *Bath 1680-1850, A social history*, Routledge & Kegan Paul, London 1981.
McCann	Timothy J. McCann, *The Correspondence of the Dukes of Richmond and Newcastle 1724–50*, Sussex Record Society, vol. 73, 1984.	Newby 1986	Evelyn Newby, 'Hoares of Bath', *Bath History*, vol. I, 1986.
		Newby	Evelyn Newby, *William Hoare of Bath RA*, exhibition catalogue, Victoria Art Gallery Bath, 1990.
Mahon	Lord Mahon (ed.), *The Letters of Philip Dormer Stanhope, Earl of Chesterfield*, 5 vols, J. B. Lippincott & Co., Philadelphia 1892.	O'Brien	Patrick O'Brien (ed.), *Urban Achievement in Early Modern Europe*, Cambridge University Press, 2001.
Mason 1968	F. N. Mason (ed.), *John Norton & Sons, merchants of London and Virginia*, David & Charles, Newton Abbot 1968.	O'Connell	Sheila O'Connell, 'Simon Gribelin, Printmaker and Metal-Engraver', *Print Quarterly*, vol. 2, 1985.

Oman	Charles Oman, *English Engraved Silver 1150–1900*, Faber & Faber, London 1978.	Saville	Alan Saville (ed.), 'Secret Comment: The diaries of Gertrude Savile 1721–1757', *Thoroton Society*, no. 41 (1997).
Ormond & Rogers	Richard Ormond & Malcolm Rogers (eds), *Dictionary of British Portraiture*, National Portrait Gallery, London 1979.	Scarisbrick	Diana Scarisbrick, *Jewellery in Britain 1066–1837*, Michael Russel, Norwich 1994.
Orrery	The Countess of Cork and Orrery (ed.), *The Orrery Papers*, 2 volumes, Duckworth & Co., London 1903.	Scott Thomson	Gladys Scott Thomson, *The Russells in Bloomsbury 1669–1771*, Jonathan Cape, London 1940.
Outing	Roger Outing, *The London Banks*; www.banknotes4U.co.uk.	Sedgwick	Romney Sedgwick, *The History of Parliament, the House of Commons 1715–54*, HMSO, London 1970.
Penn	Marjorie Penn (ed.), 'Account Books of Gertrude Savile, 1736-58', *Nottinghamshire Miscellany*, no. 4, Thoroton Society Record Series, vol. 24, 1967.	Schroder	Timothy Schroder, *British and Continental Gold and Silver in the Ashmolean Museum*, 3 vols, Ashmolean Museum, Oxford 2009.
Pevsner	Nikolaus Pevsner, *Bristol & North Somerset*, Penguin, London 1958.	Schrager	Luke Schrager 'Recent research into the missing registers', *The Silver Society Journal*, no. 10, 1998.
Philips	A. S. Phillips, *Huguenot Goldsmiths in England compiled from the Royal Bounty Lists 1687–1737*, January 1933 (copies in V&A metalwork dept. and GH).	Scott	Betty Rizzo (ed.), *The History of Sir George Ellison*, University Press of Kentucky, c.1996.
Portal	Christopher Portal, *The Reluctant Goldsmith*, Mendip Publishing, Castle Cary 1993.	Shaw-Taylor	Desmond Shaw-Taylor, *The Conversation Piece: Scenes of fashionable life*, exhibition catalogue, The Royal Collection, 2009.
Price	Jacob M. Price (ed), *Joshua Johnson's letterbook 1771–74*, London Record Society, 1979.	Sloman	Susan Sloman, *Gainsborough in Bath*, Yale University Press, 2002.
Reynolds	Graham Reynolds, *English portrait miniatures*, revised edition, Cambridge University Press, 1988.	Smith 2000	Roger Smith, 'James Cox: a revised biography', *The Burlington Magazine*, June 2000.
Rogers	Pat Rogers, *Henry Fielding*, Elek, London 1979.	Songhurst	W. J. Songhurst (ed.), *Minutes of the Grand Lodge of Freemasons of England, 1723-39*, 1913; Masonic Reprints of the Quatuor Coronati Lodge, no.2076, vol X.
Rolls	Roger Rolls, *The Hospital of the Nation*, Bird Publishing, Bath, 1988.		
Rosenfeld	Sybil Rosenfeld, *The Theatre of the London Fairs in the 18th century*, Cambridge University Press, 1960.	Southwick	Leslie Southwick, *London Silver-hilted Swords, Their makers, suppliers & allied traders, with directory*, Royal Armouries, Leeds 2001.
Rowe	Kenneth Rowe, *The Postal History and Markings of The Forwarding Agents*, Hartmann, Louisville c.1984.		
Rysbrack	Katharine Eustace, *Michael Rysbrack*, exhibition catalogue, City of Bristol Museum and Art Gallery, 1982.	Southwick 2011	Leslie Southwick, 'The Freemasons' Sword of State … ', *Arms & Armour*, vol. 8.1, 2011.
SL/SNY	Sotheby's, auction catalogues: SL (Bond Street, London), SNY (New York).	Spence	Cathryn Spence and Daniel Brown, *Thomas Robins the Elder, an introduction to his life and work*, Everything Curious, Bath 2006.
Sale	A. J. H. Sale & Vanessa Brett, 'John White: some recent research', *The Silver Society Journal*, no. 8, 1996.	Stace	Bernard Stace, *Bath Abbey Monuments*, 1993.
Saumerez-Smith	Charles Saumerez-Smith, *Eighteenth-century decoration*, Weidenfeld & Nicolson, London 1993.	Stone	Lawrence Stone, *Uncertain Unions, Marriage in England 1660–1753*, Oxford University Press, 1992.

Strong & Allen	Roy Strong & Brian Allan, *The British Portrait 1660–1960*, Antique Collectors' Club, Woodbridge 1991.
Strutt	Joseph Strutt, *A Biographical Dictionary of Engravers*, London 1785.
Sumner	Ann Sumner, 'Gainsborough's "Portrait of Lady Clarges"', *The Burlington Magazine*, October 1988.
Sundon	A. T. Thomson, *Memoirs of Viscountess Sundon*, 2 vols, London 1847.
Sutherland	Lucy Stuart Sutherland, *A London Merchant 1695–1774 (William Braund)*, Oxford University Press, London 1933; and 'The Accounts of an Eighteenth-Century Merchant: the Portuguese Ventures of William Braund', *The Economic History Review*, vol. 3.3, April 1932.
Sutton 2008	Alan Sutton (ed), *The Complete Diary of a Cotswold Lady. The Diaries of Agnes Witts 1747–1825*, 5 vols., Stroud 2008.
Tames	Richard and Sheila Tames, *A Traveller's History of Bath*, Arris, Glos 2009.
Tanner	Sarah Tanner, 'A man who never was', *The Silver Society Journal*, no. 2, 1991.
Thompson	David Thompson, *Watches*, British Museum, London 2008.
Tillyard	Stella Tillyard, *Aristocrats*, Chatto & Windus, London 1994.
Toogood	Malcolm Toogood, *Bath's Old Orchard Stret Theatre*, Cepenpark Publishing, Chippenham 2010.
Truman 1991	Charles Truman, *The Gilbert Collection of Gold Boxes*, Los Angeles County Museum of Art, 1991.
Truman 2013	Charles Truman, *The Wallace Collection Catalogue of Gold Boxes*, Wallace Collection, London 2013.
VCH	*The Victoria History of the Counties of England, Middlesex*: vol. VII, 1982.
Venn	John Venn, *Alumni Cantabrigienses*, Part I to 1751, Cambridge University Press, reprint 1974.
Vertue	George Vertue notebooks, *The Walpole Society*, vol. 26.III, 1934.
Vivian	Frances Vivian (edited by Roger White), *A life of Frederick, Prince of Wales 1707–1751*, Edwin Mellen Press, New York 2006.
Wagner	Henry Wagner, (edited by Dorothy North), 'Huguenot Wills and Administrations in England and Ireland 1617–1849', *Huguenot Society Quarto Series*, vol. LX, 2007.
Waite	Vincent Waite, 'The Bristol Hotwell' in Patrick McGrath (ed.), *Bristol in the 18th Century*, David & Charles, Newton Abbot 1972.
Waterhouse	Ellis Waterhouse, *Dictionary of British 18th century painters*, Yale University Press, 1981.
Webb	*Account books of the Webb family*, TNA, C/108/284.
Weber	Julia Weber, '*Von Moskau bis Lissabon, von Dublin bis Konstantinopel Der Handel mit Meißener Porzellan im 18. Jahrhundert (1719–1773)*', Keramos, no.216, 2013.
Wharncliffe	Lord Wharncliffe (ed.), *The Letters & Works of Lady Mary Wortley Montagu*, 2 vols, G. Bell & Sons, London 1898.
Wickes	Ledgers of George Wickes (Parker & Wakelin and Garrard & Co.), microfiche at NAL, pressmark SD.95.0050.
Whipham	Thomas Whipham, 'Behind the Wallpaper', *The Silver Society Journal*, no. 13, 2001.
White	Ian White, *Watch and Clockmakers in the City of Bath*, Antiquarian Horological Society, Wadhurst c.1996.
Williams 1945	Marjorie Williams, *Lady Luxborough goes to Bath*, Blackwell, Oxford 1945.
Williams 1976	J. Anthony Williams (ed.), *Post Reformation, Catholicism in Bath*, Catholic Record Society, vol. 66, 1976.
Wood	John Wood, *A Description of Bath 1765*, Kingsmead Reprints, Bath 1969. John Wood snr first published this work in 1742; it was revised 1749 and re-issued in 1765.
Wroughton	John Wroughton, *Stuart Bath, Life in the forgotten city 1603–1714*, The Lansdown Press, Bath 2004.
Yescombe	Edward Yescombe, 'The career of William Yescombe, Bath Attorney', *Bath History*, vol. X, 2005.
Yogev	Gedalia Yogev, *Diamonds and Coral, Anglo-Dutch Jews and 18th century trade*, Leicester University Press, 1978.
Young	Ruth Young, *Mrs Chapman's Portrait*, Bath 1926.

Picture Acknowledgements

Short form	Acknowledgement
Albert	The Albert Collection
Althorp	The Collection at Althorp
Ashmolean Museum	Ashmolean Museum, University of Oxford
Bath in Time	Bath in Time – Bath Central Library except for the following:
BPT	Bath Preservation Trust
MWH	Royal National Hospital for Rheumatic Diseases
V&A	©V&A Images/Victoria and Albert Museum
Bath	The Charter Trustees of The City of Bath
Bedford	By kind permission of the Duke of Bedford and the Trustees of the Bedford Estates.
BM	© Trustees of the British Museum
Cameron	Peter Cameron, London
Chatsworth	© Devonshire Collection, Chatsworth. Reproduced by permission of Chatsworth Settlement Trustees.
CL	Christie's: London (King St), Geneva, New York, South Kensington
Cornwall	By kind permission of the Duke of Cornwall
Courtauld	Photographic Survey, The Courtauld Institute of Art, London
Dorset RO	Reproduced by permission of the Dorset History Centre
Geffrye	Geffrye Museum, London: Purchased with the assistance of the Art Fund and the MLA/V&A Purchase Grant Fund
GH	The Worshipful Company of Goldsmiths
Gilbert	The Rosalinde and Arthur Gilbert Collection on loan to the Victoria and Albert Museum, London
Goodwood/NAS	Courtesy of the Trustees of the Goodwood Collection
Hermitage	© The State Hermitage Museum, St Petersburg
Hoare	C. Hoare & Co., London
Holburne	© The Holburne Museum
Holburne	© The Holburne Museum, on long term-loan from a private collection (p. 84)
Libson	Private collection, c/o Lowell Libson Ltd
LMA	London Metropolitan Archives, City of London
LMA/WCMPC	London Metropolitan Archives, City of London and the Worshipful Company of Makers of Playing Cards

Short form	Acknowledgement
London	Museum of London
Lodge 41	Royal Cumberland Lodge No. 41
Mellon	Yale Center for British Art, Paul Mellon Collection
Metropolitan	The Metropolitan Museum of Art, gift of Mr and Mrs Charles Wrightsman, 1976 (1976. 155.23). Image © The Metropolitan Museum of Art
Montrose/NAS	Courtesy of the Duke of Montrose
Motco	Motco Enterprises Ltd
N. Yorks RO	North Yorkshire Record Office, Northallerton. The Fairfax papers held by the North Yorkshire County Record Office
NAS	National Archives of Scotland, Edinburgh
NPG	© National Portrait Gallery, London
Northumberland/Alnwick	Collection of the Duke of Northumberland, Alnwick Castle
Northumberland/Syon	Collection of the Duke of Northumberland, Syon House
Private collections	Anonymous
Royal collection	Royal Collection Trust / © Her Majesty Queen Elizabeth II 2013
Schredds	Schredds of London
SL/ SNY	Sotheby's, London / New York
Smith	Allan Smith Antique Clocks
Spero	Simon Spero, London
Staffs RO	Reproduced courtesy of Staffordshire Record Office
Tollemache	Sir Lyonel Tollemache
V&A	© Victoria and Albert Museum, London
V&A/Schreiber	© Victoria and Albert Museum, London given by Lady Charlotte Schreiber (p. 242 top)
VAG	© Victoria Art Gallery, Bath and North East Somerset Council
W&W	Woolley & Wallis, Salisbury
Wales	© National Museum of Wales
Walpole	Courtesy of The Lewis Walpole Library, Yale University
Walters	Walters Art Museum
Wilts RO	Wiltshire and Swindon archives
Yale	Yale Center for British Art
Photographers on behalf of the author	Dan Brown, Lucilla Phelps

Endnotes

Facts and Figures (p. 12)
1 Forbes.

Introduction (p. 15)
2 Beet; Fawcett & Inskip. The family of Mary Bertrand will be the central story in a forthcoming volume of this research.
3 Dated Kingham 26 Sepr 1747, addressed to his aunt Mrs Percivall at Pendarves, near Helstone, Cornwall. The second letter is dated 14 December. I am grateful to Nancy Shawcross, Curator of Manuscripts, Rare Book & Manuscript Library, University of Pennsylvania, who sent me copies of this recently acquired correspondence, which includes the verses on Thomas Loggan [▶ n. 342].
4 Neale, pp. 26–27.
5 This does not only apply to trinkets. Royal regalia are the obvious example, but writing of diplomats in an earlier period than this research, Helen Jacobsen uses the phrase '… the centrality of luxury expenditure to the world of the power elite.' And: '… luxury consumption was of crucial importance to a career in political service at the Restoration court.' [Jacobsen, pp. 99 and 119]
6 Wickes; Clifford; Barr; Webb. TNA holds stockbooks of Willdey. V&A has the largely nineteenth-century archives of Barnard's.
7 Roger Jones, 'Flouting destiny' in *Slightly Foxed*, no. 36, 2012.

Part 1: Paul Bertrand and Mary Deards

Paul Bertrand in London (p. 27)
8 In 1598 Henry IV of France gave rights to Protestants in France (a Catholic country) under the Edict of Nantes. In 1685 Louis XIV revoked the Edict, which led many thousands of French Protestants to leave the country, however the exodus began ahead of the revocation. Although it was not the first time Protestants had emigrated, the numbers who went to countries such as England, the Low Countries, Germany and America, were vastly greater than before. Many were from the professions or were skilled craftsmen; some arrived impoverished, others were able to take with them the tools of their trade and money in valuables, if not in cash.
9 R. A. Brock, *Documents, chiefly unpublished relating to the Huguenot Emigration to Virginia and to the settlement at Manakin Town*, part 2, p. 5 notes. [Patents. Liber 6, fo. 89; researched by Brian Beet.] Paul, aged about 28, bachelor of divinity (i.e. a clergyman) and Marie Gribelin spinster, aged 18, 'who consents at the French Church, Savoy'. The register of the Savoy Church up to about 1692 is lost. The record of the marriage, dated 20 October 1685, is a Faculty Office licence, Archbishop of Canterbury, Harl. Publ. vol. 24.
10 Beet.
11 'Bertrand, Paul, minister of the Gospel, Calvert Co. 24 March 1686-7-91. To wife Mary, 100 A. "Cox-Hay" on Patuxent R.' and personal estate. IGI: Tax, Criminal & Wills – Maryland calendar wills, vol. 4, Paul Bertrand's will.
12 IGI: Lancaster County, Virginia, USA – wills 1653–1800, John Bertrand's will. Paul Bertrand's wider family has not been covered in this research.
13 In February 1700/01 there is a mystifying charitable payment of 10s to Marie Morin [or Marin] for taking care of Bertrand. She was his godmother. It is unclear why this payment was made (Paul's mother was still alive in 1714), but it may have been connected with the death of John Bertrand, whose will was proved in 1701. The child's age was given as nine years, making the window for Paul's birth 1689 to 1691, but probably nearer the earlier date, as he was 'about 40' in 1730 when he married for the second time. ['Estats d'Assistance reglés par le commité aux Protestant François refugiés, 3 fevrier 1701', *Hug. Soc.* MS 15, quarto series vol. L].
14 Isaac Griblin: Heal LG and Sun Ins, vol. 1 p. 106. However another of the same name was a glass man and japanner [Wagner p. 332]. John Bertrand: 'Whereas Mary Annamiros the wife of John Bertrand, jeweller, hath eloped from her said husband …', *London Gazette*, 19 June 1711 [4863]. A more likely relative may be John Bertrand snr 'an eminent French merchant', died aged 94, *General Evening Post*, 21 May 1743 [1509]. Jacques Bertrand is listed as 'distilleur' in the records of the Huguenot church La Patente, Soho.
15 Rigal was 'metteur en oeuvre'. He married Catherine Gillon 19 August 1704 at the Savoy chapel; was godfather to Antoine Mariot, son of Louis and Jeanne, 16 September 1717 at Threadneedle Street church. According to the will of the jeweller Denis Chirac, Anthony Rigal was his brother-in-law [Wagner].
16 The powers of the livery companies became diluted through the eighteenth century, but the Goldsmiths' Company maintain their control of the marking system for gold and silver. The scattered areas of London outside their jurisdiction, known as liberties, attracted Huguenot craftsmen.
17 Guildhall: Apprentice Indentures 1710–62, micr. series 2, card 62 vol. 21 p. 4157, 3/119. The premium was £20.
18 POB: s17330221-438. Francis Neale was naturalised in 1709, the same year as Bertrand.
19 Masons. Rate books in Southwark do not survive before the 1740s, by which time Bertrand was in Bath.
20 In 1717-18 [WAC: micr. box 187] a Benedict Prosser was in Horseshoe Court; and in 1723 a Benjamin Prosser is listed at the lodge at Goose and Grid Iron, St Paul's Churchyard [Grand Lodge].
21 WAC: rate books micr. boxes 182 and 187. Some rate books for the Savoy Liberty do not survive from before 1745.
22 WAC: Hollywell Ward poor rate. Thomas Ragsdale features in Bertrand's accounts.
23 Sun Ins, vol. 7 fo. 58: Barbara Lowe at Mr Neale's at the Golden Cross in the Strand in the precinct of the Savoy, milliner. The most famous 'Golden Cross' was an

inn, later an hotel still operating into the twentieth century, opposite Northumberland House, Charing Cross — but this is the other end of the Strand to the Savoy. It has not been discovered whether this Mr Neale had anything to do with Francis Neale, Bertrand's apprentice, or with Robert Neale who features so strongly in his bank account later. The Savoy is a considerable distance from Tower Hamlets, the address of Francis Neale snr.

24 SoG: VGM and Boyd's Marriage Index. Dufour was treasurer of the French Huguenot Hospital; see Murdoch & Vigne, pp. 30–31.

25 Mary Magdalen's sister Elizabeth was the second wife of Jean Roussel. By his first wife, Ester Helot, Jean had a son Elias, a gold box maker. Jean was probably the brother of Louis Roussel, father of Peter Russel.

26 IGI. The first christening is the evidence for Marie Bertrand, Paul's mother, being alive in 1714.

27 *London Evening Post*, 18–20 March 1735 [1142] and others.

28 Oman; O'Connell.

29 Sun Ins, vol. 1 fo. 94; and vol. 6 fo. 18, noting endorsements.

30 There is a solitary entry in Bertrand's bank account in 1739 for Simon Gribelin. As this was six years after the death of Simon snr, it may relate to a brother of Samuel, or be a clerical error.

31 Oman 1978, p. 82. The salvers bear the mark of Edward Vincent, London 1728/9. When a seal of office became redundant, in this case because of the death of George I, it was customary to melt the seal and have it remade into a piece of plate, usually either a salver or cup and cover, engraved with a depiction of the seal — in this case the Principality of Wales.

32 Vertue, p. 65; Strutt. See p. 86. Burke wrongly lists the earls, having overlooked the 3rd. GEC correctly identifies the 7th–9th earls.

33 Ancestry: Clerkenwell, Burials of Brethren and Others from 1 January 1754. I am most grateful to Stephen Porter, archivist at Charterhouse, for checking records for me.

MARRIAGE TO MARY DEARDS (p. 37)

34 SoG.

35 *London Evening Post*, 8 June 1731 [551].

36 With one exception the entries in Thomas Harrison's account relating to the Deards family are on the debit side of the ledger. The largest payments are to John Deards in 1716 (£107 16s) and 1723 (£389 10s). The sole credit entry is 'By bill on Elizabeth Deards £67 10s' on 18 November 1723.

37 *Post Man and the Historical Account*, 1 August 1700 [785]. These were the Walks near the Abbey, later described as the 'lower walks' in order to distinguish them from the 'comparatively quiet and retired gravel-walk', created later near Royal Crescent and the Circus, to which Captain Wentworth and Anne Elliot walked in Jane Austen's *Persuasion*.

38 Wood, p. 330. He also wrote: 'In building Lindsey's Assembly House we enlarg'd the Terrass Walk before it from twelve to seven and twenty feet in breadth; and the success that attended all the houses, fronting this Walk, that they forthwith began to level and plant the Grove in the manner we now see it …' [p. 246].

39 According to Wood [p. 243] '… private edifices composed of a basement story, supporting a principal and half story, were called Third Rate Houses; those composed of two stories, supporting an attick, were denominated Fourth Rate Houses.' Fifth rate houses had 'an addition of visible garrets in the roof of the third rate houses'.

40 John Hayward's business may have been carried on in some manner by his executor William Hayward, his 'good friend and kinsman, maltster' [PROB 11/641; PROB 3/30/123]. Rachel Hawley bequeathed: 'To Mrs Eliz Hayes … my fathers picture which is now in Mr William Haywards hands.' He was also related to Robert Hayes, barber and periwig maker [PROB 11/669]. John Hayward had a 'new-built tenement' near the 'upper bowling green or gravel walks' which in 1735 was bought by Thomas Bragg, a vintner, for £450 and one gold watch [information kindly supplied by Elizabeth Holland, Bath RO 0896/1].

41 North Yorks RO: Wombwell MSS, Vouchers and Accounts of the Fairfax Family 1733–52, micr.1128 & 1131.

42 *Country Journal or The Craftsman*, 27 March 1731 [247].

43 PROB 11/695, 9 September 1738.

44 Bath RO: Inrollment of Apprentices 1706–76, p. 16. Also Guildhall: Apprentice Indentures, 13/109, 4157 & 5407.

45 North Yorks RO: Wombwell MSS, Vouchers and Accounts of the Fairfax family 1733–52, ZDV (F) IV-3 (vouchers 1730s).

46 Invoices at Fairfax House dated 1754 and 1764. I am grateful to Peter Brown for this information. An invoice also survives dated 1771, for a cover to a chalice, from Peter Goullet 'working jeweller & toy-man from London in Blake Street, York' — very probably the son of the Bath jeweller.

PARTNERSHIPS (p. 45)

47 1738 *Intelligencer or Merchants Assistant*, printed for W. Meadows.

48 Two hundredweight, three quarters and 14 pounds. 1 hundredweight = 4 quarters or 112 pounds [Penn].

49 Any business relationship (if one existed) with Bertrand is unclear. On present evidence it is impossible to know if he is the same Thomas Pomfret as a man in the wine trade in London. There is an invoice at Hoare & Co. A 'wine cooper' of this name is listed at the Angell in Tower Street, St Dunstan in the East [Sun Ins, 1719, vol. 10 fo. 358 [16288].

50 Wiltshire is a common surname and references in archives may refer to more than one family. John was certainly in the family business, described as 'waggoner'. John and Walter jointly opened an account with Hoare in 1724, which John continued alone. It is possible that Thomas was a sadler and that one of his sons was apprenticed in 1747 to Roger Prosser, a tailor who kept a public house in Bath. Any possible connection with William Prosser, who worked for John Deards snr in London, has not been pursued.

51 Namier, p. 517.

52 Walter jnr was a year junior to John. In August 1740 Bertrand signed Walter snr's bank account on his behalf — surely not something Hoare would have allowed unless the bank was aware of a business connection, see p. 48 illus.

53 PROB 11/913.

54 BJ, 9 November 1747 and 20 March 1748/49. The ledgers at Hoare refer only to 'Mr Paul Bertrand'.

55 Walter snr signed a will on 17 February 1743 although he did not die until 1765; his brother John snr died in July 1743 and was buried in Weston. It is assumed that the entry in the church registers for 5 July refers to the brother of Walter, but there may have been another of the same name. Walter jnr signed off the bank account with Hoare & Co. in his father's name and took on premises in Broad Street, Bath for his waggons (today called Shire's Yard); he had been made a freeman of Bath in December 1742, described as 'common carrier' [Bath RO: Council Book 6], the fee was 10 guineas.

56 The advertisements began in August 1747, for example: 'P. Bertrand and Compy Leaving Trade, their Stock will be sold, at their shop on the Walks, at Prime Cost, the First of September and so continue 'till all is sold.' BJ, 3 January 1747/48: 'Messrs Bertrand and Compy. Having left off Trade, the greatest Variety of Jewels and Toys, with Useful and Ornamental Dresden and China Ware, Are to be Sold at Davis's India-House, Adjoining Mr Wiltshire's Long Room, on the Lower-Walks'.

57 For example there were several payments to Ann Wiltshire. Neither she nor Catherine Lovelace (the previous owner of the assembly rooms) had an account with Hoare & Co.

58 This is supported by the large sums going through John and Walter's joint account with Hoare & Co. at this time; their account was signed in 1753 as 'Walter Wiltshire & Co'. In October 1779 Walter Wiltshire listed a group of bills he was sending to Messrs Hoare. An entry in the Duchess of Somerset's cash book for 27 November 1752 reads: 'Mr Wiltshire Cash Recd at Bath £200'. This may represent winnings at the assembly room, but it seems more likely that the duchess required cash for out-of-pocket expenses, which Wiltshire was able to facilitate [Alnwick: Sy: U.IV.2a, 'Messrs Hoare & Co. Cash Book']. During an earlier visit to Bath, in September and October 1749 (the year before the duke died), the household expenses for a six-week visit amounted to £358 18s 5½d; when travelling expenses were added the total came to £410 11s 6d [Alnwick: DP D1/1/139].

59 Munting.

60 BJ, 10 June 1745. Unless there was more than one Thomas Joye in Bath, it seems he may have added to his gambling income by doing some trading [BJ, 10 June 1745].

61 Goldsmith, p. 48; the business of winding up Nash's estate is also referred to by Yescombe.

62 Nash made payments to Bertrand and to John Wiltshire between 1745 and 1749, but there is no way of knowing what the transactions in the Hoare's ledgers represent.

63 Bath RO: Acc.662. Leffever's father had been secretary to Lord Galway as ambassador to Lisbon.

64 'Leffever to Bristowe: That several years ago Mr John Wiltshire, master of one of the Rooms at Bath, and Mr John Simpson (since deceased and father of the present Defendant Charles Simpson) master of the other great Room, offer'd Mr Nash £100 a year, each of them, in lieu of his share at their EO Tables: and also very lately, within two or three months, the said John Wiltshire and Charles Simpson offer'd Mr Nash £700, that is £350 each by way of composition, or otherwise £100 ... a year, each of them, during Mr Nash's life.'

And again: 'The total of Gain during the Seasons Mr Nash was concern'd is about 8000 Guineas at Tunbridge. Mr Nash's share at a 4th is 2000; at a 5th 1600; at a 10th 800; whereof he has receiv'd only 350.'

65 Baker received substantial payments from Walter Wiltshire jnr in the years following Bertrand's retirement. For example in 1747 the following sums appear on the debit side of Wiltshire's account: £223 10s 6d; £308; in 1748: £1,095 2s, £1,244 18s 10d, £1,370 10s 9d, £1,854 9s; in 1749 £801 2s, etc. Wiltshire already had an account with the bank, opened in 1724. Donna Andrew links 'one John Wiltshire' to John Graham, a quack who spent time in Bath and whose brother married Catherine Macaulay. This could well be John (1762–1842) [▶ p. 46], son of Walter Wiltshire. He appears to have turned Graham's 'Temple of Health' in the Adelphi into a gaming house, which was destroyed by officers of the peace in 1782. Wiltshire 'was found guilty of keeping an EO table and punished'. [Andrew, p. 208]

CUSTOMER OF HOARE & CO. (p. 53)

66 John Houghton (d. 1705), quoted by Peter Earle, 'The economy of London, 1660–1730' in O'Brien.

67 Hutchings.

68 Finding these references has been a matter of luck — no attempt has been made by the present author systematically to check every page of every ledger. Sometimes cross-checking between Bertrand's shop and a customer's account reveals entries that tally, but in the case of Samuel Strode, for example, they do not.

EMPLOYEES (p. 59)

69 Information kindly supplied by the Geffrye Museum.

70 BJ, 16 April 1750.

71 Bath RO: 'Mr Roubel' is listed in the rate book at Ladymead (1766), John Roubel (1776) and Sarah Roubell (1782–89). 'I give and devise to my Sister Elizabeth Roubel the use of the two parlours on the first floor of my Messuage or Tenement in Lady Mead in the said City of Bath in which my said Sister now lives and also of the Kitchen fforwards under the said parlours and of the Garden and Outlet to my said Messuage adjoining ... under the yearly Rent of a pepper corn only if demanded and on condition of her keeping what I have as aforesaid to her devised in good repair ...' [PROB 11/1031]. Roubel may have had one of the properties that are today a row of shops fronted with the date 1736. A painting in the VAG depicts Cornwell House, a seventeenth-century building with gardens down to the river, which was in Ladymead.

72 BJ, 25 April 1748 and 19 November 1753.

73 Bath Advertiser, 25 October 1755.

74 BJ, 23 May 1768.

75 Bath RO: 1766 Rate Book 1; listed also in 1770. Bristol RO: Apprentice Book, 18 December 1758. BJ, 26 April 1770.

76 Information from Anthony Sale. Bath RO: Settlement Examinations vol. 3 1769–72 for Susanna Savage, 21 February and 28 March 1771; Overseers Accounts for St Michael's parish 1767–76, 22 February, 22 March 1771 and 5 February 1774 ; Bastardy Bond no. 14, 27 May 1773.

77 POB: t17560528-2.

78 BJ, 22 November 1756.

79 *London Gazette*, 17 February 1756 [9556]; also 27 July 1756, 15 February 1757. 'Commission of Bankrupt awarded against John Pyke, of the City Bath, Toyman, Dealer and Chapman …'. *Public Advertiser*, 4 December 1759 [7814]. It seems unlikely that he was connected with the well-known watchmakers, John Pyke (father and son), active in London *c.* 1710–80.

80 *Public Ledger or The Daily Register of Commerce and Intelligence*, 30 January 1760 [16]: the stock in trade of Mr John Pyke, Toyman, of Bath.

81 *Public Advertiser*, 20 July 1769 [10834].

PART OF BATH'S COMMUNITY (p. 65)

82 Bath CL. The line of buildings can be traced in maps to the second half of the nineteenth century. The corner was remodelled on a different alignment in 1895–97. The road was widened in 1922. Canopies were added to windows of the shops in Orange Grove, etc.

83 The Misses Walton retained their shop in Orange Grove. Wiltshire's rooms were demolished in 1805 to allow for the creation of York Street; Bridgwater House and The Huntsman's public house were built in the 1740s [Forsyth p. 208].

84 The houses are on the east side of what John Wood described as 'Berton' Street: '… the Houses intended to be erected on the West Side of it were to contain a Principal and half Story between the Plinth and Crowning; but those on the East Side were to contain two full Stories; for which Reason the Ground Rent on one Side of the Way was fixed at a third Part more than on the other … the East Side were denominated Second Rate houses.' [Wood, p. 241] Elsewhere Wood writes that the street 'is fifty Feet broad, and contains twelve Houses, seven of which are fifth Rate Structures' [Wood, p. 335]. Bertrand insured the house, as follows: 'Paul Bertrand of the City of Bath Toyman. On his new built Stone and Tiled house only Situate Barton Street in the Parish of Wallcot without the Walls of the City in my own Occupation exclusive of all of our houses or adjoining Building not exceeding Five hundred pounds … 500', Sun Ins, vol. 61, p. 29, 16 October 1744 [89152].

85 Lady Cope is listed later in Queen Square.

86 Forsyth and Lowndes both say that Hoare lived at no. 6 Edgar Buildings, however the rate books list nine houses in Edgar Buildings and show Hoare at the fourth house from the western end — i.e. no. 4. In 1864 this house and no. 8 Gay Street were in the name of W. Lewis [Bath RO: Walcot Watering Rate]. The succession of property ownership is of interest only in so far as it relates to the descendants of the goldsmith Peter Russel. A report of a 1905 exhibition (which featured portraits of the family) reads: 'Until recently Mr Lewis was the owner of 8 Gay Street, which was the property of William Hoare, though he resided principally in Edgar Buildings. These houses were left by Mr Prince Hoare, the only surviving son of William Hoare, to Mr Lewis's father and uncle, the latter receiving the Edgar Buildings property which has passed, by sale, out of the family, but 8 Gay Street has not, for it is now owned by Mr Lewis's son, to whom he gave it a few years ago. Mr Lewis is about to move from Bath to Salisbury.' William Hoare's house was put up for sale after his death in a sale conducted by Mr Plura — who in 1754 had been Bertrand's neighbour in Queen Street [Newby p. 116; *The Bath Chronicle*, 9 January 1794]. Prince Hoare owned or rented several properties including 8 Gay Street (which was lived in for a time by Mrs Piozzi, better known as Mrs Thrale, the friend of Samuel Johnson) and 1 & 2 Edgar Buildings [note 341].

87 PROB 11/999, written 18 November 1773, proved 19 July 1774.

88 Bath RO: Walcot Church Rate book for 1736 reads 'Queen Street from Barton Farm along ye upper side of ye Square'. Today Queen Street is the extension of John Street to the south of Queen Square, between Quiet Street and Trim Street; Barton Buildings runs off Old King Street. Information about its origins appears to conflict: according to Forsyth pp. 141 and 252, Barton Buildings was developed by John Wood the Younger in the 1760s and Old King Street was built 1764–70 by John Ford, a mason. Ford is listed as a ratepayer in Queen Street and is also in the Bertrand accounts. But a map dated 1740 [Bath in Time no. 18251 of Walcot Parish, Building of Bath Museum collection] shows a range of houses seemingly in a fairly developed state.

89 Mrs Noise may be connected to John Noyes; Mrs Hervey could be related to 'Mr Hervey' in the accounts – but the name is too common to give a definite identification. The name Hoare appears against several properties in Bath rate books.

90 Bath RO: Council book 5, 30 April 1733.

91 Bath RO: Council books 3 and 5, 1728–1738.

92 Neale, p. 175.

93 *BJ*, 31 October 1748.

94 Bath RO: RNHRD, 0386/1/1 p. 42.

95 Bath RO: RNHRD, 0386/1/1 pp. 119 & 144.

96 Newby 1986, p. 106.

97 Bath RO: RNHRD 0386/1/1 p. 308. Henry Wright has one listing in Bertrand's bank account in 1751.

98 This could be referring to the St Martin's Lane Academy in London, founded in 1720 and re-established by William Hogarth in 1735; artists and designers met initially at Slaughter's Coffee House in St Martin's Lane. However it is far more likely that this extract confirms the existence of an Academy of Painting in Bath, for which no records appear to have survived – see Sloman.

99 Bath RO: First Church Rate. Sun Ins, vol. 61 [89152]. Somerset RO: Walcot Churchwardens' Accounts, 2 April 1746 and 23 April 1747, quoted by Sloman.

100 Songhurst. Jean [John] Roussel was at both the masonic meetings Bertrand attended in Charing Cross, and Elias and Peter Russel were at a lodge meeting at the Goat, at the foot of the Haymarket, in 1730. 'Abra Russell' is listed at a meeting in Shorts Gardens in 1730.

101 Toogood.

102 In the 1860s the two Bath lodges came together under one roof. Royal Sussex Lodge acquired the Orchard Street Chapel in 1865 and Royal Cumberland Lodge took a sub-tenancy two years later. The hall still has one of the original theatre boxes.

103 *DNB*; Mowl.

104 Bath RO: Old Hospital Letters 0386/1/39 Misc, undated.

105 Barbeau, p. 38; Eglin, ch. 9; Munting; *DNB*.

106 Eglin, p. 213.

107 It is a printed form, with the detail of the transaction written in. I am grateful to Ann Mitchell, at Woburn, for the following: 'The document which Nash signed is a bond, an agreement to pay a financial penalty if specified conditions are not met; there is sometimes, but not always, another manuscript which accompanies

it such as a mortgage. The formal first section was in Latin until 1733 *Noverint universis per presentes me …* [Know all men by these presents that I …]. It simply states that one person is bound to pay a certain sum to another party. The second part states that if a specified action is performed then the first part will be void. By convention the bond was for a penal sum, twice the amount actually due.'

108 See Eglin pp. 116–17 on the 3rd Duke of Bedford and quoting Goldsmith re Thomond.

109 Nash's account with Hoare shows one payment of £250 from Thomond (who also banked there) in August 1738. The entry in Bertrand's account for Thomond is for June that year. Eglin (p. 116) writes more on Nash's gambling finances.

Part 2: Bath as a resort

BATH IN THE EARLY EIGHTEENTH CENTURY (p. 79)

110 *Gents Mag*, January 1733, p. 48.

111 Neale, p. 49, gives the size of the city in the 1680s. The present church of St Swithin, by Jelly & Palmer, was built 1777–80 and extended 1788. Better records survive today for Walcot parish than for SS James and Michael or for the Abbey parish.

112 Before the 1832 Reform Act several boroughs returned members to parliament even though they had a small population and few eligible voters. Once prosperous market towns or villages, over centuries their population had dwindled, but they retained their parliamentary status and could elect two members to the House of Commons. They became known as 'rotten boroughs'. Among the most infamous examples were Old Sarum, East Looe in Cornwall and Newtown on the Isle of Wight. There were also 'pocket boroughs', controlled by local landowners and members of the House of Lords to ensure that seats in parliament were held by family members and those whose political loyalty was assured.

113 Bath RO: Council Book 3.

114 Wood, p. 224.

115 This had been suggested at least as early as January 1695/96, when Council minutes record 'Sir Thos Estcourt and Wm Blathwayt Esq to make the river Avon navigable between Bath and Bristol' – a member of the Corporation was sent to London to solicit parliament. The plan is again recorded in the minutes in January 1710/11 and in August 1720.

116 Alnwick: U.1.24.m/10.

117 Countess of Bristol to her husband, 16 September 1723 [Hervey]. Elizabeth Felton (1676–1741) married Lord Bristol as his second wife in 1695; they had eleven sons and six daughters. Lord Bristol's son by his first wife died in Bath in November 1723.

118 Forsyth; Mowl; Neale; Davis & Bonsall; each quote various population and visitor figures; the figure of 12,000 was claimed by John Wood.

119 Neale, p. 47.

120 Egmont, vol. 1, p. 117, 19 November 1730.

121 Davis & Bonsall.

122 *London Evening Post*, 15 February 1747/48.

123 Barbeau, p. 108–09.

124 Hughes, p. 17.

125 Alnwick: DNP MS25, Percy letters and MS, nos. 27, 28.

126 A group of silver relating to Lord Warwick was sold SL 5 June 1997 lots 131–34, notably a basin, Simon Margas 1718/9 engraved by Joseph Sympson; footnotes refer to other sales. He was a customer of Hoare & Co.

127 Lincoln RO: Monson 28B/12/4/1.

29 March. Account of the Plate 'yesterday delivered to Mr Hoare'.

That the Gilt plate new Sterling

weighed	644 oz	10 dwt
[…] Gilt old Sterling	1362 oz	10 dwt
Other	24 oz	10 dwt
Silver new Sterling	5348 oz	
Silver old Sterling	482 oz	10 dwt
Two gold tumbers	22 oz	15 dwt
besides the above her Grace had chose out		
Silver Plate new Sterling	1531 oz	
Silver Plate old Sterling	1507 oz	5 dwt
total:	3038.5	

128 Lopato.

THE ASSEMBLY ROOMS (p. 93)

129 Two verses from a longer poem published in *Gents Mag.*, vol. 1, p. 305, July 1731.

130 Hyman.

131 Francis Fleming was bequeathed £20 by John Deards jnr, who died in 1794.

132 Fleming, vol. 3.

133 Wood, p. 225.

134 Egmont, vol. 1 p. 96, 22 April 1730.

135 Harrison's will was proved 20 February 1734/35. One of the bequests of Rachel Hawley was: 'To Mrs Eliz Hayes I give my fathers picture which is now in Mr William Haywards hands' [PROB 11/732], note 137.

136 It is unlikely that she was the same person as the 'Mrs Hayes' who is mentioned in London as a performer at the theatre in Lincoln's Inn in 1718. It is a daunting and largely fruitless task to follow up references to the name Hayes, but it is worth noting an Elizabeth Hayes, listed in London rate books in the early 1740s in the Haymarket, London, location of the Queen's Theatre, where Mary Lindsey had so often performed: *The Daily Courant* [5155] advertised a production of 'The Fair Example' at the theatre in Little Lincoln's Inn Fields, 30 April 1718 [WAC: rates for the Haymarket, micr.1871]. The theatre's cashier was Joseph Hayes, whose name appears on a receipt for 20 guineas for a silver ticket for opera at the theatre, dated 1734 [Woburn: 2/34/1; see Hume, pp. 357–58. Jos Hay[n]es features in Bertrand's bank account.

Hayes' account with Hoare & Co. in the 1720s does not help identify where she was living at the time: debit entries in 1723, 1728 and 1729 include names that might be linked to theatre or gambling (Cranston, Treherne, Woodruffe, Otto, Noon, Thos Threader, Grace Smith).

137 Robert Hayes was related to William Hayward, in turn a kinsman of the Bath toyman John Hayward [PROB 11/641].

138 TNA: C 6/397/94.

139 The Council 'agreed that a goldsmith shall be a freeman of this City … as there is no freeman of that trade Mr Hayes to be the freeman' [Council Minutes, 9 July 1700]. Hayes seems to have replaced John Sherston, who in October 1690 was elected Sergeant at Mace. Several generations of the Sherston family appear to have had dealings with the Council.

140 It is possible that Phillip Hayes was the brother of Mary Lindsey and Catherine Hayes; it is also possible

that Elizabeth became his second wife after the death of his first wife, Margaret, in 1709, but there is no evidence for these suggestions and their baptisms have not been traced. On 9 July 1700 he was made a freeman of the City, for which he paid £40 [Bath RO: Council book 3, fo. 299]. On 20 December 1706 he was fined by the London Goldsmiths' Company 'for selling substandard gold wares; ordered he pay £2 7s 0d the goods cost & £1 19s 6d charges' [GH: CR Bk 10, p. 319]. In 1708 he took a lease for 18½ years 'of the vault before his tenement in the Walks', elsewhere described as 'the Green'; In 5 October 1713 Phillip Hayes leased 'a messuage … over the way leading to Terrace Walks' for 21 years [Bath RO: Council Books 3 & 4]. Later entries in the Chamberlain's accounts (e.g. in 1718/19) record payments for 'The house late Mr Hayes £8; the hatchment there 2s 6d; the vault £1'. At least five children, including one named Katherine, were baptised at the Abbey [Bath RO: Registers of Bath Abbey, SS Peter & Paul]. See Holland; Bird.

141 TNA: C 11/1747/21, Hayes v. Regnart. The plea refers back to 1715 and William Welsh, Bristol merchant, as owner; in October 1717 Hayes entered into an agreement with Mr Regnart, who was a London surgeon.

142 LMA/Ancestry: Ms 10091/55; they were of the parish of St Paul's Covent Garden, in London at the time of the marriage. Hawley (c.1672–1743) was an Irish peer who inherited the title following the death of his grandfather in 1684. Francis Hawley was a grenadier, and saw action at Phillips-Norton in 1685; his portrait is an early depiction of British military uniform. [A transparency is at the national army museum, acc. no. 1990-08-142; see: www.britishempire.co.uk/forces/armyuniforms/britishinfantry/1stfoot1685.htm] His first wife was Lady Elizabeth Ramsay, daughter of the 3rd Earl of Dalhousie, and after her death in 1712/13 Hawley was briefly MP for Bramber, Sussex 1713–15. Samuel became 4th Baron Hawley on the death of his half-brother; he died in 1790 when the peerage became extinct [GEC]. Rachel Hawley named 'my brother Francis Hawley and William Hawley … my sisters Elizabeth Hawley and Gertrude Hawley' in her will.

143 Fawcett & Inskip, no. 1 on their diagram of properties.

144 Mary Delany's first husband, Alexander Pendarves, was a relation and neighbour to Lady Pendarves in Cornwall. Delany, series 1, vol. 1, pp. 63–69.

145 According to John Wood, the theatre was erected in 1705.

146 Fawcett 1998, p. 81.

147 Her will is dated 28 January 1744/45, proved 18 February by Samuel Hawley [PROB 11/737].

148 PROB 11/732. She was presumably the subject of Mrs Delany's letter in the passage quoted earlier.

149 Wood, p. 447.

150 The outline of what is thought to be the building appears on the 1750 Kingston map [Holland].

151 Delamain signed his will on 11 December 1710 and it was proved on 15 March 1714 – he left his estate to his two daughters, Ann and Martha. One of his executors was his servant Elizabeth Warren; the will mentions her 'fathful service' and 'the trust I repose in her in respect of her fidelity towards my said children'. The other executor was Delamain's friend Samuel Burrough, a staymaker of St Mary le Savoy in London.

The will reveals that Charles Delamain had a brother named Henry: no attempt has been made to link him to the Henry Delamain (d. 1757) who was one of Stephen Janssen's associates in the founding of the enamelling factory at York House, Battersea [Benjamin p. 40]. In the 1740s a 'Mr Delamain' performed on the London stage [Burney].

152 At the time of this litigation Pocock in, 1715, was commander of a cavalry unit in Bath in case of Jacobite rebellion. In 1716 Bath Council refused Pocock's request for 'a lease for 21 Years Of and in All that Peice or parcell of ground called the Upper Walks Situate lying and being at the North East end of the Abby Church, within this City he laying out £2000 in building a house on part of the said ground …'. [Bath Council Book 4, 31 December 1716] John Wood wrote that in 1716, 'Mr Humphrey Thayer, a wealthy druggist of London, and afterwards one of the Commissioners of the Excise, purchased the old bowling-green and abbey orchard, with a view to improve each piece of ground by building, at the expiration of the under tenant's leases [Wood, p. 227]. See the 1717 version of Joseph Gilmore's map [Wroughton, p. 58].

Brig. Gen. Pocock died in 1732 at his house 21 Leicester Fields, London, where he had lived since 1710, and his widow Elizabeth continued there until 1745. She bequeathed to St Martin-in-the-Fields a magnificent silver-gilt ewer and dish, Lewis Mettayer, London 1720/1 (now in the Cahn Collection) and a pair of silver-gilt flagons, John Hugh le Sage, London 1746/7 (now in the Gilbert Collection, V&A). Mettayer was the brother-in-law of Bertrand's uncle, Simon Gribelin [▶ p. 28]; John Hugh le Sage was in Great Suffolk Street from 1720.

153 The petitions and statements from the defendants are at TNA in the following documents: C5/356/38; C11/963/16; C11/1225/14. The defendants were: Col. John Pocock; Henry Smith; Humphrey Thayer; Thomas and Ann Hall (she was the elder daughter of Delamain); Samuel Burrows [Burrough], James and Elizabeth Ashley (formerly Warren, Burrows and Warren were Delamain's executors); Thomas Bartlett ('menial servant' to Pocock); and Thomas Harrison.

Lindsey appears to have been nervous about continuing the lease at a higher premium when she was unsure of trading conditions, and the case boiled down to disagreement over who said what, and what was agreed, in discussion over whether she would take a lease for a further year or three years. In April 1716 Pocock stated that she 'having a better summer than she expected was in treaty with the Corporation of Bath the last summer for a piece of ground on the Outward Walks in Bath whereon to build a shopp & House against the next year, but being refused a grant of such Ground she then started this pretence …'. Smith testified that 'she had purchased Mr Long's Ground'.

154 Hume 1985, pp. 62–67.

155 I am most grateful to Thelma Wilson and Olive Baldwin, authors of the entries for Mary Lindsey in the *DNB* and *Grove's Dictionary of Music*. Their advice has been generously given in lengthy correspondence. For more on Lindsey's career see Kathryn Lowerre, *Music and Musicians on the London Stage 1695–1705*, Ashgate 2009.

156 There is one small transaction (£10) for a Mary Lindsay in the ledgers of Hoare & Co. in September 1716, and a further entry in 1733 for Mrs Mary Linsey (the

clerks at the bank often used different spelling for names) this time for the more substantial sum of £300 [ledger 19 fo. 274 and ledger 34 fo. 388].

157 Burke 1837.

158 *Applebee's Weekly Journal*, 16 July 1720; *Daily Post*, 22 July 1720 [252]. *Boston Gazette* 4–11 December 1721 [107].

159 Grist; and *Daily Courant*, 23 March 1704 [604], advertising a performance at the Theatre Royal, Drury Lane.

160 Holkham: A/7, fo.151.

161 Hervey: 12 & 16 August 1721.

162 Wood, pp. 242 and 319.

163 Goldsmith, pp. 62–70. Wood also related the story, as the girl lodged with him; he was away at the time of her suicide in 1731. 'Sylvia' was Frances Braddock, a daughter of Gen. Edward Braddock.

164 Delany, vol. 1, series 1, p. 566, 17 August 1736: Mrs Pendarves to her sister, Ann Granville.

165 Catherine Hayes: PROB 11/645, written 27 November 1730, proved 20 July 1731. One of the witnesses was Edward Lloyd, possibly the man who later features in Bertrand's bank account.

Mary Lindsey: PROB 11/678, written 1 August 1732, proved 21 August 1736; Wood says she died on 11 August.

Catherine Lovelace: PROB 11/705, written 8 January 1739, codicil 17 May 1740 witnessed by Samuel Purlewent; the will was proved in London 19 September 1740 by William Robinson (possibly also in Bertrand's bank account). Wood describes Lovelace as Lindsey's maid, Fleming as her housekeeper; she may have had family ties with Thomas Harrison. She left her estate to her nephew Francis Lovelace, perhaps the son of Paul and Elizabeth Lovelace, baptised at St Ann, Blackfriars, on 28 August 1715. Paul Lovelace witnessed Thomas Harrison's signature in a ledger at Hoare's bank in July 1712.

166 This is supported by the account of the Hon. Dodington Grevile at Hoare & Co. which in 1739 shows payments to Walter Wiltshire, Mrs Lovelace and Ann Wiltshire. There are also several payments to Mrs Hayes and Eliza Hawley [ledger O fos. 258 & 278]. Perhaps the opening of Bertrand's bank account in May 1736 was linked to Lindsey's death three months later.

WHEN TO GO AND HOW TO GET THERE (p. 105)

167 Holkham: A/5 Household accounts, fo. 144. When Thomas Coke of Holkham and his wife visited Bath in May 1721, her expenses for the three-day journey amounted to £25 6s 3d.

168 Polite reminders were sent out: 'As the Payment of your Coach Duty may have slipt your Memory, therefore permit me to remind you, that your last Year's Payment determined 26th Day March 1751. John Draper.' Essex RO: Mildmay, D/DM/A7.

169 Daniel Finch to his wife Lady Essex Finch, 19 July 1680 [Hist.MSS, vol. 71 p. 81].

170 Lincoln RO: Monson 10/1A/1. *Family Household Book, the Earl of Rockingham 1715–23*, pp. 167–68.

171 'The Bath Flying Stage Coach, in two Days Will begin flying the 1st of April next, from the One Bell Inn in the Strand, and will set out Mondays, Wednesdays and Fridays, and come in Tuesdays, Thursdays and Saturdays', *Daily Advertiser*, 23 March 1745 [4426] – one of several firms that regularly advertised journey times in a variety of newspapers.

172 *BJ*, 26 August 1745. *The Public Advertiser*, 3 April 1766 advertised: 'The London Bath and Bristol Machines will set out on Sunday the 13th instant at Ten o'clock in the Evening and continue going every Sunday Tuesday and Thursday from the Swan Inn, Holborn Bridge … Insides to and from Bath in one Day £1 8s 0d to and from Bath in two Days £1 5s 0d. Children and Outsides Half Price … Inside Passages to be allowed 14 lb. Children and outsides 7 lb. Weight of Luggage …'. By the 1790s travelling time was down to 10 hours in good weather.

173 *BJ*, 27 October 1746.

174 *Farley's Bristol Newspaper*, 24 December 1726 (report dated Bath 10 December) quoted Fawcett 1995; *BJ*, 23 February 1746/47.

175 POB: t17530502-65.

176 *BJ*, 20 July 1747.

177 Hervey: 12 August 1721.

178 *The London Daily Post and General Advertiser*, 21 October 1738.

179 Hervey: 21 August 1721.

180 POB: t17210525-57 and t17220510-3. Hervey: 12 August 1721.

181 Bath RO: Avon Navigation Agreement 1735, quoted Fawcett 1995, p. 19.

182 Claydon: Sir Edmund Verney Bt, 4/7/36.

183 Dorset RO: Fox-Strangways archives, D/FAI, Box 2213 part A.

184 *Universal Spectator and Weekly Journal*, 19 April 1729 [XXIX].

185 Sources differ as to whether the marriage was in 1735 or 1736: GEC; *Read's Weekly Journal or British Gazetteer*, 17 April 1736 [606].

186 Lincoln RO: Monson 10/1A/1. *Family Household Book, the Earl of Rockingham 1715–23*.

187 Benjamin Mildmay (1672–1756) was Chief Commissioner of the Salt Duties 1714–20 and Commissioner of Excise 1720–28, when he succeeded his brother as Lord Fitzwalter; he was awarded an earldom in 1730. His accounts begin when he married, at the age of 51, the widow of the Earl of Holdernesse. Her daughter Caroline married Lord Ancram, later Marquis of Lothian. Fitzwalter's accounts include clothing and trinkets for his step-children and the Ancrams' children Lady Louisa and Lord Newbattle. Essex RO: Mildmay, D/DM/A4–8 from which A. C. Edwards transcribed many, but not all, of the entries for toyshops given here.

WHERE TO STAY (p. 115)

188 *London Evening Post*, 12 September 1732 [747]. Baron Comyns was Sir John Comyns, Baron of the Exchequer.

189 BL Hist. MSS, vol. 71, II: A. G. Finch, Rutland, p. 467.

190 Neale, pp. 39–40.

191 For example *BJ*, 24 November 1746: 'William George, grocer and chandler, is remov'd from the Parade to a shop over against the White Hart Inn in Stall Street, where he continues to sell and lett to hire as usual. China-ware, Glasses &c.'

192 Holkham: Household accounts, A/5 fo. 144 and A/7 fo. 256.

193 Hervey: 14 and 23 September 1723.
194 Mowl, p. 37.
195 Dorset RO: D/HAB/F24.
196 Neale, pp. 40 & 141; Jenkins, p. 96; Eglin, p. 151.
197 Stafford RO: D641/3/P/1/3/6 and D641/3/P/1/3/4.
198 Fawcett & Inskip.
199 Baker.
200 Cannon, p. 127.
201 Jenkins.

What to do: the daily round (p. 121)

202 Mahon, vol. 3, 2 November 1734.
203 The Duke of Beaufort's accounts show regular payments that presumably represent his subscription and other expenditure, e.g. £21 to Eliz Hayes on 15 January 1739, and £21 to Lady Hawley on 10 January 1744. [Badminton: FmJ 3/7.]
204 Penn, p. 129.
205 Defoe, vol. 2, p. 51.
206 *BJ*, 17 September 1744.
207 Mahon, vol. 3, 2 November 1734; Montagu 1805, vol. 1, p. 80. Both incidents presumably refer to the wife of the 8th Duke, Maria, née Shireburn (1692–1754).
208 Duke of Bedford: Scott Thomson, p. 195. No invoices from Bertrand were found at Woburn, and only two (for small amounts) from William Deards to the 4th Duke.
209 'Holt at 10s per Doz, Bath at 7s 6d pr Doz or 4s pr half Doz, Bristol at 6 pr Doz, Scarborough at 7.6 pr Doz or 4 pr half Doz, Pierment at 14s pr Doz, german Spar at 14 pr Doz & half Flasks 10s pr Doz. NB Fresh Holt, Bath & Bristol Water every Monday by my own Waggons.' [Lincoln RO: Thomas Ashby, ASW 2/104 vouchers. Bill to Mr Henry Lee, 12 Duke Street, Grosvenor, 26 July 1737.]
210 First quote: *BJ*, 13 January 1745/6. This must refer to Richard Rundell, father of Philip – their relationship was established by Sarah Tanner. Second quote: *BJ*, 1 June 1747 and 15 May 1749.
211 Duchess of Marlborough to Lady Cowper, 3 September 1716, quoted in *Diary of Mary Countess Cowper 1714–20*, London 1864.
212 Mahon vol. 3, 2 November 1734, writing of the friend he nicknamed 'Amoretto', the Hon. Robert Sawyer Herbert.
213 Holland: no. 38 KE.
214 NAS: GD44/51/465/4/39.
215 *Daily Advertiser*, 22 January 1745 4446]. Coindreau was listed bankrupt 'of St Martin in the Fields', *Gents Mag*, vol. 14, November 1744, p. 619.
216 Laird.
217 Thayer's (later Wiltshire's) room was 85 ft × 30 ft (approximately 26 m × 9 m); Simpson's room was 90 ft × 36 ft (approximately 27.5 m × 11 m).
218 *BJ*, 2 November 1747.
219 Lowndes. Holland (no. 20) shows another building described as a a theatre in 1743, to the south of the city.
220 *BJ*, 7 October 1745: 'The wonderful and surprizing MOOR is now at the Greyound Inn in the Market Place, Bath, who has the Gift of two Voices, one of a Man, the other of a child, which he conveys to any part of the House, and has given general Satisfaction to all who have heard him. He takes no Money till the performance is over. NB He will wait upon Gentlemen and Ladies at their Houses and Lodgings if sent for.'
221 *BJ*, 21 September 1745.

222 Saville, p. 33.
223 *Tatler*, 19–21 July 1709 [44]; 2–4 August [90]; 31 December – 2 January 1709/10 [115]. Powell came from Dublin and worked in both London and Bath. One advertisement was for performances in London 'at Punch's Opera at Litchfield Street'. Powell in 1713, TNA: C 11/1225/14. Anthony and John Powell, in Bertrand's bank account in 1740, might perhaps be related.
224 PROB 11/759, will written 1736, proved January 1747/48.
225 *Daily Journal*, 26 January 1732, 7 February 1732, 29 March 1732; again in the 1740s.
226 In July 1760, shortly before the sale of the brothers' figures, the Society for the Encouragement of Arts, Manufactures and Commerce included another kind of wax modelling among the categories they offered to students: 'for the best Models in Wax of Figures of Beasts or Birds, Fruit Flowers or Foliage (fit for Goldsmiths or any Workers in Metal) by Youths under the Age of Nineteen … fifteen guineas'. *Public Advertiser*, 2 July 1760 [8004].
227 *Original Weekly Journal*, 22 February 1718/19, quoted by Black, p. 51. Gambling at court was permitted through the Christmas season.
228 Hervey: 22 April 1723, and 18 September 1723.
229 Mahon: 2 November 1734.
230 *BJ*, 14 January 1744/45. Lord Winchilsea and his sister Isabella [pp.108 and 162–63] were two of an estimated thirty children of the 7th Earl.
231 *Weekly Journal*, 26 April 1718 [72].
232 Munting.
233 *BJ*, 5 November 1750, quoted by Eglin, p. 212.
234 Connely, p. 135.

Royalty and their retinues (p. 143)

235 *Public Advertiser*, 7 December 1754.
236 Egmont, vol. 1, p. 472.
237 *Gents Mag*., 1734.
238 See SL 20 November 1994 lot 81 for a box also decorated with a medallion of Prince Frederick.
239 Alnwick: DNP MS25, Percy Letters & MSS, no. 102. Lord Hertford's house is now the central building of Marlborough College.
240 Bird: Saturday, 26 January 1733/34.
241 *Gents Mag*.
242 *Daily Gazeteer*, London edition 4 May 1736 [266], a report written from Bath on 1 May.
243 *The London Daily Post and General Advertiser*, 21 October 1738.
244 Bath RO: City Accounts 1739/40. Chamberlain's accounts 1733–71. Council Book 5, 3 November 1738.
245 Edwards, p. 128.
246 *BJ*, 29 September 1746: 'Married Edward Godfrey Esq deputy treasurer to PofW, to Miss Miles, dau of Mr Miles Grocer to His Majesty.' Previously 1st Clerk, he was appointed Deputy Treasurer in the Prince's household, under John Hedges, in December 1734.
247 Sedgwick; McCann. Pelham was the second son of Sir Nicholas Pelham of Catsfield and Crowhurst, brother of Thomas Pelham of Lewes.
248 For example the credit balance of his account in May 1741 was £16,291 14s 3d. Large transactions included: 29 September 1737 By Ralph Bridge £9,783 6s 9d, and on the debit side: 9 November 1737 To James Colebrooke £8,759 11s. The ledgers do not reveal whether the entries are personal or official transactions.

249 Chamberlayne, Pt II Bk III pp. 207 and 248; Vivian, p. 104. He was deputy cofferer to the Household 1749-54.
250 Barr, p. 95: The account in Wickes's ledger is dated 26 October 1736. 'To a gold cup 58oz @ £3 15s 6d, £218 19s 0d; To making £80 0s 0d.; To a case £2 2s 0d; a total of £301 1s.
251 In 1729 Johann Shutz was made a Groom of the Bedchamber in the Prince's household and in 1742 Master of Robes; in 1737 he was Steward of the Duchy of Cornwall and Warden of the Stanneries. His daughter Anne Maria married Sir John Griffin. Johann's brother Augustus, whose London address was in Brook St, was Keeper of the Privy Purse in the Lord Chamberlain's office and 'Comptroller upon the Issues and Payments of the Receiver-General' in the Customs Office at a salary of £400 [IHR website; Vivian p.103; Chamberlayne, Pt II, Bk III, pp. 62, 210, 216 and 248; 1749 poll]. In the next generation, Hogarth painted 'Francis Matthew Schutz in his bed' in the late 1750s. The wills of several members of the Schutz family are summarised in Wagner.
252 His bank account shows some payments of £100 and £50 a time to Bertrand and to John Wiltshire between 1745 and 1749, but there is nothing to indicate what they represent.
253 Mrs le Grand and Edward Southwell are both mentioned in her will; the account of Sir Watkin Williams Wynn in January 1737 shows the large payment of £1,030 to Sir Edward Dering, who was a cousin; Daniel Dering, another cousin, was Auditor General to the Prince of Wales 1730. The sale of the contents of Belvedere, (Christie's 1980 and see Martha R. Severens, *Magazine Antiques*, November 1995) contained portraits of Sir John Percival and the Southwell family; Sir Edward Dering was painted by Pompeo Batoni c. 1759 (private collection, Museum of Fine Arts Boston).
254 Egmont: vol. 1, p. 1; vol. 3, p. 318; Chamberlayne, Pt II, Bk III, p. 256.
255 Delany: vol. 1, pp. 268-69.
256 Egmont: vol. 3, p. 318.
257 PROB 11/755.
258 *The Slaves of Mrs Allen and her Computation of their Value*, James Murray Robins Papers, Massachusetts Historical Society.
259 http://digital.lib.ecu.edu
260 Beet.
261 Kent, 1740.

SUMMER AT BRISTOL (p. 165)
262 Hervey: 22 April 1723, and 18 September 1723.
263 Waite.
264 Angerstein, p. 132.
265 John Taylor, watchmaker, was made a freeman on 13 July 1730, £21. The John Taylor who was apprenticed 8 November 1734 must therefore have been his son, though Taylor's will mentions no children, only his wife Elizabeth. Thomas Rogers (brother of William) was apprenticed to him in 1734 [Bath RO: Council Book 5 1728-38; Enrollment of Apprentices 1706-1776, p. 19]. Taylor's signature on his will [PROB 11/274] was witnessed by Francis and Bridget Cornish, possibly the parents of another apprentice, James Cornish. Advertisements: *Daily Advertiser*, 28 February 1744 [4092] and BJ, 25 Juy 1748.
   Ian White records one man working 1730-70 rather than two generations. See also: Bird.

266 John Kemp supplied a gold chain to Richard Hoare in 1745 for his term of office as Lord Mayor; see Brett 2007.
267 POB t17450116-16. *Daily Advertiser*, 28 February 1744 [4092]: To be Lett in Bath/The House and Shop of the late Mr John Taylor, Jeweller, deceas'd, in the Church-Yard, it being an accustom'd Shop./Enquire of Mr Ed: Kingston, Apothecary, in Bath.
268 TNA: C 108/284.

OTHER SHOPKEEPERS AND ARTISTS IN BATH (p. 171)
269 Louis Simond and Richard Warner, quoted in Tames, p. 171.
270 Sources of information about these tradesmen, who were a crucial component of Bath's success, include records of apprenticeships, freedoms, trade cards and newspaper advertisements [Bath RO and Bath CL].
271 Bath RO: Council Book 3, 9 July 1700 records a fee of £2, but Bird quotes £40; his article gives further information on the goldsmiths mentioned here, and others. Phillip Hayes had a shop in Orange Grove (the premises nearest the passageway to the Terrace).
272 Bath RO: Freemen's Book 1697-1775, listed 17 July 1733; Council Book 1632-1775 has 'Peter Goulet 13 July 1730 £31 10s; and in Book 5, 17 July 1733, Peter Goulet £10 10.
273 Beet: for Derussat.
274 BJ, 21 March 1747/48: '... at Mrs Axford's in the Grove, sets all sorts of Jewels, viz Fancy things, earrings, seals, buckles &c to the best Advantage and in the Newest Taste, And makes Mourning Rings very neat, All as cheap as in London *Arms and cyphers engrav'd on seals or plate; and money for old Gold or Silver.'
275 Bath RO: Chamberlain's Accounts, 1733-71; 1776 Schedule of Deeds.
276 BJ, 25 July 1748.
277 Songhurst. Bath RO: Council Book 1684-1711 fo. 503 '4 October 1708 Philip Masters lease near Gravel Walks also his son Philip and daughter Elizabeth'; later in the possession of James Masters. Inrollment of apprentices 1706-76, pp. 20 and 128, when Benedict was described as 'goldsmith'.
278 These include bills to Frederick, Prince of Wales, who spent £367 7s with Basnett in 1738 [Vivian, p. 966].
279 Bennet's firm latterly had an account with Walter Wiltshire at Gosling's Bank [V&A]. An invoice survives to Viscount Glenorchy, receipted by T. Hooper [NAS: GD112/21/269].
280 In February 1717/18 Philip Ditcher of Westgate St, Gent, insured 'his house being the dwelling house only of John Leader' [Sun Ins, vol. 7 fo. 307 [10468]]. Ditcher's millinery shop in the Grove was taken over by George Speren (Fawcett & Inskip).
281 *The Public Advertiser*, 19 March 1767. Tanner.
282 BJ, 28 May 1744 and 1 October 1744.
283 Bath RO: 1776 Schedule of Deeds, p. 203.
284 Joanna Davis is also noted here: Holland (M4184 Register of the Duke of Kingston, Nottingham University); Bath RO.
285 PROB 11/865. Coward's will was witnessed by Lewis Clutterbuck; he left a guinea for the purchase of a ring to the silversmith Philip Masters and a shoemaker, Lawrence Cottle.
286 I am grateful to Kate Devlin, at Alnwick, who checked current inventories on my behalf.
287 Songhurst; Bath RO.

288 Kielmansegge, p. 122.
289 Delany, vol. III, p. 466.
290 Orrery, vol. 1, p. 99: John Earl of Orrery to Counseller Kempe, Bath 16 October 1731.
291 *Post Boy*, 7 January 1721 [4909].
292 Hyman, p. 13.
293 Bird: Abbey registers. Bath RO: Inrollment of apprentices 1706–76.
294 *Public Advertiser*, 20 March 1760 [7916].
295 William Rogers is a common name, and no conclusions can be drawn from the following information. Rogers was at a shop 'fronting the Abbey Church' in 1749, presumably the property for which he paid rates in the Church Yard in Bath in 1766 (the earliest rate book available). He was not there by the first quarter of 1768. 'Wm Rogers' also paid rates on a house in Kingston Street, presumably where he lived (immediately next to 'the Duke of Kingston's Baths', later listed as Abbey House), from 1766 until 1775; by December 1776 George Williams was there.

Philip Rundell completed his apprenticeship in 1767. John Bridge was apprenticed in 1769. On 24 December 1767 there appeared in *The Public Advertiser* the following notice: 'Whereas Luke Miller, a Covenant-Servant to William Rogers, Shagreen-case Maker, in Naked-Boy Court, Ludgate Hill, has left his said Master without an Cause assigned. This is to warn all Persons not to employ the said Luke Miller, as they shall answer the same at their Peril.' Naked Boy Court was immediately behind 32 Ludgate Hill, the premises at that time of Theed & Pickett, later Rundell & Bridge. In 1773 a William Rogers is listed in the Report on Assay Offices. Rogers was bankrupt in 1775. *Lloyd's Evening Post*, 3–6 February 1775 [2747].

It seems highly unlikely that a jeweller from Bath turned into a shagreen case maker in London near the end of his career, but the coincidence of location and name is worth noting.
296 *BJ*, 30 October 1749 and other issues.
297 Sloman, p. 12.
298 V&A: 94.B.25. E 366-467-1952.
299 Bath RO: Chamberlain Account Rolls typescript, vol. 2. 'A Bill for the Chamber of Bath, 5 August 1737. To 22 Doz of Plates Engraved wth the City Arms and a Motto at 4*s* per Doz. Rd Matravers Mayor; 10 October 1738 To Mr Skinner Engraving of 5 Doz of dishes ye City arms and an inscription £1 10*s*.' Council Book 6, 9 February 1738. RNHRD, 0386/1, p.144, 3 April 1740.
300 *BJ*, 22 April 1745.
301 *BJ*, 1 October 1750.
302 Thomas Thorpe, *An Actual Survey of the City of Bath … and of Five Miles Round*, engraving published 1742.
303 Bath RO: married by special licence at Widcombe, 12 June 1743. Sloman; Fawcett 2002.
304 Bath CL: Printed by Thomas Boddely, in King's-Mead-street 1741.
305 Sloman p.19.
306 *Oxford DNB*, entry by Katherine Coombs. See also Coombs 1998 and Reynolds.
307 Spence.
308 *BJ*, 20 October 1752.
309 Sloman; Holburne 2002.
310 Bath RO: parish registers of Weston, Bath, record the burials of a James (1738) and Elizabeth (1740) Vertue.
311 Dack.

312 *London Evening Post*, 12 September 1732 [747], and others.
313 *Daily Courant*, 7 July 1721 [6150].
314 This entry on Le Normand is expanded in Brett 2014. See also Cassidy-Geiger, pp. 87–111; Giermann has a bibliography that includes research by Cornelia Hofmann and Birgit Tradler (1999). The hangings were moved to Moritzburg, the hunting lodge of the Wettin family just outside Dresden, in 1830. They were restored 1985–98. For treasure recovered from Moritzburg that had been buried during the Second World War, see SL 17 December 1999, which included the magnificent blackamoor's head, Christoph Jamnitzer, Nuremberg *c*. 1615, and the enamelled jewel casket, Johann Melchior Dinglinger, presented by him to Augustus the Strong at Christmas 1701.
315 *Daily Post*, 2 December 1736 [5374].
316 I am grateful to Wandsworth Heritage Service for checking archives on my behalf. A search of Putney Parish Register 1620–1734 and Putney Parish Rate Book for 1736 (the earliest available) found no listing for Le Normand or Levet.
317 Bosquet and Clerenbault were recorded as merchants trading with Lisbon in 1724. Anthony Clerenbault died in November 1758 aged 90 [*London Evening Post*, 4–7 November 1758 [4837]]. Le Normand's will: PROB 11/680, proved 17 December 1736. For more on these family relationships see: Brett 2014.
318 Sold from Hornby Castle, Yorks., 2–11 June 1930 lot 412, [Cassidy-Geiger note 47]. This appears to be the only known reference to Levet: if he continued working on his own account his work must be unsigned and/or unrecognised or has not survived; and as yet no archival references have been found. There seems to be little chance of identifying Levet: it is a common surname, but he may have been related to Sir Richard Levett, Lord Mayor in 1699, whose widow lived in Bath (she died 1723). The family included an India merchant named John Levett, whose brother Francis was a merchant with the Levant Company in Leghorn, then in Florida.

The monogrammed panel [▶ p. 2] is referred to in a MS annotation in the *Catalogue of the Ornamental Furniture, Works of Art and Porcelain at Welbeck Abbey*, privately printed 1897, by Richard Goulding, Librarian 1902–29. The annotation refers to it in a *Catalogue of Pictures at Welbeck*, 1747 by George Vertue for Henrietta, Dowager Countess of Oxford (which exists as a copy of 1831).
319 Montagu 1813, 1906 and 1923.
320 *St James Chronicle*, 11–14 June 1791. The 'forewoman' of the featherwork project for Montagu House was Betty Tull.
321 *Morning Post and Daily Advertiser*, 2 April 1788 [4693]. Abraham Gossett (1701–85).
322 Mary Clerembault (d. 1785) bequeathed to Catherine Bosquet two portraits by Gossett of herself and her brother John (d. 1784); now in the Royal Collection. She also bequeathed to John Robert le Cointe a feather picture by 'Mr le Nordian'. John Clerembault bequeathed £1,000 to Catherine Gossett [Wagner].
323 'On the beautiful Feather-Hangings, designed for Mrs Montagu', *Gents Mag*, June 1788.

Part 3

RETIREMENT (p. 193)

324 John Wesley, quoted by Elizabeth Robinson in a letter to Anne Donnellan, written from Bulstrode, 21 Aug 1740. 1809 letters, vol. 1., p. 115.
325 Two large payments in the bank account for South Sea Annuities, to Bennet Stevenson (£602 5s in February 1748) and Henry Wright (£1,060 in 1751) may relate to the hospital.
326 PRO 11/818.
327 *BJ*, 10 November 1755.
328 St Mary's, Ealing, was built 1733–40 to replace an earlier church destroyed in 1729 when the steeple fell in. Mary Bertrand would have known the church with a cupola (in situ 1754–1838). The church was re-modelled in the mid-nineteenth century.
329 Quoted by Hounsell.
330 Rogers, p. 205; VCH. Several residents feature in Bertrand's account. Ealing House belonged briefly to Hugh Bethel and later to William Adair (who inherited it from General Huske); the Bishop of Durham had Elm Grove; King Gould owned Pitshanger; Rochester House in Little Ealing was built for John Pearce, a London distiller whose son Zachary became Bishop of Rochester. Gunnersbury House was previously owned by Lord Hobart and was acquired as a summer residence in 1761 by Princess Amelia; she lived with her father George II until his death in 1760 and also had Richmond Park.
331 For the Perreaus: Andrew 2001.
332 Chesterfield succeeded as 5th Earl in 1773; he was cousin to the 4th Earl (best known for his letters to his illegitimate son). Dodd was painted by John Russell, 1759 (NPG): Russell, like William Hoare, is known for his pastel portraits.
333 'French draws' presumably refers to a chest of drawers but there is a chance that it could mean drawings or designs. Mary Wright may have been a connection of the surgeon Henry Wright, in Bath, but it seems more likely that she was in some way connected with Phoebe Wright (d. 1778) who ran the 'Royal School of embroidering females' in Great Newport Street. Mary Bertrand's will states that Mary Wright lived in Kings Square Court; she may have been married to William Wright, who had a house in Carlisle Street, of which Kings Square Court is now part (west of Soho Square). The enameller and goldsmith George Michael Moser is thought to have lived in the same street; his daughter Mary Moser RA (1744–1819) was a great friend of Phoebe Wright.
334 PROB 11/818. Additional writing in the margins, relating to Limited administration 14 November 1823, is largely illegible. Note the similarity between Gye (one of the witnesses) and Gyde [▶p. 94].
335 As a comparison, when Lewis Mettayer died in 1740, he bequeathed his wife £80 per annum out of his estates in Spitalfields and Pall Mall [Wagner].
336 PROB 11/999. Ealing Central Library: micr. St Mary's Ealing Baptisms and Burials 1765–1812, X001/141. Without her bank account the date of Mary Bertrand's death might not have been found, for Brian Beet and the present author were misled by the will of another Mary Bertrand of Bath, buried in Bath Abbey 'under Dr Wall's monument' in 1784, which proved to be a time-consuming red herring. However this second Mary Bertrand could perhaps be the woman who exhibited at the Royal Academy in London between 1772 and 1776: 'Miss Mary Bertrand. *A Girl asleep*. This is one of the best Things in the Exhibition. It is done in a masterly Manner, and the Lady who painted it is one of the most promising Geniuses which have lately appeared.' *Public Advertiser*, 28 April 1773 [11875].
337 It is not known whether this refers to John Isted, a bookseller and publisher, at the Golden Ball, against St Dunstan's Church, Fleet Street, or to Ambrose Isted, listed in Bertrand's bank account. It is worth noting the following remote links given by Faulkner:

> The Rev. Charles Sturgess was the son of the Rev. Charles Sturgess and Sarah, sister of Ambrose Isted Esq ... Sturgess was vicar of Ealing 1775–97. The Rectory of Chelsea was offered to Mr Sturgess, not merely because he stood in the clerical line, the nearest in family connection with the heirs of Sir Hans Sloane; but, because they had known him for more than twenty years past in their neighbourhood of Reading; the Bishop of Durham collated him to a prebend in the Church at Salisbury, expressly on account of his character and conduct being so well known to his lordship when his diocesan, indeed, his patron.

The Bishop of Durham had property at Ealing; Bertrand Russel, son of Peter Russel and Hannah Hoare was incumbent of Gainsford, Co. Durham.
338 *Daily Advertiser*, 18 April 1761. John Shuckburgh was at the Sun, near the Inner Temple Gates and 'next to Richard's Coffee House' in Fleet Street.
339 Mary Bertrand probably rented accommodation when she first went to Ealing as her name does not appear in the Ealing rate books. She made regular payments of 10 guineas to John Jackson between 1758 and 1766; he is listed at Gunnersbury in the rate books and may well be the same John Jackson who was a banker in Fleet Street, at the Angel. The partnership of Adair & Jackson appears to link two Ealing property owners. But there was another John Jackson, a jeweller at the Crown and Pearl, George Street [Heal LG].
340 John Winter, probably a connection, is listed in Ealing rate books and is commemorated in the church. The only entries on the debit side of Mary Bertrand's bank account from 1767 are to 'James Smyth's rect' (twice yearly at £46 10s). A memorial in Ealing church to James Smyth records that he was 'of Upper Grosvenor Street London and of Ealing' and that he died on 10 December 1780 aged 70 [Faulkner]; he can presumably be identified with an invoice headed 'James Smyth & Co., Perfumers, at the Civet Cat between Grosvenor Street & Brook Street in New Bond Street', dated 25 March 1757 receipted by Arthur Rothwell [V&A, E.236-1943, box GG66].
341 A copy of the 1905 catalogue is in the Victoria Art Gallery, Bath; at the time the pictures belonged to the Revd G. B. Lewis. ▶ n. 86.
342 I am most grateful to Amina Wright for telling me of this material and to Samuel Gedge for its present whereabouts: the Rare Book & Manuscript Library, University of Pennsylvania. ▶ n. 3.
343 Letter to George Montagu, 18 May 1749 [Lewis, vol. 9, p. 82].
344 Lewis, vol. 12, p. 222.
345 Bath RO.
346 Lr. 40 fo. 71.

347 Alnwick: Sy.U.1.24m 2nd parcel. In 1746 Richard Calvert bought Dresden ruffles from Cutler (3 gns) and from the silversmith Gilpin (£2 10s) [Claydon: 4/7/50].
348 Newby; *DNB*.
349 Heal LG.
350 IGI. There appears to have been a daughter, Elizabeth b. 27 April 1742, who died as an infant, then Mary, b. 18 November 1745 and Bertrand b. 20 April 1747.
351 See John Wiltshire's will, PROB/875. Mary Russel married Lt. Col. George Lewis (1735–91). Bertrand Russel, Mary's brother, was one of Lewis's executors. A portrait of Colonel Lewis by John Singleton Copley, 1794, is now in Detroit Institute of Arts, having been sold by his descendants SL 19 November 1969 lot 42. He served at the siege of Gibraltar where he was in charge of the artillery and set fire to and destroyed the floating batteries of France and Spain. He was also in the campaign against the French and Spanish in America, including Louisbourg, Bunker's Hill and Quebec.

Part 4

PAUL BERTRAND'S BANK ACCOUNT (p. 205)

352 See also Truman 1991, p. 311.
353 The attribution largely rests on the pencilled name found on the inner wood case of an etui in the Ashmolean Museum, Oxford.
354 Clifford.
355 When a mark was registered at Goldsmiths' Hall it was categorised as that of a smallworker, largeworker, goldworker, buckleworker, etc. Research is ongoing, but it seems that Bellis was a retailer not a working craftsman.
356 *Public Advertiser*, 8 January 1760 [7834].
357 *Public Advertiser*, 10 January 1761.
358 POB, t17790707-33.
359 He attended the French Lodge at the Swan in Long Acre, in 1730 [Songhurst].
360 Sun Ins, vol. 1, p. 65.
361 PROB 11/799, Southwick.
362 Mrs Bernardeau is mentioned in Bowcock's account book, 24 July 1756 [Adams & Redstone]. Wagner's listing of the 1766 will of Anne Bernardeau gives the daughter's name as Ann Holroyd.
363 They included: Samuel Bernardeau, who is mentioned alongside Daniel Chenevix at their naturalization in 1699. House of Lords, Journal Office HL/PO/JO/10 (A2A website). William Bernardeau, a turner, in Bear Street near Leicester Fields. A few yards to the east, just across Castle Street at the sign of the Coffee Mill in St Martin's Court, was Daniel Bernardeau, a cutler, who is also listed in Russell Court (James's address) which was just to the east of Covent Garden. [Murdoch. 1749 poll for both William and Daniel Bernardeau; neither is mentioned in James's will.] Daniel advertised that he made 'fine mahogany stands for china dishes' as well as bowling green bowls and oval frames.
364 A. C. Edwards, p. 134.
365 Bath RO: RNHRD, 0386/1/1.
366 PROB 11/839.
367 1749 poll. *Public Advertiser*, 14 July 1759 [7968], advertisement from the office of the Amicable Society for a Perpetual Assurance for claims following Bishop's death.
368 Songhurst.
369 Jowett 2012. Items bearing Augustus le Sage's mark are known from 1757, but he did not become a freeman of the Goldsmiths' Company until 1782. Jowett points out that in 1772 Suffolk Street was reconfigured and the Le Sage workshop then fell within Cockspur Street. Augustus's elder brother Simon le Sage was bequeathed the workshop by their father.
370 TNA: C 108/284.
371 Grimwade; Schrager.
372 POB: t17550910-21.
373 Her will [PROB 11/914] mentions her brothers, Peter and David Crucifix and their children. It is possible that she was the widow of a wine merchant, Louis Roussel, who died in 1749 and was no relation of Peter Russel [Beet].
374 GH: Apprentice Book.
375 Jowett.
376 POB: t17671209-18.
377 *The Shorter Oxford English Dictionary*, repr. 1950.
378 Sun Ins, vol. 15, fo. 85, next the Swan & Helmett agt Cripplegate Conduit.
379 Hoare: Bound tradesmen's bills. BL, H/14, 6 March 1721.
380 POB: t17420115-13: Theft of 10 China cups and Saucers, value 3s, the goods of Frederick Stanton and William Thorne.
381 Clifford, 1999.
382 *Grub Street Journal*, 14 October 1736 [355].
383 Heal Signs; Hildyard says from 1737. Cotterell had an account with Hoare October 1736–April 1737, ledger 37, fo. 27.
384 Sun Ins, vol. 005, fo. 170 [6307]: at the Angell and 4 coffins and then at the Blue Anchor & Crown near Hungerford Street.
385 Buckminster: Box 3198-3523, no. 3413.
386 Banks: 119.6.
387 *London Evening Post*, 4–6 June 1747 [3056].
388 Hartop 2010, pp. 26–30.
389 Grimwade lists Joseph Creswell registering a mark as a smallworker in 1767, at Cateaton Street. As this is near Aldermanbury, in the City, it may not be the same man. Oliver Fairclough has instead suggested that the mark IC, hitherto ascribed to John Carter, which is on the Williams Wynn service, might actually be an unrecorded mark of Joseph Creswell [Hartop 2010, p. 27].
390 Grimwade; 1749 poll; Heal LG.
391 Schroder, p. 1242.
392 Gunnis; 1749 poll; Wagner.
393 Mortimer.
394 Alcorn.
395 Grimwade; Heal LG.
396 Loomes.
397 *London Daily Post and General Advertiser*, 5 May 1740 [1725].
398 *General Advertiser*, 22 April 1751 [5153]. The Rubens is now in the National Gallery, London.
399 Culme 2000: mentioned in the trial of Samuel Drybutter in 1757. Sun Ins, vol. 15 fo. 206 [28119]: John Jacob in Bonds Stables in the Liberty of the Rolls, shagreen case maker in the house of Mrs Gibson; remov'd to the next door at the back of the Golden Lyon Tavern in Bond Stables September 1723. Although there are another two men with the same name in Bath, their dates do not align well with Bertrand. Bath RO: Council

Book from 1708 (in Gravel Walks), and 1776 Schedule of Deeds, p.179.
400 Grimwade; Wagner.
401 Ledger 37 fo. 282.
402 Grimwade; Heal LG.
403 Listed in 1749 poll; Loomes dates him from 1744 and also has Robert Leroux son of John apprenticed in 1707. See Thompson 2008, pp. 88–89; will: PROB 11/1591/38. The will of Mary Le Roux, née Bordier, from Geneva, may be of interest: proved January 1747/48 [PROB 11/759]. The main beneficiaries of her will were her grandsons Robert and James Alexander Le Roux, but there is no indication of any connection to watchmaking.
404 Philip Priestley, 'Watchcase-maker's marks in the missing register of 1739–58', *The Silver Society Journal*, no. 12, 2000. Most unusually, Le Roux advertised 'a small size Gold repeating Box and Case in one, with a Gold Dial plate not quite finished, the Hall Mark in the Box, and the Workman's Mark ALR. There was in it when lost, a Bill specifying the Weight of it, and a brass Plate belonging to the Watch.' *Daily Courant*, 12 April 1718 [5140].
405 BL, East India Office coll., H/14. Godden.
406 LMA: City Freedom papers, COL/CHD/FR/02/0266-0272.
407 PROB 11/674. *London Gazette*, 4 March 1735 [7382]. LMA: Apprenticeship papers: COL/CHD/FR/02/0541-0546 and COL/CHD/FR/02/0541-0546.
408 *London Gazette*, 4 March 1735 [7382], etc.
409 *The London Daily Post and General Advertiser*, 6 September 1735 [264].
410 *Daily Gazetteer*, 9 March 9 1737 [531]. Buckminster.
411 *Daily Post*, 13 June 1737 [5539]; *Daily Advertiser*, 12 January 1743 [3739 & 3741. *Daily Advertiser*, 14 April 1743 [3819].
412 Chatsworth.
413 *London Chronicle*, 3–5 February 1767 [1581].
414 PROB 11/929. *Public Advertiser*, 4 June 1767 [10169]; *The London Evening Post*, 17 September 1767 [6221].
415 *Baldwin's New Complete Guide*, 1768 edn; she was buried St Stephen Walbrook 2 April 1769. *Public Advertiser*, 9 May 1769 [10707], and 20 June 1769 [10805].
416 Chatsworth; Woburn; BM.
417 PROB 11/929 and 11/948. BM: Heal D,2.788.
418 PROB 11/870; BL: India Office, N/1/1 fo. 130.
419 Clifton.
420 Loomes. Although a member of the Clockmakers' Company, Mulford appears to have worked as a silversmith.

421 Sun Ins, vol. 7 fo. 84 [9354], 18 October 1717 and 22 October 1718.
422 *General Advertiser*, 13 April 1749 [451].
423 SL, 10 October 1946 lot 117; CL, 19 October 1988 lot 181.
424 BM: Heal 67.308. Grimwade. Culme 1998: in relation to Dru Drury's creditors.
425 *London Gazette* [6798].
426 Edgcumbe, p. 144. The Bellis apprenticeships were listed in the notifications of the Feast of the Sons of the Clergy – Alexander: *London Daily Post and General Advertiser*, 12 April 1740 [1706]; Samuel: *London Evening Post*, 23–25 April 1744; *London Evening Post*, 23–25 April 1745 [2725].
427 Brett 2010.
428 Alexander Bellis, described as a goldsmith of Primrose Street, married in 1754 the widow of a toy and hardwareman, George Plimmer, who had died in 1749, *London Evening Post*, 18–20 July 1754 [416]. Pars will: PROB 11/936.
429 Bath RO: rate book.
430 Heal LG.
431 *Public Advertiser*, 30–31 January 1766.
432 BM: Heal 105.82.
433 NAS: GD44/51/463.3.38.
434 SoG, Boyd's Marriage Index.
435 *London Evening Post*, 16–18 November 1738 [1718].
436 Grimwade. *Gents Mag.*, *London Gazette*, 6–10 December 1763 [1037].
437 It is possible that Turner may have started in business as a glass seller but no evidence has been found that the man who insured goods at the Two Golden Balls in Long Acre in 1719/20 is the same person, [Sun Ins, vol. 10, fo. 375 [16374], 22 January 1719/20, 7s 6d].
438 *London Daily Post and General Advertiser*, 20 March 1741 [1999].
439 POB: OA17550728.
440 POB: t17621208-28.
441 Walpole to Horace Mann, 19 May 1750.
442 *London Chronicle*, 25 September 1759 [429]: 'On Sunday the 8th instant was married at Presteigne in Radnorshire, John Evans, of Travelgwynne, in the county of Montgomery Esq; formerly High Sheriff of Radnorshire, to Miss Betty Turner, only daughter and heiress of Thomas Turner Esq: China Merchant in London, with a fortune of £10,000.'
443 Photocopy in NAL, pressmark 96.DD.39.
444 Clifton; Loomes; Chamberlayne, Pt II, Bk III, p. 213. See an orrery in the Science Museum, London.
445 NAS: GD44//51/302.59. Buckminster: Box 921–925. Fitzwalter purchased from Thomas Heath 'a set of 6-inch, full size case of mathematical instruments' [Edwards p. 21]. See: Holbrook.

Index

This index does not include all the names in Hoare & Co.'s ledgers for Paul Bertrand's account (in bold capitals on pp. 246–323). The biographical notes on those pages are indexed below and so are ledger names that appear additionally in preceding pages of the text. N.B: Cross references in the index below may refer to pp. 246–323.

Trades and professions are in capitals. Because of the overlap in job descriptions, some are grouped under broad headings such as 'Dress', 'Food and drink', 'Textiles'. Merchants, brokers and agents are indexed if their specialty is known — see e.g. 'trade destinations' or 'armed forces'. Other than Bath artists, who are listed individually, painters and printmakers are under 'Artists'.

Abercromby, Robert 250
Academy: of Painting Bath 69; Great Queen St 276
Accounts see Coke, Fitzwalter, Sondes, Rockingham, Verney; invoices
Acts of Parliament: fraud 259; gaming 49, 136–37; theatre 97; transportation 316
Adair family 196, 246, 256, 276
Adam, Robert 222
Addison, Jane 222
Adey, Daniel 267
Advertisements see retailing
Africa Company: HOUSE 211/2; DIRECTORS see Lockwood, Mann, Merle. See trade destinations
Agents see armed forces, insurance, government offices, trade destinations
Alexandre, Jean 291
Alington, Marmaduke 53, 246, 270
Allen: Eleazar & Sarah 163–64; Revd Fifield 316; Gertrude 272; John 304; Joseph 57, 211/7, 246; Philip 21/27, 246; Ralph 21/26, 68, **72**, 82, 177, 246, 304, 309; William 246, 304
Alsop, Robert **84**
Altham, Richard Annesley, 5th Baron 247
Ambassadors see embassies
Amber, Norton 278
America: map **30**; PB's family in 27–28; Annapolis 30; Florida 290, 318; Georgia Society trustees Lapottre, Smith. MARYLAND 27, 287. PHILADELPHIA 275. SOUTH CAROLINA/ Hobcaw Barony 163–64, 249, 290. VIRGINIA 29, 273, 297. See de Beaulieu, Wm Deards jnr, government offices, slavery, trade destinations
Ancram: Lady Caroline (Holdernesse), William Kerr, Lord Ancram, later 4th Marquess of Lothian. See Fitzwalter
Angerstein, R. R. 165
Anglesey, James Annesley, 5th Earl 247
Annesley see Altham, Anglesey
Anson, George 1st Baron 247
Anstey: Christopher, Miss 191
Antrobus, Daniel 315
APOTHECARIES, DOCTORS, PHYSICIANS, SURGEONS see Arbuthnot, Ayscough, Barlow, Bave, Bostock, Broxholm, Charleton, Cheyne, Cleland, Coxe, de Vic, Ditcher, Farrer, French, Galloway, Garnier, Geekie, Harrington, Howse, Jones, Lawrence, Moore, Morris, Oliver, Otway, Peirce, Pritchard, Ranby, Rayner, Regnart, Shadwell, Skrine, Street, Tessier, Winter, Woolmer, Wright. See health
Arbuthnot, John 247
ARCHITECTS, BUILDERS, MASONS, SURVEYORS see Adam, Chambers, Clement, Davis, Emes, Ewell, Ford, Gibbs, Halfpenny, Harvey, Holloway, Jacob, Jelly & Palmer, Jones, Marchant, Palmer, Reynolds, Soane, Strahan, Stride, Stuart, Vardy, Wood
Arkenside, Mark 27
ARMED FORCES (Army & Navy agents, colonial agents, contractors/suppliers/victuallers) see Adair, Franks, Gould, Graeme/Graham, Guerin, Haddock, Lamb, Linwood, Mann, Perry, Popple, Revell, Townsend; at Minorca 304. See government offices, trade destinations
Arnold: Christopher 52, 247, George 247, 267, John 52
Artaud, Stephen, William 247
ARTISTS (painters, printmakers, miniaturists) Batoni n.253; Beare 278; Capon **44**; Carter **200**; Singleton Copley n.351; Corton 61, 184; Crosby **44**; Dahl 314; Delamotte 309; Devis 258, 282; Faber **144**, **155**, 259; Ferrers 252; Frye 245; Gainsborough **84**, 174, 225, 260–61, 298, 309; Gravelot **116**; Hamilton 305; Hayman 116, 261, 274, 300; Haytley 305; Heins **126**; Hogarth **128**, 137, 157, 247, 257, 268, 275, 279, 293, 313, 319, 293, 302; Hone 52, 73; Hudson **84**, **145**, 263, 265, 273, 285, 292, 320; Hysing 155; Lacon 133; Laroon **128**; Morris **122**; Nattier **90**; Nilson **134**; Nivelon **102**; Pellegrini **101**, Philips **91**; Pond **155**; Portret 185; Ramsay 247, 256 279, 317; Raphael 33, 229; Richardson **72**, 267; Romney 285; Rubens 229; Seeman 285; Seymour 268; Shepherd **17**; Slaughter 58; Smart 296; van Diest 248, 259; van Loo 157, 302; Watson 270; Watteau 235; West 310; Wilson 273; Wootton **156–57**, 319; Wright 322; Zoffany 270; Zurich 184. See architects, chasers, engravers, enamellers, sculptors, wax modellers. Bath artists are listed individually
Arundel: Thomas 14th Earl 101; Henry 8th Baron of Wardour **202**
Ashby, Thomas n.209
Ashe, Metcalfe 49, 282, 320
Assay see marks
Assembly rooms see Bath
Assheton, Mary, Sir Ralph, 2nd Bt, 267
ATTORNEYS, NOTARIES AND LAWYERS see Alington, Annesley, Allen, Brydges, Clutterbuck, Cranmer, Craster, Geekie, Gery, Hamilton, Henley, Henshaw, Hickey, Jennings, Lamb, Nash, Neale, Pechell, Powell, Purlewent, Rous, Smith, Stanley, West, Wilbraham, Wilmott. See Acts, government offices, law, scrivener
Atwood family 117, 119, 248
AUCTIONEERS AND APPRAISERS see Cock, Ford, Langford, Margas, Prestage, Richard, Robins, Sale. See inventories
Auctions and sales see Allen, Arundel, Bellis, Bertrand, Bostock, Chandos, Coindrieau, Colebrook, Crespin, Fleury, Hubert, Lacon, Lifford, Margas, J. Neale,

Pantin, Pons, Powis, Rouse, Thomond, Turner, East India Co. See dealers, East India
Aumonier, Peter 56, 248
Avon navigation scheme 72, 81–82, 111, 292
Axford: Benjamin 172, 179; Susanna 119
Aylesford, Heneage Finch 1st Earl 252
Ayscough, Dr 149

Baker: Francis, Philip 51, 56, 248; Richard, 248
Baldwin, Thomas 79
Baltimore, Charles Calvert, 5th Baron 149, 256, 282
Bank of England: 211/5; DIRECTORS Delme, Eyles, Fauquier, Gaussen, Gould
Banks/bankers see goldsmiths. In Bath: Hayes, Harrington, PB, Wiltshire. See bills of exchange, retailing
Bankrupts see Allen, Baker, Boothby, Burgh, Burnett, Caesar, Colebrook, Creswell, Curtis, Davis, Wm Deards jnr, Dicker, Fines/Fynes, Hutcheson, Margas, Morris, Pars, Penny, Pyke, Rogers, Rous, Salomons, Shruder, Shurmer, Smith, Spurrier, Tabart, White
Banks, Joseph and family 249
Barber, Constance 104, 249
BARBERS, HAIRDRESSERS, PERIWIG & PERUKE MAKERS see Berwick, Hayes, Kirkpatrick, Trinquand
Barbot, John, Paul, 56, 63, 211/18, **214**, 249, 302
Barker, Joseph 37, 56, 203, 249, 284
Barlow, Hugh 309
Barnard, Gilbert Vane 2nd Baron 318
Barnsley, William 303
Barrear, Abraham 218
Barrington, Viscount 250, 260
Base metals: BRAZIERS AND IRONMONGERS see Burnett, Trinquand; Bath metal 39, 166. See French plate
Basnet, William 173
Bath, William Pulteney and Anna Maria, 1st Earl and Countess 250
Bath: Timelines 9, 94. Maps **20–24, 40–41**
  Assembly rooms 18–24; 21/43, 21/48, 63, 93–104, 129, 131; **19, 50, 78, 98, 187**; see p.94 for owners
  Academy of Painting 69. BANKING see PB, Harrison, Hayes, Hoare & Co., Wiltshire. BATHS & bathing 21/18 & /19 /29 /30 /54 /55, 123–5, 142; **124**. CONSTITUENCY 80; MPs: Henley, Pitt. CORPORATION 21/21, **24**, 67, 80–81, 131, 152. MEMBERS see Atwood, Cogswell, Masters, Robinson. COST OF STAY 110,114, 119, 129. DEVELOPMENT 79–83. HOSPITAL 21/12, 53, 68–**69**, 80, 131, 181 see apothecarys. FREEDOM 67, 146, 149, 171, see boxes. JOURNAL 87. MASTER OF CEREMONIES see Nash, Wade. POPULATION & VISITORS 83, 85, 88. PUMP ROOM 21/31, **124–25, 170**; band 93, 180; pumper, 267, 310. ROMAN REMAINS 21/55, 92. ROYALTY at 143–57. SEASON 55, 105. St Swithin's 21/58. See entertainment; music; shop signs; travel & transport
  Cityscapes 76, 78; Abbey 21/23, **180, 192**; Barton Street 21/1, **70**; Green Walks **64**; Guildhall **67**; Orange Grove 21/40, **60, 80, 104, 147, 182**; Terrace Walk **18–19, 39, 192**
  Inns, taverns and lodgings 115–20. Abbey house 21/24, **142**, 265; Atwood 117; Axford 119; Bear 21/13, 305; Bell Tree 21/17; Billing 110; Bush **118**; Carey 257; Chandos 21/15; Christopher 300; Crown 305; Fisher 118; Greyhound, 301; Hart (Masters) 293; Humphreys 153; Jones 119; King 119; Moore 295; Nassau house 21/39, 119; Phillips 117–19, 301; Pigott **118**; Queens Head 305; Royal Oak 313; Rummer 262; Skrine/Savil 21/16, **153**–54,

309; Stibbs 313; White Hart 21/20; Winchester House 119. See fire, food and drink
Bathe, William 61
Bathurst family, 68, 250, 265, 289
Battey, Mary 224
Bave, Dr 110, 322
Beaufort 247, 255, 264, 279; Henry Somerset 3rd Duke 251, 320; Charles Noel 4th Duke 310
Beaulieu see de Beaulieu
Bedford: 2nd Duke (d. 1711) 83, 131; 3rd Duke (d. 1732) 71, 74–**75**, 83, 268, 287, 314; 4th Duke (d. 1771) 126, 201, 233,
Bellis: Alexander 236; James 57, 63, 211/16, 214–**15**, 251, Samuel 236
Benn, William **84**
Bennet, Jane 246, Francis 174–75, 251
Benoimont, Lewis 288
Bentinck, Lady Barbara 277
Bequests see wills
Berchere, Suzanne 252
Berkeley: Lady Betty, dau of 3rd Earl 281. Elizabeth (sister of Baron Botetourt) 310
Bernardeau family 56, 68, 211/13, 215–**16**, 251
Berrisford, James 168
Bertrand: timeline 9, family tree **28**; maps 21/46, 30, 210; shop location **18**
  Mary (née Deards): marriage 37; signature **43**; as widow 66, 196–200, 251; will 30, 292. See Deards
  Paul: monument and possible portrait 26, 194; poem 132. Early life, family, training and first marriage, in America and London 27–35. Occupation in London 32. Second marriage and Bath 37–44. Will 204. Advertisements 315. Bank account 48, graph 54–55, table 56–57, **198**, 207–323, **208–09**. Invoices **42–43**, **130**, 138–39, **148, 150, 160**. Porcelain from shop **140–141, 160**. See Hoare & Co., Wiltshire family
Berwick, Peter 305
Bethel, Hugh, Sarah, Slingsby 251, 264, 276
Bickerstaff, Isaac see Steele
Bigge, Thomas 174
Bignal, James 242
Bills/notes of exchange **51**, 54, 96, **224**, 254, 267, 271, **300**
Bingley, Robert Benson 1st Baron 256
Birmingham 171
Birt, Peter 315, Samuel
Bishop: Sampson, Samuel, 36, 56, 210, 217, 251
Blachford, John **84**
Blackwellhall factors see textile
Bland: Sir John, 5th Bt 252, 314; Muriel 286
Blandford, Lady (m.2ndly William Wyndham) 147
Blathwaite/Blathwayt, William 62
Bloodworth, Col 149, **156**
Blount, Elizabeth 261
Bloxman/ Bloxom/ Bloxham (Mary Deards snr) 38, 252
Blunt, Martha 302
Boldero, John royal g/sm 153, 294
Bolingbroke, Henry St John 1st Viscount 112, 249
Bonnet, Stede 164
BOOKSELLERS, PRINTERS, PUBLISHERS, STATIONERS see Banks, Barber, Birt, Bloss, Bowyer, Chandler & Ward, Cluer/Cleudar, Dodsley, Frederick, George, Gosling, Gyles, Hammond, Isted, Jackson, Leake, Luce, Martin, Pepys, Richardson, Sayer, Shuckburgh, Speren, Wakelin, Ward
Booth, George, 2nd Earl of Warrington 321
Bosquet, Catherine, Nicholas 190–91
Bouket, Peter 255 see Buhet

350   N.B.: USE PAGES 246–323 AS A SECOND INDEX

Bow: porcelain factory 207, 215, **242–43**, 247; mill near 265
Bowcock, n. 362
Bowden, John 56, 253
Bowerbank, Revd 66
Bowles, Thomas 88
Boxes [gold, snuff, etui etc]: **16, 34, 86, 112, 120, 158, 206, 214**; freedom 149, 157, 181; to Nash 159; Pr of Orange **146**; Pr of Wales 144; tontine 308; for keeping cash 293.
   BOX AND CASE MAKERS see Allen, Barbot, Cunst, Derussat, Elliott, Fleury, Jacob, Neale, Pars, Rigal, Russel, Spicer, Spurrier. See chasers, engravers, goldsmiths, japanners, toymen; crime
Boyle: Lady Charlotte (m. 4th Duke of Devonshire) 161; Lady Dorothy see Euston
Braddock: Frances ('Sylvia') 97, 103; Gen. Edward n. 163
Bragg, Thomas n. 40
Bra[i]thwaite: George 236, 263; Richard 297
Braund, William 273
BRAZIERS see base metal
Breadalbane see Glenorchy
Brett, Edward 204, 299; Ch [?] 315
Brice, Edward 246
Bridge: John 174, 179; Ralph n. 248
Bridges, Henry 71, 254
Bridgwater, Scroop Egerton 1st Duke 74, 304
Brifaut, John 57, 254
Briscoe, Stafford 315
Bristol: 165–70, Merchant Adventurers 263, 271. Individuals linked to, see Arnold & Co., Atkins, Bathe, Baugh, Boissier, Casamayor, Colston, Coster, Creswick [Cressett], de Vic, Delamain, Gwatkin, Hobbs, Hutcheson, King, Roubel, Salmon, Smith, Taylor, Walcam, Welsh
Bristol diamonds 167; see hardstones
Bristol: Elizabeth 1st Countess (d.1741) 83, 103, 109, 117, 136; John Hervey 1st Earl (d.1751) 279; Lord John, Hon Thomas, (sons of 1st Earl) 279, 282; 3rd Earl (d. 1779) 92
Bristowe (lawyer) 51
Brooke: William Greville 7th Baron; Francis 8th Baron later 1st Earl Brooke and 1st Earl of Warwick **89**–90, 254
Broxholm, Dr 149
Browne, Col **91**; Capt Prosper 255, 312
Bruce, David 294
BRUSHMAKER Bean
Brydges see Chandos
Buck, Anne, Sir Charles 285
Buckeridge, Elizabeth 72
BUCKLEMAKER see silversmith
Buckley, Hon Mrs Elenora 125, 163
Buckworth, Sir John 2nd Bt 115
Buhet/Buker: Mary 273, Elias, Peter 255
BUILDERS see architects
Bull in a china shop 220
Bull: John 255; Lewis 19, 176
Bullock: Ann (sister of H. de Beaulieu) 163, 255; Thomas 255
Bunbury: Charles 255; Revd Sir William 279; Sarah 292
Burlington: Dorothy (née Savile) 3rd Countess 136, 158–61, 287, 291; invoices to: 138, 160, 231–**32**, 250, 268, 289. Richard Boyle, 3rd Earl 291, 297. See Boyle, Euston
Burnet, Bishop Robert 256
Burnett, Michael 256
Burrows/Burrough, Samuel n.153

CABINET MAKERS see Channon, Churchill, Cracherode, Davis, Fenton, Madden, Salmon. See carvers

Cabrier 215
Caesar/Ceesar, Charles 49, 257
Caldwall, John 179
Calendar & hallmarking 12; **82**, 107
Callard: Isaac 57, 211/15, 217–**18**, 225, 256, Paul **218**
Calvert, Felix, later Verney Bt 256. See Baltimore
Cambridge colleges: Clare 320, Downing 270
Campbell: & Currie, Colen 257, John 294
Canada: Belle Isle 321, Nova Scotia 277, 317, seige of Quebec n.351
Cardigan, George Brudenell 4th Earl, later Duke of Montagu 115
Carlingford, Theobald Taaffe 4th Earl 314
Carmichael see Hyndford
Carriers see travel
Carteret, Louisa, Fanny, 222
CARVERS & FRAMERS see Gosset, Harvey, Johnson, Ross. See cabinet makers, sculptors, wax modellers
Cary, Joseph 67
CASE MAKERS: see boxes, watch casemaker
Castaing, Elie 168, 319
Caswall, George 307
Cavendish, Lady Elizabeth 291; see Devonshire
Cawthorn, Samuel 219, 257
Ceramics: 207, auction/sale 306, 312, decoration 185, hire 117, 321; see invoices. FACTORIES see Bow, Chantilly, Chelsea, Meissen, Vauxhall (Crisp), Worcester. CHINA/EARTHENWARE MEN & WOMEN see Been, Bridges, Burnet, Cotterell, Dobson, Kendall, Margas, Mitchell, Morgan, Smith, Turner, Wicksteed, Williams. See Giles
Chadd, Richard & Robert; and Thomas Rag[s]dale 31, 180, 304
Chambers: Ephraim, Rosamund 247; Sir William 270
Chandler, Mary 54, 56, 173, 258, 312
Chandos: James Brydges 1st Duke 72, 81, 107, 117, **120**, 257, 261; agents/associates 255, 268, 270, 276, 283, 290, 292, 301, 308. Henry, 2nd Duke **156**
Channel Islands 191
Chantilly **115, 216**
Chapman: Mary, John 283; Mike (maps) **20–23**
CHAPMEN see Margas, Penny, Pyke, Rous, Shurmer. See dealers
Chardin, Sir John 296
Charleton, Rice 258
Charlotte, Queen 231
Charterhouse 35
Chartier, Isaac 270
CHASERS see Heckel, Neal, Pars. See boxes, engravers
Chatham, 1st Earl see Pitt
Cheere: Henry 296, John 248
Chelsea factory **141**, 207, 242–43, 251
Chenevix: family tree 28, maps 36, 38, timeline 9, **39, 259**. Elizabeth (née Deards) 16, 37, 90, 199–200, 217, 222, 240. Paul Daniel 37, 56, 294, 299; bank account: 234, 256. Richard 299. Invoices 165, **202**, 309; advertisements/stock 91, 133, 225, 305. See Bertrand, Deards
Chesterfield: Philip Dormer Stanhope, 4th Earl 12, 87, 125, 129, 252, 271, 283, 298; 5th Earl 196
Chesterton, G.K. 207
Cheyne, Dr George **122**, 259, 294
Child & Co. 259 see Tylney
China & chinamen see ceramics
Chirac, Denis n. 15

N.B.: USE PAGES 246–323 AS A SECOND INDEX

Chudleigh, Elizabeth (d. 1788), m. 3rd Earl of Bristol and bigamously Duke of Kingston 92
Churchill family 260; *see* Marlborough
Cibber, Colley 252
Clanricarde, Earl of 286
Clarke, Richard 130
Clavering: Alice, Sir James 321
Clayton 260; invoice to **233**. *See* Sundon
Cleland, Archibald 69
Clerembault: Anthony, Nicholas 190–91
Clergy, Sons of 263
Clerkenwell 144
Clifford, Jerenomy 291
CLOCKMAKERS *see* watchmakers
CLOTHIER /cloth *see* textiles
Clubs: Benn **84**, 285; Hell Fire 267; Wig 248
Cluer [Cleudar], J and Elizabeth 260
Clutterbuck family 261, 280
Cobb, Thomas 260
Cobham, Richard Temple, 1st Viscount 71
Cock, Christopher 229, 261, 303
Cocks family *see* Somers
Codrington, Mary, Sir William, 262, 264
Coffee houses: Galloway 275, Janeway 286, Morgan 49, 119, 320, Sheyler 119
Coindrieau, Lewis 130
Coke, Thomas (of Holkham) 101, 105, 117, 281
Cole(s): Benjamin & Martha **18**, Henry 56, 170, 262, John 262,
Colebrook family 262, 297; sale 263
Coleman, William 108
Coller, Thomas 218
Collier, Arthur 253
Collins: George 263, Richard 263
Colonies *see* individual areas, government offices
Colthurst/Coulthurst family 142, 265
Comyns, Sir John, Baron of the Exchequer 115
Cooper: Gislingham, Robert 264, 320
Cope: John (diamond cutter); Sir John 66, 251, 264, 293, 312; Mary 184, 251
Coral *see* hardstones
Cornish: Francis, Bridget 265
Corrie, John 265
Costs *see* accounts, inventories, invoices, travel
Costume and liveries *see* dress
Cottenham, Charles Pepys, 1st Earl 300
Cotterell: Jacob **20**. John 56, 211/2, **220**, 265. Cottrell [Cotterell] Dormer: Sir Clement 144–47, **145**; Sir Charles 258, Col John 246
Cottesloe, Barons 275
Courtauld: Ann, Augustine, Esther 222, 229, Samuel 270, 306
Coutts & Co. 294; *see* Chenevix
Coward: Elizabeth and Leonard, snr & jnr 21/47, 54, 56, 173, **175–76**, 261, 265
Cowper: William 191; William, 2nd Earl 87, 265
Cox, James 238, 261; John 265, 303
Craft, William Hopkins **230**
Craggs, Anne 298
Craig, John 266
Crespin, Paul 225, 261, 304
Creswell: John 37, 222, 266, Joseph 222
Creuze, 317; de la Creuze 289
Crime: burglary & theft 63, 108–9, 168, 277, 291, 297, 303; East India Company 273; fraud & forgery: 196, 264, 285,303; highwaymen/pirates 109,164; murder 214;

transportation 168, 316; treason 252, 303. VICTIMS Callard, Colebrook, Macartney, Nesbitt, Pugh, Rogers, Simpson & Ward, Shruder, Taylor, Turner. *See* Goldsmiths' warnings; society
Cromp, Thomas 92, 266
Crook, John **266**–67
Crucifix: Peter, David n.373
Cunst, Jasper 146
Curghey, John 250, 285
Currency 13–**14**
Customs & Excise 211/1; *see*, government offices
CUTLERS, RAZOR MAKERS *see* Bernardeau, Cole, Deards, Fleureau, Gopsill, Harrison, Moody, Savigny, Scrivener, Siddall, Spicer
Cuzack, Mr 314

Damareen, John Lewis *see* Demarin
Danborough, William 219
Dancers/Dancing masters *see* entertainment
Daniel, Père 126
Dartmouth, William Legge, 1st Earl 289
Dates: as written in this volume 12; timelines 9–11, 94
Davis: Charles Edward 192; John & Joanna 21/47, 90, 176–77, 267
Dealers: Hubert, Hayter; *see* auctioneers, chapmen,
Deane, William 274
Deards family: 16, 28, family trees 28, 38; maps **36**, **38**, 210; in Bath 37, 82, 85. Advertisements, lost items, purchases and stock: 37, 88, 91, 106, 111, 136, 144, 184, 225, 244, 263, 308. John snr 32, 37, 40, 222, 288; John jnr 93, 200; Mary snr 40, 250, 252, 275, 285, 301; William snr 37, 40, 93, 199, 261, 266–67, 291; William jnr 30, 214, 302. Elizabeth *see* Chenevix; Mary jnr *see* Bertrand
De Beaulieu: Henrietta 162–63
Debts *see* bankrupts, gaming, society
Decoration *see* chasing, engraving, hardstones
Defoe, Daniel 123
De Jolie, Charlotte 28–29
Delamain: Charles 21/49, 37, 94, 99–101, 167; Henry n.151
De Lamerie, Paul 151, 153, 225, 248, 252, 260, 268, 274, 279, 298, 321
Delany, Mary (née Granville, m. 1stly Pendarves) 86, 97, 103–04, 130, 144, 162, 165, 177, 191, 252, 262, 277, 281, 302, 311, 312, 316. *See* Pendarves
Delassol, Mr 73
Delaval: Anne 284, Francis 247
Deletang [De L'Etang], Peter 56, 211/4, 227, 267, 289
Delme, Peter, 267, 291
Delorane [Deloraine]: Mary, m. 1stly Henry Scott 1st Earl, 2ndly Wm Wyndham 128, 156, 268, 323
Delvin: Christopher Nugent, styled Lord Delvin 268
Demarin [Damareen], John 169, 268
Derby factory 243; *see* ceramics
Derby: Edward Stanley 11th Earl 256
Dering [Dearing]: Daniel 163; Sir Edward, 5th Bt 96, **112**, 274, 282; Mary 30, 155–56, 162–64, 268, 278, 300; Robert 162
Derussat: John Andrew 164, 171; Mrs de Rossett 164
Deskford *see* Findlater
Desse[r], William 232
Devis, William 282
De Varenne, Elizabeth (Margas) 233
De Vic, Isaac 56, 167, 269
Devonshire: William Cavendish, 2nd Duke (d. 1729) 291; 3rd Duke (d. 1755) 312; 5th Duke (d. 1811) 137, m. Georgiana (d. 1806) 255, 302

352   N.B.: USE PAGES 246–323 AS A SECOND INDEX

Dewes, Anne 165; *see* Delany
Diamonds *see* hardstones
Dicks, Robert 269
Dinglinger, Johann Melchior n. 314
Distance conversions 13
DISTILLERS *see* food and drink
Ditcher: Jane, Philip 174
Dive, Mrs Francis 163
Divorce *see* society
Dobson: Edward, John, William 269
Doctors *see* apothecaries
Dodd, William 196
Dodsley Robert 319
Doneraile, Arthur 3rd Viscount (d.1750) 156, 269, 298; *see* St Leger
Downe, Viscounts 267
Drake family 246, 270, 293, 305
Draper, John n. 180
DRAPERS *see* Textiles
Dresden: Japanisches Palais, Schloss Moritzburg 189; *see* Meissen
Dress and livery: Dresden ruffles 108, 201, mourning 172; clothes packed for Bath 108. *See* CORDWAINER Hill; HOSIER Pomfret; MANTUA MAKER Walton; MILLINERS Chandler, Ditcher, Griffith, Lowe, Neale, Sayer, Walton; PATTENMAKER Penny; SHOEMAKER Cottle n.285; STAYMAKER Burrough; TAILORS Collins, Cranmer, Graham, Howse, Jourdain, Prosser, Salmon. *See* armed forces, barbers, fans, haberdashers, lace, textiles
Drink *see* food and drink
DRUGGIST/CHEMIST *see* apothecary
Dry: Mary Jane, Rebecca 164
Dryden, John 35, 128
Dubose, Judith 164
Duesbury, William 243
Dufour, Paul 31
Duncombe: Anthony (later Baron Feversham), Jane 264, 270, 289
Dupplin *see* Kinnoull
Dupont, Lewis 57, 270
Dupré, Ann 217
Durham, Bishop of 311, 317
Duvall [Duval]: John & Peter 57, 211/27, 271
Duvivier, Lambert 271
Dyor & Antrim 293
Dysart, Lionel Tollemache, 4th Earl 135, 215, 220, 231–**32**, **244**, 265, 314, **323**. *See* Lauderdale
Ealing 196
Earthenware *see* ceramics
Earthquake 243; *see* Portugal
East India House & Company: 211/3; sales 220, 282, 306. MERCHANTS 249, 317, 318. DIRECTORS *see* Braund, Eyles, Gould & Nesbitt, Hyde, Rous, Turner. *See* trade destinations
Edict of Nantes 27
Edwards: Mary, 229, 279; John 300
Egerton, Anne 74
Egmont *see* Perceval
Egremont, Earl of 247
Elbridge, John 266
Elkington family **271**
Embassies: Berlin 284, Constantinople 35, Hamburg 274, Lisbon n. 63, 302, Prussia 257, Soissons 302, Sweden 302

Embroidery: Royal School of n. 333; Broderers' Company: Wright 244
Emes, Samuel 320
Employees: of Bennet n. 279; of Bertrand 59; of Chenevix 217, 222; of de Lamerie 279; of Hoare 52, 318, 322; of Roubel 61; of Wiltshire 322. *See* accounts, invoices
ENAMELLERS York House n. 151; *see* Allen, Craft, Duesbury, le Seur, Moser
ENGRAVERS, PRINTSELLERS *see* Bowles, Cluer, Faber, Gribelin, Cole, Kirk, Luce, Rollos, Sayer, Skinner, Sturt, Sympson, Vertue, Watson, White, Wicksteed, Lens. *See* booksellers
Engraving: 172, freedom boxes 149; on plate 34, 182, 309; removing 283; of duty stamps 262. Armorials on silver: *see* Bethel, Barrington, Clayton, Colebrook, Delme, Liddell, Osbaldeston, Pepys, St Albans, Sherrard. *See* boxes, engravers
Entertainment & sport: 121–37. Balls, dancing, royal birthdays 93, 102, 121, 131, 249. Dancers: Johnson 287, St Luce 291; lectures 131; Moor with two voices 131; Morris dancing 131; puppet shows/ wax figures 21/51, 288, 131–33; museums *see* Bridges, Rackstrow. SPORT: backsword 127; cockfighting 127; fishing 255; horse racing 101, 105, 129, 137, 229, 272; walking **126**–**128**. *See* assembly rooms, fairs, gaming, raffles
EO (evens & odds) *see* gaming
Epsom 101, 272
Ernie, John and Constantia Kyrle 271
Estcourt, Sir Thomas n. 115
Eton College 277
Etuis *see* boxes
Euston, Dorothy Boyle Countess of **158**–61; *see* Burlington
Ewell, Charles 28–29
Excise *see* customs, government posts
Exeter, Brownlow Cecil 9th Earl 317
Eyles: Frances 286, Sir John 272
Eyre: Henry 127, Sir Robert 33

Fairfax: Hon Charles Fairfax, 9th Viscount & family 40, **42**–**43**, **118**, 138, 272; Ferdinand 272
Fairs: Bartholomew 131, Leipzig 271
Family trees: Bennet/Rundell 174, Bertrand 28, Deards 38; Hoare/Russel 202; Royal 142; Wiltshire 46
Fane, Charles Fane 2nd Viscount 126
Fans **50**, **60**, **64**, **124**, 182; East India sales 282, 310; *see* Hart, Margas, Pinchbeck, Speren, Robins, Wicksteed, Loggan. FAN MAKERS Burnett, Clarke, Duvivier, Portret, Sayer. FAN STICK MAKER Lucas. *See* shop signs
Farren, Thomas 250, 302
Farrer, Dr 110
Feast of the Sons of the Clergy n.426
Featherwork, **2**, 175, **188**–**91**
Feline, Edward 56, 211/14, **222**–**24**, 273, 287; Henry 224, 273; Magdalen 224
Fenton, William 49
Ferguson, John 301
Ferrand, Elizabeth 273
Ferrers, Robert Shirley 1st Earl 112
Feversham 289; *see* Duncombe
Fielding, Henry 87, 196, 261, 310
Fiennes, Celia 81
Finch: Elizabeth (m. Sir Heneage Finch, Earl of Nottingham) 115; Frances (m. Sir John Bland) 252; Sir John (brother of 7th Earl of Winchilsea) 107; Isabella 108, 162–63 sister of: Daniel, 8th Earl 126, 136, 342 n. 230

N.B.: USE PAGES 246–323 AS A SECOND INDEX   353

Findlater: James Ogilvy, 5th Earl, Sophia (m. 5th Earl), Lord Deskford, later 6th Earl of Findlater 269, 288
Fines [Fynes], Kendall 273
Fire 154, 214, 278, 313
Fisher, Bryce [Brice] 249, 273, 290, 315
Fitz-William, Lady Anne 277
Fitzwalter, Benjamin Mildmay 1st Earl and Countess Frederica 85, 113–14, 216, 225, 244, 269, 276, 278, 280, 297
Fleming, Francis 93
Fleureau: Isaac, Francis 274
Fleury, Isaac 211/22, 273, Oliver 274
Flowers (artificial) 130
Floyer: Catherine 290, Charles 290, 318, Jane 274, Peter 274
Fogg: Catherine 289
Folkes: Sir Thomas 279
Fonnereau family: 274, 291
Food and drink: in accounts 110; in Bath 129; printing of labels 260. Bath Oliver biscuit 298, lampreys 287, mangoes 233, mineral waters 125, 167, 246, 233, pasties 186, rum 260, tea & coffee *see* Margas. *See* invoices. *See* BREWERS Calvert, Penny. CONFECTIONERS Smith. DISTILLERS Marchant, Pearce, Woolmer. GROCERS Cox, George, William, Marshall. HOP DEALERS Lant, Marchant. MALTSTERS Noyes, Penny, Stride. MEALMAN Shurmer. SUGAR MERCHANT Elbridge. VICTUALLERS Bullock, Marchant, Neale, John, Revel. VINTNERS Bragg, Cogswell, Neal. WATERS Smith. WINE COOPERS Pomfret, Viel. WINE MERCHANTS Clement, De Vic, Devaux, Hunt, Joye, Lemaitre, Linwood, Nesbitt & Gould, Pomfret, Purdie, Roussel, Russell, Standert, Thomas. *See* accounts, Bath/ inns, coffee houses
Ford, Richard 235, 273
Forgery and fraud: *see* crime
Forster & Johnson 274
Fotherby, Mary 274
Foulkes, George 240
Foundling Hospital 273
Fowler: & Rocke, Eli 275
Fox: Henry (later 1st Baron Holland) 275, 290; Stephen (later 1st Earl of Ilchester) 51, 111, 275, **300**; Fox Strangways archive 268
Frankland, Mary 164
Frederick [Fredericke], William 62, 173, 275
Frederick, Prince of Wales **156**; at Bath 146–53, 235; **225**, 298; gold boxes **146**; at Epsom 272; at Kew 315; with Quakers 275; PB's invoice 138, **148–51**. *See* Moody (cutler), Basnet (laceman), Wickes (silversmith); royal family, royal household
Freeman, Mary 258
Freemasonry: PB 31, 71; sword 294; trowel **71**. FREEMASONS *see* Barnevelt, Bennet, PB, Bishop, Bridges, Cockey, Cole, Collins, Creswell, Deards, Figes, Fleureau, Gwynn, Hamilton, Howell, Jackson, Kendrick, Kennedy, Kirkpatrick, Leake, Loubier, Masters, Moody, Morris, Nash, Nesbitt, Rainsford, Ross, St Albans, Skinner, Roussel, Russel, Shelvocke, Sherrard, Stanton, Stillingfleet, Street, Thurett, Wiltshire, Wooley, Wright
French Hospital 278
French plate: Brifaut 283, 254
Friend, William 281
Frith, Henry 33
Furnese: Anne, Catherine, Selina, daughters of Sir Robert 2nd Bt **112**

Furnishings: UPHOLDER: *See* Gibson; *see* cabinet makers, carvers, featherwork, textiles/mercers

Gagnon, Stephen 215
Galway, Henry 1st Earl n.63
Gaming: **134–136**; Acts of Parliament 49, at coffee houses 320, Groom Porter 99, in Bath and Tunbridge Wells 49, at Epsom 101, large losses 74–75, 252, Nash's involvement 73–75. GAMBLERS *see* Bedford, Bristol, Bland, Burlington, Cibber, Henley, Joye, Morris, Nash, Taaffe, Thomond, Valentine. *See* Assembly rooms, Delamain, Hayes, Lindsey
GARDENERS *see* Freeman, Meredith. Gardens *see* Inchiquin, Petre, Vauxhall
Garnier: Daniel, George, Isaac 276
Gatliffe, Sara 236
Gaudron, Marrianne 229
Gaultier family 316, Marianne 299
Gaussen, Peter **86**, 276
Gay, Robert **24**, 66, 70, 73, 81
Geekie, Alexander 276
Geneva 90
George: H 180; William n.191
Georgia Society trustees *see* Lapottre, Smith
Germain, Lady Elizabeth ('Betty', m. John Germain) 68; *see* Sackville
Germany: Berlin 284; Hamburg 274; Leipzig 271; Elector Palatine 113; Prussia 257. *See* Dresden, Poland, royal family
Gibbs, James 263, 307
Gibson, Christopher, Thomas 276
Gifts: diplomatic 146, *see* invoices
GILDERS *see* Allen, Pascall; *see* carvers
Giles, Abraham and James 231
Gillon, Catherine n. 15
Gilmore, Joseph **20**, 115, **118, 142, 153**
Gilpin, Thomas n. 347
GLASS SELLERS/GLASSMEN, *see* Gribelin, Margas, Turner
Glazby, William 272
Glenorchy, John Campbell Viscount (later 2nd Earl of Breadalbane) 263, **271, 306–07**
Glover, Mr 33
Godfrey: Benjamin 286; Charles 260; Edward 151
Godolphin: Francis 2nd Earl; Francis 2nd Baron 277
Godschall/Godskrall, Sir Robert 277
Gold: 13. *See* boxes, goldsmiths
Goldney, Samuel 174
Goldsmiths: 16; Company 211/8, printed warnings 291, beadle 219, royal 153. *See* boxes, jewellers, silversmiths, toymen, watch casemakers
GOLDSMITHS *see* Baker, Barber, Barrett, Boursin, PB, Braithwaite, Brown, Browne, Buhet, Cartwright, Cox, Cranmer, Cunst, Curtis, Dalton, Davis, Devis, Delamain, Dell, Dickinson, Dupont, Forster & Johnson, Foubert, Gribelin, Hart, Hayes, Howe, Janaway, Kemp, Lagarene, Lupart, Margas, Martin, Masters, McKenzie, Menier, Owen, Pantin, Passavant, Pons, Pugh, Rigal, Rogers, Russel, Sherston, Smith, Taylor, Thelkeld, Turmeau, Wickes, Wright
BANKER/GOLDSMITHS *see* Arnold, Atkins & Co., Barclay, Berchere, Bloxham, Boothby, Brassey & Co., Child & Co., Colebrook, Cooper, Coutts & Co., Cranmer, Drummond, Duncombe, Ewer, Fowler, Freame, Gosling, Green & Amber, Green, Hankey, Hayter, Hoare & Co., Horne & Temple, Ironside, Knight & Jackson, Lockwood, Martin, Middleton & Co., Minors,

354 N.B.: USE PAGES 246–323 AS A SECOND INDEX

Nesbitt, Paterson, Payne, Pepys, Roffrey, Sawbridge, Simpson & Ward, Snow & Denne, Sword Blade, Temple, Wallis, Wright
Goldsmith, Oliver 49, 74, 103, 159, 247
Gordon, Cosmo Gordon 3rd Duke 91, 106, 130, 216, 239, **266**, 318
Goring, Sir Charles 272
Gosling: Robert, Richard, & Sharpe 275, 277
Gosset family 191, **225**, 277
Goujon, Stephen 229
Gould, King & Nathaniel 277, 295 see Nesbitt
Goulet: Charles 171, Peter 171–72, 179, Susanna 171
Government offices: admiralty 317; apothecary general 276; armed forces 120, 295; attorney general 281; auditor's office 285; customs house 292; exchequer 267, 285, 289, 317; excise 113, 256, 263, 295, 302, 310, 317, 319; groom porter 99; Isle of Wight 283; northern province 252; pay office/paymaster general 120, 247, 276; post office 303, 308, prime minister 301; privy purse n.251; salt duties 113; speaker 279; stamp duties/office 252, 295, 302, 319; trade & plantations 271, 278, 302; treasury 263; war office 248. See armed forces, royal households
Govers, Henry 271
Gouyn, Charles 207, **242**
Grace, Edward 261
Grafton, Duke of see Euston
Graham: George 258, 277; John 56, 173, 277, n.65; Robert 290
Grain chains 37
Grandjean, Philippe 291
Green, Thomas 306
Greenway, Thomas 82
Grevile, Hon Dodington n.166
Greville see Brooke
Gribelin family 27, 29–35; Samuel **35**, 47, 56, 195, 211/20, 278; Simon 27, **32–35**, 278
Griffin, Benjamin and family 273, 278
Griffith, Rebecca 125
GROCERS see food and drink
Guerin, Isabeau and Maynard 278
Guildford, Lady **112**; see North
GUNSMITHS see Griffin, Purdey, Sale. See instruments
Gwynn, Howell 71, 278
Gye, Richard 204
Gyde, Cam 94
Gyles: John, Laurence, Isaac 279

HABERDASHERS see Arnold, Bennet, Bowden, Channing & Brent, Creswell, Marks, Moody. See dress, textiles
HAIRDRESSERS see barbers
Halfpenny: Charles, William & John 279
Halifax, George Montagu, 1st Earl (cr.1715 d.1739) 256, 285, 294 see Montagu
Hall: map **24**, John 94; Rachel 92; Thomas & Ann n.153
Hallmarking see marks
Hamilton: James 4th Duke 279; his sister-in-law Lady Archibald 161; his son Lord Anne 279; Mr 149. See Brooke, Edwards
Hammond: Henry 176; Mr 149
Hampden, Robert Trevor 1st Viscount 317
Handel, George Frederick 35, 120, 260
Hanet, Paul 218
Hanmer, Sir Thomas 4th Bt and Lady 255
Har[r]ache, Thomas 63, Pierre 278
Hardwares see base metal, cutlers, French plate
Hardstones: Bristol diamonds 167, coral 275, Pitt diamond, 264, 301. See DIAMOND CUTTERS Cope, Deletang/De L'Etang; DIAMOND MERCHANTS Franks, Salomons; DIAMOND-SETTER Roubel; LAPIDARIES Allen, Danborough, Spurrier. See jewellers, jewellery
Harford: Charles 56, 280; Richard 113–14, 280
Harland, Admiral Robert 270
Harrington family 280; William Stanhope 1st Baron, later Viscount Petersham and Earl of Harrington 252
Harris, Will **202**, 217
Harrison: Edward 250; Thomas 37, 45, 64, 83, 93–99, 129, 283
Hart, William 280
Hartley, George 257
Harvey: Felton 280; John 82, 275, 280; William 280
Hasell, Susanah 164
Hastings, Selina see Huntingdon
Hawley: Francis 2nd Baron 21/38, 96–99; Rachel 97, 99; Samuel 4th Baron 97–98. Elizabeth see Hayes
Hay see Dupplin
Hayes: Catherine (Kitty) 95, 290; Elizabeth Lady Hawley 93–9, 131, 281; Phillip 21/42, 96, 100, 171; Robert 96; Samuel 96. See assembly rooms, Hawley, Haynes
Hayne(s), Mary 118; David, Joseph, Charles 281
Hayter, William 281,
Hayward, John 39, 322; William n.40
Health/illness: advice 114, anatomical museum n.65, bathing 123, advertisements 246, 253, 261. DRUGGISTS: de Vic, Thayer; LANCET MAKER: Stanton. See apothecaries, Bath, hospitals, society
Heath, Thomas 445
Heaven: James, Thomas 94
Heckel, Augustin 146
Hedges, John n. 246
Helot [Hellet/Helst] family 28, 33; John 281
Henley, Anthony 281; Robert, later 1st Earl of Northington, 177, 281, 289
Herbert: Hon Robert Sawyer 129, Miss **91**
Herne (E.India sale fans) 282
Herring: Henrietta Maria 260; Mr (gamester) 137
Hertford see Somerset
Hervey, Mrs 66, 204. See Bristol
Hetling, Ernst von 153
Hickey, William 282
Hillan, Christian 57, 211/17, 225–27, **226–27**, 282
Hinchingbrook: Viscountess Elizabeth (mother of 4th Earl of Sandwich) 115
Hire of equipment 117, 125
Hoare & Co. **17**, 53, 57, 92, 96, 211/10; employees 52, 318. PB a/c 52, 207–323, 282; ledgers **48**, **52**, 57, **198**, **204**, 207, **208–09**. FAMILY: Henry 53, 293, 303; Richard **53**, **216**, 293, 312; Susannah 274. PURCHASES **48**, 105, 136, 139, 184, 216, **220–21**, 239, 265–66, 280, 287
Hoare, William and family 202–03; Elizabeth 198, 203; Ellen 282; Hannah 28, 240, 282; Martha 303; Mary 283; Prince 66, 199, 203, 265, 283, 296; William 56, 65–66, 68, 70, 122, 194–95, 198–99, 202–04, 283, 295–06, 302. PORTRAITS: **122**, **194**, **198**, **202**, 247, 249, 251–52, 257, 285, 286, 296;
Hobart: John Baron Hobart, later 1st Earl of Buckinghamshire n.330
Hobbs, John 82
Holder, Elizabeth 72
Holderness see Fitzwalter
Holland, John 283; see Fox, Henry
Hollingsworth see Pepys
Holroyd, Ann n. 362
Hooke, John 258
Hopkins, William 56, 283

N.B.: USE PAGES 246–323 AS A SECOND INDEX 355

Horses *see* auctions, entertainment, travel/transport
HOSIERS *see* dress
Hospitals: French Protestant 253, St Bartholomew's 72, 251, 263, 277, 292; St George's 308. *See* Bath
Hotham, Sir Charles Bt and Lady 65, 261, 283
Houghton, John, 53
Houstoun, George 285
Howse: Margaret 284, Samuel 284, William 284
Hoyle, Edmund 137
Hubert, James 56, **227**, 284; Michael 284; William 211/21, 227, 229, 267, 284, **289**
Hudson's Bay Company 249
Huguenot emigration 27
Humphreys (lodging house) 153–54, 284
Hunt, John 269
Huntingdon: Selina Hastings, m. Theophilus, 9th Earl 112, 137, 285
Huske, Lt Gen John 246, 276
Hutcheson [Hutchinson] 170, 285, 263
Hyndford: James Carmichael, 2nd earl 257

Ilchester *see* Fox
Inchiquin *see* Orkney
India warehouse 16. SHOPKEEPERS Davis, Margas, Motteux. *See* East India Company, toys
India: Calcutta 231, 233; Fort St George 318; Madras 257, 317. MERCHANT Levett
Ingleby, Sir John 3rd Bt 115
Ingram: Arthur, William 285
Instruments: Foubert's 'machine' 274, Bath Abbey organ 287. INSTRUMENT MAKERS *see* Cartwright, Heath, Margas, Marshall, Moore, Pyefinch, Scarlett, Sisson, Wright. LANCET MAKER *see* Stanton. OPTICIAN *see* Scarlett. *See* auctions, cutlers, watches
Insurance *see* Sun Fire. AGENTS *see* Allen, Boddicott
Inventories *see* Brathwaite, Kingston, Taylor. *See* accounts, auctions, crime, retailing
Invoices: Bernardeau 216; PB **42–43, 48, 130,** 138–139, **148, 150, 160**; Chenevix **202**; Coward **176**; Crook **266**; Elkington **271**; Margas **232**; Mitchell **179**; Sale **306**; Salmon **307**; Stanton & Cotterell **220**; Sutherland **314**; Tabart **323**; Thomas **315**; Turner **244**; Walton **201**; Wickes **152**; lodgings 118. *See* trade cards
Irby, Sir William 149
IRONMONGER *see* base metal
Ironside, Edward **84**, 283
Isted: Ambrose 197, 285; John 285

Jackson/& Colebrook: John 276, 285; Richard 285
Jacob: John (s/smith) 57, 211/23, **228**–29, 286, 301, John (case maker) 229, 286; John (patron) 261
Jacobite: rebellion 87, 264, 292. Followers: Astley, Benn, Caesar, Carew, Hay, Powis, Winton, Wynn. *See* crime/treason
Jamnitzer, Christoph n.314
Janssen [Jansson]: Mary 282; Stephen n.151
Japan wares: in bequests/stock *see* Margas, Spencer, Thomond, Turner, East India Company. JAPANNERS *see* Allen, Griblin
Jeffery [Jefferys], Nathaniel 200, 240
Jekyll, Sir Joseph 262
Jelly & Palmer 70
Jenning[s]: Deborah 286; Admiral Sir John 286; *see* Marlborough, Masham
Jernegan: Henry 255; Lady Mary (grandmother of 8th Lord Stafford) 119, **130**, 138, 246, 276, 322;

Jesser, John 51, 56, 286
Jewel Office 153
JEWELLERS 16; *see* Artaud, Axford, Bellis, Berchere, PB, Bertrand, Bishop, Boursin, Braithwaite, Briscoe, Brown, Callard, Cawthorn, Chadd & Ragsdale, Cox, Cole, Coles, Coller, Creswell, Creuze, Crisp, Davis, Deletang, Delamain, Demarin, Dicks, Duval, Fines, Fleureau, Forster & Johnson, Foubert, Goulet, Govers, Hughes, Kelsall, Kendrick, Lacam, Lock, Laubie, Marchant, Masters, Mayaffre, Naylor, Pantin, Pons, Poole, Pyke, Reeve, Rogers, Roubel, Satchwell, Smith, Tabart, Taylor, Thibault, Tilley, Torin, Trible, Turmeau, Webb, Wetherell & Janaway, Williams. NECKLACE MAKER/STRINGING Phillips, Wheatley. *See* goldsmiths, hardstones, toymen, watchmakers
Jewellery: value of 310, 312, 316, 321; *see* invoices
Jews/Judaica *see* religion
Johnson: Revd Gideon 163; Joshua and Thomas 287; Samuel 287
Jones: George Greenhill 56, 211/3, 229–**30**, 287; Richard 73, 82, 287
Jordan [Jorden/Jourdon/Jourdain]: Abraham 287; Anthony 224, John, Rachel 214.
Jowell, George 75, 287
Joye, Thomas 49, 287

Kandler, Charles, Frederick 42, 255
Kemp, John 53, 168, 309
Kendall: James, John, Luke 288
Kent: Henry Grey, Duke of 281; William 157
Kerr, Lady Louisa *see* Fitzwalter
Kerry: Gertrude, Countess 316
Kielmansegge, Count Frederick 176
Killigrew, William 94, 129
King, John 56, 288; Thomas & Sarah 83, 119
Kingsale, Gerald de Courcy 19th Baron 322
Kingston: Evelyn Pierrepont, 1st Duke **34**, 92; 2nd Duke **92**. Estate: 81, 92, 94, 142, 176, 266, 275, 304–05, 307; map 21/54, **24, 41,** 305
Kinnoull: Thomas Hay 7th Earl (d. 1718/19) **86**; George 8th Earl (d. 1758) 35, 86; Thomas Lord Dupplin, 9th Earl (d. 1787) 86, 270; John Hay 281
Knight & Jackson 286

Lacam, Isaac 309
LACEMEN/MERCHANTS *See* Basnet, Cole, Coward, Graham, Harford, Jennings, Tabart, Walton. ORRIS WEAVER Morell
Lacon family 131, 133, 288
Lagarene, Michel Cabaret 29
Lambert, Sir John 101
LANCET MAKER *see* cutlers, instrument makers
Langford (auctioneer) 261
Langkopf, Molling & Rasch 275
Langton, Ann, 261
LAPIDARY *see* hardstones
Lapostre/Lapautre/La Potre 289
Laprimandaye, Peter 306
Lauderdale, Elizabeth (née Murray, Countess of Dysart, widow of Sir Lionel Tollemache, m. 1st Duke 1671/2 (d. 1698)) **135**; Charles Maitland (d. 1744) and Elizabeth (1692–1778, dau of 4th Earl of Findlater) 6th Earl and Countess 115
Laurence, Richard 172
Law: Lindsey v. Pocock 101, EO proceedings 50. *See* Acts of Parliament, attorneys, crime, scriveners

Layton, Benjamin 293
Leake, James 18, 21/45, 56, 71, 87, 172, 176–78, 289
Le Cointe, John Robert n. 322
Le Despencer, Baron (Dashwood) 267
Lee, Henry n. 209
Leeds, Thomas Osborne 4th Duke of 190
Le Febure 323
Leffever [Lefevre], Roland 50, 313, 320
Le Grand: Edward 162, 289; Helena 259, 268, 280, 289, 306; William 289
Le Jeune: family 28; Mariaval **136**
Lemaitre [Le Maitre]: Mary Magdelaine 28, 31, 227; Cesar and Peter 56, 227, 289
Lennox, Lady Caroline 275
Le Normand, Nicholas **2, 188**–91
Lens, Bernard **76, 86, 184**
Le Quin (Paris) 304
Le Roux family: Abraham 230; John **230**, 289
Le Sage family 217
Le Seur/ Lechieur, Daniel 289, 312
Letter writers & diarists *see* writers
Levant Company 290
Leveridge, Richard **101**
Levett: Mr 190–91; family 290
Lewis, Lt Col George 30, 66, 199, 202
Liddell, Sir Henry 268
Liege, Francis 215
Lifford, Frederick William de Roye, 1st Earl 235
Lillie: Charles 31, 290; Edward 290
Lillo, George 272
Lincoln: Henry Pelham Clinton, 9th Earl and 2nd Duke of Newcastle under Lyne, *see* Newcastle. Lucy, m. 7th Earl 135, 153
Lindsey, Mary 93–95, 99–104. *See* Bath/assembly rooms
LINEN DRAPERS/MERCHANTS *see* textiles
Linley, Eliza 290
Lisbon *see* Portugal, trade destinations
Littleton, Mr 149
Liveries *see* dress
Lock, Mr (jeweller) 59
Lodging houses *see* Bath/inns
Loggan, Thomas **64**, **185**
Lombard, Jane 248
London Assurance Co. DIRECTORS *see* Loubier, Pearse, Rous
London: maps: **30, 36, 210–213**. Exeter Market/Exchange 30, 189, 211/17, 304; Fleet St **44**; Westminster Hall **210**. Inns: Golden Cross n.23, Swan **44–45**. LORD MAYORS *see* Barber, Benn, Delme, Eyles, Godschall, Hoare, Marshall, Perry. *See* shop signs
Londonderry: Frances 1st Countess 115, 290; Ridgeway Pitt, 3rd Earl 290
Long: Sir James 257, Sir Robert 303, Walter 290. *See* Tylney
Longbowstringmakers' Company 218
LORINER *see* Hopkins *see* spurs
Lost items *see* bills of exchange, crime, retailing
Lotteries/lottery shops 284; raffles: 274
Loubie[r]/Laubie, Louis 291
Lovelace: Catherine and family 94, 104, 253, 305
Lowe, Barbara n.23
Lucas, Robert 309
Luxborough, Henrietta, née St John, Baroness 85, 173
Lytton, Barbara and John Robinson 291, 305, 319

Macartney, General 279
Madden: John 204; Sarah 292
Mainwaring: Ambrose 292; Edward 255, 292

Malegue family 28
Maltsters *see* food and drink
Mann: Galfridus, Robert 292
Maps: America **30**; UK **38**; Bath **20–24, 40–41, 305**; London **30, 36, 210–13**. *See* Gilmore
Marchant family 137, 292
Margas: SILVERSMITHS Jacob 251, John, Simon 233. CHINAMEN 56, 130, 211/6, 231–33, **232–33**, 235, 292, 310, 317
Marin *see* Morin
Mariot: Antoine, Louis n. 15
Marks: on metals 12, 39, in Bristol 167, registration n. 355; on lost watch n.404; duty stamp 262; tradesmen's marks 262
Marlborough College n. 239
Marlborough: John Churchill, 1st Duke (d. 1722) 74, 260; Sarah, 1st Duchess (née Jennings, d. 1744) 89, 127, 165, 286, 293, 301, 311; 3rd Duke (succ. 1733, d. 1758) 156; 4th Duke 201; *see* Blandford
Marshall, Sir Henry **84**, 292; Isabella, John 310,
Martin 130; Benjamin 131
Masham: Anne, Abigail, Samuel 286, 293
Mason, John 230
Masons *see* architects
Massingberd family 250, 274
Massy, Anne 24
Masters family 21/22, 56, 149, 168, 172, 293
Mathematical instruments *see* Instruments
Mayaffre, Andrew 310
Maynard Master 225
Medicine *see* apothecaries, health, food and drink
Meissen factory 90, **140**, 214, 242, 317; *see* Dresden, retailing/advertisements, auctions
Meissonnier, Juste Auréle **92**
MERCERS *see* textiles
MERCHANT TAYLORS *see* textiles
MERCHANTS *see* trade destinations and relevant trades, e.g. snuff, textiles. Merchant and insurance companies *see* Africa, Bristol, East India, Georgia, Hudson's Bay, Levant, London Assurance, South Sea, Sun Fire Insurance; also *see* Portugal, Turkey
Methuen, Paul 261
Mettayer family 28, 33
Meux, later Massingberd 293
Meynell, Littleton Pointz 255, 312
Mildmay, Benjamin *see* Fitzwalter
MILLINERS *see* dress
Mineral waters *see* food and drink
Mineral Water Hospital [Royal National Hospital for Rheumatic Diseases (RNHRB)] *see* Bath
Mining *see* Coster, Gilbert, Langton, Townsend. *See* Bristol diamonds
Minors, Thomas 153, 194
Mitchell, Mary, 179
Models, silver **81, 105**
Mohun, Charles 4th Baron 279
Moncrief, Mary 302
Monmouth, Anne Countess of Buccleuch, widow of James 1st Duke of Monmouth 135
Monson: Theodosia, m. 2nd Baron 302
Montagu: Lady Mary (née Pierrepont, m. Edward Wortley Montagu) 37, 74, 89, 92–93, 149, 317. Elizabeth (née Robinson) 112, 125, 191, 305, 310, 318. John 2nd Duke and Duchess 53, 115, 128, 247, 276, 320. Family of Earl of Halifax: Ann 163; Barbara 294, 305; Frances 256; George 294

N.B.: USE PAGES 246–323 AS A SECOND INDEX 357

Montaigne, John 323
Montfort: Henry Bromley, 1st Baron 252
Montrose: Christian, m. 1st Duke **179**, 258, 284
Monuments: PB **26**, Coward **175**, Wiltshire **46**
Moody, George 291, 294
Moore: J. F. 249; John 295, 309; W 56
Morgan's coffee house 21/37, 49, 119
Morin/Marin, Marie 28, 295
Mornington *see* Tylney
Morris, John **122**, 295
Moseley, Elizabeth 253
Moser: George Michael, Mary **206**
Motteux, Peter **101**
Mountcashell, Edward Davys, 3rd Viscount 115
Mulford, John 56, 211/8, **234**, 296
Mundy, Philippa 293
Murray, Lady Betty 163
Music, opera, theatre: MUSIC 101, 120–21, 131. OPERA AND THEATRE: in Bath 21/12, 21/56, 97, 131, 313; in London 100, 128, 211/15 & /18 /21, 248, 261, 278, 281. *See* Baddeley, Delamain, Dillon, Handel, Hayes, Haynes, Leveridge, Lillo, Linley, Lindsey, Motteux, Ricciarelli, Quin
Muskerry, Robert Maccarty, Viscount and Earl of Clancarty 101
Mussaphia, Benjamin 271

Nash, Richard: timeline 9; map 21/11; 50, **64, 73**, 95, 252, 296, 298; and Wiltshire family 49–51; freeman 67; gaming 50, 73–**75**, 136, 165; gifts to 143–44, 146, 159; litigation 50, 282
Natural curiosities 181, 190, 274
Navy *see* armed forces
Neal[e]: Abraham 296; Daniel 297; Francis 29, 31, 296; Jacob 231, 296; James 306; John 31, 297; Robert 51, 56, 296, 310
Neave, Richard 297
Nesbitt: Arnold 74, 263, 297, 316; Robert 297
Newark, Viscount *see* Kingston
Newbattle, Viscount *see* Fitzwalter
Newcastle, Thomas Pelham, cr 1715 Duke of Newcastle upon Tyne and (in 1756) of Newcastle under Lyne **39**, 153, 303
Newland, Thomas 290
Newmarket: 37, 137, 308, 321; Jockey Club 229
Newsome, Mr 297
Nicholls, Norton 274
Nollekens, Joseph 257
Noon, Mr 101
Norfolk, Maria 8th Duchess 125, 178, 261
North, Frederick Lord (2nd Earl of Guildford) **146**
Northampton, James Compton, 5th Earl 263
Northey, William 315
Northington: *see* Henley
Northumberland, Elizabeth, née Seymour, m. Sir Hugh Smithson, later 1st Duke 89, **91**, 268, *see* Somerset
Norton: John, John & Sons 257, 297
Notes of exchange *see* bills
Nova Scotia 277
Noyes: Anne 297, Mrs 66, 204; *see* Martyn
Nugent, Robert Viscount Clare and Earl Nugent **84**, 156, 298

O'Brien: Capt; Percy Windham 252, 316
OILMEN *see* Johnson & Elliott 287
Oliver, William 69, **122**, 296, 298
Opera *see* music
OPTICIANS *see* instruments

Orange, Prince William of 83, 90, 107, 144–47, 159
Orkney, George Hamilton 1st Earl (1676–1737) 298; his daughter Anne (2nd Countess of Orkney d. 1756) 21/2, 107; her husband William O'Brien, 4th Earl Inchiquin (d. 1777) 252, 298, 316
Orrery, John Boyle 5th Earl 79, 177–78
ORRIS WEAVER *see* lace
Ownership of toys *see* invoices, wills
Oxenden, Sir George 5th Bt 257
Oxford, Robert Harley 1st Earl 190
Oxford: visit of Prince of Orange 147

Pacheco, Mr 278
Palmer: John 46; Joseph 258
Palmerston, Henry Temple 1st Viscount 68
Pantin, Lewis and family 57, **152**, 211/24, 234–**35**, 299
Parker & Wakelin **214**, 256, 273; *see* Wickes
Parker, Sir Philip 163
Parquot, Peter 31
Pars: Albart 236, Edward/Evert 211/12, **236**, 299
Pascall, James 35, 186
Passavant: John, Susanna 294, 299
PAWNBROKER *see* Doughty, Penny. *See* retailing/advertisements
Pearl stringing: *See* Phillips, M
Peirce [Pearce]: Jeremy **122**, 299, John 299
Pelham: Col James 153, 155–**57**, 299; Henry, of Stanmer 302. *See* Newcastle
Pendarves: Alexander 97; Lady 97; Mrs 132; *see* Delany
Penny: Thomas 300, William, 311
Pepys: John, Steventon, William 300
Perceval: Sir John 5th Bt (1683–1748, cr. Viscount Perceval 1723, Earl of Egmont 1733) 83, 87, 96, 156, 162, 266, 287, 289, 299, 301. His wife Catherine (née Parker) 163; his dau Catherine (Hanmer) 279; his son, later 2nd Earl of Egmont (1710/11–70, inh. 1748) 300. Philip 163
Percival: Joseph, 265, 300; Richard 15, 132, 185, 199. *See* Coster
PERFUMERS *see* Lillie 290; Smyth [Smith] 199, 310
Perreau: Robert and Daniel 196, 246, 256
Perry: John 249; Micajah **300**
PERUKE MAKER *see* barber
Phillips: Ann, Joanna 117, 119, 301; Mary 301
PHYSICIAN *see* apothecaries
Pickett, William 180
Pierrepont *see* Kingston
Pilleau, Peze 229, 268
Pigott, Aletheia **118**
Pinchbeck: Christopher 51; Jonathan (Fan Warehouse) **60**, 144; Mrs 197
Pine, J **24**
Piozzi, Hester [Thrale] n.86
Pitt diamond 264, 301
Pitt, William 1st Earl of Chatham 149, 229, 278, 301; *see* Londonderry
Pitts, Rebecca 149
Playhouse *see* music
PLAYING CARDS **88–89, 131, 133–34, 139**. MAKERS *see* Durrance, Williams
Plura, Joseph **237**, 302
Pocock: Col John 100–01, Elizabeth n.152
Pointz *see* Poyntz
Poland: King of 189; *see* Dresden, Germany
Pomfret, Thomas 45, **48**, 56, 97, 45, 139, 302. Thomas Fermor 1st Earl and Countess Henrietta 128, 149
Pons, Peter 229, 317

358   N.B.: USE PAGES 246–323 AS A SECOND INDEX

Poole: Grace, William 302. Sir Francis, 2nd Bt 295, 302, 319. Charles 302
Pope, Alexander 59, 65, **82**, 217, 247, 259, 291, 302, 312
Popple: Alured 293, 302; Henry 248, 302. Marianne 293, William 303
Porcelain *see* ceramics
Portal: Abraham 263, Lewis 236, Priscilla 254
Portland, Margaret (née Cavendish) 86, 190–91, 271, 273; her husband William Bentinck, 2nd Duke (1708–62) 265, 300
Portret, Jacob 185
Portsmouth, Elizabeth 1st Countess 163
Portugal: earthquake 165, 290, 312; Consul General 302; *see* trade destinations
Postal service 72, 109, 303, 308
Powell: Anna 279; Anthony 303; Mansel 303; Martin 100, 131, 133, 303
Poyntz [Pointz]: Margaret 311, Stephen 107, 155–57, 302, William 302
Prestage (auctioneer) 214
Preston: Charles Graham 3rd Viscount 303; his wife Anne (née Cox) 265
PRINTERS, PRINTSELLERS *see* booksellers, engravers
Prior Dobson & Williams 269
Privateer: Comyn 263, Shelvock 308
Properties: Althorp 140–41, 311; Arlington St 92; Badminton Hse 251; Barn Elms 53; Belvedere n.243; Bendish Hall 308; Benington 257; Bilby Hall 318; Bolesworth C'tle 316; Boreham 53; Brocket Hall 288; Brodsworth 271; Brookmans Pk 276; Calverley 251; Calwich Abbey 277; Cannons 120, 261; Chevening 312; Christchurch Mn 274; Clarendon Pk 289; Claverton 309; Claydon 256; Cliveden 107, 298; Cornwell Hse 296; Corsham Ct 261; Crowcombe 256; Dodington Pk 262; Doneraile Pk 269; Draycote 257; Drayton 307; Dyrham Pk 62; Rochester Hse 299; Gunnersbury Hse 196; Ealing Hse 196, 251, 276; Eardisley Pk 303; Ecton Hall 303; Erlestoke 268; Fairfax Hse 42; Ferne Hse 278; Flixton Hall 246; Fordhook 196; Frampton Ct 261; Gilling Castle 42; Grange 177, 281; Gubbins 307; Gunby 293; Gunnersbury Hse 196; Ham Hse 135; Hanbury Hall 319; Hardcott Hse 149; Helmingham Hall 135; Hill St 305; Holkham 101; Holland Hse 275; Horsmans Pl 255; Kedleston 267; Kelston Hall 280; Kempton Pk 296; King's Weston 311; Kippax 252; Knebworth 319; Lacock Abbey 314; Ladymead Hse 281; Longleat 244; Maiden Bradley 320; Maiden Earley 289; Marden Pk 260; Melbourne Hall 288; Menabilly 260; Minterne Hse 260; Montagu Hse 191, 305; Moulsham Hall 113; Mount Morris 305; New Hall 53; Newark Pk 261, 280; Newton Pk 261, 288; Nunnington Hall 303; Osterley Pk 259; Ozleworth Pk 261; Pendarves n.3; Phillis Ct 264; Piercefield Pk 296, 306; Pitshanger 196, 277; Powderham C'tle 265; Powis C'tle 303; Prior Pk 72, 177; Revesby Abbey 249; Rochester Hse 196; Rood Ashton 290; Rousham 145, 258; Sandleford Priory 305; Schomberg Hse 113; Seaton Delaval 247; Shaw Hall 107, 120; Shaw Hse 296, 310; Shockerwick **46**, 256; Shortgrove 315; South Wraxall 290; Spencer Hse 311; Stanmore Hse 270; Stourhead 53; Strawberry Hill **200**; Titchfield Abbey (Place Hse) 268; Troy Hse 256; Twickenham 312; Twisel C'tle 252; Ufton Ct 294; Wallington Hall 251; Wanstead 257; Warwick C'tle 90; Wenvoe C'tle 315; Weymouth Hse 298; Whetham 271; Whitmore Hall 255, 292; Wichnor Pk 290; Wimbledon Pk 311; Woburn Abbey 325

Prosser family 31, n. 50
PUBLISHERS *see* booksellers
Pugh, Humphrey 57, 211/10, **238**, 261, 304
Pulteney *see* Bath, Earl
Puppet shows *see* entertainment
Purdey [Purdie]: John, James, 304, William 59, 303
Pyefinch family, Henry 231–33, **232**
Pyke, John 21/47, **62–63**, 214
Pyle, Sir Seymour Bt 115

Rackstrow, Benjamin **44**, 254
Raffles: 274; *see* lotteries
Ragdale [Ragsdale] *see* Chadd
Ragg [Wragg]: Joseph, Samuel, Mrs 163–64
Ralph, James 196
Ramsay, Lady Elizabeth (dau of 3rd Earl of Dalhousie) n. 142
Ranby, Mr 162
Rashleigh, Jonathan 260
Rawlinson, Sir Thomas **84**
Rayner, Dr 69
RAZOR MAKERS *see* cutlers
Reasey, Mary 230
Reeve: George 171; Mrs (Norwich) 33
REFINERS *see* Cox, Floyer
Regnart (surgeon), n. 141
Religions: ROMAN CATHOLIC 21/17, 71, *see* Fairfax, Meredith, Petre, *see* Jacobites. JEWS / JUDAICA *see* Franks, Swartz; cup and cover 253. NON-CONFORMIST *see* Gould, Huntingdon, Stillingfleet, Wesley. QUAKER *see* Barclay, Freame, Marchant. Non-juror 294
Retailing: advertisements 37, 59, 61, 63, 88, 180–81, **183**, 185, 215, 269, 283, 317. Fitting out shops 18–19, 41; shopkeepers as bankers 45, 53; pricing stock 40. *See* auctions, crime, employees, fires, hire, individual occupations/trades, invoices, marks, shop signs, trade cards
Rhett, Col William 164
Ricciarelli, Joseph 63
Rich: John 261; Sir Robert, 4th Bt 115
Richardson, Samuel 174, 177, 258, 305
Richmond: Charles Lennox 2nd Duke, 222, 246; Sarah 2nd Duchess 249
Rigal, Anthony 29
Robellon [?], Mrs 163
Robins: Henry 261; Thomas 78, **98**, 124, **182**, **185**
Robinson family: Sara [Scott] 294, 305; Elizabeth (*see* Montagu); Matthew jnr, Matthew snr, Matthew Morris and Morris 305. Thursby (Mayor of Bath) 287; William 291, 305
Rocher, Jeanne 257
Rockingham: Lewis Watson, 1st Earl (d. 1723/4) 112, 113; Mary Finch 1st Marchioness 163; 2nd Earl (d. 1745) **112**. *See* Sondes
Rogers: Thomas 179, William 21/34, 171, 174, 179–81, 304, William jnr 180
Rokeby, Matthew Robinson 2nd Baron 305
Rollos: John, Philip 33–**34**
Roman Catholics *see* religion
Roman remains *see* Bath
Romney, Robert Marsham 2nd Baron 68
Roper, Hon Charles 317
Rosoman (Yeates & Warner) 131
Ross: Alexander 310; Joshua 35, 71, **186**; Thomas **51**, 57, 71, **108**, **182**, 186, 306
Rothwell, Arthur n. 340

Roubel, Moses and family 21/36, **58**–63, 304, 321
Roupert family 28
Roussel family, 28–31; Susanna 218. *See* Russel
Rousselet, Nicolas 31
Rowley, John 244
Royal Academy n.331
Royal Bounty 270
Royal Exchange: 211/6. DIRECTORS *see* Comyn, Cooke, Godschall, Lockwood
Royal family: 142–157; family tree 142; George I gaming 135; George II coronation 312; Pr Amelia 143–**44**, 159, 196, 258; Anne Pr Royal 90, 144, 147; Pr Caroline 108, 143, 154–57, 155; Pr Louisa of Denmark 128; Pr Mary of Hesse 107, 128, 143, 154–55, 157, 268, 302; William Duke of Cumberland 128, 131, 143. *See* Frederick, Pr of Wales; Orange, Pr of; royal households
Royal Households: members in PB a/c 156.
   KING & QUEEN clerk 303; cofferer 250; dresser to princesses 155–56, 162; gentleman pensioner 225; Duke of Cumberland's comptroller 156, 302; gent/groom/lord of the bedchamber 265, 283, 289; lady of the bedchamber 89; gent of privy chamber 307, 313; governess 156, 268; governor to children 302; groom of the stole 89; groom porter 99; master of jewel office 153, 260; master of the ceremonies 144–45; sergeant surgeon 162; table keeper 163; warden of the Stanneries n.251.
   PRINCE OF WALES auditor general n.252; cofferer 256; comptroller 156, 269, 298; deputy treasurer n. 239; governor 146; master of the robes n. 251; gent/groom/lord of the bedchamber 156, 269, 300, 315; secretary 155–57; steward 156; surveyor general 272; treasurer & receiver general 151, 156; treasury 247; yeoman of the cellar 313; Pr dowager's treasurer 315. *See* Government offices
Royal Warrant holders *see* Duval, Scarlett, Wickes, Wright
Rundell [Bridge & Rundell]: family tree 174; Eleanora, John 281, Phillip 174, 179–80, Richard, Samuel 281, Thomas 127, 311
Russel [Roussel]: timeline 9; map 36; family tree 202; advertisement 225.
   Elias 199, 217, 227; Elizabeth (*see* Chenevix); Hannah, Mary 199; Peter 36, 56, 101, 195, 199, **202–04**, **206**, 217, 239–40, 306, 101, 210
Russell: Lady Caroline **201**, **314**; Lady M 322. *See* Bedford
Russia 34, 92
Rysbrack, Michael 263, 322

Sacheverell, Henry 316
Sackville: (sons of 1st Duke of Dorset) Lord George, later Germain 307; Lord John, 278
St Albans, Charles Beauclerk 1st Duke 71, **106**
St John, Hon John 112; *see* Bolingbroke
St Leger *see* Doneraile
St Luce, Mr 291
Sale, Edward **306**–07
Sales *see* auctions
Salmon, Robert 59, Sarah 59; Lazarus **307**
SALTER Gilbert 276
Sandwich, John Montagu 4th Earl, 309; *see* Hinchingbrooke
Sargent: Birch & Co., Aufrere & Co., John 247
Satchwell, Thomas 253
Saunderson *see* Scarborough 3rd Earl
Savigny, Mr (cutler) 262
Savil *see* Skrine
Savile: Gertrude 45, 123, 133; Henry **40**

Sayer: Mary, Robert 308
Scarborough: Richard Lumley, 2nd Earl 136, 308; Thomas Lumley-Saunderson 3rd Earl 149, 151, 156
Scarborough, Yorks 93, 284
Scarlett, Edward 211/25, **239**, 308
Scarsdale, Nathaniel Curzon 1st Baron 267
Scent flask **163**
Scheemakers, Peter 270
Schultz *see* Shutz
Scientific instruments *see* instruments
Scott, George 149, 287, 294, 305
SCRIVENER Frith 33
Scudamore, Frances 251
SCULPTOR/STATUARY Cheere, Gosset, Hoare, Moore, Nollekens, Plura, Rysbrack, Scheemakers. *See* artists, monuments
Seager, William 275
Seals 68, **82**, **129**; *see* engraving
Second-hand, *see* retailing, pawnbrokers
Servants *see* accounts, crime, employees
Seymour: Lady Betty 89, **91**; *see* Northumberland; Lord George 89 *see* Somerset
Shagreen *see* boxes
Sheridan, Richard Brinsley 290
Sherrett, Peter 236
Sherston, John 171
Sheyler's coffee house 119
Shop signs BATH: Duke of Grafton's Hunter 260; Golden Flower d'Luce 62–63, 201; Golden Cannister 288; Golden Lyon 322; Grasshopper 181; Hand & Solitaire 59; Kings Arms 62, 275; Nag's Head 284; Ring & Pearl 172, 181; Two Lappets 176; Star 175. *See* Bath/inns
   LONDON: Acorn 248, 254; Angel 286; Angel & Crown 283; Archimedes & Globe 239; Bible & Ball 251; Black Lion 285; Black Spread Eagle 275; Blackmoores Head 214; Blue Balcony 307; Blue Last & Comb 29; Civet cat 310; Crown 217; Crown & Golden Ball 227; Crown & Pearl 274; Crown & Sceptres 235; Dyal 267, 272; Eagle & Pearl 255, 263; Fan & Crown 73; Fish 255; Fleur de Luce 258; Gold Angel 253; Golden Anchor 310; Golden Ball 279, 285; Golden Bottle 17, 282; Golden Cup 217, 253, 320; Golden Eagle 270; Golden Ewer 240; Golden Falcon 270; Golden Falcon & 2 Flower de Lis 300; Golden Fan 233; Golden Head 35, 231; Golden Key 318; Golden Lion 291; GR & Crown 262; Golden Ring 273; Grasshopper 280, 293; Green Man & Still 322; Hand & Fan 256; Hand & Spur 295; Hand & Snuff Box 246; Hen & Chickens 282; Indian Queen 220; King's Arms 88, 299; King's Arms & Snuffers 257; Lock & three keys 33; Maidenhead 260; Marygold 259; Mitre & Crown 277; Orrery & Globe 244; Parrot 253; Peacock 234, 265; Pearl 274; Pistol & L 215; Plume of Feathers 299; Queen's Head 283; Ring & Pearl 284; Ring & Ball 315; Rose & Crown 293; Ship 258; Spread Eagle 311; Sun & Mitre 262; Tea Table 265; Three Crowns 294; Three Kings & Spotted Dog 250; Three Rabbits 293; Three Squirrels 275, 277; Three Tunns 314; Tobacco Pipe 311; Turk's Head 249; Two Golden Balls n. 437; Unicorn 222; Unicorn & 2 Daggers 309; Vine 294; Wheatsheaf 298. *See* trade cards
Shops, management of *see* retailing
SHORTHAND WRITER *see* Edey 271
Shrewsbury, Adelaide 1st Duchess 129
Shruder, James 56, 211/26, **240–41**, 309
Shuckburgh: Ann, Diana, John 197

360   N.B.: USE PAGES 246–323 AS A SECOND INDEX

Shutz [Schultz]: Augustus 157, 301, Elizabeth 157; John **156**–57, 299, 309
Siddons, Sarah 71
SILK *see* textiles
SILVERSMITHS including bucklemakers, plateworkers, smallworkers, spoon makers: *see* Allen, Aumonier, Baker, Barbot, Barker, Bellis, Boothby, Boursin, Buker/Bouket, Bull, Callard, Cawthorn, Chadd & Ragsdale, Cooper, Courtauld, Cragg, Crespin, Creswell, Curghey, de Lamerie, Dicker, Dobson, Farren, Feline, Fleureau, Fleury, Garnier, Godfrey, Goulet, Hanet, Harache, Hart, Hillan, Holland, Hopkins, Houstoun, Innocent, Jacob, Jones, Kandler, Kendrick, Lawrence, Le Sage, Marchant, Martin, Masters, McFarlan, Mettayer, Moody, Mulford, Norris, Pantin, Parker & Wakelin, Pars, Pilleau, Prior, Dobson & Williams, Reeve, Renou, Rollos, Sardett, Shruder, Spilsbury, Whipham, White, Wickes, Willaume, Williams. *See* goldsmiths, jewellers, jewel office, watch casemakers
Simpson: Charles 94, 129, John, William 94
SINGERS *see* music
Sisson, Jonathan 262
Skinner, Jacob 51, **62**, 68, 149, 181–**82**
Skrine family 153, 260, 309; *see* Barrington, Clarges
Slater, James 267
Slavery 164, 233, 247; *see* trade destinations
Sloane: Sir Hans 163, 285; Sarah 247
Smith [Smyth]: George, James **196**, 199, 310; Elizabeth 296; Henry 100; John, Thomas 282, 310; Bath confectioner 118
Smithin, Samuel 153
Smithson *see* Northumberland
Snow & Denne 113, 310
SNUFFBOX MAKERS *see* boxes
SNUFF MEN *see* Cotterell, Crook, Desca, Gaudron, Hubert, Moody, Vertue. TOBACCONISTS AND MERCHANTS *see* Cary, Coulthurst, Gould, Hyde, Joye, Perry, Norton
Soane, Sir John 296
SOAP BOILER *see* Gwatkin
Societies: Antiquaries 253; Encouragement of Arts, Manufactures and Commerce 226; Royal Society fellows *see* Brigstock, Cheyne, Clarke, Domcke, Fauquier, Masham, Petre, Ravaud. *See* Clergy, sons of; clubs; Georgia
Society: 'quality'/middling sort 83, 85, 87; the season 105; visitors to Bath 83; behaviour/codes of conduct 85–86, 88, **102**, 132; meeting the devil 256; income 113–14, 279. DEATH: in a brothel 101, by breaking a leg 247, duelling 279, by hanging 109, 214, from smallpox 89, in a moat 261, suicide 63, 99, 103, 252, 258, 268–69, 308, of children 58, 161, 255, 318; funerals/mourning 162, 172, 175, 253, 289–90; bequests, *see* wills. DEBTS: in marriage 255, *see* bankrupts, gaming. MARRIAGE cross-class 253; gifts 89; unhappy/ divorce 161, 251, 279, 284, 294, 305; elopements 279; illegitimacy 112, 246, 251; large families 112, 250, 255, 342 n.230. Longevity 256. Substantial fortunes: 249, 262–63, 267, 179, 288, 311; hiding cash 293. *See* bankrupts, crime, gaming, health, wills
Somers [Cocks] 261
Somerset: 6th Duke (1662–1748) and Duchess (née Percy), **89**, 315; 7th Duke (1684–1749/50, styled Earl of Hertford to 1748) and Duchess (Frances, née Thynne) 83, 89–**91**, 145, 147, 161, 176, 201, 290, 318, 323; 8th Duke (1694/5–1757) 320. *See* Beaufort, Northumberland

Sondes, Catherine Tufton, Viscountess 110, 113. *See* Rockingham
South Sea Company 88, 120, **139**, 195, 211/4. DIRECTORS *see* Edwards, Fauquier, Joye, Linwood, Smith
Southwell family 163; Edward 300, 311; Lady Betty 103; Helena (le Grand) 289
Sparrow, Revd James 66
Spectaclemakers' Company 233
Spencer: Hon John 138–41, **156**, 302, 311; John Spencer 1st Earl 311
Speren, George **50**, **64**, **124**, 172, **182**, 185
Spilsbury, Francis 311
Sport *see* entertainment
Sprimont, Nicholas 225
SPUR MAKER *see* Moore. *See* Loriner
Spurrier: Isaac 311, Jonathan 311
Stamford, Mary 2nd Countess 109
Standert, Frederick 260, 290, 312
Stanhope: Philip 2nd Earl, his sisters Lucy and Jane 312. Hon John 284; Sir William 283–84, 312 (*see* Chesterfield, Hotham)
Stanley: Lady Charlotte (dau of 11th Earl of Derby) 256; Sarah (née Sloane) 163; Sir Edward 5th Bt 66, 262, 264, 312; Sir John 4th Bt 312
Stanton: Edward 312; Frederick 211/2, **220–21**, 312; William 312
STATIONERS *see* booksellers
STATUARY *see* sculptor
STAYMAKERS *see* dress
Steele, Sir Richard 101, 133
Stevenson, Bennet 119, 312
Stow, John 30, **36**, 210
Strafford, Anne 1st Countess 286
Strahan, John 82, 313
Strawberry Hill 200
Strode: Grace 89, Samuel and William 313
Strype, John 30, **36**, 210
Stuart: Prince Charles Edward 87; James 305; *see* Jacobites
Sturt: Humphrey 314; John 184, 314
Sun Fire Insurance 246, 273. *See* insurance
Sunderland, Charles Spencer 3rd Earl 311
Sundon: Charlotte, m. William Clayton 1st Baron 266, 322
Surgeons: *see* apothecaries
Sutherland, Frances **314**
Swartz, Baron 101
Swift, Jonathan 249
Sword Blade bank 307
Sylvia 'Miss': *see* Braddock
Sympson, Joseph n. 126; S 181
Syms, Mr 103

Tabart, Daniel 57, 314, 323; James 317
Tables: PB bank a/c 54–57; *see* family trees, timelines
TAILORS: *see* dress
Talbot, William Fox- 314
TALLOW CHANDLER: Lloyd 309
Tankerville, Charles Bennet 3rd Earl 248
Tanqueray, David 255
Taylor: Elizabeth 21/32, 167–**70**; John 168, 179; Robert 262
Tea & coffee: *see* food and drink
Teboe /Tibboe/Tibbault: *see* Thibault
Terrace Walk, Bath 18–19, 39–41
Tessier, Dr James 145, 291
TEXTILE trades/merchants: BLACKWELLHALL FACTORS *see* Baker, Lehook, Pointer, Scott. DRAPERS *see* Bennet, Cracherode, Marshall, Rundell. CLOTHIERS *see* Baker,

N.B.: USE PAGES 246–323 AS A SECOND INDEX

Coulthurst, Cox, Fisher, Gould, Griffin, Jesser, Neale, Wiltshire. LINEN DRAPERS & MERCHANTS *see* Arnold, Barclay, Bennet, Fonnereau, Griffith, Harford, Howse, Penny, Perry, Townsend, Turmeau. MERCERS *see* Bennet, Clutterbuck, Colebrook, Harford, Hinchliffe, Howse, Pritchard. MERCHANT TAYLORS *see* Dell, Elkington, Painter. SILK MERCHANT *see* Delme. SILK THROWSTER *see* Denne. SILK WEAVER *see* Jourdain, Woolstonecraft. STUFF SHOP *see* Bellis/Jourdain. WEAVERS *see* Cazalet, Collins, Pritchard. WOOLLEN DRAPERS *see* Baker, Barnevelt, Harford, Mann. WOOL STAPLERS *see* Mackrell, Neale. *See* armed forces, dress, haberdashers, lacemen
Thayer, Humphrey 93–100, 129
Theatre: *see* music
Thelkeld, Peter, William, Mary 314–15
Theobald, James 137, 255
Thibault, Thomas 57, 211/9, 219, 291, 295, 315
Thimbles **166**
Thomas, Evans 56, **315**
Thomond: Henry O'Brien 8th Earl 74, 315; Piercy O'Brien 316
Thorne, William 220
Thresher, John 262
Thynne *see* Brooke, Somerset, Weymouth
Tilley [Tilly], James and Margaret 47, 62, 316
Tilson, James, Thomas 316
Timbrell & Bell 281
Timelines 9, 94
Tobacco *see* snuff
Tole [Toll], Ann 266, Richard, Esther 316
Tollemache *see* Dysart, Buckminster
Tompion, Thomas 67, 92
Tonson, Mary 248
Torin [Torians/Torvano/Torriano], James Lewis, Samuel 316
Townshend: Horatio, Thomas, Viscounts 317
Toys & toyshops: meaning of 16. *See* retailing, India warehouse, invoices. TOYMEN/WOMEN *see* Allen, PB, Bellis, Bowden, Caldwall, Cartwright, Chadd & Ragsdale, Chenevix, Clarke, Cox, Creswell, Deards, Hayward, Harache, Howe, Jackson, Kirk, Lilley, Martin, Neal, Pantin, Parquot, Passavant, Pinchbeck, Plimmer, Pugh, Pyke, Rogers, Roubel, Smith, Speren, Sutherland, Taylor, Thelkeld, Triquet, Vertue, Viet & Mitchel, Vigne, Wetherell & Janaway, Wicksteed, Willdey, Wright
Tracey, Mr Justice 115
Trade cards *see* Allen, Bernardeau, Cole, Coles, Coward, Davis, Dobson, Hillan, Jackson, Jarvis, Layton, Le Quin, Owen, Phillips, Pritchard, Pugh, Pyke, Rogers, Sayer, Scarlett, Shruder, Sisson, Spicer, Stanton, Stephen, Turmeau, Walton. *See* invoices, shop signs
Trade destinations/merchants to: 54, Africa 247; America 249; Baltic 297; Bance Island 247; Dublin 249; Florida 290; Germany 249, 274–75; India 247, 318; Leghorn n.318; Lisbon 275, 320; Madras 257, 317; New York 249, 278; Nova Scotia 277, 317; Pennsylvania 249; Philadelphia 249, 275, 297; Portugal 273, 277, 289; Russia 297; Turkey 260, 264, 290, 292, 297, 307, 319; Virginia 301; West Indies 249
Travel & transport: carriers 45, 108; cost 111, cost of keeping horses 83, 119, in Bath 81, 111, 116, 144, to Bath 105–14. COACHMAKER: Cutler 308. *See* Wiltshire family
Travell, Agnes 322

Trevor: Lady Elizabeth 251; Robert Hampden 4th Baron, later Viscount Hampden 311; family 317
Trials: *see* crime
Trigau, Jacob 316, 318
Trim, George 131
Triquet, Stephen 168
Trognaux [Trigneau] 56, 318
Tucant: watchmaker 169
Tucker, Gertrude 72
Tunbridge Wells 101, 105, 168; gaming at 37, 49–51
Turet/Thuret: Isaac, Jacques 316
Turkey 35, 264; *see* trade destinations
Turmeau: Allain, Isaac, Jane 318
Turner: Elias 307; Jane 274; Thomas 56, 211/28, 241–**44**, 318; Charles, William 52, 224, 274, 318
TURNERS *see* Bernardeau, Francis, Higgons, Hutchinson, Jarvis, Neale
Turton: Jane 296
Tylney: Richard Child, Viscount Castlemain then Earl Tylney, and John 2nd Earl 257. Catherine Tylney-Long 290, m. 4th Earl of Mornington 257
TYPOGRAPHER: Luce, L 291
Tyso: John royal g/smith 153

UPHOLDER: Gibson 276. *See* furnishings
UNDERTAKER: Bennet 175. *See* society/funerals

Valuations: *see* inventories
Valuer/appraiser: *see* auctions/dealers
van Geffen, Arnoldus **105**
Vanne, Charles 295
Vardy, John 270
Vauxhall: Gardens 73, **196**, 312; factory 266
Verney, 256, Sir John (later Viscount Fermanagh) 85, 110–11, 291
Vernon: Bowater, Thomas, James 319
Vertue: George 35, 186; James **67**, 186–**87**, 319
VICTUALLER *see* food and drink
Viel, John 269
Viet & Mitchell 130
Vigne: Ferdinand 168, Thomas 319
Villiers: Catherine 266; *see* Orkney,
Vincent: Edward, George 293
VINTNERS *see* food and drink, Bath/inns

Wade: Gen. George 277, 289; William 277
Wakelin: John 259, Charlotte 319
Walcam, John **167**, 319
Wales: *see* Frederick Pr of, Royal households
Wallingford: William Knollys, styled Viscount Wallingford 246
Wallis 39
Walmersley: Catherine 301, William 319
Walpole, Horace 90, 161, **200**, 243, 269
Walton sisters 65, 197, **201**, 319
Walton, Izaak **44**
Warburton: Barbara (née Lytton), William 291, 305, 319; Revd William 72
Ward (bookseller) 312; Caesar 258; Sarah 272
Wardour, Col Tomkins **91**
WAREHOUSEMAN *see* Newberry
Warner (Yeates & Rosoman) 131
Warwick *see* Brooke
Watches and clocks **39**, 103, 167, 227, 230. WATCH CASEMAKER *see* Goujon, Helot, Hill, le Roux, Moore. CHAIN MAKER *see* Desear, Kemp.

CLOCK AND WATCH MAKERS *see* Allen, Baird, Bathe, Bradshaw, Browne, Bullock, Cabrier, Cartwright, Chandler, Cockey, Cox, Demarin, de Vic, Devis, Duval, Everell, Ewer, Fonnereau, Graham, Gribelin, Helot, Howse, Hubert, Jarvis, Jourdain, King, Laurence, Le Roux, Massey, Mulford, Pepys, Pyke, Rainsford, Reynolds, Roubel, Taylor, Threlkeld, Thuret, Tompion, Tucant, Turmeau, Vigne, Walcam, Walker, Williams. *See* retailing/advertisements, goldsmiths, instruments, invoices, jewellers, marks

Water closet: Harrington 280

Water *see* Bath; food and drink

Watson: Catherine, m. Edward Southwell 110, 311, Joel 319

Waxes 229. WAX MODELLERS, WAXWORKS *see* Cocks, Gosset, Lacon, Pars. *See* artists, entertainment, puppets

Weather, 107, 109. *See* travel

WEAVERS *see* textiles

Webb: Arthur, Peter 170, 217, 263, 269, 271, 280, 304, 307, 316, 319, 321

Webster: Abigail, Thomas 315

Weights and measures conversions 13

Welsh, William n. 141

Wesley, John 137, 195

West Indies: Antigua 296; Barbados 262, Bermuda 303, 393; Jamaica 247, 270, 275, 303; St Croix/Leeward Islands 318; St Domingo, St Kitts 214, St Vincent 296. *See* government offices, trade destinations

Westmeath: *see* Delvin

Wetherell & Janaway 286

Weymouth: Henry Thynne 1st Viscount 89; Thomas 2nd Viscount (d. 1751) 89, 298

Wharton, Philip 1st Duke 103

Wheatley, George 50, 320

Whipham, Thomas 321

White, John 301, 320

Whitmore: Richard, Sir Thomas **184**; Anne 264

Wickes, George 151–**52**, 157, 234, 266. Customers *see* Adair, Ashley, Bance, Chandos, Clarke, Coster, Creswick, Delme, Downing, Frederick, PoWales, Gilbert, Hyde, Inchiquin, Pelham, Penton, Sherrard, Whitchurch, Yeat

Wicksteed, James and family 73, 172, **183**, 187

Willaume, David 24, 33, 320

Willdey [Wildey]: George 211/5, 214, 220, 229, 230, 285, 294, 317; Judith 130, 322; Thomas 320

Williams: David 250, 320; Elizabeth 299; James 62, 321; John 321; Martha 320; Roger 321; Wm Peere 294, 299, 306, 321

Willoughby, John 75

Wills/bequests *see* Allen; Aumonier; Bertrand, Mary & Paul; Callard; Deards; Dering; Downing, Ferrand, Hawley/Hayes, Lindsey, Lombard, Margas, Roubel, Spencer, Marlborough, Willdey, Wiltshire. *See* inventories

Wiltshire: family tree **46**; timeline 9; 45–51; as carriers 45, 108, 111, 280; partners of PB 41, 45; and Nash 49–51; in London 36, 44; accounts at Hoare & Co. 45, 57; concert room 133

Ann **46**–47, 94, 104, 321; John (d. 1762) 41, 46, **51**, 71, 94, 138–39, 203, 261, 321; John (d. 1842) n. 65; Walter jnr 51, 94; Walter snr 45, 47–48, 265, 278, 321; William 44, 321. *See* Bath assembly rooms

Winchilsea: *see* Finch

Windham: *see* Wyndham

Wine: *see* food and drink

Winter: Mary 197; Dr 321

Winterton, Turnour Earls of 318

Winton: George Seton 5th Earl 316

Wirgman, Gabriel 277

Witt, Thomas 322

Wolfe, Gen. James 225

Wood: map of Bath **20, 24**; timeline 9. John snr 65, 69–70, 72–**73**, 79, 92–93, 103, 117, 120, 166, 171, 322; John jnr 72, 79, 261, 322

WOOL DRAPER AND STAPLER *see* textiles

Wootton, William 322

Worcester factory 220

Worlidge, Thomas **126**, 183, **187**, 296

Wragg [Ragg]: Joseph & Samuel 163–64

Wray: Charles **52**, 322; Sir Bourchier, 6th Bt 313

Wright: Mary 197; Phoebe n. 333; Henry 69, 71, **122**, 322; Thomas 211/11, **244**–45, 322

Writers, diarists, etc *see* Angerstein, Arkenside, Bristol, Chesterton, Cowper, Delany, Domcke, Dryden, Fielding, Fiennes, Gilbert, Goldsmith, Hickey, Houghton, Johnson, Kielmansegge, Leveridge, Lillo, Montagu, Motteux, Perceval (Egmont), Percival, Pope, Ralph, Richardson, Robinson, Scott, Sheridan, Walton, Walpole, Webb

Wyatt: James

Wyndham, William 156, 268, 323; Charles, Bt 316. *See* Delorane, Thomond

Wynn: Sir Watkin Williams 222, **235**

Yeates/Yates: 303, Richard **131**, 303, 323; William 323

Zincke, Christian Friedrich **112**, **146**